MW00654798

A Translator's Translation

of

The New Testament

A translation that has arisen out of the process of producing a source text of the New Testament for minority languages

Ellis W. Deibler, Jr.

Cummins Works
Ann Arbor, Michigan

First printing 2008

Second Printing 2008

Cummins Works, Publisher
Ann Arbor, Michigan 48104
USA

Pine Tree logo © 2008 Cummins Works

ISBN 0-9640069-4-4

TABLE OF CONTENTS

Preface... iv
Affirmation v
Introduction to "A Translator's Translation".................................. vi
About the author ix
About the development team.. ix
Note on spellings ix
Concerning the theme statements... x
Explanation of the format of this translation xi
Publisher's note xii
Matthew 1
Mark 68
Luke 107
John 170
Acts 216
Romans.. 289
1 Corinthians 325
2 Corinthians 355
Galatians.. 376
Ephesians... 389
Philippians 399
Colossians 408
1 Thessalonians... 417
2 Thessalonians... 425
1 Timothy.. 430
2 Timothy.. 438
Titus 445
Philemon 450
Hebrews 453
James 477
1 Peter... 487
2 Peter... 496
1 John.. 502
2 John.. 510
3 John.. 512
Jude 514
Revelation 517

PREFACE

In 1999, the International Conference of Wycliffe Bible Translators adopted a proposal called Vision 2025. The proposal stated our goal: to begin a Bible translation project in every language in which it is needed by the year 2025. It seems an impossible goal. Yet we believe God would have us strive to reach this goal, for His glory.

As an organization, we have realized that to reach this goal we need to be doing things differently. As for my part, I decided to create a translation of the New Testament that will help translators to recognize the problems that must be considered, so that they can handle those problems well.

Having completed this work (which is being published as **A Translation for Translators**), it was thought that a somewhat revised form of the work might be useful to others who study the Scriptures. The result is this: **A Translator's Translation**.

Its distinguishing features are:
- Short sentences
- Clear connections between clauses and sentences
- Sometimes clause order is reversed to reflect more clearly the chronological or logical order
- All abstract nouns are made into full clauses
- Most passive constructions are made active
- Most rhetorical questions have been translated by using a non-question form
- All figures of speech that we have been able to identify are stated non figuratively
- Simple vocabulary is used wherever possible
- Words are always used in their primary sense
- The implicit information that is deemed necessary to understand what the original writer intended to convey is supplied in italics.

I have based this translation on thorough scholarship, using published helps for translators, including other versions and commentaries.

One advantage in using this translation is that the implicit information, written in italics, is easily seen.

Please note that there is no implied endorsement of this translation by the Translation Department, either of the Summer Institute of Linguistics or of the Wycliffe Bible Translators or of any other publisher.

While offering this translation to Bible translators, hoping that it will enable them to complete their work in a much shorter time, I also offer it to the general public.

Ellis W. Deibler, Jr.
January 2008
Waxhaw, North Carolina

We will appreciate your comments and suggestions.
Each printing incorporates minor corrections which include your feedback.
Write to:
e-mail: ellis_deibler@sil.org
fax: (704) 843-6200

AFFIRMATION

We affirm that:

- The Scriptures of the Old and New Testaments were given by inspiration of God, and are the only infallible rule of faith and practice.

- The Scriptures were originally written in the language of the common people. They were written with the expectation that the recipients could and would understand the meaning clearly.

- Every person needs to have an opportunity to know about Jesus Christ. We believe that for people to be able to do that and to grow as believers, they need the Scriptures in the language they know best. When we attempt to translate the Scriptures into another language, we must communicate the message through the set of grammatical and lexical structures that are unique to that language. Failure to do so will almost certainly result in a translation that is not natural and will be very difficult to understand. Every language has its own forms and structures that are different from those of every other language. The set of forms and structures of English is different from the set of Hebrew and the set of Greek. Therefore we should expect that the forms used in one language —be it Biblical Hebrew or Greek or any other language— will frequently be unsuitable to convey a message, in whole and in part, in another language. Since every language is different, we should not expect that we can just substitute English words, one by one, using their primary sense only, for Greek words, assuming their primary sense in Greek is the one meant in that context. Furthermore, there is much information implicit in the Greek forms, information that the original writers expected their readers to understand, that must be made explicit to the English readers if they are to understand the message and respond to it. This translation attempts to convey a lot of that information which, after careful analysis, we have deemed to be part of the intended message.

- What we do in translation is work to try to make certain that the message survives the translation. In field situations, this translated message is then re-translated back into English (or into some other language that a consultant can handle), and then checked with the original. This is a severe test, to see that the intended message is clear. Using the understanding that has accrued over many decades of Bible translation work by several of those involved in this translation and by having several of us check it with the original Greek, we have tried to achieve this goal for A Translator's Translation.

- I hope that the readers of this translation will recognize and appreciate its clarity and communicability.

INTRODUCTION TO "A TRANSLATOR'S TRANSLATION"

As you start to look at this translation, you may very quickly be saying to yourself, "Hey, It does not look at all like any translation I know! Why do they call this a translation? It's a paraphrase!"

A Translator's Translation is not a paraphrase. A paraphrase is a rewording, in the same language, of some source text. It is not a translation because it has not been translated from one language to another. **A Translator's Translation** is a translation. It has been carefully translated from the Greek. The source text has been the latest edition of the United Bible Societies' Greek text.

Then you may ask, "So why does it look so different from other English translations?" We must remember that this translation was done primarily as a help to those who are translating the New Testament into some language which does not yet have the Scriptures. We have intended to unravel the complexities of the original text so that translators can understand the meaning clearly, and then express that meaning in the most natural way in the receptor language.

I also must explain something of the nature of language itself. Language is a system by which meaning is expressed by linguistic forms. Those forms include phonological forms, grammatical forms, lexical forms, and other forms. However, each language has its own set of forms that are peculiar to that language. Thus, we should never expect that the forms that are appropriate to express some bit of meaning in one language are the same forms that will be suitable for conveying that same meaning in another language.

For example, consider the expression, "I am thirsty." Let us look at how that concept is expressed in some other languages. I will list the country and language name, then the spelling of the words that mean "I am thirsty," and then the literal English meaning:

USA	Cheyenne	naho'ahe mahpe	I-want-water
Azerbaijan	Azerbaijani	man ichmak istayiram	I to-drink want
Papua New Guinea	Minaveha	magau ayaya	my-throat dry
Ghana	Akyode	bulef] kya m]]me	thirst is-killing-me
Indonesia	Soko Padang	ku mangkahara	I am-affected-by-dry
Mozambique	Sena	ndina nyota	I-have thirst
Pakistan	Burushaski	jaa buk yuukimi	my throat dry
		OR, jaa bisqa buumi	my spit dried-up
Kazakhstan	Kazak	men sholdep zhatyrmya	I arid am-being
India	Kolami	iir attain	water dries-me
India	Tamil	enaku tagam edukkiradu	thirst takes for-me
Papua New Guinea	Tok Pisin	nek bilong mi em i drai	my neck is dry
Papua New Guinea	Alekano	nagamikumú nivisekave	about-water, it-has sickened me
Guatemala	Cakchiquel	chaki'j nuchi'	my-mouth dry

So think about the implications: If such a universal experience as being thirsty is expressed in such completely different ways in these languages, we can be sure that every other semantic concept will have its own way of being expressed naturally in each language. So I repeat that we should NEVER expect that the natural way of expressing some Biblical concept will be the same in English or in any other language as it was in Greek.

Let me give some specific examples of what I have done in this translation, and my reasons why.

As a rule, all abstract nouns are made into full clauses. So the Greek word πίστίς 'faith' is translated as 'believe.' Why? Because 'faith' is expressing an event, not a thing. There are many hundreds, perhaps thousands, of languages in the world that do not have abstract nouns. And besides, in a passage such as Mark 2:5 where a literal translation is 'seeing their faith', the question arises, 'How can you see faith? What does it look like? What color is it?' So this translation makes clear that 'faith' is an event, not a thing, and also expresses the object of that event, because 'believe' always implies that a person believes something. So instead of 'he saw their faith' this translation has, "he realized that they believed *that he could heal the man*."

Similarly, figures of speech are spelled out. For example, in Mark 2:21-22, Jesus, as part of his reply to someone who was criticizing his disciples for their not fasting, gave two extended metaphors, one about putting patches of new cloth on old clothes and one about putting new wine in old wineskins. A translator must ask himself, "What was Jesus really trying to say?" **A Translator's Translation** tries to make clear the meaning that Jesus was really trying to convey, by including in italics the words, "*He spoke these parables to show them that if* anyone wants to live according to God*'s new message, that person should not try to obey the old traditions like abstaining from food*."

You may immediately ask, "But isn't that adding to Scripture?" The answer is, No! It is simply making clear what the original writer intended and what he expected his audience to know. We are trying to prevent the reader from getting a zero meaning or a wrong meaning. To paraphrase the injunction of Rev. 22:19, "If anyone in his translation takes away from the meaning that was intended by the original inspired authors, God will take away that person's share in the tree of life."

This translation includes a lot of implicit information in italics. Often it is cultural information that the original readers would have known and which the writers assumed their readers would know, and thus such information was part of the intended message. However, even English-speaking audiences often do not know such information. For example, in Mark 1:44, a literal translation of part of that verse is 'Go, show yourself to the priest.' **A Translator's Translation** has "Go to the priest *in Jerusalem* and show yourself to him *in order that he may examine you and verify that you are healed*." The parts in italics are crucial to understanding the passage, and they are bits of information that every Jew familiar with the Old Testament would know. But that information is not likely to be known by modern readers of English.

I have translated many passive constructions as active ones. Every event has a performer of that event, and there are hundreds if not thousands of languages which have no passive constructions. For instance, in Mark 2:5, a literal translation of the Greek is 'Your sins are forgiven.' The question arises, "By whom?" This translation makes clear exactly what Jesus' hearers understood him to be saying, by translating it "I forgive your sins."

Rhetorical questions can easily be misunderstood, because their linguistic function is to do something other than to get an answer from the listeners. For instance, in Mark 3:33, Jesus said, "Who are my mother and my brothers?" In some languages a literal translation has led the readers to understand that Jesus did not know who his mother and brothers were. To make clear what Jesus really meant, **A Translator's Translation** has, "Listen to what I have to say about my mother and my brothers."

The expression 'Son of Man', if translated literally, will almost certainly be misunderstood by many readers, and likewise will not convey what Jesus intended his listeners to understand. It was clearly a Messianic term (for example, John 12:34), a title that Jesus used often to point in the direction of meaning 'Messiah,' but one which he could use without arousing the anger of the Jewish religious leaders. **A Translator's Translation** attempts to convey the sense more clearly by using 'I, the one who came from heaven.' Note also that the first person singular 'I' is used to make clear that the speaker was referring to himself. Jesus was following the custom of most of the Biblical writers, all of whom expected their readers to know that in using a third person singular expression they were referring to themselves, but which is not the custom in English or most other languages.

Most, if not all, existing English translations have been done with varying degrees of following the rule that they will keep the forms used in the translation as close to the forms of the original as possible. Those translators believed that a translation that does not follow that principle is not a 'faithful' translation. However, it is not an appropriate principle to follow. What really matters is trying to be faithful to the meaning, of the original text, not to the forms of that original. Thus, **A Translator's Translation** has, at every point, tried to answer the question, 'Exactly what was the meaning the original writers intended and expected to convey?' I hope you enjoy this translation and that you are blessed by our attempt to make that meaning clear.

ABOUT THE AUTHOR

Ellis W. Deibler, Jr. joined Wycliffe Bible Translators and the Summer Institute of Linguistics in 1957. He has completed translation projects in the Alekano and Yaweyuha languages in Papua New Guinea. Several years later he did a complete revision of the Alekano New Testament. He has checked Bible translations, lectured and taught on principles of translation, and led translation workshops in nineteen countries, mostly in the South Pacific, Central Asia, and South Asia. He has written several books and published many articles dealing with Bible translation. He is now retired and living in Waxhaw, North Carolina.

ABOUT THE DEVELOPMENT TEAM

Martha Deibler checked the translation for clearness, ambiguities, correct exegesis, and implicit information. Martha joined Wycliffe Bible Translators in 1967 and co-translated the New Testament in Cakchiquel in Guatemala and supervised the translation projects in two more dialects of the same language. She has served for more than thirty years as a Translation Consultant.

Willis Ott developed the format of the document and advised on many exegetical and translational problems. He and his wife joined the Summer Institute of Linguistics in 1954 and completed a translation project for the Ignaciano people of Bolivia. He has served as a translation consultant in Bolivia, Botswana, Ethiopia, Guatemala, Kenya, the Democratic Republic of Congo (formerly Zaire), Peru, Mozambique and Sudan. He retired after 44 years of service with the Summer Institute of Linguistics and is now living in Waxhaw, North Carolina.

Andrew Sims is the project manager for this series, in charge of distribution, and keeping records of what books, in what form, are sent to whom and when. Andrew and his wife joined Wycliffe Bible Translators and the Summer Institute of Linguistics in 1973. They completed a translation project in a language in the Eastern Highlands of Irian (Indonesia) in 1996. He has served as a translation consultant in Indonesia and Southeast Asia. He lives in Waxhaw, North Carolina.

Donna Fedukowski has helped check the some of the implicit information. Gail Morse, Linda Boehm, Martha Deibler, Joyce Gullman, Janice Roddy, Linda Jonson, Susan Hochstetler, and several members of the Christian Reformed Church in Ann Arbor, Michigan, have edited the copy for errors and clarity.

NOTE ON SPELLINGS

We beg those who are accustomed to British spellings to overlook the American way of spelling. Aside from these normal differences, please advise us of any kind of typographical errors. We would also appreciate feedback concerning exegetical matters.

CONCERNING THE THEME STATEMENTS

In this translation, the theme statements precede each paragraph. They summarize the thematic content of that paragraph, reflecting the most prominent ideas in that paragraph. The translator should use the theme statements to make sure that the reader understands the most important parts of that paragraph. For example, a translator could rephrase the theme statement as a question to ask during a comprehension check. If the reader/listener has clearly understood the essential focus of the passage, he should be able to make an equivalent theme statement.

Example: The Translators Translation has the following theme statement for Mark 2:1-12: "By healing a paralyzed man, Jesus demonstrated his authority to forgive sins as well as to heal." Compare this theme statement with the section heading in the New Living Translation "Jesus heals a paralyzed man" or in the Jerusalem Bible "Cure of a paralytic."

The theme statements in this translation are not the same as the section headings that are included in most translations today.

Section headings in most translations often include more than one paragraph. They focus on a word, person or event mentioned in the section. These usually do not reflect the thematic focus of the section. It is my hope that the theme statements will help translators to write clear and accurate headings in the translation. But some may want to write theme statements similar to those in this translation instead of short heading that most translations use.

Translators who want to include section headings should carefully consider what to write in such headings. They should also consider where they want section headings to occur. Although there is a theme statement for every paragraph in this translation, a translator must choose where to include a section heading. For example, in **A Translator's Translation**, the letter to Philemon has nine theme statements. A translator may choose to have fewer section headings. If a translator includes several paragraphs in a section, the heading he writes should reflect the themes of those paragraphs.

A translator will also need to decide how to present the section heading. In some English translations, section headings are not complete sentences. The translator should present the section headings in the grammatical form that the speakers of the language prefer.

Observe that the theme statements do not necessarily use the simplified language that is found in the translation.

EXPLANATION OF THE FORMAT OF THIS TRANSLATION

> Scripture reference

> Theme statement

John 1:1-18

THEME: This book is about Jesus, who was eternally with God but also became a human being to reveal God to mankind.

[1] The one who expresses *what God is like* has always existed from the beginning *of everything*. He has always existed with God, and he has **God's nature**. [2] He always existed with God *before* he began *to create anything*. [3] He is the one by whom *God* caused everything to exist. He is the one who created absolutely everything. [4] He is the one who *caused everything to* live. He, who caused us people to live, *revealed to us the truth about God as* a light *reveals what is in the darkness*. [5] People do not want him to reveal *that what they do is evil* just *like* darkness *is evil*. But *just as* darkness cannot put out light, *evil people have never prevented the one who was like a light from revealing* God's truth. [1]

> Emphasized words in the Greek text are bolded.

> Implicit information is italicized.

> Alternative translations and alternative interpretations are placed in footnotes.

---

[1] OR, …But *just as* darkness cannot put out light, *evil people have never* understood the one who was like a light.

PUBLISHER'S NOTE

A Translator's Translation was created as a readable companion volume to **A Translation for Translators**, each having much the same text and implicit material. Here is one passage from Romans from the latter work. You may find it interesting to compare it with the same passage in this volume.

Romans 6:15-23

THEME: If someone should conclude that people can sin now because they are not obligated to obey the Mosaic laws, I would say, "Certainly not!" Instead, let your minds compel your bodies to act righteously.

I suppose that certain people might think about what I have just said and they might say [RHQ], "*You say that* the laws *God gave Moses* did not enable us *to stop sinning, but that God is now* treating us kindly in ways we do not deserve. ◄*That seems to mean that God permits* us to continue sinning./*Does that mean that God permits* us to continue sinning?► [RHQ]" My reply to that is no, we should certainly not continue *sinning!* [16] ◄*I want* you to remember this:/Do you not know this?► [RHQ] *Slaves* have to obey *what their masters command* [MET] *them to do*. Similarly, if you present yourselves to someone *in order to* obey him, you will be **the slaves** [MET] of the person you obey. Similarly, *if you have yielded yourselves to do the* sinful things *you desire*, you are slaves of your sinful desires [PRS], and you will be eternally separated from God. *If you have yielded yourselves* to obey *God*, you are slaves of God and you need to *live* righteously. [17] *You* were once slaves *to* your sinful *desires*. But you began to sincerely obey the new teaching [MET] that you were taught {that *people* taught you}. I thank God for that. [18] *I* also *thank God that* you have been freed {*that* he has freed you} from *being controlled by a desire to* sin and that you have become *as though you were* slaves [MET] to *living* righteously [MET]. [19] I am illustrating what I say *by talking about slavery* because your human nature prevents you from understanding *spiritual truth* easily. *In the past* you willingly did the immoral and unlawful things that *your minds compelled* your bodies to do [MET], *just like* slaves *do what their masters compel them to do*. As a result you did even more unlawful things. Now, *you need to* willingly allow *your minds to compel* your bodies to *act* righteously, [MET] in order that you will behave in a holy/pure way. [20] When you were *like* slaves *because your sinful desires compelled you to do* sinful things [MET], you were not concerned about *behaving* righteously [MET]. [21] Nevertheless, *doing* those things resulted in your being separated from God, so ◄you did not benefit at all from *doing* the *sinful* things that you are now ashamed of./what did you gain from *doing* the things that you are now ashamed of?► [RHQ] [22] But you have been freed {*God has freed you*} from *letting the desire to* sin control you. You have become *as though you were* [MET] the slaves of God. So now the result is that God has caused you to completely belong to him and, as a result, you will live eternally. [23] *What people receive for* sinning *is that they are* eternally separated from God. That is *like* wages that *people receive*. [MET] But what God gives us is a gift. What he gives us is that we live eternally because of *our relationship with* (OR, because *we are united to*) Christ Jesus our Lord.

A Translator's Translation

of

The New Testament

The Gospel that was written by
Matthew

1

Matthew 1:1-17

THEME: The genealogy of Jesus, with the names listed in three groups of fourteen generations each.

[1] *This is* the record of the ancestors of Jesus Christ, the descendant of *King* David and of Abraham, *from whom all we Jews have descended.* [2] Abraham was the father of Isaac. Isaac was the father of Jacob. Jacob was the father of Judah and Judah's *older and younger* brothers. [3] Judah was the father of Perez and Zerah, *and their mother* was Tamar. Perez was the father of Hezron. Hezron was the father of Ram. [4] Ram was the father of Amminadab. Amminadab was the father of Nahshon. Nahshon was the father of Salmon. [5] Salmon and his wife Rahab, *a non-Jewish woman*, were the parents of Boaz. Boaz was the father of Obed. *Obed's mother was* Ruth, *another non-Jewish woman*. Obed was the father of Jesse. [6] Jesse was the father of King David. David was the father of Solomon. *Solomon's mother was previously married to* Uriah. [7] Solomon was the father of Rehoboam. Rehoboam was the father of Abijah. Abijah was the father of Asaph. [8] Asaph was the father of Jehoshaphat. Jehoshaphat was the father of Jehoram. Jehoram was an ancestor of Uzziah. [9] Uzziah was the father of Jotham. Jotham was the father of Ahaz. Ahaz was the father of Hezekiah. [10] Hezekiah was the father of Manasseh. Manasseh was the father of Amon. Amon was the father of Josiah. [11] Josiah was the grandfather of Jeconiah and Jeconiah's brothers. *They lived* at the time the *Babylonian army* took the Israelites as captives to Babylon.

[12] After the Israelites were taken to Babylon, Jeconiah became the father of Shealtiel. Shealtiel was the grandfather of Zerubbabel. [13] Zerubbabel was the father of Abiud. Abiud was the father of Eliakim. [14] Eliakim was the father of Azor. Azor was the father of Zadok. Zadok was the father of Akim. [15] Akim was the father of Eliud. Eliud was the father of Eleazar. Eleazar was the father of Matthan. Matthan was the father of Jacob. [16] Jacob was the father of Joseph. Joseph was Mary's husband, and Mary was Jesus' mother. Jesus is the one who is called the Messiah.

[17] *As you can calculate, I have grouped Jesus'* ancestors *as follows:* There was *a succession of* fourteen of them from *the time when* Abraham *lived* to *the time when King* David *lived*. There was *a succession of* fourteen of them from *the time when* David *lived* to *the time when* the *Israelites were taken* away to Babylon. There was *a succession of* fourteen of them from *the time when the Israelites were taken* away to Babylon until *the time when* the Messiah *was born*.

Matthew 1:18-25

THEME: When Joseph learned that Mary was pregnant, he decided to divorce her, but an angel told him to take her as his wife because it was the power of the Holy Spirit that had enabled her to be pregnant.

[18] This is *the account of what happened just before* Jesus Christ was born. Mary, his mother, had publicly promised Joseph that she would marry him. Before they began to live

together, *Mary* found out that she was pregnant. *It was the power of* the Holy Spirit that had caused her to become pregnant. [19] Joseph, *whom people considered to be* her husband, was a man who obeyed God's commands. *One of those commands was that men must divorce women who had acted immorally. So, when Joseph learned that Mary was pregnant, assuming her pregnancy was a result of immoral behavior,* he decided to break the engagement. But because he did not want to shame her publicly, he decided to divorce her privately. [20] While he was seriously considering this, much to his surprise, in a dream he saw an angel who *had been sent by* the Lord. The angel said, "Joseph, descendant of *King* David, do not be afraid that *you would be doing wrong by marrying* Mary. Instead, *begin to treat her* as your wife, since the Holy Spirit, *not a man*, has caused her to be pregnant. [21] She will give birth to a son. It is he who will cause his people to be saved from *the guilt of* their sins. Name *the baby* Jesus, *which means 'the Lord saves people'.* [22] Long ago the Lord told the prophet *Isaiah to write about what was going to happen*. This is what Isaiah wrote: [23] "Listen, a virgin will become pregnant and will give birth to a son. He will be called Emmanuel." (Emmanuel means 'God is with us.') [24] When Joseph got up from sleep, he did what the angel whom the Lord *had sent* commanded him to do. He *began to live with Mary* as his wife. [25] But he did not have sexual relations with her until she had given birth to a son. And *when he was born, Joseph* named him Jesus.

2

Matthew 2:1-12

THEME: After some astrologers saw an unusual star, they traveled westward to find the place where the infant Jesus was. King Herod helped direct them, but then an angel told them not to go back to King Herod.

[1] Jesus was born in *the town of* Bethlehem in *the district of* Judea during the time that King Herod *the Great ruled there. Some time* after Jesus was born, some men who studied the stars, men who lived in a *country* east *of Judea,* came to Jerusalem. [2] They asked *people*, "Where is *the new* King of *you* Jews? *We believe that your new king* has been born, because we have seen the star *that we believe indicated that. We saw it while we were in our country* east *of here.* So we have come to worship him."

[3] When King Herod heard *what those men were asking*, he became worried *that this infant might be proclaimed King of the Jews to replace him. The people* of *the city of* Jerusalem *also* became worried, *because they were afraid of what King Herod might do.* [4] Then Herod gathered together all the ruling priests and men who taught the people the *Jewish* laws, and he asked them where *the prophets had predicted that* the Messiah was to be born. [5] They said to him, "*He will be born* in Bethlehem, *here* in Judea, because *long ago* the prophet *Micah wrote this that God said*: [6] You *who live in* Bethlehem, in *the province of* Judah, your town is very important, because a man from your *town* will become a ruler of my people, the Israelites.'"

[7] Then *King* Herod secretly summoned those men who studied the stars. He asked them exactly when the star *first* appeared. *By what they told him, he was able to know the approximate age of the baby.* [8] Then he *concealed what he really planned to do and* said to them, "Go to Bethlehem and inquire thoroughly *where* the infant is. When you have found him, *come back and* report to me so that I, myself, can go *there and* worship him, too."

[9] After the men heard what the king *told them*, they went *toward Bethlehem*. To their surprise, the star they had seen while they were in the eastern *country* went ahead of

them *again* until it stood above *the house* where the child was. [10] When they saw the star, they rejoiced greatly, *and followed it*. [11] They *found* the house and entered it and saw the child and his mother, Mary. They bowed down and worshiped him. Then they opened their treasure *boxes* and they gave gold, *costly* frankincense, and myrrh to him. [12] *Because* God *knew King Herod planned to kill Jesus*, in a dream he warned the men who studied the stars that they should not return to *King* Herod. So they returned to their country, *but instead of traveling back on the same road, they* went on a different road.

Matthew 2:13-21

THEME: Following an angel's instructions, Joseph took his family to Egypt to escape from Herod.

[13] After the men who studied the stars left *Bethlehem*, an angel *from* the Lord appeared to Joseph in a dream. He said, "Get up, take the child and his mother, and flee into *the country of* Egypt. Stay there until I tell you *that you should leave*, because *King* Herod is about *to send soldiers* to look for the child to kill him." [14] So Joseph got up, he took the child and his mother *that* night, and they fled into Egypt. [15] They stayed there until *King* Herod died, *and then they left Egypt*. By doing that, they fulfilled what the prophet *Hosea* wrote, which had been said by the Lord,
I have told my son to come out of Egypt.

[16] *While King* Herod *was still living*, because he realized that he had been tricked by the men who studied the stars, he became furious. Then, *assuming that Jesus was still in Bethlehem or the surrounding regions*, Herod sent *soldiers there* to kill all the boy babies two years old and younger. *Herod calculated how old the baby was* according to what the men who studied the stars told him *about when the star first appeared*. [17] *Since Bethlehem and Ramah were in the area where the descendants of Jacob's wife Rachel lived*, *when the infant boys there were killed*, it fulfilled what Jeremiah the prophet wrote:
[18] *Women* in Ramah were weeping and wailing loudly. *Women who were the descendants* of Rachel were grieving for *what happened to* their children.
Even though people tried to comfort them, they would not be comforted
because their children were dead.

[19] After Herod died *and while Joseph and his family were still in Egypt*, an angel from the Lord appeared to Joseph in Egypt in a dream. [20] He said to Joseph, "Take the child and his mother and go back to *the country of* Israel *to live*, because the people who were looking for the child *to kill him* have died." [21] So Joseph took the child and his mother and went back to Israel.

Matthew 2:22-23

THEME: Following an angel's warning, Joseph and his family returned to Nazareth, and thus a prophecy about the Messiah was fulfilled.

[22] When Joseph heard that Archaelaus now ruled in *the district of* Judea instead of his father, *King* Herod *the Great*, he was afraid to go there. Because God warned Joseph in a dream *that it was still dangerous for them to live in Judea*, he *and Mary and Jesus* went to *the district of* Galilee [23] to the town of Nazareth *to live there*. In that way, God caused to happen what had been said by the ancient prophets *about the Messiah*—that he would be called a Nazareth-man.

3

Matthew 3:1-6

THEME: John the Baptizer announced the coming of Jesus, and he baptized many people who heard his message.

[1] While *Jesus was still in Nazareth*, John, *whom the people called* the Baptizer, went to a desolate place in *the district of* Judea. [2] He was preaching *to the people who came there.* He kept saying, "*You need to* turn away from your sinful behavior, because God will soon begin to rule *over people, and he will reject you if you do not turn away from your sinful life.*" [3] John was the person who *fulfilled* what was said by Isaiah the prophet long ago,
In a desolate area, *someone will be heard* shouting *to the people who pass by*,
"Prepare *yourselves to receive* the Lord when he comes!
Make yourselves ready so that you will be prepared when he comes, just as people straighten out the road *for an important official!*"

[4] John wore *coarse* clothing made from camel's hair. And *as the prophet Elijah did long ago*, he wore a leather belt around his waist. His food was *only* grasshoppers and honey *that he found* in that desolate area. [5] *People who lived in the city of* Jerusalem, many *people who lived in other places in the district of* Judea, and many *people who lived in* the area around the Jordan *River* came to John *to hear him preach.* [6] After *they heard him tell them to turn away from their sinful behavior*, they *openly* confessed their sins, and as a result he baptized them in the Jordan River.

Matthew 3:7-10

THEME: John told the Pharisees and Sadducees that they needed to repent before he would baptize them.

[7] After John noted that many men of the Pharisee *religious group* and of the Sadducee *religious group* were coming *to him* to be baptized, he said to them, "You people are *evil like poisonous* snakes! I warn you that God will some day punish everyone who sins. And do not think that you can escape his punishment *if you do not turn from your sinful behavior!* [8] So, do the deeds that are appropriate for people who have truly turned away from their sinful behavior *before you come to me in order to be baptized!* [9] *God promised to give Abraham many descendants. In order to fulfill that promise, God does not need you!* I tell you that he can change these stones to make them descendants of Abraham. So do not start to say to yourselves, 'Since we are descendants of Abraham, *God will not punish us even though we have sinned.*' [10] *God is* ready *to punish you if you do not turn away from your sinful behavior, just as* a man does who lays his axe at the roots of a *fruit* tree *to* chop it down and throw it into the fire if it does not produce good fruit."

Matthew 3:11-12

THEME: John said that someone greater than him would soon come who would enable some of the people to change their lives and who would severely punish the others.

[11] "As for me, I *am not very important because* I baptize you *only* with water. *I baptize you* because of your feeling sorry that you have sinned. But someone else will come soon who is very great; *he will do powerful deeds. Because he is* superior to me, I am not worthy *even to do a menial task for him, such as* carrying his sandals. He will put *his* Holy Spirit *within* you *to truly change your lives*, and *he will judge others of you and punish you in* the fire *in hell.* [12] *He is like a farmer who wants to clear away the grain that is on the ground*

where it has been threshed. That farmer uses a huge fork to throw the grain into the air *to separate the wheat from the chaff,* and then he cleans up the threshing area. *Similarly,* God will *separate righteous people from the evil people, like a farmer who* gathers the wheat into his storage area, and then he will burn those *who are like* chaff with a fire that will never be put out."

Matthew 3:13-17

THEME: When John baptized Jesus, God showed that Jesus was his son by sending the Holy Spirit upon him.

[13] During that time Jesus went from *the district of* Galilee to the Jordan *River,* where John was. *He went there* to be baptized by John. [14] *When Jesus asked John to baptize him,* John objected, saying, "**I** need to be baptized by **you** *because you are superior to me. Since you are not a sinner, you* should not come to me *to be baptized by me!*" [15] But Jesus said to him, "Baptize me at this time, since in this way we *two* will do everything *that God* requires." Then John consented to baptize him.

[16] After he was baptized, Jesus immediately came up out of the water. Just then the heaven opened up and *Jesus* saw God's Spirit in the form of a dove coming down upon him. [17] Then *God* spoke from heaven, saying, "This is my Son. I love him. I am very pleased with him."

4

Matthew 4:1-11

THEME: After Jesus fasted forty days, Satan tempted him in various ways.

[1] Then Jesus was led by the Spirit into a desolate area to be tempted by the devil. [2] After he did not eat food day and night for forty days, he was hungry. [3] *Satan* the tempter came to him and said, "Since you *claim that you have a relationship with* God *as* a son *has with his father, prove it* by commanding these stones to become bread *so you can eat it!*" [4] But Jesus said *to him,* "*No! I will not change stones into bread, because* it is written *in the Scriptures, 'Eating* food *sustains* people *physically, but* it does not sustain them *spiritually.* Instead, *paying attention to* everything that God has spoken *to them is what sustains people spiritually.*'" [5] Then the devil took Jesus to *Jerusalem*, the city that is dedicated *to God*. He set him on the highest part of the Temple, [6] and said to him, "Since you *claim that you have a relationship with* God *as* a son *has with his father, prove it by* jumping down *to the ground. You will not be hurt,* because it is written *in the Scriptures, 'God* will command his angels to protect you. They will lift you up in their hands *when you are falling*, so that *you will not get hurt*. You will not *even* strike your foot on a stone.'" [7] But Jesus said, *"No! I won't jump down, because* in another place *in the Scriptures* it is written: 'Do not try to test the Lord your God *to see if he will prevent something bad from happening to you when you do something foolish!*'" [8] Then the devil took him on *top of* a very high mountain. There he showed him all the nations in the world and the magnificent things in those nations. [9] And he said to him, "I will *let you rule all these nations and* give you the magnificent things in them if you bow down and worship me." [10] But Jesus said to him, *"No, I will not worship you*, Satan, *so* go away! It is written in the Scriptures, 'It is the Lord your God whom you must worship; and you must serve only him!'" [11] Then the devil went away, and right away, angels came to Jesus and ministered to him.

Matthew 4:12-17

THEME: Jesus went to Galilee and preached that people needed to repent to belong to the group whom God would consider his people.

[12] *While* Jesus *was in Judea, John the Baptizer's disciples* told him that John had been put in prison. *So* Jesus returned to *the district of* Galilee. *While he was in Galilee, he first went to the town of Nazareth.* [13] Then he left Nazareth and went to *the town of* Capernaum *to live there. Capernaum is located* beside *Lake* Galilee in the region *which was formerly the regions* of *the tribes of* Zebulon and Naphtali. [14] *One reason he went there* was so that *these words* that were written by the prophet Isaiah might be fulfilled:

[15] *The regions of* Zebulon and Naphtali *are on* the road *which is* near Lake *Galilee and* on the eastern side of the Jordan *River. They are* the regions in *the district of* Galilee *where many* non-Jews *are living.* [16] *Although the people there will be like* people who sit in a dark place, *they will suddenly perceive clearly a new teaching, as* people who have seen a *bright* light shining on them *perceive everything clearly. The* people who are located in a dangerous region *will suddenly hear God's new teaching*, as people on whom a light shines.

[17] From that time, *while* Jesus was *in the town of Capernaum*, he began to preach this to people: "God will very soon begin to rule, *and he will judge you when he rules*. So you need to turn from your sinful behavior *so that God will not punish you*."

Matthew 4:18-22

THEME: Jesus summoned four fishermen, who immediately left their work and went with him.

[18] *One day* while Jesus was walking by Lake Galilee, he saw two men—Simon, who was *later* called Peter, and Andrew, his *younger* brother. They were casting their *fishing* net into the lake because they earned their living by catching *and selling* fish. [19] He said to them, "*Just as you have been* gathering fish, come with me and I will teach you how to gather people *to become my disciples.*" [20] They immediately left *the work they were doing with* their *fishing* nets, and they went with him.

[21] As *the three of them* walked on from there, Jesus saw two other men, James, and John, the *younger* brother of James. *They were* in their boat with Zebedee, their father, mending their *fishing* nets. Jesus told them that *they should leave their work and* go with him. [22] They immediately left their fishing boat and their father, and they went with Jesus.

Matthew 4:23-25

THEME: Jesus taught and healed many people when he was in the district of Galilee.

[23] Jesus went *with those other four men* throughout all of *the district of* Galilee. He was teaching *the people* in the buildings where we Jews worship God. He was preaching the good message that tells how to become members of the group of people whose lives God rules over. He was also healing all *the Galileans* who had diseases or illnesses. [24] When people who lived in other parts of *the district of* Syria heard what he was doing, they brought to him people who suffered from illnesses, people who suffered from many kinds of diseases, people who *suffered from* severe pains, people who were controlled by demons, people who were epileptics, and people who were paralyzed. And Jesus healed them *all*! [25] Then crowds started to go with him. *They were* people from the district of Galilee, from *the district of* Ten Towns, from Jerusalem, from other *parts of the district of* Judea, and from areas east of the Jordan *River*.

5

Matthew 5:1-12

THEME: On a hillside, Jesus taught his disciples and others what kind of people God esteems.

¹When Jesus saw the crowds, he climbed a hill. He sat down *in order to teach* his disciples, and they came near to him *to listen to him.* ²Then he began to teach them by saying,

³"*God* is pleased with people who recognize that they have a spiritual *need;*
he will allow them to be the people whose lives he rules over.
⁴*God* esteems people who mourn *because they have sinned;*
he will encourage them.
⁵*God* is pleased with people who are meek;
they will inherit the earth *that God will recreate.*
⁶*God* is pleased with people who sincerely *desire to live* righteously
just as they desire to eat and drink;
he will enable them to do all that he desires.
⁷*God* is pleased with people who act mercifully;
he will act mercifully to them.
⁸*God* is pleased with people who think only about that which pleases him;
some day they will *be where* God is and will see him.
⁹*God* is pleased with people who help others to live peacefully;
he will consider them to be his children.
¹⁰*God is pleased with* people who have evil things done to them
because they *live* righteously;
he will allow them to be where he rules over people.
¹¹*God is pleased with* you when *you endure other people*'s insults,
when *they* do evil things to you and when *they* say falsely *that* you are evil
because of your allegiance to me. ¹²*When that happens,* rejoice and be glad,
because *God will give* you a great reward in heaven. *God will think highly of you*
just as *he thought highly of* the prophets, whom your *ancestors persecuted* long ago.

Matthew 5:13-16

THEME: Jesus taught that we should live in such a way that other people will see how we live and will praise God.

¹³**You** are *able to influence* evil *people and improve the way they live—to keep them from becoming more evil, just as* salt *is able to improve the flavor of food and to preserve it from spoiling.* Salt that no longer tastes salty cannot become salty again. As a result, that salt becomes useless. People reject it, throw it on the ground, and walk on it. *In the same manner, if the way you live no longer influences people to live in a godly manner, God will reject you.* ¹⁴**You** *can enable* evil *people to perceive God's truth in the same way that* a light *enables people to perceive what is around them. Just as* everyone can see *the lights of* a city on a hill, *other people can see what you do.* ¹⁵After people light a lamp, they never put it under a basket. Instead, *they put it* on a lampstand in their houses in order that it can shine on everyone there. ¹⁶*Similarly,* you need to do *what is right* in such a manner that other people can see the good deeds you do, and as a result they will praise your Father *who is* in heaven.

Matthew 5:17-20

THEME: Jesus taught that it is important to obey all of God's commandments.

[17] "My coming to earth was not to annul the laws *God gave Moses* or what the prophets *wrote*. Instead, *I came* so that *what the authors of those books prophesied would come to pass*. So do not think any longer that I have come *to earth* in order to annul *what they wrote*. [18] Keep this in mind: *Every* point of those laws, *including those points that seem* least important, and even the smallest details, will surely be in effect until the heavens and the earth disappear and until all *that those laws say will have* come to pass. [19] Since *all God's laws are important*, those who disobey any of those commandments, *even* one of the least *important ones*, and teach people *to disobey any of those commandments*, God will say they are the least *important* of those in the place where he rules. But those who obey *those commandments* and teach *other people to obey them,* God will say they are very important among those that he rules. [20] Keep this in mind: *You assume that* the Pharisees and the men who teach our laws *faithfully obey* what God commands. But if you do not obey those laws better than they obey them, you will by no means enter the place where God rules.

Matthew 5:21-26

THEME: Jesus taught that we should not be angry and that we should quickly settle accounts with those we have wronged.

[21] "You have heard *your religious teachers say* that it was said to your ancestors, 'Do not commit murder.' *This implied that* if someone did commit murder, *the judge* would sentence him to be *executed*. [22] But what I say to you is this: *If you are* angry with someone, *God* will judge you. If you say to someone, '*You are worthless,'* the Jewish Council will judge you. If you say *to someone,* '*You are* a fool,' *God will sentence* you to be *thrown* into the fires in hell. [23] So, when you take your gift *for God* to the altar, if you remember that you have offended someone, [24] leave your gift by the altar, and first go *to the person you have offended*. Tell that person that you are sorry for what you have done, and ask that person to forgive you. Then go back and offer your gift *to God*. [25] *Also*, when a fellow citizen *takes you to court*, settle accounts with him quickly while you are walking with him on the road. Do that *while there still is time to do so,* in order that he will not take you to the judge, *because if* the judge *favors the person who is accusing you, he will declare you to be guilty and send you* to the prison guard, and the prison guard will put you in prison. [26] Keep this in mind: *If you go to prison*, you will never get out *if you do not* pay all that the judge says you owe. *And remember also that you ought to settle accounts with God before it is too late*!

Matthew 5:27-30

THEME: Jesus taught about the way to refuse to sin when we are tempted to do something wrong.

[27] "You have heard the commandment, 'Do not commit adultery.' [28] But what I say to you is this: If a man only looks at a woman desiring to have sex with her, *God considers that his thoughts* about sinning sexually are sin. [29] If because of what you see you *are tempted to* sin, *stop looking at those things! Even if you have to* gouge out one of your eyes and throw it away *to avoid sinning, do it!* It is good *that you not sin and* as a result *go to heaven, even though while you are still here on earth* you lack one *or both of* your eyes. But it is not good *that you continue to have two eyes and sin and, as a result,* God sends your whole body to hell. [30] If you are *tempted to* use one of your hands to sin, *stop using your hand. Even if you have to* cut your hand off and throw it away *to avoid sinning, do it!*

It is good *that you do not sin and as a result go to heaven, even though while you are still here on earth* you lack one *or both* of your *hands*. But it is not good *that you sin and, as a result, God* sends your whole body to hell.

Matthew 5:31-32

THEME: Jesus taught that people should not divorce their spouses.

[31] "*Moses* wrote, 'If a man is divorcing his wife, he should write a document *on which he states that he is* divorcing her.' [32] But *now listen to what* I say to you: *A man* may *divorce his wife* only if she has committed adultery *and not for any other reason*. If a man divorces his wife *for any other reason, and he has sex with another woman*, he makes his wife become one against whom he has committed adultery, *because in God's estimation she still is his wife*. Also, if a man marries a woman who is divorced *for improper reasons*, *God considers* him *guilty of* committing adultery.

Matthew 5:33-37

THEME: Jesus taught that people should not add anything to strengthen their words when they promise to do something.

[33] "You have also heard *your religious teachers say* that it was written to your ancestors, 'Make sure that you do what you promised the Lord you would do!' [34] But *now listen to what* I say to you: Never promise to do anything and then ask someone else to affirm *that what you are saying will happen. For example, do* not *promise to give something and then ask spiritual beings in* heaven *to affirm that you will do it*, because heaven is where God *sits* on his throne *to rule over people*. [35] *Also, do* not *promise to give something and then ask spiritual beings* on earth *to affirm that you will do it*, because the earth is where God rests his feet. *Also, do* not *promise to do something and ask religious authorities* in Jerusalem *to affirm that you will do it*, because Jerusalem is the city where *God*, the great King, *rules*. [36] *Also, do not promise to do something and then say that* your head *should be cut off if you do not do it*. You are not *even* able to *change the color of the hair of your head by* making one *black* hair white or one *white* hair black. [37] *If you talk about doing something,* just say 'Yes, *I will do it*,' or 'No, *I will not do it*.' *If you say* anything more than that, it is from *Satan*, the Evil One.

Matthew 5:38-42

THEME: Jesus taught that everyone should be kind to all people, even to people who mistreat us.

[38] "You have heard *your religious teachers say* that Moses wrote, '*Retaliate like this*: If *someone damages* one of your eyes, *someone should damage* one of that person's eyes. *If someone damages* one of your teeth, *someone should damage* one of that person's teeth.' [39] But *now listen to what* I say to you: Do not take revenge for evil *deeds done to you*. Instead, if someone *insults you by* striking you on one cheek, turn your other cheek toward that person *so that he can strike it also*. [40] If someone wants to sue you and take your inner garment, give him your outer garment also. [41] If a *military authority* compels you to go with him one mile *to carry his gear*, go with him two miles, *carrying his gear*. [42] Also, if someone asks you for *something*, give *him what he is asking for*. If someone requests you to lend him *something*, do not refuse *to lend it to him*.

Matthew 5:43-48

THEME: Jesus taught that we should love the people whom we would not normally love.

⁴³ "You have heard *your religious teachers say that* Moses wrote, 'Love the citizens of your country and hate your enemies.' ⁴⁴ But *now listen to what* I say to you: Love your enemies *as well as your friends*, and pray for those who cause you to suffer. ⁴⁵ Do that to imitate what *God*, your Father *who is* in heaven does. He desires that you do *as he does. He acts kindly to all people. For example, he causes* the sun to shine *equally* on both wicked *people* and good *people*, and *he sends* rain on *both* righteous *people* and on unrighteous *people.* ⁴⁶ If you love *only* those who love you, *do not expect God to* reward you *for that. This is based on the fact that all people*, even the tax collectors, *who you think are very great sinners*, love those who love them. *If you act like them, you are not any better than they are!* ⁴⁷ If you want *God* to bless only your friends, you are not acting any better than other people. Even the non-Jews, *who you think are unacceptable to God*, want God to bless their friends, *but God does not reward them for that.* ⁴⁸ *You need to love those who do not love you*, and in that way become perfect, as *God* your Father *who is* in heaven is perfect.

6

Matthew 6:1-13

THEME: Jesus taught how we should give to needy people. He also taught his disciples how to pray.

¹ "When you do your good deeds, make certain that you do not do them when other people are watching, just so that they may see you *and think highly of you.* If *you do good deeds merely so that other people may think highly of you, God*, your Father who is in heaven, will not give you any reward. ² So, whenever you give something to the poor, do not *announce it as people announce something they want others to know about* by playing a trumpet *fanfare.* That is what the hypocrites do in the synagogues and on the main roads, so that people will *see what they do and* praise them. Keep this in mind: *The praise those hypocrites get* is the *only* reward they will receive! ³ Instead *of doing as they do*, when you give something to the poor, do not let other people know it. ⁴ In that way, you will be giving to the poor secretly. *As a result, God*, your Father who observes *you* while no one else sees *you*, will reward you.

⁵ "Also, when you pray, do not do what the hypocrites do. They like to stand in the Jewish meeting places and on the corners of the main streets to pray, in order that other people will see them *and think highly of them.* Keep this in mind: *People praise them, but* that is the *only* reward they will get. ⁶ But as for you, when you pray, go into your private room and close the door in order to pray to *God*, your Father, whom no one can see. He observes you where no one else observes you, and he will reward you. ⁷ When you pray, do not repeat words over and over as the people who do not know God do *when they pray. They repeat meaningless words* because they think that if they use many words, their gods will listen to them and give them *what they ask for.* ⁸ Do not *repeat words* as they do, because *God* your Father knows what you need before you ask him. ⁹ So pray *things* like this: Father, *you who are* in heaven, we want you to be revered. ¹⁰ We want *people to let* you rule *over their lives.* We want *people who live* on the earth to do what you desire, as those who live in heaven *do what you want them to do.* ¹¹ Give us each day the food that we *need for* that day. ¹² Forgive our sins in the same way that **we** have

forgiven the people who sin against us. [13] Do not let us do wrong things when we are tempted, and rescue us when *Satan*, the evil one, tempts us to do evil things.[a]

Matthew 6:14-15

THEME: Jesus taught more about forgiving others.

[14] "*Forgive the people who sin against you*, because, if you forgive other people, *God*, your Father who is in heaven, will forgive your *sins.* [15] But if you do not forgive other people, neither will God forgive your sins.

Matthew 6:16-18

THEME: Jesus taught about fasting.

[16] "When you abstain from eating food *in order to spend time in prayer*, do not look sad as the hypocrites pretend to be. They make their faces appear sad so that people will see they are fasting *and will think highly of them*. Keep this in mind: *Their being thought of highly for fasting is the only* reward those people will get! [17] Instead, *each of* **you**, when you abstain from food, should comb your hair and wash your face *as usual* [18] in order that other people will not notice that you are fasting *because you will look as you always do*. But *God*, your Father, whom no one can see, *will observe that you are fasting. God* your Father sees *you* even though no one else sees *you*, and he will reward you.

Matthew 6:19-21

THEME: Jesus taught that we should do deeds that please God. That will be like putting treasures in heaven.

[19] "Do not *selfishly* accumulate large quantities of money and material goods for yourselves on *this* earth, since *the earth is where everything perishes. For example*, on earth termites ruin things, and things rust, and thieves enter *buildings* and steal things. [20] Instead, do *deeds that will please God. Your doing such deeds will be like* storing treasures in heaven. *Nothing perishes in heaven*. There, no termites ruin *things*, nothing rusts, and thieves do not enter buildings and steal. [21] *Remember that* the things *you think are the most* valuable are *the things* you will be constantly concerned about. *So you who want to store up treasures in heaven*, you *need to be* constantly thinking *about God and heaven, instead of thinking about your earthly possessions.*

Matthew 6:22-23

THEME: Jesus taught that we should be generous with what we possess.

[22] "Your eyes are *like* a lamp for your body, because they enable you to see things. So if your eyes are healthy, you are able to see everything well. *In the same way, if you are generous with your money and other possessions, you will be able to know much of what God wants you to know.* [23] But if your eyes are bad, you are not able to see things well. And if that continues, the time will come when you will not be able to see at all. You will be in complete darkness. *In the same way, if you continue to be greedy, you will be in spiritual darkness. If greediness consumes you, all that you do will be evil.*

---

[a]   Some Greek manuscripts add, "For the authority to rule, and the power to rule, is yours forever, and people should praise you forever."

Matthew 6:24

THEME: Jesus taught that we should not try to serve God and accumulate money at the same time.

²⁴ "No one is able to serve two *different* bosses *simultaneously.* If *he tried to do that,* he would hate one of them and love the other one, or he would be loyal to one of them and despise the other one. *In the same way,* you cannot *devote your life to* worshipping God and *worshipping* money and material goods *at the same time.*

Matthew 6:25-34

THEME: Jesus taught that we should not worry about having enough food and clothes.

²⁵ "Since *you should be concerned about what God thinks is important and not about material goods,* I tell you that you should not worry about *things you need in order to* live. *Do not worry* about whether you will have *enough food* to eat, and *things* to drink, or *enough* clothes to wear. It is important to have *sufficient* food *and drink* and clothing, but the way you conduct your life is much more important. ²⁶ Look at the birds. They do not plant *seeds, and they do not* harvest *crops* or gather *produce* into barns. *They always have food to eat because God,* your Father, who is in heaven, provides food for them. And **you** are certainly worth a lot more than birds! *So be assured that God will supply what you need!* ²⁷ None of you can, by means of worrying, *add time to your life. You cannot* add *even* one minute to your life! *So you should not worry about things such as food and clothing!*

²⁸ "You should also not worry about *whether you will have enough* clothes *to wear.* Think about the way flowers *grow* in the fields. They do not work *to earn money, and they do not make their own clothes.* ²⁹ But I tell you that even though *King* Solomon, who *lived long ago, wore very beautiful clothes,* his clothes were not as beautiful as one of those *flowers.* ³⁰ God makes the wild plants very beautiful, *but they grow* in the field *for only a short time.* One day they grow, later they dry up, and eventually they are thrown into an oven *to be burned to make heat for baking bread. But you are more important to God than wild plants are, and you live much longer.* So God will certainly provide clothes for you. *Why do* **you** trust him so little? ³¹ Because of God's caring for you, do not worry and say, 'Will we have anything to eat?' or 'Will we have anything to drink?' or 'Will we have clothes to wear?' ³² Those who do not know God are always worrying about such things. But **God,** your Father who is in heaven, knows that you need all those things, *so you shouldn't worry about them.* ³³ Instead, the most important thing you should be concerned about is to let *God* completely direct your life, and to strive *to live* righteously. *If you do that,* God will give you all the things you need. ³⁴ So *on any given day* do not be worried about what will happen to you the next day, because *when* that day comes, *you* will be concerned about *what happens during* that day. You will have enough to be concerned about each day. *So do not worry ahead of time.*

7

Matthew 7:1-5

THEME: Jesus taught that we should not condemn others for their faults if we have faults ourselves.

[1] "Do not talk about how sinfully others have acted, in order that God will not say how sinfully you have acted. [2] If you condemn *other people*, *God* will condemn you. To the same extent that you condemn others, you will be condemned. [3] None of you should be concerned *about someone else's small faults. That would be like noticing* a speck in that person's eye. But you should *be concerned about your own big faults. They are like* planks in your own eye, which you do not notice. [4] You should not say to other people *about their minor faults*, 'Let me remove the specks from your eyes!' if a plank is still in your own eye. [5] You hypocrite, *stop committing your own sins*! *That will be like* removing the plank from your own eye. Then, as a result, you will have the spiritual insight you need to help others get rid of the *faults that are like* specks in their eyes.

Matthew 7:6

THEME: Jesus taught that we should not teach spiritual truth to those who will not appreciate it.

[6] "You do not give holy things to dogs *that would ignore those things* and attack you. You do not throw pearls in front of hogs, *because they would just ignore them* and trample them. *Similarly*, do not give *precious spiritual truth to people who you know will not value it but instead would do evil things to you.*

Matthew 7:7-11

THEME: Jesus taught that God is ready to give good things to us if we persist in prayer.

[7] "Keep asking *God for what you need. If you do that, he* will give it to you. Confidently keep *expecting God to give you the things you need, and he will give them to you. It will be like* looking for what you need and finding it. Continue *praying persistently to God. Then God will answer you. It will be like* knocking *on a door*. And *God* will open the way for you *to get what you pray for.* [8] Remember that *God* will give *good* things to everyone who continues to ask *him for them. He* will give things to whoever confidently continues asking. *He* will open *the way* for people *to get the things they keep persistently praying for.*

[9] No man among you would give a stone to his son if his son were to ask for bread. [10] Likewise, no man would give a *poisonous* snake to his son if his son would ask for a fish. [11] Even though you people are evil, you know how to give good things to your children. So *God*, your Father who is in heaven*,* will certainly give good things to those who ask him.

Matthew 7:12

THEME: Jesus taught that we should treat others as we would like them to treat us.

[12] "In whatever *good* manner you want others to act toward you, that is the manner **you** should act toward them. This command of mine *sums up all the instructions that Moses wrote in* the laws *God gave him* and *also what* the prophets *wrote long ago*.

Matthew 7:13-14

THEME: Jesus taught that we should try to walk on the narrow road that leads to heaven.

¹³⁻¹⁴ "It is difficult to go where people live eternally *with God in heaven*! *It is like* going along a narrow road that leads to a narrow gateway. Not many people find that way. *The way* that most *people take* is easy, *but it results in their being punished in hell. That way is like a* wide road that people walk on until they reach the wide gateway, but that road and that gateway lead to where *they* will be destroyed. Many people enter that gateway. So *I am telling you to leave the wide road and* enter the narrow gateway *to heaven.*

Matthew 7:15-20

THEME: Jesus taught about how to recognize false prophets.

¹⁵ "Beware of people who come to you and say falsely that they are telling you *what God has said. They seem to be harmless, but they are extremely harmful. They are like* wolves that have covered themselves with sheepskins *to make people believe that they are sheep*, but they actually are wolves that attack people. ¹⁶ *So how will you know that those people are false?* Well, by seeing what kind of fruit plants produce, you know *what kind of plants* they are. *For example, since thorn bushes cannot produce grapes*, no one can pick grapes from thorn bushes. And *since thistles cannot produce figs*, no one can pick figs from thistles. ¹⁷ *Here is another example*: All good fruit trees produce good fruit, but all rotten trees produce worthless fruit. ¹⁸ No good fruit tree is able to produce worthless fruit, and no rotten tree is able to produce good fruit. ¹⁹ *And*, all the trees that do not produce good fruit are chopped down and burned in the fire *to get rid of them. Similarly, false prophets will be thrown into the fires of hell.* ²⁰ By seeing what kind of fruit *plants* produce, you know *what kind of plants* they are. *In the same way, when you see what the people who come to you do, you will know if they are false prophets.*

Matthew 7:21-23

THEME: Jesus warned that he will reject those who do not do what God desires.

²¹ "*Many* people pretend that they are under my authority, *habitually* calling me 'Lord'. *Even so,* some of them will not go to heaven where God rules, *because they do not do what he desires. Only* those people who do what my Father, who is in heaven, desires *will go there.* ²² On the day *that God judges everyone*, many *people, trying to tell me that they deserve to go to heaven*, will say to me, 'Lord, we spoke God's message as your representatives! As your representatives we expelled demons from *people!* And as your representatives, we did many miracles!' ²³ Then I will declare to them, 'I have never said that you are *my friends.* Go away from me, you who do what is evil!'

Matthew 7:24-27

THEME: Jesus warned that undesirable things would happen to those who did not obey his teaching.

²⁴ "So then, anyone who hears what I say and does what I command, will be like a wise man who built his house on rock. ²⁵ *Even though* the rain came down and the river flooded, and the winds blew and beat against that house, it did not fall down because it was built on a solid foundation. ²⁶ On the other hand, anyone who hears what I say but does not **obey** what I say will be like a foolish man who built his house on the sand. ²⁷ When the rain fell and the river flooded, and the winds blew and beat against that house, it crashed

down and broke completely apart, *because it was built on the sand. So it is important for you to obey what I teach you.*"

Matthew 7:28-29

THEME: The crowds were amazed at Jesus, because he taught with his own authority.

²⁸ When Jesus finished saying all those things, the crowd *who had heard him was* amazed at the *new* teaching he had taught them. ²⁹ The reason they were amazed was that he was teaching as a person does who has *his own* authority. He was not teaching like the men who taught the *Jewish* laws, *who just repeated what other people had taught them.*

8

Matthew 8:1-4

THEME: Jesus healed a leper and made it possible for him to associate with people again.

¹ When Jesus went down from the hillside, large crowds followed him. ² *After he left the crowds*, a man who had leprosy unexpectedly came and knelt before him. He said *to Jesus*, "Lord, *please heal me, because I know* you are able to heal me if you are willing to!" ³ Then Jesus, *disregarding the religious law that forbade people to come close to lepers*, stretched out his hand and touched the man. He said *to him*, "I am willing to *heal you*, and I heal you *now*!" Immediately, the man was healed from his leprosy. ⁴ Then Jesus said to him, "Make sure that you do not report *your healing immediately* to anyone *other than the local priest.* Show yourself to him *so that he can examine you and verify that you no longer have leprosy.* After the priest tells *the local people,* they will know that *you have been healed, and you will be able to associate with them again.* Then go to *the Temple in Jerusalem* and take to the priests *the offering* that Moses commanded *that people who have been healed from leprosy should take so* that *they can* offer it *as* a sacrifice to God."

Matthew 8:5-13

THEME: Jesus healed from a distance a Roman officer's servant because the officer had a strong faith in him.

⁵ When Jesus went to Capernaum, a *Roman* officer who was in charge of one hundred soldiers came to him. He begged Jesus *to help him.* ⁶ He said *to him*, "Sir, my servant is lying *in bed* at home and is paralyzed with severe pain." ⁷ Jesus said *to him*, "I will go *to your house* and heal him." ⁸ But the officer said *to him*, "Sir, *do not bother to go. Since I am a non-Jew*, I am not worthy for you, *a Jew*, to come into my house *and associate with me.* Instead, *just* say *that* my servant *is healed,* and he will be healed. ⁹ *I believe this* because, **as for me, I** am a man under the authority of others, and I also have soldiers under my authority. When I say to one of them 'Go!', he goes. When I say to another 'Come!' he comes. When I say to my slave, 'Do this!' he does it. *And I believe that you speak with a similar kind of authority.*" ¹⁰ When Jesus heard this, he marveled. He said to the crowd that was walking with him, "Listen to this: I have never before found anyone who has as firm a faith *in me as this non-Jewish man has.* Not even in Israel, *where I would expect people to believe in me*, have I found anyone who has the kind of faith in me that he has! ¹¹ I tell you truly that many *other non-Jewish people will believe in me as this Roman officer* does. They will come from *distant countries, including* those *far* to the east and *far* to the west, and they will sit down to eat with Abraham, Isaac, and Jacob in heaven, where God rules. ¹² But *the Jews who should have allowed* God to rule over them will be sent to *hell, where*

there *is* total darkness. And as a result, they will weep *because of their suffering* and will grind their teeth *because of their severe pain*." [13] Then Jesus said to the officer, "Go *home. What you believed—that I would heal your servant from a distance—will happen.*" *Then the officer went home and found out that* his servant was healed at the exact time *Jesus told him that*.

Matthew 8:14-15

THEME: Jesus healed Peter's mother-in-law.

[14] When Jesus *and some of his disciples* went to the home of Peter, Jesus saw Peter's mother-in-law. She was lying on a bed because she had a fever. [15] He touched her hand, and as a result, *immediately* her temperature was back to normal. Then she got up and served them *some food*.

Matthew 8:16-17

THEME: Jesus healed many sick people, and expelled demons from other people.

[16] That evening *when the Jewish day of rest ended and people were free to travel*, many people who were controlled by demons *and people who were sick were* brought to Jesus. He caused the demons to leave just by speaking to them, and he healed all the people who were sick. [17] By doing this, he fulfilled the words that had been said by the prophet Isaiah *about the Messiah*: 'He healed people who had sicknesses and he cured them of their diseases.'

Matthew 8:18-22

THEME: Jesus told a man what to expect if he went with Jesus. He told another man to follow Jesus immediately, not wait until later.

[18] Jesus saw the crowd around him, but *he needed to rest*, so he told *his disciples to take him by boat* to the other side *of the lake*. [19] *As they were walking toward the boat*, a man who taught the *Jewish* laws came to him and said, "Teacher, I will go with you wherever you go." [20] *So that the man might know what he could expect if he went with him*, Jesus said to him, "Foxes have holes *in the ground in which to live*, and birds have nests, but *even though I* am the one who came from heaven, I do not have a home where I can sleep." [21] Another man who was one of Jesus' disciples said to him, "Sir, permit me first to go *home. After* my father *dies I will* bury him, *and then I will come with you*." [22] But Jesus said to him, "Come with me *now*! *Those who do not have eternal life are* dead *in God's sight*. Let those people *do the work of* burying people who die, *instead of your doing it*!"

Matthew 8:23-27

THEME: The disciples were amazed when Jesus calmed a storm on the lake.

[23] Then Jesus got into the boat. The disciples also got *in, and they started skirting around Lake Galilee*. [24] Suddenly strong winds blew on the lake, and very high waves were splashing into the boat and filling it. But **Jesus** was sleeping. [25] They went and woke him up, and said *to him*, "Sir, rescue *us*! We are about to drown!" [26] He said *to them*, "*You shouldn't* be afraid! *Why do* you have such little faith *in me? In spite of all you have seen me do,* do you not believe *that I can rescue you*?" Then he got up and rebuked the wind and told the waves to calm down. And *the wind stopped blowing and the lake* became calm. [27] *As a result*, they were amazed, and they said *to one another*, "This man is

certainly an *extraordinary* person! *All things are under his control!* Even the winds and the waves obey him!"

Matthew 8:28-34

THEME: Jesus expelled some demons from two men.

[28] When *Jesus and the disciples* came to the *east* side *of the lake*, they arrived in the region where the Gadarenes *lived. Jesus got out of the boat and began walking on the road. Then* two men who were controlled by demons came out of the burial caves *where they were living.* Because they were extremely violent *and attacked people*, no one dared to travel on the road *near where they were living.* [29] Suddenly, they shouted *to Jesus*, "You are the Son of God! *Since* you have nothing in common with us, *leave us alone!* Have you come here to torture us before the time *God has appointed to punish us*?" [30] There was a large herd of pigs rooting for food not far away. [31] So the demons begged Jesus, saying, "Since you are going to cast us out of the men, send us into the herd of pigs!" [32] Jesus said *to them*, "*If that is what you want*, go!" So the demons left *the two men* and entered the pigs. Suddenly, the whole herd *of pigs* rushed down the steep bank into the lake and drowned. [33] The men who were tending the pigs *became afraid and* ran into the town and reported everything *that had happened*, including what had happened to the two men who had been controlled by demons. [34] Then *it seemed as if* all *the people who lived in* that town went to meet Jesus. When they saw him *and the man who had been controlled by the demons*, they begged Jesus to leave their region *because they were afraid he might destroy more things than just the pigs.*

9

Matthew 9:1-8

THEME: Jesus showed he had power to forgive sins as well as to heal a paralyzed man.

[1] Jesus *and his disciples* got into the boat. They skirted around *the lake,* and he went to *Capernaum*, the town where he *was living.* [2] *Some men* brought to him a man who was paralyzed and who was lying on a sleeping pad. When Jesus perceived that they believed *he could heal* the paralyzed man, he said to him, "Young man, be encouraged! I forgive your sins." [3] Some of the men who taught the *Jewish* laws said among themselves, "*He claims he can forgive sins! That means he claims to be equal with God!* He is insulting God!" [4] Jesus knew what they were thinking. So he said, "You should not think evil *thoughts, saying it is wrong for me to claim that I am God.* [5] It would *not* be risky *for someone* to say *to this man*, 'I forgive your sins', *because no one could see whether or not his sins were really forgiven. But no one, without having the power to heal,* would say *to him*, '*Get* up and walk!' *because people could easily see whether he was healed or not.* [6] *So I am going to do something* in order that you may know that *God* has authorized *me*, the one who came from heaven, to forgive the sins *of people while I am* on the earth, *as well as to heal people.*" Then he said to the paralyzed man, "Get up, pick up your sleeping pad, and go home!" [7] And *immediately* the man got up, *picked up his sleeping pad*, and went home! [8] When the crowds saw this, they were awestruck. They praised God for giving authority to a human being *to do* such *things.*

Matthew 9:9-13

THEME: Jesus invited Matthew to go with him, and told the Pharisees that they needed to repent.

⁹ As Jesus was going away from there, he saw **me**, a man named Matthew. I was sitting at a table, where I collected taxes for *the Roman government.* He said to me, "Come with me *and become my disciple!*" So I got up and went with him. ¹⁰ *Then I invited* Jesus and his disciples *to my home for a meal.* While *they* were sitting and eating in my home, many tax collectors and *other people who were considered to be habitual* sinners came unexpectedly to eat with us. ¹¹ When the Pharisees saw *that, they came* to us disciples and said, "*It is disgusting to us that* your teacher, *who claims to be righteous,* eats with tax collectors and *other* sinners!" ¹² Jesus heard what *they said*, so he told them *this parable*: "*It is* people who are sick who need a doctor, not those who are well." *What he meant by that was that it was people who knew that they were sinners who were coming to him to get spiritual help.* ¹³ He continued by saying, "You need to learn what these words that *God said* mean: 'I want you to *act* mercifully *to people,* and not *just to offer* sacrifices.' Keep in mind that it is not that I came *from heaven* to invite *people who think they are* righteous *to turn away from their sinful lives and come to me.* On the contrary*, I came to invite people who know they are* sinners *to turn from their sins and come to me.*"

Matthew 9:14-17

THEME: Jesus illustrated why it was not appropriate for his disciples to fast, and that living according to his new message was better than following the old traditions like fasting.

¹⁴ Later the disciples of John *the Baptizer* came to Jesus and asked him, "We and the Pharisees *often* abstain from food *to show we wanted to please God*, but your disciples do not do that. Why *do they not*?" ¹⁵ *Jesus wanted to show them and the Pharisees that it was not appropriate for his disciples to abstain from food and mourn while he was still with them.* So he *gave them this illustration*: "When the bridegroom is with *his friends at the time of the wedding*, his friends certainly do not mourn, do they? *They do not mourn because they are not sad then. But when* the bridegroom is taken from them, they will abstain from food, *because then they will be sad.*"

¹⁶ *Jesus wanted to show that those who desire to live in accordance with his new message should not be forced to obey the old religious traditions like fasting. So he said to them*, "People do not sew a patch of unshrunken cloth on an old garment *to mend a hole.* If they did that, *when they washed the garment*, the patch would *shrink* and tear the garment, and the hole would become bigger. ¹⁷ Neither does anyone pour freshly-*squeezed* grape juice into old skin bags *to store it.* If anyone did that, those skin bags would tear *because they would not stretch when the juice ferments and expands. They* would be ruined, and the wine would be spilled *on the ground.* Instead, *people* put new grape juice into new skin bags, *and the bags will stretch when the juice ferments.* As a result, both *the wine and the bags* are preserved."

Matthew 9:18-26

THEME: Jesus healed a woman who had constant hemorrhaging. He also caused a young girl to become alive again.

¹⁸ While Jesus was saying that, *a man named Jairus,* a leader of the Jewish meeting place came. He bowed down before Jesus *to show respect.* Then he said, "My daughter just died! But if you come and lay your hand on her, she will live *again!*" ¹⁹ So Jesus got up and he and *we* disciples went with the man. ²⁰⁻²¹ Then a woman who *had been suffering*

constant vaginal bleeding for twelve years came near Jesus. She was saying to herself, "*I want Jesus to heal me without anyone finding out that I have this problem of bleeding.* So if I *touch him* or even if I just touch his garment, I will be healed *without anyone finding out about it.*" So she came behind him and touched the tassel of his garment. ²² Then Jesus turned around *to see who had touched him.* And when he saw the woman, he said to her, "Be encouraged, dear woman. Because you believed *that I could heal you, I* have healed you." The woman was healed at that very moment.

²³ Then Jesus *and some of us disciples* came to Jairus' house. Jesus heard the flute players *playing funeral music,* and the crowd *that had gathered were* wailing loudly *because the girl had died.* ²⁴ *Knowing that he would cause her to live again*, he said *to them*, "*Stop the funeral music and wailing* and go away, because the girl is not dead! She is *just* sleeping!" *The people laughed at him, because they knew she was dead.* ²⁵ But Jesus told them to get out of the house. Then he went into *the room where the girl was lying.* He took hold of her hand and she *became alive again and* got up. ²⁶ And the *people of that* whole region heard about it.

Matthew 9:27-31

THEME: Jesus healed two blind men.

²⁷ As Jesus went away from there, two blind men followed him and shouted, "Have mercy on us *and heal our eyes, you who are the Messiah*, the Descendant of *King* David!" ²⁸ Jesus went into *his own* house, and then the blind men went in, too. Jesus said to them, "Do you believe that I am able *to heal your eyes*?" They said to him, "Yes, Lord!" ²⁹ Then he touched their eyes and he said *to them*, "Because you believe *that I can heal your eyes*, I am healing them *right now*!" ³⁰ And they were able to see! Then Jesus told them sternly, "Be sure you do not tell anybody *what I did for you*!" ³¹ But they went out and reported it throughout that whole region.

Matthew 9:32-34

THEME: Jesus expelled a demon, but the Pharisees accused him of doing such things by Satan's power.

³² When Jesus *and we disciples* left *his house*, some people brought to him a man who was unable to speak because he was controlled by a demon. ³³ After Jesus had expelled the demon, the man who had been unable to speak began to speak! The crowd *who saw this* marveled. They said, "Never before have *we seen* anything *as marvelous* as this happen in Israel!" ³⁴ But the Pharisees said, "It is *Satan*, who rules the demons, who *enables this man to* expel demons *from people.*"

Matthew 9:35-38

THEME: Jesus told his disciples to pray that God would send more workers to tell his message to those who were ready to respond.

³⁵ Then *we* went *with* Jesus through many of the cities and towns *in the district of Galilee.* He was teaching in the *Jewish meeting places* and preaching the good message about how God rules *over people's lives.* He also was healing the *people who had* various diseases and illnesses. ³⁶ When he saw the crowd of people, he pitied them because they were harassed and dejected. *They were* like sheep that do not have a shepherd. ³⁷ Then he gave *this illustration to us* disciples: "*The people who are ready to receive my message are like a* field that is ready to be harvested. But there are only a few *of you who are teaching people my message.* ³⁸ So pray and ask the Lord *God* to send *more* workers *who*

will gather people together and teach them my message, just as a landowner sends workers into his field to gather the harvest."

10

Matthew 10:1-15

THEME: Jesus selected twelve apostles and instructed them before sending them out to various places.

[1] He told *us* twelve disciples to come to him. Then he gave *us* the power to expel evil spirits *that controlled people.* He also enabled *us* to heal all people who had diseases or who were sick. [2] The following men are the twelve *whom he called* apostles.[b] Simon—*to whom he gave the new name* Peter, Andrew—Peter's *younger* brother, James—the son of Zebedee, John—the *younger* brother of James, [3] Philip, Bartholomew, Thomas, *me*—Matthew, the tax collector, James—the *son* of Alpheus, Thaddeus, [4] Simon—a member of the party *that wanted to overthrow the Roman government,* and Judas Iscariot—who *later* enabled *the Jewish leaders* to seize Jesus.

[5] When Jesus was *about to* send *us* twelve *apostles to tell his message in various places,* he gave *us* these instructions: "Do not go where the non-Jews live or into the towns *where the* Samaritans live, *since they hate you.* [6] Instead, go to the people of Israel who have *gone away from God like* sheep that have gone away *from their shepherd* and have gotten lost. [7] When you go *to them,* proclaim to them that God will soon begin to rule over people. [8] Heal sick people, cause dead people to become alive, heal people who have leprosy, and cause demons to leave people *who are controlled by them.* Do not charge *for helping people because God* did not charge anything *for helping you.* [9-10] Do not take any money with you, nor a knapsack. Do not take *an extra* shirt, nor sandals *in addition to what you are wearing,* nor a walking stick. Every worker deserves to get pay *from the people for whom he works, so you deserve to receive food and a place to stay from the people to whom you go.* [11-12] In whatever town or village you enter, find out which person is worthy *that you should stay in his home.* And as you go into that house, *ask God to* bless the people *who live there.* Stay in that home until you leave *that town or village.* [13] If the people who live in that house are worthy *of being blessed, God* will bless them. If the people who live in that house are not worthy *of being blessed, God* will bless you *instead of them.* [14] If the people *who live in any house or town* do not welcome you *to their home or town,* nor listen to your message, leave that house or town. And as you leave, shake off the dust from your feet. *That will be a warning to them that God will punish them for rejecting your message.* [15] Note this carefully: *At the time when God* judges *all people, he* will punish *the people who lived in* Sodom and Gomorrah, *the ancient cities which God destroyed because their people were extremely wicked.* But God will punish **very** severely *the people in* any town *who refuse to hear your message.*"

Matthew 10:16-25

THEME: Jesus warned his disciples about their religious leaders, and he told them to endure when they were persecuted by men who refused to accept the new message.

[16] "Take note: After I send you out, *you will be as defenseless* as sheep in the midst of *people who are as dangerous as* wolves. You, *on your part, should* wisely *stay away from*

---

[b] The word 'apostles' means 'messengers'.

such people, as you stay away from poisonous snakes. You should be as harmless as doves are. [17] Also, I warn you about *their religious leaders*. They will arrest you and take you to the religious councils *to put you on trial and punish you because of your being my disciples*. You will be whipped *in* their meeting places. [18] *And* because *you teach* about me, you will be taken to governors and kings *to be put on trial and punished*. As a result, you will testify to those rulers and to *other* non-Jews *about what I have done*. [19] When *the religious leaders* arrest you, do not be worried about what you will say *to them*, because at that very time *the* Holy Spirit will tell you the words you should say. [20] It is not that you *will decide what to* say. Instead, you will say what the Spirit of your *heavenly* Father tells *you to say*. [21] *You will be taken* to the authorities to be killed *because of your faith in me. For example*, people will do that to their brothers, and fathers will do that to their children. Children will rebel against their parents and cause *them* to be killed. [22] Many people will hate you *because you believe in me*. Nevertheless, *many people* will keep on believing in me until they die. They are the people *God* will take to live with him. [23] When people in one town cause you to suffer, escape to another town *and tell the people there about me*. Note this: *You need to tell others about me now* because *I*, the one who came down from heaven, will certainly return *to earth* before you have finished going from one town to another town throughout Israel *and telling people about me*.

[24] "A disciple should not *expect to be* greater than his teacher, and servants *are not* superior to their master. [25] You do not *expect that* people will *treat* a disciple better than *they treat* his teacher, or that *they will treat* a servant *better than they treat* his master. *In the same way, since I am your teacher and master, you can expect that people will mistreat you, because they have mistreated me*. The most you can expect is that people *will treat you as they treat me. I am like* the ruler of a household. But people *have insulted me by* calling *me* Beelzebub, *the ruler of the demons*. So they *will* certainly *insult you more, you who are only like* members of my household!

Matthew 10:26-33

THEME: Jesus instructed his disciples not to fear those who would persecute them.

[26] "Do not be afraid of *people who insult you and do evil things to you. God wants* everything that is unknown now to be revealed. *He does* not *want his truth* to remain hidden and kept secret. [27] *So, instead of being afraid*, what I say to you *privately as people talk privately* at night, tell *publicly as people do* during the daytime. What I *say to you privately as people do when they* whisper to you, proclaim publicly. [28] Do not be afraid of people who *are able to* kill your body but are not able to destroy your soul. Instead, fear *God, because* he is able to destroy both a *person's* body and a *person's* soul in hell. [29] *Think about the* sparrows. *They have so little value* that *you* can buy two of them for *only* one small coin. But when *any* sparrow falls to the ground *and dies, God*, who is your *heavenly* Father, knows it, *because he knows everything*. [30] *He knows everything about you too*. He even knows how many hairs you have on your head! [31] *God* values **you** much more than he values sparrows. So do not be afraid *of people who threaten to kill you*!

[32] If people, *without being afraid, are willing to* tell others *that they are my disciples*, I will acknowledge before my Father who is in heaven *that they are my disciples*. [33] But if they are afraid to say in front of others that they are *my disciples*, I will tell my Father who is in heaven *that* they are not *my disciples*.

Matthew 10:34-39

THEME: Jesus instructed his disciples that they should be willing to suffer because of their faith in him.

[34] "Do not think that I came to earth to cause *people* to live together harmoniously. The result of my coming is that *some of those who follow me* will be killed. [35] Because I came *to earth, people who do not believe in me* will oppose *those who do believe in me. For example*, some sons will oppose their fathers, some daughters will oppose their mothers, and some daughters-in-law will oppose their mothers-in-law. [36] *This shows that sometimes* a person's enemies will be members of his own household. [37] Those who love their fathers or mothers more than *they love* me are not worthy *to have a relationship with me*. And those who love their sons or daughters more than *they love* me are not worthy *to belong to me.* [38] *Prisoners who are going to be executed are each forced to* carry a cross *to the place where they will be nailed to it.* Those who are not *willing to allow others to hurt and disgrace them like that because of being my disciple*s are not worthy to belong to me. [39] Those who *deny that they believe in me because they are afraid of being killed* will not live *with God eternally,* but those who *confess that they believe in* me and, *as a result are* killed, will live *with God eternally.*

Matthew 10:40-11:1

THEME: Jesus instructed his apostles about the people whom God rewards, and then he sent them to various towns.

[40] "*God,* the one who sent me, *considers that* everyone who welcomes you is welcoming me *at the same time*, and *he considers that* everyone who welcomes me welcomes *him.* [41] Those who welcome *someone because they know* that person is a prophet they will receive the *same* reward prophets *receive from God. Likewise*, those who welcome a person *because they know* that person is righteous they will receive the reward righteous people *receive from God.* [42] *Note this*: Suppose people *see that you are thirsty and* give you a drink of cold water because they know that you are one of my disciples. Those who do that will certainly be rewarded *by God. They might consider that what they did* is insignificant, *but God will consider it very significant.*"

11

[1] When Jesus had finished instructing *us* twelve disciples *what about what we should do, he sent us to various Israelite towns.* Then he went to teach and preach in *other Israelite* towns *in that area.*

Matthew 11:2-15

THEME: Jesus showed the messengers sent by John the Baptizer that he was the Messiah. Then he told the people that John was the man like Elijah who was to prepare the way for the Messiah.

[2] While John *the Baptizer* was in prison, he heard what *the man whom he thought was* the Messiah was doing. So he sent *some of* his disciples *to him* in order [3] to ask him, "Are **you** the *Messiah* who *the prophets prophesied* would come, or is it **someone else** that we should expect *to come*?" [4] *After they asked* Jesus *that question*, he answered them, "Go back and report to John what you hear *me telling people* and what you see *me doing.* [5] *I am enabling* blind people to see and lame people to walk. *I am* healing *people* who have leprosy. *I am enabling* deaf people to hear and dead people to become alive again.

I am telling poor people *God's* good message. ⁶ *Also, tell John that God* is pleased with those who do not stop believing in me *because what I do is not what they expected the Messiah to do."*

⁷ When John's disciples had gone away, Jesus began to talk to the crowd of people about John. He said to them, "*Think about* what sort of person you went to see in the desolate area *when you went there to see John. You did not go there to listen to a man who constantly changed his message, as* a reed that is blown by the wind *constantly* waves back and forth. ⁸ Then what *kind of person* did you go *there* to see? *Did you go there to see* a man who was dressed in expensive clothes? *No! You know very well that* people who wear beautiful clothes reside in kings' palaces, *not in desolate areas.* ⁹ Then what *kind of person* did you go to see? *Did you go there to see John because he was* a prophet? Yes! But I tell you that *John* is more *important* than an *ordinary* prophet. ¹⁰ **He** is the one about whom these words that God said to the Messiah have been written *in Scripture:*

Listen! I am going to send my messenger ahead of you to prepare *the people* for your coming.

¹¹ Note this: Of all the people who have ever lived, no one is greater *in God's estimation* than John the Baptizer. However, *God considers* all those who let God rule their lives to be greater than *John*, even if they are insignificant *people.* ¹² From the time John the Baptizer *preached* until now, people who have *allowed* God to rule their lives have been violently attacked and made to suffer.ᶜ Violent men have utterly exerted themselves to try to *rule the people over whom God rules.* ¹³ *All of what I am saying about John is confirmed by the fact that* the writers of Scripture foretold *about God ruling people's lives*, until John the Baptizer came. ¹⁴ *Even though most of you are unwilling to believe what I am saying, I will tell this truth to* anyone who is willing to believe *it:* John is *the man who is like* Elijah. He is the one who *one of the prophets said* would come *to prepare the people to welcome the Messiah.* ¹⁵ If you want to understand this, you must think *carefully about what I have just said."*

Matthew 11:16-19

THEME: Jesus rebuked the people who refused to believe both him and John the Baptizer.

¹⁶ "Let me describe *you* people who have heard what John *the Baptizer* and I have taught. You are like children who are *playing games* in an open area. *Some of the children* are calling to the others, saying, ¹⁷ 'We played *happy music* on the flute for you, but you did not dance! Then we sang sad funeral songs for you, but you did not cry!' ¹⁸ *In the same way, you are dissatisfied with both John and me!* When John came *and preached to you*, he did not eat *good food* or drink *wine, like most people do.* But you *rejected him* saying, 'A demon is controlling him!' ¹⁹ *In contrast, I,* the one who came from heaven, eat *the same* food and drink *wine as other people do.* But you *reject me*, saying, 'Look *at that man!* He eats too much food and drinks too much wine, and he associates with tax collectors and *other* sinners!' But those *who really think about* what *John* and I have done will realize that what we do *shows a lot of* wisdom.

ᶜ   OR, …people have very eagerly been asking God to take control of their lives.
   OR, …Jewish people who have thought I would become their king have been extremely
   eager to be included in my kingdom.

Matthew 11:20-24

THEME: Jesus explained why the people of Corazin, Bethsaida, and Capernaum would be punished more severely than the people of Tyre, Sidon, and Sodom.

[20] *The people who lived in* the towns *in the area where Jesus went saw him* perform many miracles. But they were not sorry that they had sinned, and they did not stop sinning. So Jesus began to reproach them *by saying to them,* [21] "You *people who live in the towns of* Chorazin and Bethsaida will suffer terribly *in hell*! *I* did great miracles among you, *but you did not turn from your sinful behavior.* If the miracles I did among you had been done in *the ancient cities of* Tyre and Sidon, the *wicked people who lived there* long ago would have sat in ashes, wearing coarse cloth *to show that they were sorry for their sins.* [22] So note this: *God will punish the wicked people who lived in the cities of* Tyre and Sidon, but he will punish you **even more** severely on the final day when he judges *all people.* [23] *I also have something to say to* you *people who live in the town of* Capernaum. Do not *think that* you will be honored in heaven! *No way! After you die, God* will send you down into the place where *sinful people* will be punished *forever! God destroyed the ancient city of* Sodom *because the people who lived in that city were extremely wicked.* If *I* had performed in *Sodom* the miracles I performed in your town, *the people there would have turned away from their wicked behavior and* their *city* would still be in existence today. But you, *although I did miracles in your town, did not turn from your wicked behavior.* [24] So note this: *God* will punish *the people who lived in the city of* Sodom, but he will punish you *even* more severely on the final day when *he* judges *all people.*"

Matthew 11:25-30

THEME: Jesus thanked God for revealing his truth to uneducated people, and he urged the people to come to him to get rid of the burden of trying to obey religious laws.

[25] At that time Jesus prayed, "Father, you rule over *everything in* heaven and *on* the earth. I thank you that you have prevented *people who think they* are wise *because of being* well educated from *knowing* these things. *Instead,* you have revealed them to *people who accept your truth as readily as* little children *do.* [26] Yes, Father, *you have done that* because it seemed good to you *to do* so."

[27] *Then Jesus said to the people there who wanted him to teach them,* "God, my Father, has revealed to me all the things *I need to know for my work.* Only my Father knows *who* I *really am.* Furthermore, only *I* and those *people* to whom I wish to reveal him know *what God* my Father *is like.* [28] Come to me, all you people who are very weary *of trying to obey all the many laws that your religious teachers tell you to obey.* I will enable you to quit *trying to obey all those laws.* [29-30] Let me *help* you *carry those loads, just as two oxen that have* a yoke *on their necks help each other pull a heavy load.* It will not be difficult for you to do the things I ask you to do for me. Since I am gentle and humble, accept what I teach *about what God wants you to do. And as a result, you will quit worrying about obeying all the religious laws, and* your spirits will be at peace."

12

Matthew 12:1-8

THEME: Jesus showed the religious leaders that the Scriptures indicated that God permitted some people to disobey religious laws when they needed food. He also showed that he had the authority from God to tell people what was right to do on the Sabbath.

¹ During that period of time, on a Jewish day of rest, Jesus *and we* disciples were walking through some grain fields. And because *we* were hungry, *we* began to pick some of the heads of grain and eat them. *The laws of Moses permitted people to do that if they were hungry.* ² Some Pharisees saw *us do what they considered to be work.* So they said to Jesus, *accusing him,* "Look! Your disciples are doing *work* that *our* laws do not permit *us* to do on our day of rest!" ³ *Jesus wanted to show them that the record in the Scriptures indicated that God permitted people to disobey certain religious laws when they needed food. So* he said to them, "*It is written in the Scriptures* what *our revered ancestor King* David did when he and the men with him were hungry. You have read about that, *but you do not think about what it implies!* ⁴ David entered *the courtyard of God's* tent *and asked for some food. The high priest gave him* the bread that had been presented *to God.* According to the laws *of Moses,* only priests were permitted to eat that bread, but David and the men who were with him ate it. *And God did not consider that what they did was wrong!* ⁵ Also, think about the laws *that Moses wrote.* He said that *even though* the priests, *by working* in the Temple on the Jewish day of rest, are not obeying *the laws about* the Jewish day of rest, they are not guilty. You have surely read that, *but you do not understand what it means.* ⁶ Note this: *God allows men to work in* the Temple *on our rest day because that work must be done. But in addition,* I tell you that *I have* more *authority than the authority of* the Temple. *So, it is more important for you to obey my teachings than to obey your traditions about our rest day.* ⁷ *You should think about* these words *of God in the Scriptures:* 'I want you to *act* mercifully toward people, and not *just* offer sacrifices.' If you understood what that means, you would not condemn *my disciples,* who have done no wrong. ⁸ And I want you to know that *I,* the one who came from heaven, have *the* authority *to determine what is right for my disciples to do on* the day of rest!"

Matthew 12:9-14

THEME: Jesus healed a man on the Sabbath. At the same time, he told the Pharisees that they were mistaken in thinking that it was wrong to heal a person on the Sabbath.

⁹ After Jesus left *there that day,* he went into a building *where we Jews* worship God. ¹⁰ *He saw* a man with a shriveled hand there. *Since the Pharisees thought that Jesus would be disobeying the tradition about not working on the day of rest if he healed the man, one of* them asked him, "Does *God* permit *us* to heal *people* on our rest day?" *They asked that question* so that they might accuse him *if he healed someone on the day of rest.* ¹¹ He replied to them, "Would anyone among you who has *only* one sheep that falls into a hole on the rest day *just leave it there? Certainly not!* You would take hold of it and lift it out right away, *and that would be acceptable work on our rest day, too!* ¹² *Since* sheep are valuable, *their owners may work on our rest day in order to rescue them. So, since* people are more valuable than sheep, it is certainly right for us to do something good *by healing another person any day, including our* day of rest!" ¹³ Then he said to the man, "Stretch out your hand!" The man stretched it out, and it became normal like the other hand! ¹⁴ Then the Pharisees left *the meeting house. They feared that the people would reject their traditions and would accept Jesus' teaching instead. So* they met together to plan how they could kill him.

Matthew 12:15-21

THEME: Jesus explained that his acting humbly when he healed people was a fulfillment of prophecy.

[15] Because Jesus knew *that the Pharisees were plotting to kill him,* he *took us disciples and* went away from there. Crowds, *including many sick people,* followed him, *wanting him to heal them,* and he healed them all. [16] But he told them firmly that they should not tell *other people yet* who he was. [17] *By acting humbly like that,* he fulfilled what Isaiah the prophet said *long ago about the Messiah. Isaiah wrote that God said*:

[18] Take note of my servant whom I have chosen, the one I love and in whom I am pleased. I will put my Spirit in him, and he will proclaim that the non-Jews will be judged justly. [19] He will not quarrel *with people,* neither will he shout. He will not *teach with* a loud voice in the *main* streets. [20] Until he has justly judged *the people who trust in him and* has declared them not guilty, he will not destroy *anyone who is as weak as* a smashed stalk, nor will he silence *anyone who is as helpless as* a smoldering *linen* wick. [21] As a result, the non-Jews will confidently expect *that he will do great things for them.*

Matthew 12:22-32

THEME: Jesus refuted the argument that he was expelling demons by Satan's power, and he warned that making such statements is an unforgivable sin against the Holy Spirit.

[22] *One day, while Jesus was in his house in Capernaum, some men* brought to *Jesus* a man *who, because of being* controlled by a demon, was blind and unable to speak. *Jesus* healed him *by expelling the demon.* As a result, the man *began to* talk and *was able to* see. [23] All the crowd *who saw it* marveled. They began asking *each other,* "Could this be the *Messiah, the* Descendant of *King* David*, whom we have been expecting*?" [24] Because the Pharisees *and the men who taught the Jewish laws* heard *that the people thought that Jesus might be the Messiah because he had cast out the demon,* they said, "*It is not God, but* Beelzebul, the ruler of the demons, who enables *this man* to expel demons *from people*!" [25] But Jesus knew what *the Pharisees* were thinking *and saying.* So, *in order to show them that what they said did not make sense,* he said to them, "If *the people in* one nation fight against each other, *they* will destroy their nation. If *people who live in* the same city or house fight each other, they will certainly not remain *as one group or family.* [26] *In the same way*, if Satan were expelling his own *demons, it would be as though* he was fighting against himself. His rule over them would *certainly* not last! [27] Furthermore, if *it is true that* Satan enables **me** to expel demons, is it also true that your disciples *who* expel demons *do so* by *Satan's* power? *No!* So they will show you that you *are not thinking logically.* [28] But since it is God's Spirit who *enables* me to expel demons, *you should recognize that* God has sent me to start to rule *over people's lives.*

[29] "*I will cite another example that illustrates why I am able to expel demons.* A person cannot go into the house of a strong man *like Satan* and carry off his possessions if he does not first bind the strong man. Then he will be able to steal *the things in that man's* house.

[30] "*No one can be neutral.* Those who do not acknowledge *that the Holy Spirit enables* me *to expel demons* are opposing me, and those who do not gather *people to become* my *disciples* are causing *those people* to go away *from me.*

[31] "You *are saying that it not the Holy Spirit who is enabling me to expel demons.* So I will say this to you: *If those who offend and slander other people in any way are then sorry and ask God to forgive them, God* will forgive them. But *God* will not forgive people who discredit what the Holy Spirit does. [32] *God is willing to* forgive people who criticize *me, the*

one who came from heaven. But *I warn you,* those who say evil things about what the Holy Spirit *does* will not be forgiven. *God* will not forgive them now, and he will never forgive them."

Matthew 12:33-37

THEME: Jesus said that we can judge what people are like by seeing what they do.

[33] "Think about this: You can know whether *a person is good and what that person says is good, in the same way that you* can know whether a tree and the fruit it produces are good. *You can also know whether a person and what that person says is evil, in the same way that you can know* whether a tree and its fruit are blighted. *People can know the evil character of you Pharisees by listening to your accusations against me.* [34] *What* you *teach harms people spiritually just like poisonous* snakes *harm them physically!* You are not able to speak good things because you are evil. Evil people *like you* speak what comes from all that is in their *hearts.* [35] Good people *speak good things. That is like* taking good things out of storehouses where they are stored. But evil people *speak evil things. That is like* taking evil things out of storehouses where they are stored. [36] I tell you that on the judgment day people will have to give an account to *God* for every useless word they have spoken, *and they will be judged accordingly.* [37] *God* will either declare you righteous based on the words you have spoken, or he will condemn you, based on what you have said."

Matthew 12:38-42

THEME: Jesus told the Jewish leaders that the only miracle they would see him do would be one like God did for Jonah.

[38] Then some of the Pharisees and men who taught the *Jewish* laws responded *to what Jesus was teaching* by saying to him, "Teacher, we want to see you *perform* a miracle *that would prove to us that God sent you.*" [39] Then Jesus said to them, "*You* people who *have already seen me perform miracles* are evil, and you do not faithfully worship God! You want *me to perform* a miracle *that would prove to you that God sent me*, but *God will enable* you to see only one miracle. It will be *like* what happened to Jonah the prophet. [40] Jonah was in the stomach of a huge fish for three days and nights *before God caused him to live again.* Similarly, for three days and nights I, the one who came from heaven, will be in a place *where dead people are, and then God will cause me to live again.* [41] When *God* judges *all people*, the people who lived in Nineveh will stand *before him* with *you* people who *have seen me perform miracles. The people of Nineveh* turned from their sinful ways as a result of *hearing what* Jonah preached. *Jonah was important, but I*, who am more important than Jonah, *have come and preached to you, but you haven't turned from your sinful ways. So* when *God* judges *all people, you* will be condemned. [42] The queen *from Sheba, south of Israel, who lived long ago,* traveled a long distance to hear *King* Solomon's wisdom. But now *I, a man* who *is much* greater *and wiser* than Solomon, am here, *but you haven't listened to what I have told you.* So at the time when *God* judges *all people,* the queen from *Sheba* will stand *before him, along* with you people, and she will condemn you."

Matthew 12:43-45

THEME: Jesus taught that those who have had evil spirits expelled from them need to have their lives controlled by the Holy Spirit.

[43] "*Sometimes* when an evil spirit leaves a person, it wanders around in desolate areas, seeking *someone in whom it can* rest. If it does not find anyone, [44] it says *to itself*, 'I will return to the person in whom I used to live.' So it goes back *and finds that the Spirit of*

God is not in control of that person's *life. The person's life is like* a house that has been swept clean and everything put in order, *but it is* empty. ⁴⁵ Then *this evil spirit* goes and gets seven other spirits that are *even* more evil, and they *all* enter *that person* and *start* living there. *So, although* that person's condition *was bad* before, it becomes much worse. That is what *you* wicked people who *have heard me teach* will experience."

Matthew 12:46-50

THEME: Jesus said that those who do God's will are as important to Jesus as his own relatives are.

⁴⁶ While Jesus was still speaking to the crowds, his mother and his brothers *arrived.* They stood outside *the house*, wanting to speak with him. ⁴⁷ Someone said to him, "Your mother and your *younger* brothers are standing outside *the house*, wanting to talk to you." ⁴⁸ Then Jesus said to the person who told him *that, "I will tell you something about* those *I consider to be like* my mother and my brothers." ⁴⁹ He then pointed toward *us* disciples and said, "These are people whom *I love as much as I love* my mother and my brothers. ⁵⁰ Those who do what *God* my Father *who is* in heaven wants are *as dear to me as* my brother, my sister, or my mother."

13

Matthew 13:1-9

THEME: Jesus taught a parable about different kinds of soil.

¹ That same day, Jesus along *with us* disciples left the house *where he was teaching and went* to Lake *Galilee.* He sat down there, ² and a very large crowd gathered around him to *listen to his teaching. So, in order to not be crowded by the people,* he got into a boat and sat down *to teach them.* The crowd stood on the shore *and was listening.* ³ He was telling them many parables. *One of the parables* he told them was this: "Listen! A man went out *to his field* to sow *some seeds.* ⁴ As he was scattering *them over the soil,* some *of the* seeds fell on the path. Then some birds came and ate those seeds. ⁵ Other *seeds* fell on ground where there was not much soil *on top of the* rock. Those seeds sprouted very soon, *because the sun quickly warmed* the shallow *moist* soil. ⁶ But when *the young plants came up, the soil dried quickly and* the plants were scorched by the sun. They withered because they did not have *deep* roots. ⁷ Other seeds fell on *ground that contained roots of* thorny *weeds.* The thorny *weeds* grew *together with the young plants,* and *they* crowded out *the plants.* ⁸ *But* other seeds fell on good soil, and *the plants grew and* produced *a lot of* grain. Some *plants produced* one hundred times *as many seeds as were planted.* Some *plants produced* sixty times *as much.* Some *plants produced* thirty times *as much.* ⁹ If you want to understand this, you should consider *carefully what I have just said.*"

Matthew 13:10-17

THEME: Jesus told the disciples why he taught them using parables.

¹⁰ *We* disciples approached Jesus and said to him, "Why do you use **parables** when you speak to the crowd?" ¹¹ He answered *us* by saying, "God is revealing to you what he did not reveal before, about *how he wants to* rule *over peoples' lives.* But he has not revealed it to others. ¹² Those who *think about what I say and* understand *it,* God will enable them to understand more. But those who do not *think carefully about what I say* will forget even what they already know. ¹³ That is why I use parables when I speak to people, because

although they see *what I do*, they do not perceive *what it means*, and although they hear *what I say*, they do not really understand *what it means*. [14] What these people do completely fulfills what *God told* the prophet Isaiah *to say long ago to the people who did not try to understand what he said,*

> You will hear *what I say*, but you will not understand it. You will keep seeing *what I do*, but you will not understand *its significance*.

[15] *God also said to Isaiah,*

> These people have become unresponsive *to what they see me do and to what they hear me say*. They listen unwillingly *to what I say*, and they do not observe *what I do*. If it were not so, they would perceive *what I am doing*, they would understand *what I say to them*, and they would turn *away from their sinful lives* and turn *to me,* and I would save them *from being punished for their sins*.

[16] But as for **you**, God is pleased with you because you have seen *the things I have done* and because you understand *what I say*. [17] Note this: Many prophets and righteous people *who lived long ago* longed to see what you are seeing *me do*, but they did not see it. They longed to hear the things you have been hearing *me say*, but they did not hear them."

Matthew 13:18-23

THEME: Jesus explained that the parable about the kinds of soil illustrates four different ways people respond to his teaching.

[18] "*Since God wants* **you** *to understand my teaching,* listen as I *explain* the parable about the man who sowed *seeds in various kinds of soil.* [19] The people who hear about how God rules over people's lives and do not understand *what they have heard* are *like* the path where *some of* the seeds fell. *Satan*, the Evil One, comes and causes these people to forget what they have heard. [20] *Some people are like the* shallow soil on top of rock. When they hear God's message, they **immediately** accept it with joy. [21] *But because it does not penetrate deeply into their hearts, they* believe it for *only* a *short* time. *They are like the plants that* did not have *deep* roots. When they are treated badly and caused to suffer *because of their allegiance to me,* they soon stop believing my message. [22] *Some people are like the soil that had the roots of* thorny *weeds* in it. They hear God's message, but they desire to be rich, *so they* worry *only* about material things. As a result, they forget *God's* message and they do not do the things that God wants them to do. [23] But *some people are like the* good soil where *some of the seeds* fell. *Just as the plants that grew in this soil* produced a lot of grain, *these people* hear my message and understand it. *Some of them* do many things *that please God, some do* even more *things that please God, and some do* very many *things that please God*."

Matthew 13:24-30

THEME: Jesus told a parable about wheat and weeds.

[24] Jesus also told the crowd a parable, *by which he tried to explain that although* God is a king, *he will not immediately judge and punish all the wicked people.* Jesus said, "*God* is like a landowner *who sent his servants* to sow good *wheat* seed in his field. [25] While those servants were sleeping *and not watching the field*, an enemy of the landowner came and scattered weed *seeds* in the midst of the wheat. Then he left. [26] After *the seeds* sprouted and the green plants *grew*, the heads of grain began to form. But the weeds also grew. [27] So the servants of the landowner came and said to him, 'Sir, you *gave us good seeds and those are the ones we planted* in your field. So where did the weeds come from?' [28] The landowner said to them, '*My* enemy did this.' His servants said to him, 'So, do you wish us to pull up *the weeds and* put them in a pile?' [29] He said *to them,* 'No, *do not do*

that, because you might pull up *some of* the wheat at the same time. [30] Let the wheat and the weeds grow together until harvest *time*. At that time I will say to the reapers, 'First gather the weeds, and tie them into bundles to be burned. Then gather the wheat *and put it* into my barns.'"

Matthew 13:31-33

THEME: Jesus illustrated the effects of people letting God rule their lives.

[31] Jesus also told this parable: "The *number of people over whose* lives God rules *will continue to grow.*[d] *It is very much* like the way mustard seeds grow after a man plants them in his field. [32] Although mustard seeds are among the smallest of all the seeds *that people plant, here in Israel* they become large plants. When the plants have fully grown, they are larger than the other garden plants. They become shrubs that are large enough for the birds to build nests in their branches."

[33] Jesus also told this parable: "*The way people who let* God rule their lives *can influence the world* is like yeast that a woman mixed with about fifty pounds of flour. *That small amount of yeast made* the whole batch of dough swell up."

Matthew 13:34-35

THEME: Jesus' use of parables fulfilled a prophecy in Scripture.

[34] Jesus told the crowd parables *to teach them* all these things. In speaking to them he habitually used such illustrations. [35] By doing that, *Jesus* fulfilled what *God told one of* the prophets to write *long ago,*
     I will speak in parables; I will tell *parables to teach* what I have kept secret since
     I created the world.

Matthew 13:36-43

THEME: Jesus explained the parable about wheat and weeds. The wheat represents those who obey God, and the weeds represent those who disobey God. The reaping represents judgment.

[36] After Jesus dismissed the crowds, he went into the house. Then *we* disciples approached him and said, "Explain to us the parable about the weeds *that grew* in the wheat field." [37] He answered, "The one who sows the good seed represents *me*, the one who came down from heaven. [38] The field represents the world, *where people live.* The seeds *that grew* well represent the people who let God rule their lives. The weeds represent the people who do what *the devil*, the Evil One, *tells them to do.* [39] The enemy who sowed the weed seeds represents the devil. The *time when the grain will be* harvested represents the time when the world will end. The reapers represent the angels. [40] The weeds are gathered and burned. That represents *the judging of people, which God will do* at the end of the world. *It will be like this:* [41] I, the one who came down from heaven, will send my angels and they will gather *from everywhere the people* who cause others to quit believing in me, and all those who disobey *God's* commands. [42] They will throw those people into the fires of *hell.* There they will weep and grind their teeth *because of the great pain they are suffering.* [43] *But God's* brightness will shine *on* the people who have conducted their lives as he wanted them to. It will shine *on them as brightly* as the sun *shines.* It will shine on them in the place where *God*, their Father, rules over them. If you want to understand this, you need to think *carefully* about what I have just said."

---

d   OR, …*God's influence in the lives of people* whose lives he rules over *will continue to increase.*

Matthew 13:44-50

THEME: Jesus illustrated the value of letting God rule our lives.

[44] "*What people do who begin to allow* God to rule over their lives is like *what a certain man did to acquire a treasure. He found* a treasure buried in a field, and then hid it *by burying it again in order that no one else would find it*. Being very happy *to have found something so valuable, he went and* sold all his possessions *to obtain money to buy the field the treasure was in*. He then went and bought the field, *and so he was able to acquire that treasure*.

[45] "Also, what *people do who begin to allow* God to rule over their lives is like *what* a merchant *did who was* looking for good quality pearls *to buy*. [46] When he found one very costly pearl *which was for sale*, he sold all his possessions *to acquire enough money to buy that pearl*. Then he *went and* bought it.

[47] "What God *will do to people who falsely say they are letting him* rule their lives is like what certain *fishermen* did *with the fish they caught* in a lake, using a large net. They caught all classes *of fish, both edible fish and worthless ones*. [48] When the net was full, the *fishermen* pulled it up onto the shore. Then they sat there and put the edible *fish* into buckets, and threw the worthless ones away. [49] *What they did in separating the good fish from the bad ones* is like *what will happen to people* when the world ends. The angels will come *to where God is judging people* and will separate the wicked *people* from the righteous *ones*. [50] They will throw the wicked people into the fire *in hell*. And those people will weep and gnash their teeth *because of the intense pain they are suffering*."

Matthew 13:51-52

THEME: Jesus illustrated the value of understanding his parables.

[51] *Then Jesus asked us*, "Do you understand all these *parables I have told you*?" We said to him, [52] "Yes, *we understand them*." Then he said to us, "Because *you understand all these parables, you will understand the following parable: You, along with* all the other *people who trust in me,* will teach people what *you heard me say* about God's rule over people's lives. *You will add that to what you formerly learned. You will be* like a head of a household who takes both new things and old things out of his storage room."

Matthew 13:53-58

THEME: Jesus did not do many miracles in Nazareth because they rejected him as the Messiah.

[53] When Jesus had finished *telling* these parables, he took *us* and left that *area*. [54] We went to *Nazareth*, his home town. *On the Jewish day of rest* he began to teach the people in the synagogue. The result was that the people there were astonished. But *some* said, "*This man is just an ordinary person like us! So* how is it that he knows so much and understands so much? And how is it that he is able to do *such* miracles? [55] He is *just* the son of the carpenter *that lived here!* His mother is Mary, and his *younger* brothers are James, Joseph, Simon and Judas! And his sisters *also live* here in our *town*. So how is he able to do all these *miracles*?" [57] The people were unable to accept *the idea that* he *was the Messiah. So* Jesus said to them, "*People* honor *me and other* prophets *everywhere else we go,* but in *our* home towns *we're* not *honored*, and *even* our own families do not honor us!" [58] And Jesus did not perform many miracles there because the people did not believe *that he was the Messiah*.

14

Matthew 14:1-13a

THEME: Herod had John the Baptizer imprisoned and then killed because John criticized Herod for marrying his brother's wife.

[1] During that time Herod *Antipas*, the ruler, heard reports about Jesus *performing miracles.* [2] He said to his servants: "That must be John the Baptizer. He must have risen from the dead, and that's why he has power to perform miracles." [3-4] The reason *Herod had these thoughts about John was this: Herod had married* Herodias, the wife of his brother Philip, *while Philip was still living. So* John had been saying to him, "*What* you *did by* marrying *your brother's wife while your brother is still alive* is against *God's* law!" Then, to *please* Herodias, Herod *told his soldiers* to arrest John. They bound him with chains and put him in prison. [5] Herod wanted to kill John, but he was afraid that the people *who had accepted John's teaching would riot if he did that*, because they believed John was a prophet.

[6] But when Herod *gave a party to celebrate* his birthday, the daughter of Herodias danced for *his guests*. This pleased Herod. [7] So he promised to give her whatever she asked for, and he asked God to punish him if he did not do what he had promised. [8] *So Herodias' daughter went and asked her mother what to ask for*. Her mother told her to ask for John the Baptizer's head. *So* her daughter *went back and* said *to Herod*: "*Cut off* the head of John the Baptizer and *please* bring it here on a platter *so my mother can know for sure he is dead*!" [9] The king was distressed *because he knew it would be very wrong for him to do that. But* because he had taken an oath *in front of* his guests *when he made that promise*, and *he did not want* them *to think that he would break his promise*, he commanded that *the girl* be given *what she requested*. [10] He sent *the executioner to go to* the prison and cut off John's head. [11] *The executioner did that, and* put John's head on a platter and gave it to the girl. Then the girl took it to her mother. [12] John's disciples then went *to the prison*, took John's body and buried it, and they reported to Jesus *what had happened*. [13] After Jesus heard that, he took *just us disciples* with him and *we* went by boat *on Lake Galilee* to an uninhabited place.

Matthew 14:13b-21

THEME: Jesus miraculously fed more than 5000 people.

After the crowds heard *that we had gone to an uninhabited place*, they *left their towns and* followed on foot. [14] When Jesus came *to the shore,* he saw a large crowd of people *who had gathered there, waiting for him*. He felt sorry for them, and he healed those *among them who were* sick.

[15] When it was *nearly* evening, we disciples came to him and said, "This is a place where nobody lives, and it is very late. Dismiss the crowds so they can go into the *nearby* towns. *Have them do that so they can* buy food for themselves." [16] But Jesus said *to us*, "They do not need to leave *to get food. Instead*, you *yourselves* give them something to eat!" [17] *We* said to him, "But we have only five loaves of bread and two *cooked* fish here!" [18] He said *to us*, "Bring them to me!" [19] He told the people *who were gathered there* to sit on the grass. Then he took the five flat loaves and the two fish. He looked up toward heaven, thanked *God for them,* and broke *them into pieces*. Then he gave them to *us* disciples, and *we* distributed them to the crowd. [20] All *the people in the crowd* ate until they had enough to eat. Then we *disciples* gathered the pieces that were left over, *and we* filled twelve baskets with them! [21] Those that ate were about five thousand men. *We did* not count *the* women and children!

Matthew 14:22-33

THEME: Jesus walked on Lake Galilee, and then Peter tried to do the same.

²² Right after that happened, Jesus ordered *us* disciples to get in the boat and to go ahead of him further around *the lake* while he dismissed the crowds. ²³ After he dismissed them, he went up into the hills to pray by himself. When it was evening, he was *still* there alone. ²⁴ *By this time we* were already many hundred meters from the shore. The boat was being severely tossed by the waves because the wind was *blowing* against *it*. ²⁵ *Then Jesus came down from the hill to the lake.* Some time between three and six in the morning he walked on the water toward our *boat*. ²⁶ When we disciples saw him walking on the water, we thought that he must be a ghost. We were terrified, and we screamed out in fear. ²⁷ Immediately Jesus said to us, "Hang in there! It is I! Do not be afraid!" ²⁸ Peter said to him, "Lord, if it is you, tell me to walk on the water to you!" ²⁹ Jesus said, "Come!" So Peter got out of the boat. He walked on the water toward Jesus. ³⁰ But when he saw the *waves being tossed* by the strong wind, he became afraid. He began to sink, and cried out, "Lord, save me!" ³¹ Immediately Jesus stretched out his hand and grabbed him. He said to Peter, "You only trust a little bit *in my power*! Why did you doubt *me and start sinking*?" ³² Then Jesus and Peter got in the boat, and the wind *immediately* stopped blowing. ³³ All of us disciples who were in the boat worshipped Jesus and said, "Truly you are the Son of God!"

Matthew 14:34-36

THEME: Jesus healed many sick people in the region of Genessaret.

³⁴ When we had gone further around *the lake in the boat*, we came to the shore at *the town of* Gennesaret. ³⁵ The men of that area recognized Jesus. So they sent *people to inform those who lived* in that whole surrounding region *that Jesus was in their area. So the people* brought to Jesus all the sick people *who lived in that region*. ³⁶ *The sick people* kept begging him to allow them to touch *him or* just to touch the tassel of his robe *so that they would be healed*. And all who touched *him or his robe* were healed.

15

Matthew 15:1-9

THEME: Jesus rebuked the religious leaders for ignoring God's commands in order to uphold their own religious traditions.

¹ Then *some* Pharisees and men who taught the *Jewish* laws came from *the city of* Jerusalem *to talk to* Jesus. They said, ² "We think it is disgusting that your disciples disobey the traditions of our ancestors! They do not perform the proper ritual of washing their hands before they eat!" ³ Jesus answered them, "What is really disgusting is that **you** refuse to obey God's commands *just* so you can follow your own traditions. ⁴ God gave these *two* commands: 'Honor your father and your mother,' and 'Anyone who speaks evil about his father or mother must be executed.' ⁵ But **you** tell people, 'You can say to your father or mother, "What I was going to give to you *to help provide for you*, I have now *promised* to give *to God*." ⁶ And if you do that, you think you do not need to give anything to your parents. In *this way*, *by teaching people* your traditions, you disregard what God commanded. ⁷ You only pretend to be good! Isaiah prophesied accurately about you *also when he quoted what God said about your ancestors. God said,* ⁸ 'These people talk *as if*

they honor me, but their hearts are not in it at all. [9] It is useless for them to worship me, because they teach what people thought up *as if I myself had commanded it.*'"

Matthew 15:10-11

THEME: Jesus said that people are defiled by the words that come out of their mouths, rather than by any kind of food that they eat.

[10] Then Jesus *again* summoned the crowd to come *nearer* to him. Then he said to them, "Listen to *what I am about to tell you,* and *try to* understand. [11] Nothing that a person puts into his mouth *to eat* causes *God to consider* that person to be unacceptable. Instead, it is *the words* that come" out of people's mouths that cause *God to reject them.*"

Matthew 15:12-20

THEME: Jesus explained that people's inner thoughts are what make them unacceptable to God.

[12] Later we disciples went to Jesus and said, "Do you know that the Pharisees heard what you said, and they felt offended?" [13] Then, *to teach us what God would do to the Pharisees*, Jesus told *us this parable*: "My Father in heaven *will get rid of* all *those who teach things that are not in line with his truth, just as a farmer* gets rid of plants he did not plant by pulling them up along with their roots. [14] Do not pay any attention to *the Pharisees*. They *do not help people who do not know God's truth* to *understand it, just as* blind guides *do not help* blind *people to perceive where they should go.* If a blind person *tries to* lead *another* blind person, they will both fall into a hole. *Similarly, both the Pharisees and their disciples will end up in hell.*"

[15] Peter said to Jesus, "Explain to us the parable *about what a person eats.*" [16] He said *to them*, "I am disappointed that even **you,** *who should understand what I teach*, **still** do not understand! [17] You ought to understand that all *the food that people* eat enters their stomachs, and later the refuse passes out *of their bodies. Because food does not alter what we think and desire, what we eat does not cause God to consider us unacceptable to him.* [18] *You should know that* what comes out of *people's* mouths, *meaning everything that they say*, comes from their hearts. Many of the *things they say* cause *God to consider* them as unacceptable *to him.* [19] It is people's innermost beings that *cause them* to think things that are evil, to commit murder, to *commit* adultery, to commit other sexual sins, to steal, to testify falsely, and to speak evil about *others.* [20] It is these things that cause *God to consider* people as unacceptable *to him.* To eat with unwashed hands does not cause *God to consider* people unacceptable."

Matthew 15:21-28

THEME: Jesus healed a non-Jewish woman's daughter after testing the mother's faith in him.

[21] After Jesus *took us and* left *the district of* Galilee, we went into the region *where the cities of* Tyre and Sidon *are located.* [22] A woman *from the group of people called* Canaanites who live in that region came *to the place Jesus was staying.* She kept shouting *to him*, "Lord, you are the descendant of *King* David, *you are the Messiah*! Have pity on me *and my daughter*! She is suffering very much because a demon controls her." [23] But Jesus did not answer her at all. *We* disciples came to him, and *knowing that the woman was not a Jew,* we said to him, "Tell her to leave, because she keeps *bothering us* by yelling behind us!" [24] But Jesus said *to her*, "I have been sent to *help* only the Israelite people *at this time. They are like* sheep that have gotten lost, *because they do not know the way to heaven.*" [25] But she came *closer* to Jesus and knelt down in front of him *to*

worship him. She pled, "Lord, help me!" [26] Then, *to suggest to her that he needed to help the Jews first and not the non-Jews, whom the Jews called dogs,* he told her, "It is not good *for someone* to take food *that has been prepared for* the children and throw it to the *little* dogs." [27] *But to show that she believed that non-Jews could also receive help from God*, she said *to Jesus*, "Sir, *what you say is* correct, but even the *little* dogs eat the crumbs that fall to the floor *when* their masters *sit at* their tables *and eat!*" [28] Then Jesus said to her, "O woman, *because* you believe firmly *in me, I* will *heal your daughter* as you desire!" At that moment *the demon left* her daughter, *and she* was healed.

Matthew 15:29-31

THEME: Jesus healed many people on a hillside near Lake Galilee.

[29] After Jesus, along *with us disciples,* departed from that area, we went *back* to Lake Galilee *and walked* along it. Then Jesus climbed the hill *near there* and sat down *to teach the people.* [30] Crowds came and brought to him lame, crippled, blind people, those who were unable to talk, and many others *who had various sicknesses.* They laid them in front of Jesus *so that he would heal them.* And he healed them. [31] The crowd saw *him heal* people who couldn't talk, crippled people, lame people, and blind people, and they were amazed. They said, "Praise God *who rules over us who live in* Israel!"

Matthew 15:32-39

THEME: Jesus miraculously fed over 4,000 people.

[32] A couple of days later, Jesus called us disciples to him and said *to us*, "This crowd *of people* has been with me for three days and have nothing *left* to eat. I feel sorry for them. I do not want to send them away *while they are still* hungry, because they might faint on the way *home.*" [33] We disciples said to him, "In this place where nobody lives we can't possibly obtain enough food to feed such a large crowd!" [34] Jesus asked us, "How many small loaves do you have?" We said to him, "*We have* seven small loaves and a few small fish." [35] He told the people to sit on the ground. [36] Then he took the seven small loaves and the fish. After he thanked *God for them*, he broke them *into pieces* and he kept giving *them* to us. Then we *kept distributing* them to the crowd. [37-38] *Because Jesus made the food multiply miraculously*, all *those people* ate and had *plenty to* satisfy *them.* There were four thousand men *who ate*, but no *one counted* the women and the children *who also ate.* Then we *disciples* collected the pieces of food that were left over, and we filled seven large baskets *with them.*

[39] After Jesus dismissed the crowd he, *along with us,* got in the boat, and we sailed *around the lake* to the region called Magadan.

16

Matthew 16:1-4

THEME: Jesus again told the religious leaders that the only miracle he would do for them was one like God did for Jonah.

[1] *Some* Pharisees and Sadducees came to *Jesus* and asked him *to perform* a miracle that would prove *that* God *had sent him.* [2] He answered them, "*In this country*, in the evening you say, '*It will be* nice weather *tomorrow*, because the sky is red.' [3] *Early* in the morning *you say*, 'It will be stormy weather today, because the sky is red, and dark clouds have

formed.' You understand how to predict *the weather by looking at the sky*, but you can't *seem to look at what is happening* now *and by that* understand *what God is doing.* ⁴ *You* evil people have seen me *perform miracles* but you do not faithfully worship God. You want to see *me perform* a miracle *that would prove that God has sent me*. But *God* will *enable you to see* only one miracle. It will be *like* what happened to Jonah, *the prophet, who was inside a huge fish for three days and then came out of it to live again*." Then Jesus left them and sailed away, *along with us disciples.*

Matthew 16:5-12

THEME: Jesus rebuked the disciples for worrying about not having enough food.

⁵ *We* forgot to take bread when *we* sailed to another edge of *the lake.* ⁶ *Then* Jesus said to us, "Beware *that you do not accept* the yeast that the Pharisees and Sadducees *distribute.*" ⁷ Then, *not realizing that he was speaking figuratively*, we said to one another, "*He must have said that* because we forgot to bring any bread!" ⁸ Because Jesus knew what *we were saying*, he said *to us*, "I am disappointed that you are discussing among yourselves, *thinking* that *it was because* you did not bring any bread *that I talked about the yeast of the Pharisees and Sadducees.* You believe only a little *what I am able to do for you.* ⁹ Do you not yet understand *that I can provide miraculously for you if you need food*? Do you not remember that five thousand *people ate when I multiplied the* five small loaves *and the two fish? And after everyone had enough to eat,* you collected *twelve* baskets *of leftover pieces!* ¹⁰ *Do you not remember that* four thousand *people ate when I multiplied the* seven small loaves *and a few fish?* And *after everyone had enough to eat,* you collected *seven* large baskets *of leftover pieces!* ¹¹ You should have understood that I was not speaking about *real* bread *that contains yeast*. What *I was saying* was that you should *not accept what* the Pharisees and Sadducees *say, because it would affect you like* yeast *affects dough.*" ¹² Then we understood that he was not talking about the yeast that is *in* bread. Instead, *he was talking* about the *wrong* teaching of the Pharisees and Sadducees.

Matthew 16:13-20

THEME: Jesus commented on the implications of Peter's recognition of Jesus being the Messiah.

¹³ When Jesus came with *us* disciples to the region near *the town of* Caesarea Philippi, he asked us, "Who do people say that I, the one who came from heaven, *really* am?" ¹⁴ We answered, "Some *people* say *you are* John the Baptizer, *who has come back to life again*. Others say *you are the prophet* Elijah, *who has returned from heaven as God promised. Still* others *say that you are the prophet* Jeremiah or one of the *other* prophets *who lived long ago, who have come back to life again.*" ¹⁵ Jesus said to us, "*What about* **you**? Who do you say that I am?" ¹⁶ Simon Peter said to him, "**You** are the Messiah! You are the Son of the all-powerful God." ¹⁷ Then Jesus said to him, "Simon, son of Jonah, *God* is pleased with you. What you just said was not revealed to you by any human. Instead, *it was* my Father, *who lives* in heaven, *who revealed this to you.* ¹⁸ I will **also** tell you this: You are Peter, *which means rock. You are like* a rock. The teaching that you *and your fellow apostles give will be like a foundation on which*[e] I will create congregations of people who *believe in* me. And the demons *who live* where the dead people, people who lived evil lives, now live will not be able to *come and* prevent *me from doing* that." ¹⁹ Then, *saying to Peter what he later told all of us*, "I will enable you to have authority over the groups of people over whose lives *God* rules. Whatever you forbid regarding those people, it will

---

[e] OR, ...Because of what you do...

have been forbidden by God. Whatever you permit regarding them, it will have been permitted by God." ²⁰ Then Jesus warned *us* disciples strongly not to tell anyone *at that time* that he was the Messiah.

Matthew 16:21-23

THEME: Jesus began to teach the disciples about his coming death and resurrection.

²¹ From that time Jesus began to teach *us* disciples that it was necessary for him to go to *the city of* Jerusalem. *He said that* there the ruling elders, the chief priests and the men who taught the *Jewish* laws would cause him to suffer and be killed. Then on the third day *after that* he would become alive again. ²² *Because Peter assumed that the Messiah would not suffer and die*, he took Jesus aside and began to rebuke him *for talking about suffering and dying.* He said, "Lord, may *God* never permit that to happen to you! That must certainly not happen!" ²³ Then Jesus turned *to look at* Peter, and he said to him, "Stop talking to me *like that*! *Stop saying what* Satan *would say, and stop* trying to prevent *from happening what God has planned*! You are a hindrance to me, because you are not thinking like God thinks. Instead, *you are thinking* like people *think*!"

Matthew 16:24-28

THEME: Jesus taught the disciples more about what they would face as his disciples, and about his coming again.

²⁴ Then Jesus said to *us* disciples, "If any one *of you* wants to be my disciple, you must not do *only* what you yourself desire *to do. You* must be willing to *let people hurt you and disgrace you. That is like what is done to criminals who are forced to* carry a cross *to the place where they will be crucified. That is what anyone who wants to* be my disciple *must do.* ²⁵ *You must do that*, because those who try to save their lives *by denying they belong to me when people want to kill them for believing in me* will not live *eternally*, but those who are killed *because of being my disciples* will live *with God eternally*. ²⁶ People *might* get everything *they want* in this world, but *if they do not become my disciples,* they would really be gaining nothing, *because* they would not get eternal life! There is absolutely nothing that people can give *to God* that would enable them to gain eternal life. ²⁷ *Listen carefully: I*, the one who came from heaven, *will leave this earth, but I* am going to return, with the angels of heaven accompanying me. At that time I will have the glorious radiance that my Father has, and I will reward everyone according to what they did *when they were living on earth*. ²⁸ Listen carefully! Some of you who are here now will see *me*, the one who came from heaven, when I return to rule. You will see this before you die!"

17

Matthew 17:1-8

THEME: Jesus' appearance changed while Moses and Elijah talked with him on a mountain.

¹ A week after Jesus *said that*, he took Peter, James, and John, the *younger* brother of James, and led them up a high mountain where they were away from other people. ² *While they were there, the three disciples* saw that Jesus' appearance was changed. His face shone like the sun, and his clothing *shone and* became as brilliant as light. ³ Suddenly Moses and Elijah, *who were important prophets long ago*, appeared and started talking with him. ⁴ Peter *saw them and* said to Jesus, "Lord, it is wonderful for us to be here! If you want *me to*, I will make three shelters, one for you, one for Moses, and one for Elijah."

[5] While Peter was speaking, a bright cloud *appeared and* covered them. *They heard God* speaking *about Jesus from* inside the cloud. He said *to them,* "This is my Son. *I* love him. He pleases me very much. *So* you must listen to him!" [6] When the three disciples heard *God speaking,* they were exceedingly afraid. *As a result,* they prostrated themselves on the ground. [7] Jesus went to them and touched them *and* said *to them,* "Stand up! Stop being afraid!" [8] And when they looked up, they saw that Jesus was the only one *still there.*

Matthew 17:9-13

THEME: Jesus explained that John the Baptizer fulfilled the prophecy about Elijah returning.

[9] When they were walking down the mountain, Jesus commanded them, "Do not tell anyone what you saw *on the mountain top* until *God has caused me,* the one who has come from heaven, to become alive again after I die." [10] *Since those three disciples had just seen Elijah and he did not do anything to prepare people for the coming of the Messiah,* they asked Jesus, "If *what you say is true,* why do the men who teach the *Jewish* laws say that it is necessary for Elijah to come *back to earth* before *the Messiah comes*?" [11] Jesus answered *them,* "It is true that *God promised that* Elijah would come to prepare all *the people for the Messiah's coming.* [12] But note this: Elijah's *representative* has already come *and our leaders have seen him,* but they did not recognize him *as the one who would come before the Messiah.* Instead, they treated him *badly,* just as they desired. And those same rulers will soon treat *me,* the one who came from heaven, in the same manner." [13] Then the three disciples understood that he was referring to John the Baptizer *when he was talking about Elijah.*

Matthew 17:14-20

THEME: Jesus healed an epileptic boy, and he rebuked his disciples for not having enough faith to do miracles.

[14] When *Jesus and the three disciples* returned to the *rest of us disciples* and to the crowd *that had gathered,* a man approached Jesus and knelt before him. [15] He said *to him,* "Sir, have mercy on my son and *heal him!* He has epilepsy and suffers very much. *Because of this illness,* he has fallen in the fire and in the water many times. [16] I brought him to your disciples *so they might heal him,* but they were not able to." [17] Jesus responded *by saying to everyone who had gathered there,* "You who have seen how I help people do not believe *that you can do anything! Your minds* are distorted. How long do I have to be with you *before you* are *able to do what I do*? How long *do* I have to endure your *lack of faith*? Bring the boy here to me!" [18] When *they brought him to Jesus,* Jesus rebuked the demon *that was causing the epilepsy. As a consequence,* the demon came out of the boy, and the boy was healed from that time onward. [19] *Later, some of us* disciples approached Jesus. We asked him privately, "Why were **we** not able to expel the demon?" [20] He answered us, "It is because you did not believe very much *in God's power.* Keep this in mind: Mustard seeds *are very small, but in this area they grow and produce large plants. In the same way,* if your faith grows until you truly believe *that God will do what you ask him to,* you will be able to do anything! You *could even* say to this hill, 'Move from here to there!' and it would go *where you told it to go.*"[f]

---

[f] Some Greek manuscripts add v. 21, "But this kind of demon will leave only if you have first prayed and fasted."

Matthew 17:22-23

THEME: Jesus again predicted his death and resurrection.

[22] When *we disciples* had gathered together in *the district of* Galilee, Jesus said to us, "*I, the one who came from heaven to earth,* will soon be handed over to the authorities. [23] They will kill me. But *God* will cause me to become alive again on the third day after I am killed." *When we heard that*, we became very sad.

Matthew 17:24-27

THEME: Jesus arranged for a miracle so Peter could pay the temple tax.

[24] When we came to Capernaum, the men who collect taxes *for the Temple* approached Peter and said to *him*, "Your teacher pays the *Temple* tax, does he not?" [25] He answered *them*, "Yes, *he does pay it.*" When we came into *Jesus'* house, *before Peter began to talk about paying taxes*, Jesus said *to him*, "Simon, from whom do you think rulers collect revenue or taxes? *Do they collect taxes* from the citizens of their own *country*, or from citizens of countries *they have conquered?*" [26] Peter answered *him*, "From *citizens of* other *countries*." Then Jesus said to him, "So citizens of their own *country* do not need to *pay taxes.* [27] But, *even though the Temple is mine, pay the tax for us* so that we will not offend *the tax collectors. In order to get the money to pay it*, go *down* to the lake. Cast your *fish line and* hook, and take the first fish you catch. When you open its mouth, you will find a silver coin *worth enough to pay the tax* for you and me. Take that coin and give *it* to the tax collectors."

18

Matthew 18:1-5

THEME: Jesus showed that being great in God's sight means being as humble as a child.

[1] About that time we disciples approached Jesus and said, "Who *among us will be* the most important when God *makes you* king?" [2] Jesus called a child to come, and he placed that child in our midst. [3] He said, "Keep this in mind: If you do not change *the way you think* and become *humble* as little children, you will surely not go to the place where God rules. [4] The people who become as humble as this child *or any child* is, will be the most important among those over whom God rules. [5] Also, when those who, *out of love* for me, welcome *a* child like this one, *God considers* that they are welcoming me."

Matthew 18:6-9

THEME: Jesus taught that we need to take severe measures to keep from sinning when we are tempted.

[6] "If you cause someone who believes in me to sin, *even if it is someone who is socially unimportant like* this little child, *God will severely punish you.* If a heavy stone were fastened around your neck and you were thrown into the deep waters of the sea, *everyone would consider such punishment to be severe. But God will punish* you *even* more severely *than that if you cause someone to sin!* [7] How horrible it will be for anyone who causes others to stop believing in me. *God will punish such a person eternally*. It is inevitable that there will be *those who* cause others to stop believing in me. But it will be horrible for everyone who does that. [8] So, if you *are tempted to use* one of your hands or

feet to sin, *stop using that hand or foot! Even if you have to* cut it off *to avoid sinning, do it!* It is good *that you not sin and* go where you will live *with God eternally, even though while you are still here on earth* you are maimed or lame and do not have a hand or a foot. But it is not good that you continue to have your two hands or two feet *and do the sin you are tempted to do and, as a result,* you are thrown into *hell,* where there is eternal fire burning. [9] If, because of what you see you *are tempted* to sin, *stop looking at those things! Even if you have to* gouge out one of your eyes and throw it away *to avoid sinning, do it!* It is good *that you not sin and later* go where you will live *with God eternally, even though while you are still here on earth* you have only one eye. But it is not good that you continue to have your two eyes *and do the sin you are tempted to do. It would be very bad for* you to be thrown into hell, where there is eternal fire burning!

Matthew 18:10-14

THEME: Jesus taught that God is deeply concerned if even one person goes astray from him.

[10] "Make an effort to not despise *even* one of these children. I tell you truly that *since* the angels *live* in heaven *in the presence of* my Father, *they will report to him if you mistreat the children.*[9] [12] What do you think *you would do in the following situation*? If you had one hundred sheep and one of them got lost, you would surely leave the ninety-nine sheep *that are* on the hill and go and search for the lost one, wouldn't you? [13] If you found it, I affirm to you that you would rejoice very much. You would be happy that ninety-nine sheep did not stray away, but you would rejoice even more *because you had found* the sheep that had strayed away. [14] In the same way *that the shepherd does not want one of the sheep to stray away,* so God, your Father in heaven, does not want *even* one of these children to go to hell."

Matthew 18:15-20

THEME: Jesus taught about what we should do if someone sins against us and about agreeing when we pray.

[15] "If a fellow believer sins *against you,* go *to him,* and when you two are alone, reprove him *for sinning against you.* If that person listens to you *and says he is sorry for having sinned against you,* you will have restored *your friendship with* that person. [16] If that person will not listen to you *nor say he is sorry for having sinned against you,* go get one or two other people *who will listen to what you both have to say.* Have them go with you so that *what is written in the Scriptures might happen:* 'When one person accuses another in *some matter,* it should be confirmed by *at least* two or three people *before that person can be declared* guilty.' [17] If the one who has sinned against you will not listen to them *or feel sorry for having sinned against you,* tell that to the congregation *so that they can rebuke him.* If that person will not listen to the congregation *or feel sorry for having sinned against you,* exclude him *from being a member of your congregation, just* as you *would exclude* pagans, tax collectors, *and others who do not believe in God and who sin greatly.* [18] Keep this in mind: *Whatever* you decide on earth *about punishing* or *not punishing a member of your congregation* is what has also been decided by *God* in heaven. [19] Also note this: If *at least* two of you *who live* here on earth agree together about whatever you ask God for, God, my Father *who is* in heaven, will give you what you ask. [20] *This is true,* because wherever *at least* two or three of you assemble because you believe in me, I am *spiritually* present with you. *I will hear what you ask for and I will ask God to do it for you.*"

---

[9] Some Greek manuscripts add v. 11, "And I, the one who came from heaven, have come to save those who are on their way to hell."

Matthew 18:21-35

THEME: Jesus told a parable to illustrate the need for forgiving others.

²¹ Then Peter approached *Jesus* and said to him, "How many times must I forgive a fellow believer who *keeps on* sinning against me? *If he keeps asking me to forgive him, must I forgive him* as many as seven times?" ²² Jesus said to him, "I tell you *that the number of times you must forgive someone is* not just up to seven, but *you must forgive him* limitlessly. ²³ *In order to illustrate* why *you should do this, I will tell you a story in which* God, *who cares for* the people whose lives he rules over, is compared to a king *and his officials.* That king told *some of his servants that he wanted* his officials to pay what they owed him. ²⁴ *So those officials were brought to* settle *their accounts with him. One of the officials* owed the king several million dollars. ²⁵ But because he did not have *enough money* to pay *what he owed*, the king demanded that he, his wife, his children and all he possessed be sold *to pay his debt.* ²⁶ Then that official, *knowing that he did not have the money to pay that huge debt*, fell *on his knees in front of the king* and he begged him saying, 'Be patient with me, and I will pay you all of it, *eventually.*' ²⁷ The king, *knowing that the official could never pay all that huge debt*, felt sorry for him. So he canceled his debt and released him. ²⁸ Then this official went to another one of the king's officials who owed him a bit less than a year's wages. He grabbed him *by the throat*, started choking him, and said to him, 'Pay back what you owe *me!*' ²⁹ That official fell *on his knees* and begged him saying, 'Be patient with me, and I will pay you all of it, *eventually.*' ³⁰ But this official kept refusing *to cancel that small debt the man owed him.* Instead, he had *that official* put in prison *to stay there* until he could pay back all the money he owed him. ³¹ When the *king's* other officials learned that this had happened, they felt very distressed. So they went to the king and reported in detail what had happened. ³² Then the king summoned the official *who had owed him several million dollars.* He said to him, 'You wicked servant! I canceled that huge debt *you owed me* because you begged me *to do so!* ³³ *So* you should have been merciful *and canceled your fellow official's debt*, just as I was merciful to you *and canceled your debt!*' ³⁴ The king was very angry. He handed this official over to some jailers who would torture him severely until he paid all of the debt that he owed." ³⁵ *Then Jesus continued by saying,* "That is what my Father in heaven will do to you if you do not *feel merciful and* sincerely forgive fellow believers *who sin against you.*"

19

Matthew 19:1-12

THEME: Jesus taught them God's view of divorce, and about abstaining from marriage to give more time to serve God.

¹ After Jesus had said that, he *took us* and left *the district of* Galilee and went to the part of Judea *that is located* on the *east* side of the Jordan *River.* ² Large crowds followed him there, and he healed *the sick among* them.

³ *Some* Pharisees approached him and said to him, "Does *our Jewish* law permit *a man* to divorce his wife for any reason whatever?" *They asked that* in order to be able to criticize him, *whether he answered "Yes," or "No."* ⁴ Jesus said *to them*, "*Since* you have read *the Scriptures, you should know* that at the time *God first* created *people*, 'he made *one* man, and he made *one* woman *to be that man's wife.*' ⁵ That explains why *God said*, '*When* a man *and woman marry*, they should no longer live with their fathers and mothers. *Instead*, the two of them shall live together, and they shall become *so closely united that they are like* one person.' ⁶ Consequently, *although they functioned as* two *separate people before*,

they now *become as* one. Since that is true, a man must not separate *from his wife* whom God has joined to him, *because it is God's plan for them to remain together*."

[7] The Pharisees then said to him, "That is true. So why did Moses command that *a man who wanted to divorce* his wife should just give her a paper *stating his reason for* divorcing her and then send her away?" [8] He said to them, "It was because *your ancestors* stubbornly *wanted their own ways* that Moses allowed them to divorce their wives, *and you are no different from them*. But, when God first created a man and a woman, *he did not intend for them to separate*. [9] I'm telling you emphatically that *since God considers that a marriage lasts until either the husband or the wife dies, he considers that* any man who divorces his wife and marries another woman is committing adultery, unless *his first wife* has committed adultery." [10] We disciples said to him, "If that is true, it is better for men never to marry!" [11] Then he said to us, "Not every man is able to accept this teaching. Only the men whom God enables *to accept it are able to do so*. [12] There are men who *do not want to marry because they are* sexually defective since birth. There are other men *who do not want to marry* because they have been castrated. There are other *men who choose not to marry* so they can serve God better *and spend more time telling people about how* God wants to rule people's lives. You who are able to understand *what I have said about marriage* should accept it *and obey it*."

Matthew 19:13-15

THEME: Jesus rebuked the disciples for trying to prevent children from coming to him.

[13] Then *some* children were brought to Jesus for him to lay his hands on them and pray *for them*. But we disciples scolded the people *for bringing their children to Jesus because we thought Jesus did not want to take the time to be with children*. [14] *When Jesus saw us scolding them*, he said to us, "Let the children come to me, and do not stop them! It is people who are *humble and trusting* like they are who can experience God's rule *in their lives*." [15] Jesus then laid his hands on the children *and asked God to bless them*. Then he left there.

Matthew 19:16-22

THEME: A rich young man went away sad because Jesus told him to sell all his possessions.

[16] *As Jesus was walking along, a young* man approached him and said *to him*, "Teacher, what good *deeds* must I do in order to live *with God* eternally?" [17] Jesus said to him, "Consider *what you are implying about who I am when* you ask **me** about what is good. There is only one who is good and who *really knows what is good. That being is God. But in order to answer your question* about *desiring to* live *with God eternally, I will say to you*, 'Obey the commandments *God gave Moses*.'" [18] The man asked Jesus, "Which *commandments must I obey?*" Jesus answered *him*, "Do not commit murder, do not commit adultery, do not steal, do not testify falsely, [19] honor your father and mother, and love people you come in contact with as *much as you love* yourself." [20] *Supposing that he might not be able to live with God eternally even though he had kept those commandments*, the young man said to Jesus, "I have always obeyed all those commandments. What else must I do *to live with God eternally*?" [21] Jesus said to him, "If you desire to be all that God intends you to be, go *home*, sell everything you have and give *the money* to the poor. *The result will be that* you will have *spiritual* riches in heaven. Then come and be my disciple!" [22] When the young man heard those words, he went away feeling sad, because he was very rich *and he did not want to give away everything he owned*.

Matthew 19:23-30

THEME: Jesus taught how difficult it is for rich people to let God rule their lives, but he added that there are rewards for those who leave family and possessions for his sake.

²³ Then Jesus said to *us* disciples, "Keep this in mind: It is very difficult for rich people *to decide* to let God rule their *lives*. ²⁴ Note this also: It is impossible for a camel to go through the eye of a needle. It is *almost* as difficult for rich people *to decide* to let God rule their *lives*." ²⁵ When *we* disciples heard this, we became exceedingly astounded. *We thought that rich people were the ones God blesses the most. So we said to him*, "If that is so, it does not seem likely that anyone will be saved!" ²⁶ *When Jesus heard us say that*, he looked intently at us, and *then* he said to us, "*Yes*, it is impossible for people *to save themselves*. But *God can save them, because* everything is possible for God!" ²⁷ Then Peter said to him, "You know that we have left everything behind and have become your disciples. So what benefit will **we** get *for doing that*?" ²⁸ Jesus said to us, "Keep this in mind: *You will get many benefits*. When *God* makes *the* new *earth* and when *I*, who came down to earth, sit on my magnificent throne, those of **you** who have accompanied me will each sit on a throne, and you will judge *the people of* the twelve tribes of Israel. ²⁹ *God will reward* those who, because of being my *disciples,* have left *behind* a house or plot of ground, *their* brothers, *their* sisters, their father, their mother, their children *or any other family members. God* will give them a hundred times *as many benefits as they have given up*. And they will live *with God* eternally. ³⁰ But many *people who consider themselves to* be important *now* will be unimportant *at that future time*, and many *who consider themselves to be* unimportant *now will be* important *at that time*."

20

Matthew 20:1-16

THEME: Jesus told a parable to illustrate how God will reward those who serve him.

¹ "*In order to illustrate how God rewards people*, I will compare God, as he rules his people, with the owner of an estate. Early in the morning the owner of the estate went to where *people who wanted work gathered.* He went there to hire laborers to work in his vineyard. ² He promised the men he hired that he would pay them the standard wage *for work*ing one day. Then he sent them to his vineyards. ³ At nine o'clock *that same morning* he went back *to the market*. There he saw more men who did not have work. ⁴ He said to them, 'Go to my vineyard as other men have done *and work there*. I will pay you whatever is a just *wage.' So they also went to his vineyard and began to work.* ⁵ At noon and at three o'clock he again went *to the market* and found *other laborers whom he promised to pay a fair wage.* ⁶ At five o'clock he went *to the market again* and saw other *men* standing *there who were not working*. He said to them, 'Why are you standing here all day and not working?' ⁷ They said to him, 'Because no one has hired us.' He said to them, '*I'll hire you.* Go to my vineyard as other men have done *and work there.' So they went.*

⁸ "When evening came, the owner of the vineyard said to his manager, 'Tell the men to come so that you can give them their wages. First, pay the men who started working last, and pay last the men who started working first.' ⁹ The *manager* paid that standard wage to each of the men who did not start working until five o'clock *in the afternoon*. ¹⁰ When the men who had begun working early *in the morning* went *to get their wages*, they assumed that they would receive more than the standard wage. But they also were given only the standard wage. ¹¹ So they complained to the owner of the vineyard *because they thought their payment was unfair.* ¹² They said *to him*, 'You're not being fair! The men who started

working after *all of the rest of us started only* worked for one hour! You have *paid* them the same *wage* as *you paid* us! But we worked hard *all* day, *including in the* hottest part of the day!' [13] The owner of the vineyard said to one of those *who complained*, 'Friend, I did not treat you unfairly. You agreed with me *to work the whole day* for the standard wage. [14] *Stop complaining to me!* Take your wages and go! I desire to give the same wage I gave you to the men who began working after all of you *had begun working.* [15] I certainly have a right to *spend my money* as I desire, *including paying those laborers what I desire to pay them.* You shouldn't be envious about my being generous!'" [16] *Then Jesus said to us*, "In the same way, *God will reward* well *some* people who *seem to be* less important now, and he will not reward *some* who *seem* more important *now.*"

Matthew 20:17-19

THEME: For the third time Jesus predicted his death and resurrection.

[17] When Jesus was walking *on the road* up to Jerusalem, *accompanied by us* twelve *disciples*, he took us to a place by ourselves *to talk to us privately.* Then he said to us, [18] "Listen carefully! We are *now* going up to Jerusalem. *While we are there, someone* will enable the chief priests and the men who teach the *Jewish* law to seize *me*, the one who came from heaven, *and they will put me on trial.* They will condemn me *and say* that I should be killed. [19] *Then they* will put me in the hands of non-Jews so that they can make fun of me, whip me, *and kill me by* nailing me to a cross. But on the third day *after that, God* will cause me to live again."

Matthew 20:20-28

THEME: Jesus taught that greatness in God's sight means humbly serving others as Jesus did.

[20] Then the mother of James and John brought her two sons to Jesus. She bowed down before Jesus and asked him to do her a favor. [21] Jesus said to her, "What do you want *me to do for you*?" She said to him, "Permit these two sons of mine to sit next to you[h] *and rule with you* when you become king." [22] Jesus said to *her and her sons*, "You do not understand what you are asking for! Can you suffer like I am about to suffer?" *James and John* answered him, "Yes, we are able *to do that.*" [23] Then Jesus said to them, "Yes, you will suffer as I will suffer. But I am not the one who chooses the ones who *will* sit next to me *and rule with me.* God, my Father, will give those places to the ones **he** appoints."

[24] When we ten *other disciples* heard *what James and John had requested,* we became angry with them *because we also wanted to rule with Jesus in the highest positions.* [25] *So* Jesus called all of us together and said *to us*, "You know that those who rule the non-Jews *enjoy* showing that they are powerful. Their chief rulers *enjoy* commanding the people under them. [26] You *should* not be like them. On the contrary, everyone among you who wants *God to consider* him great must become *like* a servant to *the rest of* you. [27] And everyone among you who wants *God to consider him* to be the most important must become *like* a slave for *the rest of* you. [28] *You should imitate me. Even though I am* the one who came from heaven, I did not come to be served. On the contrary, *I came in order* to serve *others* and to allow myself to be killed, so that *my death would be like* a payment to rescue many *people from being punished for their sins.*"

---

[h] OR, …Permit these two sons of mine to sit next to you at your right side and at your left side…

Matthew 20:29-34

THEME: Jesus healed two blind men.

²⁹ As we were leaving *the town of* Jericho, a large crowd of people followed *us.* ³⁰ *As we walked along we saw* two blind men sitting alongside the road. When they heard that Jesus was passing by, they yelled *to him,* "Lord, Descendant of *King* David, *you are the Messiah!* Take pity on us!" ³¹ *People in* the crowd scolded them *and* told them to be quiet. But the blind men yelled even louder, "Lord, Descendant of *King* David, *you are the Messiah!* Take pity on us!" ³² Jesus stopped and called them *to come to him. Then* he said *to them,* "What do you want me to do for you?" ³³ They said to him, "Lord, heal our eyes *so we can see!"* ³⁴ Jesus *felt* sorry *for them and* touched their eyes. Immediately they were able to see, and they went with Jesus.

21

Matthew 21:1-11

THEME: Jesus entered Jerusalem humbly on a donkey, but with great acclaim by the crowd.

¹ As *we* approached Jerusalem, *we came* near *the village of* Bethphage, near Olive *Tree* Hill. Jesus said to two *of his* disciples, "Go to the village just ahead of you. As soon as you enter *it,* you will see a donkey and her foal that are tied *up.* Untie them and bring them *here* to me. ³ If anyone says anything to you *about your doing that,* tell *him,* 'The Lord needs them.' He will *then allow you to* lead them away." ⁴ When all this happened, what was written by a prophet was fulfilled. The prophet wrote, "Tell the people who live in Jerusalem, 'Look! Your king is coming to you! He will come humbly. *The evidence that he is humble will be that he will be* riding on a colt, the offspring of a donkey.'"

⁶ So the *two* disciples went and did what Jesus told them to do. ⁷ They brought the donkey and its colt *to Jesus.* They placed their cloaks on them. Jesus *mounted the colt* and sat on the cloaks. ⁸ Then a large crowd spread *some of* their clothing on the road, and other *people* cut off branches from *palm* trees and spread them on the road. *They did those things to decorate the road to honor Jesus.* ⁹ The crowds that walked in front of him and those who walked behind him were shouting things like, "Praise the *Messiah,* the descendant of *King* David!", "May the Lord *God* bless *this one* who comes as *God's* representative and with *God's* authority!", "Praise God, who is in the highest *heaven!"* ¹⁰ As Jesus entered Jerusalem, a crowd of people from all *over the city* became excited and were saying, "Why *are they honoring* this man *like that?"* ¹¹ The crowd *that was already following him* said, "This is Jesus, the prophet from Nazareth in Galilee!"

Matthew 21:12-17

THEME: Jesus chased buyers and sellers from the temple, and he rebuked the Jewish leaders for objecting to children praising him.

¹² Then Jesus went into the Temple *courtyard* and chased out all of those who were buying and selling there. He also overturned the tables of those who were giving *Temple tax* money in exchange for *Roman* coins, and he overturned the seats of those who were selling pigeons *for sacrifices.* ¹³ Then he said to them, "It is written *in the Scriptures that God said,* '*I want* my house to be called a place where *people* pray', but **you** bandits have made it your hideout!"

[14] After that, *many* blind and lame *people* came to Jesus in the Temple *to be healed*, and he healed them. [15] The high priests and the men who taught the *Jewish* laws saw the wonderful deeds that Jesus did. *They also saw and* heard the children shouting in the Temple, "We praise the *Messiah*, the descendant of *King* David!" Those men were indignant *because they did not believe that Jesus was the Messiah.* [16] *They thought that Jesus should not be allowing the children to say that,* so they asked him, "*How can you tolerate* this? Do you hear what these *children* are shouting?" Then Jesus said to them, "Yes, *I hear them, but* if you *remembered what* you have read *in the Scriptures about children praising me, you would know that God is pleased with them. The psalmist* wrote, *saying to God,* 'You have taught infants and other children to praise you perfectly.'"

[17] Then Jesus left the city. We *disciples* went *with him* to *the town of* Bethany, and we slept there *that night*.

Matthew 21:18-22

THEME: Jesus taught the disciples a lesson from what happened to a fig tree.

[18] Early *the next morning,* when we were returning to the city, *Jesus* was hungry. [19] He saw a fig tree near the road. *So he went over to it to pick some figs to eat.* But when he got close, he saw that there were no *figs on the tree.* There were only leaves on it. So *to illustrate how God would punish the nation of Israel,* he said to the fig tree, "May you never again produce figs!" As a result, the fig tree withered that night. [20] *The next day* when we disciples saw *what had happened to the tree,* we marveled, and we said *to Jesus,* "How is it that the fig tree withered so quickly?" [21] Jesus said to us, "Keep *this* in mind: If you believe *that God has power to do what you ask him to* and you do not doubt *that,* you will be able to do *things like what I have* done to this fig tree. You will even be able to do *marvelous deeds like* saying to a nearby hill, 'Uproot yourself and throw yourself into the sea' and it will happen! [22] In addition *to that,* whenever you ask *God for something* when you pray *to him,* if you believe *that he will give it to you, he* will."

Matthew 21:23-27

THEME: Jesus refused to state the basis for his authority because the Jewish leaders refused to admit where John the Baptizer's authority came from.

[23] After that, Jesus went into the Temple *courtyard.* While he was teaching *the people,* the chief priests and the elders of the Jewish Council approached him. They asked, "By what authority are you doing these things? Who authorized you to do what you did *here yesterday*?" [24] Jesus said to them, "**I** also will ask **you** a question, and if you answer me, I will tell you who authorized me to do these things. [25] Where did John *the Baptizer* get *his authority to* baptize *those who came to him*? *Did he get it* from God or from people?" The chief priests and elders debated among themselves *as to what they should answer. They said to each other,* "If we say, '*It was* from God', he will say to us, 'Then why did you not believe *John's message*?' [26] If we say, 'It was from people', we are afraid that the crowd *will react violently,* because all *the people* believe that John was a prophet *sent by God.*" [27] So they answered Jesus, "We do not know *where John got his authority.*" Then **he** said to them, "*Because you did not answer my question,* I won't tell you who authorized me to do the things I did *here yesterday.*"

Matthew 21:28-32

THEME: Jesus rebuked the religious leaders and said that God would accept notorious sinners before he would accept them.

²⁸ *Then Jesus said to the chief priests and elders*, "Tell me what you think *about what I am about to tell you*. There was a man who had two sons. He went to his older son and said, 'My son, go and work in my vineyard today!' ²⁹ But the son said *to his father*, 'I do not want to *go and work in the vineyard today!*' But later he changed his mind and went to the vineyard *and worked*. ³⁰ Then the father approached his younger son and said what he had said to the older one. That son said, 'Sir, I will *go and work in the vineyard today.*' But he did not go. ³¹ So which of the two sons did what their father desired?" The men answered, "The older son." Jesus *explained to them what that parable meant* by saying, "Keep this in mind: *Other people, including* tax collectors and prostitutes, *whom you think are very sinful*, will enter where God rules before you *Jewish leaders* will. ³² *I say this to you* because, even though John *the Baptizer* explained to you how to live righteously, you did not believe his message. But tax collectors and prostitutes believed his *message, and they turned away from their sinful behavior*. In contrast **you,** even though you saw what they did, refused to turn away from your sinful behavior, and you did not believe *John's message*."

Matthew 21:33-46

THEME: Jesus told a parable about the Jewish religious leaders rejecting him as Messiah.

³³ "Listen to another parable *I will tell you*. There was a landowner who planted a vineyard. He built a fence around it. He dug a hole in the ground *inside the fence*. He placed *in the hole* a stone tank to *collect the juice that would be* pressed out of the grapes. He also built a lookout tower. He rented the vineyard to some men *to care for it and to give him some of the grapes in return*. Then he went away to another country. ³⁴ When the time came to harvest the grapes, the landowner sent some of his servants to the renters to get his share of the grapes *that the vineyard had produced*. ³⁵ But the renters seized the servants. They beat one of them, they killed another one, and another one they stoned *to death*. ³⁶ *So the landowner* sent more servants than *he had sent* the first *time*. The renters treated those servants the same way that *they had treated the others*. ³⁷ Later, *knowing this, the landowner* sent his son to *the renters to get his share of the grapes*. When he sent him, he said *to himself*, 'They will certainly respect my son *and give him some of the grapes*.' ³⁸ But when the renters saw *that* his son *had arrived*, they said to each other, 'This is the man who will inherit *this vineyard!* Let's join together and kill him and divide the property *among ourselves*.' ³⁹ So they grabbed him, dragged him outside the vineyard, and killed him. ⁴⁰ *Now I ask you*, when the landowner returns to his vineyard, what *do you think* he will do to those renters?" ⁴¹ *The chief priests and elders* replied, "He will thoroughly destroy those wicked *renters*! Then he will rent the vineyard to others. They will give him *his share of* the grapes when they are ripe." ⁴² Jesus said to them, "*That is right, so you need to think carefully about these words which* you have read in the Scriptures,

The builders rejected a certain stone. *But others put* that same stone *in its proper place, and it* has become the most important stone in the building. The Lord has done this, and we marvel as we look at it.

⁴³ "So, *because you reject me*, I am going to tell you this: God will no longer let you *Jews* be the people over whom he rules. Instead, he will let *non-Jews* be the people over whom he rules, and they will do what he asks them to do. ⁴⁴ *The important stone in the building represents me, the Messiah, and those who reject me are like people who fall on this stone*. Anyone who falls on this stone will be broken to pieces, and it will crush anyone on whom it falls."

[45] When the chief priests and the *elders who were* Pharisees heard this parable, they realized that he was accusing them *because they did not believe he was the Messiah.* [46] They wanted to seize him, but *they did not try to do so* for fear of *what* the crowds *would do,* because *the crowds* considered Jesus to be a prophet.

22

Matthew 22:1-14

THEME: Jesus told a parable about a wedding feast to illustrate what happens to people who do not accept him as the Messiah.

[1] Then Jesus told *the Jewish leaders* other parables *in order to illustrate what happens to the people who do not accept him as the King God promised to send. This is one of those parables:* [2] "*God is like* a king who *told his servants to* make a wedding feast for his son. [3] *When* the feast *was ready*, the king sent his servants to tell the people whom he had invited that it was time for them to come. *The servants did that.* But the people who had been invited did not want to come. [4] So he sent other servants *to again tell the people whom he had invited that they should come.* He said *to those servants,* 'Say to the people whom I invited *to come to the feast,* "This is what the king says to you, 'I inform you that I have prepared the meal. The oxen and the fattened calves have been butchered. Everything is ready. It is time *now for you to* come to the wedding feast!'" [5] *But* the people disregarded *what the servants said.* Some of them went to their own fields. Others went to their places of business. [6] The rest of them seized the king's servants, mistreated them, and killed them. [7] *When the king heard what had happened,* he became furious. He commanded his soldiers to go and kill those murderers and burn their cities. [8] *After his soldiers had done that,* the king said to his other servants, 'I have prepared the *wedding* feast, but the people I invited do not deserve to *come to it because they did not consider it an honor to have been invited.* [9] So, go to the intersections of the main streets. Tell whomever you find to come to the *wedding* feast.' [10] So the servants went there, and they gathered everyone they saw *who wanted to come to the feast.* They gathered *both people that were considered* to be evil and *those that were considered to be* good. They brought them into the hall where the wedding *feast took place, and* the hall was filled.

[11] But when the king went *into the hall* to see the guests who were there, he saw someone who was not wearing clothes *that are provided for guests to wear* at a wedding *feast.* [12] The king said to him, 'Friend, you should never have come in here, because you are not wearing the clothes *that are appropriate to wear* at a wedding *feast!*' The man did not say anything, *because he did not know what to say.* [13] Then the king said to his attendants, 'Tie this person's feet and hands and throw him outside where there is total darkness. People who are there cry out *because they are suffering* and they gnash their teeth *because of their severe pain.*'" [14] *Then Jesus said, "The point of this story is that God* has invited many *to come to him,* but only a few people are the ones whom he has chosen *to be there.*"

Matthew 22:15-22

THEME: Jesus taught his critics that they needed to give to God and to the government what they each required.

[15] After Jesus said that, the Pharisees met together to plan how they could cause him to say something that would enable them to arrest him. [16] They sent to him some of their disciples, *who thought that the Israelites should pay only the tax the Jewish authorities*

required them to pay. They also sent some members of the party that supported Herod. *The members of that party thought that the Israelites should pay only the tax the Roman government required them to pay. Those who were sent came and* said to Jesus, "Teacher, we know that you are truthful and that you teach the truth about what God wants *us to do.* We also know that you do not change what you teach because of what someone says about you, even if it is an important person who does not like what you teach. ¹⁷ So, tell us what you think *about this matter.* Is it right that we pay taxes to the Roman government, or not?" ¹⁸ But Jesus knew that their intent was evil—*that they were wanting him to say something that would get him in trouble with either the Jewish authorities or the Roman authorities.* So he said *to them,* "You are pretending to ask a legitimate question, but you just want me to say something for which you can accuse me. ¹⁹ Show me *one of* the coins with which the *Roman tax* is paid." So they showed him *a coin called* a denarius. ²⁰ He said to them, "Whose picture is *on* this *coin*? And *whose* name *is on it?*" ²¹ They answered, "*It has the picture and name of* Caesar, *the head of the Roman government.*" Then he said to them, "Okay, give to the government what they *require*, and give to God what he *requires*." ²² When the men heard Jesus say that, they marveled *that his answer did not enable anyone to accuse him.* Then they left Jesus.

Matthew 22:23-33

THEME: Jesus showed from the Scriptures that the spirits of God's people are alive after death.

²³ During that same day some Sadducees came to Jesus. *They are a Jewish sect whose members do not* believe that people will become alive again after they die. They *wanted to* ask *Jesus* a question. ²⁴ *In order to discredit the idea that dead people will live again*, they said *to him,* "Teacher, Moses wrote *in the Scriptures,* 'If a man dies who did not have any children, his brother must marry the *dead man's* widow so that she can have a child by him. The child *will be considered* the descendant of the man *who died, and in that way the dead man will have descendants.*' ²⁵ Well, there were seven boys in a family *living* near us. The oldest one married. He *and his wife* did not have any children, and he died. So the second brother married the widow. *But he also died without having a child.* ²⁶ The same thing *happened to* the third *brother,* and also to the other four *brothers, who one by one married this same woman.* ²⁷ Last of all, the widow also died. ²⁸ So, at the time when people are raised from the dead, which of the seven *brothers do you think* will be her husband? Keep in mind that they had all been married to her." ²⁹ Jesus replied to them, "You are certainly wrong *in your thinking.* You do not know *what is written in* the Scriptures. *You* also *do not know that* God has *the* power *to make people alive again.* ³⁰ The fact is that *the woman will not be the wife of any of them, because* after *God causes all dead* people *to* live again, no one will be married. Instead, *people* will be like the angels in heaven, *who do not marry.* ³¹ But as to dead people becoming alive again, God said something about that. I'm sure you have read it. *Long after Abraham, Isaac, and Jacob had died, God said to Moses,* ³² 'I am God, the one whom Abraham *worships* and the one whom Isaac *worships* and the one whom Jacob worships.' *Abraham, Isaac and Jacob died long before Moses lived, but God said that they were still worshiping him, so we know their spirits were still alive!* God is *surely* not one who is *worshipped by* dead *people! He is the God whom* living *people worship, because he keeps their spirits alive after they have died!*"

³³ When the crowds of people heard *Jesus teach* that, they were amazed.

Matthew 22:34-40

THEME: Jesus told his critics that the greatest commandments were to love God and to love others.

[34] But when the Pharisees heard that Jesus had answered the Sadducees in such a way that the Sadducees could not *think of a way to* respond to him, the Pharisees gathered together to *plan what they would say to him. Then they approached him.* [35] One of them, who was an expert in the laws *of the Jews,* wanted to see if Jesus *could answer* his question well *or if he would say something wrong.* He asked him, [36] "Teacher, which commandment in the laws *that God gave Moses* is the most important?" [37] Jesus *quoted Scripture as he replied,* "'You must love the Lord your God with all your heart. *Show your love for him* in all your desires, in all your emotions, and in all your thoughts.' [38] That is the most important commandment *in the laws that God gave Moses.* [39] The next most important commandment *that everyone must surely obey* is: 'You must love the people you come in contact with as much as *you love* yourself.' [40] These two commandments are the basis of every law *Moses wrote in the Scriptures* and also of all that the prophets *wrote.*"

Matthew 22:41-46

THEME: Jesus showed that the Messiah must be greater than King David, and not just his descendant.

[41] While the Pharisees were still gathered together *near* Jesus, he asked them, [42] "What do you think about the Messiah? Whose descendant is he?" They said to him, "*He is* the descendant of *King* David." [43] Jesus said to them, "*If the Messiah is King David's descendant*, then David should not have called him 'Lord' when David was saying *what* the *Holy* Spirit *prompted him to* say. [44] *David wrote this in the Scriptures about the Messiah*: 'God said to my Lord, "Sit *here beside me* on my right, *where I will greatly honor you. Sit here* while I completely defeat your enemies." [45] So, since *King* David called *the Messiah* 'my Lord', *the Messiah* cannot be *just someone* descended from David. *He must be much greater than David!*" [46] No one *who heard what Jesus said* was able to think of even one word to say to him *in response.* And after that, no one else ever dared to ask him another question *to try to trap him.*

23

Matthew 23:1-12

THEME: Jesus warned the people against the hypocritical behavior of the religious leaders.

[1] Then Jesus said to the crowd and to us his disciples, [2] "**Moses** was the *renowned* teacher who taught *the people the laws God gave him.* Now, the Pharisees and the men who teach our *Jewish* laws have made **themselves** the ones who interpret those laws. [3] Consequently, you should do **whatever they tell you that you must do.** But do not do what they do, because they themselves do not do what they tell *you that you must do.* [4] They *require you to obey many rules that are difficult to obey.* But **they themselves** do *not help anyone obey those laws. It is* as if they are tying up loads that are hard to carry and putting them on your shoulders *for you to carry. But they* do not want to lift *even the slightest load* that they *could lift with* one finger. Whatever they do, they do it to be seen by other people. *For example,* they make extra wide the tiny boxes containing portions of Scripture that they wear on their arms. They enlarge the tassels on their robes, *to make*

others think that they are pious. ⁶ *They want people to honor them. For example*, at dinner parties they look for seats where the most important people sit. In the places of worship *they want to sit* in the seats where the pious people sit. ⁷Also, *they want people to* greet them *respectfully* in the market places and to honor them by calling them 'Teacher'. ⁸But **you** *who are my disciples* should not allow people to address you *honorably* as 'Rabbi', *which means 'teacher'. I am the* only one who is *really* your teacher, which means that you are all *equal, like* brothers and sisters, *and none of you should act superior to another, as the Pharisees do.* ⁹Do not *honor anyone* on earth *by* addressing him as 'Father', because God, your Father in heaven, is the only *spiritual* father of all of you. ¹⁰Do not *allow people to* call you 'Instructors', because I, the Messiah, am the one instructor who *teaches all of* you. ¹¹In contrast, everyone among you who wants to be important *in God's estimation* must serve others as **servants** do. ¹² *God* will humble those who exalt themselves. And *he* will exalt those who humble themselves."

Matthew 23:13

THEME: Jesus warned the religious leaders about preventing people from letting God rule their lives.

¹³ *Then Jesus said to the religious leaders,* "You men who teach the *Jewish* law and you Pharisees are hypocrites! How terrible it will be for *you, because by teaching what is false,* you *prevent people who are thinking about letting* God rule their lives *from doing that. What you are doing is like* closing a gate *so that people who* want to enter *a city cannot go in.* As for **you,** *you do not let* God *rule your lives. Neither do you allow* other people *to let God rule their lives. That is like* not going into a *house* yourselves or allowing others to enter it."ⁱ

Matthew 23:15

THEME: Jesus also warned the religious leaders about zealously encouraging others to believe what they teach.

¹⁵ "You are hypocrites, you men who teach the *Jewish* laws and you Pharisees! Your punishment will be terrible, because you exert yourselves very much to get *even* one person to believe what you teach. For instance, you travel across seas and lands *to distant places* to do that. And *as a result of your false teaching*, when one person *believes what you teach*, you make that person much more *deserving to go to hell* than you yourselves *deserve to.*

Matthew 23:16-22

THEME: Jesus rebuked the religious leaders about their silly ideas about supporting their promises with oaths.

¹⁶ "You *Jewish leaders,* your punishment will be terrible! You are *like people who are* blind who are trying to lead others. You say, '*In the case of* those who promise to *do* something and then ask the Temple *to affirm what they have promised*, it means nothing *if they fail to do what* they have promised. But if they ask the gold that is in the Temple *to affirm what they have promised*, they have to do what they promised.' ¹⁷You are fools, and you are

---

ⁱ   Some Greek manuscripts add v. 14, "You teachers of our laws and you Pharisees will suffer terribly in hell. You are hypocrites because you swindle the houses *and property* of widows. Then you pretend you are good, as you pray long prayers publicly. *God* will *certainly* punish you very severely."

like people who are blind! The gold *that is in the Temple* is important, but *the Temple* is even more important because it is **the Temple** that the gold is in that sets the gold apart for a special use for God. [18] Also, *you say,* 'In the case of those who promise to *do* something and then ask *the altar to affirm what they have promised,* it means nothing *if they fail to do what they have promised.* But if they ask the gift *that* they have put on the altar *to support what they have promised,* they have to do *what they promised.'* [19] *You are like people who are* blind. The gift *that is offered* on the altar is important, but the altar is even more important because it is **the altar** on which the offering is placed that sets it apart for a special use for God. [20] So, those who promise to do something, and then ask the altar *to affirm what they have promised* are asking everything on the altar *to support what they promised.* [21] Those who promise to do something, and then ask the Temple *to affirm what they promised,* are asking that *God,* to whom the Temple belongs, *will affirm what they have promised.* [22] Those who promise to do something and then ask heaven *to affirm what they promised* are asking the throne of God and *God,* who sits on that throne, *to affirm what they promised.*

Matthew 23:23-24

THEME: Jesus also rebuked the religious leaders about paying attention to unimportant laws and at the same time ignoring important ones.

[23] "You men who teach the *Jewish* laws and you Pharisees, your punishment will be terrible! You are hypocrites because, *even though* you give *to God* a tenth of *the herbs you produce, such as* mint, dill, and cummin, you do not *obey God's* laws that are more important. *For instance, you do not act* justly toward others, you do not show mercy to people, and you are not trustworthy. It is good to *give a tenth of your herbs* to God, but you should also *obey* these other *more important laws.* [24] You *leaders are like* blind people *who are trying to lead others. According to your laws, you* say that touching gnats and camels makes you unacceptable to God. What you are doing is as though you are straining a gnat *out of a jar of water so that you do not swallow it,* and *at the same time* you are swallowing a camel!

Matthew 23:25-26

THEME: Jesus also rebuked the religious leaders about being greedy and selfish.

[25] "You men who teach people the *Jewish* laws and you Pharisees, your punishment will be terrible! You are hypocrites! You are greedy and selfish, but you *make yourselves appear holy. You are like* cups and plates that have been cleaned on the outside, but on the inside *are very filthy.* [26] You blind Pharisees! First you must *stop being greedy and selfish. Then you will be able to do what* is *righteous. That will be like* cleaning the inside of a cup first. Then when you clean the outside *of the cup, the cup will truly be clean.*

Matthew 23:27-28

THEME: Jesus rebuked the religious leaders for being hypocrites and pretending to be righteous.

[27] "You men who teach the *Jewish* laws and you Pharisees, your punishment will be terrible! You are hypocrites! You are like tombs that are whitewashed *so that people can see them and avoid touching them.* The outside surfaces are beautiful, but inside they are full of dead people's bones and filth. [28] You are *like those tombs.* When people look at you, they think you are righteous, but in your hearts you are hypocrites and you disobey *God's* commands.

Matthew 23:29-36

THEME: Jesus accused the religious leaders of being guilty of killing all the prophets.

[29] "You men who teach the *Jewish* laws and you Pharisees are hypocrites! Your punishment will be terrible! You rebuild the tombs of the *prophets whom others killed long ago*. You decorate the monuments *that honor* righteous *people*. [30] You say, 'If we had *lived* when our ancestors *lived*, we would not have helped those who killed the prophets.' [31] Thus *you recognize that you should honor the prophets, but you refuse to accept my message from God. In that way,* you testify against yourselves that you are descendants and disciples of those who killed the prophets. [32] **You** are as ready to commit murder as your ancestors were! [33] *You people are so wicked*! You are *as dangerous as poisonous* snakes! You *foolishly* think that you will escape being punished in hell! [34] Take note that this is why I will send prophets, wise men, and other men who will teach you *my message*. You will kill some of them by nailing them to crosses, and you will kill some in other ways. You will whip some of them in the places where you worship and *you will* chase them from city to city. [35] As a result, God will consider **you** to be guilty for killing all the righteous *people*, including killing *Adam's son* Abel, who was a righteous man, and Zachariah, the son of Barachiah, whom you *are guilty of* killing *in the holy place* between the Temple and the altar, and for killing *all the prophets* who lived between *the times that those two men lived*. [36] Take note of this: You people who have observed my ministry, it is you whom *God* will punish *for killing all* those *prophets*!

Matthew 23:37-39

THEME: Jesus expressed his sorrow about what would happen to Jerusalem.

[37] "O *people of* Jerusalem, you killed the prophets *who lived long ago*, and you killed *others* whom *God* sent to you. You stoned them *to death*! Many times I wanted to gather you together *to protect you,* like a hen gathers her young chicks under her wings. But you did not want *me to do that.* [38] So listen to this: Your city will become an uninhabited place. [39] Keep this in mind: You will see me again only when *I return* and you say *about me*, 'God is truly pleased with this man who comes with God's authority.'"

24

Matthew 24:1-2

THEME: Jesus told his disciples that Jerusalem would be destroyed.

[1] Jesus left the Temple *courtyard.* As he was walking along, *we* disciples came to him to ask him to note *how beautiful* the Temple buildings *were.* [2] He said to us, "These buildings that you are looking at *are wonderful, but* I want to tell you *something about them. They will be completely destroyed.* Every stone *in these buildings* will be thrown down. Not one stone will be left on top of another."

Matthew 24:3-14

THEME: Jesus told his disciples about the distressing things that would happen before his return.

[3] *Later*, as Jesus was sitting alone on *the slope of* Olive *Tree* Hill, *we* disciples went to him and asked him, "When will this happen *to the buildings of the Temple*? Also, tell us what

will happen to indicate that you are *about to* come again, and *to indicate* that this world is ending?"

[4] Jesus replied, "*All I will say is,* be sure that no one deceives you *about what will happen*! [5] Many *people* will come and say that they have my authority. They will say, 'I am the Messiah', and they will deceive many *people.* [6] You will hear about wars *that are close* and wars that are far away, but do not let that trouble you. Keep in mind that *God has said* those things must happen. But *when they happen*, it will not mean that the end *of the world* has come! [7] *Various* countries will fight each other, and *various* governments *will also fight* against each other. There will be famines and earthquakes in various places. [8] These things will happen first. Then there will be other things that *will precede my return. What will happen will be as painful as a woman's* birth pains.

[9] "At that time, *people who oppose you* will take you to *the authorities who* will mistreat you and kill you. You will be hated by *people who live in* all nations because you *believe in* me. [10] Also, many *people* will stop believing *in me because of the suffering they will experience.* They will betray each other and will hate each other. [11] Many will come saying they are prophets, but they will be lying, and they will deceive many people. [12] Because there will be more and more *people* who will disobey *God's* laws, many *people* will no longer love *their fellow believers.* [13] But *all* those who keep on *believing in me* to the end *of their lives* will be saved. [14] Furthermore, the good message about my ruling over people's lives will be preached in every part of the world, in order that people of all ethnic groups may hear it. Then the end *of the world* will come.

Matthew 24:15-22

THEME: Jesus told his disciples about the suffering that would come when Jerusalem was about to be destroyed.

[15] "*But before the world ends,* the disgusting person who will defile *the* holy *Temple* and cause people to abandon it will stand in the Temple. Daniel the prophet spoke *and wrote* about that *long ago.* May everyone who reads *this* pay attention *to the following warning from me:* [16] When you see that happen *in the Temple*, those *of you* who are in Judea must flee to the *higher* hills! [17] Those who are outside their houses must not go back into their houses to get things *before they flee.* [18] Those who are *working* in a field should not turn back to get their outer clothing *before they flee.* [19] *I feel* very sorry for women who will be pregnant and women who will be nursing *their babies* in those days, *because it will be very difficult for them to run away!* [20] Pray that you will not have to flee in the winter *when it will be hard to travel. People who think that God never allows anyone to do any work on* our day of rest *will not help you as you flee, so* pray also that you will not have to flee on such a day, [21] because there will be great suffering *when those things happen.* There has never been such great suffering since *God* created the world, and *there* will never be *suffering like that again.* [22] If *God had not decided to* shorten that time *of great suffering*, everyone would die. But *he has decided to* shorten it because *he is concerned* about the *people* whom *he* has chosen.

Matthew 24:23-28

THEME: Jesus warned his disciples not to believe false reports about his return because everyone will see him when he comes.

[23-24] "*At that time* people will appear *who will* falsely *say they are* the Messiah or *that they are* prophets. They will perform many kinds of miracles in order to deceive people. They will even try *to see* if *it is* possible to deceive *you people whom God has* chosen. So at that time, if someone says to you, 'Look, here *is* the Messiah!' or *if someone says,* 'There

is the Messiah!' do not believe it! [25] Take note *that* I have warned you about *all this* before *it happens.* [26] So if someone says to you, 'Look, *the Messiah* is in the desolate area!' do not go there. *Likewise, if someone says to you,* 'Look, he is in a secret room!' do not believe *that person,* [27] because just as lightning flashes from the east to the west *and people everywhere can* see it, when *I,* the one who came from heaven, return again, *everyone will see me.* [28] *My return will be as obvious as the fact that* wherever you see vultures gathering, you know there will be an animal carcass there.[j]

Matthew 24:29-31

THEME: Jesus told his disciples what will happen at the time of his return.

[29] "Immediately after the time of great suffering of those days, *the universe will become dark.* The sun will become dark. The moon will not shine. The stars will fall from the sky. And the powerful *objects* in the sky will be shaken.[k] [30] After that, *something will be seen* in the sky that indicates that *I,* the one who came from heaven, *am returning to the earth.* Then *unbelieving people from* all ethnic groups of the earth will *mourn for fear of being punished by God.* They will see *me,* the one who came from heaven, coming on the clouds with power and great glory *as I return to the earth.* [31] I will send my angels *to the earth* from everywhere in the heavens. *They will be* playing trumpets loudly. *Then* from throughout the whole earth they will gather the people I have chosen.

Matthew 24:32-35

THEME: Jesus told his disciples how to know when the time of his return was near.

[32] "Now *I want you to* learn something from *how* fig trees *grow. In this area,* when the branches *of a fig tree* become tender and its leaves begin to sprout, you know that summer is near. [33] In the same way, when you see all these things *I have just described happening,* **you** will know that *the time of my return* is very close. [34] Keep this in mind: All of these events will happen before all the people who have observed the things I have done have died. [35] *You can be certain that these* things I have told *you* about will happen. That they will happen is more *certain* than the earth and sky continuing to exist.

Matthew 24:36-44

THEME: Jesus told his disciples to be ready because they do not know the time of his return.

[36] "But neither I, nor any other person, nor any angel in heaven, knows either the day or the hour *when the things I have told you about will happen.* **Only** *God, my* Father, *knows.* [37-39] It's like what happened when Noah lived. Until the flood came, *the people* did not know *there was any danger* to them. Before the flood waters covered the earth, *the people* were eating and drinking *as usual,* and they got married *as usual.* They were doing all this until the day Noah *and his family* entered the big boat. And then the flood came and drowned all *those who were not in the boat.* Similarly, *the unbelieving people will not know* when *I, the one who came from heaven,* will return *and they will not* be *expecting me.* [40] When *I return, I will not take all people up to heaven. I will take only those who trust in me. For instance,* two *people* will be in the fields. One of them will be taken up *to heaven* and the other *person* will be left *here to be punished.* [41] Similarly, two *women* will be at the mill grinding grain. One of them will be taken up *to heaven* and the other will be left. [42] So,

---

[j] OR, Just like the vultures gather together **wherever** there is an animal carcass, *God will punish sinful people* **wherever** *they are.*

[k] OR, ...And the spiritual beings in space will be deposed.

because you do not know what day *I, your Lord, will return to the earth*, you need to be ready *for me to return at any time.* [43] You know that if the owners of a house knew at what time in the night thieves would come, they would be awake and prevent the thieves from breaking in. In the same way I *will come just as unexpectedly as thieves.* [44] So **you** need to be ready *for my return*, because *I, the one who came from heaven, will return to the earth* at a time when you do not expect *me to come.*

Matthew 24:45-51

THEME: Jesus told a parable to warn his disciples not to act wickedly, thinking he would not return soon.

[45] "Think about what every faithful and wise servant is like. The house owner appoints one servant to supervise the other servants. He tells him to give them food at the proper times. *Then he leaves on a long trip.* [46] If the servant is doing that *work* when the house owner returns*, the house owner* will be very pleased with him. [47] Keep this in mind: The house owner will appoint *that one servant* to be the supervisor of **all his possessions**. [48] But a wicked servant might say to himself, 'The owner *has been away* for a long time, *so he probably* will not return soon *and find out what I am doing.*' [49] *So he* will begin to beat the other servants and eat and drink with those who are drunk. [50] *Then* the house owner will come back at a time when the servant does not expect him. [51] He will punish that servant severely[I] and will put him *in the place* where the ones who only pretend to be good servants are put. In that place the people cry and grind their teeth *because of their intense suffering.*"

25

Matthew 25:1-13

THEME: Jesus taught in a parable that his disciples should always be ready for his return.

[1] *Jesus continued by saying, "I will tell you something else about the time when I return from* heaven as king. *What will happen to people who say they know me will be* like *what happened to* ten virgins who took their lanterns and went to the place where they would meet a bridegroom *and go to his wedding celebration.* [2] Five of the virgins were foolish and five of them were wise. [3] The *virgins* who were foolish took their lanterns, but they did not take any *extra olive* oil *for the* lanterns. [4] But the *virgins* who were wise took oil in their flasks as well as in their lanterns. [5] The bridegroom was delayed, *and it became late.* So all the virgins became sleepy and fell asleep. [6] In the middle of the night someone *woke them up by* shouting, 'Hey! The bridegroom *is arriving!* Go outside and meet him!' [7] So all the virgins got up and trimmed their lantern wicks *so they would burn properly.* [8] The foolish virgins said to the wise ones, 'Give us some of your *olive* oil because our lamps are about to go out!' [9] The wise virgins replied, 'No, because there might not be enough oil for our lamps and for yours. Go to a store and buy some for yourselves!' [10] But while *the foolish virgins* were going to buy *some oil*, the bridegroom arrived. So the *wise virgins*, who were ready, went with him to the wedding hall *where the bride was waiting.* Then the door was closed. [11] Later, the rest of the virgins came *to the hall* and called *to the bridegroom*, 'Sir, open *the door* for us!' [12] But he said *to them*, 'The truth is that I do not know you, so *I will not open the door for you!*'" [13] *Then Jesus continued by saying, "So, in order that that this*

[I]   OR, He will cut that servant into two pieces…

will not happen to you, keep expecting *my return,* because you do not know when *it will be.*"

Matthew 25:14-30

THEME: Jesus told a parable to teach his disciples about making good use of what God has given them.

¹⁴ "*When I return from heaven as king, I will deal with those who say they have been serving me like* a man who was about to go on a long journey dealt with his servants. He called them together and gave them each some of his wealth *to invest and gain more money for him.* ¹⁵ He gave them money according to their ability *to do something with it. For example*, he gave one servant five thousand dollars, he gave another two thousand dollars, and he gave another one thousand dollars. Then he left on his journey. ¹⁶ The servant who had received five thousand dollars went immediately and used that money to gain five thousand dollars more. ¹⁷ Similarly, the servant who had *received* two thousand dollars gained two *thousand dollars* more. ¹⁸ But the servant who had received one *thousand dollars* went and dug a hole in the ground and hid the money there *to keep it safe.*

¹⁹ "After a long time the servants' boss returned. He *called them together to* find out what they had done with his money. ²⁰ The servant who had received five thousand dollars brought two *bags, each containing* five thousand dollars. He said, 'Boss, you gave me five thousand dollars to invest. Look, I have gained five thousand more!' ²¹ His boss replied, '*You are a very* good and faithful servant! *You have* done *very* well! You have faithfully handled a small *amount of money,* so I will put you in charge of a lot of things. Come and be happy with me!'

²² "The servant who had *received* two thousand dollars also came and said, 'Boss, you gave me two thousand dollars to invest. Look, I have gained two thousand more!' ²³ His boss replied, 'You are a *very* good and faithful servant! You have done very well! You have faithfully handled a small *amount of money,* so I will put you in charge of a lot of things. Come and be happy with me!'

²⁴ "Then the man who had received one thousand dollars came. He said, 'Boss, *I was afraid of you.* I knew that you are a man who does not do foolish things with his money. *You even* take *from others money* that does not really belong to you*, like a farmer who* harvests *grain from another man's field* where he did not *even* do the planting. ²⁵ So *because* I was afraid *of what you would do to me if I did not make a profit*, I went out and hid your thousand dollars in the ground *to keep it safe.* Here, this is *the money* that belongs to you!' ²⁶ His boss replied, 'You wicked, lazy servant! You knew that *I* take *from others money* that does not really belong to me*, like a farmer who* harvests *grain from another man's field* where he did not even do the planting! ²⁷ So then you should have at least put my money *on deposit* in a bank, so that when I returned I would get it back with the interest *it earned*!' ²⁸ *Then the boss said to his other servants*, 'Take the thousand dollars from him and give it to *the servant* who has the ten thousand dollars! ²⁹ To those who *use well what* they have *received, God* will give more, and they will have plenty. But from those who *do* not *use well what they have received,* even what they *already* have will be taken away. ³⁰ Furthermore, throw that worthless servant outside, into the darkness, where he will be *with those who are* wailing and gnashing their teeth *because of their intense suffering.*

Matthew 25:31-46

THEME: Jesus told a parable about how he will judge between those who have shown kindness to others and those who have not.

[31] "When I, the one who came from heaven, come again, I will come with all my radiance and *bring* all my angels with me. Then I will sit as a king on my wonderful throne *to judge people.* [32] People from all nations will be gathered in front of me, and I will separate them, one from another, as a shepherd separates his sheep from his goats. [33] I will put *the righteous people* on my right and *the unrighteous ones on my left, as a* shepherd puts sheep *on one side* and goats *on the other side.*

[34] "Then I will say to those on my right, 'You people whom my Father has blessed, come! From the time he created the world, he has been preparing to allow you to *receive the blessings he will give to all those* who let him rule their lives. *Now is the time for* you to receive *those blessings!* [35] *They belong to you,* because you gave me something to eat when I was hungry.[m] You gave me something to drink when I was thirsty. When I was a stranger *in your town,* you invited me *to stay* in *your houses.* [36] When I needed clothes, you gave me some. When I was sick, you took care of me. When I was in prison, you came to visit me.'

[37] "Then the righteous people will reply, 'Lord, when did we see you hungry and we gave you something to eat? When were you thirsty and we gave you something to drink? [38] When were you a stranger *in our town* and we invited you *to stay* in *our houses*? When did you need clothes and we gave you some? [39] When were you sick or in prison and we came to visit you?'

[40] "I will reply, 'The truth is that whatever you did for any one of your fellow believers, even an unimportant one, *it was as though* you did it for me.'

[41] "Then I will say to those on my left, 'You people whom God has cursed, leave me! Go into the eternal fire that God has prepared for the devil and his angels! [42] *This is right,* because you did not give me anything to eat when I was hungry. You did not give me anything to drink when I was thirsty. [43] You did not invite me into *your homes* when I was a stranger *in your town.* You did not give me any clothes when I needed them. You did not take care of me when I was sick or in prison.'

[44] "They will answer, 'Lord, when were you hungry or thirsty or a stranger or needing clothes or sick or in prison, and we did not help you?'

[45] "I will reply, 'The truth is that whenever you did not do anything to help any one of *my people, even if they were* unimportant people, *it was as though* you did not do anything *to help* me.'

[46] "Then those *on my left* will go away to the place where *they* will be punished eternally, but the righteous people will go to where they will live forever *with God.*"

---

[m] OR, *They belong to you.* It is as though you gave me something to eat when I was hungry.

26

Matthew 26:1-5

THEME: Jesus told his disciples of his coming arrest. The Jewish leaders planned how to seize Jesus.

[1] When Jesus had finished *saying* all those things, he said to *us* disciples, [2] "You know that two days from now *we will celebrate* the Passover *festival. At that time* I, the one who came from heaven, will be put into the hands of those who will nail me to a cross."

[3] At the same time the chief priests and the Jewish elders gathered in the home of the high priest, whose name was Caiaphas. [4] *There* they plotted how they could seize Jesus in some deceitful way so that they could have him executed. [5] But they said, "*We must* not *do it* during the *Passover* festival, because *if we do it then*, the people might riot."

Matthew 26:6-13

THEME: Jesus commended a woman for showing her appreciation of him.

[6] While *we* were *with* Jesus in *the village of* Bethany in the home of Simon, whom *Jesus had healed of* leprosy, [7] a woman came to him. She *was carrying* a stone jar *containing* very expensive perfume. *To show how much she appreciated* Jesus, she poured the perfume on his head as he was eating. [8] When *we* disciples saw that, *some of us* were angry. *One of us* said, "It is terrible that this perfume *was* wasted! [9] *We* could have sold it and gotten a lot of money for it! Then the money could have been given to poor people." Jesus knew *what we were saying. So he* said to us, "You should not be bothering this woman! She has done a beautiful thing to me. [11] *Keep in mind that* you will always have poor people among you, *so you can help them whenever you want to*. But I will not always be with you, *so it is good that she showed her appreciation for me now!* [12] When she poured this perfume on my body, *it was as if she knew that I am going to die soon. And it is as if she* has anointed my body for burial. [13] I will tell you this: Wherever the good message *about me* is preached throughout the world, those who preach it will tell what this woman has done, *and as a result* she will *always* be remembered."

Matthew 26:14-16

THEME: Judas agreed to betray Jesus for thirty silver coins.

[14] Then Judas Iscariot, *even though he was* one of *us* twelve *disciples*, went to the chief priests. [15] He asked them, "If I enable you to seize *Jesus*, how much *money* are you willing to give me?" They *agreed to give him* thirty silver coins. So they counted out the coins and *gave them* to him. [16] From that time Judas watched for an opportunity to enable them to seize *Jesus*.

Matthew 26:17-25

THEME: Two disciples prepared the Passover meal. During the meal, Jesus said that Judas would betray him.

[17] On the first day *of the week-long festival* of Unleavened Bread, *we* disciples went to Jesus and asked, "Where do you want us to prepare *the meal for* the Passover *celebration* so that *we can* eat *it with* you?" [18] *In reply* he *gave instructions to two disciples about where they should go. He* said *to them*, "Go into *the city* to a man *with whom I have*

previously arranged this. Tell him that the teacher says, 'The time I *told you about* is near. I am going to celebrate the Passover with my disciples at your house, *and I have sent these two to prepare the meal.*'" [19] So the *two* disciples did as Jesus told them. They *went and* prepared the Passover *meal in that man's house.*

[20] When it was evening, Jesus was eating the meal with *us* twelve disciples. [21] While we were eating, he said *to us,* "Listen carefully to this: One of you is going to enable *my enemies* to seize me." [22] *We* were very sad. We began to say to him, one after the other, "Lord, I'm not the one, am I?" [23] He replied, "The one who will enable my enemies to seize me is the one of you who is dipping bread into *the sauce in* the dish along with me. [24] *It is certain that* I, the one who came from heaven, will *die,* because that is what *the prophets* have written about me. But there will be terrible punishment for the man who enables *my enemies* to seize me! It would be better for that man if he had never been born!" [25] Then Judas, the one who was going to betray him, said, "Teacher, I'm not the one, am I?" Jesus replied, "Yes, it is you."

Matthew 26:26-30

THEME: Jesus gave the disciples the bread and wine to symbolize his coming death.

[26] While we were eating, Jesus took *a small loaf of* bread and thanked God for it. He broke it *into pieces* and gave it to *us* disciples, and said, "Take this *bread and* eat *it. It represents*[n] my body." [27] Later he took a cup *of wine* and thanked *God for it.* Then he gave it to us, saying, "Drink some *of the wine in this cup,* all of you. [28] *The wine in* this cup *represents* my blood,[o] which will soon flow *from my body when I die. With* this blood I *will sign* the new agreement *that God is making* to forgive the sins of many *people.* [29] Note this carefully: I will not drink wine in this way anymore until the time when I drink it with you with a new *meaning. That will happen* when my Father *enables me to begin* to rule as king."

[30] After we sang a hymn, we started out towards Olive *Tree* Hill.

Matthew 26:31-35

THEME: Jesus prophesied that Peter would deny three times that he knew Jesus.

[31] *On the way,* Jesus told us, "This night all of you will desert me because of *what will happen to* me! *This is certain to happen* because *these words that God said* are written in *the Scriptures:* 'I will *cause* the shepherd to be killed, and *all* the sheep will be scattered.' [32] But after I have *died and* become alive again, I will go ahead of you to *the district of* Galilee *and meet you there.*" [33] Peter replied, "Perhaps all *the other disciples* will desert you *when they see what happens to you,* but I *certainly* will never *leave you!*" [34] Jesus replied to him, "The truth is that this very *night,* before the rooster crows, you will say three times that you do not know me!" [35] Peter said to him, "Even if I am killed *while defending you,* I will never say that I do not know you!" All *the rest of us* disciples also said the same *thing.*

---

[n] OR, …*Then he gave it to his disciples* and said, "This bread *is* my body, which *I am about to sacrifice* for you.

[o] OR, …*Then he gave it to his disciples,* saying, [28] "*The wine in* this cup *is* my blood…

Matthew 26:36-46

THEME: While the disciples slept, Jesus prayed that God would spare him from the coming suffering.

³⁶ Then Jesus went with us to a place called Gethsemane. There he said to *most of* us, "Stay here while I go over there and pray." ³⁷ He took Peter, James, and John with him. He became extremely distressed, ³⁸ and said to them, "I am very sorrowful, so much so that *I feel as if my sorrow is about to* kill me! Remain here and stay awake with me!" ³⁹ After going a little further, he threw himself face down *on the ground.* He prayed, "My Father, if it is possible, let me not have to endure the suffering *that is coming* now. But do not do as I want. Instead, do as you want!" ⁴⁰ Then he returned to the *three* disciples and saw that they were sleeping. He *woke* Peter and said to him, "I am disappointed that you *men fell asleep and* were not able to stay awake with me for just one hour! ⁴¹ You must keep alert and pray so that you can resist when you are tempted. You want *to do what I tell you*, but you are not able *to actually do it.*"

⁴² He went away a second time. He prayed, "My Father, if it is necessary for me to suffer, may what you want be done!"

⁴³ When he returned to the *three disciples*, he saw that they were asleep *again*. They couldn't keep their eyes open. ⁴⁴ So he left them and went away again. He prayed the third time, saying the same thing *he had prayed before*. ⁴⁵ Then he returned to the disciples. He *woke them up and* said to them, "I am disappointed that you are still sleeping and resting! *Look! Someone* is about to enable sinful *men* to seize *me*, the one who came from heaven! ⁴⁶ Get up! Let's go *to meet them*! Here comes the one who is enabling them to seize me!"

Matthew 26:47-56

THEME: Judas enabled men to seize Jesus. Jesus ridiculed them, but the disciples fled.

⁴⁷ While *Jesus* was still speaking, Judas *arrived. Even though he was* one of *us* twelve *disciples*, he came *to enable Jesus' enemies to seize him*. A large crowd carrying swords and clubs was with him. They had been sent by the chief priests and elders. ⁴⁸ Judas had *previously* arranged to give them a signal, saying, "The man whom I will kiss is the one *you want*. Seize him!" ⁴⁹ He immediately went to Jesus and said, "Greetings, Teacher!" Then he kissed Jesus *on the cheek.* ⁵⁰ Jesus replied, "Friend, is it *to kiss me* that you have come here?"ᵖ Then *the men who came with Judas* stepped forward and seized Jesus. ⁵¹ Suddenly, one of the men who was with Jesus drew his sword and struck the servant of the high priest *to kill him, but only* cut off his ear. ⁵² Jesus said to him, "Put your sword back in its sheath! All those who try to kill others with a sword will themselves be killed with swords! ⁵³ Do you not think that if I asked my Father, he would immediately send more than twelve armies of angels to help me? ⁵⁴ *But if I did that, what the prophets* have written in the Scriptures *about what will happen to the Messiah* would not be fulfilled."

⁵⁵ At that time Jesus said to the crowd *that was arresting him*, "It is ridiculous that you have come *here* to seize me with swords and clubs, as *if I were* a bandit! Day after day I sat in the Temple *courtyard,* teaching *the people*. Why did you not arrest me *then*? ⁵⁶ But all this is happening to fulfill what the prophets *have written in* the Scriptures *about me*." Then all of us disciples deserted Jesus and ran away.

ᵖ OR, Jesus replied, "Friend, do what you have come for!"

Matthew 26:57-68

THEME: Jesus was put on trial before the Jewish Council.

[57] The men who had seized Jesus took him to *the house where* Caiaphas, the high priest *lived.* The men who taught the *Jewish* laws and the elders had already gathered *there.* [58] Peter followed *Jesus* at a distance. He came to the high priest's courtyard. He entered *the courtyard* and sat down with the guards to see what would happen.

[59] The chief priests and the rest of the *Jewish* Council were trying to find people who would tell lies about Jesus so that they could *convince the Roman authorities to* execute him. [60] But even though many people spoke lies about him, they did not find anyone *who said anything that was useful.* Finally two men came forward [61] and said, "This man said, 'I am able to destroy God's Temple and to rebuild it in three days.'" [62] Then the high priest stood up and said to Jesus, "Aren't you going to reply? What *do you say about* these accusations?" [63] But Jesus remained silent. Then the high priest said to him, "I command you to tell us *the truth,* knowing the all-powerful God *is listening to you*: Are you the Messiah, the Son of God?"[q] [64] Jesus replied, "Yes, *it is as* you say. But I will also say this to all of you: The day *will come when* you will see *me,* the one who came from heaven, sitting beside Almighty *God,* and ruling. You will also see me coming on the clouds from heaven!"

[65] At that, the high priest tore his outer garment. *That was the custom to show he was shocked to hear Jesus say he was equal to God.* Then he said, "This man has just insulted God! He claims to be equal with God! We certainly do not need anyone else to testify *against him*! You heard what he said against God! [66] What is your decision?" *The Jewish leaders* replied, *"According to our laws*, he *is guilty and* deserves to be executed!" [67] Then *some of them* spat in his face. *Others* struck him with their fists. Others, *after they blindfolded him,* slapped him [68] and said, *"Since you claim to be* the Messiah, tell us who hit you!"

Matthew 26:69-75

THEME: Peter denied three times that he knew Jesus.

[69] Peter was sitting outside in the courtyard. A servant girl came up to him *and looked at him.* She said, "You also were with Jesus, *that man* from Galilee!" [70] But in front of everyone there, he denied it. He said, "I do not know what you are talking about!" [71] Then he went out to the gateway of the courtyard. Another servant girl saw him and said to the people who were standing nearby, "This man was with Jesus, *the man* from Nazareth." [72] But *Peter* again denied it. He said, "May God punish me *if I am lying*! *I tell you,* I do not even know that man!" [73] After a little while, the people who were standing there approached Peter and said to him, "It is certain that you are one of those *who were with that man.* We can tell from your accent that you *are from Galilee*." [74] Then Peter began to proclaim loudly that God should curse him *if he was lying.* He asked God in heaven to witness *that he was telling the truth* and said, "I do not know that man!" Immediately a rooster crowed. [75] Then Peter remembered the words Jesus had spoken *to him,* "Before the rooster crows, you will deny three times *that you know* me." And he went out *of the courtyard,* crying bitterly.

---

[q] Literally, "Are you the Christ, the Son of God?"

27

Matthew 27:1-2

THEME: The Jewish religious leaders took Jesus to the Roman governor.

¹ Very early the next morning all the chief priests and Jewish elders decided how *to arrange for the Romans* to execute Jesus. ² They tied his hands and took him to Pilate, the *Roman* governor.

Matthew 27:3-10

THEME: After Judas returned the money and hanged himself, the Jewish leaders bought a field with the money, in fulfillment of prophecy.

³ When Judas, the one who had enabled Jesus' enemies to seize him, realized that they had decided to have Jesus executed, he was very sorry *about what he had done*. He took the thirty coins back to the chief priests and elders, ⁴ and said, "I have sinned. I have betrayed a man who has not done anything wrong." They replied, "That means nothing to us. That's your problem!" ⁵ So Judas *took* the money *and* threw it inside the Temple. Then he went away and hanged himself.

⁶ *Later* the high priests *found* the coins. They picked them up and said, "This is money we paid *to have a man killed*, and our law does not *allow such money* to be put into the *Temple* treasury." ⁷ So they decided to use the money to buy the field where ground was dug for making pots. *They began to use that ground as a cemetery* for burying foreigners *who died in Jerusalem*. ⁸ That is why that field is still called 'The field of blood.' ⁹ *By buying that field*, they fulfilled these words that the prophet Jeremiah wrote *long ago*,

They took the thirty silver coins; that was what the leaders of Israel decided *that he was worth*; ¹⁰ and with that money they bought the field where clay was dug for potters. They did that as the Lord had commanded.ʳ

Matthew 27:11-26

THEME: Jesus was put on trial before the governor.

¹¹ Jesus stood in front of the governor. The governor asked him, "Do you *claim to be* the king of the Jews?" Jesus replied, "*It is* as you have *just* said."

¹² When he was accused by the chief priests and elders about various things, he did not answer. ¹³ So Pilate said to him, "You hear how many accusations they are making against you; *have you no reply?*" ¹⁴ But *even though he was not guilty*, Jesus did not say anything. He did not reply to any of the things about which they were accusing him. The governor was very surprised at that.

¹⁵ It was the governor's custom *each year* during the *Passover* celebration to release *one person who was in prison. He released* whatever prisoner the people wanted. ¹⁶ At that time there was *in Jerusalem* a well-known prisoner whose name was Barabbas. ¹⁷ So when the crowd gathered, Pilate asked them, "Which *prisoner* would you like me to release for you: Barabbas, or Jesus, whom *some of you* claim to be the Messiah?" ¹⁸ He

---

ʳ Matthew refers very loosely to passages in Jeremiah and Zechariah. The Greek text says 'as the Lord commanded me' but the word 'me' does not make sense in this passage, so this translation omits it.

asked that question because he realized that the chief priests *wanted to have Jesus executed.* They had brought Jesus to him *only* because they were jealous of Jesus. *And he thought the crowd would prefer that he release Jesus.*

[19] While Pilate was sitting on the platform *where he made* judicial *decisions,* his wife sent him *this message*: "Early this morning I had a bad dream because of that man. So do not condemn that righteous man!"

[20] But the chief priests and elders persuaded the crowd to ask *Pilate to* release Barabbas, and to *order* that Jesus be executed. [21] So when the governor asked them, "Which of the two men do you want me to release for you?" they replied, "Barabbas!" [22] Pilate asked *in astonishment*, "So what shall I do with Jesus who *some of you* say is the Messiah?" They all answered, "*Sentence* him *to* be crucified!" [23] Pilate replied, "Why? What crime has he committed?" But they shouted even louder, "*Have* him crucified!"

[24] Pilate realized that he was accomplishing nothing and that instead, the people were starting to riot. So he took *a basin of* water and washed his hands in front of the crowd. He said, "*By washing my hands I am showing you that* if this man dies, it is *your* fault, *not mine!*" [25] And all the people answered, "The guilt for causing his death will be on us, and it will be on our children, too!" [26] Then he had Barabbas released for them. But he *had* Jesus whipped. And then he turned Jesus over to *the soldiers* to be crucified.

Matthew 27:27-31

THEME: The soldiers made fun of Jesus before taking him to be crucified.

[27] Then the governor's soldiers took Jesus into the government headquarters. The whole cohort of soldiers gathered around him. [28] They pulled off *his clothes,* and *pretending he was a king, they* put a purple robe on him. [29] They *took some branches with* thorns and wove them to make a crown and put it on his head. They put in his right hand a reed *like a staff that a king would hold*. Then they knelt in front of him and made fun of him, saying, "Hooray for the king of the Jews!" [30] They kept spitting on him. They took the staff and kept striking him on the head with it. [31] When they had finished ridiculing him, they pulled off the robe and put his own clothes on him. Then they led him away to *the place where they* would nail him to a cross.

Matthew 27:32-44

THEME: Jesus was crucified, along with two bandits.

[32] *After Jesus carried his cross* a short distance, *the soldiers* saw a man named Simon, *who was* from *the city of* Cyrene. They forced him to carry the cross for Jesus. [33] They came to a place called Golgotha, which means 'the place *like* a skull.' [34] When *they got there,* they mixed something that tasted very bitter with some wine. They gave it to *Jesus* to drink *so that he would not feel so much pain when they nailed him on the cross.* But when he tasted it, he refused to drink it. *Some soldiers took his clothes,* [35] and then they nailed him to the cross. Afterwards, they divided his clothes among themselves by gambling with something like dice *to decide which piece of clothing each one would get.* [36] Then the soldiers sat down there to guard him *to keep anyone from trying to rescue him.* [37] They fastened *to the cross* above Jesus' head a *sign that stated* why *they* were nailing him to the cross. *But all* it said was, 'This is Jesus, the king of the Jews.' [38] They also crucified two bandits. One was nailed to a cross on the right side *of Jesus* and one to a cross on the left side. [39] The people who were passing by insulted him by shaking their heads *as if he were an evil man*. [40] They said, "You *said you* would destroy the Temple,

and then you would build it again in three days! *So if you could do that*, you *should be able to* save yourself! If you are the man who is also God,^s come down from the cross!"

⁴¹ In the same way, the chief priests, the men who taught the *Jewish* laws, and the elders made fun of him. They said, ⁴² "He *claims to have* saved others *from their sicknesses*, but he can't help himself! He *says he* is the king of Israel. So he should come down from the cross. Then we would believe him! ⁴³ He *says that he* trusts in God, and that he is the man who is also God.' So if God is pleased with him, God should rescue him now!" ⁴⁴ And the *two* bandits who had been crucified with him also insulted him in the same way.

Matthew 27:45-56

THEME: When Jesus died at about three o'clock, several unusual events occurred.

⁴⁵ At noon it became dark over the whole land, *and it stayed dark* until three o'clock *in the afternoon*. ⁴⁶ At about three o'clock Jesus shouted loudly, "Eli, Eli, lama sabachthani?" That means, 'My God, my God, why have you deserted me?' ⁴⁷ When some of the people standing there heard *the word 'Eli', misunderstanding it*, they said, "He is calling for *the prophet* Elijah!" ⁴⁸ Immediately one of them ran and got a sponge. Then he put the sponge on *the tip of* a reed, soaked it in some sour wine, and *held it up* for *Jesus* to suck out *the wine that was in it*. ⁴⁹ But the other *people there* said, "Wait! Let's see if Elijah comes to save him!" ⁵⁰ Then after Jesus shouted out loudly again, he *died*, giving his spirit over *to God*. ⁵¹ At that moment the *heavy thick* curtain *that closed off the most holy place* in the Temple split into two pieces from top to bottom. *That signified that ordinary people could now go into the presence of God.* The earth shook, and *some large* rocks split open. ⁵² *Some* tombs opened up, and the bodies of many godly people who had died became alive again. ⁵³ They came out of the tombs, and after Jesus became alive again, they went into Jerusalem and appeared to many people *there*.

⁵⁴ The officer who supervised the soldiers *who nailed Jesus to the cross was standing nearby*. His soldiers who had been on guard *were also there*. When they *felt* the earthquake and saw the *other* things that happened, they were terrified. They exclaimed, "Truly he was both man and God!"^t

⁵⁵ Many women were there, watching from a distance. They were women who had accompanied Jesus from *the district of* Galilee in order to provide for his needs. ⁵⁶ Among these women were Mary from *the village of* Magdala, *another* Mary who was the mother of James and Joseph, and the mother of James and John.

Matthew 27:57-61

THEME: Jesus was buried.

⁵⁷ When it was *almost* evening, a rich man named Joseph came *there*. He was from *the town of* Arimathea. He also was a disciple of Jesus. ⁵⁸ He then went to Pilate and asked for permission *to take* the body of Jesus *and bury it*. Pilate ordered that *he* be allowed to take *the body*. ⁵⁹ So Joseph *and others* took the body and wrapped it in a clean linen cloth. ⁶⁰ Then they placed it in Joseph's own new tomb that had been dug out of the rock *cliff*. They rolled a huge *circular flat* stone in front of the entrance to the tomb. Then they left. ⁶¹ Mary from Magdala and the other Mary were sitting there opposite the tomb, *watching*.

---

^s   Literally, "If you are the Son of God…"

^t   Literally, "a Son of God"

Matthew 27:62-66

THEME: The religious leaders arranged for Jesus' tomb to be sealed and guarded.

[62] The next day was Saturday, the Jewish day of rest. The chief priests and *some of* the Pharisees went to Pilate [63] and said, "Sir, we remember that while that deceiver was still alive, he said, 'Three days after *I die* I will become alive again.' [64] So we ask you to order that the tomb be guarded for three days. If you do not do that, his disciples may come and steal the body. Then they will tell people that he has risen from the dead. If *people are deceived by that*, it will be worse than the way he deceived people before *by saying he was the Messiah*." [65] Pilate replied, "You *can* take some soldiers. Go to the tomb and make it as secure as you know how." [66] So they went and made the tomb secure by *fastening a cord from* the stone *that was in front of the entrance to the rock cliff on each side* and sealing it. They also *left some soldiers there to* guard *the tomb*.

28

Matthew 28:1-10

THEME: After an angel appeared to several women and showed them the tomb was empty, Jesus appeared to them.

[1] After the Jewish day of rest *ended*, on Sunday morning at dawn Mary from Magdala and the other Mary went to look at the tomb. [2] Suddenly there was a strong earthquake. *At the same time* an angel from God came down from heaven. He *went to the tomb and* rolled the stone away *from the entrance so that everyone could see the tomb was empty*. Then he sat on the stone. [3] His appearance was *as bright* as lightning, and his clothes were as white as snow. [4] The guards shook with fear. Then they became *completely immobile*, as though they were dead.

[5] The angel said to the two women, "**You** should not be afraid! I know that you are looking for Jesus, who was crucified. [6] He is not here! He has been raised *from the dead*, just as *he* told you *would happen*! Come and see the place where his body lay! [7] Then go quickly and tell his disciples, 'He has risen from the dead! He will go ahead of you to Galilee. You will see him there.' *Pay attention to what* I have told you!"

[8] So the women left the tomb quickly. They were afraid, but they were *also* very joyful. They ran to tell us disciples *what had happened*. [9] Suddenly, *as they were running*, Jesus appeared to them and said, "Greetings!" The women came close to him. They knelt down and clasped his feet and worshiped him. [10] Then Jesus said to them, "Don't be afraid! Go and tell all my disciples that they should go to Galilee. They will see me there."

Matthew 28:11-15

THEME: What the guards were told to tell people about why Jesus' body was gone.

[11] While the women were going, some of the soldiers who had been guarding *the tomb* went into the city. They reported to the chief priests everything that had happened. [12] So the chief priests and Jewish elders met together and made a plan *to explain why the tomb was empty*. They gave the soldiers a lot of money *as a bribe*, [13] and said, "Tell people, 'His disciples came during the night and stole his *body* while we were sleeping.' [14] If the governor hears about this, we will make sure he does not get angry *and punish you. So you won't have to worry*." [15] So the soldiers took the money and did as they were told. And this story has been spread among the Jews to the very day *I am writing* this.

Matthew 28:16-20

THEME: Jesus appeared to the apostles in Galilee and gave them final instructions.

[16] *Later we* eleven *disciples* went to Galilee. We went to the mountain where Jesus had told *us* to go. [17] We saw him *there* and worshiped him. But some of *us* doubted *that it was really Jesus, and that he had become alive again.* [18] Then Jesus came *close* to *us* and said, "My Father has given me all authority over everything and everyone in heaven and on earth. [19] So go, and *using my authority, teach my message to* people of all ethnic groups so that they may become my disciples. Baptize them *to be under the authority of* my Father, and of me, his Son, and of the Holy Spirit. [20] Teach them to obey everything I have commanded you. And remember that I will be with you always, until the end of *this* age."

The Gospel that was written by

Mark

1

Mark 1:1-8

THEME: The good message about Jesus the Messiah, the Son of God, began when John, the Baptizer, just as was prophesied long ago, announced the coming of Jesus.

[1-2] *This is* the good message about Jesus Christ, the Son of God.[a] *What I want to tell you* begins just as the prophet Isaiah *said it would begin, when* he wrote down *these words that God said to his Son:*

Listen! I am going to send my messenger ahead of you to prepare *the people for your coming.* [3] He will call out to people *who pass by where he is* in the desolate area, 'Prepare *yourselves to receive* the Lord when he comes! *Make yourselves ready so that you will be prepared* when he comes, *just as people* straighten out the road *for an important official.*'

[4] *John was that messenger whom Isaiah predicted would come. People called John* 'The Baptizer'. In the desolate area near the Jordan River he kept telling people, "If you want God to forgive you for your sins, you must turn away from your sinful behavior *before you ask me* to baptize *you!*" [5] A great number of people who lived *in the city of* Jerusalem and *elsewhere* in *the district of* Judea were going out to where John was. There, *after hearing John's message,* they *responded by* confessing their sins. Then John baptized them in the Jordan River. [6] John wore *coarse* clothing made of camel's hair. *As the prophet Elijah did long ago,* he wore a leather belt around his waist; and what he ate was *only* grasshoppers and honey *that he found* in that desolate area. [7] *This is what* he was preaching: "Very shortly a man will come who is very great. *I am nothing compared to him. Because he is so superior to me,* I am not even worthy to *serve him like a slave* by stooping down and untying his sandals. [8] I use *only* water when I baptize you *because you say you want to change your lives,* but he will put *his* Holy Spirit *within* you *to truly change your lives.*"

Mark 1:9-13

THEME: God showed Jesus to be the Son of God by God's Spirit descending upon him; by God himself declaring it; by Satan testing him; and by angels taking care of him.

[9] During the time *when John was preaching,* Jesus came from *the town of* Nazareth, *which is in the district* of Galilee. He went to *where John was preaching,* and John baptized him in the Jordan *River.* [10] Immediately after Jesus came up out of the water, he saw heaven opened up *and he saw* the Spirit *of God* in the form of a dove descending on him. [11] And *God* spoke to Jesus from heaven saying, "You are my Son, the one whom I love dearly. I am very pleased with you." [12] Right away the Spirit *of God* sent Jesus into a desolate area. [13] He was there for forty days, and during that time he was tempted by Satan. Wild animals were *there* also. But angels took care of him.

---

[a] OR, *This is* the good message about Jesus Christ, the Man who was also God.

Mark 1:14-15

THEME: After John was arrested, Jesus came and preached the good message from God.

[14] Later, after John *the Baptizer* was put in prison *for rebuking the governor Herod Antipas for his sins*, Jesus went to *the district of* Galilee. There he was preaching the good message that came from God. [15] He was repeatedly saying, "Now is the time when God will begin to rule people's lives *in a new way*. So turn away from your sins! Believe the good message *in order to become those whose lives he will rule!*"

Mark 1:16-20

THEME: Jesus showed his authority when he summoned four men and they immediately followed him.

[16] *One day*, while Jesus was walking along by Lake Galilee, he saw two men, Simon and Andrew, the *younger* brother of Simon. They were casting their *fishing* net into the lake because they earned their living by catching *and selling* fish. [17] Then Jesus said to them, "*Just as you have been* gathering fish, come with me and I will *teach* you how to gather people *to become my disciples*." [18] Immediately they left *the work they were doing with* their *fishing* nets, and they went with him. [19] After they had gone on a little further, Jesus saw two other men, James and John, the *younger* brother of James. They were the sons of *a man named* Zebedee. They were both in a boat mending fishing nets. [20] As soon as Jesus saw them, he told them that *they should leave their work and* go with him. So they left their father, *who remained* in the boat with the hired servants, and went away with Jesus.

Mark 1:21-28

THEME: People were amazed as a result of Jesus expelling a demon from a man.

[21] *Later* Jesus *and those disciples* arrived at *the town of* Capernaum. On the next Jewish day of rest, after Jesus had entered the Jewish meeting place, he began teaching *the people who had gathered there*. [22] They were continually amazed at the way he taught. *He did not just teach what others had taught*, like the men who teach the *Jewish* laws did. *They habitually just repeated what other people had taught*. Instead, he taught with *his own* authority. [23] Suddenly, *while he was teaching*, a man who had an evil spirit in him *appeared* in their meeting place, and he shouted, [24]"Jesus, from Nazareth, *since we evil spirits* have nothing in common with you, *don't interfere with us*! Don't destroy us *now*! I know who you are! You are the Holy One *who has come* from God!" [25] Jesus rebuked *the evil spirit*, saying, "Be quiet! And come out *of the man*!" [26] The evil spirit shook the man hard. He screamed loudly, and then he came out of the man *and left*. [27] All the people *who were there* were amazed. And they discussed this among themselves, *exclaiming*, "This is amazing! Not only does he teach in a new and authoritative way, but the evil spirits obey him *when he commands them*!" [28] The people very soon told *many others* throughout the whole *district* of Galilee what Jesus *had done*.

Mark 1:29-31

THEME: Jesus healed Simon's mother-in-law.

[29] After they left the Jewish meeting place, *Jesus, Simon, and Andrew*, along with James and John, went directly to the house of Simon and Andrew. [30] Simon's mother-in-law was lying in bed because she had a fever. Right away someone told Jesus about her *being*

sick. ³¹ He went to her and helped her up by taking hold of her hand. She recovered *at once* from the fever, *and she got up and* served them *some food.*

Mark 1:32-34

THEME: Jesus healed many people and expelled many evil spirits from people.

³² That evening, after the sun had gone down *and restrictions about travel on the Jewish day of rest were ended,* some people brought to Jesus many people who were sick and others who were controlled by demons. ³³ *It seemed as though* everyone *who lived in* the town was gathered at the doorway *of Simon's house.* ³⁴ Jesus healed many people who were ill with various diseases. He also expelled many demons. He did not allow the demons to tell people *about him,* because they knew he *had come from God, and for various reasons he did not want everyone to know that yet.*

Mark 1:35-39

THEME: Jesus traveled throughout Galilee preaching and expelling evil spirits from people.

³⁵ Jesus arose very early *the next morning* while it was still dark. He left *the house* and went *out of town* to an uninhabited place and began to pray. ³⁶ Simon and his companions searched for him, *wanting him to go back to town to help other people.* When they found him, they said to him, ³⁷"*Come back to the town with us, because* many people *in town* are looking for you!" ³⁸ He said to them, "*No,* let's go on to the neighboring towns so that I can preach there also, because the reason that I came *into the world* was to *preach to many people!*" ³⁹ So they went throughout *the district of* Galilee. *As they did so, on each Jewish rest day* he preached in places where we Jews worship God. He was also expelling evil spirits from people.

Mark 1:40-45

THEME: Jesus cured a leper and arranged for him to be able to associate with people again.

⁴⁰ *One day* a man who had leprosy came to Jesus. He knelt down in front of Jesus and pleaded with him saying, "*Please heal me, because I know* you are able to heal me if you are willing to!" ⁴¹ Jesus felt very sorry for him. *So he ignored the religious law that forbade healthy people to come close to lepers,* and he stretched out his hand and touched the man. Then he said to him, "I am willing *to heal you,* and I heal you *now!*" ⁴² Immediately the man was healed! He no longer had leprosy! ⁴³ Jesus spoke sternly to him before he sent him away. ⁴⁴ Jesus said to him, "Make sure that you do not report *your healing immediately* to anyone *other than* the local priest. Show yourself to him *so that he can examine you and verify that you no longer have leprosy.* After the priest tells *the local people,* they will know that *you have been healed, and you will be able to associate with them again.* Then go to *the Temple in Jerusalem* and take to the priests *the offering* that Moses commanded *that people who have been healed from leprosy should take so* that *they can* offer it *as a* sacrifice to God." ⁴⁵ The man went *and presented himself to the priest. But then* he began to tell many people about *how Jesus had healed him.* As a result, Jesus was no longer able to enter any town publicly *because the crowds would surround him.* Instead, he remained outside *the towns* in places *where no people lived.* But people kept coming to him from all over that region.

2

Mark 2:1-12

THEME: By healing a paralyzed man Jesus demonstrated his authority to forgive sins as well as to heal.

¹ *Jesus and his disciples* returned to Capernaum. A few days later, because people heard that Jesus was in *his* house, ² many people gathered there. As a result, *after they filled the house* there was no longer space to stand *in the house or* around the doorway *outside*. Jesus preached *God's* message to them. ³ Some people came to the house bringing a man who was paralyzed. Four men carried *him on a sleeping pad.* ⁴ They were not able to bring the man to Jesus because there was a large crowd there. So they *went up the steps to the flat roof and* removed *some of* the tiles *above* where Jesus was. Then, after making a *big* hole in the roof, they lowered *by ropes* the sleeping pad on which the paralyzed man lay. They lowered *it through the hole, down in front of Jesus.* ⁵ When Jesus perceived that they believed *he could heal the* paralyzed man, he said to him, "Young man, *I* forgive your sins!" ⁶ There were some men who taught *the Jewish* laws sitting there, and they started deliberating within themselves like this: ⁷ "Who does this man think he is, talking like that! He is insulting God! Nobody can forgive sins! Only God can forgive sins!" ⁸ Jesus knew right away within himself that they were deliberating like that within themselves. So he said to them, "You shouldn't question within yourselves *whether I have the right to forgive this man's sins.* ⁹ It would *not* be risky *for someone* to tell this man who is paralyzed, 'I forgive your sins,' *because no one could see whether or not his sins were really forgiven. But no one, if he did not have the power to heal, would* say to him, 'Get up, pick up your stretcher, and walk away', *because people could easily see whether he was healed or not.* ¹⁰ So I am going to do something in order that you may know that *God* has authorized *me*, the one who came from heaven, to forgive the sins *of people, as well as to heal people, while I am* on the earth." Then he said to the paralyzed man, ¹¹ "To you I say, 'Get up, pick up your sleeping pad, and go home!'" ¹² The man got up immediately! He picked up the sleeping pad, and went away, while all the people *there* were watching. They were all amazed, and they praised God and said, "Never before have we seen anything like what happened just now!"

Mark 2:13-17

THEME: Jesus invited Levi to be his disciple, and refuted those who objected to his associating with such people.

¹³ Jesus left *Capernaum* again and walked *with his disciples* alongside Lake *Galilee*. A large crowd came to him, and then he taught them. ¹⁴ As he walked on *towards the town*, he saw a man named Levi, whose father's name was Alphaeus. He was sitting in his office where he collected taxes *for the Roman government*. Jesus said to him, "Come with me *and become my disciple*!" So he got up and went with Jesus.

¹⁵ *Later*, Jesus was eating a meal in Levi's house. Many tax collectors and *other* people who were *considered to be habitual* sinners were eating with Jesus and his disciples. *That* was not surprising, for there were many people like them who were going *everywhere* with Jesus. ¹⁶ Some *men who taught the Jewish* laws who were also there and who were members of the Pharisee *sect* saw Jesus eating with tax collectors and *other*s who were considered to be sinners. So they said to his disciples, "*It is disgusting that* he eats with tax collectors and *other* sinners!" ¹⁷ When Jesus heard what *they were saying*, he said to the men who taught the *Jewish* laws, "*It is* people who are sick who need a doctor, not

those who are well." *What he meant by that was that it was people who knew that they were sinners who were coming to him to get spiritual help.* And he said, "I did not come *from heaven* to invite *people who think* they are righteous *to turn from their sinful behavior and come to me.* On the contrary, *I came from heaven to invite* people *who know they* are sinners *to turn from their sins and come to me.*"

Mark 2:18-22

THEME: Jesus told them it was inappropriate for his disciples to show sorrow by fasting while he was with them, and that requiring people to perform rituals like fasting was inconsistent with the new way of life he was bringing.

[18] The disciples of John *the Baptizer* and some men who belonged to the Pharisee *sect* used to fast, abstaining from food *to show they wanted to please God.* One day, some people came *to Jesus* and asked him *critically*, "The Pharisees and the disciples of John fast, but your disciples don't do that. Why *don't they?*" [19] *Jesus wanted them to understand that it was not appropriate for his disciples to be sad and abstain from food* while he was still with them. So he said to them, "When the bridegroom is with *his friends at the time of the wedding*, his friends certainly don't abstain from food, do they? *No!* During the time he is with them, they will not abstain from food, *because they* will be happy together. [20] *But* some day he will be taken away from them. Then, in those days, they will abstain from food, *because they will be sad.*"

[21] *Jesus wanted to show that those who desire to live in accordance with his new message should not be forced to obey the old religious traditions like fasting. So he said to them*, "No one sews a patch of unshrunken cloth on an old garment *to mend a hole.* If they did that, *when they washed the garment, the patch would shrink* and the new *piece of cloth* would tear more of the old cloth. As a result, the hole would become bigger! [22] *Neither does anyone* put freshly-*squeezed* wine into old skin bags *to store it.* If anyone did that, the wine would burst the skin bags *because they would not stretch when the wine ferments and expands.* As a result, both the wine and the skin bags would be ruined! On the contrary, new wine must be put into new skin bags!"

Mark 2:23-28

THEME: When the Pharisees complained about Jesus' disciples plucking grain on the Sabbath day Jesus replied that there was Scriptural precedent for ignoring religious laws if there was a physical need, and that he is able to decide what people should do on the Sabbath.

[23] On one Jewish day of rest Jesus was walking through some grain fields with his disciples. As they were walking *along*, the disciples began to pick some of the heads of grain. *They rubbed them in their hands to remove the chaff, and were eating the grain. The law of Moses permitted people to do that if they were hungry.* [24] Some of the Pharisees *saw them doing what they considered to be work, so they* said to him, "Look! They shouldn't be doing *work* that *our* laws do not permit *us to do* on our day of rest!" [25] *Jesus wanted to show them that the record in the Scriptures indicated that God permitted people to disobey certain religious laws when they needed food. So he said to them*, "*It is written in the Scriptures* what *our revered ancestor King* David did when he needed food and both he and the men with him were hungry. You have read about that, *but you don't think about what it implies.* [26] During the time Abiathar was high priest, David entered the courtyard of God's tent *and asked for some bread. The high priest gave him* the bread that had been presented to God. It was permitted in Moses' law that only the priests could eat that bread! But David ate some of it. Then he also gave some of it to the men who were with him. *And God did not consider that what David did was wrong!*" [27] Jesus said to them further, "*God* established the day of rest to benefit people! He did not

create people to *obey the rules of* the day of rest! [28] And *think about this*: *I am* the one who came from heaven. So *I* have the authority *to determine is right for my disciples to do on* the day of rest!"

3

Mark 3:1-6

THEME: After Jesus healed a man with a withered arm on the Sabbath, Jewish leaders began to plan to kill him.

[1] *On another Jewish day of rest*, Jesus entered the Jewish meeting house again. There was a man there whose hand was shriveled. [2] *Some men of the Pharisee sect* watched Jesus to see whether he would heal the man on the day of rest. They did this so that, if he healed the man, they would accuse him of disobeying *their laws and working on the day of rest*. [3] Jesus said to the man with the shriveled hand, "Stand up here *in front of everyone*!" *So the man stood up.* [4] Then Jesus said *to the Pharisees*, "Do the laws *God gave Moses* permit *people* to do good on the day of rest, or *do they permit people* to harm *others*? *Do they permit us* to save *a person's* life *on the day of rest* or to let *him* die *by refusing to help him?*" But they did not reply. [5] He looked all around at them angrily; he was very distressed that they were stubbornly *not wanting to help the man*. So he said to the man, "Stretch out your hand!" When the man stretched out his hand, it became normal again!

[6] Then the Pharisees *decided to get rid of Jesus. So* after they left *the meeting house*, they *immediately met with some of* the Jews who supported Herod *Antipas,* the ruler of *the district of* Galilee. Together they planned how they could kill Jesus.

Mark 3:7-12

THEME: Many people came from various areas to hear Jesus, because he had healed many.

[7] Jesus and his disciples left *there* and went to an area further along *the shore of* Lake *Galilee to get away from the people*. But a great crowd of people followed him. They were people who came from *the district of* Galilee, [8] from Jerusalem, from *other towns in the district of* Judea, from *the district of* Idumea, from *the region on* the east side of the Jordan *River*, and from *the region* around *the cities of* Tyre and Sidon. This great crowd of people came to him because they heard about what he was doing. [9-10] Since he had healed many people, many *other* people who had various illnesses pushed forward in order that by touching him *they would be healed*. So he told his disciples that they should get a small boat ready for him *to get in and teach from it*. He wanted to do that to prevent the crowd from crushing him *when they pushed forward to touch him*. [11] Whenever the evil spirits saw Jesus, *they caused the people whom they controlled* to fall down in front of Jesus *in recognition of Jesus' power*. They exclaimed, "You are the Son of God!"[b] [12] He strongly commanded the *evil spirits* that they should not tell anyone who he was.

---

[b]   OR, …Then they exclaimed, "You are the Man who is also God!"

Mark 3:13-19

THEME: Jesus appointed the twelve apostles.

[13] Later Jesus went *with many other people* up into the hills. After he picked out *from among them* the men whom he wanted, they came *close* to him. [14] He appointed twelve of them in order that they might be with him and in order that he might send them out to preach. He called them apostles. [15] He also gave them power to expel evil spirits from people. [16] Specifically, he appointed these twelve: Simon, to whom he gave the *new* name Peter; Andrew, Peter's *younger* brother; [17] James, *the son* of Zebedee; and John, the *younger* brother of James, to *both of* whom he added the *new* name, 'Thunder *Men*' *because of their fiery zeal;* [18] Philip; Bartholomew; Matthew, *whose other name was Levi;* Thomas; *another* James, the *son* of Alphaeus; Thaddeus; Simon, a *member of the* party *that wanted* to overthrow *the Roman government;* [19] and Judas Iscariot, who *later* enabled *the Jewish leaders to* seize Jesus.

Mark 3:20-30

THEME: Jesus explained why the claim that he was expelling evil spirits by Satan's power was ridiculous, and that such a claim was an unforgivable sin.

[20] Jesus along with his disciples went to the house where he was staying *in Capernaum*. Again a crowd gathered where he was. There were many people crowding around him, so that he and his disciples had no time to eat or *to do anything else.* [21] After his relatives heard about this, they went to take him home with them because they were saying that he was insane.

[22] *Around that time* some men who taught the *Jewish* laws came down from Jerusalem. *They heard that Jesus was expelling demons.* So they were telling people, "He is controlled by Beelzebul, the ruler of the evil spirits. *Beelzebul is the one who* enables *this man* to expel demons *from people*!" [23] Jesus summoned them, and *then he spoke to them in parables to enable them to realize that Satan would not oppose his own evil spirits. He also wanted them to realize that by expelling evil spirits, he was demonstrating that he was much more powerful than Satan.* So he said, "*It is ridiculous* to suggest that Satan would expel his own *evil spirits*! [24] If *people who live in the same* nation fight one another, they will cease to be a single group under one ruler. [25] And if *people who live in the same* house fight each other, they will certainly not remain *as one family.* [26] In the same way, if Satan and his *evil spirits* were fighting one another, instead of remaining strong, he would become powerless. [27] Contrary to *what you say about me*, a person cannot go into the house of a strong man *like Satan* and carry off his possessions if he does not first bind the strong man. Then he will be able to steal *the things in that man's* house." [28] *Jesus also said*, "Consider this carefully! People may sin in many ways and they may say evil things about God, *but if they then are sorry and ask God to forgiven them*, God will forgive them. [29] But anyone who says evil things about what the Holy Spirit *does* will never be forgiven. That person is eternally guilty of sin."

[30] Jesus told them that because *they refused to admit that the Holy* Spirit was helping him to expel demons. Instead, they were saying, "An evil spirit is controlling him!"

Mark 3:31-35

THEME: Jesus told them that those who obey God were as dear to him as his close relatives.

[31] Jesus' mother and his brothers arrived. While they stood outside, they sent *someone inside* in order to call him *outside*. [32] A crowd was seated around Jesus, and one of them said to him, "Your mother and your brothers and sisters are outside, and they are looking

for you!" [33] Jesus replied, "*Let me tell you something about those I consider to be like* my mother and my brothers!" [34] After he looked around at the *disciples* who were seated around him *in a circle*, he said, "Look here! *I love these men as much as I love* my mother and my brothers. [35] Those who habitually do what God wants are *as dear to me as* my brother, my sister, or my mother!"

4

Mark 4:1-25

THEME: Jesus taught the crowds by parables about the various ways that people who hear his message react.

[1] Another time Jesus began to teach people alongside Lake *Galilee. Meanwhile*, a very large crowd gathered around him. So*, in order not to be jostled by the crowd,* he got into a boat on the lake *and* sat in it *in order to teach the crowd from the boat*. The people were gathered on the shore close to the lake. [2] He taught them many parables. While he was teaching them, he told them *this*: [3] "Consider *well the meaning of this illustration*: A man went out *to his field* to plant *some seeds*. [4] As he was scattering them *over the soil*, some *of the* seeds fell on the path. Then some birds came and ate those seeds. [5] Other *seeds* fell on ground where there was not much soil *on top of rock*. Those *seeds* sprouted very soon, *because the sun quickly warmed* the shallow *moist* soil. [6] But when *the young plants came up*, they were scorched by the sun, and they withered because they did not have *deep* roots. [7] Other seeds fell on *ground that contained roots of* thorny *weeds. The* thorny *weeds* grew *together with the plants,* and *they* crowded out *the plants. So the plants* produced no grain. [8] But other seeds fell on good soil, and *the plants* grew *and* produced *a lot of* grain. *Some plants produced* thirty times *as many seeds as were planted. Some* plants *produced* sixty times *as much. Some plants produced* one hundred times *as much*." [9] Then Jesus said, "If you want to understand this, you should consider *carefully what I have just said*."

[10] *Later*, when only the twelve *disciples* and a few *other* people were with him, they asked him about the parables. [11] He said to them, "God is revealing to you what he did not reveal before, about *how he wants to* rule *over people's lives*. It is to you that *I* am making this known. But I tell about this *only* in parables to those who have not *yet invited God to rule their lives*. [12] As a result, *they are like the people about whom God said:*
> Although they see *what I do*, they do not perceive *what it means*. Although they hear *what I say*, they do not understand *what it means*. So they don't turn away *from their sinful behavior in order that I might* forgive them.

[13] He also said to them, "*I am disappointed that* you do not understand this parable! If you don't understand this, you certainly won't understand any of the *other* parables! *Nevertheless, I will explain it to you.* [14] *In the illustration that I told you*, the man who planted *seeds represents someone who declares* God's message. [15] *Some people are like* the path on which *some of the seeds fell*. When these people hear *the message*, Satan comes at once and causes them to forget what they have heard. [16] *Some people are like the* shallow soil on top of rock. When they hear *God's* message, they **immediately** accept it with joy. [17] But *because it does not penetrate deeply into their hearts, they* believe it for *only* a *short* time. *They are like the plants that* did not have *deep* roots. When they are treated badly or caused to suffer because of their faith, they soon stop believing *God's message*. [18] *Some people are like* the *soil that had roots of* thorny *weeds* in it. They hear God's message, [19] but they desire to be rich, and they desire *to own many* other things. *So they* worry *only* about material things. The result is that they forget *God's* message and

they don't do the things that God wants them to do. [20] *But some people are like* the good soil where *some of the seeds* fell. *Just as the plants that grew in that soil* produced a lot of grain, *these people* hear God's message and accept it. *Some of them do* many things *that please God, some do* even more *things that please God, and some do* very many *things that please God."*

[21] He also told them *another parable*, saying, "*People* certainly don't bring a lamp *into a house* and then *light* it and put it under a basket or under a bed. Instead, they put it on a lampstand *where it lights the house.* [22] *In* the same way, there are some parts of *God's message* that *people* do not know. *But God intends for people* to understand all the things that are not known *to them now.* [23] If you want to understand this, you should consider *carefully what you have just heard."*

[24] Then he said to them, "Consider carefully what you hear *me say to you*, for *God* will let you *understand* to the same degree that you *carefully consider what I say. He* will let you *understand* even more than that. [25] Those who *consider what I say* and understand it, *God* will enable them to understand more. But those who do not *consider carefully what I say*, they will forget even what they already know."

Mark 4:26-34

THEME: Jesus told them two parables to show them how the number of people who will submit to God's rule over their lives will greatly increase.

[26] Jesus also said, "God *has the power to change* people who let him rule their lives. *I will illustrate how that can happen.* A man planted seeds in the ground. [27] Afterwards he slept each night and rose each day *without worrying about the seeds.* Meanwhile, the seeds sprouted and grew in a way that he did not understand, because by itself *the soil caused the plants to grow and produce grain.* [28] First the stalks *appeared.* Then the heads *appeared.* Then the full kernels in the heads *appeared.* [29] As soon as the grain was ripe, he sent *people* to harvest it because it was time to harvest *the grain."*

[30] Jesus also said *with a parable*, "Let me tell you how the number of people whose lives God rules *will continue to grow.*[c] *I hope* this parable will show this to you. [31] *You know what happens to* mustard seeds when they are planted. Although mustard seeds are among the smallest of seeds, *here in Israel* they become large plants. [32] After they are planted, they grow up and become larger than the other garden plants. They put out big enough branches that birds are able to make nests in their shade."

[33] Jesus used many such parables when he talked to the people about God. If they were able to understand *some parables, he kept telling them more.* [34] He used parables when he spoke to them. But he explained all *the parables* to his own disciples when he was alone with them.

Mark 4:35-41

THEME: While Jesus and his disciples crossed the sea in a boat and while Jesus slept, a storm arose, so the disciples woke him and he calmed the storm.

[35] On that same day, when the sun was setting, Jesus said to *his disciples*, "Let's cross over to the opposite side *of the lake."* [36] So they left the crowd, *got in* the boat where Jesus *already* was, and left. *Other people* went with them in other boats. [37] A strong wind came

---

[c] OR, …The people whose lives God rules will continue to have more and more influence in this world.

up and the waves started coming into the boat! The boat was soon nearly filled *with water*! [38] Jesus was in the back part of the boat, asleep, *with his head* on a cushion. So they woke him up and said to him, "Teacher! Aren't you concerned? We're going to drown!" [39] So Jesus got up and rebuked the wind. Then he said to the lake, "Be quiet! Be still!" *Immediately* the wind stopped blowing and *the lake* became very calm. [40] He said to the disciples, "*You should not* have been afraid *like that!* Don't you yet believe *that I can protect you*?" [41] They were very awestruck. They said to one another, "What kind of man is he? *All things are under his control!* Even the wind and the waves obey him!"

5

Mark 5:1-20

THEME: Jesus expelled evil spirits from a Gerasene man and then allowed them to enter a herd of pigs, which then ran down a hill and drowned. As a result the local people asked Jesus to leave the area.

[1] Jesus and his disciples arrived on the *east* side of Lake *Galilee*, in the region where the Gerasenes *lived*. [2] There was a man in that region controlled by evil spirits. [3] *Because that man was violent and people were afraid of him*, they had tied him up many times. *As he grew more violent*, no one was able to tie him up any longer, not even with chains, [4] because he would break the chains whenever he was bound with them. He would also smash the iron shackles whenever they were fastened *on his feet*. [5] He lived in one of the burial caves. Night and day he would scream among the caves and in the hills. He would also cut himself with *sharp* stones. On that day he came out of the caves. [6] As Jesus *and his disciples got* out of the boat, he saw Jesus from a distance, and immediately ran to Jesus and knelt before him. [7-8] Then Jesus said to the evil spirit, "You evil spirit, come out of this man!" *But the evil spirit did not leave quickly*. It shouted very loudly, "Jesus, Son of the great God in heaven, since we have nothing in common, *leave me alone!* I ask you to promise before God that you will not torture me *now*!" [9] *So, in order to expel the demon more easily*, Jesus asked him, "What is your name?" He replied, "My name is Mob because there are many of us *evil spirits in this man*." [10] Then the evil spirits fervently kept begging Jesus not to send them out of the region. [11] *At the same time*, a large herd of pigs was rooting for food on the nearby hillside. [12] So the evil spirits pleaded with Jesus, "Allow us to go to the pigs and enter them!" [13] He gave them his permission. So the evil spirits left the man and entered the pigs. The herd, *which numbered* about 2000, rushed down the steep bank into the lake, and they drowned in the lake!

[14] The men who were tending the pigs ran and reported in the town and the country villages *what had happened. Many people* went to see what had happened. [15] They came to *the place where* Jesus *was* and saw the man who had *previously* been controlled by evil spirits. He was sitting there, clothed and in his right mind. *Then* they became afraid *because they thought he might destroy more of their property.*[d] [16] The people who had seen what happened described *to the others* what had happened to the man who was *previously* controlled by evil spirits. They also described *what had happened to* the pigs. [17] Then the people begged Jesus to leave their region *because they were afraid he might destroy more things than just the pigs*.

[18] As Jesus got in the boat *to leave*, the man *previously* controlled by the evil spirits begged Jesus, "*Please* let me go with you!" [19] But Jesus did not let him go with him. On the

---

[d] OR, ...*As a result* they became afraid *because they realized that Jesus must be very powerful.*

contrary, he said to him, "Go home to your family and tell them how much the Lord *God* has done for you, and tell them how *God* was kind to you." ²⁰ So the man went *and traveled around the district of* the Ten Towns. He told people how much Jesus had done for him. And all the people *who heard about it* were amazed.

Mark 5:21-43

THEME: Jesus cured a woman who had been suffering from hemorrhaging and brought Jairus' daughter back to life.

²¹ Jesus *and his disciples* went in a boat back around Lake *Galilee to where they were previously*. When they arrived at the shore of the lake, a large crowd gathered around Jesus. ²² One of the leaders of the Jewish meeting place came there. His name was Jairus. When he saw Jesus, he prostrated himself at his feet. ²³ Then he pleaded with Jesus earnestly, "My daughter is *sick and* nearly dead! Please come *to my house* and lay your hands on her so she will be healed and not die!" ²⁴ So Jesus *and the disciples* went with him.

A large crowd followed *Jesus* and *many* pushed close to him. ²⁵ There was a woman *in the crowd* who had been suffering from *constant vaginal* bleeding for twelve years. ²⁶ She had suffered a lot from the treatment of many doctors. But although she had spent all *her money* to pay the doctors, they had not helped her. Instead, she had become worse. ²⁷ After she heard that Jesus *healed people*, she came *to where he was and pushed* in the crowd *close* behind Jesus. ²⁸ She did that thinking, "If I touch *him or* even if I touch his clothes, I will be healed." So she touched Jesus' clothes. ²⁹ At once her bleeding stopped. At the same time, she sensed within her *body* that she had been healed. ³⁰ Jesus *also* immediately sensed within himself that his power had *healed someone*. So he turned around in the crowd and asked, "Who touched my clothes?" ³¹ *One of* his disciples replied, "You can see that many people are crowding close to you! So *we are surprised* that you ask 'Who touched me?' *because probably many people touched you!*" ³² But Jesus kept looking around to see who had done it. ³³ The woman was very afraid and trembling. *She thought that Jesus might be angry because she* had violated the law that women who had such a problem should not touch other people. But, she knew *Jesus had healed her*. So she prostrated herself before him. Then she told him truthfully *about what she had done*. ³⁴ He said to her, "Dear woman, because you *have* believed *that I could heal you*, I have healed you. You may go home with peace *in your heart, and I promise that* you will not be sick *this way anymore*."

³⁵ While Jesus was still talking *to her*, some people arrived who had come from Jairus' house. They said *to Jairus*, "Your daughter has died. So it is useless to bother the teacher any longer *by urging him to go to your house*." ³⁶ But when Jesus heard what these men said, he said to Jairus, "Don't lose hope! Just believe *that she will live again!*" ³⁷⁻³⁸ Then he allowed only *his three closest disciples*, Peter, James, and John, to go with him *to Jairus' house*. He did not allow any other people to go with him. After they came to the house, Jesus saw that the people there were in turmoil. They were weeping and wailing loudly. ³⁹ He entered the house and said to them, knowing that *he was going to cause her to live again*, "Why are you making such a disturbance? Stop crying, for the child isn't dead! She is *just* sleeping!" ⁴⁰ The people laughed at him, *because they knew she was dead*. But he sent all the other people outside the house. Then he took the child's father and mother and the *three disciples* who were with him. He went into *the room* where the child was *lying*. ⁴¹ He took hold of the child's hand and said to her *in her own language*, "Talitha, koum!" That means, "Little girl, get up!" ⁴² At once the girl got up and walked around. (*It was not surprising that she could walk*, because she was twelve years old.) *When this happened*, they were *all* very astonished. ⁴³ Jesus ordered them strictly, "Don't tell anyone about *what I have done!*" Afterwards he told them to bring her something to eat.

6

Mark 6:1-6a

THEME: Jesus taught in the synagogue and the people who heard him were amazed and offended.

¹ Jesus left *Capernaum* and went to his home town, *Nazareth*. His disciples went with him. ² On the Jewish day of rest, *he entered* the Jewish meeting house and taught the people. Many who were listening to him were astonished. *But some* were saying, "This man *is just an ordinary person like us! So* how is it that he knows so much and understands so much? And how is it that he is able to perform *such* miracles! ³ He is *just an ordinary* carpenter! *We know him and his family! We know* Mary his mother! *We know* his brothers James, Joses, Judas and Simon! And his sisters also live *here* in our *town*!" The people were unable to accept *the idea that he was the Messiah.* ⁴ So Jesus said to them, "*People* honor *me and other* prophets *everywhere else we go,* but in our home towns *we're* not *honored,* and *even* our relatives and *the people who live in* our own houses don't *honor us*!"

⁵ *So*, although he healed a few sick people there by touching them, he *decided* not to perform many *other* miracles *in Nazareth because the people there did not believe he was the Messiah.* ⁶ He was amazed that they did not believe *in him.*

Mark 6:6b-13

THEME: Jesus began to send out his disciples two-by-two and gave them power and instructions.

Jesus *and his disciples* went from town to town *in that region* teaching the people. ⁷ *One day* he summoned the twelve *disciples* and *told them* he was going to send them out two-by-two *to teach people in various towns.* He gave them power *to expel* evil spirits. ⁸⁻⁹ He also instructed them to wear sandals and to take along a walking stick while traveling. He told them not to take food, nor a *travelers'* bag, nor any money for their journey. He also did not allow them to take extra clothing. *He wanted the people who heard their message to give them what they needed.* ¹⁰ *He also instructed them*, "When you enter a town, *if someone invites you to stay in his house*, accept the invitation. *Eat and sleep* in that same house until you leave the town. ¹¹ Wherever the people do not welcome you or listen to your message, shake off the dust from your feet as you leave *that place. Do that* as a warning to them *that rejecting your message will bring punishment from God.*" ¹² *So* the disciples went out *to various towns and* were preaching that people should stop their sinful behavior. ¹³ They were also expelling many evil spirits from people, and they were anointing many sick people with *olive* oil and healing them.

Mark 6:14-29

THEME: King Herod heard about Jesus and wondered if he were John, the Baptizer, returned to life after King Herod had ordered him executed due to the maneuvers of Herod's wife, Herodias.

¹⁴ *King* Herod *Antipas* heard about *what* Jesus *was doing*, because many people were talking *about it*. Some people were saying *about Jesus*, "*He must be* John the Baptizer. He has risen from the dead! That's why he has *God's* power to perform these miracles!" ¹⁵ Others were saying *about Jesus*, "He is *the prophet* Elijah, *whom God promised to send back to earth again*." Others were saying *about Jesus*, "*No*, he is a *different* prophet, like one of the *other* prophets *who lived long ago*." ¹⁶ Having heard *what the people were*

saying, Herod himself repeatedly said, "The man *performing those miracles* must be John! I *had* his head cut off, but he has become alive again *to get revenge for my killing him*!" ¹⁷ The reason *King Herod concluded that John wanted revenge is as follows: Some time before* this, Herod married Herodias, while she was *still* the wife of his brother, Philip. ¹⁸ *Then* John kept telling Herod, "*What* you *did by* marrying your brother's wife *while your brother is still alive* is against *God's* law!" Then, because Herodias *urged him to put John in* prison, Herod himself sent *soldiers who* seized John and put him in prison. ¹⁹ But because Herodias wanted to get *further* revenge on John, she wanted him executed. But she could not do that because *while John was in prison,* Herod kept John safe *from her.* ²⁰ Herod did this because he respected John. He knew that John was a righteous and holy man. The king did not know what he should do, but he liked to listen to John. ²¹ But Herod's birthday gave *Herodias* the opportunity *to have John executed*. To celebrate his birthday Herod invited the *main* government officials, the *main* army leaders and the most important men in *the district of* Galilee to come and eat and celebrate with him. ²² *While they were eating*, Herodias' daughter came into the room and, by dancing, she pleased *King* Herod and his guests. So the king said to her, "Ask me for whatever you desire and I'll give it to you!" ²³ He also said to her, "Whatever you ask, I'll give it to you! I will even give you up to half of what I own and rule, if you ask for it! May God punish me *if I don't do what I have promised*!" ²⁴ The girl immediately left the room and went to her mother. She *told her mother what the king had said, and* asked her, "What shall I ask for?" Her mother replied, "*Ask the king to give you* the head of John the Baptizer!" ²⁵ The girl quickly entered the room again. She went to the king and said, "I want you to have the head of John the Baptizer *cut off and* given to me at once on a platter, *so my mother can know he is dead*!" ²⁶ The king became very distressed when he heard what she asked for, *because he did not want John to be killed. But he couldn't refuse what she requested because he had promised that he would give her anything she asked for, and because his guests had heard him p*romise that. ²⁷ So the king at once ordered the executioner to go and *cut off* John's head and bring it *to the girl*. The executioner went to the prison and cut off John's head. ²⁸ He put it on a platter, brought it back, and gave it to the girl. And the girl took it to her mother. ²⁹ After John's disciples heard what happened, they went *to the prison* and took John's body, and they buried it in a burial cave.

Mark 6:30-34

THEME: The apostles returned to Jesus to report what they had done. Then they all went off to a lonely place, but many people followed them.

³⁰ The *twelve* apostles returned to Jesus *from the places where they had gone*. They reported to him what they had done and what they had taught. ³¹ He said to them, "Come *with me* to a place where we can be alone and rest a little while!" He said this because many people were continually coming and going, with the result that *Jesus and* his disciples did not have time to eat *or do anything* else. ³² So they went away by themselves in a boat to an uninhabited place. ³³ *But* many people saw them leaving. They also recognized *Jesus and the disciples, and they saw where they were going*. So they ran *ahead on land* from all the *nearby* towns to the place *where Jesus and his disciples were going*. They actually arrived there before *Jesus and the disciples*. ³⁴ As Jesus *and his disciples* got out of the boat, Jesus saw this great crowd. He felt sorry for them because they were *confused*, like sheep that do not have a shepherd, and he started to teach them many things.

Mark 6:35-44

THEME: When it became late in the afternoon the people became hungry and there was no place to obtain food; as a result, Jesus miraculously provided food for them.

[35] Late in the afternoon the disciples came to him and said, "This is a place where nobody lives, and it is very late. [36] So dismiss the people so that they can go to the surrounding villages and other places where they can buy themselves something to eat!" [37] But he replied to them, "*No,* you *yourselves* give them something to eat!" They answered him, "*There is no way* we can buy enough bread to feed *this crowd,* even if we had as much money as a man earns by working two hundred days!" [38] But he replied to them, "How many loaves of bread do you have? Go and find out!" They went and found out and then they told him, "We have *only* five flat loaves and two *cooked* fish!" [39] He instructed *the disciples to tell* all the people to sit down on the green grass in groups. [40] So the people sat in groups. There were 50 people in some groups and 100 people in other groups. [41] Jesus took the five flat loaves and the two fish. He looked up towards heaven and thanked *God for them.* Then he broke them *into pieces* and gave them to the disciples for them to distribute to the people. [42] All *the people* ate until they were satisfied. [43] The disciples then collected twelve baskets full of *leftover* pieces *of bread* and fish. [44] There were approximately five thousand men who ate *the bread and fish. They did not even count the women and children.*

Mark 6:45-52

THEME: Jesus sent his disciples ahead of him to Bethsaida by boat while he stayed to pray. Later he saw that they were in difficulty due to a wind blowing against them so he went to them, walking on the water.

[45] Right away Jesus told his disciples to get in the boat and go ahead of him to *the town of* Bethsaida*, which was* further around *Lake Galilee.* He *stayed and* dismissed the many people who were there. [46] After he said good-bye to them, he went up into the hills to pray. [47] When it was evening, the *disciples'* boat was in the middle of the lake and Jesus was by himself on the land. [48] He saw that the wind was *blowing* against them as they rowed, so they were having great difficulty. He approached them early in the morning, when it was still dark, by walking on the water. He intended to walk past them. [49] They saw him walking on the water, but they thought he was a ghost. They screamed [50] because they were all terrified when they saw him. But he immediately talked to them and said, "Be calm! It is I! Don't be afraid!" [51] He got in the boat *and sat down* with them, and *immediately* the wind stopped blowing. They were completely amazed *about what he had done.* [52] *Although they had seen Jesus multiply* the loaves *of bread and the fish,* they did not understand *from that how powerful he was, as they should have.* They were not thinking!

Mark 6:53-56

THEME: As soon as Jesus and his disciples reached land and disembarked, people began to come to Jesus, bringing sick people in order that he might heal them, and he healed all who touched him.

[53] When they had gone further around *the lake in the boat,* they came to the shore at *the town of* Gennesaret. Then they anchored the boat there. [54] As soon as they got out of the boat, *the people there* recognized Jesus. [55] So they ran throughout the whole district *to tell others that Jesus was there.* Then the people *placed* those who were sick on stretchers and carried them to any place where they heard *people say* that Jesus was. [56] In whatever village, town or other place he entered, they would bring to the marketplaces those who were sick. Then the *sick people* would beg Jesus to let them touch *him or* even the tassel

of his garment *so that they would be healed*. And all who touched *him or his garment* were healed.

7

Mark 7:1-23

THEME: Some Pharisees and scribes criticized Jesus about his disciples disobeying the traditions of the elders. Jesus showed that their attitudes and practices were mistaken.

[1] *One day* some Pharisees and some men who taught the *Jewish* laws gathered around Jesus. They had come from *the city of* Jerusalem *to investigate him*. [2-4] The Pharisees and all of the *other* Jews *strictly* observe the traditions that their ancestors *taught. For example, they refuse to* eat until they first wash their hands *with a special ritual*, especially after they *return* from *buying things in* the marketplace. They think that God will be angry with them if they don't do that, *because some person or thing unacceptable to God might have touched it*. There are many other such *traditions* that they accept and try to obey. For instance, they wash *in a special way* their cups, pots, kettles, containers, and beds *to keep from being rejected by God*.

[5] Well, those Pharisees and men who taught the *Jewish* laws saw that some of his disciples were eating food with hands that they had not washed using the special ritual. So they questioned Jesus, saying, "Your disciples disobey the traditions of our ancestors! You shouldn't *let them* eat without washing their hands using our special ritual!" [6] Jesus said to them, "Isaiah *rebuked your ancestors*, and his words also describe you very well, you who only pretend to be good! He wrote these words *that God said*:

These people talk *as if they* honor me, but their hearts are not in it at all. [7] It is useless for them to worship me, because they teach what people thought up *as if I myself had commanded it.*

[8] You, *like your ancestors*, refuse *to obey* God's commands. Instead, you follow only the traditions that your ancestors *taught*." [9] Jesus also said to them, "*You think* you are clever in refusing to do what God commanded *just* so you can obey your own traditions! [10] *For example,* Moses *wrote God's* command, 'Honor your fathers and your mothers'. He also wrote, '*Anyone* who speaks evil about his father or mother must be executed.' [11-12] But **you** tell people that it is all right if they no *longer help their* parents. *You tell them that it is all right* for them to promise to give their things to God *instead of giving them to their parents*. You allow them to say to their father and mother, 'What I was going to give to you *to help provide for you, I have now promised to* give to God. So *I can't help you any longer!*' As a result, you are *actually telling people* they no longer have to help their parents! [13] And by doing that, you disregard what God commanded! You teach your own traditions to others *and tell them strongly that they should obey them*! And you do many other things like that."

[14] Then Jesus again summoned the crowd *to come closer to him*. He said to them, "Listen to me, all of you! *Try to* understand *what I am about to tell you.* [15] Nothing that enters our bodies from without causes *God to* consider us to be unacceptable. On the contrary, it is that which comes from people's hearts that causes God to reject them."[e]

[17] After Jesus had left the crowd and then entered a house with the disciples, they questioned him about the parable *that he had just spoken*. [18] He replied to them, "*I am*

---

[e] Some Greek manuscripts add v. 16, "If you want to understand what I am saying, you must think carefully about it!"

disappointed that even **you,** *who should understand what I teach,* don't understand *what the parable means*! You ought to understand that nothing that *enters our bodies from* without can cause *God to* consider us unacceptable to him. [19] Instead of entering *and ruining* our souls, it goes into our stomachs, and afterwards the refuse passes out *of our bodies*." By saying this, Jesus was declaring that people *can eat* any food without causing *God* to reject them. [20] He also said, "It is what comes from people's innermost beings that causes *God* to consider them unacceptable. [21] Specifically, it is people's hearts *that cause them to* think things that are evil, to commit sexual sins, to steal, to murder, [22] to *commit* adultery, to *be* greedy, to *do* malicious *acts*, to deceive *others*, to *behave* indecently, to envy, to speak evil about others, to *be* proud, and to *do* foolish *things*. [23] People think *these thoughts* and then they do these evil actions, and that is what causes *God to* consider them unacceptable to him."

Mark 7:24-30

THEME: Jesus went to the region around Tyre to be away from people, but they learned of it, and a woman came to ask him to expel an evil spirit from her daughter.

[24] After Jesus *and his disciples* left *the district of* Galilee, they went to the region around *the city of* Tyre. While he stayed at a certain house, he did not want anyone to know *it*, but people soon found out *he was there.* [25] A certain woman, whose daughter was controlled by an evil spirit, heard about Jesus. At once she came to him and prostrated herself at his feet. [26] This woman *was not a Jew.* She was born in *the region around the part* of *the district of* Syria *called* Phoenicia. *Her ancestors came* from the country of Greece. She pleaded with Jesus to expel the evil spirit from her daughter. [27] But he *wanted to test her faith. So, suggesting that he should help the Jews first, and not the non-Jews, whom some Jews called dogs*, he said to her, "First let the children eat all they want, because it is not good *for someone* to take the food *that has been prepared* for the children and throw it to the *little* dogs." [28] But *to show that she believed that non-Jews could also receive help from God*, she replied to him, "Sir, *what you say is* correct, but even the little dogs that lie under the table eat the crumbs that the children *drop*." [29] *Jesus* said to her, "Because of what you have said, *you have shown me that* you believe *in what I can do for you*. So I will help you. Now you may go *home, since I have caused* the evil spirit to leave your daughter." [30] The woman returned to her house and saw that her child was lying *quietly* on the bed, and that the evil spirit had left.

Mark 7:31-37

THEME: When Jesus went back to Lake Galilee, some people brought a deaf-mute man to Jesus and asked him to heal the man, which he did.

[31] Jesus *and his disciples* left the region around Tyre and went *north* through *the city of* Sidon, then *toward the east* through the district of the Ten Towns, and then *south* to *the towns near* Lake Galilee. [32] *There*, people brought to him a man who was deaf and who could hardly talk. They begged *Jesus* to lay his hands on him *to heal him.* [33] *So Jesus* took him away from the crowd *so that the two of them could be* alone. Then he put *one of* his fingers into *each of* the man's ears. After he spat *on his fingers*, he touched the man's tongue *with his fingers*. [34] Then he looked up toward heaven, he sighed *because he was concerned for the man,* and then *in his own language* he said to the man's *ears*, "Ephphatha!" which means "Open up!" [35] At once the man could hear plainly. He also started to speak clearly because Jesus healed *what was causing him to be unable to speak*. [36] Jesus told *the people* not to tell anyone *what he had done*. But, although he ordered them *and others* repeatedly *not to tell anyone about it*, they kept talking about it very much. [37] *People who heard about it* were utterly amazed and were saying

enthusiastically, "Everything he has done is wonderful! *Besides doing other amazing things*, he heals deaf people and people who cannot talk!"

8

Mark 8:1-10

THEME: Again Jesus provided food miraculously for a great crowd who gathered to hear him and became hungry.

[1] During those days, a large crowd of people gathered *again*. *After a couple days had passed* they had no food to eat. So Jesus called his disciples to him and said to them, [2] "These people have been with me for three days[f] and have nothing *left* to eat. I feel sorry for them. [3] If I send them away *while they are still* hungry, some of them will faint on the way home, because some of them have come from far away." [4] *Knowing he was suggesting that they give the people something to eat*, his disciples replied, "We can't possibly find food *to satisfy* this crowd, here in this place where nobody lives!" [5] Jesus asked them, "How many loaves of bread do you have?" They replied, "*We have* seven." [6] Jesus told the people to sit down on the ground!" Then he took the seven flat loaves, and after he thanked *God for them*, he broke them *into pieces* and gave them to his disciples for them to distribute to the people. [7] *They found that* they *also* had a few small *dried* fish. So, after he thanked God for these, he told the disciples, "Distribute these also." After they distributed *the bread and fish to the crowd*, [8] the people ate and had *plenty to* satisfy *them*. *The disciples* collected the leftover pieces. *They* filled seven large baskets *with them*. [9] *They estimated that* there were about four thousand people *who ate on that day*. [10] Then Jesus dismissed the crowd. Immediately after that, he got in the boat along with his disciples, and they *went around the lake* to the district of Dalmanutha.

Mark 8:11-21

THEME: Jesus rebuked those who insisted on him performing more miracles, and rebuked the disciples when they worried about not having enough food with them.

[11] *In those days some* Pharisees came to Jesus. They asked him *to perform* a miracle that would prove *that* God *had sent him*. They wanted to *find a way by which they could* convince the people to reject him. *So* they started to argue with him. [12] Jesus sighed deeply within himself, and then he said, "I am disgusted that, *even though* you people have seen how I *heal people*, you keep asking me to perform miracles! Note this: I will certainly not do *such* a miracle for you people!" [13] Then he left them.

He got into the boat again, along *with his disciples*, and they went further around *the lake*. [14] The disciples had forgotten to bring along *enough* bread. They had only one flat loaf with them in the boat. [15] *As they were going*, Jesus warned them against *the attitudes of the* Pharisees and Herod *Antipas*. He said, "Be careful! Beware of the yeast of the Pharisees and the yeast of Herod!" [16] *Not realizing that he was speaking figuratively*, they said to one another, "*He must have said that* because we don't have *enough* bread." [17] Jesus knew what *they were discussing among themselves*. So he said to them, "I am disappointed that you are thinking that *it was because* you do not have *enough* bread *that I talked about the yeast of the Pharisees and Herod*! Do you not yet perceive or understand *that I can provide miraculously for you if you need food*? You are not thinking! [18] I am also

---

[f] OR, This is the third day that these people have been with me…

disappointed that, although you have eyes, you don't *understand what you* see! You have ears, but you don't understand *what I say*!" *Then he asked*, "Don't you remember [19] *that* five thousand *people ate* when I broke the five flat loaves *into pieces and multiplied them*? *Not only was everyone satisfied but there was food left over!* How many baskets full of pieces of bread *that were left over* did you collect?" They replied, "*We collected* twelve *baskets full.*" [20] Then he asked, "*Don't you remember that* four thousand *people ate when I multiplied* the seven *flat loaveş*? *Again, after everyone had plenty to eat*, how many baskets did you collect that were full *of pieces of bread that were left over*?" They replied, "Seven." [21] Then he kept saying to them, "*I am disappointed that* you do not yet understand *that you should never worry about not having enough food!*"

Mark 8:22-26

THEME: Jesus healed a blind man.

[22] They arrived *in the boat at the town of* Bethsaida. People brought a blind man to Jesus and earnestly requested that Jesus touch him *to heal him.* [23] Jesus took the blind man's hand, led him outside the town, put saliva on the man's eyes, put his hands on the man, and then he asked him, "Do you see anything?" [24] The man looked up and then he said, "*Yes,* I see people walking around, but I can't see them *clearly. They look* like trees!" [25] Then Jesus again touched the blind man's eyes. The man looked intently, and at that moment he was completely healed! He could see everything clearly. [26] Jesus said to him, "Don't go into the town! *First go straight home and tell the people there about what I did!*" Then he sent the man home.

Mark 8:27-30

THEME: Jesus asked his disciples what people were saying about who he was and what they thought.

[27] Jesus and the disciples *left Bethsaida and* went to the villages near *the town of* Caesarea Philippi. On the way he questioned them, "Who do people say that I *really* am?" [28] They replied, "*Some say you are* John the Baptizer, *who has come back to life again. Others say you are the prophet* Elijah *who has returned from heaven as God promised. And others say that you are one of the other former* prophets *who have come back to life again.*" [29] He asked them, "What about you? Who do **you** say that I am?" Peter replied to him, "You are the Messiah!" [30] Then Jesus warned them strongly not to tell anyone *yet that he was the Messiah.*

Mark 8:31-33

THEME: Jesus spoke plainly to his disciples about his coming death and resurrection.

[31] Then Jesus began to teach them, "*Even though* I am the one who came from heaven, it is necessary that I suffer very much. It is also necessary that I be rejected by the elders, the chief priests, and the men who teach the *Jewish* laws, and that I be killed. But on the third day after that, I will become alive again." [32] He said this to them clearly. But Peter took Jesus aside and then, *because he assumed the Messiah would never die*, he began to rebuke Jesus *for talking about dying.* [33] Jesus turned around and looked at his disciples. Then he rebuked Peter, saying, "Stop talking to me *like that*! *Stop saying what* Satan *would say*! You are not thinking like God thinks. Instead, *you are thinking* like people *think*!"

Mark 8:34-9:1

THEME: Jesus explained to the crowd and his disciples what is required if anyone wants to be Jesus' disciple.

³⁴ Then he summoned the crowd along with the disciples *so that they might listen to him.* He told them, "If any one *of you* wants to be my disciple, you must not do *only* what you yourself desire *to do.* You must *be willing to let people hurt you and disgrace you. That is like what is done to criminals* who are forced to carry a cross *to the place where they will be crucified. That is what anyone who wants to* be my disciple *must do.* ³⁵ *You must do that,* because those who try to save their lives *by denying they belong to me when people want to kill them for believing in me* will not live *eternally.* But those who are killed because of being my *disciples* and *because of telling others my* good message will live *forever with me.* ³⁶ People might get everything *they want* in this world, but *if they don't become my disciples,* they would really be gaining nothing *because* they would not get eternal life! ³⁷ *Keep in mind that* there is absolutely nothing that people can give *to God* that would enable them to gain eternal life! ³⁸ Note this: Those who refuse *to say they belong to* me and reject what I say in these days when many people have turned away *from God* and are very sinful, *I,* the one who came from heaven, will also refuse *to say that they belong to me* when I come back with the holy angels accompanying me. *At that time* I will have the glorious radiance that my Father has!"

9

¹ He also said to *his disciples*, "Listen carefully! Some of you who are here now will see God ruling powerfully *in many ways.* You will see it before you die!"

Mark 9:2-8

THEME: Jesus took Peter, James and John up a high mountain where his appearance changed and Moses and Elijah appeared and talked with Jesus.

² A week after Jesus *said that,* he took Peter, James and *James' brother* John and led them up a high mountain where they were away from other people. *While they were* there, *the three disciples* saw that Jesus' appearance was changed. ³ His clothes became dazzling white; they were whiter than anyone on earth could make them by bleaching them. ⁴ *Two prophets who had lived long ago,* Moses and Elijah, appeared and began conversing with Jesus. ⁵ *After a short time,* Peter *interrupted by* exclaiming, "Teacher, it is wonderful for us to be here! Allow us to make three shelters, one for you, one for Moses, and one for Elijah!" ⁶ *He said this because he wanted to say something, but* he did not know what to say, because he and the other *two disciples* were completely awestruck. ⁷ Then a *bright* cloud *appeared and* covered them. *God* spoke to them from the cloud saying, "This is my Son. *I* love him. *So* you must listen to him!" ⁸ When *the three disciples* looked around, they saw that suddenly Jesus was alone with them, and that there was no longer anyone *else* there.

Mark 9:9-13

THEME: Jesus told them that the one like Elijah has already come and been cruelly and unjustly treated, but that the Messiah would also be evilly treated.

⁹ When they were walking down the mountain, Jesus told them not to tell anyone *yet* what had just happened to him. He said, "You may tell them after *I,* the one who came from heaven, rise from the dead." ¹⁰ So they did not tell others about it *for a long time.* But they

discussed among themselves what it meant when he said that he would rise from the dead.

[11] *The three disciples had just seen Elijah, but Elijah had not done anything to prepare people to accept Jesus. So* they asked Jesus, "*If what you say is true*, why do the men who teach the *Jewish* laws say that it is necessary for Elijah to come before *the Messiah comes*?" [12-13] *Jesus wanted them to know that John the Baptizer was the one who represented Elijah. So* he answered them, "It is true that *God promised that* Elijah would come to prepare all *the people for the Messiah's coming. Well,* Elijah's representative has already come, and our leaders treated him very badly, just as they wanted to do, just as *the prophets* prophesied long ago. But I also want you to consider what *the prophets* wrote about *me*, the one who came from heaven. They wrote that I would suffer and that *many people* would reject me."

Mark 9:14-29

THEME: Jesus expelled an evil spirit and later explained to the disciples why they had failed to do that.

[14] *Jesus and the three disciples* returned to where the *other* disciples were. They saw a large crowd around the other disciples, and *some* men who taught the *Jewish* laws arguing with them. [15] The crowd was very surprised *to see* Jesus. So they ran to him and greeted him. [16] He asked them, "What are you arguing about?" [17] A man in the crowd answered him, "Teacher, I brought my son *here so that* you *would heal hi*m. There is an evil spirit in him *that makes him* unable to talk. [18] Whenever the spirit attacks him, it throws him down. He foams at the mouth, he grinds his teeth together, and he becomes stiff. I asked your disciples to expel the spirit, but they were not able to do it." [19] Jesus replied by saying to the people, "*You who have seen how I help people* do not believe *that you can do anything!* How long do I have to be with you *before you are able to do what I do*? How long do I have to endure your *lack of faith*? Bring the boy to me!" [20] So they brought the boy to Jesus. As soon as the evil spirit saw Jesus, it shook the boy severely, and the boy fell on the ground. He rolled around, and he foamed at the mouth. [21] Jesus asked the boy's father, "How long has he been like this?" He replied, "*This started to happen* when he was a child. [22] *The spirit not only does this*, but also he often throws him in the fire or in the water to kill him. But pity us and help us, if you can!" [23] Jesus exclaimed to him, "*Don't say* 'If you can', for *I* can do anything for people who believe *in me*!" [24] Immediately the child's father shouted, "I believe *that you can help me, but I don't believe strongly*. Help me to believe more strongly!" [25] Because *Jesus wanted to heal the boy before* the crowd got bigger, he rebuked the evil spirit, saying, "You evil spirit, you who are *causing this boy to be* deaf and unable to talk, I command you to come out of him and never enter him again!" [26] The evil spirit shouted, it shook the boy violently, and then it came out of the boy. The boy did not move. He seemed like a corpse. So many of the people there said, "He's dead!" [27] However, Jesus took him by the hand and helped him get up. Then the boy stood up. *He was healed!* [28] Later, when Jesus and his disciples were alone in a house, one of them asked him, "Why were not we able to expel *the evil spirit*?" [29] He said to them, "You can expel this kind *of evil spirit* only by praying *for God's authority to do it*. There is no other way that you can do it."

Mark 9:30-32

THEME: Jesus was teaching his disciples that he would be handed over to other men, killed and become alive again; but they did not understand what he was saying.

[30] After *Jesus and his disciples* left that *district*, they traveled through *the district of* Galilee. Jesus did not want anyone *else* to know that he was in their area [31] *lest they interrupt him*

as he taught his disciples. He was telling them, "*Some day I*, the one who came from heaven, will be handed over to the authorities. They will kill me. But on the third day after I am killed, I will become alive again!" [32] But *the disciples* did not understand what *Jesus* was saying. *And* they were afraid to ask him *about it.*

Mark 9:33-37

THEME: Jesus taught his disciples by illustration about what kind of person God considers important.

[33] *Jesus and his disciples* returned to *the town of* Capernaum. When they were in the house, he asked them, "What were you discussing while we were traveling on the road?" [34] But they did not reply. *They were ashamed* to reply because, while they were traveling, they had been arguing with each other about which one of them *would be* the most important *when Jesus became king.* [35] He sat down, summoned the twelve disciples *to come to him*, and then he said to them, "If anyone wants *God to consider him* to be the most important person of all, he must *consider himself* to be the least important person of all, and he must serve everyone *else.*" [36] Then he brought a child near. He took the child in his arms and said to *the disciples*, [37]"*God considers that* those who, *out of love* for me, welcome a child like this one, are welcoming me. So it is as though they are also welcoming *God,* who sent me."

Mark 9:38-41

THEME: Jesus taught his disciples about who is for him and who is against him.

[38] John said to Jesus, "Teacher, we saw a man who was expelling demons, *claiming he had* authority from you *to do that.* So we told him to stop doing it because he is not one of us *disciples.*" [39] Jesus said, "Don't tell him not to *do that.* For no one will speak evilly about me just after he performs a miracle while saying that I *have told him to do it.* [40] Furthermore, those who are not opposing us are trying to *achieve the same goals that* we are. [41] Also note this: Those *who belong to me who help you in any way, even* if they *just* give you a cup of water to drink because you follow *me*, the Messiah, will certainly be rewarded *by God!*"

Mark 9:42-48

THEME: Jesus taught his disciples about sin and its result.

[42] *Jesus also said*, "But if you cause someone who believes in me to sin, *even if it is someone who is socially unimportant like* this little child, *God will severely punish you.* If a heavy stone were tied around your neck and you were thrown into the sea, *everyone would consider such punishment* to be *severe. But God will punish* you *even* more severely *if you cause someone to sin.* [43] *So*, if you are *tempted to use one of your hands to sin, stop using that hand*! *Even if you have to* cut your hand off *to avoid sinning, do it*! It is good *that you do not sin and* that you go where you will live *with God eternally, even though* you lack one of your hands *while you are here on earth.* But it is not good that you continue to have your two hands *and do the sin you are tempted to do and, as a result,* you go to hell. There the fires never go out![9] [45] If you are *tempted to use* one of your feet to sin, *stop using that foot*! *Even if you have* to cut your foot off *to avoid sinning, do it*! It is good *that you do not sin and* that you go where you will live *with God eternally, even*

---

[9] Some Greek manuscripts add here for v. 44, "In that place people suffer forever, and the fires never go out."

though you lack one of your feet *while you are here on earth*. But is not good that you continue to have your two feet *and do the sin you are tempted to do and, as a result*, you are thrown into hell.[h] [47] If because of what you see you are tempted to sin, *stop looking at those things*! *Even if you have to* gouge out one of your eyes *to avoid sinning, do it*! It is good *that you do not sin and* that you go to *live eternally in* the place where God rules, *even though* you lack one of your eyes *while you are here on earth*. But it is not good that you continue to have your two eyes *and do the sin you are tempted to do and, as a result,* you are thrown into hell. [48] In that place people suffer forever and the fires never go out."

Mark 9:49-50

THEME: Jesus taught that we must endure trials to remain useful to God.

[49]"*You must endure difficulties in order that God will be pleased with you. Your difficulties are like* a fire that makes things pure. *Your enduring is also like* people putting salt on sacrifices to make them pure. [50] Salt is useful *to put on food*, but you cannot make salt to taste salty again if it becomes flavorless. Similarly, you *must remain useful to God, because no one can make you useful to God again if you become useless*. You must also live peacefully with each other."

10

Mark 10:1-12

THEME: Some Pharisees asked him if the law permitted a man to divorce his wife. Jesus answered and supported his answer from Scripture.

[1] Jesus left that place[i] *with his disciples,* and they went through *the district of* Judea and on across *to the east side of* the Jordan *River*. When crowds gathered around him again, he taught them again, as he customarily did. [2] *While he was teaching them, some* Pharisees approached him and asked him, "Does *our Jewish* law permit a man to divorce his wife?" They asked that in order to be able to criticize him, *whether he answered "yes" or "no."* [3] He answered them, "What did Moses command your *ancestors about a man divorcing his wife*?" [4] *One of* them replied, "Moses permitted a man to write on paper *his reason* for divorcing his wife, *give this paper to her*, and then send her away." [5] Jesus said to them, "It was because your *ancestors* stubbornly *wanted their own ways* that Moses wrote that law for *them,* and you *are just like they were!* [6] *Remember that Moses also wrote that* when *God* first created *people*, he made *one* man, and he made *one* woman *to be that man's wife*. [7] That explains why *God said,* 'When a man *and woman marry*, they should no longer live with their fathers and mothers. [8] *Instead,* the two of them shall live together, and they shall become so *closely united that they are like* one person. Consequently, *although they functioned as* two *separate people before*, they now *become as* one.' [9] Since that is true, a man must not separate *from his wife* whom God has joined to him, *because it is God's plan for them to remain together*!"

[10] When Jesus and his disciples were alone in a house, they asked him again about this. [11] He said to them, "*Since God considers that a marriage lasts until either the husband or the wife dies, he considers that* any man who divorces his wife and marries another

---

[h]   Some Greek manuscripts add here for v. 46 as they did in v. 44, "In that place people suffer forever, and the fires never go out."

[i]   OR, Jesus left Capernaum…

woman is committing adultery if he marries another woman, *even* if he divorces his first wife. [12] *And he considers that* a woman who divorces her husband and marries another man is *also* committing adultery."

Mark 10:13-16

THEME: Jesus became indignant when he saw his disciples scolding people for bringing children for him to bless.

[13] *One day*, some people were bringing children to Jesus for him to lay his hands on them *and bless them*. But the disciples scolded them *because they thought Jesus did not want to be bothered spending time with children.* [14] When Jesus saw that, he became angry. He said to the *disciples*, "Let the children come to me! Don't stop them! It is people who *are humble and trusting* like they are who can experience God's rule *in their lives.* [15] Note this: Those who do not *trustingly* allow God to direct *their lives*, as children *do*, will not enter the place where God rules." [16] Then he took the children in his arms and laid his hands on them *and asked God to* bless them.

Mark 10:17-31

THEME: After a man asked Jesus what he should do in order to live eternally, Jesus told him to sell all his possessions.

[17] As Jesus was beginning to travel *again, accompanied by his disciples*, a young man ran up to him. He knelt before Jesus and asked him, "Good teacher, what must I do to have eternal life?" [18] Jesus said to him, "Only God is good! No one *else* is good. So you should consider carefully *what you are implying by* calling me good.[j] [19] *But to answer your question*, you know the commandments *God gave Moses, such as* 'do not commit murder; do not commit adultery; do not steal, do not testify falsely, do not cheat anyone, honor your father and mother'." [20] The man said to him, "Teacher, I have obeyed **all those** commandments ever since I was young. *So is there something else I haven't done?*" [21] Jesus looked at him and loved him. He said to him, "There is one thing that you have not *yet done*. You must go *home*, sell all that you possess, and then give *the money* to the poor. *The result will be that* you will have *spiritual* riches in heaven. Then come and be my disciple!" [22] The man became disappointed when he heard that, and he went away feeling sad, because he was very rich *and he did not want to give away all his possessions.* [23] Jesus looked around *at the people*. Then he exclaimed to his disciples, "It is very difficult for people who are wealthy *to decide* to let God rule their *lives!*" [24] The disciples were surprised at what he said. *They thought that God favored the rich people, so if God did not save them, he wouldn't save anyone.* So Jesus replied again to them, "My dear friends, it is very difficult for people to decide to let God rule their lives. [25] It is impossible for a camel to go through the eye of a needle. It is *almost* as difficult for rich people *to decide* to let God rule their *lives.*" [26] The disciples were very astonished. So they said to one another,[k] "If that is so, it is unlikely that anyone will be saved!" [27] Jesus looked at them and *then* he said, "*Yes*, it is impossible for people *to save themselves*! But God certainly can *save them*, because God can do anything!" [28] Peter exclaimed, "You know that we have left everything *behind* and have become your disciples. *So what about us?*" [29] Jesus replied, "Keep this in mind: Those who have left *their* houses, *their* brothers, *their* sisters, *their* father, *their* mother, *their* children or *their* plots of ground to *be* my *disciples* and to

---

[j] OR, ...You should consider carefully *your words, since you are implying that I am God by* calling me good!

[k] OR, ...So they said to him...

proclaim the good news, ³⁰ will receive in this life a hundred times as much *as they left behind. That will include* houses, and *people as dear as* brothers and sisters and mothers and children, and plots of ground. Furthermore, although *people* will persecute them *here on earth because they believe in me,* in the future age *they will have* eternal life. ³¹ But many *people* who *consider themselves to* be important *now* will be unimportant *at that future time,* and many who *consider themselves to* be unimportant *now will be* important *at that time!"*

Mark 10:32-34

THEME: As they were traveling toward Jerusalem, Jesus took the disciples aside and began to tell them again about what was going to happen to him.

³² *Some days later as they continued to travel,* Jesus was walking ahead of his disciples on the road that leads up to Jerusalem. *The disciples* were astonished *that he was going to Jerusalem where there were many people who opposed him,* and the other people who were with them were afraid *about what would happen to him in Jerusalem. Along the way* he took the twelve *disciples aside.* Then he began to tell them again about what was going to happen to him, saying, ³³"Listen carefully! We are going up to Jerusalem. *While we are there, someone* will enable the chief priests to seize me, the one who came from heaven. *They will put me on trial* with the help of the men who teach the *Jewish* law. They will condemn me *and declare* that I should be killed. *Then they* will put me in the hands of non-Jews, ³⁴ who will make fun of me. They will spit on me. They will whip me. *Then* they will kill me. But on the third day after *that,* I will become alive again!"

Mark 10:35-45

THEME: Jesus rebuked his disciples for wanting the most important positions when he became king.

³⁵ *Along the way* James and John approached Jesus and they said to him, "Teacher, we want you to do for us what we will ask you to do!" ³⁶ He said to them, "What do you want me to do for you?" ³⁷ They said to him, "In your glorious *kingdom, let* us sit next to you[1] and *let us rule with you."* ³⁸ But Jesus said to them, "You don't understand what you are asking for. Can you suffer like I am about to suffer? Can you endure being killed as I will be killed?" ³⁹ They said to him, "*Yes,* we are able *to do that!"* Then Jesus said to them, "Yes, you will suffer like I will suffer, and you will be killed as I will be killed. ⁴⁰ But I am not the one who chooses the ones who *will* sit next to me *and rule with me. God* will give those places to the ones *he* appoints."

⁴¹ The *other* ten *disciples* later heard what James and John *had requested. As a result,* they became angry *because they also wanted to rule with Jesus in the highest positions.* ⁴² *Then, after* Jesus called them all together, he said to them, "You know that those who rule the non-Jews *enjoy* showing that they are powerful. Their chief rulers *enjoy* commanding the people under them. ⁴³ But don't be like them! On the contrary, everyone among you who wants *God to consider him* great must become *like* a servant to *the rest of* you. ⁴⁴ And everyone among you who wants *God to consider him* to be the most important must become *like* a slave for *the rest of* you. ⁴⁵ *You should imitate me. Even though I am* the one who came from heaven, I did not come to be served. On the contrary, *I came in order* to serve *others,* and to allow myself to be killed, so that *my death would be like* a payment to rescue many *people from being punished for their sins."*

---

[1] Literally, "Let us sit one at your right hand and one at your left."

Mark 10:46-52

THEME: After a blind man called out and asked Jesus to have mercy on him, Jesus healed him.

⁴⁶ *On the way to Jerusalem*, Jesus and the disciples came to *the town of* Jericho. *Afterwards*, while they were leaving Jericho along with a great crowd, a blind man who was a *habitual* beggar was sitting beside the road. *His name was* Bartimaeus *and* his father's *name was* Timaeus. ⁴⁷ When he heard *people say* that Jesus from Nazareth *was passing by*, he shouted, "Jesus! *You who are the Messiah* descended from *King* David, take pity on me!" ⁴⁸ Many *people* scolded him *and* told him to be quiet. But he shouted even louder, "*You who are the Messiah* descended from *King* David, take pity on me!" ⁴⁹ Jesus stopped and he said *to the people*, "Tell him *to come over here!*" They summoned the blind man, saying, "Jesus is calling you! So cheer up and get up *and come!*" ⁵⁰ He threw aside his cloak as he jumped up, and he came to Jesus. ⁵¹ Jesus asked him, "What do you want me to do for you?" The blind man said to him, "Sir, enable me to see *again!*" ⁵² Jesus said to him, "*I am* healing you *because* of your faith *in me*. So you may go!" Immediately he was able to see! And he went with Jesus along the road.

11

Mark 11:1-11

THEME: Two disciples brought a young donkey to Jesus; then Jesus mounted it and rode to Jerusalem with people shouting praise to him.

¹ As they approached Jerusalem, they came near *the villages of* Bethphage and Bethany, near Olive *Tree* Hill, Jesus spoke to two of his disciples. ² He said to them, "Go to the village just ahead of you. As soon as you enter it, you will see a donkey tied *up* that no one has ever ridden. Untie it and bring it *to me*. ³ If anyone says to you, 'Why are you doing that?', say, ' The Lord needs it. He will *have someone* bring it back here as soon as *he no longer needs it*.'" ⁴ So *the two disciples* went and they found a young donkey. It was tied close to the door *of a house*, which was beside the street. Then they untied it. ⁵ Some of the *people there* said to them, "Why are you untying the donkey?" ⁶ They told them what Jesus had said. So the people permitted them *to take the donkey*. ⁷ They brought the donkey to Jesus. *The disciples* threw their cloaks on it *for him to sit on*. ⁸ Many people spread their cloaks on the road *to honor Jesus as a king*. Others, *in order to honor him*, spread along the road branches that they cut from *palm trees* in the fields *beside the road*. ⁹ The people who were going in front of him and those following behind him were all shouting things like, "Praise God!", and "May the Lord *God* bless *this one* who comes as his representative." ¹⁰ "May *God* bless you when you rule *like* our ancestor *King* David ruled!" "Praise God, who is in the highest *heaven!*"

¹¹ He entered Jerusalem, and then he went into the Temple *courtyard*. After he looked around at everything *there*, he left *the city* because it was already late *in the afternoon*. He returned to *the town of* Bethany with the twelve *disciples and slept* there.

Mark 11:12-14

THEME: Jesus cursed a fig tree as a sign of what would happen to the people of Israel.

¹² The next day, as *Jesus and his disciples* were leaving Bethany, *Jesus* was hungry. ¹³ He saw from a distance a fig tree with all its leaves, so he went to see if he could find any *figs* on it. But when he came to it, he found only leaves *on it*. That was because it was not yet

time when *normal fig trees have ripe* figs. [14] *But, to illustrate how God would punish the nation of Israel*, he said to the tree, "No one shall ever eat figs from you again *because you will no longer bear any*!" The disciples heard what he said.

Mark 11:15-19

THEME: Jesus expelled those who were buying and selling goods in the temple and taught that the temple was to be a place of prayer. These actions angered the priests and scribes who, then, looked for a way to kill Jesus.

[15] Jesus and his disciples went *back* to Jerusalem. He entered the Temple *courtyard and began to chase out those* who were buying and selling there. He also overturned the tables of those who were giving *Temple tax money* in exchange for *Roman* coins, he overturned the seats of those who were selling pigeons *for sacrifices*, [16] and he would not allow anyone who was carrying anything for sale to go through the Temple *area*. [17] Then as he taught the people, he said to them, "*You know* that it is written *in the Scriptures that God said*, '*I want* my house to be called a place where *people from* all nations can pray', but you bandits have made it your hideout!" [18] The chief priests and the men who taught the *Jewish* laws heard *later about what Jesus had done*. So they planned how they might kill him, *but they knew that would be difficult* because they realized that the crowd was amazed at what he was teaching, and they feared *that the people would soon decide that Jesus had more authority over the Temple than they did*.[m] [19] That evening, *Jesus and h*is *disciples* left the city *and again slept in Bethany*.

Mark 11:20-25

THEME: When Jesus and his disciples passed the fig tree that Jesus had cursed, they saw that it had withered. Jesus used this as an illustration for trusting that God would answer prayer.

[20] *The next* morning while they were going along *the road toward Jerusalem*, they saw that the fig tree *Jesus had cursed* had withered completely. [21] Peter remembered *what Jesus had said to the fig tree* and he exclaimed to Jesus, "Teacher, look! The fig tree you cursed has withered!" [22] Jesus replied, "*You shouldn't be surprised that God did what I asked!* You must trust that God *will do whatever you ask him to do*! [23] *Also* keep *this* in mind: If anyone says to a hill *like* this one, 'Uproot yourself and throw yourself into the sea!' and if he does not doubt *that what he asks for will happen*—if he believes that what he asks for will happen—it will happen. [24] So, I tell you, whenever you ask God for something when you pray, believe that you have received it, and *God* will do it for you. [25] Now, *I tell you this also*: Whenever you are praying, if you have a grudge against anyone *because they have harmed you*, forgive them, in order that your Father in heaven will *likewise* forgive your sins."[n]

Mark 11:27-33

THEME: The chief priests, scribes and elders asked Jesus by what authority he was doing these things. He, then, asked them a question that they would not answer; so he did not answer theirs.

[27] Jesus and his disciples arrived in the Temple *courtyard* in Jerusalem again. While Jesus was walking *there, a group consisting of* chief priests, *some* men who taught the *Jewish* laws, and elders came to him and they said to him, [28]"By what authority are you doing

---

[m] OR, …*they feared what the people might do if they tried to arrest Jesus*.

[n] Some Greek manuscripts add v. 26, "But if you do not forgive others, your Father who is in heaven will *similarly* not forgive your sins."

these things? Who authorized you to do things *like those you did here yesterday*?" [29] Jesus said to them, "**I** will ask **you** one question. If you answer me, I will tell you who authorized me to do these things. [30] Where did John *the Baptizer* get *his authority to* baptize *those who came to him*? *Did he get it* from God or from people?" [31] They debated among themselves *as to what they should answer. They said to each other*, "*If we say*, 'It was from God', he will say *to us*, 'Then why did you not believe *John's message*?' [32] On the other hand, if we say, 'It was from people,' *what might happen to us*?" They were afraid *to say that about where John got his authority, because they knew* the people *there would be very angry with them if they did. They knew that* all *those people* truly believed that John was a prophet *sent by God*. [33] So they answered Jesus, "We don't know *where John got his authority*." Then Jesus said to them, "*Because you did not answer my question*, I will not tell you who authorized me to do the things I did *here yesterday*."

12

Mark 12:1-12

THEME: After Jesus told the Jewish leaders a parable, they realized he was accusing them of wanting to kill him, but they feared how the people would react if they arrested Jesus.

[1] Then Jesus told those Jewish leaders a parable. He wanted to show what God would do to those who rejected the former prophets and himself. He said, "A certain man planted a vineyard. He built a fence around it. He made a stone tank to collect the juice that would be pressed out of the grapes. He also built a lookout tower. He rented the vineyard to some men to care for it and to give him some of the grapes in return. Then he went away to another country. [2] When the time came to harvest the grapes, he sent a servant to the renters in order to receive from them his share of the grapes that the vineyard had produced. [3] But they grabbed him and beat him, and they did not give him any grapes, and they sent him away. [4] Later, the owner sent another servant to them. But they bashed in his head and mistreated him. [5] Still later the owner sent another servant. That one they killed. The owner sent many other servants, and the renters mistreated them also. Some they beat and some they killed. [6] The man still had one other person with him. He had his son with him, whom he loved very much. So, finally he sent his son to them because he thought that they would respect him and give him his share of the grapes. [7] But when the son arrived, the renters said to each other, 'Look! This is the man who will inherit the vineyard! Let's join together and kill him so that this vineyard will be ours!' [8] They grabbed him and killed him. Then they threw his body outside the vineyard. [9] So what will the owner of the vineyard do? He will come and kill those renters. And he will rent the vineyard to others. [10] Now think carefully about these words that you have read in the Scriptures,

The builders rejected a certain stone. *But others put* that same stone *in its proper place, and it* has become the most important stone in the building! [11] The Lord has done this, and we marvel as we look at it.

[12] Then *the Jewish leaders* realized that he was accusing them when he told the parable *about what the wicked renters did*. So they wanted to seize him. But they were afraid of *what* the crowds *would do if they did that*. So they left him and went away.

Mark 12:13-17

THEME: The Jewish leaders failed in their attempt to trap Jesus by their question of whether they should pay taxes to the Roman government.

[13] The *Jewish leaders* sent to *Jesus* some Pharisees *who thought that the Jews should pay only the tax that their own authorities required people to pay*. They also sent some members of the party that supported Herod *Antipas and the Roman government*. They wanted to make Jesus say something wrong *that would make one of those groups very angry with him.* [14] After they arrived, they said to him *deceivingly*, "Teacher, we know that you *are* truthful and that you teach the truth about what God wants *us to do*. We also know that you don't change what you teach because of what someone says about you, even if it is an important person who does not like what you teach. So *tell us what you think about this matter:* Is it right that we pay taxes to the Roman government, or not? Should we pay the taxes or shouldn't we?" [15] Jesus knew that they did not really want to know *what God wanted them to do*. So he said to them, "I *know that* you are *just* trying to make me say something wrong for which you can accuse me. *But I will answer your question anyway.* Bring me a coin so that I can *ask you something after I* look at it." [16] So they brought *him* a coin, and he asked them, "Whose picture is *on* this *coin*? And *whose* name *is on it?*" They replied, "*It has the picture and name* of Caesar, *the head of the Roman government.*" [17] Then Jesus said to them, "*Okay*, give to the government what they *require*, and give to God what he *requires.*" *The answer he gave did not allow them to accuse him, so they were frustrated. But* they were *also* amazed at *what* he *said.*

Mark 12:18-27

THEME: Jesus showed from Scripture that the Sadducees were wrong in ridiculing the idea of life after death.

[18] *Some* Sadducees came to Jesus. They are a Jewish sect who do not believe that people will become alive again after they die. They *wanted to* ask *Jesus* a question. *In order to discredit the idea that dead people will live again,* they said *to him,* [19]"Teacher, Moses wrote for us *Jews* that if a man who has no children dies, his brother must marry *the dead man's* widow so that she can have a child by him. The child *will be considered to be* the descendant of the man *who died, and in that way the dead man will have descendants.* [20] *Well,* there were seven boys in one family. The oldest one married a woman, but *he and his wife* did not have any children. Later he died. [21] The second *brother married the widow, but he also died without having a child.* The third *brother did* like *his other brothers did. He married the widow and died without having a child.* [22] Although all seven *brothers, one by one, married that woman*, they had no children *and one by one they died*. Afterwards, the woman died, too. [23] *So,* at the time when people are raised from the dead, whose wife *do you think that woman* will be then? Keep in mind that she was married to all seven *brothers!*" [24] Jesus replied to them, "Your *thinking* is certainly wrong. You don't know *what is written in* the Scriptures *about this. You also don't know that* God has *the* power *to make people alive again.* [25] *That woman will not be the wife of any of them, because* after *God causes* all dead people *to* live again, no one will be married. Instead, *people* will be like the angels in heaven, *who do not marry.* [26] But as to people becoming alive again after they die, in the book that Moses *wrote, he said something about people who have died* that I am sure you have read. *When Moses was looking at* the *burning* bush, God said to him, 'I am the God whom Abraham *worships* and the God whom Isaac *worships* and the God whom Jacob *worships.*' [27] *Abraham, Isaac, and Jacob died long before Moses lived. But God said they were still worshiping him, so we know their spirits were still alive!* God is *surely* not one whom dead *people worship!* He is the

God *whom* living *people worship, because he keeps their spirits alive even after they have died!* So your *claim that* dead people do not become alive again is very wrong."

Mark 12:28-34

THEME: Jesus commended a scribe who accepted Jesus' assessment of the two greatest commandments, after which they asked Jesus no more questions to trap him.

[28] A man who taught the *Jewish* laws heard their discussion. He knew that Jesus had answered the question well. So he stepped forward and asked Jesus, "Which *of God's* commandments is the most important?" [29] Jesus answered, "The most important commandment is this: 'Listen, you people of Israel! *You must worship* the Lord, our God, your only Lord. [30] *You must love him with all your heart! Show your love for him* in all your desires, in all your emotions, in all your thoughts, and in all that you do!' [31] The next *most important commandment* is: 'You must love people you come in contact with as much as *you love* yourself.' No other commandment is more important than those *two*!" [32] The man said to Jesus, "Teacher, you have answered well. You correctly said that he is the only God and that there is no other God *we must* worship. [33] *You have* also *said correctly that* we *should* love *God* with all our heart; and *that we should show our love for him* in all our thoughts, and in all that we do. *And you have said correctly that we must* love people with whom we come in contact as much as *we love* ourselves. *And you have also correctly said that doing these things pleases God* more than giving him burnt offerings or *other* sacrifices." [34] Jesus realized that this man had answered wisely. So he said to him, "*I perceive that* you will soon *decide to let* God rule your life." After that, *the Jewish leaders* were afraid to ask him any more questions *like that to try to trap him.*

Mark 12:35-37

THEME: Jesus showed from Scripture that the Messiah must be David's Lord as well as his descendant.

[35] *Later*, while Jesus was teaching in the Temple *courtyard*, he said *to the people*, "The men who teach our *Jewish* laws must be wrong when they say that the Messiah is *merely* a descendant of *King* David. [36] The Holy Spirit prompted David himself to say *about the Messiah*,

God said to my Lord, 'Sit *here beside me* on my right, *where I will greatly honor you. Sit here* while I completely defeat your enemies.'

[37] King David himself calls *the Messiah* 'my Lord.' So *the Messiah* cannot be *just someone* descended from *David. He must be much greater than David!*" Many people listened to him gladly *as he taught those things.*

Mark 12:38-40

THEME: Jesus warned them about the scribes' hypocritical actions.

[38] While Jesus was teaching *the people*, he said to them, "Beware that you *don't act like* the men who teach our *Jewish* laws. They like to put on long robes and walk around *to show people how important they are. They* also *like people to* greet them *respectfully* in the market places. [39] In the places of worship, *they like to sit in* the in the area where the pious people sit. At festivals, *they like to sit in* the seats where the most important people sit. [40] They swindle the houses *and property* of widows. *Then* they pretend *they are good,* as they pray long prayers *publicly. God* will *certainly* punish them very severely!"

Mark 12:41-44

THEME: Jesus told them that a poor widow's tiny offering was worth more in God's sight than large amounts of money from rich people.

[41] *Later,* Jesus sat down *in the Temple courtyard* opposite the boxes in which people put offerings. *As he was sitting there,* he watched all the people putting money in the boxes. Many rich people put in large amounts *of money.* [42] Then a poor widow came along and put in two *small* copper coins, which had a very small value. [43-44] He gathered his disciples around him and said to them, "The truth is that these other people have a lot of money, *but* they gave *only a small part of it.* But this woman, who is very poor, has put in all the money she had to pay for the things she needs! So *God considers that* this poor widow has put more money into the box than all *the other people.*"

13

Mark 13:1-2

THEME: Jesus prophesied that the temple would be completely destroyed.

[1] While Jesus was leaving the Temple *area,* one of his disciples said to him, "Teacher, look at how marvelous *these* huge stones *are* and how wonderful *these* buildings *are!*" [2] Jesus said to him, "*Yes,* these buildings that you are looking *at are wonderful,* but *I want to tell you something about* them. *They will be completely destroyed.* Every stone *in these buildings* will be thrown down. Not one stone will be left on top of another."

Mark 13:3-37

THEME: Jesus taught his disciples about the events that would precede his return.

[3] After they arrived on Olive *Tree* Hill across *the valley* from the Temple, Jesus sat down. When Peter, James, John, and Andrew were alone with him, they asked him, [4]"When will this happen *to the buildings of the Temple*? Tell us what will happen to indicate that *God* is about to finish doing all these things *that he has planned.*" [5] Jesus replied to them, "*All I will say is,* be sure that no one deceives you! [6] Many *people* will come and say that they have my authority. They will say, 'I am *the Messiah,*' and they will deceive many *people.* [7] Whenever you hear about wars *that are close* or wars that are far away, don't be troubled. *God has said* those things must happen. But *when they happen, it will not mean that the end of the world has come!* [8] *Various* countries will fight each other, and *various* governments *will also fight* against each other. There will be earthquakes in various places, and there will be famines. These things will happen first. Then there will be other things *that will precede my return. What will happen will be as painful as* birth pains.

[9] "Be ready for *what people will do to you at that time.* Because *you believe in* me, you will be arrested and put on trial before the religious councils. In the places where you gather to worship, you will be beaten. You will be put *on trial* before high government authorities. As a result, you will be able to tell them *about me.* [10] My good message must be proclaimed to all people-groups before *God finishes all that he has planned.* [11] And when people arrest you to prosecute you *because of your faith* in me, don't worry beforehand about what you will say. Instead, say what *God* puts into your mind at that time. Then it will not be *just* you who will be speaking. It will be the Holy Spirit *who will be speaking through you.* [12] *And there will also be other evil things that will* happen: People *who do not believe in me* will help others seize their brothers *and sisters* and have them killed. Parents *will betray* their

children, and children will betray their parents and have them killed. ¹³ *In general*, most people will hate you because *you believe in* me. But *all* you who keep on *believing in me to the end of your life* will be saved.

¹⁴ "*During that time* the disgusting *person described by the prophet Daniel* will enter the Temple. He will defile *the Temple* when he enters it and will cause people to abandon it. When you see him standing *there* where he shouldn't be, *you should run away quickly!* (May everyone who is reading this pay attention to *this warning from Jesus!*) At that time those *of you* who are in Judea must flee to the *higher* hills. ¹⁵ Those who are outside their houses must not go back into their houses to get anything *before they flee.* ¹⁶ Those who are *working* in a field must not turn back to get their outer clothing *before they flee.* ¹⁷ *I feel very sorry for* women who will be pregnant and women who will be nursing *their babies* in those days, *because it will be very difficult for them to run away*!

¹⁸⁻¹⁹ In the final days there will be great suffering. There has never been such suffering since the time when God first created the world until now; and *there* will never be *suffering like that again.* So pray that *this painful time* will not happen in winter *when it will be hard to travel.* ²⁰ If the Lord *God* had not *decided to* shorten that time *of suffering*, everyone would die. But he has *decided to* shorten it because *he is concerned* about *you* whom he has chosen. ²¹⁻²² *At that time people* will appear *who will* falsely *say they are* the Messiah or *that they are* prophets. They will perform many kinds of miracles in order to deceive people. They will try *to see if it is* possible to deceive *you people whom God has* chosen. So at that time if someone says to you, 'Look, here is the Messiah!' or *if someone says*, 'Look, there he is!' don't believe it! ²³ Be alert! *Remember that* I have warned you about all this before *it happens*!

²⁴ "After that time of great suffering, the sun will become dark, the moon will not shine, ²⁵ the stars will fall from the sky, and the powerful *objects* in the sky will be shaken.º ²⁶ Then people will see *me*, the one who came from heaven, coming in the clouds with great power and glory. ²⁷ Then I will send out the angels to gather *the people* whom I have chosen from everywhere, *and that includes* the most remote places on earth.

²⁸ "*Now I want you to* learn something from *how* fig trees *grow. In this area*, when the branches *of a fig tree* become tender and its leaves begin to sprout, you know that summer is near. ²⁹ In the same way, when you see the things *I have just described* happening, **you** will know that *the time of my return* is very close. *It will be as though I am* already at the door. ³⁰ Keep this in mind: All of these events will happen before all the people who have observed the things I have done have died. ³¹ You can *be certain that these things that* I have told *you* about will happen. That they will happen is more *certain* than that the earth and sky will continue to exist. ³² But neither I, nor any other person, nor any angel in heaven knows the day and the hour *when the things I have told you about will happen*. Only God, *my* Father, *knows.* ³³ So be ready, *like people who are waiting for an important man to come*, because you don't know the time *when all these events will happen!* ³⁴ When a man who wants to travel *to a distant place* is *about to* leave his house, he tells his servants that they should manage the house. *He tells* each one what he should do. Then he tells the doorkeeper to be ready *for his return.* ³⁵ *That man must always be* ready, *because he does not know whether* his master will return in the evening, at midnight, when the rooster crows, or at dawn. *In the same way*, you also must *always* be ready, because you don't know *when I will* return. ³⁶ *May it not happen that* when I come suddenly, I will find that you are not ready! ³⁷ These words that I am saying to you *disciples,* I am saying to everyone *who believes in me: Always* be ready!" *That is what Jesus warned his disciples.*

º OR, ...and the spiritual beings in space will be deposed.

14

Mark 14:1-2

THEME: The Jewish leaders planned how they could arrest Jesus without starting a riot.

[1] It was only two days before *the people started to celebrate the one-week festival called* Passover. *During those days they also celebrated* the festival of Unleavened Bread. The chief priests and the men who taught the *Jewish* laws were seeking a way to seize Jesus in some deceitful way, so that they could have him executed. [2] But they were saying *to one another*, "*We must* not *do it* during the *Passover* festival, because *if we do it then,* the people might riot!"

Mark 14:3-11

THEME: Jesus commended a woman who extravagantly anointed Jesus in anticipation of his death. The high priests agreed to pay Judas if he would help them seize Jesus.

[3] Jesus was in *the village of* Bethany in the house of Simon, who *had been healed of* leprosy. While they were eating, a woman came. *She was carrying* a stone jar that contained very expensive perfume *called* nard. She opened the jar and poured the perfume on Jesus' head. [4] One of the people *who were present* became angry and said to the others, "It is terrible that *she* wasted that perfume! *We* could have sold it for a huge amount of money,[p] and then *the money* could have been given to poor people!" So he rebuked her. [6] But Jesus said, "Stop scolding her! You shouldn't bother her, because she has done a beautiful thing to me. [7] You will always have poor people among you. So you can help them whenever you want to. But I will not always *be with* you. *So it is good that she showed her appreciation for me now.* [8] *It is appropriate that she did* what she was able to do. *It is as if she knew that I am going to die soon* and has anointed my body for burial. [9] I will tell you this: Wherever the good message *about me* is preached throughout the world, those who preach it will tell what this woman has done, *and as a result* she will *always* be remembered."

[10] Then Judas Iscariot went to the chief priests to *talk to them about* helping them to seize *Jesus*. He did that *even though* he was one of the twelve *disciples!* [11] When they heard *what he was willing to do*, they were *very* happy. They promised to give him money *for doing that. Judas agreed, so they gave him the money*. Then he *began* watching for an opportunity to enable them to seize *Jesus*.

Mark 14:12-17

THEME: Two disciples followed Jesus' instructions and prepared the Passover meal.

[12] On the first day of *the week-long festival of* Unleavened Bread, *the day* when the lambs *for the* Passover *celebration* were killed, Jesus' disciples said to him, "Where do you want us to go and prepare *the meal for* the Passover celebration so that *we can eat it with* you?" [13] So he *chose* two of his disciples *to prepare everything. He* said to them, "Go into the city. A man carrying a large jar of water will meet you. Follow him. [14] When he enters *a house*, say to the owner of the house, '*Our* teacher says *we should ask you to please* show *us* the room he arranged *with you* where he can eat the Passover *meal* with *us,* his disciples. Please show us the room that he *arranged with you about*.' [15] He will show you a

---

[p] OR, …*We* could have sold it for as much money as I could earn in a year!

large room on the upper *floor of the house.* It will be furnished and ready *for us to eat a meal in it.* Prepare the meal for us there." [16] So the *two* disciples left. They went into the city and found *everything* just as *Jesus* had told them. They prepared the *meal for* the Passover *celebration and then returned to Jesus and the other disciples.* [17] When it was evening, Jesus came *to this house,* along with the twelve *disciples.*

Mark 14:18-26

THEME: During the Passover meal, Jesus prophesied that one disciple would betray him. Then he gave them the bread and wine. He said these represented his body and blood which would be sacrificed.

[18] As they were *all* sitting there and eating, Jesus said, "Listen carefully to this: One of you is going to enable *my enemies* to seize me, one of you who is eating with me *right now!*" [19] The disciples became very sad, and they said to him, *one* after the other, " I'm not the one, am I?" [20] He said to them, "It is one of *you* twelve *disciples,* the one who is dipping *bread* into the *sauce in the* dish along with me. [21] *It is certain that I,* the one who came from heaven, will die, because that is what *the prophets* have written about me. But it will be terrible for the man who enables *my enemies* to seize me! It would be better for that man if he had never been born!"

[22] While they were eating, *Jesus* took *a flat loaf of* bread and thanked God for it. He broke it *into pieces* and gave it to them and said, "Take this *bread and eat it. It represents* my body.[q] *Take it.*" [23] Later he took a cup *of wine* and thanked *God for it.* Then he gave it to them and, as they all drank from it, [24] he said to them, "*The wine in* this cup *represents* my blood,[r] which will soon flow *from my body when I die. With* this blood I *will sign* the new agreement *that God is making to cancel the sins* of many *people.* [25] Note this: I will not drink wine in this way anymore until the time when I drink it with a new *meaning. That will happen* when God *enables me to begin* to rule as king." [26] After they sang a hymn, they started out towards Olive *Tree* Hill.

Mark 14:27-31

THEME: Jesus predicted that Peter would deny three times that he knew Jesus.

[27] *On the way,* Jesus said to them, "All of you are going to desert me. *This is certain to happen,* because *these words that God said* are written *in the Scriptures*: 'I will *cause* the shepherd to be killed, and *all* the sheep will be scattered.' [28] But after I have *died and* become alive again, I will go ahead of you to *the district of* Galilee *and meet you there.*" [29] Then Peter said to him, "Perhaps all the *other disciples* will desert you, *but not I*! I will not *desert you!*" [30] Jesus said to him, "The truth is that this very night, before the rooster crows a second time, you will say three times that you don't know me!" [31] But *Peter* replied strongly, "Even if I am killed *as I defend* you, I will never say that I don't know you!" And all *the other disciples* said the same *thing.*

---

[q] OR, ...*Then he gave it to his disciples* and said, "This bread *is* my body, which I *am about to sacrifice* for you.

[r] OR, ...*Then he gave it to his disciples,* [24] saying, "*The wine in* this cup *is* my blood...

Mark 14:32-42

THEME: While the disciples slept, Jesus prayed that God would spare him from the coming suffering but concluded by expressing his desire that God's will be done.

³² Then *Jesus and* the disciples came to a place called Gethsemane. There he said to *most of* them, "Stay here while I pray!" ³³ He took Peter, James, and John with him. He became extremely distressed, and said to them, ³⁴"I am very sorrowful, so much so that *I feel as if my sorrow is about to* kill me. *You men* stay here and keep awake!" ³⁵ After going a little further, he threw himself on the ground. Then he prayed that if it were possible, he would not *have to suffer*. ³⁶ He said, "O my Father, since you are able to do everything, rescue me so that I do not have to go through the suffering that is coming now! But, don't *do* what I want. Instead, *do* what you want!" ³⁷ Then he returned *to the three disciples* and saw that they were sleeping. He *woke them up and* said, "Simon! *I am disappointed that* you *fell asleep and* were not able to stay awake for just one hour!" ³⁸ *And he said to all three of them*, "You must keep awake and pray so that you can resist when you are tempted. You want *to do what I tell you*, but you are not able *to actually do it*." ³⁹ Then he went away again and prayed again what he prayed before. ⁴⁰ When he returned, he found that they were sleeping again because they were very sleepy, so sleepy that they couldn't keep their eyes open. *Because they were ashamed*, they did not know what to say to him *when he awakened them*. ⁴¹ *Then he went and prayed again*. He returned a third time; *and he found them sleeping again*. He *woke them and* said to them, "I am disappointed that you are sleeping again and resting! *You have slept* enough. The time *for me to suffer* is about to begin. Look! *Someone* is about to enable sinful *men* to seize *me*, the one who came from heaven. ⁴² *So*, get up! Let's go *to meet them*! Look! Here comes the one who is enabling them to seize me!"

Mark 14:43-49

THEME: Judas betrayed Jesus.

⁴³ While *Jesus* was still speaking, Judas *arrived. Even though he was* one of *Jesus'* twelve *disciples*, he came *to enable Jesus' enemies to seize him*. A crowd carrying swords and clubs was with him. They had been sent by the *leaders of* the Jewish Council. ⁴⁴ Judas had *previously* arranged to give them a signal, saying, "The man whom I will kiss is the one *you want*. Seize him and *guard him* carefully as you lead him away." ⁴⁵ So when Judas arrived, he immediately went to Jesus and said, "My teacher!" And he kissed Jesus *on the cheek*. ⁴⁶ Then *the crowd* seized Jesus. ⁴⁷ But one of the *disciples* who was standing nearby drew his sword and struck the servant of the high priest *to kill him, but he only* cut off his ear.
⁴⁸⁻⁴⁹ Jesus said to them, "It is ridiculous that you have come *here* to seize me with swords and clubs, as *if I were* a bandit! Day after day I was with you in the Temple *courtyard* teaching *the people*! Why did you not seize me then? *But this is happening* in order to fulfill *what the prophets have written in* the Scriptures *about me*."

Mark 14:50-52

THEME: Mark ran away.

⁵⁰ All *the disciples immediately* left him and ran away. ⁵¹ *At that time, I was* following Jesus. *I was* wearing only a linen cloth around my body. *The soldiers* seized me. ⁵² But, *as I pulled away from them*, I left^s behind the linen cloth *in their hands* and ran away naked.

Mark 14:53-65

THEME: After the high priest asked Jesus if he was the Messiah, Jesus said he was the son of God, the Messiah, after which the Jewish Council decided Jesus must die.

⁵³ *The men who had seized* Jesus took him to *the house where* the high priest *lived*. All of the Jewish Council were gathering *there*. ⁵⁴ Peter followed *Jesus* at a distance. He went into the high priest's courtyard, and sat there with the guards, warming himself beside a fire. ⁵⁵ The chief priests and the rest of the *Jewish* council *had already* tried to find people who would tell *lies* about Jesus *so that they could convince the Roman authorities* to execute him. But they did not succeed, ⁵⁶ because, although many people spoke lies about him, they contradicted each other. ⁵⁷ *Finally*, some stood up and accused him falsely by saying, ⁵⁸"We heard him say, 'I will destroy this Temple that was built by men, and then in three days I will build another *temple* without help from anyone else'." ⁵⁹ But, the words that *some of* these men said also did not agree with *what others said*.

⁶⁰ Then the high priest stood in front of Jesus and said to him, "Aren't you going to reply? What *do you say about* these accusations?" ⁶¹ But Jesus remained silent and made no reply. Then the high priest *tried again*. He asked him, "Are you the Messiah, the Son of God?"^t ⁶² Jesus said, "I am. Furthermore, you will see *me*, the man who came from heaven, sitting beside almighty God, and ruling. *You will also see me* coming down through the clouds from heaven!" ⁶³ *At that*, the high priest tore his outer garment. *That was the custom to show he was shocked to hear Jesus say he was equal to God*. Then he said, "We certainly don't need any *more* people to testify *against this man*! ⁶⁴ You have heard what he said against God! *He claims to be equal with God*! So what is your decision?" They all said that Jesus was guilty and deserved to be executed. ⁶⁵ Then some of them began spitting on Jesus. They put a blindfold on him and began striking him and saying to him, "*If you are* a prophet, tell us *who hit you*!" And those who were guarding him struck Jesus with their hands.

Mark 14:66-72

THEME: As Jesus had prophesied, Peter denied three times that he knew Jesus.

⁶⁶ While Peter was outside in the courtyard *of the high priest's house*, one of the girls who worked for the high priest came. ⁶⁷ When she saw Peter warming himself *beside the fire*, she looked at him closely. Then she said, "You also were with Jesus, *that man* from Nazareth!" ⁶⁸ But he denied it by saying, "I don't know or understand what you are talking about!" Then he went *out* to the gate *of the courtyard*.^u ⁶⁹ Another servant girl saw him there and said the same thing. *She told* the people who were standing nearby, "This man is one of those *who was with that man they arrested*." ⁷⁰ But he denied it again. After a little

---

^s OR, *At that time, there was* a young man following Jesus. *He was* wearing only a linen cloth around his body. The soldiers seized him. ⁵² But, he left…

^t OR, …He asked him, "Are you the Messiah? Do you say you are the Man who is also God?"

^u Some Greek manuscripts add, "And a rooster crowed."

while, those who were standing there said to Peter again, "*The way you speak* shows that you also are from Galilee. So it is certain that you are one of those *who accompanied Jesus!*" [71] But *Peter* began to proclaim loudly that God should curse him if he was lying. He asked God in heaven to witness that he was telling the truth and said, "I don't know the man you are talking about!" [72] Immediately the rooster crowed a second time. Then Peter remembered what Jesus had said to him, "Before the rooster crows a second time, you will deny three times *that you know* me." *And* he began to cry.

15

Mark 15:1-5

THEME: In the presence of Pilate, the governor, Jesus refused to answer accusations against him.

[1] Very early in the morning the chief priests met together with *the rest of* the Jewish council to decide *how to accu*se Jesus before the Roman governor. They tied Jesus' hands and took him to Pilate, *the Roman governor, and they began accusing him, saying "Jesus is claiming that he is a king!*" [2] Pilate asked *Jesus*, "Do you *claim to be* the king of the Jews?" Jesus answered him, "*It is* as you have *just* said." [3] Then the chief priests accused *Jesus* of many things. [4] So Pilate asked him again, "Don't you have anything to reply? Listen to all the accusations they are bringing against you!" [5] But *even though Jesus was not guilty*, he did not say anything more. Pilate was surprised at that.

Mark 15:6-15

THEME: At the crowd's insistence, Pilate released a criminal and gave orders that Jesus should be crucified.

[6] It was *the governor's* custom *each year* during the *Passover* celebration to release *one person who was in prison. He would release whatever* prisoner the people requested. [7] Well, *at that time* there was a man called Barrabas who had been *put in prison with some others. They had murdered some soldiers when they rebelled against the Roman government.* [8] A crowd approached *Pilate* and asked him *to release someone*, just like he customarily did for them *during the Passover celebration*. [9] Pilate answered them, "Would you like me to release for you the *man who you* Jews *say is your* king?" [10] He asked this because he realized what the chief priests were doing. They were accusing Jesus out of jealousy *because many people were becoming his disciples*. [11] But the chief priests urged the crowd *to request* that Pilate release Barrabas for them instead *of Jesus*. [12] Pilate said to them, "*If I release Barrabas*, what do you want me to do with the man who *some of* you Jews say is *your* king?" [13] They shouted, "*Have* him crucified!" [14] Then Pilate said to them, "Why? What crime has he committed?" But they shouted even louder, "*Have* him crucified!" [15] So because Pilate wanted to please the crowd, he released Barrabas for them. Then, after *he* had Jesus whipped, *he turned him over to the soldiers* to be crucified.

Mark 15:16-20

THEME: The soldiers ridiculed Jesus as being a king.

[16] The soldiers took Jesus into the *courtyard of the* palace *where Pilate lived*. That place was the government headquarters. Then they summoned the whole cohort of soldiers *who were on duty there*. [17] *After the soldiers gathered* together, *in order to ridicule* Jesus *by*

pretending he was a king, they put a purple robe on *him.* Then they *took some branches with* thorns and wove them to make a crown, and put it on his head. [18] Then they greeted him *like they would greet a king,* saying, "Hooray for the King of the Jews!" [19] They repeatedly struck his head with a reed and spat on him. By kneeling down, they *pretended to* honor him. [20] When they had finished ridiculing him, they pulled off the purple robe. They put his own clothes on him and led him outside *of the city* to nail him to a cross.

Mark 15:21-24

THEME: After they crucified Jesus, the soldiers gambled for his clothing.

[21] *After Jesus carried his cross for a while, he was unable to carry it any further.* Then a man named Simon from *the city of* Cyrene *came along.* He was the father of Alexander and Rufus. He was passing by as he was returning to *Jerusalem* from out in the countryside. *The soldiers* forced Simon to carry the cross *for Jesus.* [22] And they made Jesus, *along with Simon,* go to a place *called* Golgotha, which means 'the place *like* a skull'. [23] Then they tried to give Jesus wine that was mixed with *medicine called* myrrh. *They wanted him to drink it so that he would not feel so much pain when they crucified him.* But he did not drink it. [24] *Some* of the *soldiers took his clothes,* and then they nailed him to the cross. Afterwards, they divided his clothes among themselves by gambling with *something like* dice, *to decide* which *piece of clothing* each one would get.

Mark 15:25-32

THEME: People passing by, as well as the Jewish leaders and two criminals crucified with Jesus, insulted him.

[25] It was nine o'clock in the morning when they crucified him. [26] *They attached to the cross above Jesus' head* a sign that stated why *they* were nailing him to the cross. *But all* it said was, "The king of the Jews." [27] They also crucified two men who were bandits. They nailed one to a cross on the right side *of Jesus* and one to a cross on the left side.[v] [29] The people who were passing by insulted him by shaking their heads as *if he were an evil man.* They said, "Aha! You *said you* would destroy the Temple and then you would build it again in three days.' [30] *If you could do that, then* rescue yourself by coming down from the cross!" [31] The chief priests, along with the men who taught the *Jewish* laws, also *wanted to* make fun of Jesus. So they said to each other, "He *claims to have* saved others *from their sicknesses,* but he can't help himself! [32] He says he is the Messiah, the king of Israel.' *If what he says is true,* he should come down from the cross! Then we will believe *him*!" The men who had been crucified with him also insulted him.

Mark 15:33-41

THEME: As several women who had accompanied Jesus watched, he died, after which the temple curtain split into two parts and the Roman officer pronounced that Jesus was the son of God.

[33] At noon the whole land became dark, *and it stayed dark* until three o'clock in the afternoon. [34] At three o'clock Jesus shouted loudly, "Eloi, Eloi, lama sabachthani?" which means, "My God, My God, why have you deserted me?" [35] When some of the people who were standing there heard *the word 'Eloi', misunderstanding it,* they said, "Listen! He is calling for *the prophet* Elijah!" [36] One *of them* ran, got a reed, and put a sponge on it. He

---

[v] Some Greek manuscripts add verse 28, "In that way, the words that Isaiah wrote in the Scriptures proved to be true, 'They accused him, saying he was a criminal.'"

dipped it in sour wine, and held it up for *Jesus* to suck out *the wine that was in* it. *While he was doing that, someone* said, "Wait! Let's see whether Elijah will come to take him down *from the cross*!" ³⁷ And then, after Jesus shouted loudly, he stopped breathing *and died.* ³⁸ *At that moment* the *heavy thick* curtain *that closed off the most holy place* in the Temple split into two pieces from top to bottom. *That signified that ordinary people could now go into the presence of God.* ³⁹ The officer who supervised the soldiers *who nailed Jesus to the cross* was standing in front of Jesus. When he saw how *Jesus* died, he exclaimed, "Truly this man was sent by God!"ʷ ⁴⁰⁻⁴¹ There were also some women *there*, watching from a distance. They had accompanied Jesus when he was in *the district of* Galilee and provided what he needed. They had come with him to Jerusalem. Among them were Mary from *the town of* Magdala, *another* Mary who was the mother of the younger James and of Joses, and Salome.

Mark 15:42-47

THEME: Two women watched as Joseph and others buried Jesus' body in a cave after getting permission from Pilate.

⁴²⁻⁴³ When it was *almost* evening, *a man named* Joseph from *the town of* Arimathea *came.* He was a member of the *Jewish* council *whom everyone* respected. He was also one of those who had been waiting expectantly for *the time when* God *would send* his king to begin to rule. *He knew that, according to Jewish law, people's bodies had to be buried on the day they died. Now the day Jesus died* was the day when *people* prepared *things for the* Jewish day of rest, which would start *when the sun set.* So Joseph had enough courage to go to Pilate to ask for permission *to take* the body of Jesus *down from the cross and bury it immediately.* ⁴⁴ Pilate was surprised *to hear that* Jesus was already dead. So he summoned the officer in charge of the soldiers *who crucified Jesus*, and asked him if *Jesus* had already died. ⁴⁵ When the officer told *Pilate that Jesus was dead*, Pilate allowed Joseph *to take away* the body. ⁴⁶ After Joseph bought a linen cloth, he *and others* took *Jesus' body* down *from the cross.* They wrapped it in the linen cloth and laid it in a tomb that had been dug out of the rock *cliff.* Then they rolled a *huge circular flat* stone in front of the entrance to the tomb. ⁴⁷ Mary *from the village of* Magdala and Mary the mother of Joses were watching where they laid Jesus' *body.*

16

Mark 16:1-8

THEME: Two days later several women were astonished to find Jesus' tomb empty.

¹ On *Saturd*ay evening when the Jewish day of rest had ended, Mary *from the village of* Magdala, Mary the mother of the *younger* James, and Salome bought fragrant ointment. *The Jews had a custom of* anointing bodies *before they buried them, and the women wanted to follow this custom.* ² So very early on Sunday, *just* after sunrise, they took *the fragrant ointment* and started toward the tomb. ³ *On the way* they were saying to each other, "Who will roll away for us the stone *that blocks* the entrance to the tomb?" ⁴ *After they arrived*, they looked up and saw that the stone had already been rolled away. *They were surprised,* because it was a huge stone. ⁵ They entered the tomb and saw *an angel who looked like* a young man, sitting at the right side *of the c*ave. He was wearing a white robe. They were astonished! ⁶ The young man said to them, "Don't be astonished! *I know*

ʷ OR, …Truly this man was the Son of God.

you are looking for Jesus of Nazareth, who was crucified. He has become alive again! He is not here! Look! *Here is* the place where they laid his *body*. [7] But *don't stay here*. Instead, go and tell his disciples. And especially *be sure* to tell Peter. Tell them, '*Jesus* is going ahead of you to Galilee, and you will see him there, just as he told you!" [8] The women went outside and ran from the tomb. They were trembling *with fear*, and they were astonished. But they did not say anything to anyone *about this* while they were going, because they were afraid.

[The end of Mark's Gospel was lost or destroyed long ago. Then someone wrote verses 9-20 from what he remembered about those events. That ending is given below.]

Mark 16:9-14

THEME: Jesus rebuked the disciples for not believing the reports of his being alive again.

[[9] When Jesus became alive *again* early on Sunday morning, he appeared first to Mary *from the village of* Magdala. She was the woman from whom he had expelled seven evil spirits. [10] She went to those who had accompanied *Jesus*, while they were mourning and crying. She told them *what she had seen*. [11] But when she told them that Jesus was alive again and that she had seen him, they refused to believe it. [12] Later *that day*, Jesus appeared to two of *his disciples* while they were walking *from Jerusalem* to *their homes in* the *surrounding* area. *But they did not recognize him at first because* he looked very different. [13] *After they recognized him*, those two went back *to Jerusalem* and told his other *followers what had happened*, but they *still* did not believe it. [14] Later he appeared to the eleven *apostles* while they were eating. He rebuked them for stubbornly refusing to believe the reports of those who saw him after he had become alive again.

Mark 16:15-20

THEME: Miracles began to happen after Jesus instructed his disciples to preach the gospel everywhere and he told them that they would be able to perform miracles.

[15] *Later* he said to them, "Go into the whole world and preach the good message to everyone! [16] Everyone who believes *your message* and who is baptized will be saved. But everyone who does not believe it will be condemned. [17] Those who believe *my good message* will perform miracles. For example, by my power they will expel evil spirits. They will speak in languages that they have not learned. [18] If they *accidentally* pick up snakes or drink any poisonous *liquid*, they will not be hurt. *Whenever* they put their hands on sick *people in order that God will heal them*, those sick people will become well."

[19] After the Lord Jesus had said this to *the disciples, God* took him up into heaven. Then he sat down on his throne beside God *to rule with him*. [20] *As for the disciples*, they went out *from Jerusalem* and preached everywhere. *Wherever they went*, the Lord enabled them to perform miracles, and *by doing that*, he confirmed that God's message is true.]

The Gospel that was written by

Luke

1

Luke 1:1-4

THEME: Luke told Theophilus why he was writing about all that Jesus did.

¹⁻² My noble *friend* Theophilus, many people saw the things *Jesus* did while he was with us, from the time he started *his ministry*. They served God *by teaching people* the message *about the Lord Jesus*. Many of those who heard what they taught wrote down for us accounts of the things *Jesus did from the time* he began *his ministry*. ³ I myself have studied carefully these accounts. So I decided it would be good for me also to write for you an accurate account of these matters. ⁴ I want you to know the truth about what others have taught you.

Luke 1:5-25

THEME: An angel told Zechariah that his wife Elizabeth would bear a son, John.

⁵ When King Herod *the Great* ruled the district of Judea, there was a *Jewish* priest named Zechariah. He belonged to the *group of priests called* the Abijah group. He and his wife Elizabeth were both descended from the *first priest of Israel*, Aaron. ⁶ *God considered that* both of them were righteous, because they constantly obeyed without fault everything that God had commanded. ⁷ But they had no children, because Elizabeth was unable to bear children. Furthermore, she and her husband were very old.

⁸ One day *Zechariah's* group was doing their work *in the Temple in Jerusalem*, and he was serving as a priest in God's presence. ⁹ Following their custom, *the other priests* chose him by lot to enter the Lord's temple and burn incense. ¹⁰ While he was burning the incense, many people were outside *in the courtyard*, praying. ¹¹ Then an angel whom God had *sent* appeared to him. The angel was standing at the right side of the place *where the priests burned* incense. ¹² When Zechariah saw the angel, he was startled and became very afraid. ¹³ But the angel said to him, "Zechariah, do not be afraid! When you prayed *asking God for a son,*[a] *God* heard what you prayed. *So* your wife Elizabeth shall bear a son for you. You must name him John. ¹⁴ He will cause you to be very happy, and many other people will also be happy because he is born. ¹⁵ God will consider him to be very important. He must never drink wine or any other alcoholic drink, *in order that he will be completely dedicated to God*. He will be controlled by the Holy Spirit from the time he is born. ¹⁶ He will *persuade* many people in Israel to turn away *from their sins and please* the Lord their God. ¹⁷ As *God's* Spirit enables him *to preach* powerfully as *the prophet* Elijah did, he will precede *the Messiah*. He will cause parents to act *peacefully* toward their children *again*. He will cause *many* people who do not obey *God to hear and obey* the wise things that righteous people *tell them*. He will do this in order to make *many* people ready when the Lord *comes*."

---

[a] OR, *...that God would send the Messiah...*

[18] Then Zechariah said to the angel, "I am very old, and my wife is also so old *that she cannot bear a child. So* I cannot *believe* that what you said *will happen*!"

[19] Then the angel said to him, "I am *God's chief angel*, Gabriel! *I do what God tells me because* I constantly stand in God's presence! *He* sent me to tell you this good message *about what will happen to you.* [20] What I have told you will certainly happen at the time *God decides*, but you did not believe my words. So now *God will cause* you to be unable to talk until your son is born!"

[21] While *Zechariah and the angel* were talking, the people *in the courtyard* were waiting for Zechariah *to come out.* They wondered, "Why is he staying in the Temple for such a long time?" [22] When he came out, he was not able to speak to them. Because he couldn't talk, he made motions with his hands *to try to convey what had happened.* Then they realized he had seen a vision *from God* while he was in the Temple.

[23] When Zechariah's time to work *as a priest in the Temple* was finished, he *left Jerusal*em and returned to his home.

[24] Some time later his wife Elizabeth became pregnant. She did not go out of her house for five months, *because she knew that people would laugh at her during that time if she told them she was pregnant.* [25] But she said to herself, "God has enabled me to become pregnant. At this time he has pitied me so that I will no longer be ashamed *at not having any children!*"

Luke 1:26-38

THEME: An angel told a virgin named Mary that she would bear a son, Jesus.

[26] When Elizabeth had been *pregnant for almost* six months, God sent the angel Gabriel again. [27] *This time* he went to *the town* of Nazareth in *the district of* Galilee, to a virgin whose name was Mary. *Her parents* had promised her in marriage to a man named Joseph, who was descended from *King* David. [28] The angel said to her, "Greetings! God is with you and *is going to* greatly bless you!" [29] But Mary was greatly confused *when she heard* that. She wondered what *the angel meant* by those words. [30] Then the angel said to her, "Mary, God is very pleased with you, so don't be afraid. [31] You will become pregnant and bear a son, and you must name him Jesus. [32] He will become great. *People will* call him the Son of God.[b] God, the Lord, will make him a king as his ancestor *King* David was. [33] He will be the king of *the* Jews, the descendants of *your ancestor* Jacob, forever. He will rule as king forever!"

[34] Then Mary said to the angel, "I am a virgin, so how can I *have a baby*?" [35] The angel replied, "The Holy Spirit will come to you and the power of God will be on you *to enable you to become pregnant.* So the child *you will* bear will give himself completely to obey God, and *people* will say that he is the Son of God. [36] *I also need to tell you something else.* Your cousin Elizabeth is very old, and *people* said that she could not bear any children. But she has been *pregnant for almost* six months, and will bear a son! [37] *You should not be surprised at that*, because God can do everything!" [38] Then Mary said, "All right, I want to serve God, so may what you have said about me come true!" Then the angel left her.

---

[b] OR, He will become great. *People will* call him the Man who is also God.

Luke 1:39-45

THEME: Mary visited Elizabeth.

[39] Very soon after that, Mary got ready and went quickly to a town in the highlands of Judea. [40] She entered Zechariah's house and greeted *his wife* Elizabeth. [41] As soon as Elizabeth heard Mary greet her, the baby leaped inside *Elizabeth's* womb. The Holy Spirit took complete control of Elizabeth, [42] and she said loudly *to Mary*, "*God* has blessed you *more than any other* woman, and *he has* blessed the child you will bear! [43] I am not worthy that *God would allow you* to visit me! You will be the mother of my Lord! [44] *I realized this because* as soon as I heard you greet me, the baby inside my womb leaped because he was so happy *that you had come*! [45] *God* is pleased with you *because* you believed that what God told you would come true."

Luke 1:46-56

THEME: Mary praised God.

[46] Then Mary *praised God by* singing,
"Oh, how I praise God!
[47] I rejoice in my inner being because God is the one who saves me.
[48] I was only his lowly servant girl, but he did not forget me.
So from now on, people living in all future time will say that God was pleased with me,
[49] because *they will* hear about the things that God, the mighty one, has done for me.
He is awesome!
[50] He acts mercifully from one generation to the next toward those who respect him.
[51] He shows *people* that he is very powerful. He scatters those who think proudly
within their hearts.
[52] He sends mighty kings away and does not let them rule any more,
but he honors those who are oppressed.[c]
[53] He gives good things to eat to those who are hungry,
but he sends away the rich people without giving them anything.
[54-55] He promised to Abraham and all our other ancestors who descended
from him that he would act mercifully toward them forever.
And now he has remembered what he promised.
So he has helped me and all the other people of Israel who serve him."

[56] Mary stayed with Elizabeth for about three months. Then she returned to her home.

Luke 1:57-66

THEME: What happened when John was born.

[57] When it was time for Elizabeth to give birth to her child, she bore a son. [58] Her neighbors and relatives heard how God had greatly blessed her, so they were happy along with *Elizabeth.* [59] Seven days later they gathered together for the *ceremony for* circumcising the baby *to show that he belonged to God.* Since his father's name was Zechariah, they wanted to give the baby the same name. [60] But his mother said, "No, *his name will not be Zechariah*! His name will be John!" [61] *So* they said to her, "*John* is not the name of any of your relatives, *so you shouldn't give him that name*! [62] Then they made motions with their hands to his father, *for him* to indicate what name **he** wanted to give to his son. [63] *So* he signaled for them to *give him* a tablet *to write on. When they gave him one*, he wrote *on it,*

---

c   OR, …but he honors those who are humble.

"His name is John." All those *who were there* were surprised! [64] Immediately Zechariah was able to speak again, and he praised God. [65] All their neighbors were awestruck! They told other people who lived all over the highlands of Judea about what had happened. [66] Everyone who heard about it kept thinking about it. They were saying, 'We wonder what work *the child* will do *for God when* he *grows up*." They wondered that because *from what had happened they were sure that* God would be helping him *in a powerful way*.

Luke 1:67-80

THEME: Zechariah praised God and predicted what his son would do.

[67] *After the birth of his son*, Zechariah was completely directed by the Holy Spirit as he spoke these words that came from God:

[68] Let's praise the Lord, the God whom *we people* of Israel *worship*,
because he has come to set *us*, his people, free *from our enemies*.
[69] He is sending us someone who will powerfully save us,
someone who is *descended from King* David, who served God *well*.
[70] Long ago God caused his prophets to say that he would do that.
[71] *He* will rescue us from our enemies.
He also will *save us* from the power of all those who hate us.
[72] *He will do this because* he has not forgotten what he promised our ancestors.
He made an agreement that he would act mercifully to us, their *descendants*.
[73] That is what he strongly promised our ancestor Abraham that he would do.
[74] God told him that he would rescue us from the power of our enemies,
    that he would enable us to serve him without being afraid,
        [75] that he *would cause us* to be completely dedicated to him,
    and that he would enable us to *live* righteously all of our lives."

[76] *Then Zechariah said this to* his little son:
"My child, *people* will say that you are a prophet whom God *has sent*;
    you will begin *your work* before the Lord comes;[d]
    you will prepare *people so that they will be ready* for him.
[77] You will tell *God's* people how *he* will forgive them
    and save them *from being punished for* their sins.
[78] Our God will do that because he is very kind to us.
Just as a new day starts when the sun rises, *God will do that new thing for us
    when the Messiah* comes to us from heaven.
[79] *People who do* not know God *are like* those who sit in the darkness.
They are afraid they will soon die.
But when the Messiah tells us God's message, it will be like causing such people
    to see a bright light.
He will guide us so that we will be living peacefully."

[80] *Later*, Zechariah's son grew up and became spiritually strong. Then he lived in a desolate region until he began to preach to the Israelite people.

---

[d] Or, …My child, people will say that you are a prophet whom God *has sent*, because you will begin *your work* before the Messiah comes.

2

Luke 2:1-7

THEME: Jesus was born in Bethlehem.

¹About that time the Emperor Augustus ordered that *a census be taken* of all the people who lived in countries *controlled* by the Roman *government, so the government could collect taxes from them.* ²That was the first time they took a census in *the province of* Syria*, which included the district of Judea.* They did this while Quirinius was the governor of the province. ³Every person had to go to the town where his *ancestors* lived, so *the officials* could write down their names. ⁴So, because Joseph was a descendant of *King* David, he went up from Nazareth, the town in Galilee *where he lived*, to *the town of* Bethlehem, in Judea. That was the town where *King* David *grew up.* ⁵Joseph went with Mary, who *was considered to be* his wife, who was now pregnant. They went so that they could put his name and Mary's name *in the record book.* ⁶⁻⁷When they arrived *in Bethlehem*, there was no place for them to stay in the house where travelers stay. *So they stayed in a cattle shed.* When the time for Mary to give birth arrived, she gave birth to her first son there. She wrapped him in strips of cloth and placed him in a trough where *people* put food for the animals.

Luke 2:8-20

THEME: Responding to the angel's announcement, shepherds went to see Jesus.

⁸That night, there were *some* shepherds who were taking care of their sheep *as usual* in the fields near *Bethlehem.* ⁹An angel from God appeared to them, and a great light from God shone on them and around them. *So* they became very afraid. ¹⁰But the angel said to them, "Don't be afraid! I have come to tell you good news, which will *make you* very happy! This message is for everyone *to hear*! ¹¹*The message is that* today a baby has been born in *Bethlehem*, the town where *King* David *grew up.* That baby will *eventually* save you *from the guilt of your sins*! He will be the Messiah, *your* Lord! ¹²I will tell you how *you will recognize him.*ᵉ *In Bethlehem* you will find a baby who has been wrapped in strips of cloth and placed in a trough where *people* put food for the animals."

¹³Suddenly a large group of angels from heaven appeared and joined the other angel. They all praised God, singing, ¹⁴"May *all the angels* in the highest heaven praise God! And on the earth may the people to whom God has shown his favor have peace *with him*!"

¹⁵After the angels left them *and returned* to heaven, the shepherds said to each other, "Let's go to Bethlehem to see this *wonderful* thing that has happened, which God has told us about!" ¹⁶So they went quickly. They found the *place where* Mary and Joseph *were staying*, and *they saw* the baby lying in the trough where *people* put food for the animals. ¹⁷Then they told *Mary and Joseph and others* what *the angel* had told them about this child. ¹⁸Everyone who heard what the shepherds said to them was amazed. ¹⁹But Mary *did not talk to others about what the angels said*; she just kept thinking very much about it. ²⁰The shepherds returned *to their sheep.* They kept praising God very much for all the things they had heard and seen, *because* everything *happened* just like *the angels* told them.

ᵉ OR, …He will be the Messiah, *your* Lord! ¹²I will tell you how you will know that what I say is true.

Luke 2:21-24

THEME: They circumcised Jesus and presented him to the Lord.

²¹ Seven days later, when *the priests* circumcised the baby, *his parents* named him Jesus. That was the name the angel *told them to* give him before Mary became pregnant.

²²⁻²⁴ It had been written by Moses *long ago* in a law that God gave him, that when a woman gave birth to her first son, the parents had to take him *to the Temple* in Jerusalem to dedicate him to God. So when the time came for them to do those rituals so that *God would consider* them pure again, Mary and Joseph took Jesus there. God had commanded in his law that if the first child *of a couple* was a boy, his parents should offer as a sacrifice to God two turtledoves or two young pigeons. *So Joseph and Mary gave the priest two birds so he could offer them.*

Luke 2:25-35

THEME: Simeon prophesied about what Jesus would do.

²⁵ At that time there was an *old* man in Jerusalem whose name was Simeon. He habitually did what was pleasing to God and he obeyed God's laws. The Holy Spirit was *directing* him as he was waiting for *God to* encourage the Israelite *people by sending the Messiah.* ²⁶ The Holy Spirit *previously* revealed to him that he would see God's *promised* Messiah before he died. ²⁷ When Joseph and Mary brought their baby Jesus *to the Temple* in order to perform the rituals that *God had commanded* in his laws, the Spirit led Simeon to enter the Temple *courtyard, and revealed to him that Jesus was the Messiah.* ²⁸ So he took Jesus up in his arms and praised God, saying,

²⁹⁻³²"Lord, you promised me that I would see the *one who would enable* you
to save *people* of all people-groups *from the guilt of their sins.*
He will be *like* a light that will reveal *your truth* to non-Jews,
and he will cause *people* to think highly of your people, the Israelite people.
Since I have now seen this one you promised to send,
now let me die peacefully."

³³ His parents marveled about what *Simeon* said about *Jesus.* Then Simeon blessed them, and said to Mary, ³⁴"Note what I say: *God* has determined that because of this child, many Israelite people will *turn away from God*, and many others will turn to God. Although he will be like a sign *to warn people, many* people will oppose him. ³⁵ As a result, he will make clear the *evil* thoughts of many people. *Furthermore, the cruel things they will do to him will be like* a sword that will pierce your heart."

Luke 2:36-38

THEME: Anna praised God for Jesus and told others about him.

³⁶ There was also *in the Temple courtyard* a very old woman named Anna. She was a prophetess. Her father Phanuel was a member of the tribe of Asher. After she had been married seven years, her husband died. ³⁷ After that, she lived until she was eighty-four years old, and she was still a widow. She stayed in the Temple *area* all the time, night and day, worshiping God by abstaining from food and praying. ³⁸ *While Joseph and Mary and the baby were* still *in the Temple*, Anna came to them. She thanked God *for the baby.* Then she spoke about Jesus to many people who were expecting *God to send the Messiah* to set *the people of* Jerusalem free *from their enemies.*

Luke 2:39-40

THEME: Jesus grew up in Nazareth.

³⁹ *Some time* after Joseph and Mary had finished performing the rituals that God required of *the parents of a first son,* they returned to their own town, Nazareth, in the district of Galilee. ⁴⁰ As the child grew up, he became strong and very wise, and God was very pleased with him.

Luke 2:41-52

THEME: What Jesus did in the Temple when he was a boy.

⁴¹ Every year Jesus' parents went to Jerusalem to *celebrate* the Passover festival. ⁴² So when Jesus was twelve years old, they went up *to Jerusalem* as usual. ⁴³ When the celebration ended, his parents started to return home, but Jesus stayed in Jerusalem. *His parents* did not realize *Jesus stayed there.* ⁴⁴ They thought he was with the other people who were traveling with them. They walked all day. Then they started to look for him among their relatives and friends. ⁴⁵ They did not find him, so they returned to Jerusalem to search for him. ⁴⁶ Two days later, they found him. He was in the Temple *courtyard,* sitting with the *Jewish* religious teachers. He was listening to what they said, and he was asking them questions. ⁴⁷ Everyone who heard what he *said* was amazed at how much he understood and *how well* he answered *the questions that the teachers asked.* ⁴⁸ When his parents saw him, they were very surprised. His mother said to him, "My son, why have you done this to us? Your father and I have been very worried as we have been searching for you!" ⁴⁹ He said to them, *speaking about the Temple being God his Father's house,* "I am surprised that you did *not know* where to find me. You should have known that it was necessary for me to be in my Father's house!" ⁵⁰ But they did not understand *the meaning of* what he said to them. ⁵¹ Then he returned with them down to Nazareth. He always obeyed them. But his mother kept thinking about all those things.

⁵² *As the years passed,* Jesus continued to become wiser and he grew taller. God and people continued to approve of him more and more.

3

Luke 3:1-20

THEME: What John the Baptizer preached.

¹ When the Emperor Tiberius had been ruling *the Roman Empire* for fifteen years, and while Pontius Pilate was the governor of *the district of* Judea, and Herod *Antipas* was ruling *the district of* Galilee, and his brother Philip was ruling *the districts of* Iturea and Trachonitis, and Lysanius was ruling *the district of* Abilene, ² and while Annas and Caiaphas were the high priests *in Jerusalem,* God gave messages to Zechariah's son John while he was living in the desolate region. ³ *So* John went all over the area close to the Jordan *River.* He kept telling people, "If you want *God* to forgive you for your sins, you must turn away from your sinful behavior *before you ask me* to baptize *you!*"

⁴ John was the one who *fulfilled* these words that the prophet Isaiah had written in a scroll *long ago*:
In a desolate area, someone will be heard shouting *to the people who pass by,*
"Prepare yourselves *to receive* the Lord when he comes!
Make yourselves ready so that you will be prepared when he comes,

just as people straighten out the road *for an important official*!
[5] *Just as people* level off all the places where the land is high,
and just *as they* fill all the ravines,
and *just as people* make the road straight wherever it is crooked,
and *just as people* make smooth the bumps in the road,
you need to remove all the obstacles that prevent God from blessing you.
[6] *God wants* people everywhere to understand how he can save *people.*

[7] Although large groups of people came to John to be baptized, *he knew that many of them were not sincere.* So he kept saying to them, "You *people are evil like* poisonous snakes! *I* warn you that *God* will some day punish *everyone* who sins. And don't think that you can escape *his punishment if you do not turn from your sinful behavior!* [8] So do the deeds that are appropriate for people who have truly turned from their sinful behavior! *God promised to give Abraham many* descendants. In order to fulfill that promise, God does not need you! I tell you that he can change these stones to make them descendants of Abraham! So don't start to say to yourselves, '*We* are descendants of Abraham, *so God will not punish us, even though we have* sinned!' [9] *God is ready to punish you if you do not turn away from your sinful behavior.* just *like a man* who lays his axe at the roots *of a fruit* tree *to chop it down and throw it into the fire if it does not produce good fruit.*"

[10] *Then various* ones in the crowd asked him, "What shall we do *to escape God's punishment*?" [11] He answered them, "If any of you has two shirts, you should give one of them to someone who has no shirt. If any of you has *plenty of* food, you should give some to those who have no food." [12] *Some* tax collectors came *and asked* to be baptized. They asked him, "Teacher, what shall we do *to please God*?" [13] He said to them, "Do not take from the people any more money than *the Roman government* tells you to take!" [14] Some soldiers asked him, "What about us? What should we do *to please God*?" He said to them, "Do not *say to anyone, 'If you do not give me* some money, you'll be sorry," and don't take *people to court and* falsely accuse them of doing something wrong!' And be content with your wages."

[15] People were expecting *that the Messiah would come soon.* Because of that, many of them wondered about John. *Some of them asked him* if he was the Messiah. [16] John replied to them all, "No, *I am not.* I used *only* water when I baptized you. But *the Messiah* will soon come! He is far greater than I am. *He is so great that* I am not worthy to *be like his slave and* untie his sandals *like* a slave would do! He will put *his* Holy Spirit within you *to truly change your lives*, and *he will judge others of you and punish you in* the fire *in hell.* [17] He *is like a farmer who wants to* clear away the grain on the ground where it has been threshed. That farmer *uses* a huge fork *to throw the grain into the air* to separate the wheat from the chaff, and then he cleans up the threshing area. *Similarly, God* will *separate righteous people from the evil people, like the farmer who* gathers the wheat into his storage area, and then he will burn *those who are as useless as* chaff with a fire that will burn forever."

[18] John kept telling them many things to urge them *to turn to God*, as he told them the good message *from God.* [19] He also rebuked *the ruler of the district*, Herod *Antipas. He rebuked him* for *marrying* Herodias, his brother's wife, *while his brother was still alive*, and for doing many other evil things. [20] But Herod *had* John put in prison. That was another evil thing he did.

Luke 3:21-22

THEME: John baptized Jesus.

²¹ *But before John was put in prison*, when he was baptizing many people, after he baptized Jesus and Jesus was praying, the sky opened. ²² Then the Holy Spirit, resembling a dove, descended upon *Jesus*. And *God* spoke to Jesus from heaven, saying, "You are my son, the one whom I love dearly. I am very pleased with you!"

Luke 3:23-38

THEME: The list of Jesus' ancestors.

²³ When Jesus began *his work for God*, he was about thirty years old. *People* thought he was *the son* of Joseph. *Joseph was* the son of Heli. ²⁴ *Heli was the son* of Matthat. *Matthat was the son* of Levi. *Levi was the son* of Melchi. *Melchi was the son* of Jannai. *Jannai was the son* of Joseph. ²⁵ *Joseph was the son* of Mattathias. *Mattathias was the son* of Amos. *Amos was the son* of Nahum. *Nahum was the son* of Esli. *Esli was the son* of Naggai. ²⁶ *Naggai was the son* of Maath. *Maath was the son* of Mattathias. *Mattathias was the son* of Semein. *Semein was the son* of Josech. *Josech was the son* of Joda. ²⁷ *Joda was the son* of Joanan. *Joanan was the son* of Rhesa. *Rhesa was the son* of Zerubbabel. *Zerubbabel was the son* of Shelatiel. *Shealtiel was the son* of Neri. ²⁸ *Neri was the son* of Melchi. *Melchi was the son* of Addi. *Addi was the son* of Cosam. *Cosam was the son* of Elmadam. *Elmadam was the son* of Er. ²⁹ *Er was the son* of Joshua. *Joshua was the son* of Eliezer. *Eliezer was the son* of Jorim. *Jorim was the son* of Matthat. *Matthat was the son* of Levi. ³⁰ *Levi was the son* of Simeon. *Simeon was the son* of Judah. *Judah was the son* of Joseph. *Joseph was the son* of Jonam. *Jonam was the son* of Eliakim. ³¹ *Eliakim was the son* of Melea. *Melea was the son* of Menna. *Menna was the son* of Mattatha. *Mattatha was the son* of Nathan. *Nathan was the son* of David. ³² *David was the son* of Jesse. *Jesse was the son* of Obed. *Obed was the son* of Boaz. *Boaz was the son* of Sala. *Sala was the son* of Nahshon. ³³ *Nahshon was the son* of Amminadab. *Amminadab was the son* of Admin. *Admin was the son* of Arni. *Arni was the son* of Hezron. *Hezron was the son* of Perez. *Perez was the son* of Judah. ³⁴ *Judah was the son* of Jacob. *Jacob was the son* of Isaac. *Isaac was the son* of Abraham. *Abraham was the son* of Terah. *Terah was the son* of Nahor. ³⁵ *Nahor was the son* of Serug. *Serug was the son* of Reu. *Reu was the son* of Peleg. *Peleg was the son* of Eber. *Eber was the son* of Shelah. ³⁶ *Shelah was the son* of Cainan. *Cainan was the son* of Arphaxad. *Arphaxad was the son* of Shem. *Shem was the son* of Noah. *Noah was the son* of Lamech. ³⁷ *Lamech was the son* of Methuselah. *Methuselah was the son* of Enoch. *Enoch was the son* of Jared. *Jared was the son* of Mahalaleel. *Mahalaleel was the son* of Cainan. ³⁸ *Cainan was the son* of Enos. *Enos was the son* of Seth. *Seth was the son* of Adam. *Adam was the man* God created.

4

Luke 4:1-13

THEME: Jesus refused to do the things Satan suggested to him.

¹ Jesus left the Jordan *River valley under the* complete control of the Holy Spirit. ² For forty days the Spirit led him around in the desolate area. During that time Jesus, being tempted by the devil, did not eat anything. When that time ended, he was *very* hungry. ³ Then the devil said to Jesus, "Since you *claim that you have a relationship with* God as a son *has with his father, prove it by* telling these stones to become bread *so that you can eat them!*"

[4] Jesus replied, *"No! I will not change stones into bread, because it is written in the Scriptures that eating* food sustains people physically, but it does not *sustain them spiritually. They also need food for their spirits."* [5] Then the devil took him on top of *a high mountain* and showed him in an instant all the nations in the world. [6] Then he said to Jesus, "I will give you the authority *to rule* all these areas and will make you famous. *I can do this* because *God* has permitted me *to control these areas*, and I can allow anyone I desire to rule them! [7] So if you worship me, I will *let* you *rule* them all!" [8] But Jesus replied, *"No, I won't worship you, because* it is written *in the Scriptures*, 'It is the Lord your God whom you must worship, and you must serve only him!'"

[9] Then the devil took *Jesus* to Jerusalem. He set him on the highest part of the Temple and said to him, "Since you *claim that you have a relationship with God as a son has with his father, prove it by* jumping down from here.[f] [10] *You will not be hurt*, because it is written *in the Scriptures*, 'God will command his angels to protect you.' [11] They will lift you up in their hands *when you are falling*, so that *you will not get hurt.* You will not *even* strike your foot on a stone.'" [12] But Jesus replied, *"No, I won't do that, because* it is written *in the Scriptures*, 'Do not try to test the Lord your God *to see if he will prevent something bad from happening to you when you do something foolish'*."

[13] Then, after the devil had finished trying to tempt *Jesus* in many ways, he left him. He wanted to try to tempt him later at an appropriate time.

Luke 4:14-15

THEME: Jesus began his work in the district of Galilee.

[14] As the Spirit empowered him, Jesus returned to *the district of* Galilee. *People* throughout all that region heard about what he *was doing.* [15] He taught *people* in their meeting halls. *As a result*, everyone praised him.

Luke 4:16-30

THEME: The people of Jesus' home town tried to kill him after he rebuked them for rejecting him.

[16] Then *Jesus* went to Nazareth, *the town* where he grew up. On the Jewish day of rest he went to the Jewish meeting place, as he usually did. He stood up *to indicate that he wanted* to read *Scriptures* to them. [17] *Someone* gave to him a scroll containing *the words* the prophet Isaiah *had written.* He opened the scroll and found the place from which he *wanted to* read. *He read these words*:
> [18] The Spirit of the Lord *God* is upon me.
> He has appointed me to declare God's good news
>   to the poor.
> He has sent me *here* to proclaim that
>   God will set free those whom *Satan*
>   has captured, and
> he will *enable me to give sight to* those
>   who are blind.
> He will enable me to free people
>   who have been oppressed
> [19] And he sent me to declare that now is the time

---

[f] OR, …Since you claim that you are the man who is also God, prove it by throwing yourself down from here.

when the Lord *God* will *act* favorably *toward people.*

²⁰ Then he rolled up the scroll and gave it back to the attendant, and sat down *to teach the people*. Everyone in the synagogue was looking intently at him. ²¹ He said to them, "Today as you have been hearing *me speak, I am beginning* to fulfill this Scripture passage." ²² *At first* everyone there spoke well about him, and they were amazed at the charming words he spoke. *But then some of* them said, "He is *only* Joseph's son, *so why should we listen to what he says?*" ²³ He said to them, "Surely *some of* you will quote to me the proverb that says, 'Doctor, heal yourself!' *What you will mean is,* 'People told us you did miracles in *the town of* Capernaum, *but we don't know if those reports are true. So* do miracles here in your own home town, too!'" ²⁴ Then he said, "It is certainly true that *people* do not accept *the message of* a prophet when he speaks in his home town, *just as you are not accepting my message now.* ²⁵ But think about this: There were many widows in Israel during the time *the prophet* Elijah *lived. During that time*, because of there being no rain for three years and six months, there was a great famine throughout the country. ²⁶ But *God* did not send Elijah to *help* any of those *Jewish* widows. *God sent him* to *the town of* Zarepath near *the city of* Sidon, to *help* a *non-Jewish* widow. ²⁷ There were also many *Jewish* lepers in Israel during the time the prophet Elisha *lived.* But *Elisha* did not heal any of them. He healed only Naaman, a *non-Jewish* man from Syria." ²⁸ When all the people in the synagogue heard him say **that**, they were very angry, *because they realized he was inferring that he similarly would help non-Jewish people instead of helping Jews*. ²⁹ So they all got up and shoved him out of the town. They took him to the top of the hill outside their town in order to throw him off the cliff *and kill him.* ³⁰ But he *simply* walked through their midst and went away.

Luke 4:31-37

THEME: Jesus expelled an evil spirit.

³¹ *One day* he went *with his disciples* down to Capernaum, a town in *the district of* Galilee. On the next Jewish day of rest, he taught the people *in the Jewish meeting place.* ³² They were continually amazed at what he was teaching, because *he spoke with authority.* ³³ *That day*[g] there was a man there who was controlled by an evil spirit. That man shouted very loudly, ³⁴"Hey! Jesus, from Nazareth! *We evil spirits* have nothing in common with you, *so don't interfere with us*! Don't destroy us *now*! I know who you are. You are the Holy One *who has come* from God!" ³⁵ Jesus rebuked *the evil spirit*, saying, "Be quiet! And come out *of the man*!" The demon threw the man down on the ground in the midst of the people. But without harming the man, the demon left him. ³⁶ The people were all amazed. They said to each other, "His words to the demons *have great power*! He speaks to them like he knows that they must obey him, and as a result they leave people!" ³⁷ The people were telling everyone in *every village* in the surrounding region what Jesus *had done.*

Luke 4:38-41

THEME: Jesus healed Simon's mother-in-law and many others.

³⁸ Jesus *and his disciples* left the Jewish meeting place and went into Simon's house. Simon's mother-in-law was sick and had a high fever, so *others in Simon's family* asked Jesus to *heal* her. ³⁹ He bent over her and rebuked the fever. At once she became well! She got up and served them *some food.*

---

^g OR, *In the Jewish worship place* on one of those Jewish days of rest…

⁴⁰When the sun was setting *that day, and the restriction about not traveling on the Jewish day of rest was ended,* many people whose *friends or relatives* were sick or who had various diseases brought them to Jesus. He put his hands on them and healed *all of* them. ⁴¹He also was *expelling demons* from many people. As the demons left those people, they shouted to Jesus, "You are the Son of God!"ʰ But he rebuked those demons and would not allow them to tell *people about him,* because they knew he was the Messiah, and *for various reasons he did not want everyone to know that yet.*

Luke 4:42-44

THEME: Jesus told them he had to preach in other towns.

⁴²*Early* the next morning *Jesus* left that house and went to an uninhabited place *to pray.* Many people searched for him, and when they found him they kept urging him not to leave them. ⁴³But he said to them, "I must tell *people* in other towns also the good message about how God wants to rule their lives, because that is what *God* sent me to do." ⁴⁴So he kept preaching in the Jewish meeting places *in various towns* in Judea.

5

Luke 5:1-11

THEME: Jesus chose some fishermen to be his disciples.

¹One day while many people were crowding around him to hear the message from God, Jesus was standing on the shore of Lake Gennesaret, *which is also called Lake Galilee.* ²He saw two *fishing* boats at the edge of the lake. The fishermen had gone out of the boats and were washing their *fishing* nets *on the shore.* One of the boats belonged to Simon. ³Jesus got in that boat and asked Simon to push the boat a little bit away from the shore *so that he could speak to the crowd more easily. Jesus* sat in the boat and taught the people *who were on the shore.* ⁴After he finished speaking *to them,* he said to Simon, "Push the boat out to where the water is deep. Then let your nets down *into the water* to catch *some fish!*" ⁵Simon replied, "Master, we worked hard all night but we did not catch a single fish! But because you tell me to do it, I will let down the nets." ⁶When Peter *and the men with him* had done that, they caught so many fish that their nets were breaking. ⁷They motioned to their partners in the other boat to come and help them. So they came and filled both the boats *with fish from the net.* The result was that the boats were so full that they began to sink. ⁸⁻⁹Simon and all the men who were with him were amazed at how many fish they had taken. James and John, the two sons of Zebedee, who were Simon's partners, were among those who were amazed. When Simon, *whose other name was* Peter, saw *the fish, feeling ashamed to be in the presence of someone who obviously had God's power,* he prostrated himself before Jesus and said, "Lord, you should go away from me, because I am a sinful man!" ¹⁰But Jesus said to Simon, "Don't be afraid! *Until now you have been gathering fish,* but from now on you will gather people *to become my disciples.*" ¹¹So after they brought the boats to the shore, they left their business *in the hands of others* and went with Jesus.

ʰ OR, ...You are the Man who is also God!

Luke 5:12-16

THEME: Jesus healed a leper and enabled him to associate with people again.

¹² While *Jesus* was in one of the cities *there in Galilee*, there was a man there who was very severely affected by leprosy. When he saw Jesus, he prostrated himself before him and, *wanting Jesus to heal him*, pleaded with him, "Lord, *please heal me, because* you are able to heal me if you are willing to!" ¹³ *Then Jesus, disregarding the religious law that forbade people to come close to lepers*, reached out his hand and touched the man. He said, "I am willing *to heal you*; and I heal you now!" Immediately the man *was healed*. He was no longer a leper! ¹⁴ Then Jesus told him, "Make sure that you do not report *your healing immediately. First, find a local* priest and show yourself to him *so that he can examine you and verify that you no longer have leprosy*. After the priest tells *the local people,* they will know that *you have been healed, and you will be able to associate with them again. Then go to the Temple in Jerusalem* and take to the priests *the offering* that Moses commanded *that people who have been healed from leprosy should offer.*" ¹⁵ But many people heard the man's report of what *Jesus had done*. The result was that large crowds came to Jesus to hear his *message* and to be healed of their sicknesses. ¹⁶ But he often would go away from them to the desolate area and pray.

Luke 5:17-26

THEME: By healing a paralyzed man Jesus showed he had authority to forgive sins too.

¹⁷ One day when *Jesus* was teaching, some men from the Pharisee *sect* were sitting there. Some of them were men who taught the *Jewish* laws. They had come from many villages in Galilee and also from Jerusalem and from *other* villages in Judea. *At that time while God was giving Jesus power to heal people,* ¹⁸ several men brought on a sleeping pad a man who was paralyzed. They wanted to bring him into *the house* and lay him in front of Jesus. ¹⁹ But there was no way to do that because of the large crowd of people, so they went up *the steps* onto the roof. *They tied ropes to the sleeping pad,* and after *removing some of* the tiles *on the roof*, they lowered the man *on* the sleeping pad. They lowered him through the opening into the midst of the crowd in front of Jesus. ²⁰ When Jesus perceived that they believed *he could heal the man*, he said to him, "My friend, *I* forgive your sins!" ²¹ The men who taught the *Jewish* laws and the rest of the Pharisees began to question within themselves, "Who does this man *think he is, saying* that? He is insulting God! Nobody can forgive sins! Only God can forgive sins!" ²² Jesus perceived what they were thinking. So he said to them, "You should not question within yourselves *about what I said. But consider this*: ²³ It would *not* be risky *for someone* to say *to this man, 'I* forgive your sins,' *because no one could see whether or not his sins were really forgiven. But no one, without having the power to heal,* would say to *him, '*Get up and walk! *because people could easily see whether he was healed or not.* ²⁴ So I am going to do something* in order that you may know that *God* has authorized *me, the one who came from heaven*, to forgive the sins *of people as well as to heal people while I am on* the earth." Then he said to the man who was paralyzed, "To you I say, 'Get up, pick up your sleeping pad, and go home!'" ²⁵ Immediately the man *was healed*! He got up in front of them. He picked up the *sleeping pad* on which he had been lying, and he went home, praising God. ²⁶ All the people *there* were amazed! They praised God and were completely awestruck. They kept saying, "We have seen wonderful things today!"

Luke 5:27-32

THEME: Jesus answered criticism about associating with sinful people.

[27] Then *Jesus* left *the town* and saw a man who collected taxes *for the Roman government*. His name was Levi. He was sitting in the booth where he collected the taxes. Jesus said to him, "Come with me *and become my disciple!*" [28] So Levi left his work and went with Jesus.

[29] Afterwards, Levi prepared a big feast in his own house *for Jesus and his disciples*. There was a large group of tax collectors and others eating together with them. [30] The men who were there who taught the *Jewish* laws, ones who belonged to the Pharisee *sect*, complained to Jesus' disciples, saying, "*It is disgusting that* you are eating with tax collectors and *other* sinners!" [31] Then, *to indicate that it was those who knew they had sinned who were coming to him for help*, Jesus said to them, "*It is* people who are sick who need a doctor, not those who are well. [32] *In the same way*, I did not come *from heaven* to invite *those who think they are* righteous *to come to me*. On the contrary, *I came to invite those who know they are* sinners to turn from their sinful behavior *and come to me*."

Luke 5:33-39

THEME: Jesus explained that people could not follow both their old customs and his new teaching.

[33] *Those Jewish leaders* said to Jesus, "The disciples of John *the Baptizer* often abstain from food *to show they want to please God*, and the disciples of the Pharisees do that too. But your disciples keep on eating and drinking! *Why don't they abstain from food like the others?*" [34] *To show them that it was not appropriate for his disciples to be sad and abstain from food while he was still with them*, Jesus said to them, "When the bridegroom is with *his friends at the time of the wedding*, you certainly don't make his friends abstain from food, do you? *No, you don't.* [35] *But* some day he will be taken away from them. Then, at that time, his friends will abstain from food, *because they will be sad*."

[36] Then Jesus told them two parables *to show them that those who desire to live according to God's new message should not be forced to obey the old religious traditions like fasting, and that those who know only the old traditions are not eager to accept new ones*. He said, "People never tear a piece of cloth from a new garment and attach it to an old garment *to mend it*. If they did that, not only would they ruin the new garment by tearing it, but the new piece of cloth would not match the old garment. [37] Neither does anyone put freshly-*squeezed* wine into old skin bags *to store it*. If anyone did that, the new wine would burst the skin bags because they would not stretch *when the wine ferments and expands*. *Then* the skin bags would be ruined, and *the wine* would *also* be spilled. [38] On the contrary, new wine must be put into new wineskins.

[39] Furthermore, those who have drunk *only* old wine *are content with that*. They do not want to drink the new wine, because they say, 'The old wine is *just* fine!'"

6

Luke 6:1-11

THEME: Jesus explained why he had authority to decide what his disciples should do on the Sabbath day.

¹ On one Jewish day of rest, while Jesus was walking through some grain fields with his disciples, they picked some of the heads of grain. They rubbed them in their hands *to separate the grains from the husks*, and ate the grain. *The law of Moses permitted people to do that if they were hungry.* ² Some Pharisees *who were watching* said to Jesus, "You should not be doing *work* that *our* laws do not permit *us* to do on our day of rest!" ³ *Jesus wanted to show them that the record in Scriptures indicated that God permitted people to disobey certain religious laws when they needed food. So* he replied, "*It is written in the Scriptures* what *our revered ancestor, King* David did when he and the men with him were hungry. You have read about that, *but you don't think about what it implies.* ⁴ David entered the courtyard of God's tent *and asked for some food. The high priest gave him* the bread that the priests had presented to God. It was permitted *in Moses' law* that only the priests could eat that bread. But David ate some, and he gave some to the men who were with him. *And God did not consider what David did was wrong!*" ⁵ Jesus also said to them, "*Since I am* the one who came from heaven, *I* have the authority *to determine what is right for my disciples to do on* the day of rest!"

⁶ Another Jewish day of rest Jesus entered a Jewish meeting house and taught the people. There was a man there whose right hand was shriveled. ⁷ The men who taught the *Jewish* laws and the Pharisees *who were there* watched Jesus, to see if he would heal the man on the day of rest. They did this so that, *if he healed the man*, they would accuse him *of disobeying their laws by working on the day of rest.* ⁸ But Jesus knew what they were thinking, so he said to the man with the shriveled hand, "Come and stand here *in front of everyone*!" So the man got up and stood there. ⁹ Then Jesus said to them, "I ask you this: Do the laws *God gave Moses* permit *people* to do what is good on the day of rest, or *do they permit people* to harm *others*? *Do they permit us* to save *a person's* life *on the day of rest,* or to let *him* die *by refusing to help him?*" ¹⁰ *They refused to answer him. So* after he looked around at them all, he said to the man, "Stretch out your *withered* hand!" The man did that, and his hand became all right again! ¹¹ But they were very angry, and they discussed with one another what they could do to *get rid of* Jesus.

Luke 6:12-16

THEME: Jesus chose twelve apostles.

¹² About that time *Jesus* went up into the hills to pray. He prayed to God all night. ¹³ The next day he summoned all his disciples. From them he chose twelve men, whom he called apostles. ¹⁴ They were Simon, to whom he gave the *new* name, Peter; Andrew, Peter's *younger* brother; James and *his younger brother* John; Philip; Bartholomew; ¹⁵ *Levi, whose other name was* Matthew; Thomas; *another* James, the *son* of Alpheus; Simon, who belonged to the party *that encouraged people to* rebel *against the Roman government;* ¹⁶ Judas, the son of *another* James; and Judas Iscariot[i], the one who later enabled the Jewish leaders to seize *Jesus.*

---

[i] OR, …Judas from the town of Kerioth…

Luke 6:17-26

THEME: Jesus taught them which people God would be pleased with and which people he would be displeased with.

¹⁷*Jesus* came down from the hills with his disciples and stood on a level area. There was a great crowd of his disciples there. There was also a large group of people who had come from Jerusalem and from many *other towns in the district of* Judea, and from the coastal areas near *the cities of* Tyre and Sidon. ¹⁸ They came to hear Jesus talk to them and for him to heal them from their diseases. He also healed those whom evil spirits had troubled. ¹⁹ Everyone *in the crowd* tried to touch him, because he was healing everyone by *God's* power. ²⁰ He looked at his disciples and said,

"*God* is pleased with you *who know* that you lack what *he wants you to have;*
he will allow you to be the people whose lives he rules over.
²¹"*God* is pleased with you who sincerely desire to receive what *he wants you to have*;
he will give you what you need, until you are satisfied.
"*God* is pleased with you that grieve now *because of sin.*
Later you will be joyful.
²²"*God* is pleased with you when *other* people hate you, when they will not let you join
with them, when they insult you, when they say you are evil because *you believe in*
me, the one who came from heaven. ²³ When that happens, rejoice! Jump up and
down for joy! *God will give* you a great reward in heaven! *When they do these things
to you, it will prove you are God's servants.*ʲ Don't forget that their ancestors did the
same things to the prophets *who served God faithfully*!
²⁴"But there will be terrible punishment for you that are rich;
the happiness you have received *from your riches* is all that you will get.
²⁵ There will be terrible punishment for you who *think you* have all you need *from God*
now: You will *realize* you lack a lot of *what God* wants.
"There will be terrible punishment for you who are joyful now:
You will *later* be very sad.
²⁶ When most people speak well about you, trouble is ahead for you:
It will prove you are not God's servants, because your ancestors used to speak well
about those who falsely *claimed they were* prophets.

Luke 6:27-36

THEME: Jesus taught how we should act toward those who are not kind to us.

²⁷"But I say this to each of you who are listening *to what I say*: Love your enemies *as well
as your friends*! Do good things for those who hate you! ²⁸ *Ask God to* bless those who
curse you! Pray for those who mistreat you! ²⁹ If someone *insults one of you by* striking you
on one of your cheeks, turn your face *so he can strike* the other cheek *also*. If *a bandit*
wants to take away your coat, let him have your shirt too. ³⁰ Give something to everyone
who asks you *for something*. If someone takes away things that belong to you, do not ask
him to return them. ³¹ In whatever way you want others to act toward you, that is the way
you should act toward **them**.

³²"If you love *only* those who love you, do not *expect God* to praise you for *doing that,
because* even sinners love those who love them. ³³ If you do good things *only* for those
who do good things for you, do not *expect God* to reward you *for doing that, because* even
sinners act that way. ³⁴ If you lend *things or money only* to those who you expect will give

---

ʲ OR, …*God will give* you a great reward in heaven! *People have always treated God's servants like
that.*

something back to you, do not *expect that God* will reward you *for doing that*! Even sinners lend to other sinners, because they expect them to pay everything back. [35] Instead, love your enemies! Do good things for them! Lend to them, and do not expect them to pay anything back! *If you do that, God will give* you a great reward. And you will be *acting like* his children *should*. Remember that God is kind to people who are not grateful and to people who are wicked, *and he expects you to be like that too.* [36] Act mercifully toward others, just as your Father *in heaven acts* mercifully *toward you.*

Luke 6:37-42

THEME: Jesus taught that we should not decide how God should punish others.

[37]"Do not say how sinfully others have acted, and then *God* will not say how sinfully you have acted. Do *not condemn others*, and then *he* will not condemn you. Forgive others *for the evil things they have done to you*, and then *God* will forgive you. [38] Give *good things to others*, and then *God* will give *good* things to you. It will be *as though God is putting things in a basket* for you: He will give you a full amount, pressed down in the basket, which he will shake *so he can put more in*, and it will spill over the sides! *Remember that* the way you act *toward others* will be the way *God* will act toward you!"

[39]"He also told *his disciples* this parable *to show them they should be like him, and not be like the Jewish religious leaders*: "You certainly would not *expect* a blind man to lead another blind man. If he tried to do that, they would both probably fall into a hole. *I am your teacher, and you disciples should be like me.* [40] A disciple should not *expect to be* greater than his teacher. But if a student is fully trained, the student can become like his teacher. *So you should be content to be like me.*

[41]"None of you should be concerned about *someone else's small faults*. That would be *like* noticing a speck in that person's eye. But you should be concerned about *your own big faults. They are like* planks in your own eye, *which you do not notice.* [42] You should not say 'Friend, let me take out that speck in your eye!' when you do not notice the plank in your own eye! *If you do that*, you are a hypocrite! You should first *stop committing your own sins. That will be like* removing the plank from your own eye. Then, as a result, you will have the spiritual insight you need to help others get rid of the *faults that are like* specks in their eyes.

Luke 6:43-45

THEME: Jesus taught that what people do reflects their inner thoughts.

[43]"*People are like trees*. Healthy trees do not bear bad fruit,[k] and unhealthy trees do not bear good fruit. [44] *Just as you* can tell if a tree is good or bad by looking at its fruit, *you can tell which people are good and which are bad by looking at the way they conduct their lives. For example, since thorn bushes cannot produce figs*, no one can pick figs from thorn bushes. And *since bramble bushes cannot produce grapes*, no one can *pick* grapes from bramble bushes. [45] *In the same way*, good people will live in a good way because they have a lot of good *thoughts* within themselves, and evil people will live in an evil way because they have a lot of evil *thoughts* within themselves. People speak *and act* according to what is in their hearts.

---

k   OR, …Healthy trees bear only good fruit…

Luke 6:46-49

THEME: Jesus taught why it is necessary to obey his teaching, not just listen to it.

⁴⁶"*Since people should obey what their masters tell them*, it is disgraceful that you say I am your master but you don't do what I tell you! ⁴⁷ Some people come to me and hear my messages and obey them. I will tell you what they are like. ⁴⁸ They are like a man who dug deep *into the ground to prepare to build his house*. He made sure the foundation was on solid ground. Then when there was a flood, the water tried to wash away the house. But the river could not shake the house, because it was built on a solid *foundation*. ⁴⁹ But some people hear my messages but do not obey them. They are like a man who built a house on top of the ground without *digging* a foundation. When the river flooded, the house collapsed immediately and was completely ruined. *So it is important for you to obey what I teach you.*"

7

Luke 7:1-10

THEME: Jesus healed a man without going to his house because the man's master believed Jesus could do that.

¹ After Jesus finished saying this to the people, he went *along with his disciples* to *the town of* Capernaum. ² There was a Roman army officer there who had a slave whom he highly esteemed. This slave was so sick that he was about to die. ³ When the officer heard about Jesus, he *summoned* some Jewish elders and told them to go to Jesus and ask him to come and heal his slave. ⁴ When they came to where Jesus was, they earnestly asked Jesus *to return with them*. They said, "This officer deserves that you do this *for him*, ⁵ because he loves us *Jewish* people, and he *paid the money to* build a synagogue for us." ⁶ So Jesus went with them. When he was near the *officer's* house, the officer *decided that it was not necessary for Jesus to come to his house. So he* summoned some friends. He *told them to* go to Jesus and tell him this: "Sir, don't bother to come. *Since I am a non-Jew*, I am not worthy for you, *a Jew*, to come into my house *and associate with me*. ⁷ I did not feel worthy to come to you, *either*. But *please* command *that* my servant *be healed*, and he will become well! ⁸ *I believe this* because, as for me, there are people who have authority over me *and I obey them*. I also have soldiers under my *authority*. When I say to one of them, 'Go!' he goes. When I say to another 'Come!' he comes. When I say to my slave, 'Do this!' he does it. *And I believe that you speak with a similar kind of authority.*" ⁹ When *the officer's friends arrived and* told that to Jesus, he marveled. Then he turned and said to the crowd that was accompanying him, "I tell you, I have never before found anyone who has a firm faith *in me like this non-Jewish man has*. No one from Israel, *where I would expect people believe in me*, has the kind of faith in me that he has!" ¹⁰ When those men returned to the officer's house, they found that the slave was well.

Luke 7:11-17

THEME: Jesus caused a widow's son to become alive again.

¹¹ Soon after that, Jesus went to a town called Nain. His disciples and a large crowd *of other people* went with him. ¹² As they approached the town gate, the corpse of a young man who had just died was being carried out *on a stretcher*. His mother was a widow, and he was her only son. A large group of people from the town were accompanying them. ¹³ When the Lord saw her, he pitied her. He said to her, "Don't cry!" ¹⁴ Then, *ignoring the*

Jewish laws about not coming near a corpse, he came close and touched the stretcher *on which the body was lying*. So the men carrying it stood still. He said, "Young man, I say to you, get up!" [15] The man sat up and began to talk! Jesus returned him to his mother *to care for her*. [16] Then everyone *there* was awestruck. They praised God, saying, "A great prophet has come among us!" They also said, "God has come to help his people!" [17] *Then they* reported what Jesus *had done* throughout all of Judea and other nearby areas.

Luke 7:18-35

THEME: Jesus taught about his ministry and the ministry of John the Baptizer.

[18] The disciples of John *the Baptizer went to the prison where John was, and* told him about those things. [19] So *one day* John summoned two *of his disciples* and *told them* to go to the Lord and ask him: "Are you *the Messiah who the prophets prophesied would come,* or is it someone else that we should expect *to come*?" [20] When those two men came to Jesus, they said, "John the Baptizer sent us to ask you this: Are you *the Messiah that* we are expecting *God* to send, or shall we look for someone else?" [21] At that very time Jesus was healing many people of their diseases and *other* sicknesses, he was *casting out* evil spirits, and he was causing many blind people to be able to see. [22] So he answered those two men, "Go back and report to John what you have seen *me doing* and what you have heard *me telling people. I am enabling* blind people to see. *I am enabling* lame people to walk. *I am* healing people who have leprosy. *I am enabling* deaf people to hear. *I am* raising people from the dead, *and I am* telling *God's* good message to poor people. [23] *Also tell John that God* is pleased with those who don't stop believing in me *because what I do is not what they expect the Messiah to do*."

[24] When the men whom John had sent left, Jesus began to talk to the crowd of people about John. He said to them, "*Think about* what sort of person you went to see in the desolate area *when you went there to see John. You did not go there to listen to a man who constantly changed the nature of his message, like* a reed that is blown back and forth by the wind. [25] Then what kind of man did you go there to see? Was he a man who wore expensive clothes? No! *You know very well that* people who wear beautiful clothes and live in luxury are in kings' palaces, *not in the desolate areas*! [26] Then what *kind of person* did you go to see? *Did you go there to see John because he was* a prophet? Yes! But I will tell you that *John is* more *important* than an *ordinary* prophet. [27] He is the one about whom *these words* that God said to the Messiah have been written *in Scripture*:

Listen! I am going to send my messenger ahead of you to prepare *the people* for your coming.

[28] I tell you that of all the people who have ever lived, no one is greater *in God's sight* than John. However, *God considers* all those who have let God rule their lives to be greater than *John, even if they are* insignificant *people*."

[29] When they heard *what Jesus said,* all the people, including tax collectors, *whom many people despised*, agreed that God's way was right.[1] By *letting* John baptize them, *they had* agreed *that what* God *required people to do in order be saved* was right. [30] But the Pharisees and the men who taught the *Jewish* laws did not *let* John baptize them, because they rejected God's will *for their lives*.

[31] *Then Jesus also said,* "*Many of* you people have heard what *John and I* have taught. I will illustrate what you are like. [32] You are like children who are *playing games* in an open area. *Some of them* are calling to *the others*, saying, "We played happy music for you on

---

[1] OR, …When all the people heard *what John preached*, they agreed that God's way was right, including tax collectors, *whom everyone despised*.

the flute, but you did not dance! Then we sang sad funeral songs for you, but you did not cry!" [33] *In the same way, you are dissatisfied with both* John the Baptizer *and me!* When John came and *preached to you*, he did not eat *ordinary* food or drink wine, *like most people do*. But you *rejected him* saying, 'A demon is controlling him!' [34] In *contrast*, I, the one who came from heaven, eat *the same food* and drink *wine as others do*. But you *reject me,* saying, 'Look! *This man* eats too much food and drinks too much wine, and he associates with tax collectors and *other* sinners!' [35] But those who are *truly God's* children realize that *what John and I do shows a lot of* wisdom."

Luke 7:36-50

THEME: Jesus told why he appreciated the sinful woman pouring perfume on his feet.

[36] *One day* one of the Pharisees *named Simon* invited Jesus to eat a meal with him. So Jesus went to the man's house and sat down *to eat.* [37] There was a woman in that city *who many people knew had been* a prostitute. She heard that Jesus was *reclining while* eating in the Pharisee's house. So she went there, taking a stone jar that contained perfume. [38] She stood behind *Jesus'* feet. As she was crying *because she was sorry for her sins, her tears fell on Jesus' feet.* Then she wiped his feet with her hair, and kissed his feet, and anointed them with the perfume. [39] When the Pharisee who had invited *Jesus* saw that, he thought within himself, "*Prophets know about other people's lives, so* if Jesus were a prophet, he would have known who this woman is who is touching him, and what kind of a person she is. He would have known that she is a prostitute!" [40] Then Jesus said to him, "Simon, there is something I want to tell you." He replied, "Teacher, what is it?" [41] Jesus replied, "Two people owed some money to a moneylender. One owed him five hundred silver coins, and the other owed him fifty silver coins. [42] Neither of them was able to pay back *what he owed*, so the man *in great kindness* said they did not have to pay back anything. So, which of those two men will love that man more?" [43] Simon replied, "I suppose the one who owed the most money and did not have to pay it back *will love him more*." Jesus said to him, "That is correct." [44] Then he turned toward the woman, and said to Simon, "Think about *what* this woman *has done!* When I entered your house, you *did not follow our custom of welcoming guests by* giving me any water *to wash* my feet, but this woman has wet my feet with her tears and then wiped them with her hair! [45] You did not *follow our custom of greeting by* kissing me, but since I came in she hasn't stopped kissing my feet! [46] You did not *follow our custom of welcoming guests by* anointing my head with *olive* oil, but she has anointed my feet with fragrant perfume. [47] So I will tell you that even though she has sinned very much, she has been forgiven. *By what she has done she has shown that* she loves *me* very much. But a person who has *sinned* just a little bit, but whom *I* have forgiven, will love *me just a little bit*." [48] Then he said to the woman, "I *have* forgiven *you for* your sins." [49] Then those who were eating with him said among themselves, "This man must *think he is God*, saying that he can forgive *people for* their sins!" [50] But Jesus said to the woman, "Because you have trusted *in me, God* has saved you *from the guilt of your sins.* May *God* give you inner peace as you go!"

8

Luke 8:1-3

THEME: The list of women who helped Jesus.

[1] Soon after that, Jesus went, along with his twelve *disciples,* through various cities and villages. As they went, he was telling people the good message about how God wants to

have complete control *over their lives.* ²Some women from whom he had expelled evil spirits and healed of diseases also *went with him.* These included Mary, the woman from *the village of* Magdala, from whom *he had expelled* seven evil spirits; ³Joanna, the wife of Chuza, who was one of *King* Herod *Antipas'* officials; Susanna; and many others. They were providing some of their own funds *to help Jesus and his disciples.*

Luke 8:4-8

THEME: The story about four different kinds of soil.

⁴A great crowd of people came to Jesus from many towns. He told them this parable: ⁵"A man went out *to his field* to sow *some* seeds. As he was scattering them over the soil, some *of the seeds* fell on the path. Then *people* walked on those seeds, and birds ate them. ⁶Some *of the seeds* fell on rock *on which there was a thin layer of soil.* As soon as the seeds grew, the plants dried up because they had no moisture. ⁷Some *of the seeds* fell on *ground that contained roots of* thorny *weeds.* The thorny weeds grew *together* with the young plants, and *they* crowded out *the plants.* ⁸But some of the seeds fell on good soil and grew *well. Each seed later* produced a hundred *grains.*" Then Jesus shouted to them, "If you want to understand this, you must consider *carefully what I have just said*!"

Luke 8:9-15

THEME: Jesus explained that the story represented different ways people respond to his teaching.

⁹Jesus' disciples *later* asked him about the meaning of the parable *he had just told.* ¹⁰He said, "God is revealing to you what he did not reveal before, about *how he wants to* rule *over peoples' lives.* But when I am telling other people about *those things, I tell them* only in parables. The result will be *like a prophet predicted long ago,*
They will see *what I am doing*, but will not perceive *what it means.*
They will hear *what I am saying*, but will not understand *it.*

¹¹So this is the meaning of that parable: The seeds *represent* God's message. ¹²*Some people are like* the path on which some of *the seeds fell.* When these people hear God's message, the devil comes and causes them to forget what they have heard. As a result, they don't believe it, and will not be saved. ¹³*Some people are like* the *soil with* rock *underneath.* When they hear *God's* message, they accept it joyfully. *But because it does not penetrate deeply into their hearts,* they believe it for *only* a *short* time. *They are like the plants that* did not have *deep* roots. When life gets difficult for them, they stop believing *God's message.* ¹⁴*Some people are like* the *soil that had roots of* thorny *weeds* in it. They are people who accept *God's message*, but later on they worry about things and try to become rich and enjoy *things that give them* a lot of pleasure. So they don't become *spiritually* mature. ¹⁵But *some people are like* the good soil. They hear *God's* message and accept it. They *become* good, honest people, and they persevere in doing things *that please God.*

Luke 8:16-18

THEME: Jesus explained the need to make his truth clear to others.

¹⁶"After people light a lamp, they don't cover it with a basket or put it under a bed. Instead, they put it on a lampstand, so that those who enter *the house* can see *things from* its light. *In the same way, you must tell God's truth to others so they can know what I can do for them.* ¹⁷*God wants to* make clear all *of his truth* that was not clear previously. *He intends for his people* to tell *others* openly all *of the truth he* has not revealed before. ¹⁸So listen

carefully *to what I tell you*, because *God* will enable those who accept *my truth* to understand *even* more. But *God* will cause those who do not accept *my truth* to not understand even *the little* that they think they have *understood.*"

Luke 8:19-21

THEME: Jesus told them that some people are as dear to him as his own relatives.

[19] *One day Jesus'* mother and his *younger* brothers came to see him, but they could not get near him because there was a large crowd *around him in the house.* [20] Someone told him, "Your mother and your brothers are standing outside, wanting to see you." [21] He replied, "Those who hear God's message and obey it are *as dear to me* as my mother and my brothers."

Luke 8:22-25

THEME: Jesus calmed a storm.

[22] One day Jesus got into a boat with his disciples. He said to them, "Let's go *around to* the other side of the lake." So they started to go. [23] As they were sailing, he fell asleep. A big windstorm came down on the lake. Soon the boat was filling with water, and they were in danger. [24] His disciples went and woke him up. They said *to him*, "Master! Master! We are going to drown!" He got up and rebuked the wind and told the waves to be calm. The wind *immediately* stopped blowing and the waves calmed down. *The lake* became calm. [25] He said to them, "I *am disappointed that* you did not trust me *to help you!*" They were afraid. They were also amazed. They said to one another, "What kind of man is this? He *not only commands people, but* when he commands the wind and the water, they also obey him!"

Luke 8:26-39

THEME: Jesus expelled many demons from a man.

[26] Jesus and his disciples arrived at the region near Gerasa, a *town* which *was on the eastern* side of Lake *Galilee.* [27] *There was* a man *in that region* in whom demons lived.[m] *He was* from the town *of Gerasa.* For a long time he had not worn clothes. He did not live in a house. Instead, he lived in burial caves. [28-29] Many times *demons* attacked him. *People* tried to guard him *so that he would not injure others.* They fastened chains on his hands and shackles on his feet, but he would break the chains and shackles. Then the demons would send him away to the desolate area.

When Jesus stepped out of the boat onto the shore, the man saw him. He *ran to Jesus* and prostrated himself before him. Then Jesus commanded, "You evil spirit, come out of that man!" But it *did not leave immediately. Instead, it* caused the man to shout very loudly, "Jesus, Son of the great God in heaven, since we have nothing in common, *leave me alone!* I beg you, do not torture me *now!*" [30] *In order to expel the demon more easily,* Jesus asked *the demon*, "What is your name?" He replied, "My name is Mob." *He said that* because many demons had entered that man. [31] *The demons* kept begging *Jesus* not to order them to go into the deep place where God punishes demons. [32] There was a large herd of pigs rooting for food on the hillside. The demons begged Jesus that he give them permission to enter the pigs. So he did. [33] The demons left the man and entered the pigs. Then the herd *of pigs* rushed down the steep bank into the lake and drowned.

---

[m] OR, In that area there was a man from that town whom demons controlled.

[34] When the men who were tending the pigs saw what happened, they ran! They told people inside the town and outside the town what had happened. [35] So people went out to see what had happened. When they came to where Jesus was, they saw that the man from whom Jesus had *expelled* the demons was sitting at the feet of Jesus, *listening to him*. He had clothes on, and he was in his right mind. Then those people became afraid *because they thought he would destroy more of their property*.[n] [36] The people who had seen what happened told those *who had just arrived* how *Jesus* had healed the man whom demons were controlling *before*. [37] Then *those people and* many other people from the area near Gerasa asked Jesus to leave their area. They were very afraid of *what else Jesus would do to them*. So *Jesus and the disciples* got into the boat to go back across the lake. [38] The man from whom he had *expelled* the demons begged him saying, *"Please, let me go with you!"* But *Jesus refused. Instead* he said to him, [39]*"No, I want you to* go home and tell people how much God has done for you!" Then he sent him away. So he went away and told people throughout the town how much Jesus had done for him.

Luke 8:40-56

THEME: Jesus caused a young girl to become alive again and healed a woman who had been bleeding for years.

[40] When *Jesus and the disciples* returned *to Capernaum*, a crowd of people who had been waiting for him welcomed him. [41] Just then a man named Jairus, who was one of the leaders of the Jewish meeting place *there*, came near and prostrated himself at Jesus' feet. He pleaded with Jesus, "Please come to my house, [42] because my only daughter, who is about twelve years old, is dying!"

As Jesus went with him, many people crowded close to Jesus. [43] Then a woman came near. She had been suffering from constant *vaginal* bleeding for twelve years, but no one could heal her. [44] She came behind *Jesus* and touched the fringe of his robe *in order to be healed*. At once her bleeding stopped. [45] Jesus said, "Who touched me?" When everyone said they had not touched him, Peter said, "Lord, there is a great crowd of people around you and pressing against you, *so any one of them might have touched you!*" [46] But Jesus said, "No, I know that someone *deliberately* touched me, *because* my power has healed someone *who touched me*." [47] When the woman realized that she could not prevent Jesus from knowing *she was healed*, her body began to shake.[o] *She was afraid that because she had disobeyed the law that a woman with such a condition should not touch others, Jesus might scold her for doing that.* She prostrated herself before him. As the other people were listening, she told why she had touched him and how she had been healed immediately. [48] *Jesus* said to her, "My dear woman, because you believed *that I could heal you, I* have healed you. Go *from here, and may you experience God's* peace."

[49] While he was still talking *to her*, a man from Jairus' house came and said to Jairus, "Your daughter has died. So it is useless for you to bother the teacher any longer *by urging him to go to your house!*" [50] But when Jesus heard that, he said to Jairus, "Don't *think that the situation* is hopeless! Just believe that *I can help her. If you do that*, she will live again." [51] When they arrived outside the house, he allowed only Peter, John, James, and the girl's mother and father to go in the house with him. [52] All the people *there* were crying and beating their breasts *in grief*. But, *knowing that he would cause the girl to live again*, he said to them, "Stop crying! She is not dead! She is *just* sleeping!" [53] The people laughed at him, because they knew *the girl* was dead. [54] But *Jesus* took hold of her hand

---

[n]   OR, …Then those people became afraid *because they realized he must be very powerful.*
[o]   OR, When the woman realized that she could not prevent the people from knowing *that she had touched him*, her body began to shake.

and called to her saying, "Child, get up!" ⁵⁵ At once her spirit returned *to her body* and she got up. Jesus told *them* to give her something to eat. ⁵⁶ Her parents were amazed, but Jesus told them not to tell anyone *else yet* what had happened.

9

Luke 9:1-6

THEME: Jesus sent out his apostles to teach and heal people.

¹ *One day* Jesus summoned his twelve *apostles*, and gave them power to expel all *kinds of* demons and to heal *people with* diseases. He gave them authority to do that. ² *Before he* sent them out to heal people and to tell people *what it meant to let* God have complete control *over their lives*, ³ he said to them, "Do not take things for your journey. Don't take a walking stick or a *traveler's* bag or food or money. Don't take an extra shirt. ⁴ Whenever you enter some house *to lodge there*, stay in that house until you leave that town. ⁵ *In towns* where the people do not welcome you, *you should not continue to stay there. I want you to* leave those towns. And as you leave, shake off the dust from your feet. *Do that as a* warning to them *that rejecting your message will bring punishment from God.*" ⁶ Then they left and traveled through many villages. Everywhere *they went*, they told people God's good message and healed sick people.

Luke 9:7-11

THEME: Herod was uncertain about who was doing those miracles.

⁷ Herod *Antipas*, the ruler of *that* district, heard about the things *Jesus and his disciples* were doing. *He had previously commanded his soldiers to execute John the Baptizer, so now* he was perplexed, because some people were saying that John had become alive again *and was doing those miracles.* ⁸ Others were saying that *the prophet* Elijah had appeared *again*. Others were saying that one of the *other* former prophets had become alive again *and was doing those miracles.* ⁹ But Herod said, "*It cannot be John who is doing these things, because* I *had* his head cut off. So who is *doing these miracles* that I am hearing about?" And he kept wanting to see *Jesus.*

¹⁰ When the apostles returned *from traveling to various towns*, they told Jesus the things they had done. Then he took them and they went by themselves *by boat* to a town called Bethsaida. ¹¹ But when the crowds *of people who had been with Jesus* found out about that, they followed him *on land. When they got to where he was*, he welcomed them. He taught them about how God is going to some day rule as king. He also healed the sick people.

Luke 9:12-17

THEME: Jesus fed over 5,000 people miraculously.

¹² Late in the afternoon the twelve *apostles* came to him and said, "This is a place where nobody lives, so dismiss the people so that they can go to the surrounding villages and other places where they can get some food and find places to stay." ¹³ But he said to them, "*No, you yourselves* give them something to eat!" They replied, "We have only five small loaves of bread and two *cooked* fish. Are you going to *give* us *the money* to go somewhere and buy food for all these people?" ¹⁴ There were about five thousand men *there*. He replied to the disciples, "*No, just* tell the people to sit down. Tell them to sit in

groups, with about fifty people in each group." ¹⁵ After they told the people that, they all sat down. ¹⁶ Then he took the five small loaves and the two fish. He looked up towards heaven and thanked *God for them*. Then he broke them *into pieces* and gave them to the disciples for them to distribute to the crowd. ¹⁷ All *the people in the crowd* ate until they all had enough to eat.. Then *the disciples* collected twelve baskets full of the broken pieces that were left over!

Luke 9:18-27

THEME: After Peter expressed his belief that Jesus was the Messiah, Jesus predicted his own death and resurrection.

¹⁸ *One day* Jesus was praying in a place where only the disciples were with him. He asked them, "Who *do the people* say that I *really* am?" ¹⁹ They replied, "*Some say you are* John the Baptizer, *who has come back to life again*. Others say you are *the prophet* Elijah *who has returned from heaven as God promised*. Others say you are one of the *other* prophets who lived long ago who has come back to life again." ²⁰ He asked them, "What about you? Who do **you** say that I am?" Peter replied, "You are the Messiah, who *has come from* God." ²¹ Then Jesus warned them strongly not to tell that to anyone *yet*. ²² Then he said, "*Even though I am* the one who came from heaven, it is necessary that I suffer very much. It is also necessary that I be rejected by the elders and the chief priests and the men who teach the *Jewish* laws and that I be killed. Then on the third day *after that* I will become alive again."

²³ Then he said to all of them, "If any one *of you* wants to be my disciple, you must not do *only* what you yourself desire *to do*. You must be willing each day *to let others hurt you and disgrace you. That is like what is done to criminals who are forced* to carry crosses *to the place where they will be crucified. That is what anyone who wants to* be my disciple *must do.* ²⁴ You must do that, because those who try to save their lives *by denying they belong to me when people want to kill them for believing in me* will not live *eternally*, but those who are killed because of being my *disciples* will live *forever with me.* ²⁵ People might get everything *they want* in this world, but they are really gaining nothing if they don't get eternal life by *becoming my disciples*! ²⁶ Those who reject my message *and* refuse to say *they belong* to me, *I*, the one who came from heaven, will also refuse to say *they belong to me* when I come back with the holy angels and have the glorious brightness that my Father has. ²⁷ But listen carefully! Some of you who are here now will see God ruling *in many powerful ways*. You will see it before you die!"

Luke 9:28-36

THEME: Jesus talked with Moses and Elijah.

²⁸ About a week after *Jesus* said those things, he took Peter, James, and *James' brother* John and led them up a mountain so that he could pray *there*. ²⁹ As he was praying, his face appeared very different to them. His clothes became as bright as lightning. ³⁰⁻³¹ Suddenly, two men appeared who had the brightness *of heaven* surrounding them. They were *prophets who had lived long ago*, Moses and Elijah. They started talking with Jesus about how he *would accomplish what God had planned* when he died *very soon* in Jerusalem. ³² Peter and the other *disciples* who were with him were sound asleep. When they woke up, they saw *Jesus'* brightness. They also saw the two men standing with him. ³³ As *Moses and Elijah* were starting to leave Jesus, Peter said to him, "Master, it is wonderful for us to be here! Allow us to make three shelters, one for you, one for Moses, and one for Elijah!" But he really did not realize what he was saying. ³⁴ As he was saying that, a *bright* cloud appeared and covered them. The disciples were afraid as the cloud surrounded them. ³⁵ *God* spoke to them from the cloud, saying, "This is my Son. He is the

one whom *I* have chosen *to do a great work for me. So* you must listen to him!" ³⁶ After *God* finished saying that, *the three disciples* saw that only Jesus was there. They did not tell anyone what they had seen until much later.

Luke 9:37-43a

THEME: Jesus expelled a demon from a boy.

³⁷ The next day, after they had come down from the mountain, a large crowd *of people* met Jesus. ³⁸ Then a man from the crowd exclaimed, "Teacher, I plead with you, *do something to help* my son! He is my only child! ³⁹ At various times an evil spirit suddenly seizes him and *causes* him to scream. The evil spirit shakes him violently and causes him to foam at the mouth. It does not leave until my child is completely exhausted. ⁴⁰ I pleaded with your disciples *who were here* for them to expel *the evil spirit*, but they were not able to do it!" ⁴¹ Jesus replied *by saying to everyone who had gathered there*, "*You who have seen how I help people* do not believe *that you can do anything!* Your *thinking* is wrong! How long do I have to be with you *before you are able to do what I do*? *How long do I have to* endure your *lack of faith?* Bring your son here *to me*!" ⁴² While they were bringing the boy to Jesus, the demon attacked the boy, threw him to the ground, and shook him severely. But Jesus rebuked the evil spirit and healed the boy. Then he returned him to his father's *care*. ⁴³ All the people *there* were amazed at the great *power* of God.

Luke 9:43b-45

THEME: Jesus predicted his arrest.

While they were all amazed at all the miracles *Jesus* was doing, he said to his disciples, ⁴⁴ "Think carefully about what I am about to tell you: *Even though* I am the one who came from heaven, *I will soon* be handed over to the authorities." ⁴⁵ But *the disciples* did not understand what *Jesus* was saying; *God* prevented them from understanding it, so that they would not know *yet* what he meant. And they were afraid to ask him about *what he had said*.

Luke 9:46-48

THEME: Jesus told his disciples who is really great in God's sight.

⁴⁶ The disciples began to argue among themselves about which one of them would be the greatest *when Jesus became king*. ⁴⁷ But Jesus perceived what they were thinking. So he brought a young child to his side. ⁴⁸ He said to *the disciples*, "Those who, *out of love* for me,ᵖ welcome a little child, *God considers that* they are welcoming me. And those who welcome me, *God considers* that they are welcoming him, the one who sent me. Remember that those among you who think of themselves as being very unimportant will be the ones *God considers* to be great."

Luke 9:49-50

THEME: Jesus told them not to forbid others from expelling demons.

⁴⁹ John replied to *Jesus*, "Master, we saw a man who was expelling demons, *claiming he had* authority from you to do that. So we told him to stop doing it, because he is not one of us *disciples*." ⁵⁰ But Jesus said to him *and the other disciples*, "Don't tell him not to *do that*.

ᵖ OR, …because they want to behave like me…

Remember that those who are not opposing you are trying to *achieve the same goals that you are!*"

Luke 9:51-56

THEME: People in a Samaritan town refused to welcome Jesus.

[51] When it was almost time for *God* to take him up to heaven, *Jesus* firmly resolved to go to Jerusalem. [52] He sent some messengers to go ahead of him, and they entered a village in *the district of* Samaria to prepare for him *to go there.* [53] But *the Samaritans did not like the Jews because of their insisting that it was necessary to go to Jerusalem to worship God. So* since Jesus had firmly resolved to go to Jerusalem, they would not let him come *to their village.* [54] When two of his disciples, James and John, heard about that, they said, "Lord, do you want us to pray that *God* will send fire down from heaven, *as the prophet Elijah did long ago,* and destroy those people?" [55] But Jesus turned and rebuked them *for saying that.* [56] So they went to a different village.

Luke 9:57-62

THEME: Jesus told three people what it would cost them if they became his disciples.

[57] As Jesus and the disciples were walking along the road, one man said to him, "I will go with you wherever you go!" [58] *In order that the man might know what he could expect if he went with him,* Jesus said to him, "Foxes have holes *in the ground in which to live,* and birds have nests, but *even though* I am the one who came from heaven, I do not have a home where I can sleep!" [59] Jesus told another man, "Come with me!" But the man said, "Sir, let me go *home* first. *After* my father *dies,* I will bury him *and then I will come with you.*" [60] But Jesus said to him, "*Those who do not have eternal life are* dead *in God's sight.* Let those people *do the work of* burying people who die. As for you, you go and tell people about how God wants to have complete control *over people's lives*!" [61] Someone else said, "Lord, I will come with you and be your disciple, but first let me go home to say good-bye to my relatives." [62] Jesus said to him, "Anyone who is plowing his field should not look back *to see what he has done. He must look forward to what is ahead. In* the same way, *anyone who continues to be concerned about the family and other things he has left behind* is not fit *to serve me and tell others about how* God wants to rule *people's lives.*"

10

Luke 10:1-12

THEME: Jesus instructed seventy-two other disciples before sending them out.

[1] After that, the Lord *Jesus* appointed seventy-two other *people.* He *prepared to* send them out, two by two, to every town and village where he intended to go. [2] He said to them, "The *people who are ready to receive your mess*age are like a field *of grain* that is ready to be harvested. But there are not many people *to bring them to God.* So pray and ask the Lord *God* to send *more* workers *who will gather people together and teach them my message, just as a landowner sends workers* into his field *to gather the* harvest. [3] Start going, but *remember that* I am sending you out *to tell my message to people who will try to get rid of you. You will be* like lambs among wolves. [4] Don't take along *any money in* a purse. Don't take a traveler's bag. Don't take *extra* sandals. Don't *spend a lot of time* greeting people along the way. [5] Whenever you enter a house *to lodge there,* first say to those people, 'May *God give inner* peace to *you people in* this house!' [6] If people who *live* there *are*

desiring to have God's peace, they will experience the *inner* peace you are *offering them.*
If people who *live* there *are not desiring to have God's* peace, you *will experience God's*
inner peace, *but they will not.* [7] *If they welcome you,* stay in that same house *until you*
leave that village. Don't move around from one house to another. Eat and drink whatever
they provide for you. A worker deserves to get pay *from the people for whom he works, so*
you deserve to receive food and a place to stay from the people to whom you go.
[8] Whenever you enter a town and the people *there* welcome you, eat what *they* provide for
you. [9] Heal the people there who are sick. Tell them, 'It is almost *time for* God to send his
king to rule *your lives.'* [10] But if you enter a town whose *people* don't welcome you, go into
its *main* streets and say, [11] '*Since you have refused to hear our message, we will not only*
leave, we will also shake off the dust of your town that clings to our sandals, to warn you
that God will reject you. But *we want you to know that* it is almost *the time for* God to start
to rule!' [12] I will tell you this: On the *final* day when *God judges everyone*, he will punish the
wicked people who long ago lived in Sodom, *the city that he destroyed because its people*
were so wicked. But he will punish *even* more severely the people of that town *who*
refused to hear your message!"

Luke 10:13-16

THEME: Jesus warned the unbelievers in three towns.

[13] "*You people who live in the towns of* Chorazin and Bethsaida *will suffer terrible*
punishment! I did great miracles in your cities *to show God's power, but you did not turn*
from your sinful behavior. If the miracles I did among you had been done in *the ancient*
cities of Tyre and Sidon, the wicked people who lived there would have *shown they were*
sorry for their sins by sitting on the ground wearing coarse cloth and putting ashes on their
heads. [14] *But they did not have the opportunity you have, so when God punishes people,*
he will punish the wicked people who lived in Tyre and Sidon, but he will punish you more
severely *than that because you did not pay attention to my message*! [15] *I also have*
something to say to you *people who live in the town of* Capernaum. Don't *think that God*
will honor you in heaven! *No way! On the contrary*, after you die, God will send you down
to the place where *sinful people* will be punished *forever*!"

[16] *Jesus also said to the disciples*, "God will consider that* those who listen to your
message are listening to me, and that those who reject your *message* are rejecting me.
And *he will consider that* those who reject me are rejecting the one who sent me."

Luke 10:17-24

THEME: Jesus commented on their ministry after the seventy-two returned.

[17] The seventy-two *people whom Jesus appointed went and did as he told them to*. When
they returned, they were very joyful. They said, "Lord, *people did what we told them to do!*
But demons also obeyed us when by your authority *we commanded them to leave*
people!" [18] He replied, "*When those demons were obeying you, because God had enabled*
you to defeat them, it was as though I saw Satan fall from heaven *as suddenly and quickly*
as lightning *strikes*! [19] Listen! I have given you authority so that if you *accidentally* walk on
poisonous snakes and scorpions, *they will not hurt you*. I have given you authority to
defeat our enemy, *Satan*. Nothing shall hurt you. [20] But *although* you can rejoice that evil
spirits obey you, you should rejoice *more* that your names have been written in heaven,
because you will be with God forever."

[21] At that time the Holy Spirit caused *Jesus* to be very happy. He said, "Father, you rule
over *everything in* heaven and *on* the earth! I thank you that you have prevented *people*
who think they are wise *because* of *being* well educated from *knowing* these things.

Instead, you have revealed them to *people who accept your truth as readily as* little children *do.* Yes, Father, *you have done that* because it seemed good to you *to do* so." [22] *Jesus also said to the 72 disciples,* "*God,* my Father, has revealed to me all the things *I need to know for my work.* Only my Father knows who I *really* am. Furthermore, only I and those *people* to whom I wish to reveal him know what *God* my Father is *like.*"

[23] Then when his disciples were alone with him, he turned toward them and said, "*God* is pleased with you who have seen *the things I have done*! [24] I want you to know that many prophets and kings *who lived long ago* desired to see the things you are seeing *me do,* but they did not *see* them. They longed to hear the things you have been hearing *me say,* but they did not hear them."

Luke 10:25-37 (Mt. 22:34-40; Mk. 12:28-31)

THEME: Jesus taught that we must show our love to everyone, even ones we don't like to associate with.

[25] *One day as Jesus was teaching people,* a man who was had studied carefully the laws *God gave Moses* was there. He wanted to ask Jesus a difficult question. So he stood up and asked, "Teacher, what shall I do in order to live *with God* forever?" [26] Jesus said to him, "You have read what *Moses* has written in the law *God gave him.* What did Moses write about that?" [27] The man replied, "*He wrote that* we must love the Lord our God with all our hearts. *We must show our love for him* in all our desires, in all our emotions, in all we do and in all our thoughts. *He* also *wrote that we must love* people we come in contact with as much as *we love* ourselves." [28] Jesus replied, "You have answered *your question* correctly. If you do all that *continually,* you will live *with God forever.*"

[29] But the man wanted to defend *the way* he *acted toward people he came in contact with.*[q] So he said to Jesus, "Which people that I come in contact with *should I love*?" [30] Jesus replied *by telling him this illustration*: "A *Jewish* man was once going down along the road from Jerusalem to Jericho. Bandits attacked him. They took away *most of* the man's clothes *and everything else he had,* and they beat him until he was half dead. Then they left him. [31] It happened that a *Jewish* priest was going along that road. When he saw that man, *instead of helping him,* he passed by on the other side *of the road.* [32] In the same way, a man who worked in the temple *in Jerusalem* came to that place and saw the man. But he also passed by on the other side *of the road.* [33] Then a man from Samaria came along that road to where the man was lying. *People from Samaria despise Jews. But* when he saw that man, he pitied him. [34] He went close to him and put some *olive* oil and wine on the wounds *to help heal them.* He wound strips of cloth *around the wounds.* He placed the man on his own donkey and took him to an inn and took care of him. [35] The next morning he gave two silver coins to the innkeeper and said, 'Take care of this man. If you spend more than this amount *to care for him,* I will pay you back when I return.'" [36] Then Jesus said, "Three people saw the man whom bandits attacked. Which one of them *acted in a loving way toward* that man?" [37] The man who studied the Scriptures replied, "The one who took pity on him." Jesus said to him, "You go and act like that *toward* everyone *you can help*!"

---

[q] OR, …to defend why he *had asked a question that Jesus answered so simply.*

Luke 10:38-42

THEME: Jesus rebuked Martha for being too concerned about household chores.

[38] As Jesus and his disciples continued to travel, they entered a village *near Jerusalem.* A woman whose name was Martha invited them to come to her house. [39] Her *younger* sister, whose name was Mary, was sitting near Jesus. She was listening to what he was teaching. [40] But Martha was very much concerned about preparing *the meal.* She went to Jesus and said, "Lord, you don't seem to care that my sister has left me to prepare everything by myself! Tell her that she should help me!" [41] But the Lord replied, "Martha, Martha, you are very worried about many things. [42] But only one thing is truly necessary, and that is, *to listen to what I am teaching.* Mary has decided to *do that,* and that is better. No one will take away from her *the blessing she is receiving from doing that.*"

11

Luke 11:1-13 (Mt. 6:9-13; 7:7-11)

THEME: Jesus taught his disciples various things about prayer.

[1] One day Jesus was somewhere praying. When he finished *praying,* one of his disciples said to him, "Lord, teach us *what to say when* we pray, as John *the Baptizer* taught his disciples!" [2] He said to them, "When you pray, say *things like this*: 'Father, we want you to be revered. *We want people to let you* rule over their lives. [3] Give us each day the food that we need. [4] Forgive us *for* the wrong things we have done, because we forgive people for the wrong things they do to us. Do not let us do wrong things when we are tempted.'"

[5] Then he said to them, "Suppose one of you goes to the house of a friend at midnight. Suppose you *stand outside and* call out to him, 'My friend, please lend me three buns! [6] Another friend of mine who is traveling has just arrived *at my house,* but I have no food *ready* to give him!' [7] Suppose he answers you from inside *the house,* 'Don't bother me! *We* have locked the door and all my family are in bed. *So* I cannot get up and give you anything!' [8] I will tell you that even if he does not *want to* get up and give you *any food,* to avoid being ashamed *for not helping you* because you are his friend, he certainly will get up and give you whatever you need.[r] [9] So I tell you this: Keep asking *God for what you need.* If you do that, *he* will give it to you. Confidently keep expecting *God to give you the things you need,* and *he* will give them to you. *It will be like* looking for what you need and finding it. Keep on *praying urgently to God. Then God will answer you. It will be like* knocking *on a door.* And *God* will open *the way* for you *to get what you pray for.* [10] Remember that *God* will give *good* things to everyone who continues to ask *him for them. He* will give things to whoever confidently keeps asking. *He* will open *the way* for people *to get the things they keep urgently praying for.* [11] If one of you had a son who asked you for a fish *to eat,* you certainly wouldn't give him a *poisonous* snake instead! [12] If he asked you for an egg, you would certainly not give him a scorpion. [13] Even though you people are evil, you know how to give good things to your children. So your Father in heaven will certainly *give good things* to those who ask him, *including* giving the Holy Spirit, *who is the best gift.*"

---

[r] OR, I will tell you that he certainly will get up and give you whatever you need if you ask him again and again shamelessly. *He will do it even though he would not do it* just because you are his friend.

Luke 11:14-28

THEME: Jesus taught people various things about demons.

¹⁴ *One day there was a man there who, because of being controlled by* a demon, was unable to speak. After Jesus *expelled* the demon, the man began to talk. *Most of* the people *there* were amazed. ¹⁵ But some of them said, "It is Beelzebul, the ruler of the demons, who enables *this man* to expel demons!" ¹⁶ Other *people there* asked him to perform a miracle *to prove he had come* from God. They wanted to trap him *into not being able to perform a miracle or into doing something ridiculous.* ¹⁷ But he knew what they were thinking. So he said to them, "If *the people in* one nation fight against each other, *they* will destroy their nation. If *the people in* one house are divided, they will cease to remain as one *family.* ¹⁸ *In the same way*, if Satan *and his demons* were fighting against each other, his rule over them would *certainly* not last! *I say this* because you are saying that I am expelling demons by *the power of* the ruler of *his own demons*! ¹⁹ Furthermore, if *it is true that* Satan enables **me** to expel demons, *is it also true that* your disciples *who* expel demons *do so* by *Satan's* power? *No, certainly not*! So they will show that you *are not thinking logically.* ²⁰ But since it is by the power of God *that I expel demons,* I am showing you *that the power of* God to rule *people's lives* has come to you."

²¹ Then, *to show that by expelling evil spirits he was making it clear that he was much more powerful than Satan, Jesus said,* "When a strong man who has many weapons guards his own house, no one can steal the things in his house. ²² But when someone else who is stronger attacks that man and subdues him, he is able to take away the weapons in which the man trusted. Then he can take from that man's house anything he *wants to.* ²³ *No one can be neutral.* Those who do not acknowledge *that the Holy Spirit enables* me *to expel demons* are opposing me, and those who do not gather *people to become* my *disciples* are causing *those people* to go away *from me*."

²⁴ *Then Jesus said this*: "*Sometimes when* an evil spirit leaves someone, it wanders around in desolate areas seeking *someone in whom it can* rest. If it does not find anyone, it says *to itself,* 'I will return to the person in whom I used to live!' ²⁵ So it goes back and finds that *the Spirit of God is not in control of that person's life. The person's life is like* a house that has been swept clean and everything put in order, *but a house that is empty.* ²⁶ Then *this evil spirit* goes and gets seven other spirits that are *even* more evil, and they *all* enter *that person* and *start* living there. *So, although* that person's condition *was bad* before, it becomes much worse."

²⁷ When Jesus said that, a woman who was listening called out *to him,* "*God is* pleased with the woman who gave birth to you and let you nurse *at her breasts*!" ²⁸ But he replied, "God *is* much more pleased with those who hear his message and obey it!"

Luke 11:29-36

THEME: Jesus rebuked the people for wanting more miracles.

²⁹ When the group of people around *Jesus* got larger, he said, "*Many of* you people who have been observing my ministry are evil. You want *me to perform* a miracle *to prove I have come from God,* but the only miracle that *I* will perform for you is one *like happened to* Jonah. ³⁰ *After Jonah was inside a huge fish for three days, God performed* a miracle *to bring* Jonah *back to life again. Jonah went and testified about that* to the people in *the city of* Nineveh. *God will perform* a similar miracle *for me,* the one who came from heaven. *When you people have seen that miracle, you will believe my message.* ³¹ The queen from *Sheba, far* south *of Israel, who lived long ago,* traveled a long distance to hear *King* Solomon's wisdom. But now *I, a man* who *is much* greater *and wiser* than Solomon, am here, *but you haven't listened to what I have told you.* So at the time when *God* judges *all*

people, the queen from *Sheba* will stand *before him, along* with you people, and will condemn you. [32] The people who lived in Nineveh turned from their sinful ways when Jonah preached to them. But now I, who am greater than Jonah, have come *and preached to you, but you haven't turned from your sinful ways.* So, at the time God judges *all people,* the people who lived in Nineveh will stand there with you and condemn you."

[33] *Then, to show them that they did not need more miracles, they needed only to understand better what he had already told them,* he said to them, "People who light a lamp don't then hide it, or put it under a basket. Instead, they put it on a lampstand so that those who enter *the house* can see *things from* its light. *Similarly, I have not concealed God's truth. I have revealed it to you.* [34] Your eyes are like a lamp for your body, because they enable you to see things. If your eyes are healthy, you are able to see everything well. *In the same way, if you accept my teaching, you will be able to know all God wants you to know.* But if your eyes are bad, you aren't able to see anything. It is like being in darkness. *And in the same way, if you don't accept my teaching, you will not be able to know all the things God wants you to know.* [35] So, *you don't need to see more miracles. You need to think carefully about what I have already* told you, so that the things you have heard from others do not cause you to remain in spiritual darkness. [36] If you *live completely in accordance with God's truth, you will be able to know everything God wants you to know. It will be like* being in a room with a lamp shining brightly, enabling you to see everything clearly."

Luke 11:37-54 (Mt. 23:1-36; Mk. 12:38-40)

THEME: Jesus rebuked the Jewish leaders for only pretending to be good.

[37] While Jesus finished saying those things, a Pharisee invited him to eat a meal with him. So Jesus went to *his house* and ate with him. [38] The Pharisee was surprised when he saw that Jesus did not wash his hands before eating *according to the Pharisees' ritual. The Pharisees washed their hands in a certain way to be cleansed from anything that might have contaminated them. They were afraid that God might reject them if they* might have *touched something unacceptable to God.* [39] The Lord *Jesus* said to Him, "You Pharisees are *concerned about things that are outside your bodies, not with what is in your hearts.* You wash the outside of cups and dishes *before you eat because you think that doing that will make you acceptable to God,* but within yourselves you are very greedy and wicked. [40] You foolish people! *God* is concerned about things that are outside *our bodies,* but he is certainly also concerned about what is in our hearts! [41] Give *money* to those who are poor. *Give according to what you know within* your *hearts that you should give.* Then you *will be surprised, realizing that* you will be acceptable *to God without having to perform all those rituals about washing.*

[42] But there will be terrible punishment for you Pharisees! You give to God a tenth of *all you produce, even* the various herbs you grow, but you don't *remember that you must act* justly *toward others* and love God! It is good to *give a tenth of your income to God,* but you ought to do these other things also! [43] There will be terrible punishment for you Pharisees, because you like *to sit in* the best seats in our meeting places *so people will think highly of you,* and you like people to greet you *respectfully* in the market places. [44] There will be terrible punishment for you, because you are like ground where there is no marker *to indicate there is a* grave *underneath.* People walk there but they can't see *what is rotten down below! In the same way, people who see you don't realize how polluted you are within yourselves.*"

[45] One of those who taught the *Jewish* laws replied, "Teacher, by saying this you are criticizing us *also!*" [46] Jesus said, "It will be terrible also for you who teach the *Jewish* laws! You require people *to obey many rules that are difficult to obey. That is like making them*

carry heavy burdens on their backs. But you yourselves don't obey the laws *that you require others to obey.*[s] ⁴⁷ There will be terrible punishment for you! You decorate the tombs of the prophets whom your ancestors killed, *but you don't live according to what the prophets taught.* ⁴⁸ So you are declaring that you approve of what your ancestors did. They killed the prophets, and you *are not honoring them*! *You just* decorate their tombs! ⁴⁹ So God in his wisdom said, 'I will send prophets and apostles *to you Jews. You* will kill some of them and cause some of them to suffer greatly. ⁵⁰ *As a result, I* will consider that many of you people *who have observed my Son's ministry* will be guilty *of murder, as if you had* killed all the prophets that have been killed, from the time I created the world, ⁵¹ starting from *Adam's son Cain* killing *his brother* Abel and continuing until they killed the prophet Zechariah *in the holy place* between the altar and the temple.' Yes, what I am saying *is true. God* will punish you people who have observed my ministry, you people whom *he* considers to be guilty for *killing* all those prophets! ⁵² There will be terrible punishment for you men who teach the *Jewish* laws, because you have *not let people* know *God's truth*! *It is as though you are* taking away a key *to a house.* You are not going into *the house* yourselves, and you are not letting other people enter it, either."

⁵³ After Jesus finished saying those things, he left there. Then the men who taught the *Jewish* laws and the Pharisees began to act in a very hostile way toward him. They tried to make him say what he thought about many things. ⁵⁴ They kept waiting for him to say something *wrong* for which they could accuse him.

12

Luke 12:1-3

THEME: Jesus warned the people not to be like the Pharisees.

¹ While they were doing that, many thousands of people gathered *around Jesus.* There were so many that they were stepping on each other. Then he said to his disciples, "Beware of *becoming* hypocrites *like* the Pharisees. Their *evil influence spreads to others like* yeast *spreads its influence in dough.* ² People will not be able to keep concealing the things that *they or other* people try to conceal now. *God* will *some day* cause *everyone* to know the things that they hide now. ³ All the things you say in the dark *secretly, some day* will be heard in the daylight. The things you have whispered among yourselves in your rooms will be proclaimed publicly."

Luke 12:4-12

THEME: Jesus told them not to be afraid to tell others of their faith in him.

⁴ "My friends, listen *carefully*! Do not be afraid of people who *are able to* kill you, but after they kill you, there is nothing more they can do *to hurt you*! ⁵ But I will warn you about the one you should truly be afraid of. You should be afraid of *God*, because he not only has *the power to* cause people to die, he has the power to throw them into hell afterward! Yes, he is truly the one you should be afraid of! ⁶ *Think about* the sparrows. *They have so little value* that *you* can buy five of them for only two small coins. But God never forgets one of them! ⁷ You are more valuable *to God* than many sparrows. So don't be afraid *of what people can do to you*! *God* even knows how many hairs there are on each of your heads,

---

s   OR, …But you do not do anything to help those people to obey those rules.

so that if you lose one hair, he knows about it. So nothing bad can happen to you without his knowing it.

[8] I want to tell you also that if people, *without being afraid, are willing to* tell others *that they are my disciples*, I, the one who came from heaven, will acknowledge before *God that they are my disciples. I will do that in the hearing of* God's angels. [9] But if they *are* afraid to say in front of others that they are *my disciples*, I will say, in the hearing of God's angels, that they are not *my disciples*. [10] *I will tell you* also that *God is willing to* forgive people who say bad things about me, the one who came from heaven, but *he* will not forgive anyone who says evil things about what the Holy Spirit *does*. [11] *So* when people ask you in Jewish worship houses and in the presence of rulers and other authorities *about your trusting in me*, don't worry about how you will answer them *when they accuse you*, or worry about what you should say, [12] because the Holy Spirit will tell you at that very time what you should say."

Luke 12:13-21

THEME: Jesus warned them about being greedy.

[13] Then one of the people in the crowd said to *Jesus*, "Teacher, tell my *older* brother to divide my father's property and give me *the part that belongs* to me!" [14] But Jesus replied to him, "Man, no one appointed me to settle *matters when people are* disputing about property!" [15] Then he said to the whole crowd, "Guard yourselves very carefully, so that you do not desire other people's things in any way! No one can make his life secure by obtaining a lot of possessions."

[16] Then he told them this illustration: "There was a certain rich man in whose fields abundant crops grew. [17] *So* he said *to himself*, 'I don't know what to do, because I don't have any place *big enough* to store all my crops!' [18] Then he said to himself, '*I know* what I will do! I will tear down my grain bins and then build larger ones! Then I will store all my wheat and other goods in *the big new bins*. [19] *Then* I will say to myself, "Now I have plenty of things stored up. *They will last* for many years. *So now* I will take life easy. I will eat and drink *all I want to* and be happy *for a long time!*"' [20] But God said to him, 'You foolish *man*! Tonight you will die! Then all *the goods* you have saved up *for yourself* will *belong to someone else, not to* you!'"

[21] *Then Jesus ended this illustration by saying*, "That is what will happen to those who store up goods just for themselves but do not value the things *that God considers* valuable."[t]

Luke 12:22-34

THEME: Jesus told his disciples not to worry about the things they need.

[22] Then *Jesus* said to his disciples, "So I want to tell you this: Don't worry about *things you need* in order to live. Don't worry about *whether you will have enough food* to eat or *enough clothes* to wear. [23] It is important to have sufficient food and clothing, but the way you conduct your lives is much more important. [24] Think about the birds: They don't plant *seeds*, and they don't harvest *crops*. They don't have rooms or buildings in which to store crops. But God provides food for them. *And* **you** are certainly much more valuable than birds. *So God will certainly provide what you need!* [25] There isn't a one of you who can lengthen his lifespan a little bit by worrying about it! [26] So, since you cannot do small things

---

[t] That is the foolishness of everyone who stores up goods just for their own *personal use* but do not *do things for others that will result in* God *rewarding them* richly *in heaven*.

like that, you certainly should not worry about other things *you need to have in order to live*! ²⁷ Think about the way flowers grow *in the fields*. They don't work *to earn money*, and they don't make their own clothes. But I tell you that *even though King* Solomon, *who lived long ago, wore very beautiful clothes*, his clothes were not as beautiful as one of those *flowers*. ²⁸ God makes the flowers beautiful, but they grow in the fields for only a short time. Then *they are cut at the same time the other grass* is cut, and thrown into an oven *to be burned to make heat for baking* bread. *So they really aren't worth very much. But you are very precious to* God, *and he* will *care for you* much more *than he cares for the grass by filling it with beautiful flowers*. So he will certainly provide clothes for you, who *live much longer than the grass. Why do you* trust him so little?²⁹ Don't always be concerned about having enough to eat and drink, and don't be worrying about those things. ³⁰ Those who don't know God are always worried about such things. But your Father *in heaven* knows you need those things, *so you shouldn't worry about them*. ³¹ Instead, be concerned about letting *God* completely direct *your life*. Then *he* will also give you enough of the things *you need*.

³²"*You who are my disciples are like a* small flock of sheep, *and I am like your shepherd*. So you should not be afraid. Your Father *in heaven* wants to let you rule with him *in heaven*. ³³ *So now* sell the things you own. Give *the money you get for those things* to poor people. *If you do that, it will be as though* you are providing for yourselves purses that will not wear out, and *God will give* you a treasure in heaven that will always be safe. There, no thief can come near *to steal it*, and no termite can destroy it. ³⁴ Remember that *the things* you *think are the most* valuable are *the things* you will be constantly concerned about.

Luke 12:35-48

THEME: Jesus told them they should be ready for his return.

³⁵"Be always ready *for doing God's work*, like *people* who have put on their work clothes and are ready, with their lamps burning all night. ³⁶ Be *ready for me to return*, like servants who are waiting for their master to return after being at a wedding feast *for several days*. They are *waiting to* open the door for him and *start working for him again* as soon as he arrives and knocks at the door. ³⁷ If those servants are awake when he returns, *he will* be very pleased with them. I will tell you this: He will put on *the kind of clothes* that servants wear and tell them to sit down, and he will serve them a meal. ³⁸ *Even* if he comes between midnight and sunrise, if he finds his servants *awake and* ready *for him*, he will be very pleased with them. ³⁹ But you must also remember this: If owners of a house knew what time the thief was coming, they *would stay awake and* would not allow the house to be broken into *and their goods to be stolen*. ⁴⁰ In the same way, you must be ready *for me to return*, because I, the one who came from heaven, will come *again* at a time when you don't expect *me to come*."

⁴¹ Peter said, "Lord, are you speaking this illustration *just* for us, or for everyone *else also*?" ⁴² The Lord replied, "*I am saying it for you and for anyone else* who is like a faithful and wise manager in his master's house. His boss appoints him to *supervise affairs in his house* and to give all the *other* servants their food at the proper time. *Then he leaves on a long trip*. ⁴³ If the servant is doing that work when his master returns, *his master* will be very pleased with him. ⁴⁴ I tell you this: His master will appoint him to supervise all of his affairs *permanently*. ⁴⁵ But that servant might say to himself, 'My master has been *away* for a long time, *so he probably will* not return soon *and find out what I am doing*.' *Then he might* start to beat the *other* servants, both male and female ones. *He might also start* to overeat and get drunk. ⁴⁶ *If he does that, and if* his master returns on a day he does not know about, at a time when the servant does not expect him, then his master will punish him severely and put him *in the place where he puts all* those who don't *serve him*

faithfully. [47] Every servant who knows what his master wants him to do but who does not get himself ready and does not do what his master desires will be beaten severely. [48] But every *servant* who did not know *what his master wanted* him to do, and who did things for which he deserved to be punished, will be beaten lightly. *God will treat his people the same way, because he* expects a lot from those people whom *he* has allowed *to understand a lot.* People who entrust things *to others' care* expect those people *to care for those things* very well. Similarly, *God* expects a lot from those people whom he has allowed *to understand a lot.* Furthermore, he expects the most from people to whom he has given the most *ability.*

Luke 12:49-53

THEME: Jesus warned them that they would face opposition even within their own families.

[49] "I came to earth to cause *trials, which will purify you as* fire *purifies metal.* I wish that the time for *God* to purify you were already begun.[u] [50] I must soon suffer greatly. I am feeling great stress, and I will continue feeling distress until my suffering is finished. [51] Do you think that as a result of my coming to earth, people will live together harmoniously? No! I must tell you, *that is not what will happen! Instead, people* will be divided. [52] Because some people in one house *will believe in me and some will not*, they will be divided. Three people in one house *who do not believe in me* will oppose two *who do believe*, or two *who do not believe in me* will oppose three *who do believe.* [53] A man will oppose his son, or a son will oppose his father. A woman will oppose her daughter, or a daughter will oppose her mother. A woman will oppose her daughter-in-law, or a daughter-in-law will oppose her mother-in-law."

Luke 12:54-59

THEME: Jesus told the people they needed to settle their relationship with God before it was too late.

[54] He *also* said to the crowds, "*In this country*, when you see a *dark* cloud forming in the west, you immediately say, 'It is going to rain!', and that's what happens. [55] *In this region,* when the wind blows from the south, you say, 'It is going to be a very hot day!', and that is what happens. [56] You hypocrites! By observing the clouds and the wind, you are able to discern what is happening regarding *the weather*. It is disgusting that you are not able to discern *what God is doing* at this present time!

[57] Each of you ought to determine now what is the right thing for you to do *while you still have time to do it*! [58] *If you don't, God will punish you. It will be like what happens when* someone takes one of you to court to make accusations against you. You should try to settle things with him while you are still on the way to the court. If he forces you to go to the judge, the judge will decide you are guilty and will put you into the hands of the court officer. Then that officer will throw you into prison. [59] I tell you that if you go to prison, you will never get out, *because you will never be able to* pay every bit *of what the judge says you owe. My point is that you ought to settle accounts with God before you die, too.*"

---

[u] OR, I came to earth to cause divisions. I wish that the time when divisions will be caused were already begun.

13

Luke 13:1-5

THEME: Jesus warned the people that God would punish them if they did not turn from their sinful lives.

¹Some people who were *listening to Jesus* at that time told him about some people from *the district of* Galilee *who had gone to Jerusalem.* Pilate, *the Roman governor,* had *ordered soldiers to* kill them while they were offering sacrifices *in the Temple there.* ²Jesus replied to them, "Do you think *that happened to those* people from Galilee *because* they were more sinful than all the other people from Galilee? ³I assure you, *that was* not so! But instead of *being concerned about them, you need to remember that God* will similarly punish you *eternally if you* don't turn from your sinful behavior. ⁴Or, *consider* the eighteen people who died when the tower at Siloam *outside Jerusalem* fell on them. Do you think *that happened to them because* they were more sinful than all the other people who lived in Jerusalem? ⁵I assure you, *that was* not so! But instead, you *need to realize that God* will similarly punish you *eternally* if you don't turn from your sinful behavior!"

Luke 13:6-9

THEME: Jesus warned that he would punish the Jews for not showing their appreciation for God's blessings.

⁶Then Jesus told them this illustration *to show how God would treat the Jews whom he continually blessed, but who did not do things that please him*: "A man planted a fig tree on his farmland. Each year he came to it looking for figs, but there were no figs. ⁷Then he said to the gardener, 'Look *here*! I have been looking for fruit on this fig tree every year for the past three years, but there have been no figs. Cut it down! It is just using up the nutrients in the soil for nothing!' ⁸But the man replied to the owner, 'Sir, let it alone for another year. I will dig around it and put manure around it. ⁹If it bears fruit next year, *we will allow it to keep growing.* If it does not bear fruit next year, you can cut it down.'"

Luke 13:10-17

THEME: Jesus told a synagogue leader he was being hypocritical regarding working on the Sabbath.

¹⁰One Jewish day of rest, *Jesus* was teaching people in one of the Jewish meeting places. ¹¹There was a woman there whom an evil spirit had crippled for eighteen years. She was always bent over; she couldn't stand up straight. ¹²When Jesus saw her, he called her over to him and said to her, "Woman, *I am* freeing you from your illness!" ¹³He put his hands on her. Immediately she stood up straight, and she praised God! ¹⁴But the man in charge of the synagogue was angry because Jesus had healed her on the Jewish day of rest. *He considered that healing was doing work.* So he said to the people, "There are six days *each week* in which *our Jewish* laws permit people to work. *If you need healing*, **those are the days** to come *to the synagogue* and be healed. Don't come on our Jewish day of rest!" ¹⁵Then the Lord replied to him, "You *and your fellow religious leaders are* hypocrites! On our Jewish day of rest, *just like on every other day*, each of you unties his ox or donkey, and then leads it from the food trough to where it can drink water. *That is work, too!* ¹⁶This woman *is more important than an animal; she is a Jew*, descended from Abraham! But Satan has *kept her crippled* for eighteen years, *as though* he had tied her *and not let her escape*! So it is certainly right for me to free her, *even if this* is a Jewish

day of rest!" ¹⁷ After he said that, all the people *there* who opposed him were ashamed. But all the *other* people *there* were happy about all the wonderful things he was doing.

Luke 13:18-21 (Mt. 13:31-33; Mk. 4:30-32)

THEME: Jesus gave two illustrations about God's rule over people's lives.

¹⁸ Then he said, "Let me tell you how *the number of people who let* God rule *their lives will increase*. I will tell you what I can compare it to. ¹⁹ It's like a *tiny* mustard seed that a man planted in his field. It grew until it became *big, like* a tree. It was *so big that* birds built nests in its branches."

²⁰ Then he said, "I will tell you something else, to illustrate how the people who let God rule *their lives can influence their society more and more*. ²¹ It's like *a little bit of* yeast that a woman mixed with about fifty pounds of flour. *That small amount of yeast made* the whole batch of dough swell up."

Luke 13:22-30 (Mt. 7:13-14, 21-23)

THEME: Jesus warns that not all people will go to heaven who think they will.

²² *Jesus* continued traveling *with the disciples* through various towns and villages, on the way to Jerusalem. As they went, he was teaching *the people*. ²³ Someone asked him, "Lord, will there be only a few people who are saved?" He replied to them, "*There will not be many, because* the way *to heaven* is *like* a narrow door. ²⁴ *So*, try hard to enter that narrow doorway, because I tell you that many will try to enter *heaven by some other way*, but they will not be able to get in. ²⁵ *God is like* the owner of a house. *Some day* he will lock the door. Then *some of* you will begin to stand outside the door and knock. You will say, 'Lord, open the door for us!' But he will reply, '*No, because* I don't know you or where you are from!' ²⁶ Then you will say, '*You must have forgotten!* We ate *meals* with you, and you taught *people* in the streets of our *towns*!' ²⁷ But he will say, '*I will tell you again*, I don't know you or where you are from. You *are* wicked people! Get away from here!'" ²⁸ Then Jesus continued by saying, "*From where God will send you*, you will see Abraham and Isaac and Jacob in the distance. All the prophets *who lived long ago will also be there*, in the kingdom where God *is ruling*. But you will be outside, crying and grinding your teeth *because you will have severe pain*! ²⁹ Furthermore, many *non-Jewish* people will *be inside*. There will be ones who have come from *lands to* the north, east, south, and west. They will be feasting in God's kingdom. ³⁰ Think about this: Some people who are not *considered* important *now*, God will make very important *then*, and some people who *are considered* very important *now*, God will make unimportant *then*."

Luke 13:31-35 (Mt. 23:37-39)

THEME: Jesus stated that it was necessary for him as a prophet to die in Jerusalem.

³¹ At that very time, some Pharisees came and said to Jesus, "Leave this area, because *the ruler* Herod *Antipas* wants to kill you!" ³² He replied to them, "Herod is *as cruel as* a fox, *but also as insignificant as a fox. So I don't worry about him. But to show him that no one can harm me until it is the time and place God has determined*, go tell him this *message from me*: 'Listen! I am expelling demons and performing miracles today, and *I will continue* doing it for a short time. After that, I will finish my work. ³³ But I must continue my trip *to Jerusalem* during the coming days, because *they killed many other* prophets there, and *since I am also a prophet*, no other place is appropriate for people to kill *me*.'"

[34] *Then Jesus said*, "O *people of* Jerusalem! You killed the prophets *who lived long ago, and you killed others* whom *God* sent to you! You stoned them *to death*! Many times I wanted to gather you together *to protect you*, like a hen gathers her young chicks under her wings. But you did not want *me to do that*. [35] So listen to this: Your city is going to be abandoned.[v] I will also tell you this: I *will enter your city only once more. After that*, you will not see me until the time *I return and* you say *about me*, 'God is truly pleased with this man who comes with God's authority!'"

14

Luke 14:1-6

THEME: Jesus told the Jewish leaders that they were being hypocritical about helping people on the Sabbath.

[1] One Jewish day of rest, Jesus went to eat at the house of an important Pharisee. Some *men who studied the Jewish* laws and other Pharisees who were there were watching him carefully *to see if he would do something for which they could accuse him.* [2] Unexpectedly, there was a man in front of Jesus whose arms and legs were swollen. [3] Jesus said to them, "Is it permitted in *our* Jewish laws to heal *someone* on our Jewish day of rest, or not?" [4] *They knew their law permitted it, but they thought healing was work, which they thought was wrong to do on the Jewish day of rest.*[w] So they did not reply. Then Jesus put his hands on the man and healed him. Then he told him to go *home.* [5] Then he said to the rest of them, "If you had a son or an ox that fell into a well on our day of rest, would you immediately *work to* pull him out, *or would you let him stay there until the next day*?" [6] *They knew that they would immediately work to pull it out, even on their day of rest, so they could not justly say that it was wrong to heal the man on that day.* Therefore they said nothing.

Luke 14:7-11

THEME: Jesus taught that we should not try to make ourselves seem important.

[7] Jesus noticed that those people who had been invited *to the meal* chose *to sit in* the places where important *people usually sit.* So he gave *this advice* to them: [8]"When someone invites one of you to a wedding feast, don't sit in a place where important people sit. Perhaps the man *giving the feast* has invited a man more important than you. [9] *When that man comes*, the man who invited both of you will come to you and say to you, 'Let this man take your seat!' Then you will have to take the most undesirable seat, and you will be ashamed. [10] Instead, when you are invited *to a feast*, go and sit in the most undesirable seat. Then when the man who invited everyone comes, he will say to you, 'Friend, sit in a better seat!' Then all the people who are eating with you will see that he is honoring you. [11] Also, *remember this*: *God* will humble those who exalt themselves. And *he* will exalt those who humble themselves."

---

[v] OR, So listen to this: *God* will no longer protect your temple.

[w] OR, *They knew their law permitted it, but they did not want to agree with him that it was good to heal on the Sabbath.*

Luke 14:12-14

THEME: Jesus taught that we should share with others who cannot repay us.

[12] *Jesus* also said to *the Pharisee* who had invited him to the meal, "When you invite people to a midday or evening meal, do not invite your friends or your family or your other relatives or your rich neighbors. They can later invite **you** *for a meal.* In that way they will repay you. [13] Instead, when you give a feast, invite poor *people*, crippled *people*, lame *people*, or blind *people*. [14] They will be unable to repay you. But God will bless you! He will repay you *at the time* when *he causes* righteous people to rise from the dead."

Luke 14:15-24

THEME: Jesus taught that many Jews would reject God's invitation to come to him.

[15] One of those who were eating with him heard him say that. He said to Jesus, "God *has truly* blessed *us Jews* who will eat *with the Messiah* when he starts to rule!" [16] But *to show that many Jews whom God had invited would not accept God's invitation*, Jesus replied to him, "A man once *decided to prepare* a large feast. He invited many people to come. [17] When the day for the feast arrived, he sent his servant to tell those whom he had invited, 'Come *now*, because everything is ready!' [18] But *when the servant did that*, all of the people *whom he had invited* began to give excuses for not wanting to come. The first *man the servant went to* said, 'I have just bought a field, and I must go there and see it. Please *ask your master to* forgive me for not coming!' [19] Another person said, 'I have just bought five pair of oxen, and I must go to examine them. Please *ask your master to* forgive me for not coming!' [20] Another person said, 'I have just been married. So I cannot come.' [21] So the servant returned to his master and reported what *everyone had said*. The owner of the house was angry *because the reasons they gave for not c*oming were ridiculous. He said to his servant, 'Go out quickly to the streets and alleys of the city *and find* poor and crippled and blind and lame *people, and bring* **them** here into *my house*!' [22] *After the servant went and did that*, he *came back and* said, 'Sir, I have done what you told me to do, but there is still room *for more people*.' [23] So his master said to him, 'Then go *outside of the city* and search for people along the highways. Search also along the narrow roads with hedges beside them, *where homeless people may be staying*. Strongly urge the people in those places to come to *my house*. I want it to be filled *with people*!'"

[24] *Then Jesus said*, "I tell you this: Very few of the *Jewish* people will enjoy my feast, even though *I* invited them *first to eat it with me when I become king*."

Luke 14:25-33

THEME: Jesus warned that it would be difficult to be his disciple.

[25] Large groups of people were traveling with *Jesus*. He turned and said to them, [26] "If anyone comes to me who loves his father and mother and wife and children and brothers and sisters *more than he loves me*, he cannot be my disciple. Yes, he must even love me more than he loves his own life! [27] *People who are ready to execute a prisoner make him* carry his cross *to the place where others will nail him* on it. Only those who are willing *to allow others to hurt them and disgrace them* like that because of being my disciples, and who are willing to obey my teaching, can be my disciples. [28] *I will illustrate*. If one of you desired to build a tower, he would surely first sit down and determine how much it would cost! Then he would determine whether he had enough money to complete it. [29] *If he did not do that*, if he laid the foundation and wasn't able to finish *the rest of the tower*, everyone who saw it would make fun of him. [30] They would say, 'This man started to build *a tower*, but he wasn't able to finish it!' [31] Or, if a king decided to *send his army to* war

against another king, he would surely first sit down *with his advisors*. They would determine whether *his army*, which had only ten thousand soldiers, could defeat the *other army*, which had twenty thousand soldiers, and was about to attack his *army*. ³²If he *decided* he couldn't *defeat that army*, while the other army was still a long distance away, he would send messengers to ask *the other king*, 'What must I do to have peace with your country?' ³³So, in the same way, if any one of you does not first decide that you are *willing to* give up all that you have, you cannot be my disciple."

Luke 14:34-35

THEME: Jesus warned about losing our usefulness to God.

³⁴*Jesus also said,* "You are like salt, which is useful *to put on food*. But salt certainly cannot be made to taste salty again if it stops tasting salty! ³⁵*If that happens*, it is not good for the soil or even for the manure heap. *People* throw it away. *The same thing will happen to you if you become useless to God*. If you want to understand what I just said, you must consider *carefully* what you have heard!"

15

Luke 15:1-10

THEME: Jesus taught that God is pleased when people turn from their sinful behavior.

¹Many tax collectors and *others whom people considered to be* habitual sinners kept coming to him to listen to him teach. ²The Pharisees and men who taught the *Jewish* laws *who were there* started to grumble, saying, "This man welcomes sinners and he also *defiles himself by eating* with them!" ³So Jesus told them this parable: ⁴"Suppose one of you had a hundred sheep. If one of them were lost, you would certainly leave the ninety-nine sheep in the pasture and go and search for the one lost sheep until you found it. ⁵When you found it, you would lay it on your shoulders and be happy. ⁶When you brought it home, you would call together your friends and neighbors and say to them, 'Be happy with me, because I have found my sheep that was lost!' ⁷I tell you that in the same way *God* will be very happy about each and every sinner who turns from doing evil. He has no *need to* be happy about ninety-nine people who *think they* are righteous and think they do not need to turn from doing evil.

⁸Or, suppose a woman has ten *very valuable* silver coins. If she loses one of them, she will certainly light a lamp and sweep the floor and search carefully until she finds it. ⁹When she finds it, she will call together her friends and neighbors and say, 'Be happy with me, *because* I have found the coin that I lost!' ¹⁰I tell you that in the same way the angels will be happy about *even* one sinner who turns from doing evil."

Luke 15:11-32

THEME: Jesus taught the Jewish leaders that they also ought to be glad when people turn from their sinful ways.

¹¹Then *he told them this parable to compare what the Pharisees and teachers of the Jewish law thought about those who turn from their sinful behavior, with what God thinks about such people*. He said, "A certain man had two sons. ¹²One day the younger son said to his father, 'Father, *I don't want to wait until you die*. Give me right now the share of your property that belongs to me!' So the man divided his property between his two sons.

[13] A few days later, the younger son *sold his share*. He gathered his money and other things together and went to a country far away. There he spent all his money foolishly in reckless living. [14] After he had spent all his money, there was a great famine throughout that country. And soon he did not have enough to eat. [15] So he went to one of the landowners in that area and asked for work. The man sent him to work taking care of the pigs in his field. [16] *Because he was very hungry*, he would have been glad to eat the bean pods that the pigs ate. But no one gave him anything. [17] Finally he thought clearly about what he had done. He said to himself, 'All of my father's hired servants have plenty of food! They have more than they can eat, but here I am, dying from hunger! [18] So I will leave here and go back to my father. I will say to him, 'Father, I have sinned against God and against you. [19] I am no longer worthy of *you* calling me your son. Just hire me to be like one of the other hired servants.' [20] So he left there and went back to his father's house. But while he was still some distance from the house, his father saw him. He felt pity toward him, and ran to his son and embraced him and kissed him *on the cheek*. [21] His son said to him, 'Father, I have sinned against God and against you. I am no longer worthy of *you* calling me your son.' [22] But his father said to his servants, 'Go quickly and bring me the best robe *in the house*! Then put it on my son. Put a ring on his finger *to show that I am honoring him again as my son*! Put sandals on his feet *to show I don't consider him as a slave*! [23] Then bring the fat calf and kill it *and cook it*! We must eat and celebrate, [24] because this is my son! *It is as though* he was dead and is alive again! *It is as though* he was lost and now has been found!' So they did that, and they all began to celebrate.

[25] While all that was happening, his older son was out *working* in the field. When he came near to the house, he heard *the sound of* music and dancing. [26] He called one of the servants and asked what was happening. [27] The servant said to him, 'Your *younger* brother has come *home*! Your father had *us* kill the fat calf *to celebrate,* because your brother has returned safe and sound.' [28] *But* the older brother was angry and refused to enter *the house*. So his father came out and pleaded with him *to come in*. [29] But he replied to his father, 'Listen! For many years I have worked for you like a slave. I always obeyed everything you told me to do. But you never even gave me a young goat, so that I could *kill it and cook it and* celebrate with my friends. [30] But this son of yours spent all the *money he got from* what you gave him. He spent it *to pay for sleeping with* prostitutes! Now he has returned home, *but it is not fair that you have told* your *servants* to kill the fat calf *and cook it* for him!' [31] But his father said to him, 'My son, you have always been with me, and all my property *that I did not give to your brother* has been yours. [32] But *it is as though* your brother was dead and is alive again! *It is as though* he was lost and now he has been found! So it is fitting for us to be happy and celebrate!'"

16

Luke 16:1-13

THEME: Jesus taught that we should handle our money in ways that are pleasing to God.

[1] *Jesus* also said to his disciples, "Once there was a rich man who had a household manager. One day *someone* told him that *the manager* was managing the rich man's money badly. [2] So he summoned *the manager* and said to him, 'It is terrible what they are saying about you! Turn over to me a *written* account of *the funds* you have been managing, because you can no longer be my *household* manager!' [3] Then the manager said to himself, 'My master is going to fire me, so I don't know what to do. I'm not strong enough to *work by* digging ditches, and I'm ashamed to beg *for money*.' [4] *Suddenly he had an idea.* 'I know what I will do, so that people will take me into their houses *and provide for*

me after I lose my job!' ⁵So *one by one* he summoned the people who owed his master money. He asked the first one, 'How much do you owe my master?' ⁶The man replied, 'Eight hundred gallons of olive oil.' The manager said to him, 'Take your bill and sit down and quickly change it to 400 *gallons*!' ⁷He said to another man, 'How much do you owe?' The man replied, 'A thousand bushels of wheat.' The manager said to him, 'Take your bill and change it to eight hundred *bushels*!' *He did similar things for the others who owed his master money.* ⁸When his master *heard what the manager had done*, he admired the dishonest manager for the clever thing he had done. *The truth* is that the ungodly people in this world act more wisely toward other people than godly people act. ⁹*So* I tell you this: Use the money you have *here* on earth to help others so that they will become your friends. Then when *you die and* you can't *take* any money with you, *your friends* will welcome you into a home *in heaven* that will last forever.

¹⁰People who faithfully manage small *matters* will also faithfully manage important *matters*. People who are dishonest in *the way they handle* small *matters* will be dishonest *in the way they handle* important *matters*. ¹¹So if you have not faithfully handled the money *God has given you here* on earth, he will certainly not allow you to possess the true *spiritual* riches *in heaven*! ¹²And if you have not faithfully managed things that belong to other people, *God* will certainly not allow you to receive *treasures in heaven that* would belong to you! ¹³No servant is able to serve two *different* bosses *simultaneously. If he tried to do that*, he would hate one of them and love the other one, or he would be loyal to one of them and despise the other one. *In the same way*, you cannot *devote your life* to worshipping God and *worshipping* money and material goods *at the same time*."

Luke 16:14-18

THEME: Jesus taught that God's laws are permanent.

¹⁴There were some Pharisees *there*. They loved money. When they heard Jesus say that, they ridiculed him. ¹⁵But he said to them, "You try to make other people think you are righteous, but God knows your hearts. *So he will reject you. Keep in mind that many* things that people think highly of, God thinks are detestable.

¹⁶The laws *God gave Moses* and what the prophets *wrote* were *in effect* until John *the Baptizer* came. Since then *I* have been preaching about how God wants to *rule people's lives in a new way*, and many people are *accepting that message and* very eagerly asking God to take control of *their lives. But that does not mean God has set aside the laws he established previously*. ¹⁷All of God's laws, *even those that seem* insignificant, are more permanent than heaven and earth.

¹⁸*For example, since God considers that a marriage lasts until either the husband or the wife dies, he considers that* any man who divorces his wife and marries another woman is committing adultery. *He* also *considers that* any man who marries a woman who has been divorced by her husband is committing adultery."

Luke 16:19-31

THEME: Jesus warned what would happen to those who did not share their possessions with poor people.

¹⁹*Jesus also said*, "Once there was a rich man who wore *expensive* purple and linen *garments*. He ate luxuriously every day. ²⁰And every day a poor man named Lazarus was laid at the gate of the rich man's *house*. Lazarus' body was covered with sores. ²¹He *was so hungry that he* wanted to eat the scraps *of food* that fell from the table where the rich man *ate*. Furthermore, *to make things worse*, dogs came and licked his sores.

²² *Eventually* the poor man died. Then the angels took him to *start feasting* next to his *great ancestor* Abraham. The rich man also died, and his body was buried. ²³ In the place where dead people wait *for God to judge them*, he was suffering great pain. He looked up and saw Abraham in the distance, and he saw Lazarus sitting close to Abraham. ²⁴ So he shouted, 'Father Abraham, I am suffering very much in this fire! So, *please* pity me, and send Lazarus *here* so that he can dip his finger in water *and touch* my tongue to cool it!' ²⁵ But Abraham replied, 'Son, remember that while you were alive *on earth* you enjoyed *many* good things. But Lazarus was miserable. Now *it is fair that* he is happy here, and you are suffering. ²⁶ Besides, there is a huge ravine between you and us. So those who want to go from here to where you are, are not able to. Furthermore, no one can cross from there to where we are.' ²⁷ Then the rich man said, 'In that case, father *Abraham*, I ask you to send *Lazarus* to my father's house. ²⁸ I have five brothers *who live there*. Tell him to warn them *to turn away from their sinful behavior so that* they don't also come to this place, where we are suffering great pain!' ²⁹ But Abraham replied, '*No, I don't need to do that, because your brothers* are able to *go to the Jewish meeting places where the priests* read what Moses and the prophets *wrote*. Let them listen to what Moses and the prophets *wrote*!' ³⁰ But the rich man replied, 'No, father Abraham, *that won't be enough*! But if someone from the dead goes back to them *and warns them*, they will turn from their sinful behavior.' ³¹ *Abraham* said to him, 'No, *that is not true*! If they don't listen to *the words* Moses and the prophets *wrote*, even if someone would rise from among the dead *and go and warn them*, they would not be convinced *that they should turn from their lives of sin.*'"

17

Luke 17:1-4

THEME: Jesus warned about God punishing those who caused others to sin.

¹ *One day Jesus* said to his disciples, "Things that will tempt *people* to sin are certain to happen, but it will be terrible for anyone who causes them to happen! ² Suppose you caused one of these people who *don't believe in me very strongly* to sin. If a huge stone were fastened around your neck and you were thrown into the sea, *that would be considered a severe punishment, but God will punish* you even more severely *if you cause someone to sin*! ³ Be careful *how you act*. If you *know about* a fellow believer who sins, you should rebuke him. If he *says that he* is sorry for having sinned *and asks you to forgive him*, forgive him. ⁴ Even if he sins against you seven times in one day, if he comes to you each time and says 'I am sorry for what I did', you must keep forgiving him."

Luke 17:5-6

THEME: Jesus taught them what big things they could accomplish if they had true faith.

⁵ *One day* the apostles said to the Lord, "Help us to trust *in God*ˣ more strongly!" ⁶ The Lord replied, "Mustard *seeds are very small, but in this area they* grow and produce large plants. *In the same way*, if your faith grows until you truly believe that God *will do what you ask him to, you will be able to accomplish big things.* You could *even* say to this mulberry tree, 'Pull yourself out *with your roots* and plant yourself in the sea!' and it would obey you!"

ˣ OR, …trust *in you*…

Luke 17:7-10

THEME: Jesus taught that we should serve God faithfully without expecting to be thanked.

[7] *Jesus also said*, "Suppose one of you had a servant who was plowing *your fields* or taking care of your sheep. After he comes into the house from the field, you would not say, 'Sit down and eat immediately!' [8] No! Instead, you would say to him, 'Put on your apron and prepare a meal for me! Then serve it to me so I can eat and drink it! Afterwards you can eat and drink.' [9] You will not *need to* thank your servant for doing the work that you had told him to do! [10] In the same way, when you have done everything *God* has told you to do, you should say, 'We are not worthy *of being thanked*. We are only God's servants. We have only done the things he told us to do.'"

Luke 17:11-19

THEME: Jesus healed ten lepers, but only a non-Jewish one thanked him.

[11] As *Jesus and his disciples* were walking along the road to Jerusalem, they were going through *the region* between *the districts of* Samaria and Galilee. [12] As they entered one village, ten lepers came near the road. *Because lepers were not permitted to come near other people*, they stood at some distance [13] and called out, "Jesus, Master, pity us *and heal us*!" [14] When he saw them, he said *to them*, "*Each of you* should go and show yourself to the priest *in your home area so he can see if you are healed*." As they were going *there*, they were healed. [15] Then one of them, when he saw that he was healed, turned back, praising God loudly. [16] He *came to Jesus*, prostrated himself at Jesus' feet, and thanked him. This man was a Samaritan, *not a Jew*. [17] Then Jesus said, "*I* healed ten *lepers*! Why did the other nine not come back? [18] I am disappointed that this non-Jewish man was the only one who returned to thank God; none of the others came back to me!" [19] Then he said to the man, "Get up and continue on your journey. *God has saved you and* healed you because you trusted *in me*."

Luke 17:20-21

THEME: Jesus taught that God's rule is within our lives.

[20] *One day* some Pharisees asked *Jesus*, "When is God *going* to rule as king?" He replied, "God's rule is not something people will be able to see with their eyes. [21] And people will not be able to say, 'Look! He is *ruling* here!' or 'He is *ruling* there!' because, *contrary to what you think*, God's ruling is within people's hearts."[y]

Luke 17:22-37

THEME: Jesus told his disciples that without warning he would return and judge people.

[22] *Jesus* said to his disciples, "There will be a time when you will want to see me, the one who came from heaven, *ruling powerfully*. But you will not see that. [23] *Some* people will say to you, 'Look, *the Messiah* is over there!' or *they will say* 'Look, he is here!' When they say that, don't believe them. Don't follow them *to go see the Messiah*. [24] Because when the lightning flashes and lights up the sky from one side to the other, *everyone can see it. In the same way* at the time when *I*, the one who came from heaven, come back again, *everyone will see me*. [25] But before that happens, I must *endure* great suffering.[z] And

---

[y] OR, …because God is already ruling among you, *contrary to what you think*.

[z] OR, But before that happens, I must suffer in many ways.

people will reject me, *even though* they *have observed me doing good for people.* ²⁶ But when I, the one who came from heaven, *come again, life* will be just like it was when Noah *lived.* ²⁷ *At that time* people ate and drank *as usual*, and they got married *as usual*, up until the day Noah *and his family* entered the big boat. And then the flood came and destroyed all those *who were not in the boat.* ²⁸ In the same way, when Lot *lived in Sodom, people there* ate and drank *as usual*. They bought things and they sold things. They planted *crops* and they built *houses as usual.* ²⁹ But on the day Lot *and his family* left Sodom, fire and *burning* sulfur came down from the sky and destroyed all those *who stayed in the city.* ³⁰ It will be the same way when I, the one who came from heaven, return to earth. ³¹ On that day, those who are outside their houses, with all the things they own inside *the house*, must not go *inside* to take them away, *because there won't be enough time to do that.* Similarly, those who are working in a field must not turn back *to get anything*; *they must flee quickly.* ³² Remember Lot's wife! *Because she turned back and wanted to get some of her things from Sodom, she died immediately and became a pillar of salt.* ³³ Anyone who wants to hold onto his life *and his possessions* will not *receive eternal* life. But anyone who is *willing to* die *for my sake* will live *eternally.* ³⁴ I will tell you this: On the night *when I return*, there will be two people *sleeping* in one bed. The one *who believes in me* will be taken *to heaven,* and the other one will be left *behind and punished.* ³⁵ Two women will be grinding grain together; one will be taken and the other left *behind.*"ᵃᵃ ³⁷ *His disciples* said to him, "Lord, where *will this happen*?" He replied to them, "Wherever there is an animal carcass, the vultures will gather *to eat it. Similarly, wherever there are people who are spiritually dead, God will punish them.*"

18

Luke 18:1-8

THEME: Jesus taught about continuing to believe that God will answer prayer.

¹ *Jesus* told *his disciples* a parable to teach them that they always ought to pray confidently and not be discouraged *if God does not immediately answer their prayers.* ² He said, "In a certain city there was a judge who did not revere God, and did not care about people, either. ³ There was a widow in that city who kept coming to him, saying, 'Please make a fair decision in *the dispute between me and* the man who is opposing me *in court!*' ⁴ For a long time the judge refused *to help her.* But later he said to himself, 'I don't revere God and I don't care about people, ⁵ but this widow keeps bothering me! So I will *settle her case and show* what she is *asking for* is right. *If I don't do that*, she will exhaust me by continually coming to me!'" ⁶ Then the Lord *Jesus* said, "*Even though* the judge was not a righteous man, think carefully about what he said! ⁷ *In the same way*, God will certainly vindicate you. He will do this for you whom he has chosen. *He will do this for you* who pray earnestly to him night and day, asking *for his help.* He may delay *helping you,* ⁸ but I tell you, *some day* he will show that what you did was right, and he will do it quickly. But when I, the one who came from heaven, return to earth, there may not be *many people who will still* be trusting *that I will vindicate them.*"ᵇᵇ

ᵃᵃ Some Greek manuscripts add verse. 36, "Two men will be working in a field; God will take one and leave the other behind."

ᵇᵇ OR, …there may not be *many people who will still* be trusting *in me, the one who came from heaven.*

Luke 18:9-14

THEME: Jesus taught about not thinking we are better than others in God's sight.

[9] *Jesus* also told a parable *to warn* people who mistakenly thought that they were doing things that made them acceptable to God and who despised other people. [10] *He said this*: "Two men went up to the Temple *in Jerusalem* to pray. One was a Pharisee. The other was a tax collector. [11] The Pharisee stood and prayed silently, 'God, I thank you that I am not like other men. *Some* extort money *from others*; some treat others unjustly; some commit adultery. *I don't do such things. And I am certainly not* like this tax collector *who cheats people*! [12] *Our law says that we should* abstain from food *once a week*, but I do more than that! I fast twice a week! I give *you* ten percent of all I earn.' [13] But the tax collector stood far *from the other people in the Temple courtyard because he felt very unworthy*. He would not even look up toward heaven. Instead, he beat on his chest *to show he was sorry for his sins*. He said, 'God, I am a sinner; be merciful to me *and forgive me*!'" [14] *Then Jesus said*, "I tell you that as the tax collector went home, the record of his sins was erased. *Remember this*: *God* will humble all those who exalt themselves, but *he* will exalt those who humble themselves."

Luke 18:15-17

THEME: Jesus taught about accepting God's rule in our lives as easily as little children do.

[15] *One day when many people were coming to Jesus*, they were also bringing small children. They wanted him to put his hands on *the children and bless them*. When the disciples saw that, they rebuked *those who were bringing them*. [16] But Jesus called the children *to come to him*. He said, "Let the children come to me, and don't stop them! It is people who are *humble and trusting* like they are who can experience God ruling *their lives*. [17] Note this: Those who do not *trustingly* allow God to direct *their lives,* as children *do*, will not enter the place where God rules."

Luke 18:18-30 (Mt. 19:16-29; Mk. 10:17-30)

THEME: Jesus taught that rich people do not easily let God rule their lives.

[18] A *Jewish* leader asked *Jesus*, "Good teacher, what shall I do in order to have eternal life?" [19] Jesus said to him, "Only God is good! No one *else* is good! So you should consider carefully what *you are implying by* calling me good! [cc] [20] *But to answer your question*, you know the commandments *God gave Moses. He commanded such things as* 'do not commit adultery, do not commit murder*, do not steal, do not testify falsely *about what you have seen or heard*, honor your father and mother.'" [21] The man said, "I have obeyed **all those** commandments ever since I was young! *So is there something else I haven't done?*" [22] When Jesus heard *him say* that, he replied to him, "*Yes,* there is one thing you haven't *done* yet. Sell all your possessions. Then give *the money* to poor people. *The result will be that* you will have *spiritual* riches in heaven. Then come and be my disciple!" [23] The man went away sad when he heard that, because he was very rich *and he did not want to give everything away.* [24] Jesus looked at him *as the man left*, and he said, "It is very difficult for those who are wealthy *to decide* to let God rule their *lives.* [25] *You would say* it is impossible for a camel to go through the eye of a needle. It is *almost* as difficult for rich people *to decide* to let God rule their *lives.*" [26] *The Jews thought that God favored rich people, so they thought that if God did not save rich people, he wouldn't save others,*

[cc] OR, …You should consider carefully *your words, since you are implying that I am God by* calling me good!

either. So *one of the disciples* who heard him say that replied, "If that is so, it is unlikely that anyone will be saved!" [27]But he said, "*Yes*, it is impossible for people *to save themselves. But God can save them, because* God can do anything!" [28]Then Peter said, "*You know that we have left our homes* and have become your disciples. *So what about us?*"[dd] [29]He said to them, "Keep this in mind: Those who have left *their* homes, *their* wives, *their* brothers, *their* parents, *their* children, *or any other family members, to tell others* about how God wants to rule *people's lives,* [30]will receive in this life many times as much *as they left*. And in the future age they will have eternal life."

Luke 18:31-34 (Mt. 20:17-19; Mk. 10:32-34)

THEME: Jesus again predicted his death and resurrection.

[31]*Jesus* took the twelve *disciples* to a place by themselves and said to them, "Listen carefully! We are *now* going up to Jerusalem. *While we are there,* everything that the prophets have written about *me, the one who came from heaven,* will be fulfilled. [32]*My enemies* will put me into the hands of non-Jews. *The non-Jews* will make fun of me and mistreat me and spit on me. [33]They will whip me, and *then* they will kill me. But on the third day *after that* I will become alive again." [34]But *the disciples* did not understand any of those things that *he said. Something* prevented them from understanding the meaning of what *he* was telling *them*.

Luke 18:35-43

THEME: Jesus healed a blind man.

[35]As *Jesus and his disciples* came near *the town of* Jericho, a blind man was sitting beside the road. *He was* begging *for money*. [36]When he heard the crowd passing by, he asked someone, "What is happening?" [37]They told him, "Jesus, *the man* from Nazareth, is passing by." [38]He shouted, "Jesus, *you who are the Messiah* descended from *King* David, take pity on me!" [39]Those who were *walking* at the front *of the crowd* scolded him *and* told him to be quiet. But he shouted even louder, "You who are the *Messiah* descended from *King* David, take pity on me!" [40]Jesus stopped and told *people* to bring the man to him. When *the blind man* came near, Jesus asked him, [41]"What do you want me to do for you?" He replied, "Lord, enable me to see *again*!" [42]Jesus said to him, "*Then* see! Because you have trusted *in me, I* have healed you!" [43]Immediately he was able to see. And he went with *Jesus*, praising God. And when all the people *who were going with him* saw it, they also praised God.

19

Luke 19:1-10

THEME: Zacchaeus changed his way of life after talking with Jesus.

[1]They entered Jericho and were going through the town. [2]There was a man *there* named Zacchaeus. He was a chief tax collector, who was rich. [3]He tried to see Jesus, but he was very short and there was a big crowd of people *near Jesus*. So he wasn't able to see him. [4]So he ran further ahead *along the road* Jesus was walking on. He climbed a sycamore-fig tree to see Jesus. [5]When Jesus got there, he looked up and said to him, "Zacchaeus,

---

[dd] OR, *…So will God accept us?*

come down quickly, because *God wants* me to go *with you* to your house and stay there *tonight*!" ⁶So he came down quickly. *He took Jesus to his house* and welcomed him joyfully. ⁷The people *who saw Jesus go there* grumbled saying, "He has gone to be the guest of a man who is a sinner!" ⁸Then Zacchaeus stood up *while they were eating* and said to the Lord *Jesus,* "Lord, I want you to know that I am going to give half of what I own to poor people. And as for the people I have cheated, I will pay them back four times the amount *I have gotten from them by cheating.*" ⁹Jesus said to him, "Today *God* has forgiven *you and the other people in* this house, because you also *have shown you have trusted in God as* your ancestor Abraham *did.* ¹⁰Remember this: *I,* the one who came from heaven, came to seek and save *people like you* who have *gone astray from God, just like a shepherd who searches for his* lost *sheep.*"

Luke 19:11-27 (Mt. 25:14-30)

THEME: Jesus taught about being willing to take risks in using what he has given us.

¹¹They were coming near to Jerusalem, and the people *going with Jesus* who heard him say those things thought that as soon as *he got to Jerusalem* he would become their king. ¹²*So* he told them this parable: "A prince prepared to go a distant country to be made a king *by the Emperor. He intended* to return later. ¹³*Before he left*, he summoned ten of his servants and gave each of them a coin worth three months' wages. He said to them, 'Do business with these coins until I return!' *Then he left.* ¹⁴But *many of* his fellow-citizens hated him. So they sent some messengers after him to tell *the Emperor*, 'We don't want this man to be our king!' ¹⁵But *the Emperor* made him king anyway. *Later* the *new king* returned. Then he gave an order to summon the servants to whom he had given the coins. He wanted to know how much they had gained by doing business with the coins. ¹⁶The first man came *to him* and said, 'Sir, with your one coin *I* have earned ten more *coins*!' ¹⁷He said to this man, '*You are a* good servant! *You have* done *very* well! Because you have *handled* faithfully a small amount *of money, I will give you* authority *to rule* ten cities.' ¹⁸Then the second servant came and said, 'Sir, with your one coin *I* have earned five more *coins*!' ¹⁹He said to that servant similarly, '*Good! I will give you authority to rule* five cities.' ²⁰Then another servant came. He said, 'Sir, here is your coin. I wrapped it in a napkin and put it away, *so that nothing would happen to it.* ²¹I did that *because* I was afraid *of what you would do to me if the business failed. I know* you are a man who does not do foolish things with your money. You *even* take *from others money* that does not really belong to you*, like a farmer who* harvests grain *from another man's field* where he did not *even* do the planting.' ²²He said to that servant, 'You wicked servant! I will condemn you by the very words you *have just spoken*! You know that I don't do foolish things with my money. *You said* I *even* take *from others money* that does not really belong to me, *like a farmer who* harvests grain *from another man's field* where he did not *even* do the planting. ²³So you should at least have given my money to money lenders! Then when I returned I could have collected that amount plus the interest *it would have earned*!' ²⁴Then *the king* said to those who were standing near, 'Take the coin from him and give it to *the servant* who has ten coins!' ²⁵They protested, 'But Sir, he already has ten *coins*!' ²⁶*But the king said*, 'I tell you this: To those who *use well what* they have *received*, more will be given. But from those who *do* not *use well what they have received*, even what they *already* have will be taken away. ²⁷Now, *as for* those enemies of mine who did not want me to rule over them, bring them here and execute them while I am watching!'"

Luke 19:28-40 (Mt. 21:1-9; Mk. 11:1-10; Jn. 12:12-15)

THEME: Jesus entered Jerusalem humbly, but like a king.

²⁸ After *Jesus* said those things, he *continued on the road* up to Jerusalem, going ahead of the disciples. ²⁹ When they got near *the villages of* Bethphage and Bethany, near the hill called Olive *Tree* Hill, ³⁰ he said to two of *his* disciples, "Go to the village just ahead *of you.* As you enter *it* you will see tied up a young animal that no one has ever ridden. Untie it and bring it *to me.* ³¹ If anyone asks you, 'Why are you untying it?' say *to him*, 'The Lord needs it.'" ³² *So* the *two disciples* went *to the village* and found the *animal* just as he had told them. ³³ As they were untying it, its owners said to them, "Why are you two untying that young animal?" ³⁴ They replied, "The Lord needs it." *So the owners said they could take it.* ³⁵ The *two disciples* brought *the animal* to Jesus. They threw their cloaks on the animal's back *for him to sit on,* and helped Jesus get on it. ³⁶ Then, as he rode along, *others* spread their cloaks on the road *to honor him.* ³⁷ As they came near *Jerusalem*, on the road that descends from Olive *Tree* Hill, the whole crowd of his disciples began to rejoice and praise God loudly for all the great miracles they had seen *Jesus do.* ³⁸ They were saying, "May the Lord *God* bless our king who comes representing him! May there be peace *between God* in heaven *and us his people*! May *everyone* praise God!" ³⁹ Some of the Pharisees who were in the crowd said to him, "Teacher, rebuke your disciples *for saying things like that*!" ⁴⁰ He replied, "I tell you this: If these people would be silent, the stones themselves would shout *to praise me*!"

Luke 19:41-44

THEME: Jesus prophesied that Jerusalem would be destroyed.

⁴¹ When *Jesus* came near Jerusalem and saw the city, he cried about *its people.* ⁴² He said, "*My disciples know what they need to do* to have peace *with God*; I wish that even today *the rest of* you people knew it. But now you are unable to know it. ⁴³ I want you to know this: Soon *your enemies* will come and will set up a barricade around your *city.* They will surround *the city* and attack *it* on all sides. ⁴⁴ They will *break through* the walls *and* destroy everything. They will smash you and your children. *When they finish destroying everything*, there will not be one stone left on top of another. *All this will happen* because you did not recognize the *Messiah* when he came to *save* you!"

Luke 19:45-48

THEME: Jesus expelled the merchants from the Temple courtyard and taught there.

⁴⁵ *Jesus entered Jerusalem and* went into the Temple *courtyard.* He saw in that place those who were selling *things,* ⁴⁶ and he began to chase them out. He said to them, "It is written *in the Scriptures that God said,* '*I want* my house to be a place where people pray'; but **you** bandits have made it a cave where you can *hide*!"

⁴⁷ Each day *during that week Jesus* was teaching people in the Temple *courtyard.* The chief priests and the men who taught the *Jewish* laws and *other Jewish* leaders tried to find a way to kill him. ⁴⁸ But they did not find any way to do it, because all the people there listened eagerly to him *and would have resisted them if they had tried to hurt him.*

20

Luke 20:1-8

THEME: Jesus refused to answer their question about his authority.

¹One day *during that week Jesus* was teaching the people in the Temple *courtyard* and telling them *God's* good message. As he was doing that, the chief priests, the men who taught the *Jewish* laws, and *the* elders came to him. ²They said to him, "Tell us, by what authority are you doing these things? Who authorized you to do things *like you did here yesterday*?" ³He replied, "I will also ask you a question. Tell me, ⁴where did John *the Baptizer* get *his authority to* baptize *those who came to him*? *Did he get it* from God or from people?" ⁵They discussed this among themselves. They said, "*If we say, 'It was* from God,' he will say to us, '*Then* why did you not believe *John's message*?' ⁶But if we say, 'It was *from* people,' the people *here* will stone us *to death*, because they *all* believe that John was a prophet *from God*." ⁷So they replied, "We don't know where *John got his authority*." ⁸Then Jesus said to them, "*Because you did not answer my question*, I will not tell you who authorized me to do those things *here yesterday*."

Luke 20:9-18

THEME: Jesus told a parable about how God would punish those who reject him.

⁹Then Jesus told the people this parable *to illustrate what God would do to the Jews who rejected the former prophets and himself*: "A *certain* man planted a vineyard. He rented the vineyard to some men *to care for it and to give him some of the grapes in return*. Then he went to another country and stayed there several years. ¹⁰When the time came to harvest the grapes, he sent a servant to the renters. He expected that they would give him some of the grapes that the vineyard had produced. But they beat the servant and did not give him any grapes. They *just* sent him away. ¹¹*Later, the owner* sent another servant. But they beat him and mistreated him *also*. They sent him away without giving him any grapes. ¹²*Still later, the owner* sent yet another servant. That one they wounded and threw him out *of the vineyard*. ¹³So the owner of the vineyard said to himself, 'I don't know what to do *about those men*!' *Then he had an idea. He said to himself*, 'I will send my son, *whom I* love *very much*. Perhaps they will respect him *and give him my share of the grapes*.' ¹⁴*So he sent his son*, but when the renters saw him *coming*, they said to each other, 'Here *comes* the man who will *some day* inherit *the vineyard*! Let's kill him so that this vineyard will be ours!' ¹⁵So they dragged him outside the vineyard, and they killed him.

Now, *do you know* what the owner of the vineyard will do to those men who were taking care of *the* vineyard? ¹⁶He will come and kill those renters! Then he will rent the vineyard to others." When they heard that, they said, "*We would* not do anything like that!" ¹⁷But Jesus looked directly at them and said, "You can say that, *but think about* the meaning of these words that are written *in the Scriptures*:

The builders rejected a certain stone. *But others put* that same stone *in its proper place, and it* has become the most important stone in the building.

¹⁸*That stone represents me, the Messiah*, and those who reject me are *like people who fall on this stone*. This stone will break to pieces everyone who falls on it, and it will crush anyone on whom it falls."

Luke 20:19-26

THEME: Jesus foiled their attempts to trap him when they asked a question about paying taxes.

[19] The chief priests and the men who taught the *Jewish* laws realized that he was accusing them when he told the parable *about what the wicked renters did.* So they immediately tried to find a way to seize him, but *they did not seize him, because* they were afraid of *what* the people *there would do if they did that.* [20] So they watched him carefully. They also hired spies who pretended to be sincere. *But* they really wanted to get him to say something for *which they could accuse* him. They wanted to be able to turn him over to the authority of the governor *of the province. But they also knew the Jews were disgusted with having to pay taxes to the government.* [21] So they asked him, "Teacher, we know you speak and teach what is right. You tell the truth even if important people don't like it. You teach truthfully what God wants us to do. [22] *So tell us what you think about this matter:* Is it right that we pay taxes to the Roman government, or not?" [23] But he knew they were trying to trick him *to get him into trouble, either with the Jews, who hated to pay those taxes, or with the Roman government.* So he said to them, [24] "Show me a *Roman* coin. *Then tell me* whose picture *they have* put on it, and *whose* name is on it." They *showed him a coin and* said, "It has the picture and name of Caesar, *the head of the Roman government.*" [25] He said to them, "In that case, give to the government what they *require,* and give to God what he *requires.*" [26] While the people were there, the *spies* were unable to find fault with him for what he said. They were amazed at his answer. So they said nothing.

Luke 20:27-40

THEME: Jesus foiled their attempt to trap him with a question they asked him about the resurrection.

[27] Some Sadducees came to *Jesus.* They are a Jewish sect who do not believe that people will become alive again after they die. [28] They *wanted to* ask *Jesus* a question *in order to discredit the idea that dead people will live again.* They said *to him,* "Teacher, Moses wrote for us *Jews,* that if a man dies who had a wife but had no children, his brother should marry the *dead man's* widow so that she can have a child by him. People *will consider that the child is* the descendant of the man *who died, and in that way the dead man will have descendants.* [29] Well, there were seven boys in one family. The oldest one married a woman, but he and his wife did not have any children. Later he died. [30] The second *brother followed this law and married the widow, but the same thing happened to him.* [31] Then the third *brother* married her, *but the same thing happened again.* All seven *brothers, one by one, married that woman, but* they had no children, and *one by one* they died. [32] Afterwards, the woman died, too. [33] Therefore, *if it is true that there will be a time* when people are raised from the dead, whose wife *do you think that woman* will be *then? Keep in mind that* she was married to all seven brothers!" [34] Jesus replied to them, "Men who live here in this world take wives, or *their parents* choose wives *for them.* [35] But those whom God considers worthy of being in heaven after they become alive again will not be married. [36] *You need to know also that* they cannot die any more, because they will be *immortal* like angels. *The fact that God has caused* them to be alive again *will show* that they are God's children. [37] But *as to people* becoming alive again after they die, Moses wrote something about that. In the place where *he wrote about* the *burning* bush, he mentions the Lord as being the God whom Abraham *worships* and the God whom Isaac *worships* and the God whom Jacob *worships.* [38] It is not dead people who worship God. It is living people who worship him. *Abraham, Isaac and Jacob died long before Moses lived, but God said that they were still worshiping him, so we know their spirits were still alive!* All *people* who are alive *again after they die continue to live to honor him!*"

³⁹ Some of the men who taught the *Jewish* laws replied, "Teacher, you have given a very good answer!" ⁴⁰ After that, they no longer dared to ask him any more questions *like that to try to trap him.*

Luke 20:41-44 (Mt. 22:41-45; Mk. 12:35-37)

THEME: Jesus showed them that the Messiah must be greater than King David.

⁴¹ *Later* he said to them, "*I will prove to you that* people *are wrong who* say the Messiah is *merely* a descendant of *King* David. ⁴² David himself wrote in the book of Psalms *about the Messiah*,

God said to my Lord,

Sit *here beside me* on my right, *where I will highly honor you.*

⁴³ *Sit here* while I completely defeat your enemies.'

⁴⁴ King David calls *the Messiah* 'my Lord'! So *the Messiah* cannot be *just someone* descended from David. *He must be much greater than David, isn't that right?*"

Luke 20:45-47 (Mt. 23:1-36; Mk. 12:38-40)

THEME: Jesus warned them not to show off like the teachers of the Jewish law did.

⁴⁵ While all the *other* people were listening, *Jesus* said to his disciples, ⁴⁶"Beware that *you don't act like* the men who teach our *Jewish* laws. They like to put on long robes and walk around *to show people how important they are. They* also like *people to* greet them *respectfully* in the market places. They like *to sit in* the most important places in our Jewish meeting places. At dinner parties *they like to sit in* the seats where the most honored people sit. ⁴⁷ They swindle the houses *and property* of widows. *Then* they pretend they are good, as they pray *long* prayers *publicly. God* will *certainly* punish them very severely."

21

Luke 21:1-4

THEME: Jesus taught that God commends people who give to him sacrificially.

¹ *Jesus* looked up *from where he was sitting* and saw rich people putting their gifts into the *offering* boxes *in the Temple courtyard.* ² He also saw a poor widow putting in two *small* copper coins. ³⁻⁴ He said *to his disciples*, "The truth is that these rich people have a lot of money, *but* they gave *only a small part of it.* But this woman, who is very poor, has put in all the money she had to pay for the things she needs! So *God considers that* this poor widow has put more money into the box than all the others."

Luke 21:5-19

THEME: Jesus warned them about the terrible things that will happen before he returns.

⁵ Some *of Jesus' disciples* talked about the Temple. *They commented about* the beautiful stones *used in building the Temple* and the other decorations that *people* had given, decorations *that were on the walls.* But he said, ⁶"*I want to tell you something about* these things you are looking at. *They will be destroyed completely.* Every stone *in these buildings* will be thrown down. Not one stone will be left on top of another."

[7] *Later* they asked him, "Teacher, when will that happen? What will happen to indicate that the things *you just told us* are about to take place?" [8] He said, "*All I will say is*, be sure that you aren't deceived *about these things*! Many *people* will come and say that they have my authority. They will say, 'I am *the Messiah*!' They will also *say* 'It is now the time *for God to rule*!' Do not follow them *to become their disciples*! [9] Also, whenever you hear about wars and riots, don't be terrified. Keep in mind that *God has said* those things must happen. But *when they happen*, it will not mean that *the world* will end right away!"

[10] Then he said to them, "*Groups in various* countries will fight each other, and *various* governments *will also fight* against each other. [11] There will be big earthquakes, and in various places there will be famines and plagues. Terrifying things will occur. There will also be unusual things happening in the sky. [12] But before all these things happen, you will be persecuted and arrested. *Some of* you will be put *on trial* in the places where you gather to worship, and *you will be thrown* into prison. You will be put on trial in front of high government authorities because of being my *disciples*. [13] That will be a time for you to tell *them about me*. [14] So determine within yourselves not to be thinking beforehand what you will say to defend yourselves, [15] because I will give you wisdom *to know* what to say. As a result, none of your enemies will be able to oppose what you say or refute you. [16] *And there will also be other evil things that will happen*: Even your parents and brothers and *other* relatives and friends *who do not believe in me* will betray you, and some of you will be killed. [17] *In general,* most people will hate you because *you believe in* me. [18] But your souls will be absolutely safe. [19] By enduring *all these things people will do to you*, you will preserve your *eternal* life.

Luke 21:20-24

THEME: Jesus predicted that Jerusalem would be destroyed.

[20] "But when you see that Jerusalem has been surrounded by the armies of *your enemies*, you will know that it is the time for them to completely destroy *this city*. [21] At that time those *of you* who are in Judea must flee to the *higher* hills. Those who are in this city must leave *quickly*. Those who are in the nearby countryside must not go back into the city *to get any of their possessions before they flee*. [22] *You must obey what I tell you* because, in order for all the things that are written *in Scripture* to be fulfilled, *God* will very severely punish *the people who stay in this city*. [23] *I feel* very sorry for women *in this city* who will be pregnant, and women who will be nursing *their babies* in those days, *because it will be very difficult for them to run away*! *I feel sorry because* the people in this *land* will suffer greatly *when God punishes them*. [24] Many of them will be killed with swords. *Others will be captured* and taken to *other* countries. Non-Jewish people will trample over Jerusalem until the time *that God has determined for them to rule the city* is ended.

Luke 21:25-28

THEME: Jesus told them about the frightening things that will happen before he returns.

[25] "There will also be strange things that will *happen to* the sun, the moon, and the stars. In *many* nations on the earth, *people* will be very frightened, and they will be anxious *when they hear* the ocean roaring and *see the huge* waves. [26] People will faint from fear as they wait for what will happen in the world. *They will be afraid* because the powerful *objects* in the sky will be shaken. [27] Then they will see *me*, the one who came from heaven, coming in a cloud with power and great glory. [28] So when these things *I have just described* begin to happen, stand up *straight and* be brave, because it will be close to the time when *God* will free you *from all suffering*."

Luke 21:29-33

THEME: Jesus taught them how to know when his return was near.

[29] *Then* he told them this parable: "Think about the fig tree, and all the *other* trees. [30] As soon as you see their leaves starting to sprout, you know that summer is near. [31] In the same way, when you see these things *I have just described* happening, **you** will know that it is almost time for God to truly rule as king. [32] Keep this in mind: All the things *I have just described* will happen before all the people who have observed the things that I have done have died. [33] *You can be certain that these things* I have told *you* about will happen. That they will happen is more *certain* than that the earth and sky will continue to exist.

Luke 21:34-38

THEME: Jesus taught them how to be ready for his return.

[34]"But be on guard. Don't be getting drunk with carousing, or let worries *concerning* your lives distract you. *If you do those things, you might be suddenly surprised by my return*, like a trap *suddenly catches an animal in it.* [35] *Keep in mind that my return will surprise* everyone all over the earth. [36] So be ready at all times. Pray that you will be able to endure without being afraid of all these *difficult* things that will happen, so that you will then stand *confidently* before me, the one who came from heaven."

[37] Each day *during that week Jesus* taught the people in the Temple *courtyard in Jerusalem.* But at night he *and his disciples* left *the city* and stayed on Olive *Tree* Hill. [38] Early *each* morning many people came to the Temple *courtyard* to listen to him.

22

Luke 22:1-6

THEME: Judas agreed to put Jesus into his enemies' hands.

[1] It was now almost time to celebrate the festival of Unleavened Bread, which *began with* the Passover feast. [2] The chief priests and the men who taught the *Jewish* laws were seeking a way to kill Jesus. *But they wanted to do it secretly*, because they were afraid that if they did not do it secretly, the people *might riot.*

[3] Then *even though* Judas, who was called *the man from the village of* Kerioth, was one of the twelve *disciples,* Satan entered him. [4] He went and conferred with the chief priests and the officers of the Temple guards and discussed with them how he could enable them to seize *Jesus.* [5] They were happy *that he wanted to do that.* They offered to give him money *for doing it.* [6] So he agreed, *and they gave him the money.* Then he tried to find an opportunity to enable them to seize *Jesus* when there was no crowd around.

Luke 22:7-13

THEME: Jesus arranged for his disciples to prepare the Passover meal.

[7] Then there came the day during the *first part of the week-long festival* of Unleavened Bread when *the* lambs *for the* Passover *celebration* had to be killed. [8] So Jesus said to Peter and John, "Go and prepare the meal for the Passover *celebration.*" [9] They replied to him, "Where do you want us to prepare it?" [10] He said to *the two of* them, "Listen carefully. When you *two* enter the city, a man carrying a jar of water will meet you. Follow him.

When he enters *a house,* [11] tell the owner of the house, '*Our* teacher says *we should* ask *you to please* show *us* the room *that he arranged with you* where he can eat the Passover *meal* with *us,* his disciples.' [12] He will show you a large room that is on the upper *floor of the house.* It will be all set up *for a meal.* Prepare the meal for us there." [13] So *the two disciples* went *into the city.* They found everything to be just as *Jesus* had told them. So they prepared *the meal for* the Passover *celebration there.*

Luke 22:14-23

THEME: Jesus told them how they should remember his death for them.

[14] When it was time *to eat the meal,* Jesus *came and* sat down with the *twelve* apostles. [15] He said to them, "I have greatly desired to eat this Passover *meal* with you before I suffer *and die.* [16] I want you to know that I will not eat *the Passover meal* again until all those whose lives God rules completely realize *what it represents.*" [17] Then he took a cup *of wine* and thanked *God for it.* Then he said, "Take this, and each of you drink some of it. [18] I want you to know that *from now on* I will not drink wine until God makes me king." [19] Then he took some bread and thanked God for it. He broke it *into pieces* and gave it to them *to eat.* He said, "This *bread represents* my body, which *I* am about to sacrifice for you. Keep on *eating bread* this way *regularly* to remember what I *have done for you.*" [20] Similarly, after *they had eaten* the meal, he took *another* cup *of wine.* He said, "*The wine in* this cup *represents* my blood, which will soon flow *from my body when I die. With* this blood *I will sign* the new agreement *that God is making with* you. [21] But *note that* the one who will enable my enemies to seize me is eating right here with me! [22] *It is certain that I,* the one who came from heaven, will die, because that is what *God* has planned. But there will be terrible punishment for the man who enables *my enemies* to seize me!" [23] Then they began to ask one another, "Which of us would do such a thing?"

Luke 22:24-30

THEME: Jesus taught them that they should imitate him by serving each other humbly.

[24] *The apostles* began to argue among themselves saying, "Which one of us *will be* the greatest *when Jesus becomes king*?" [25] So Jesus said to them, "The kings of the non-Jews *enjoy* showing that they are powerful. *Yet* they give *themselves* the title, 'ones who help the people.' [26] But you should not be like them! Instead, those who want *God to consider* them the greatest should *act as though they were* the youngest, *since the youngest are expected to serve the older ones.* Whoever is a leader should be one who serves *the others.* [27] Think about who is the most important one. It is certainly the one who *just sits* at the table, not those who serve *the meal.* But I, *your leader,* have been *an example for you by* serving you *while being* among you.

[28] "You are the ones who have stayed with me during all my troubles. [29] So now, just as my Father has appointed me to rule as a king, I am appointing you [30] so that you can sit and eat *and rule* with me when I become king. You will sit on thrones to judge *the people of* the twelve tribes of Israel.

Luke 22:31-34

THEME: Jesus predicted that Peter would say three times that he did not know Jesus.

[31] "Simon, Simon, listen! Satan has asked *God to let him test you all,* and God has given *him permission. Satan wants to separate those among you who will keep believing in me*

from those who will not keep believing in me,^{ee} just like a man sifts wheat *to separate the grain from the chaff.* ³² But I have prayed for you, Simon, that you will not completely stop believing in me. So when you restore your relationship with me, help your fellow apostles *to trust in me more!*" ³³ Peter said to him, "Lord, I am ready to go with you if they put you in prison, or **even** to die with you!" ³⁴ Jesus replied, "Peter, I want you to know that this night, before the rooster crows, you will say three times that you don't know me!"

Luke 22:35-38

THEME: Jesus warned his disciples that they would soon face opposition.

³⁵ Then *Jesus* asked all of them, "After I sent you out *to other villages, and you went* without taking any money or a *traveling* bag or *extra* sandals, you did not lack anything, did you?" They replied, "*That's right, we did not lack* anything." ³⁶ Then, *to show them that now many people would oppose them,* he said to them,^{ff} "Now *things will be different. So* whoever among you has some money should take it with him. Likewise, he should take a carrying bag. Whoever does not have a sword should sell his coat and buy a sword. ³⁷ Because, I now tell you, *something must happen to me to fulfill these words that a prophet* wrote: 'He was treated as *though he were* a criminal.' Keep in mind that everything that is written about me *in the Scriptures* must be fulfilled." ³⁸ The disciples said, "Lord, look! We have two swords!" *Realizing they did not understand the meaning of what he said*, he replied to them, "That is enough *talk about swords!*"

Luke 22:39-46

THEME: Jesus prayed alone intensely.

³⁹ As *Jesus* left *the city*, he went, as he usually did, to Olive *Tree* Hill. His disciples went with him. ⁴⁰ When he came to the place *where he often spent the night*, he said to them, "Pray that *God will help you* whenever you are tempted." ⁴¹ Then he went from them a distance of about thirty yards.^{gg} He knelt and prayed, ⁴²"*My* Father, if you are willing, grant that I don't have to *undergo* these terrible things *that are about to happen to me*. But don't do what I want. Instead, do what you want!" ⁴³ Then an angel from heaven appeared to him and strengthened him. ⁴⁴ He was greatly distressed. So he prayed more earnestly. His sweat fell down on the ground as though it was large drops of blood. ⁴⁵ When he got up from praying, he returned to his disciples and found that they were sleeping. They were exhausted because they were so sorrowful. ⁴⁶ He *woke them up and* said to them, "I am disappointed that you are sleeping! Get up! Pray that *God will help you* whenever you are tempted!"

Luke 22:47-53

THEME: Jesus' enemies captured him.

⁴⁷ While *Jesus* was still speaking, a crowd approached. Judas, *even though he was* one of the twelve *disciples*, was leading them. He came close to Jesus and kissed him *on the cheek to signal to those with him which one was Jesus.* ⁴⁸ Jesus said to him, "Judas, I am disappointed that it is by kissing me^{hh} that you are enabling *my enemies* to seize me, the

---

^{ee} OR, …*Satan wants to give you all such severe trials that you will not believe in me any longer. He wants to shake you*…

^{ff} OR, Then, *to show them that they needed to be prepared to protect themselves,* he said to them…

^{gg} OR, Then he went from them as far as someone can throw a stone.

^{hh} OR, …*Judas, is it by kissing me as though you loved me*…

one who came from heaven!" ⁴⁹When the *disciples* who were around Jesus realized what was going to happen, they said, "Lord, shall we strike *them* with our swords?" ⁵⁰One of them *drew his sword and* struck the servant of the high priest *to kill him, but only* cut off his right ear. ⁵¹But Jesus said, "Don't *do* any more of that!" He touched the *servant's* ear and healed him. ⁵²⁻⁵³Then Jesus said to the chief priests, the officers of the Temple guards, and *the Jewish* elders who had come to *seize* him, "It is ridiculous that you have come *here* with swords and clubs to capture me, as *if I were* a bandit! Day after day *I was with you* in the Temple *courtyard, and* you did not seize me! But this is the time *God is allowing* you *to do what you want.* It is also the time that *God is allowing Satan, who rules in* the darkness, *to do what he wants.*"

Luke 22:54-62

THEME: Peter said three times that he did not know Jesus.

⁵⁴They seized *Jesus* and led him away. They brought him to the high priest's house, and Peter followed *them* at a distance. ⁵⁵They kindled a fire in the middle of the courtyard and sat down together. Peter sat among them. ⁵⁶As the light *from the fire* shone *on his face, a* female servant saw him and looked intently at him. She said, "This man was also with *the man they have arrested!*" ⁵⁷But he denied it, saying, "Woman, I don't know him!" ⁵⁸A little later someone else saw Peter and said, "You also are one of those who *were with* the man *they arrested*!" But Peter said, "Man, I am not *one of them!*" ⁵⁹About an hour later someone else said emphatically *about Peter*, "*The way* this man *speaks shows he* is from Galilee. Certainly this man was also with the man *they arrested!*" ⁶⁰But Peter said, "Man, I do not know what you are talking about!" Immediately, while he was still speaking, a rooster crowed. ⁶¹The Lord *Jesus* turned around and looked right at Peter. Then Peter remembered what the Lord had said to him, "This night, before the rooster crows, you will deny three times *that you know* me." ⁶²And he went out *of the courtyard* and cried very bitterly.

Luke 22:63-65

THEME: The soldiers made fun of Jesus.

⁶³The men who were guarding Jesus made fun of him and beat him. ⁶⁴They put a blindfold on him and *beat him again. Then* they said to him, "*You say* you are a prophet, *so prove it by* telling us who it was that struck you!" ⁶⁵They said many other evil things about him, insulting him.

Luke 22:66-71

THEME: The Jewish leaders asked Jesus about his identity.

⁶⁶At dawn *the next morning*, many of the *Jewish* leaders gathered together. The group included the chief priests and the men who taught the *Jewish* laws. They took Jesus to the Jewish Council. There they said to him, ⁶⁷"If you are the Messiah, tell us!" But he replied, "If I tell you that, you won't believe me. ⁶⁸If I ask you *what you think about the Messiah*, you won't answer me. ⁶⁹But some day you will see *me*, the one who came from heaven, sitting next to almighty God and ruling!" ⁷⁰Then they all said, "If that is so, are *you saying that* you are the Son of God?"ⁱⁱ He said to them, "*Yes*, it is just as you say." ⁷¹Then they said *to each other*, "We certainly don't need any more people to testify *against him*! We ourselves have heard him say *that he is equal with God*!"

ⁱⁱ OR, Then they said, "If that is so, are *you saying that* you are the Man who is also God?"

23

Luke 23:1-5

THEME: They accused Jesus before Pilate, the Roman governor.

¹ Then the whole group got up and took him to Pilate, *the Roman governor.* ² They began to accuse him, saying, "We have determined that this fellow has caused political trouble in our country. He has been *telling people* not to pay taxes to the Roman government. Also, he says he is the Messiah, a king!" ³ Pilate asked him, "Do you *claim to be* the king of the Jews?" He replied, "*It is* as you have *just* said." ⁴ Pilate said to the chief priests and *the rest of* the crowd, "I do not conclude that this man is guilty of any crime." ⁵ But they kept insisting, saying, "He is inciting the people *to riot*! He has been teaching his ideas all over Judea! He started *doing it* in Galilee and now he is doing it here!"

Luke 23:6-12

THEME: After Pilate sent Jesus to Herod, Jesus refused to answer Herod's questions.

⁶ When Pilate heard that, he asked, "Is this man from *the district of* Galilee?" ⁷ When they told him that Jesus was *from Galilee, which was the district* Herod *Antipas* ruled, *he told them* to take Jesus to Herod *Antipas*, because Herod was in Jerusalem at that time. ⁸ *So they did*. When Herod saw Jesus, he was very happy. He *had heard about Jesus*, and he had been hoping for a long time that he could see Jesus perform a miracle. ⁹ So he asked Jesus many questions, but Jesus did not reply *to any of them.* ¹⁰ The chief priests and men who taught the *Jewish* laws stood near him, making strong accusations against him. ¹¹ Then Herod and his soldiers made fun of *Jesus*. They put gorgeous clothes on him *to mock him as being a king*. Then Herod sent him back to Pilate. ¹² Until that time Herod and Pilate had been very hostile to each other, but that very day they became friends.

Luke 23:13-25

THEME: Pilate was unsuccessful in his efforts to set Jesus free.

¹³ Pilate then gathered together the chief priests and other *Jewish* leaders and the crowd *that was still there.* ¹⁴ He said to them, "You brought this man to me, saying he had caused trouble among the people. But *I want you to know that* after having examined him in your presence, I do not conclude that he is guilty of any of the things you are accusing him about. ¹⁵ *Obviously* Herod did not *conclude that* either, because he sent him back to me *without punishing him. So it* is clear that this man has not done anything for which we should kill him. ¹⁶ So I will *have him* whipped and then released."ʲʲ ¹⁸ But the whole crowd shouted, "Execute this man! Release Barrabas for us!" ¹⁹ (Barrabas was a man who had tried to persuade people in the city to rebel *against the Roman government. While doing that,* he had murdered *someone*. So he had been put in prison, *where he was waiting to be executed.*) ²⁰ Because Pilate wanted to release Jesus, he tried to persuade the crowd again. ²¹ But they kept shouting, "*Have* him killed by being nailed to a cross! Have him crucified!" ²² He *spoke to them* a third time and asked them, "Why? What crime has he committed? I have concluded that he has done nothing for which he deserves to die. So I will *have* him whipped and then released." ²³ But they kept insisting. They shouted loudly that *Jesus* should be crucified. Finally, because they continued to shout *so loudly,* ²⁴ Pilate

---

ʲʲ   Some Greek manuscripts add v 17, "Every year at the *Passover* festival *Pilate* had to release one prisoner for the people."

decided to do what they requested. ²⁵ The man who had been put in prison because he had rebelled *against the government* and committed murder, he released! That was the man the crowd had asked him *to release*. He put Jesus into the hands *of the soldiers*, to do what *the crowd* wanted.

Luke 23:26-31

THEME: The soldiers nailed Jesus to a cross.

²⁶ As the soldiers were taking *Jesus* away, they seized a man named Simon, *who was* from *the city of* Cyrene *in Africa*. He was returning *to Jerusalem* from out in the countryside. They *took from Jesus the cross that he had been carrying and* put it on Simon's shoulders, and *told him to* carry it behind Jesus. ²⁷ A large crowd followed Jesus. The crowd included many women who were beating their breasts *in sorrow*, and wailing for him. ²⁸ But Jesus turned to them and said, "You women of Jerusalem, don't cry for me! Instead, cry because of *what is going to happen to* yourselves and your children! ²⁹ I want you to know that there will soon be a time when people will say, 'Women who have never given birth to children or nursed babies are fortunate!' ³⁰ Then, *so they will not have to endure great suffering when their enemies destroy this city*, they will say to the mountains, 'Fall down on us!' And people will say to the hills, 'Cover us!' ³¹ *I am innocent. I am like* a living tree *that people don't try to burn. But the people of Jerusalem deserve to be punished. They are like* dry wood that is ready to *burn*. So if they *nail me to the cross, God* will certainly do much worse things to them!"

Luke 23:32-49

THEME: The things that happened when Jesus died.

³² Two other men who were criminals were also being led away. They were going to be executed *with Jesus*. ³³ When they came to the place which is called 'The Skull', they nailed *Jesus* to a cross *after removing his clothes*. They did the same thing to the two criminals. They put one at *Jesus'* right *side* and one at his left *side*. ³⁴ Jesus said, "*My* Father, forgive them, because they do not realize *whom* they are doing *this to*." Then *the soldiers* divided his clothing by gambling with something like dice, *to decide which piece of clothing each one would get*. ³⁵ Many people stood nearby, watching. And the *Jewish* leaders made fun of *Jesus*, saying, "He *said that he* saved other people! If he is the Messiah, the one God has chosen, he should save himself!" ³⁶ The soldiers also made fun of his *claim to be a king*. They came up to him and offered him some sour wine. ³⁷ They said to him, "If you are the king of the Jews, save yourself!" ³⁸ *They* also *fastened on the cross* above his head a sign *that stated* why *they* were nailing him to the cross. *But all it said was*, 'This is the King of the Jews'.

³⁹ One of the criminals who was hanging *on a cross* began to insult him, saying, "Since you *said that you* are the Messiah, *you must have power!* So save yourself, and save us, too!" ⁴⁰ But the other *criminal* rebuked him, saying, "You should be afraid of God's *punishment!* They are punishing him *and us* in the same way. ⁴¹ They have justly decided that we *two* must die. They are punishing us as we deserve *for the evil things we did*. But this man has done nothing wrong!" ⁴² Then he said, "Jesus, *please* remember me *and take care of me* when you become king!" ⁴³ Jesus replied, "I want you to know that today you will be with me in the place where everyone is happy!"^{kk}

---

^{kk} OR, ...today you will be with me in Paradise.

⁴⁴ *Then it* was about noontime. It became dark over the whole land, *and it stayed dark* until three o'clock in the afternoon. ⁴⁵ There was no light from the sun. Then the *thick* curtain *that closed off the most holy place* in the Temple split into two pieces. *That signified that ordinary people could now go into the presence of God.* ⁴⁶ *As that happened*, Jesus shouted loudly, "Father, I put my spirit into your care!" When he said that, he stopped breathing *and died.*

⁴⁷ When the officer *who was supervising the execution* saw what happened, he praised God *for the way Jesus died,* saying, "*I am* sure that this man had done nothing wrong!" ⁴⁸ When the crowd of people who had gathered to see those events saw what happened, they returned *to their homes*, beating their breasts *in sorrow.* ⁴⁹ All of Jesus' friends, including the women who had come with him from Galilee, stood at a distance and saw everything that happened.

Luke 23:50-56

THEME: Joseph and others buried Jesus while some women watched.

⁵⁰ There was a man named Joseph who *came there.* He was from *the town of* Arimathea in Judea. He was a good and a righteous man, and was a member of the *Jewish* Council. ⁵¹ But he had not agreed with the other Council members in their decision *to kill Jesus* and with their *plan of how to* do it. He was waiting expectantly for *the time when* God *would send* his king to begin to rule. ⁵² He went to Pilate and asked *for permission to take* Jesus' body *and bury it. After Pilate gave him permission,* ⁵³ he *and some others* took *Jesus' body* down *from the cross.* They wrapped it in a linen cloth. Then they put his body in a tomb that he had *hired others to* dig out of a rock *cliff.* No one had ever put a body in it before. ⁵⁴ *They had to do it quickly because* that was *Friday*, the day when *people* prepared *things for the Jewish day of rest.* The day of rest was about to start *at sunset, so they had to finish the burial before sunset.* ⁵⁵ The women who had come with *Jesus* from Galilee followed *Joseph and the men who were with him.* They saw the tomb, and they saw how the men laid *Jesus'* body *inside it, and they saw the men roll a huge stone across the entrance.* ⁵⁶ Then the women returned to the houses *where they were staying. The following evening* they prepared spices and ointments to put *on Jesus' body*, but on the Jewish day of rest they rested, according to what *Moses* had commanded.

24

Luke 24:1-12

THEME: Some women discovered that Jesus had become alive again.

¹ Before dawn on Sunday those women went to the tomb. They took with them the spices that they had prepared *to put on Jesus' body.* ² They discovered that the stone had been rolled away from *the entrance to* the tomb. ³ They went in the tomb, but the body of the Lord Jesus was not there! ⁴ They did not know what to think about that. Then suddenly two men stood by them wearing bright shining clothes! ⁵ The *women* were frightened. As they prostrated themselves on the ground, the two men said to them, "You shouldn't be seeking someone who is alive in *a place where they bury* the dead! ⁶ He is not here; he has risen from the dead! Remember that while he was still with you in Galilee he said to you, ⁷ "*Even though* I am the one who came from heaven, *someone* will enable sinful men to seize me. They will *kill me by* nailing me to a cross. But on the third day *after that,* I will become alive *again.*'" ⁸ The *women* remembered those words. ⁹ So they left the tomb and went to the eleven *apostles* and his other *disciples* and told them those things. ¹⁰ The ones

who kept telling those things to the apostles were Mary from *the village of* Magdala, Joanna, Mary who was the mother of James, and the other women *who were* with them. [11] But they thought that what the women *said* was nonsense. They did not believe what the women said. [12] But Peter got up and ran to the tomb *anyway*. He stooped down *and looked inside*. He saw the linen cloths *in which Jesus' body had been wrapped. The cloths were* by themselves." So, wondering what had happened, he went to where he was staying.[mm]

Luke 24:13-35

THEME: Jesus appeared to two disciples as they were walking to Emmaus.

[13] That same day two of *Jesus' disciples* were walking to a village named Emmaus. It was about seven miles from Jerusalem. [14] They were talking with each other about all the things that had happened *to Jesus*. [15] While they were talking and discussing those things, Jesus himself approached them and started walking with them. [16] But *something* prevented them from recognizing him. [17] *Jesus* said to them, "What have you two been talking about while you were walking?" They stopped, and their faces looked very sad. [18] One of them, whose name was Cleopas, said, "You must be the only person who is visiting Jerusalem *for the Passover festival* who does not know the events that have happened there in recent days!" [19] He said to them, "What events?" They replied, "*The things that happened* to Jesus, *the man* from Nazareth, who was a prophet. Many people saw him *perform* great miracles, and God *enabled him* to teach wonderful *messages!* [20] But our chief priests and leaders handed him over *to the Roman authorities. The authorities* sentenced him to die, and they killed him by nailing him to a cross. [21] We were hoping that he was the one who would free *us* Israelites *from our enemies!* But *this does not seem possible now, because* three days have *already* passed since that happened. [22] On the other hand, some women from our group amazed us. Early this morning they went to the tomb, [23] but Jesus' body was not there! They came *back* and said that they had seen some angels in a vision. The angels said that he was alive! [24] Then some of those who were with us went to the tomb. They saw that things were just as the women had reported. But they did not see *Jesus*." [25] He said to them, "*You two* foolish *men! You are* so slow to believe all that the prophets have written *about the Messiah!* [26] *You should certainly have known that* it was necessary that the Messiah should suffer all those things *and die*, and then enter his glorious *home in heaven!*" [27] Then he explained to them all the things that *the prophets* had written in the Scriptures about himself. He started with what Moses *wrote* and what all the *other* prophets *wrote*.

[28] They came near to the village to *which the two men* were going. He indicated that he would go further, [29] but they urged him *to not do that*. They said, "Stay with us *tonight*, because it is late in the afternoon and it will soon be dark." So he went in *the house* to stay with them. [30] When they sat down to eat, he took some bread and *asked God to* bless it. He broke it and gave *some pieces* to them. [31] And then *God* enabled them to recognize him. But *immediately* he disappeared! [32] They said to each other, "*While we were walking* along the road and he talked with us and *enabled* us to understand the Scriptures, we *became so excited that it was as though* a fire was burning within us! *We shouldn't stay here; we should go tell others what happened!*" [33] So they left immediately and returned to Jerusalem. There they found the eleven *apostles* and others who had gathered together with them. [34] They told *those two men*, "It is true that the Lord has become alive again, and

---

" OR, ...He saw the linen sheets in which they had wrapped Jesus' body. He did not see anything else.

[mm] Many Greek manuscripts do not include verse 12.

he has appeared to Simon!" ³⁵ Then those two *men* told *the others* what had happened *as they were walking* along the road. They also *told them how* they both recognized him as he broke some bread *for them*.

Luke 24:36-49

THEME: Jesus appeared to many of his disciples and taught them more and gave them other instructions.

³⁶ As they were saying that, Jesus himself *suddenly* appeared among them. He said to them, "*May God give* you *inner* peace!" ³⁷ They were startled and afraid, *because* they thought they were seeing a ghost! ³⁸ He said to them, "You shouldn't be alarmed! And you should not be doubting *that I am alive*! ³⁹ Look at *the wounds in* my hands and my feet! You can touch me and see *my body*. Then you can see that it is really I myself. *You can tell that I am really alive* because ghosts don't have bodies, as you see that I have!" ⁴⁰ After he said that, he showed them *the wounds in* his hands and his feet. ⁴¹ They were joyful and amazed, *but* they still did not believe *that he was really alive.*ⁿⁿ *So* he said to them, "Do you have anything here to eat?" ⁴² *So* they gave him a piece of broiled fish. ⁴³ While they were watching, he took it and ate it.

⁴⁴ Then he said to them, "*I will repeat* what I told you while I was still with you: Everything that was written about me by Moses and the other prophets and in the Psalms must be fulfilled!" ⁴⁵ Then he enabled them to understand *the things that had been written about him in* the Scriptures. ⁴⁶ He said to them, "This is what they wrote: The Messiah will suffer *and die*, but on the third day *after that* he will become alive again. ⁴⁷ *They* also *wrote that the message that people* must turn from their sinful ways for *God* to forgive their sins must be preached *everywhere. They wrote that his followers should preach that message, claiming* his authority. They wrote that they should start *preaching* it in Jerusalem and then *go and* preach it to all ethnic groups, *everywhere*. ⁴⁸ You *apostles* must tell people that you know that those things *that happened to me* are true. ⁴⁹ And I want you to know that I will send the *Holy Spirit* to you, as my Father promised *he would do*. But you must stay in this city until God fills you with the power *of his Spirit.*"

Luke 24:50-53

THEME: Jesus left his disciples and returned to heaven.

⁵⁰ Then *Jesus* led them outside *the city* until they came near *the village of* Bethany. There he lifted up his hands and blessed them. ⁵¹ As he was doing that, he left them *and went up to heaven*. ⁵² They worshipped him. And then they returned to Jerusalem very joyfully. ⁵³ Each day they went into the Temple *courtyard*, and spent a lot of time praising God.

ⁿⁿ OR, ...*but* they still did not believe *that he was the one they were seeing.*

The Gospel that was written by
John

1

John 1:1-18

THEME: This book is about Jesus, who was eternally with God but also became a human being to reveal God to mankind.

[1] The one who expresses *what God is like* has always existed from the beginning *of everything*. He has always existed with God, and he has **God's nature**. [2] He always existed with God *before* he began *to create anything*. [3] He is the one by whom *God* caused everything to exist. He is the one who created absolutely everything. [4] He is the one who *caused everything to* live. He, who caused us people to live, *revealed to us the truth about God, as* a light *reveals what is in the darkness.* [5] People do not want him to reveal *that what they do is evil,* just *like* darkness *is evil.* But *just as* darkness cannot put out light, *evil people have never prevented the one who was like a light from revealing God's truth.*[a]

[6] God sent a man whose name was John. [7] He came to tell people *about the one who was like* a light. John came to show that everything that the *one who was like a light* said was true, in order that he could enable all people to believe *in the one who was like a light.* [8] John himself was not the *one who was like a* light. Instead, he came to tell others about that *one who was like a* light. [9] *While John was doing that*, the one who was truly *like* a light was *about to* come into the world. He was the one who enables all people *to know about God, as* a light enables *people to know what is in the darkness.*

[10] Although the one *who was like a light* was *here* on the earth, and although he was the one through whom *God* created everything, *most* people did not realize who he *was.*[b] [11] Although he came to the land that belonged to him *because he created it, most of* his own people, *the Jews*, rejected him. [12] But as for those *of us who welcomed him, God* authorized *that we would have a relationship with* him *like* children *have a relationship with their father*. We were people who believed *that what he said* about himself *was true.* [13] We became *like God's children*, not because our ancestors *belonged to God,* or because of someone's sexual desires, nor because some man desired to have children like himself. Instead, it was God who caused us to become *like* his children.

[14] The one who expresses *what God is like* became a human being, and he lived among us *for a while.* As a result, we saw how wonderful he is. He came from *God* his father, and there was no other person as wonderful as he. He was wonderful because he always acted in kindness toward us, in ways we did not deserve, and he always *spoke* truthfully to us *about God.*

[15] *One day* when John was telling people about him, *he saw Jesus.* Then John shouted to them, "I told you *previously* that someone will come later who is more important than I am, since he existed *long* before me. ***This** is the man I was talking about!*"

---

[a] OR, …*evil people have never* understood the one who was like a light.

[b] OR, …*most* people did not accept him.

[16] We have all benefited very much from what he has done. Again and again, he acted in kindness toward us, in ways we did not deserve. [17] Moses proclaimed *God's* laws *to our ancestors*. But what Jesus Christ did for us *was much better*. He acted in kindness toward us and told us the truth *about God*. [18] No one has ever seen God. But God's only Son, *Jesus*, who has always had a very close relationship with God, has told us about God.

John 1:19-28

THEME: When religious authorities asked John about his identity, he said he was preparing people for the coming of the Messiah, who was much more important than himself.

[19] The Jewish *leaders* in Jerusalem sent some *Jewish* priests and Levites[c] *to* John to ask him some questions. They said to him, "What do you *claim about* yourself?" [20] So John told them the truth, and he told them clearly. He said, "I am not the Messiah!" [21] Then they asked him, "Then what *do you say about yourself*? Are you *the prophet* Elijah *who was prophesied to return before the Messiah*?" He replied, "No, I am not." Then they asked him, "Are you the prophet *like Moses that God promised to send*?" He replied, "No." [22] So they asked him, "Then who do you *claim to be*? *Tell us* so we can *go back and* report to those who sent us. What do you say about yourself?" [23] John replied, "I am the one *the prophet Isaiah said* would proclaim *this new message* loudly *to the people who would pass by* in this desolate area: 'Prepare *yourselves to receive* the Lord when he comes, *just as people prepare* a road *for an important official'*."

[24] Some of those people *who were questioning* John were ones who had been sent by the Pharisee *religious group*. [25] They asked John, "Since *you say* you are not the Messiah, nor *the prophet* Elijah, nor the prophet *like Moses*, *what authority* do you have? *Furthermore*, why are you baptizing *Jews, treating them as though they were non-Jews who wanted to become Jews*?" [26] John replied, "I am *just* baptizing people with water *to prepare them to welcome the Messiah*. But *right now* someone is standing among you whom you people do not know. [27] He *will preach to you* after I *am gone*. *He is so important that* I am not worthy to *serve him as a slave by* untying his sandals."

[28] Those things happened at *a place called* Bethany, on the *east* side of the Jordan *River*, where John was baptizing people.

John 1:29-34

THEME: John the Baptizer announced that Jesus was the one who would become a sacrifice to remove guilt for sin, and how God had confirmed that Jesus was the Son of God.

[29] The next day John saw Jesus coming toward him. He said to the people, "Look! Here is the *man whom* God *has appointed to be a sacrifice*, *like* the lambs *that the people of Israel sacrificed! By sacrificing himself* he will *make it possible for everyone in* the world to be no longer *guilty for having* sinned. [30] He is the one about whom I said *before*, 'Someone will come later who is more important than I am, since he existed *long* before me.' [31] I myself did not *previously* recognize that he *was the Messiah*. But *now I know who he is*, and I have baptized people with water to enable *you people of* Israel to recognize who he is."

[32-34] *Later*, John spoke clearly *what God had shown him about Jesus*. He said, "I myself did not know *previously* that he *was the Messiah*. However, *God*, sent me to baptize people with water*, people who said they wanted to turn from their sinful ways. While I was doing that,* God told me, 'The man on whom you will see my Spirit descend and remain is the one who will put the Holy Spirit within you *to truly change your lives*.' I saw *God's* Spirit as

---

[c]   OR, …sent some men who worked in the temple…

he was descending from heaven in the form of a dove. The Spirit rested on Jesus. I saw *that happen*, and I tell you that he is the Son of God."[d]

John 1:35-42

THEME: After John declared again that Jesus would be a sacrifice to remove guilt for sin, four men decided to become Jesus' disciples.

[35] The next day John was at the same place again with two of us[e] disciples. [36] When he saw Jesus passing by, he said, "Look! There is the man God *has appointed to be a sacrifice, like* the lambs *the people of Israel have sacrificed!*" [37] When we heard John say this, we went with Jesus. [38] Jesus turned around and saw us coming behind him. So he asked us, "What do you want?" We replied, "Teacher, *tell us* where you are staying, *because we want to talk with you.*" [39] He replied, "Come *with me*, and you will see *where I am staying*!" So we went with him and saw where he was staying. We stayed with him until about 4 o'clock.[f]

[40] One of us two who heard what John had said and who went with Jesus was Andrew, Simon Peter's *younger* brother. [41] *After Andrew left Jesus*, the first thing he did was to find his own *older* brother Simon and say to him, "We have found the Messiah!"[g] [42] Then he took Simon to Jesus. Jesus looked intently at him, and then said, "You are Simon. Your father's name is John. *I* will give you the name Cephas." *Cephas is an Aramaic name that means 'solid rock'. It* means *the same in Greek as the name* Peter.

John 1:43-51

THEME: Jesus told Nathaniel that he knew about him supernaturally, but that he would do things that were more surprising than that.

[43] The next day *Jesus* decided to leave *the Jordan River valley*. He went to *the district of* Galilee and found a man named Philip. Jesus said to him, "Come with me!" [44] Philip and Andrew and Peter were all from *the town of* Bethsaida. [45] Then Philip *searched for* Nathaniel and found him, and said to him, "We have met *the Messiah*, the one Moses *wrote about*! The prophets also *prophesied that he would come*. He is Jesus, from *the town of* Nazareth. His father's name is Joseph." [46] Nathaniel replied, "Nazareth? Can anything good come from *such an unimportant place*?" Philip replied, "Come and see!" [47] When Jesus saw Nathaniel approaching, he said about Nathaniel, "Here is an example of a good Israelite! He never deceives anyone!" [48] Nathaniel asked him, "How do you know what I *am like*?" Jesus replied, "I saw you before Philip called you, when you were *by yourself* under the fig tree." [49] Then Nathaniel declared, "Teacher, you *must be* the Son of God![h] You are the King of Israel *we have been waiting for*!" [50] Jesus replied to him, "You believe *those things about me* because I told you I saw you when you were under the fig tree. *I was able to see you supernaturally, even though I was far away from you.* But you

---

[d] OR, ...he is the Man who is also God.

[e] Many commentaries suggest that John, the writer, was one of the two disciples. This seems to follow John's pattern of never referring to himself in the first person in this gospel. But it seems clear that John intended his readers to know that he was referring to himself. So this translation suggests that it would be very appropriate to use first person pronouns whenever it is clear that John was present as a participant.

[f] OR, ...We stayed with him from about 4 PM until the next day.

[g] The Greek text says "We have found the Messiah." 'Messiah' is the Hebrew word which, translated into Greek, is 'Christ'. Both 'Christ' and 'Messiah' mean: 'God's chosen king/savior.'

[h] OR, ...you *must be* the Man who is also God!

will see *me do* things that are more surprising than that!" [51] Then Jesus said to him, "Listen to this carefully: *Just like what your ancestor Jacob saw long ago in a vision*, some day you will see heaven opened up, and you will see the God's angels ascending from me and descending on me, the one who came from heaven."

2

John 2:1-11

THEME: In Cana Jesus did his first miracle, turning water into delicious wine.

[1] Two days later there was a wedding *celebration* in *the town of* Cana, in Galilee. Jesus' mother was there; [2] Jesus and *we* his disciples *were also there, because* we had been invited also. [3] When the guests had drunk all the wine *that was there*, Jesus' mother said to him, "The wine is all gone; *can you do something about that?*" [4] Jesus said to her, "Woman, don't *tell* me *what to do. Let me take care of it.* It is not yet time *to show* that I am *the Messiah by working miracles*." [5] Then Jesus' mother said to the servants, "Do whatever he tells you!" [6] There were six *empty* stone jars there. The Jews *put water in them* to use for washing things *to make them acceptable to God*. Each jar held 20 to 30 gallons. [7] Jesus said to the servants, "Fill the jars with water!" So they filled the jars to the brim. [8] Then he told them, "Now, ladle out some *of it* and take it to the master of ceremonies." So the servants did that. [9] The master of ceremonies tasted the water, which had now become wine. He did not know where the wine had come from, but the servants who had ladled out the wine knew. *The wine was delicious!* So he called the bridegroom over, [10] and said to him, "Everyone *else* serves the best wine first. Then when the guests have drunk so much *that they can't tell the difference, they serve* the cheap wine. But you *have not done what others do.* You have kept the best wine until now!" [11] That was the first miracle that Jesus did. He did it in Cana, in *the district of* Galilee. By doing it he showed how awesome he is, and as a result, *we* his disciples believed that he *truly was the Messiah*.

John 2:12

THEME: Jesus and others went to Capernaum and stayed there several days.

[12] Jesus then went down to *the city of* Capernaum with his mother and *younger* brothers and *us* his disciples. We stayed there several days.

John 2:13-25

THEME: After Jesus expelled the merchants from the temple, the Jewish leaders wanted him to do a miracle to show by what authority he did that. He told them metaphorically that he would become alive again three days after he died.

[13] Later, when it was almost time for the Jewish Passover *celebration*, Jesus *and we disciples* went up to Jerusalem. [14] There, in the Temple *courtyard,* he saw some men who were selling cattle, sheep, and pigeons *for sacrifices*. He also saw men who were sitting at tables, *making a big profit as they* gave people *Temple tax* coins in exchange for *their Roman* coins. [15] Then Jesus made a whip from some cords and *used it to* chase out the sheep and cattle from the Temple *courtyard*. By overturning their tables he scattered the coins of the men who were exchanging the coins. [16] He said to those who were selling doves, "Take these doves away *from here*! Stop *defiling* my Father's Temple *by* making it a market!" [17] Then *we* disciples remembered that these words had been written *in the*

Scriptures, prophesying what the Messiah would say to God: "Others will strongly oppose me because of my passionate desire for *people to respect* your Temple."

[18] So *one of* the Jewish *leaders* replied to him, "What miracle will you perform to show us that *you have authority from God* to do these things?" [19] Jesus replied to them, "If you destroy this temple, I will build it again in three days." [20] So the Jewish *leaders* said, "We have been building this Temple for forty-six years *and it is not finished yet*! So there is no way **you** can build it within three days!" [21] But when Jesus said that about the temple, *he was really talking about* his own body. [22] *Later*, after Jesus had *died and had* come back to life again, *we* his disciples remembered the words he had said. As a result, we believed *what had been prophesied in* the Scriptures *about the Messiah becoming alive again*, and we believed that what Jesus said *was true*.

[23] While Jesus was in Jerusalem at the Passover celebration, many people came to believe *that he was the Messiah* because they saw the miracles he was performing. [24] But he did not let them tell him what he should do *as the Messiah*, because he knew within himself what they were all *thinking*. [25] He did not need anyone to tell him what others were thinking, because he already knew what they were *thinking and wanting*.

3

John 3:1-15

THEME: Jesus told Nicodemus that people needed to be born again spiritually to have eternal life.

[1] There was a man named Nicodemus, who was a member of the Jewish religious council. He belonged to the Pharisee *religious sect*. [2] He went to see Jesus at night, *to talk to him about God's kingdom*. He said to Jesus, "Teacher, *we believe that* you are a teacher who has come from God. *We believe this because* we know that someone could perform the miracles you are doing only if God were helping him." [3] Jesus replied to him, "Listen to this carefully: Unless people are born again and *have a new life from God,* they cannot experience God ruling *their lives*." [4] Then Nicodemus said to him, "No one can be born when he is old! There is no way someone can enter his mother's womb and be born a second time!" [5] Jesus answered, "Note this: Being born naturally is not *enough*; people need to also be born *spiritually* by God's Spirit. If that does not happen, they cannot experience God ruling *their lives*. [6] If someone is born as a result of what humans *do*, that person becomes a human being. But those who are born *again* as a result of what *God's* Spirit *does receive a new* spiritual *nature from God*. [7] Don't be surprised about my telling you that you must be born again *and have a new life from God*. [8] *Let me illustrate*. The wind blows wherever it wants to. You hear its sound, but you do not know where the wind comes from or where it is going. Similarly, those *who do not know God cannot understand* how people are born again as a result of what God's Spirit *does*." [9] Nicodemus replied to him, "How can that happen?" [10] Jesus replied to him, "You are a *well-known* teacher among *us* Israelite people, so I am surprised that you don't understand these things! [11] Listen to this carefully: My disciples and I tell you about the things that we have seen and know *are true*, but you don't admit that what we are saying *is true*.[i] [12] I have told you about the things *that happen here* on earth that are true, but you don't believe me. So if I tell you about things *that happen* in heaven, you certainly won't believe me! [13] I am the

---

[i]   OR, …I tell you about the things that I have seen and know *are true*, but you don't admit that what I am saying *is true*.

only one who has gone up to heaven; no one else has gone up there. I am also the one who came down from heaven. *So I know what happens there.* [14] *Long ago when the Israelite people rebelled against God* in the desolate area, *God sent poisonous snakes to bite them.* But when Moses lifted up *on a pole* the *model of a* poisonous snake, *everyone who looked at that model was healed from their snake bites.* In the same way, *even though* I am the one who came from heaven, *some day people* will lift me up *on a cross to kill me.* [15] As a result, everyone who believes in me will have eternal life."[j]

John 3:16-21

THEME: God sent his Son into the world to save everyone who trusts in him.

[16] God loved us people in the world so much that he gave his only Son *as a sacrifice for us*, in order that everyone who believes in him would not be separated from God forever. Instead, they would have eternal life. [17] When God sent his Son into the world, his purpose was not to punish the *people in* the world for their sins. Instead, he sent him to save them *from being punished for their sins.* [18] Everyone who trusts in his Son, *God says that they* will not be punished. But God has already *said* that he will punish everyone who does not trust in his Son, because they have not trusted in what his only Son *has done for them.* [19] The *one who was like a* light *to reveal God's truth to us* came into the world. But people loved doing what was *evil, like* darkness *is evil*, instead of loving the *one who was like a* light. That is the reason *God will* judge people *and condemn them.* [20] Everyone who does what is evil hates the *one who is like a* light, and they will not come to the *one who is like a* light, because *the one who is like a light* would show that their deeds *are evil, and he would rebuke them.* [21] But those who live according to *God's* truth come to the *one who is like a* light, in order that people may see clearly that the things they have done they did them because *they have depended* on God.

John 3:22-36

THEME: When many people began to become Jesus' disciples, John the Baptizer declared that Jesus was greater then he was.

[22] Sometime later Jesus and we disciples went to Judea district. We stayed there and he *directed us as we* baptized people.

[23] John *the Baptizer* was also baptizing people. He was doing that at *the village of* Aenon near *the town of* Salim, because there were many springs in that area. *Many* people kept coming *to John,* and he was baptizing them. [24] That happened before John was put in prison. [25] Some of John's disciples and a certain Jew started arguing about the Jewish rituals of washing things *to make them acceptable to God.* [26] Then those disciples went to John and said to him, "Teacher, *do you remember* the man who was with you when you were baptizing people on the other side of the Jordan River? He is the one you were telling us about. Well, now he is baptizing people, and many people are going to him *instead of coming to us*!" [27] John replied, "A person can become *important* only if God permits it. *So you should not be jealous about Jesus being popular*! [28] You yourselves can verify what I said. I told you that I am not the Messiah. Instead, I *told you* that *God* sent me to prepare the way for him. [29] *Let me illustrate*: *He is like a bridegroom, and I am like his friend.* The friend of the bridegroom stands outside and waits *for him to come.* That friend is very happy when he hears the bridegroom's voice *when he arrives.* In the same way,

---

[j]   Some people think that what Jesus told Nicodemus continues through v. 21, but the best evidence suggests that vv. 16-21 are John's comments.

I am very happy *about what you have told me.* ³⁰ It is necessary for Jesus to become more important *by making more disciples than I have,* and for me to become less *important."*

³¹ *Jesus* came from heaven. He is more important than anyone else. Those who are born from *parents here* on earth are just humans, and they speak about things *that happen here* on the earth. But since he came from heaven, his *words are* more important than anyone else's. ³² He tells people what he has seen and what he heard *in heaven,* but very few people listen to what he says. ³³ Those who have accepted what he has said verify that what God has said is true. ³⁴ *We know it is true* because *Jesus,* the one God sent, speaks the message of God. *That is also true* because God causes his Spirit to live *in Jesus* to completely *direct everything he says and does.* ³⁵ God loves his Son, and has caused him to have control over everything. ³⁶ Those who trust in *God's* Son have eternal life. But those who reject God's Son will never have *eternal* life. Instead, God is angry with them *and he will surely punish them.*

4

John 4:1-30

THEME: While Jesus talked with a Samaritan woman, he showed by his God-given knowledge of her personal life that he is the life-giving Messiah.

¹⁻² *At that time, many people were asking* Jesus to baptize them. He did not baptize people; it was *we* his disciples who were doing the baptizing. But when some of the Pharisees heard *that* Jesus was making more disciples than John *the Baptizer* and that he was baptizing them, *they became very jealous.* ³ When the Lord *Jesus* heard about that, *so that the Pharisees would not cause trouble for him,* he left Judea and went again *with us disciples* to Galilee.

⁴ *He decided* it was necessary for him to travel through *the district of* Samaria. ⁵ So we arrived at a town named Sychar, in Samaria. That was near the plot of ground that *our ancestor* Jacob had given to his son Joseph *long ago.* ⁶⁻⁸ The well that *used to* belong to Jacob was on that plot of ground. Jesus was tired from walking. So while *we* disciples went into the town to buy some food, he sat down alongside the well. It was about noontime. A woman who *lived there* in Samaria came to get some water *from the well.* Jesus said to her, "Will you give me *from the well* some water to drink?" The *woman knew that* Jews did not like *to touch things that belong to* Samaritans,ᵏ ⁹ so the woman said to him, "You are a Jew, and I am from Samaria. Furthermore, I am a woman. So *I am surprised* that you are asking me for a drink *of water!*" ¹⁰ Jesus replied to her, "If you knew what God *wanted to* give you, and if you knew who I am, the one who is asking you for a drink, you would have asked me, and I would have given you water that gives life." ¹¹ She *thought he was talking about water in a stream. So she* said to him, "Sir, you don't have a bucket *or a rope with which to get water,* and the well is deep. So *since you can't get water from this well,* where can you get that life-giving water? ¹² Our ancestor Jacob left us this well. He drank water from it, and there was *enough good water* so that his sons and his flocks of sheep drank from it also. *Do you claim* to be greater than Jacob, *and because of that, you can give us life-giving water?*" ¹³ Jesus replied to her, "Everyone who drinks water from this *well* will later become thirsty again. ¹⁴ But those who drink the water that I will give them will never be thirsty again. On the contrary, the water that I give them will become in their inner beings like a spring of water that will enable them to have eternal

---

ᵏ OR, …Jews did not like to associate with Samaritans…

life." [15] The woman *did not understand that Jesus was speaking figuratively about something that would sustain her spiritually. So she* said to him, "Sir, give me that kind of water so that I will not get thirsty again, and so that I won't have to keep returning here to get water!"

[16] *Jesus knew she did not understand, but he wanted to show her by his God-given knowledge of her personal life that because he was the Messiah he could take care of her spiritual need. So* he said to her, "Woman, go and call your husband, and bring him here!" [17] She replied, "I don't have a husband!" Jesus said to her, "You said that you don't have a husband, and that is true. [18] It is also true that you have had five husbands, *one by one*. And the man you are living with now is not your husband! What you have said is very true."

[19] The woman said to him, "Sir, I perceive you must be a prophet *because you are* able *to know people's secrets*. [20] But *let me ask you a different question*: Our ancestors worshipped God here on Mount *Gerazim*, but you *Jews* say that Jerusalem is the place where we must worship *God. So which group is right?*" [21] Jesus said to her, "Woman, believe me *when I say that* there will come a time when it will not *matter whether* you worship *God our* Father on this mountain or in Jerusalem *or somewhere else*. [22] You *people from Samaria* do not know the one you are worshipping. But we *Jews* know whom we worship, because it is from *us* Jews that *God has sent the one who* will save people *from the guilt of their sins*. [23] However, there will be a time when those who genuinely worship God will worship him as *God's* Spirit *directs* and *according to God's* truth. In fact, that time has already come. Those are the kind of worshippers my Father seeks. [24] God is a spiritual being. So it is necessary that those who worship him must worship him as his Spirit *directs* and *according to God's* truth." [25] The woman said to him, "I know that the Messiah is coming. When he comes, he will tell us everything *we need to know*." ('Messiah' and 'Christ' *both mean God's promised king*.) [26] Jesus said to her, "I, the one speaking to you, am *the Messiah*!"

[27] Just then *we* disciples returned *from town. Since it was contrary to our custom for Jewish religious teachers to converse with a woman they did not know*, we were surprised that he was talking to a woman. However, none of us asked her, "What do you want?" and none of us asked him, "Why are you talking with her?"

[28] The woman left her water jar there and went into the town. She said to the people there, [29] "Come and see a man who *was able to* tell me all about my past life, *even though I never met him before*! Could this man be the Messiah?" [30] So *many people* left the town and started going to where Jesus was.

John 4:31-38

THEME: Jesus told his disciples that what sustained him was doing his Father's will, which meant convincing non-Jewish people to believe in him.

[31] Meanwhile, we disciples were urging him, "Teacher, eat *some of the food we brought*!" [32] But he said to us, "I have food to eat that you do not know anything about!" [33] So we started saying each other, "Surely no one has brought him any food *when we were not here*!" [34] Jesus said to us, "Doing what *my Father* who sent me wants *me to do* and finishing the work he *gave me to do* is *what sustains* me *like* food *does*. [35] *At this time of the year* you are saying,[l] 'There are four months left before we harvest *the crops*.' But I say to you, look carefully *at the non-Jewish people around here. God says, 'People are ready to accept my message, like crops in* fields that are ready for people to harvest. [36] *If*

---

[l]   OR, ...your ancestors used to say...

you enable them to accept my message, I will reward you, *as an owner of a field* pays those who harvest the crops. Because of your work, people will gain eternal life.' *I have been telling people God's message. That is like* a man who plants seeds. *You will help people to accept my message. That will be like* harvesting crops. *When that happens*, both you and I will rejoice. ³⁷ As a result, this saying will become true: One person plants *seeds,* but others harvest *the crops.* ³⁸ I am sending you *to enable people to accept my message, but you will not be the first ones who tell them God's message.* Others *previously* worked hard *to tell people God's message*, and now you will be harvesting the results of their work."

John 4:39-42

THEME: Many Samaritans believed that Jesus was the Messiah.

³⁹ Many of the Samaritan people who *lived* in that town believed that Jesus *was the Messiah* because they heard what that woman said *about Jesus*: "That man *was able to* tell me all about my past!" ⁴⁰ So when those Samaritans came to him, they urged him to stay with them. So we stayed there two days. ⁴¹ Many more of them believed *that he was the Messiah* because of his message. ⁴² They told the woman, "We believe in Jesus *now*, but not *just* because of what you told us. Now we have heard *his message* ourselves. And now we know that this man truly is the one who can save all of us *people in the* world *from the guilt of our sins.*"

John 4:43-54

THEME: After Jesus healed an official's son, the official and his family believed that Jesus is the Messiah.

⁴³⁻⁴⁴ Jesus had said *previously* that people did not honor prophets *like himself when they tried to teach people* in their own home area. So, two days later, Jesus and *we* disciples left that area and we went to *his own area in* Galilee *district, because he knew that people there wouldn't think very highly of him, and as a result the Jewish leaders would not be jealous.* ⁴⁵ However, when we arrived in Galilee*, many* of the people there welcomed him, because they had been in Jerusalem during the *Passover* celebration, and had seen all the things he did there. ⁴⁶ Jesus went again to *the town of* Cana in Galilee. That was where he *previously* turned water into wine. There was one of the king's officials who lived in *the city of* Capernaum, whose son was very sick. ⁴⁷ When that man heard that Jesus had returned to Galilee from Judea, he went to Jesus *in Cana* and pleaded with him, "Please come down *to Capernaum* and heal my son, who is about to die!" ⁴⁸ Jesus said to him, "You people will never believe *my message* if you don't see *me perform* various miracles!" ⁴⁹ But the official said to him, "Sir, *I believe that you came from God. So please* come down *to my home* before my son dies!" ⁵⁰ Jesus said to him, "Then you may go *home.* Your son will not die!" The man believed what Jesus said, and left. ⁵¹ *The next day* while he was on the way home, his servants met him. They told him, "Your child is going to live!" ⁵² He asked them, "At what time did my son start to become well?" They said to him, "His fever ceased yesterday *afternoon* at one o'clock." ⁵³ Then the boy's father realized that that was the time Jesus told him, "Your son will not die." So he and all the people in his house believed *that Jesus was the Messiah.*

⁵⁴ That was the second miracle that Jesus performed in Galilee, after he had returned from Judea.

5

John 5:1-13

THEME: The Jewish leaders did not like the fact that Jesus healed a paralyzed man on the Sabbath day.

[1] Some time later, Jesus went up to Jerusalem when the Jews were having *another* celebration. [2] At one of the gates *into the city* called the Sheep Gate, there is a pool. In our language we call it Bethzatha. *Around the pool* were five open areas with roofs over them. [3] Many people were lying there. They were people who were blind, lame, or paralyzed.[m] [5] One of those who was there had been paralyzed for thirty-eight years. [6] Jesus saw him lying there and found out that the man had been like that for a long time. He said to the man, "Do you want to be healed?" [7] The paralyzed man replied to him, "*Yes*, sir, *I want to be healed, but* there is no one to help me get down into the pool when the water stirs. While I am trying to get *to the pool,* someone else always gets there before me." [8] Jesus said to him, "Get up! Then pick up your mat and walk!" [9] The man immediately was healed. He picked up his mat and started walking!

The day on which this happened was a Jewish day of rest. [10] So the Jewish *leaders* said to the man who had been healed, "Today is the Sabbath day, and *in our Jewish* law *it is written that people should not work on the Sabbath*, so you should not be carrying your mat!" [11] The man replied to them, "The man who healed me, he himself said to me, 'Pick up your mat and walk!'" [12] They asked him, "Who is the man who said to you, 'Pick it up and walk!'?" [13] But since Jesus had disappeared in the crowd *without him finding out Jesus' name*, he did not know who it was *who had healed him.*

John 5:14-18

THEME: The Jewish leaders became very angry with Jesus for saying that he was the Son of God.

[14] Later, Jesus saw the man when he was in the Temple *courtyard.* He *found out Jesus' name, and* Jesus said to him, "Listen! You are healed! So stop sinning! If you don't stop sinning, something will happen to you that will be worse *than the paralysis you had before*!" [15] The man went away and told the Jewish *leaders* that it was Jesus who had healed him. [16] So the Jewish *leaders* started to harass Jesus, because Jesus was doing these things on the Sabbath day. [17] Then Jesus replied to them, "My Father has always been working every day, *including the Sabbath day*, up till now. I am doing the same thing!" [18] For that reason the Jewish *leaders* sought even harder for a way to kill him. They wanted to kill him because *they considered* that he was disobeying their rules about the Sabbath day. Also, by saying God was his Father, he was making himself equal with God, *and they thought they should kill anyone who said such things.*

---

[m] Some very old Greek manuscripts add these words which include v. 4: "They were waiting for the water in the pool to stir. From time to time God would *send down* an angel, and the angel would stir the water. Then the first person who got down into the water after the water was stirred would be healed of whatever disease that person had."

John 5:19-45

THEME: Jesus replied to their objections by stating five reasons why they should believe he was the Son of God.

[19] Jesus replied to them by saying, "Listen to this carefully: I can do nothing by my own *authority*. I do only the *kind of* things that I see *my* Father doing. Whatever kinds of things my Father is doing, those are the things I am doing. [20] *My* Father loves me, and he shows me everything he is doing. He will show me *the miracles he wants me to do* that will be greater than the ones *you have already seen me do*, so that you may be amazed. [21] *For example*, just as *my* Father causes people who have died to rise up and be alive again, I will give *eternal* life to everyone I want to. [22] Furthermore, *my* Father is not the one who judges people *concerning their sins*. Instead, he has given to me the work of judging people, [23] in order that all people may honor me, just as they honor *my* Father. *My* Father *considers that* anyone who does not honor me is not honoring *him*, the one who sent me. [24] Listen to this carefully: Those who hear my message and believe that *God* is the one who sent me have eternal life. *God will* not condemn them. They are no longer separated from God. Instead, they have *new* life *from God*.

[25] Listen to this carefully: There will be a time when those who are separated from God will hear the voice of me, the Son of God.[n] In fact, that time is here already. Those who hear *and pay attention to my message* will have *eternal* life. [26] *My* Father has *power to* make things live. Similarly, he has given me the *power to enable* people to live *eternally*. [27] Because I am the one who came from heaven, he has also given me the authority to judge people *concerning their sins*. [28] Don't be surprised about that, because there will be a time when all people who have died will hear my voice [29] and they will become alive again. Those who have lived good *lives* will rise *from their graves* and live forever. But those who have lived evil lives will rise, and I will condemn them. [30] I do not do anything *like that* by my own authority. I judge people only according to what I hear *my Father tell me*. I will judge people fairly, because I do not want to please only myself. Instead, I want to please *my Father*, who sent me.

[31] If I were the *only* one to tell people about myself, *they could rightly say that* what I say is not true. [32] But there is someone else who tells people about me. And I know that what he tells people about me is true. [33] As for you, when you sent messengers to John *the Baptizer to ask about me*, he told the truth *about me*. [34] I don't *need* people to tell others *about me*. But instead, I am reminding *you about what John told people about me,* in order that you will *believe it and* be saved. [35] *John's message about me* was *like* a lamp that shines brightly.[o] For a short while you were willing to be made happy *by that message*.

[36] But there is something else that tells you about me. *It should prove who I am* more than what John *said about me*. The miracles that *my* Father told me to do, the miracles that I am performing, show people that my Father sent me. [37] Furthermore, *my* Father, who sent me, tells people about me. You have never heard his voice or seen him. [38] Furthermore, you have not believed in *me*, the one he sent. So you have not *believed* his message in your hearts. [39] You carefully study the Scriptures, because you think that by *studying* them you will *find the way to* have eternal life. And those Scriptures tell people about me! [40] But you refuse to believe in me in order that you may have *eternal* life.

[41] It does not *matter to* me whether people praise me. [42] But you *want people to praise you*. I know that within yourselves you do not love God. [43] Although I have come to earth with

---

[n] OR, …There will be a time when those who are spiritually dead will hear the voice of me, the Man who is also God.

[o] OR, John was *like* a lamp that shines brightly.

my Father's authority, you do not accept me. But if someone else comes with his own authority, you accept **him**! [44] You accept your praising each other, but you don't try to do things that will result in God himself praising you. So there is no way you can believe *in me*!

[45] But don't think that I am the one who will accuse you while *my* Father is listening! No, it is Moses who will accuse you! You thought that he would *defend you*. [46] He wrote about me, so if you had believed what Moses *wrote*, you would have believed what I *said*! [47] But since you did not believe what he wrote *about me*, there is no way you will believe what I say!"

6

John 6:1-15

THEME: Jesus miraculously fed more than 5,000 people.

[1] Some time later, near the time of the Jewish Passover celebration, Jesus went *with us disciples by boat* and crossed to the eastern shore of Lake Galilee. This lake is *also called* Lake Tiberias. [2] A large crowd of people kept following him *on land* because they had been seeing the miracles he performed *by healing* sick people. [3] Jesus went up on the hillside and sat down with *us* disciples *to teach us*. [4] Then he looked up and saw a great crowd of people coming toward him. [5] He said to Philip, "Where will we buy food for all these people to eat?" [6] He asked this only to find out if Philip believed what *Jesus could do*, because Jesus already knew what **he himself** was going to do. [7] Philip replied to him, "*Even if we had* the amount of money a man earns in eight months, that would not be enough to buy bread so that each person could have a little bit!" [8] Another one of *us* disciples, Andrew, who was Simon Peter's *younger* brother, said, [9] "There is a boy here who has five small barley loaves and two *cooked* fish. But they will not help much among so many people!" [10] Jesus said, "Tell the people to sit down!" There was plenty of grass there, so they all sat down. There were about five thousand men *among those* who sat down. [11] Then Jesus took the small flat loaves and the fish and thanked *God* for them. Then he *gave them to us, and we* distributed the bread and the fish to all the people sitting on the ground. *Because God caused the food to keep increasing*, everyone ate as much as they wanted. [12] When everyone had all the food they wanted, he said to *us* disciples, "Gather up the pieces that are left over. Don't let anything be wasted!" [13] So we gathered up the pieces of the small flat loaves that were left over by those who had eaten. We filled twelve baskets with those pieces!

[14] After the people saw that miracle Jesus had just performed, *many of* them started to say, "Surely this is the prophet *like Moses* that *God promised* to send to the world!" [15] So because Jesus realized that they were about to come and seize him to make him *their* king, he left them again and went up into the hills by himself.

John 6:16-24

THEME: Jesus miraculously walked on the water.

[16] When it was evening, *we* disciples went down to Lake *Galilee*. [17] When it became dark and Jesus had still not joined us, *we* got into a boat and went across the lake towards Capernaum. [18] A strong wind started to blow and made the water very rough. [19] After we had rowed three or four miles, we saw Jesus coming near the boat; he was walking on the water! So we were terrified! [20] But he said to us, "Don't be afraid! It is I!" [21] We were glad to

take him into the boat. As soon as *we* did that, the boat reached the shore where *we* were going!

[22] The next day the crowd of people that had stayed on the other side of the lake *were perplexed about how Jesus had left that area.* They knew there had been only one boat there *the previous day.* They knew that we had gone away in that boat by ourselves. They knew Jesus had not gone with us. [23] Then some *men came* from *the city of* Tiberias in boats. *They were hoping to take some of the crowd back to Tiberias.* They arrived near the place where the people had eaten the food after Jesus had given thanks *and caused it to multiply.* [24] When the crowd realized that neither Jesus nor we disciples were there, *some of* them got into those boats and they sailed to Capernaum to find Jesus.

John 6:25-59

THEME: *Jesus taught them figuratively of the need for them to take for themselves the benefits of his sacrificing himself and shedding his blood to atone for their sins.*

[25] When they found him *in Capernaum* further around the lake, they asked him, "Teacher, *since you did not come in a boat,* when *and how* did you get here?" [26] Jesus replied to them, "Listen to this carefully: Do you know why you are looking for me? It is not because you *have realized who I really am* as a result of seeing me. No, you are looking for me *only* because you had plenty of bread to eat *after I provided it for you by performing a miracle.* [27] Stop desiring food that will soon spoil! Instead, desire to get *spiritual* food that will last forever! Yearn for eternal life! That is what I, the one who came from heaven, will give you. God *my* Father has shown that he approves of my *doing that.*"

[28] Then the people asked him, "What things should we do *to please* God?" [29] Jesus replied, "What God *wants you* to do is this: He wants you to believe that *I am* the one he has sent." [30] So they said to him, "Then perform *another* miracle so that we may see it and believe *you came from God.* What miracle do you *want to* perform? [31] Our ancestors ate the *food called* manna *that God provided for them by a miracle,* in the desolate area. This is written *in the Scriptures* about *what Moses caused to happen:* 'He gave them food from heaven to eat.' *Will you perform a miracle like that?*"

[32] So Jesus said to them, "The truth is that it was not Moses who gave your *ancestors* that food from heaven. No, it was my Father *who gave it to them. And my Father is the one* who gives you the true food from heaven. [33] The true bread from God came down from heaven, and he is the one who will give *eternal* life to *the people of* the world."

[34] *Not understanding what he meant,* they said to him, "Sir, give us that kind of bread **all the time!**" [35] Jesus said to them, "*Just as* food *sustains physical life,* I am the *one who enables you to have spiritual* life. Those who *eat ordinary food and ordinary drink will later be hungry and thirsty.* But those who come to me *to receive that life* will never again *lack anything spiritually.* [36] I told you before that you have seen my *miracles, but after seeing them, instead of understanding who I am,* you have not believed in me. [37] All the people that *my* Father entrusts to me will come to me, and I will certainly welcome anyone who comes to me. [38] When I came down from heaven, it was not to do what I wanted. Instead, I came to do what *my Father,* who sent me, wanted. [39] What the one who sent me wanted was that I would keep forever all those whom he entrusted to me. He wanted me to cause all of them to become alive again on the day *when I judge everyone.* [40] *Long ago in the desolate area, when those who were bitten by snakes looked at the bronze replica of a snake, they were healed.* What my Father wants is that *similarly* everyone who looks at *what I have done* and believes in me will have eternal life. I will cause them to become alive again on the day *when I judge everyone.*"

41 The Jewish *leaders* began to grumble about him because he said, "I am the one who is
like true bread who came down from heaven." 42 They said, "This man is Jesus, the son of
Joseph! We know *the names of* both his father and his mother. *He certainly did not come*
from heaven, so he is *lying* by saying, 'I came from heaven'!" 43 Jesus replied to them,
"Stop grumbling among yourselves *about what I just said*! 44 *My* Father, who sent me,
makes people want to come to me. No others will come to me *to receive eternal life*.
Those who come to me are the only ones who will believe in me. I will raise them *from the*
dead on the *judgment* day. 45 *One of the prophets* wrote *about all those who will trust in*
me, 'God will teach them all.' Everyone who listens to what *my* Father *says* and learns
from him will believe in me. 46 I came from God. I am the only one who has seen *my*
Father. No one else has seen him. 47 Listen to this carefully: Everyone who believes *my*
message has eternal life. 48 *Just as* food *sustains your physical life*, I am the *one who*
enables you to have spiritual life. 49 Even though your ancestors ate the manna *while they*
were traveling in the desolate area, they died *anyway*. 50 But the bread *I am talking about*
is something that came down from heaven. If people eat that bread, their spirits will never
die. 51 I am the one who came down from heaven to enable people to have *spiritual* life. If
people take what I will give them, they will live forever. What I will give them is my flesh,
which I will give to *all the people in* the world in order that they may have *spiritual* life."

52 Then the Jewish *leaders* began to argue among themselves. They said, "There is no
way this man can give us his flesh to eat!" 53 So, *speaking figuratively of the need for them*
to accept for themselves the benefits of his sacrificing himself and shedding his blood to
atone for their sins, Jesus said to them, "Listen carefully to this: *Although* I am the one
who came from heaven, if you do not eat my flesh and drink my blood, you will not have
eternal life. 54 Those who eat my flesh and drink my blood will have eternal life, and I will
cause them to become alive again at the *judgment* day, 55 because my flesh and my blood
are truly spiritual food. 56 Those who eat my flesh and drink my blood will have a close
relationship with me, and I will have a close relationship with them. 57 *My* Father, who is
the *source of everything that* lives, sent me, and I live because *my* Father has *given me*
life. Similarly those who eat my *flesh* will live *eternally* because of what I *do for them*.
58 *I am* the true bread that came down from heaven. Although our ancestors ate *manna*,
they later died *anyway.* But those who eat this bread will live forever." 59 He said this while
he was teaching people in the Jewish meeting place in Capernaum.

John 6:60-71

THEME: Some of Jesus' disciples left him because of this teaching.

60 After they heard him say that, many of his disciples said, "What he is teaching is
repulsive; it is very difficult for anyone to accept it." 61 Jesus was aware that his disciples
were grumbling about it, so he said to them, "I am sorry that this is offending you.
62 *Perhaps you will believe my message* if you see me, the one who came from heaven,
ascending *there* to where I was before![p] 63 *God's* Spirit is the one who gives people *eternal*
life. Human efforts are no help at all *for giving people eternal life*. The message I have
spoken to you *gives spiritual* life.[q] 64 But there are some of you who do not believe *my*
message." *Jesus said that* because he knew from the time he started *his ministry* which of
them would not believe his message. He also knew who would enable his enemies to
seize him.

---

[p] OR, *What will you think if you see me*, the one who came from heaven, ascending *there* to where I was before?

[q] OR, …The message I have spoken to you comes from God's Spirit and gives eternal life.

⁶⁵ Then he continued by saying, "That is why I told you that only those whom my Father has enabled *to believe in me* will come to me *and receive eternal life*."

⁶⁶ From that *time,* many of his disciples left him and no longer went with him. ⁶⁷ So he said to *us* twelve *apostles,* "You don't want to leave me also, do you?" ⁶⁸ Simon Peter replied to him, "Lord, *we won't leave you, because* there is no other person *like you* to whom we can go! You have the message about eternal life! ⁶⁹ We have come to believe for certain that you are the holy one *who has come* from God!" ⁷⁰ Then Jesus replied to us, "*You are saying that as though all* you twelve whom I have chosen believe that. But one of you is *under the control of* Satan!" ⁷¹ He was talking about Judas, the *son* of Simon, from Kerioth *village. Even though* Judas was one of us twelve *apostles,* he was about to enable Jesus' enemies to seize him.

7

John 7:1-9

THEME: Jesus rejected his younger brothers' suggestion that he go immediately to Jerusalem.

¹ After those things happened, Jesus went around in Galilee. He did not want to travel in Judea, because he knew the Jewish *leaders there* were wanting to kill him. ² But when the time of the Jewish celebration *called* 'Celebration of *Living in* Shelters' was near, ³ Jesus' *younger* brothers said to him, "*Since many people* here *have left you,* you should leave and go to Judea *and perform* some miracles there, so that your disciples may see them! ⁴ No one who wants to become famous does things secretly. *You say* you are doing these miracles, *so do some miracles there* so everyone can see them!" ⁵ *They said this critically,* because even *though they were* his own *younger* brothers, they did not believe he *was from God.* ⁶ So Jesus said to them, "It is not yet time for me *to go to the celebration.* For you, any time is right *to go to the celebration.* ⁷ *The people who don't belong to God* cannot hate you, but they hate me because I tell them that what they are doing is evil. ⁸ You go ahead to the celebration. I am not going up *to Jerusalem* to the celebration *yet,* because now is not the right time for me *to go.*" ⁹ After he said that, Jesus stayed *a little longer* in Galilee.

John 7:10-13

THEME: Jesus went to the celebration.

¹⁰ However, *a few days* after his *younger* brothers left to go up to the celebration, he went also. He went with *us* disciples, but no others went with us. ¹¹ At the celebration, the Jewish *leaders* were looking for him. They were asking people, "Has Jesus come?" ¹² Among the crowds, many people were whispering about Jesus. Some were saying, "He is a good man!" But others were saying instead, "No! He is deceiving the crowds!" ¹³ But no one was saying it out in the open, because they were afraid of the Jewish *leaders.*

John 7:14-36

THEME: After Jesus taught people, the Jewish leaders wanted to arrest him, but many others believed he was the Messiah.

¹⁴ In the middle of the days of the celebration, Jesus went to the Temple *courtyard* and began to teach people. ¹⁵ The Jewish *elders* were amazed *at what he was saying.* They said, "This man never studied *in one of our religious schools!* So how can he have learned

so much about the Scriptures?" [16] Jesus replied to them, "What I teach does not come from myself. It comes from *God,* the one who sent me. [17] Those who choose to do what God wants will find out whether what I teach comes from God or whether I am speaking with only my own *authority.* [18] Those who speak with only their own *authority* do that just so others will honor them. But I am *doing things so that others* will honor the one who sent me, and I am someone who speaks the truth. I never lie. [19] *Think about* the laws that Moses gave you. None of you *completely* obeys those laws. So why are you trying to kill me, *saying I don't obey the laws concerning the Jewish day of rest*?"

[20] Someone in the crowd answered, "*By saying this you show that* a demon is controlling you! Certainly no one is trying to kill you!" [21] Jesus replied to them, "Because I did a miracle *of healing someone on the Jewish day of rest*, you are all shocked. [22] Moses gave you *a law that you must* circumcise *the male children and that you must do that exactly seven days after they are born. Actually,* it was your ancestors, *Abraham and Isaac and Jacob,* not Moses, who *started that ritual.* But because of that law, you sometimes circumcise them on the Jewish day of rest, *but that is working, too!* [23] You *sometimes* circumcise boys on our Jewish day of rest so that *you* don't disobey the law of Moses, so it is ridiculous that you are angry with me, saying *I worked* on the Jewish day of rest by healing a man! *Healing someone is far more helpful than circumcising a baby boy!* [24] Stop decidingaccording to what you see *whether my healing this man is wrong*! Instead, decide according to what is really the right action *to help people*!"

[25] Some of the people from Jerusalem were saying, "This is the man they are trying to kill! [26] He is saying these things publicly, but our *Jewish* rulers are not saying anything to *oppose* him. Is that because they have decided he is truly the Messiah? [27] But *he can't be the Messiah, because* we know where this man came from. When the Messiah really comes, no one will know where he comes from."

[28] *They said that because they thought Jesus was born in Nazareth.* So while Jesus was teaching *people* in the Temple *courtyard,* he shouted, "Yes, *you say that* you know me, and *you think* you know where I am from. But I have come here not with my own authority. Instead, *God* is the one who truly sent me. You do not know him. [29] But I know him, because I have come from him. He is the one who sent me!"

[30] Then they tried to seize him *because he said he had come from God.* But no one put their hands on him *to do that,* because it was not yet the time *for him to die.* [31] But many of the crowd believed that he *had come from God.* They said, "When the Messiah comes, he certainly will not do more miracles than this man has done, will he?" [32] The Pharisees heard them whispering these things about him. So they and the chief priests sent some Temple guards to seize him.

[33] Then Jesus said, "I will be with you for only a short time. Then I will return to the one who sent me. [34] Then you will search for me, but you will not find me. And you will not be able to come to the place where I am." [35] So the Jewish *leaders* said to themselves, "Where is this man about to go with the result that we will not be able to find him? *Some Jewish people have* dispersed *and live* among Greek people. He is not intending to go *and live among them* and teach **them**, is he? [36] When he said 'You will search for me, but you will not be able to find me,' and when he said 'You will not be able to come to the place where I am,' what *did he mean*?"

John 7:37-53

THEME: Many people were divided after Jesus said that the Spirit would produce eternal life within those who come to him.

[37] On each of the seven days of the celebration, the high priest poured out some water on the altar in the Temple to remember how God provided water for the people in the desolate area long ago. But the water he poured did not help anyone who was thirsty. So on the last day of the festival, which was the most important day, Jesus stood up *in the Temple courtyard* and said with a loud voice, "Those who are thirsty should come to **me** to drink *what I will give them.* [38] Just as the Scriptures teach, streams of water shall flow out from the inner beings of those who believe in me, and that water will cause them to live eternally." [39] When Jesus said that, he was referring to *God's* Spirit, whom those who believed in Jesus would receive later. Up to that time God had not sent the Spirit *to live within believers*, because Jesus had not yet *died and returned to his* glorious *home in heaven, from where he would send the Spirit.*

[40] When some of the crowd heard those words, they said, "Surely this man is the prophet *whom God promised to send, the one who would be like Moses!*" [41] Others said, "He is the Messiah!" But others, *thinking Jesus was born in Galilee*, said, "The Messiah will not come from Galilee, will he? [42] *It is written* in the Scriptures that the Messiah will come from *King* David's family, and be born in Bethlehem, where *King* David lived!" [43] So the people were divided because of *what they thought about* Jesus. [44] Some people wanted to seize him, but no one laid hands on him *to do that.*

[45] So the Temple guards returned to the chief priests and the Pharisees, *the ones who had sent them to arrest Jesus.* They said to the guards, "Why did you not *seize him and* bring him *here?*" [46] They replied, "No one ever spoke such *amazing things* as this man does!" [47] Then the Pharisees replied, "Has *he* deceived you, too? [48] None of our rulers nor any of us Pharisees have believed that he *is the Messiah!* [49] Not one! But, on the contrary, some of this crowd *have believed in him.* They don't know *the true teachings of* our laws! They will go to hell *for listening to him!*"

[50] Then Nicodemus spoke. He was the one who earlier went to Jesus *at night.* He was also a member of the Jewish council. He said to *the rest of the Council members,* [51] "We haven't listened to what he says to find out what he is doing. Is it permitted in our *Jewish* law for us to say, before questioning someone, that we must punish him?" [52] They replied to him, "You talk like another *disgusting person* from Galilee! Read *what they have written in the Scriptures!* You will find that no prophet comes from Galilee, *like he does!*"[r] [[53] Then they all left and went to their own homes.

---

[r] Some of the oldest Greek manuscripts do not include the sentences that are now marked as 7:53-8:11. Some manuscripts have those sentences at the end of John's Gospel and others have them at the end of Luke's Gospel.

8

John 8:1-11

THEME: Jesus evaded a trap about condemning a woman who had been caught committing adultery.

¹But Jesus went *with us disciples* to Olive *Tree* Hill, *and we stayed near there that night.* ²Early the next morning, we returned to the Temple *courtyard*. Many people gathered around him, so he sat down to teach them. ³Then men who taught the *Jewish* laws and some of the Pharisee *religious group* brought a woman to him. *They* had *arranged to* seize her while she was having sex with a man who was not her husband. They made her stand up in front of the group *that was listening to Jesus,* ⁴and then they said to Jesus, "Teacher, *we* seized this woman while she was having sex with a man who is not her husband. ⁵Moses commanded us in the laws *he gave us* that we should stone such women *to death*. So what do you say *we should do*?" ⁶They asked this question as a trap so they could accuse him. *If he said they should not kill her, they would shame him for disobeying the law of Moses. If he said they should kill her, they could accuse him to the Roman governor.*

But Jesus bent down and wrote something on the ground with his finger. ⁷While they continued to question him, he stood up and said to them, "Whichever one of you has never sinned can be the first one to start throwing stones at her." ⁸Then he stooped down and wrote *some more* on the ground. ⁹After they heard what he said, those *who were questioning him* went away, one by one, the older ones first *and then the younger ones, knowing they were all sinners*. Finally only Jesus was there, along with the woman. ¹⁰Jesus stood up and asked her, "Woman, where are they? Has no one said you must die for your sin?" ¹¹She said, "No, sir, no one." Then Jesus said, "I don't condemn you either. Go *home* now, and do not continue your sinful *life* any longer!"]

John 8:12-20

THEME: Jesus replied to the Pharisees' objection to his claim to be like a light for the people of the world.

¹²Jesus spoke to the people again. He said, "I am *like* a light for *all the people in* the world. *Just as a light reveals what has been in the darkness, I reveal God's truth to them.* Those who walk in the darkness *are unaware of what is around them.* But those who become my disciples will always be aware *of God's truth*. They will have my light *which shows them how to have eternal* life." ¹³So the Pharisees said to him, "You are just telling about yourself! *There is no one else to verify these things you say about yourself*, so *we* don't *need to accept that* what you say is true." ¹⁴Jesus replied, "Even if I were the *only one to* say these things about myself, what I say is true, because I know that I came from *heaven*, and I know that I am going *back to heaven*. But **you** do not know where I came from or where I am going. ¹⁵**You** judge people according to human standards. *The reason* I am *here is* not to *judge and* condemn people *for their sins*. ¹⁶But if I did judge *people*, what I decided would be correct, because I am not the *only* one *who will decide those things*. I and the one who sent me will both decide. ¹⁷*Moses* wrote in your law that if *at least* two people testify that *some event has happened, people should consider* what they say is true. ¹⁸I am telling you about myself, and the other one who is telling you about me is *my* Father who sent me. *So you should believe that what we declare is true*."

¹⁹Then they asked him, "*If you have a* father *we can question about you*, where is he?" Jesus replied, "You don't know *who* I *really am*. If you knew who I *really am*, you would

also know who my Father is." [20] He said these things when he was in the Temple *courtyard*, near the place where the people put their offerings. *This was also very close to the place where the Jewish council met.* But no one seized him to arrest him, because it was not yet time *for him to suffer and die.*

John 8:21-30

THEME: Jesus replied to the Pharisees' continued rejection of Jesus' claims about himself.

[21] Jesus said to them additionally, "I *will soon be* going away. Then *at the end of your life* you will seek me, but you will die *without God forgiving* your sins. Where I will go, you will not be able to come." [22] So the Jewish *leaders* said among themselves, "Is he going to kill himself? Is that the reason he said, 'Where I go, you will not be able to come?'" [23] But Jesus continued by saying to them, "You were born here in this world, but I came from heaven. You belong to those who are opposed to God. I do not belong to them. [24] I told you that you will die *without God forgiving* your sins. If you do not believe I am *who I say that I am*, you will die *without God forgiving* your sins."

[25] So they said to him, "You! Who do you think you are?" Jesus said to them, "Ever since I began *teaching,* I have been telling you who I am! [26] I could judge you and say *you are guilty of* many things. But instead, *I will say only* what the one who sent me tells me to say. *What he says* is true, and I tell the people in the world what I have heard from him."

[27] They did not understand that he was talking about his Father *in heaven.* [28] So Jesus said, "I am the one who came down from heaven, but when you lift me up *on a cross to kill me*, you will know who I am. You will also know that I do not do anything on my own *authority*. Instead, I say just what *my* Father has taught me. [29] He is the one who sent me, and he helps me. Because I always say what pleases him, he has never abandoned me." [30] As Jesus was saying these things, many people believed he *was the Messiah.*

John 8:31-59

THEME: Jesus told his critics which people were true believers like Abraham and which ones really were serving Satan.

[31] Then Jesus said to the Jews who *said they* had come to believe in him, "If you continue to *live in accordance with* my message, you will truly be my disciples. [32] Then you will know *God's* truth, and as a result of *your believing his* truth, he will free you *from being controlled by the one who has made you his slaves.*" [33] They replied to him, "We are descendants of Abraham. We have never been anyone's slaves. So why do you say *we will* be freed *from being someone's slaves*?" [34] Jesus replied, "Listen carefully to what I am going to tell you. All those who continue to sin are *forced to obey* their sinful desires, *just as* slaves *are forced to obey their master.* [35] A slave is not a permanent member of a family. But a son is a member of a family forever. *Similarly, you say you are members of God's family because you are descendants of Abraham, but really, because you are like slaves of your sinful desires, you are no longer permanent members of God's family.* [36] So if you allow me to free you, you will truly be free. [37] I know you are Abraham's descendants. But you are trying to kill me because *you are not* letting my message continue *to change* your inner beings. [38] I am telling you what I saw when I was with *my* Father. But **you** do the things you have heard from **your** father."

[39] They replied to him, "Abraham is our ancestor." Jesus said to them, "If you were Abraham's descendants, *your character would be like Abraham's character, and* you would do *good* things like Abraham did. [40] I have been telling you the truth I heard from

God, but you are trying to kill me. Abraham did not do things like that. ⁴¹ No, you are doing the things your *real* father does."

They said to him, "*We don't know about you, but* **we** are not illegitimate children. And *spiritually*, we have only one Father. That is God." ⁴² Jesus said to them, "If God were your father, you would love me, because I came from God, and now I have come here *to this world*. My coming was not because I *appointed* myself. He sent me. ⁴³ And I will tell you why you don't understand what I say. It is because you don't want to accept my message. ⁴⁴ You belong to your father, the devil, and you desire to do what he wants. He has *caused people to become* murderers from the time when he first *sinned*. He has abandoned *God's* truth because he is a liar by nature. Whenever he lies, he is speaking according to his *nature*, because he is a liar and is the one who originates all lies. ⁴⁵ But because I tell you the truth, you don't believe me! ⁴⁶ *Since I have never sinned*, none of you can show that I have sinned. So, since I tell you the truth, there is no good reason for your not believing me! ⁴⁷ Those who belong to God habitually obey God's message. You don't belong to God; so you don't obey his message."

⁴⁸ The Jewish *leaders* replied to him, "We are certainly right by saying you *believe what is false as* the Samaritans *do,* and that a demon *controls* you!" ⁴⁹ Jesus replied, "A demon does not *control* me! I honor my Father, and you don't honor me! ⁵⁰ I am not trying to honor myself. There is someone else who desires *to honor me*, and he is the one who will judge *whether it is I who am telling the truth or whether it is you who are telling the truth*. ⁵¹ But the truth is that anyone who obeys what I say will never die!"

⁵² Then the Jewish *leaders, thinking he was talking about ordinary death and not about spiritual death*, said to him, "Now we are sure that a demon *controls* you! Abraham and the prophets died *long ago*! But you say that anyone who obeys what you teach will never die! ⁵³ You are certainly not greater than our ancestor Abraham! He died, and all the prophets died, so who do you think you are *by saying something like that*?" ⁵⁴ Jesus replied, "If I were honoring myself, that would be worthless. My Father is the one you say is your God. He is the one who honors me. ⁵⁵ Although you don't know him, I know him *and have a close relationship with him*. If I said that I did not know him, I would be a liar like you are. But I know him, and I obey what he says. ⁵⁶ Your ancestor Abraham was happy when he thought about what I would *do during* my life. *It was as though* he saw that, and was happy."

⁵⁷ Then the Jewish *leaders* said to him, "You aren't fifty years old yet! So you certainly did not see Abraham, *because he died long ago*!" ⁵⁸ Jesus said to them, "The truth is that I existed before Abraham was born!" ⁵⁹ So, *because they were very angry about Jesus intimating that he had eternally existed with God*, they picked up stones to throw at him *to kill him*. But *Jesus* caused them not to be able to see him, and he left the Temple courtyard.

9

John 9:1-12

THEME: Jesus healed a man who was born blind.

¹ As Jesus walked along *with us,* he saw a man who had been blind from the time he was born. ² We disciples asked him, "Teacher, was this man blind from birth because his parents sinned or because he himself sinned?" ³ Jesus replied, "His being blind was not because he or his parents sinned. Instead, *he has been blind* in order that *people can* see the power of God as a result of *what will now happen* to him. ⁴ While there is still time,

I must do the work that the one who sent me *wants me to do. Just as daytime is followed by* nighttime when people do not work, *at the end of our lives it is too late for us to do what God wants.* [5] While I am still *living* in this world, I am the *one who enables people to know about God, like a* light enables the people in this world *to see what is in the darkness.*"

[6] After he said that, he spat on the ground. He made *a little bit of* mud with the saliva, and put it on the man's eyes. [7] Then he said to him, "Go and wash in Siloam pool!" (That name means 'sent;' *just as they sent the water by a channel into the pool, God sent Jesus*). So the man went and washed *in the pool*, and when he went home he was able to see! [8] His neighbors and others who previously had seen him when he was begging said, "He is the man who used to sit here and beg, isn't he?" [9] Some said, "Yes, he is." Others said, "No, *he isn't.* But it is a man who looks like him!" But the man himself said, "Yes, I am that man!" [10] So they said to him, "How is it that now you can see?". [11] He replied, "The man whose name is Jesus made some mud and put it on my eyes. Then he told me to go to Siloam *pool* and wash. So I went there and washed, and then I could see." [12] They said to him, "Where is that man *now*?" He said, "I don't know."

John 9:13-41

THEME: The Pharisees investigated the healing of the blind man.

[13] They took to the Pharisees the man who was previously blind. [14] The day on which Jesus made the mud and enabled the man to see again was a Jewish day of rest. *The Pharisees considered that healing someone was work, and their rules did not permit people to do any work on the Sabbath day.* [15] So the Pharisees also asked him, "How did you become able to see?" He said to them, "The man put mud on my eyes. Then I washed, and now I can see!" [16] So some of the Pharisees said, "Since this man *Jesus* disobeys *our rules about working on* the Jewish day of rest, he is *certainly* not from God." But others said, "If he was a sinner, he could certainly not do such miracles!" So they were divided. [17] So they said to the blind man again, "You are the man whom he enabled to see. What do you yourself say about him?" The man said, "*I think* he is a prophet!" *So they told him to go.*

[18] The Jewish *leaders* still did not believe that the man was blind when he was born, and that he was *now* able to see. So they sent someone to bring the man's parents. [19] *When they got there, the Jewish leaders* asked them, "Is that man your son? Do you say that he was blind when he was born? *If that is true*, how is he now able to see?" [20] His parents replied, "We know that he is our son. We know that he was blind when he was born. [21] But we do not know how he is able to see. We also do not know who enabled him to see. Ask our son! He is old enough *to answer questions from authorities like you*! He can tell you himself!" [22] The Jewish *leaders* had previously declared that they would not allow anyone who declared that Jesus was the Messiah to *enter* their synagogues. His parents *knew that, so* they were afraid of the Jewish *leaders.* [23] That is the reason they said, "He is old enough *to answer questions*, so ask him!"

[24] So they sent someone to bring back to them the man who had been blind. *When he got there*, the *Jewish leaders* said to him, "Knowing that God *is listening*, tell the truth! We know that the man who healed you is a sinner." [25] He replied, "I don't know if he is a sinner or not. But one thing I do know is that I was blind, but now I can see!" [26] So they said to him, "What did he do to you? How did he enable you to see?" [27] He replied, "I told you that already, but you did not pay attention! Why do you want to hear me tell you again? Do you also want to become his disciples?" [28] Then they insulted him angrily. They said, "**You** are that man's disciple, but **we** are Moses' disciples! [29] We know that God spoke to Moses; but this man, we don't know where he is from or where he *gets any authority* from!" [30] The man replied, "That is very surprising! You *say* you don't know where he *gets any authority*. But he enabled me to see! [31] We know that God does not help sinners *who ask God to help*

them. Instead, he listens to *and helps* godly people who pray. He listens to people who do what God wants. ³² No one has ever enabled a man to see who was blind from birth *like I was*. That has never happened since the world began! ³³ So if this man had not come from God, he wouldn't be able to do anything *like that*!" ³⁴ They replied to him, "You bastard!^s Do you think **you** are qualified to teach **us**?" Then they threw him out *of the synagogue*.

³⁵ Jesus heard that they had thrown that man out. He found the man and said to him, "Do you believe that the one who came down from heaven *is the Messiah*?" ³⁶ The man answered, "Sir, who is he? *Tell me*, in order that I may believe in him." ³⁷ Jesus said to him, "You have seen him. *In fact it is I*, the one who is speaking to you." ³⁸ The man said, "Lord, I believe *you are the Messiah*!" Then he *knelt down before* Jesus and worshipped him.

³⁹ Jesus said, "I have come into this world to judge *people*. The result will be that *those who realize they do not know God's truth will perceive it. That is like enabling* those who are blind to see. But the result will also be that people who *falsely think they understand God's truth will never understand it. That is like people* who are blind remaining blind permanently." ⁴⁰ Some of the Pharisees who were with him heard him say that, and said to him, "You are not suggesting that we are *like* blind people, are you?" ⁴¹ Jesus said to them, "If you *realized that you did not yet know God's truth, but you wanted to, then you would be like* blind people *who wanted to see. God would be able to* forgive your sins. But you are now *falsely* claiming that you *know God's truth, so you are like people who are blind, who claim they* can see. *Because of that, God is not able to* forgive your sins."

10

John 10:1-21

THEME: *Jesus explained why he is like a good shepherd.*

¹ *Jesus continued by saying to us,* "Listen carefully to what I say. Anyone who does not enter *the sheep pen* through the gate, if he climbs in some other way, he is a thief or a bandit. ² The man who enters *the pen* through the gate is the shepherd of the sheep. ³ The man who watches the gate at *night* opens the gate for him. The sheep recognize his voice. He summons his own sheep by *calling out* the names *he has given* them. Then he leads them outside *the pen*. ⁴ After he has brought out all his own *sheep*, he goes in front of them. His sheep follow him because they recognize his voice. ⁵ But they will never follow a stranger. Instead, they will run away from him, because they do not recognize a stranger's voice."

⁶ Jesus said that to illustrate *the difference between himself and the Pharisees, who were deceiving the people*. But they did not understand what he was telling them. ⁷ So Jesus spoke to them again. He said, "Listen carefully to what I am saying. I am *like* a gate for the sheep *to enter the sheepfold, because I am the one who allows people to enter God's presence*. ⁸ All of *your religious leaders* who have come previously *without my authority* are *like* thieves and bandits *because they act violently and dishonestly for their own benefit*. But *just as* sheep do not *obey strangers, God's people do not* pay attention to them. ⁹ I am *like* a gate. *God* will save all those who come *to him* by *trusting in* me. *Just as* sheep go in and out *through the gate safely* to find pasture, *I will provide for them and*

protect them. ¹⁰ Thieves come *to a sheep pen* only to steal or kill or destroy *sheep. Similarly, your religious leaders injure God's people spiritually.* But I have come in order that people may have *spiritual* life,[t] and that they may have abundantly *all they need to sustain them spiritually.*

¹¹ I am *like* a good shepherd. A good shepherd *is willing to* die to save the sheep. *In the same way I am ready to sacrifice myself to save those who belong to me.* ¹² A worker whom someone has hired *to look after the sheep* is not *like* the shepherd or the one who owns the sheep. So when a worker sees a wolf coming, he leaves the sheep and runs away. Then the wolf attacks the flock of sheep and *seizes one sheep and* causes *the others* to scatter. ¹³ The worker runs away because he is *only* a man whom someone has hired. He is not *really* concerned about *what happens to* the sheep. *Similarly your religious teachers don't really care what happens to you.* ¹⁴ I am *like* a good shepherd. *Just as a good shepherd knows his* sheep, I know those who belong to me, and they know me ¹⁵ in the same way as *my* Father knows me and I know *my* Father. Furthermore, I am *ready to* sacrifice myself for *those who belong to me.* ¹⁶ And I have other people *who are not Jews* who *will some day* belong to me. They will be *like* sheep from another sheep pen. I must bring them *to God* also.[u] They will pay attention to what I say, and eventually *all those who belong to me* will be *like* one flock, and *I* will be *like* their one shepherd. ¹⁷ The reason *my* Father loves me is that I will sacrifice my life. But *after I do that,* I will become alive again. ¹⁸ No one is causing me to die. Instead, I *have chosen to* sacrifice myself. I have authority to sacrifice myself and I have authority to become alive again. That is what my Father has commanded me to do."

¹⁹ After hearing these words *that Jesus said,* the Jews were divided again. ²⁰ Many of them said, "A demon is *controlling* him and has caused him to become crazy. It is useless to listen to him!" ²¹ But others said, "What he is saying is not something a man whom a demon is controlling would say. And no demon could enable a blind man to see *like Jesus did!*"

John 10:22-42

THEME: The Jewish leaders tried to kill or arrest Jesus for claiming he was equal with God.

²² Then it was time for the celebration *to remember when our ancestors* rededicated *the Temple in Jerusalem.* It was in winter. ²³ Jesus was in the Temple *courtyard,* walking in *the place that people called King* Solomon's porch. ²⁴ The Jewish *leaders* gathered around him and said, "How long will you keep us from knowing for sure *if you are the Messiah?* If you are the Messiah, tell us clearly!" ²⁵ Jesus answered them, "I have been telling you *that I am the Messiah,* but you do not believe me! You should know who I am because of the miracles I do with my Father's authority. ²⁶ But instead, you do not believe in me because you do not belong to *me. You are like* sheep *who belong to a different shepherd.* ²⁷ *Just as sheep* pay attention to the voice *of their true shepherd, my people pay attention to me.* I know them, and they have become my disciples. ²⁸ I will give them eternal life. No one will separate them from me, not ever. No one shall ever pull them away from belonging to me. ²⁹ *Those* that my Father has given to me are more precious than anything else.[v] So no one can pull them away from belonging to me. ³⁰ *My* father and I are equal."

³¹ The Jewish *leaders* again picked up stones to throw at him *and kill him because they were angry at his saying he was equal with God.* ³² But Jesus said to them, "You have

---

[t] OR, ...But I have come in order that people may have *eternal* life...

[u] OR, ...I must bring them *to myself.*

[v] OR, My Father, who has given them to me, is greater than anything that opposes them.

seen me perform many miracles that my Father *told me to do. You should realize from seeing them that I am equal with God.* So, for which of these miracles are you wanting to stone me to death?" [33] The Jewish *leaders* replied, "It's not because you performed a great miracle. Instead, *we are wanting to* stone you to death because you are dishonoring God. You are just a man, but you are saying you are God!" [34] Jesus replied to them, "In the Scriptures it is written *what God said to the rulers whom he had appointed*, 'I have said that you are *like* gods.' [35] God said that *to those leaders when he appointed them. No one objected to that.* And no one can set aside anything that is in Scripture. [36] But I am the one *my* Father set apart to completely belong to him. He sent me here into this world. So you should not say that I am doing wrong by saying that I am God![w] [37] If I were not doing the miracles my Father *told me to do, I would not expect* you to believe in me. [38] But because I perform these miracles, believe *what* these miracles *show about me*, even though you do not believe what I *say.* If you do that, then you will know and understand that *my* Father has a close relationship with me, and I have a close relationship with *my* Father."

[39] After they heard that, they tried to seize him again, but he got away from them.

[40] Then Jesus went *along with us* back across *to the east side of* the Jordan *River.* We went to the place where John was previously baptizing *people.* We stayed there *for a few weeks,* [41] and many people came to him. They were saying, "John never performed a miracle, *but this man has performed many miracles*! Everything John said about this man is true!" [42] Many people *who came* there believed *that he was the Messiah.*

11

John 11:1-16

THEME: Jesus' friend Lazarus died.

[1] *One time* there was a man whose name was Lazarus who was *very* sick. He lived in *the village of* Bethany, where his *older* sisters Mary and Martha lived. [2] Mary was the woman who *later* poured perfume on the feet of the Lord *Jesus*, and then wiped his feet with her hair. [3] So the two sisters sent *someone to tell* Jesus *about Lazarus*, saying 'Lord, the one you love *very much* is very sick.' [4] *They hoped that Jesus would come*, but when Jesus heard the message, he said, "The *purpose of his* being sick is not that he would die. Instead, the purpose is *that people may realize* how great God is, and that people may honor me, God's son, because of *what I will do.*" [5] Jesus loved Martha and her *younger* sister *Mary* and Lazarus. [6] But when Jesus heard that Lazarus was sick, he stayed *where he was* for two more days.

[7] Then he said to us disciples, "Let's go back to Judea." [8] We said, "Teacher, just a short while ago the Jewish *leaders* wanted to stone you to death. So *we don't think you should* go back there again!" [9] *To show us that nothing bad could happen to him until the time God had chosen*, Jesus replied, "There are twelve hours in the daytime, *which is enough time to do what God wants us to do.* People who walk in the daytime will not stumble *over things they can't see*, because they see things by the light from the sun. [10] It is when people walk in the nighttime that they stumble over things, because they have no light."

[11] After he said that, he told us, "Our friend Lazarus has gone to sleep. But I will go there to wake him up." [12] So we said to him, "Lord, if he is sleeping, he will get well. *So you don't*

---

[w] OR, …You should not be angry with me for saying *I am equal with God when I say* I am the Man who is also God.

need to risk your life by going there." [13] Jesus was speaking *figuratively* about Lazarus' death, but we thought he was talking about really being asleep. [14] So then he told us plainly, "Lazarus is dead. [15] But for your sake I am glad I wasn't there *when he died*, because I want you to believe *more firmly that I am the Messiah*. So now, *instead of staying here,* let's go to him." [16] Then Thomas, who was called 'The Twin', said to the rest of us disciples, "Let's all go, so that we may die with him *when his enemies kill him.*"

John 11:17-40

THEME: Lazarus' sisters expressed disappointment that Jesus did not come and heal Lazarus before he died.

[17] When we arrived *close to Bethany*, Jesus found out that Lazarus *had died and had been buried and his body had* been in the tomb for four days. [18] Bethany is less than two miles from Jerusalem. [19] Many Jews had come *from Jerusalem* to console Martha and Mary concerning *the death of* their *younger* brother. [20] When Martha heard *someone say* that Jesus was coming, she went *along the road* to meet him. But Mary stayed in the house. [21] When Martha *got to where Jesus was*, she said to him, "Lord, if you had been here, my brother would not have died *because you would have healed him*! [22] But I know that even now God will do for you whatever you ask *concerning my brother.*" [23] Jesus said to her, "Your brother will become alive again!" [24] Martha said to him, "I know that he will become alive again when all people become alive again on the *Judgment* day." [25] Jesus said to her, "I am the one who *enables people to* become alive again and who *causes people to* live *eternally*. Those who believe in me, even if they die, they will live *again*. [26] Furthermore, all those who believe in me while they are alive, *their souls* will not die *forever*. Do you believe that?" [27] She said to him, "Yes, Lord! I believe that you are the Messiah, the Son of God.[x] You are the one *God promised to send* into the world!"

[28] After saying that, she returned *to the house* and took her *younger* sister Mary aside and said to her, "The Teacher is close *to our village*, and he wants to talk to you." [29] When Mary heard that, she got up quickly and went to him. [30] Jesus had not yet entered the village; he was still at the place where Martha met him. [31] The Jews who were in the house with Mary, consoling her, saw Mary get up quickly and go outside. So they followed her, thinking she was going to the tomb *where they had buried Lazarus*, in order to cry there.

[32] When Mary got to where Jesus was and saw him, she prostrated herself at his feet and said, "Lord, if you had been here, my brother would not have died!" [33] When Jesus saw her crying, and saw that the Jews who had come with her were also crying, in his spirit he was very angry *that Satan had caused Lazarus to die,* and was very disturbed.[y] [34] He said, "Where have you buried his body?" *Martha and Mary* said to him, "Lord, come and see." [35] Jesus began to cry. [36] Then *some of* the Jews said, "Look how much he loved Lazarus!" [37] But some others said, "He enabled a blind man to see. So he should have been able to *heal this man so that* he wouldn't die!"

[38] Within himself Jesus was again very angry[z] *about Lazarus dying*. He came to the tomb. It was a cave. The entrance had been covered with a large stone. [39] Jesus said, "Take away the stone!" Martha, *who, as I mentioned before, was an older* sister of the man who had died, said, "Lord, his *body* has been *in the tomb* for four days, so now there will be a bad smell!" [40] Jesus said to her, "I told you that if you believed *in me*, you would see how great God is! Have *you forgotten that?*"

---

[x] OR, ...the Man who is also God.

[y] OR, ...he was very troubled.

[z] OR, ...very troubled...

John 11:41-48

THEME: Jesus caused Lazarus to be alive again.

⁴¹ So they took away the stone. Then Jesus looked up *toward heaven* and said, "My Father, I thank you that you heard me *when I prayed about this earlier.* ⁴² I know that you always hear me *when I pray.* But instead *of just praying silently,* I said that for the sake of the people who are standing here. I want them to believe that you sent me." ⁴³ After he said that, he shouted, "Lazarus, come out!" ⁴⁴ The man who *had been* dead came out! The strips of cloth were still wrapped around his *hands and feet,* and a cloth was still around his face, *but he came out*! Jesus said to them, "Take off the cloths so that he can walk easily!" *So they did that.*

⁴⁵ As a result, many of the Jews who had come to *see* Mary and who had seen what Jesus did, believed *he was the Messiah.* ⁴⁶ But some of the *others* went to the Pharisees and told them what Jesus had done. ⁴⁷ So the chief priests and the Pharisees gathered all the members of the *Jewish* Council together. They started saying *to each other*, "What are we going to do *about Jesus*? He is performing many miracles! ⁴⁸ If we allow him to keep *doing this*, everyone will believe that he *is the Messiah, and they will make him their king.* Then the Roman *army* will come and destroy our Temple and our whole nation of Israel!"

John 11:49-57

THEME: The Jewish leaders decided to kill Jesus.

⁴⁹ One of the *Jewish Council* members was Caiaphas. He was the Jewish high priest that year. *Hinting that they should get rid of Jesus*, he said to them, "You *talk as though you* don't know anything! ⁵⁰ You don't realize that it would be much better for us if one man died for the sake of the people, rather than *the Romans kill* all the *people of our Jewish* nation." ⁵¹ He said that not because he thought of it himself. Instead, since he was the high priest that year, he was prophesying that Jesus would die for the whole *Jewish* nation. ⁵² But he was also prophesying that Jesus would die, not just for the Jews, but for all the people living in other lands who *would belong* to God, to unite *all of them into* one *group*. ⁵³ So from that day the *Jewish leaders* started to make plans how they could kill Jesus.

⁵⁴ Because of that, Jesus no longer traveled around publicly among the Jewish people. Instead, he left *Jerusalem* along with us disciples and went to a village called Ephraim, in an area near the desolate region. We stayed there *for a while.*

⁵⁵ When it was almost time for the Jewish Passover *celebration*, many *Jews* went up to Jerusalem from other places in the country. They went there to perform the rituals to make themselves acceptable *to God* before the Passover *celebration started.* ⁵⁶⁻⁵⁷ The Jewish chief priests and Pharisees issued an order that if anyone found out where Jesus was, that person should report it to them so that they could seize him. *Because of that, the people supposed that* Jesus would probably not *come to the celebration*. But they kept looking for him, and as they were standing in the Temple *courtyard* they were saying to each other, "What do you think? He won't come to the celebration, will he?"

12

John 12:1-8

THEME: Lazarus' sister Mary poured perfume on Jesus' feet.

[1] Six days before the Passover *celebration started*, Jesus, along with us, arrived in *the village of* Bethany. That was where Lazarus lived. He was the man Jesus *previously* raised from the dead. [2] There they gave a dinner to *honor* Jesus. Martha served the meal. *Her younger brother* Lazarus was among the people who were *reclining and* eating with him. [3] Then Mary took *a bottle* of expensive perfume *called* nard and poured it on Jesus' feet *to honor him*. Then she wiped his feet with her hair. The whole house was filled with the *beautiful* smell of the perfume.

[4] But one of his disciples, Judas Iscariot[aa], objected. He was the one who later enabled Jesus' enemies to seize him. [5] He said, "We should have sold this perfume and given *the money* to poor people! We could have gotten three hundred days' wages for it!" [6] He said that, not because he cared about the poor people, but instead because he was a thief. He was the one who kept the bag *containing the money that people gave to help Jesus and us his disciples*, and he often stole some of the money that *people* put into it. [7] Then Jesus said, "Don't bother her! Let her save *the rest of this perfume* until the day they will bury me *after I die.* [8] There will always be poor people among you, *so you can help them whenever you want to.* But I will not be with you much longer, *so it is good that she showed her appreciation for me now.*"

John 12:9-11

THEME: The Jewish leaders decided to kill Lazarus, too.

[9] A large crowd of Jews heard that Jesus was there *in Bethany*. So they came, not only *to see* Jesus but also to see Lazarus, the man he had raised from the dead. [10] So the chief priests decided to kill Lazarus also, [11] because many of the Jews were *deserting them and* going to Jesus and believing in him because of *Jesus causing* Lazarus *to be alive again*.

John 12:12-19

THEME: Jesus entered Jerusalem as a king, but a humble one.

[12] The next day the huge crowd of people that had come *to Jerusalem* for the *Passover* celebration heard that Jesus was coming. [13] So they *cut* branches from some palm trees and took the branches out *of the city* to *wave them when they* met him. Some of them were shouting, "Praise God! May the Lord *God* bless the one who is coming with his authority!" *Some other people where shouting, "May God bless* the King of Israel!" [14] When Jesus *came near to Jerusalem,* he got a young donkey and sat on it *as he rode into the city.* By doing this *he fulfilled* what had been written *in Scripture,*

[15] You people of Jerusalem, don't be afraid!
Look! Your king is coming!
He is riding on a donkey's colt!

[16] At first we disciples did not understand those things. But after Jesus had returned to heaven, we realized that *a prophet* had written those things about him, and that *by* doing those things for him *the people had fulfilled what the prophet prophesied.*

[aa] OR, ...Judas, the man from *the village of* Kerioth...

[17] The crowd that was with him continued to tell other people that he called Lazarus to come out of the tomb, *and that Lazarus had then become alive again.* [18] Because of that, many people, having heard that he had performed this miracle, went to meet him. [19] So the Pharisees said to each other, "It is obvious that we are making no progress *in trying to stop him*! *It looks like* everyone is becoming a disciple of his!"

John 12:20-28a

THEME: Jesus told some Greeks what people who wanted to be his disciples had to be ready to do.

[20] Among those who went up *to Jerusalem* to worship *God* during the *Passover* celebration were some Greeks. [21] They came to Philip, who was from *the town of* Bethsaida in *the province of* Galilee. They *wanted him* to do something for them. They said, "Sir, we would like to talk with Jesus." [22] So after Philip went and told that to Andrew, they both went and told Jesus. [23] Then, *to show them he must die in order to give eternal life to non-Jews like those Greeks*, Jesus replied to them, "It is time for *God* to honor me, the one who came from heaven. *That will happen when I die.* [24] Listen to this carefully: *My life is like a seed.* If *someone* does not plant a kernel of grain in the ground, it does not change. It remains only one *seed.* But if it changes *after it is planted in the ground, it will grow and* produce many seeds. [25] Anyone who strongly wants to keep on living *here on earth* will surely lose his life forever. But anyone who is willing to die *for my sake* will surely gain eternal life. [26] If *any of these Greeks or* anyone *else* wants to serve me, they must become my disciples. Then, *after they die*, they will be where I am, *in heaven.* My Father will honor all those who serve me.

[27] "Now I am disturbed in my inner being. I don't know what to say. Should I say, '*My* Father, save me from the *suffering and death that I am facing*'? No, *I should not say that, because* the reason I came *into this world* was that I would *suffer* now. [28] My Father, show how great you are!"

John 12:28b-36a

THEME: God encouraged Jesus about his coming death by a voice from heaven.

Then *God* spoke from heaven, saying, "I have already shown how great *I am,* and I will do it again!" [29] The crowd that was there heard it. *Some* said it was thunder. Others said an angel had spoken to him. [30] Jesus replied to them, "The voice you heard speaking *was God's voice, but* it was not for my benefit. It was for your benefit! [31] Now is the time for *God* to judge *the people in* the world. Now is the time when *I* will destroy *the power of Satan,* the one who rules this world. [32] But as for me, when I am lifted up from the ground *on a cross, I will make a way for* gathering everyone to myself." [33] He said this to show us the way in which he was going to die.

[34] *Someone in* the crowd answered him, "We understand from the Scriptures that the Messiah will live forever. So why do you say that the one who came from heaven, *who is the Messiah,* will be lifted up on a cross? What kind of man who came from heaven are you *talking about*?"[bb] [35] Then Jesus said to them, "*My message is like* a light for you. *I* will be with you for only a little while longer. Live and act *as you should* while I am still with you*, because suddenly you will have no more opportunity to hear my message!* You don't want to be like someone upon whom it suddenly becomes dark and he can't see where he

---

[bb] OR, ...That's not the kind of Messiah we are expecting!

is going any more! [36] Believe in my message while you still have an opportunity to do it, so that you may become people who have my truth within you!"

John 12:36b-43

THEME: Most of the Jewish leaders continued to reject Jesus' message.

After he said those things, Jesus left them and hid from them. [37] Although he had done many miracles while people were watching, *most of* them refused to believe he *was the Messiah.* [38] *Their stubbornness and refusal to believe was similar to the stubbornness of the people that* the prophet Isaiah wrote about *long ago,*

Lord, hardly anyone has believed our message!
Most people refused to accept it,
even though you showed them your power!

[39] That was the reason they refused to believe. *It was like* Isaiah wrote somewhere else *that God said,*

[40] They have *refused to understand; they acted as though they were* blind people!
They were insensible in their inner beings!
As a result, they have not perceived *my truth*!
They have not understood it in their inner beings!
They have not turned *from their sinful lives,*
and because of that, I cannot help them!

[41] Isaiah wrote that because *it was as though* he saw *ahead of time* how great Jesus would be, and he prophesied *those things* about him.

[42] Although most of the Jewish *leaders* did not believe Jesus was *the Messiah,* some of them believed in him. But they would not tell anyone that they believed in him, because *they were afraid that if they said that*, the Pharisees would not let them worship in the synagogues. [43] They wanted people to praise them more than they wanted God to praise them.

John 12:44-50

THEME: Jesus warned that God would condemn those who rejected his message.

[44] *Another day, when* Jesus *was teaching the people, he* shouted, "Those who believe in me, they are not believing in *me alone.* Instead, *it is the same as* their believing in the one who sent me. [45] When they see me *and what I am doing, it is as though* they are seeing the one who sent me. [46] I have come into the world *to show people God's truth,* as a light *shows people what is around them.* I have come in order that people who believe in me will not remain *ignorant of God's truth, as those who are* in the darkness *are ignorant of what is around them.*

[47] "As for those who hear my message but do not obey it, I am not *the one who* judges them. *The main reason* I came *into the world* was not to judge *the people of* the world. Instead, I came to save them *from being punished for their sins.* [48] There is something that will judge those who reject me and do not accept my message. On the judgment day *God* will condemn them *because they rejected* the message that I have told them. [49] I have not said things from my own *authority.* Instead, *my* Father, the one who sent me, instructed me what to say and how I should say it. [50] I know that *paying attention to* what he has instructed us *leads to* eternal life. So whatever I say is just what *my* Father has told me to say."

13

John 13:1-17

THEME: Jesus washed the disciples' feet as an example of humble service to each other.

¹When it was the evening before the Passover celebration, Jesus knew that it was time for him to leave this world and *to return* to *his* Father *in heaven*. He loved us who *were his disciples.* He knew *we would continue to live here* in this world, so now he *showed us* how completely he loved us. ²We were eating *the Passover meal.* The devil had already suggested to Judas Iscariot,^cc the son of Simon, that he should betray Jesus. ³But Jesus knew that his Father had given to him complete authority *to control the situation.* He knew he had come from God and would soon return to God. ⁴*But before he left us, he wanted to show us how we should love each other. So* he got up from where he was eating. He took off his *outer* cloak and wrapped a *long* towel around his waist *as a slave would do.* ⁵Then he poured some water in a basin. He began to wash our feet, and then dry them with the towel that he had wrapped around himself.

⁶When he came to Simon Peter, he said to Jesus, "Lord, it is not right for **you** to *humble yourself by* washing **my** feet!" ⁷Jesus replied to him, "Now you don't understand *the meaning of* what I am doing, but you will understand later." ⁸Peter said, "I will never, ever, *allow you to* wash **my** feet!" Jesus replied to him, "If I don't wash you, you cannot continue to be my *disciple.*" ⁹So Simon Peter said to him, "Lord, *in that case,* don't wash just my feet. Wash my hands and my head, *too!*" ¹⁰*Then, to show him that after God had cleansed people from the guilty of their sins, they needed only for God to forgive their daily sins,* Jesus said to him, "Those who have recently bathed need only to have their feet washed, *because they get dirty very quickly on the dusty roads.* The *rest of their bodies are* clean. Similarly I have made you *disciples* free *from the guilt of your sins,* although not all of you are free from guilt." ¹¹He knew which one *of us* was going to betray him. That is the reason he said, "Not all of you are free from guilt."

¹²After he finished washing our feet, he put his cloak back on. Then he sat down and said to us, "Do you understand what I have done for you? ¹³You *show you respect me by* calling me 'Teacher' and 'Lord'. You are right to say that, because I am your teacher and your Lord. ¹⁴But if I, who am your teacher and your Lord, have washed your feet, you ought to *serve each other by doing things like* washing each other's feet. ¹⁵I have made myself an example for you to show you how to *humbly serve each other* as I have done for you. ¹⁶Listen to this carefully: A servant is not greater than his master. A messenger is not greater than the one who has sent him. *So, since you are not greater than I am, you should not be proud and unwilling to serve each other.* ¹⁷Since you now know these things, *God will* be pleased with you if you do them.

John 13:18-30

THEME: Jesus predicted that one of them would betray him to his enemies.

¹⁸"I am not saying *that God will bless* all of you. I knew *what all of you were like when* I chose you. But *I also chose the one who will betray me,* in order that what is written in Scripture might be fulfilled: 'The one who is *acting like he is my friend by* eating with me has become my enemy.'

---

^cc OR, …Judas, the man from *the village of* Kerioth…

¹⁹"I am telling you *about someone betraying me* before it happens, in order that when it happens you may continue to believe that I am *who I say I am.* ²⁰Listen to this carefully: Those who accept any one of you whom I am sending out, *God will consider that* they are accepting me. And those who accept me, *God will consider that* they are accepting *him, the* who sent me."

²¹After Jesus said this: he was very troubled within himself. He solemnly declared, "Listen to this carefully: One of you is going to enable *my enemies* to seize me." ²²We looked at each other. We had no way *of knowing* whom he was talking about. ²³I, the *man other people call* 'the one Jesus loved', was sitting very close to Jesus. ²⁴Simon Peter motioned to me to indicate that I should ask Jesus whom he was talking about. ²⁵So I leaned close to Jesus and asked him, "Lord, who is it?" ²⁶Jesus answered, "It is the one to whom I will give this piece of bread after I dip it *in the sauce in the dish.*" Then, *to show us that he knew who would enable his enemies to seize him,* after he dipped the bread *in the sauce,* he gave it to *Judas Iscariot.* ²⁷As soon as *Judas ate* the bread, Satan took control of him. Then Jesus said to him, "What you are going to do, do quickly." ²⁸But none of the rest of us who were sitting there knew why Jesus said that to him. ²⁹Since Judas took care of the money *people gave us to help us,* some thought Jesus was telling him to *go and* buy some things we needed for the *Passover* celebration. *Some thought he was telling him* to give some money to poor people. ³⁰As soon as Judas had eaten the bread, he left. It was dark *outside,* and it was dark *in his soul, too.*

John 13:31-35

THEME: Jesus commanded his disciples that they should love each other.

³¹After Judas left, Jesus said, "Now *my Father* will show how wonderful I, the one who came from heaven, am. And *as a result of what* I *do,* people will see how great God is. ³²Since people will see how awesome God is as a result of what I *do,* God himself will show people how awesome I am. And he will do that very soon.

³³"*You whom I love as though you were* my children, I will continue with you only a short time longer. Then you will look for me, but I will not be here. Just as I told the Jewish *leaders,* I am telling you now, that where I am going, you cannot come *yet.* ³⁴Now I am giving you a new commandment: you must love each other. You must love each other just the way I have loved you. ³⁵If you keep loving each other, everyone *who is aware of your love* will know that you are my disciples."

John 13:36-38

THEME: Jesus also prophesied that Peter would deny three times that he knew Jesus.

³⁶Simon Peter said to him, "Lord, where are you going?" Jesus replied, "The place where I am going, you cannot come with me now, but you will come there later." ³⁷Peter said, "Lord, why can't I come with you now? I *am ready* to die for you!" ³⁸Jesus answered, "*You say* that you *are ready* to die for me. But the truth is that before the rooster crows *early tomorrow morning,* you will say three times that you don't *know* me!"

14

John 14:1-14

THEME: Jesus encouraged his disciples and told them that he is the only way to the Father.

[1] *Jesus continued by saying to us,* "Stop being worried. Keep on trusting in God; also keep trusting in me.[dd] [2] Where my Father is *in heaven* there is plenty of room *for all of you*! If that were not true, I would have told you. I am about to go *there* to prepare a place for you. [3] And because I will go *there* and prepare a place for you, I will return and take you to be with me. I will do that so that you may also be where I am. [4] You know the road to the place where I am going."

[5] Thomas said to him, "Lord, we do not know where you are going. *So* how can we know the road?" [6] Jesus said to him, "I am the road *to where my Father is*. I am the *one who reveals* the truth *about God,* and the *one who gives eternal* life *to people.* I am the only one who can *enable people* to come to *my* Father. There is no other way. [7] If you *really* knew who I was, you would have known my Father also. From now on, you know him, and *it is as though* you have seen him."

[8] Philip said to him, "Lord, show us your Father and that will be enough for us!" [9] Jesus said to him, "Philip, I have been with you for a long time. So surely you should know who I *really am*! Those who have seen me, *it is as though* they have seen *my* Father. So why do you say, 'Show us *your* Father'? [10] Don't you believe that I have a close relationship with *my* Father, and that *my* Father has a close relationship with me? The message that I tell you comes from my Father, who has a close relationship with me. The message does not come from me. He is enabling me to *teach these things, and* to perform the miracles he *wants me to perform.* [11] Believe that I have a close relationship with *my* Father and that *my* Father has a close relationship with me. If you do not believe that just because of what I say, believe it because of the miracles themselves. [12] Listen to this carefully: *You* who trust in me will do the *kinds of* miracles *that I have done. Because of what I will do for you* after I go to my Father, you will be able to do *miracles* that will be greater than *the ones I have done.*[ee] [13] And whatever you, using my authority, ask me to do, I will do it, in order that I can show you how great *my* Father is. [14] Anything you ask *my Father to do, anything you ask* with my *authority,* I will do.

John 14:15-31

THEME: Jesus promised to send the Holy Spirit to them.

[15] "If you love me, you will do what I have commanded you. [16] Then I myself will request *my* Father, and he will send you someone else who will encourage you.[ff] [17] *I am talking about* the Spirit, who *will teach you God's* truth. He will be with you forever. Those who are opposed to God cannot receive him, because they cannot understand what he *does,* and they cannot know who he is. But you know who he is, because he is with you and he will be inside you. [18] *When I leave you*, I will not let you be alone.[gg] *When I send the Spirit, it*

[dd] OR, …You are trusting in God; also keep trusting in me.

[ee] OR, …After I go to my Father, you will be able to do *miracles* that will be greater than *the ones I have done because I will send God's Spirit to you.*

[ff] OR, …who will be like a legal counsel for you.

[gg] OR, …I will not let you be helpless.

will be like I am coming back to you.^{hh} ¹⁹ Soon those who do not belong to God will not see me anymore. But *when the Spirit comes to you, it will be as though* you will be seeing me again. Because I will be alive again, you also will have *eternal* life. ²⁰ At that time you will know that I have a close relationship with my Father, and you will have a close relationship with me, and I will have a close relationship with you. ²¹ Those who have accepted my commands and obey them are the people who love me. My Father will love those who love me. I also will love them, and I will fully reveal to them *what I am like.*"

²² Then Judas spoke to him. He was not Judas Iscariot, *but instead a disciple whose other name was Thaddeus.* He said, "Lord, what has happened so that you can fully reveal to us what you are like, and not reveal that to those who do not belong to God?" ²³ Jesus replied to him, "Those who love me will obey what I have told them. My Father will *also* love them. It is **those** people whom my Father and I will *be able to* come to and have a personal relationship with. ²⁴ But those who do not love me will not obey what I have told them. *So I cannot reveal to them what I am really like.*

"These words that I am telling you have not come just from me. They came from *my* Father, the one who sent me. ²⁵ I have told you all these things while I am still with you. ²⁶ But *my* Father will send the Holy Spirit. He is the one who will encourage you.ⁱⁱ He will come with my authority. He will teach you all of *God's truth that you need to know.* He will also cause you to remember all the things I have told you. ²⁷ As I leave you, I am causing you to have *inner* peace. This *inner* peace comes from **me.** I am not causing you to have something that those who do not belong to God can give you. *So* stop being worried, and do not be afraid.

²⁸ You heard me say to you, 'I am going away, but *later* I will come back to you.' If you loved me, you would be glad that I am going back to *my* Father, because *my* Father is greater than I am, *and there he will honor me and will send the Spirit to you.* ²⁹ I have told you *these things now* before they happen, so that when they happen you will believe *that what I said is true.* ³⁰ I will not *be able to* talk to you much longer, because what happens to me will be as though *Satan,* the ruler of this world, is coming *to attack me.* But he has no *control over what happens to* me. ³¹ Instead, the people who do not belong to God must learn *from what happens to me* that I love *my* Father, and I am doing the things he has commanded me to do. Now, let's get up and leave here."

15

John 15:1-17

THEME: Jesus taught them that they needed to remain closely united to him in order to live in a way that would please God.

¹ *Jesus talked to us as we were walking along. Speaking figuratively of the need for us to conduct our lives in a way that God wants us to, he said, "I am like a genuine vine, not like those Jewish leaders who do not teach the truth. My father is like a gardener who works to* take care of a vineyard. ² *Just as a gardener cuts off the branches that bear no grapes, God gets rid of those who do not please him even though they say they belong to him.* Those branches that bear fruit, *the gardener* trims so that they may bear more grapes. *Similarly, my Father disciplines those who conduct their lives as he wants them to.* ³ You

---

^{hh} OR, …*When I rise from the dead,* I will come back to you.

ⁱⁱ OR, …He is the one who will be like a legal counsel for you.

are already *like* the branches *that a gardener* trims, because *you have believed* the message I have told you. ⁴ Remain having a close relationship with me. *If you do that*, I will remain having a close relationship with you. A branch *of a vine* cannot bear fruit *if it is cut off and left* by itself. To bear fruit, it must remain attached to the vine. Similarly, you *cannot conduct your lives the way God wants you to* if you do not remain united to me.

⁵ "I am *like* a vine. You are *like* the branches. All those who remain having a close relationship with me and I with whom I remain having a close relationship, will *do much that pleases God, like vines that* bear much fruit. *Remember that* you can do nothing *that truly pleases God* without my *help.* ⁶ A gardener cuts off and throws away useless branches. Then, after they dry up, *he* picks them up and throws them into a fire and burns them. Similarly, everyone who does not remain having a close relationship with me, *God* will get rid of. ⁷ If you remain having a close relationship with me and you keep *living in accordance with* my message, you can ask *God to do* anything *for you*, and he will do it. ⁸ The way you honor my Father is by doing much that pleases him, and by doing that you will show that you are my disciples.

⁹ "I have loved you in the same way that *my* Father has loved me. Now keep conducting your lives in *a way that is appropriate for those whom* I love. ¹⁰ If you obey what I have commanded you, you will be living in *a way that is appropriate for those whom* I love, just as I have obeyed what my Father has commanded me and I live *in a way that is appropriate for someone* **he** loves. ¹¹ I have told you these things so that you may be joyful as I *am joyful*, and that you may be completely joyful. ¹² What I am commanding you is this: Love each other just like I have loved you. ¹³ The best way that people can show they love someone else is to die for that person. There is no way you can love someone in a greater way than that. ¹⁴ You *show that you* are my friends if you keep doing what I have commanded you. ¹⁵ I will no longer call you my servants, because servants do not know *why* their masters *want them to* do things. Instead, I have said you are my friends, because I, *acting like a friend,* have revealed to you **everything** my Father has told me. ¹⁶ You did not decide to become my *disciples.* Instead, I chose you, so that you would do many things that please him. The results of what you do will last *forever*. I also chose you so that *my* Father will do for you whatever you, using my authority, ask him to do. ¹⁷ *I repeat what* I have commanded you: Love each other.

John 15:18-16:4

THEME: Jesus taught them that those who were opposed to God would hate them, too.

¹⁸ "The people who are opposed to God will hate you. When that happens, remember that they hated me first. ¹⁹ If you belonged to those who are opposed to God, they would love *you like they love* those who belong to their group. But you do not belong to those who are opposed to God. Instead, I chose you so that you would separate yourselves from them. That is why those who are opposed to God hate you. ²⁰ Remember these words that I told you: 'No servant is greater than his master.' *That means you, my servants, cannot expect people to treat you better than they treat me*. So, since they have persecuted me, they will persecute you also. If they had paid attention to the things I taught them, they would pay attention to what you teach them. ²¹ They will treat you like that because you *belong to* me, and because they do not know the one who sent me. ²² If I had not come and spoken *God's message* to them, they would not be guilty *of rejecting me and my message*. But now *I have come and told them God's message, so* they will have no excuse *when God judges them* for their sins. ²³ As to all those who hate me, *it is as though* they hate my Father as well. ²⁴ If I had not done among them the *miracles* that no one else ever did, they would not be guilty of the sin *of rejecting me*. But now, *although they have seen those miracles,* they have hated both me and my Father. ²⁵ But this has happened in order that

these words that have been written in their Scriptures might be fulfilled: 'They hated me for no *good* reason.'

²⁶ "*Later* I will send to you from *my* Father the one who will encourage you.ʲʲ He is the Spirit *who will teach you God's* truth. He will come from my Father. He will tell people about me. ²⁷ But you *disciples* must also tell people about me, because you have been with me from the time when I started *my ministry*."

16

¹ *Jesus continued by saying to us*, "I have told you these things in order that you will not stop trusting in me *when people persecute you*. ² They will not let you worship in their synagogues. In fact, there will be a time when anyone who kills you will think he is doing God a favor *by doing that*. ³ They will do such things because they have never known who I *really am*, nor who *my* Father *is*. ⁴ I have told you these things in order that when *they start to persecute you*, you will remember that I warned you. I did not tell you these things when you first started *to accompany me* because I was with you, *and they were causing trouble for me, not for you.*

John 16:5-15

THEME: Jesus told them some things that the Holy Spirit would do.

⁵ "Now I am *about to* return to the one who sent me. But *I am disappointed that* none of you is asking me, 'Where are you going?' ⁶ Instead, because I have told you these things, you are very sad. ⁷ But the truth is that it is good for you that I am going away, because if I don't go away, the *Holy Spirit,* who will encourage you, will not come to you. But when I go, I will send him to you. ⁸ When he comes, he will prove that those who do not belong to God *are wrong about what is* sinful and about who is really righteous and about whom *God will* judge *and condemn for their sins*. ⁹ *He will tell people their greatest* sin is that they do not believe in me. ¹⁰ *He will tell people that* because I am going *back* to my Father, and you will no longer see me, *you will know that I am the one who was truly* righteous. ¹¹ *He will tell people that the fact* that *God* has already determined that *he* will punish *Satan*, the one who rules this world, shows that *some day God* will also punish *those who do not belong to him.*

¹² "I have many more things *I would like* to tell you, but you are not able to accept them now. ¹³ But *God's* Spirit is the one who will teach you *God's* truth. When he comes, he will guide you so that you *understand* all *spiritual* truth. He will not speak from his own *authority*. Instead, it is the things that he hears *my Father say* that he will tell you. He will also tell you about things that will happen *later*. ¹⁴ He will honor me by taking my *truth* and revealing it to you. ¹⁵ Everything that *my* Father has is mine. That is why I said that the Spirit is able to take my truth and reveal it to you.

John 16:16-33

THEME: Jesus told them that after he left they would be sad, but that they would later be joyful when they saw him again.

¹⁶ "After a short time *I will leave you, and* you will not see me. Then a short time *after that* you will see me *again*." ¹⁷ *So* some of us said to each other, "What does he mean by

---

ʲʲ OR, ...the one who will be like a legal counsel for you.

saying 'After a short time you will not see me,' and 'A short time after that you will see me again'? And *what does he mean by* 'Because I am going back to *my* Father'?" [18] We kept asking each other, "What *does he mean by* saying 'After a little while'? We don't understand what he is saying."

[19] Jesus realized that we wanted to ask him *about that*. So he said to us, "You are asking each other *what I meant* when I said, 'After a short time you will not see me, and then a short time *after that* you will see me *again*.' [20] Listen to this carefully: *After I die*, those who oppose God will be happy, but you will be sad. But *later* you will stop being sad and you will become joyful. [21] A woman who is about to bear a child feels pain because that is *what happens* at that time. But after her baby is born, she forgets that pain, because she is very joyful that her child has been born. [22] It will be the same with you. Now *I will die and* you will be sad. But after that, I will see you again. Then you will be joyful, and no one will be able to stop you from being joyful. [23] When that happens, you will not ask **me** any questions *about anything.* Listen to this carefully: *After that happens, my* Father will do for you anything you ask, because of your relationship with me. [24] Up to the present time you have not asked *God to do* anything for you because of your relationship with me. Now keep asking *him for things that you need. If you do that*, you will receive them, and then you will be completely joyful.

[25] "Although I have been speaking these things using figurative language, there will soon be a time when I will no longer use that kind of language. Instead, I will tell you plainly about my Father.[kk] [26] At that time, you will ask *him for things* because you belong to me. I will not *need to* ask *my* Father to do what you ask. [27] *My* Father himself loves you because you have loved me and because you have believed that I came from God, *so he wants you to ask* **him**.[ll] [28] I came from *my* Father into this world. Now I will be leaving this world and going *back* to my Father."

[29] Then we, his disciples, said, "Now you are speaking plainly, without using figurative language. [30] Now we understand that you know everything. You don't need anyone to ask you questions *about anything, because you know what we want to ask before we ask you.* That *also* leads us to believe that you came from God."

[31] Jesus replied to us, "**Now** you say that you believe *that I came from God.* [32] But listen! There will soon be a time, and that time is already here, when you will all run away! Each of you will run away to your own home. You will leave me, and I will be alone. But I will not *really* be alone *at that time*, because *my* Father is always with me. [33] I have told you these things in order that you may have *inner* peace because of your relationship with me. In this world you will have trouble. But be courageous! I have defeated those who are opposed to me, and *you can defeat them too*!"

17

John 17:1-5

THEME: Jesus prayed that God would honor him.

[1] After Jesus said those things, he looked *up* toward heaven. Then he prayed, "My Father, it is now the time *for me to suffer and die.* Honor me *as I do that*, in order that I may honor you. [2] You gave me authority over all people, in order that I might enable all those whom

---

[kk] OR, …Instead, I will tell you plainly what my Father *wants*.

[ll] OR, …so he does not need anyone to persuade **him** to help you.

you chose *to come* to me to have eternal life. ³ *The way for people* to have eternal life is for them to know that you are the only true God, and to know that I, Jesus, am the Messiah, the one you have sent. ⁴ I have honored you here on this earth by completing all the work you gave me to do. ⁵ My Father, now honor me when I am with you *again,* by causing me to have the greatness I had when I was with you before the world began.

John 17:6-19

THEME: Jesus prayed that God would protect his disciples.

⁶ I have revealed *what* you *are like* to the people you brought to me from among those who do not belong to you. Those *who came to me* belonged to you, and you brought them to me. Now they have obeyed your message. ⁷ Now they know that everything you have given me, *your message and your work,* comes from you. ⁸ I gave them the message you gave me, and they have accepted it. They now know for certain that I came from you. They now believe that you sent me. ⁹ I am praying for them. I am not praying for those *who do not belong to you.* Instead, *I am praying* for those whom you have brought to me, because they belong to you. ¹⁰ All *the disciples* that I have belong to you, and all those who belong to you also belong to me. They have shown how great I am. ¹¹ I will not be *staying* in the world any longer. I will be coming back to you. They, however, will be *here* in the world *among those who are opposed to you.* My Holy Father, protect them by your power, the power that you gave me, in order that they may be united as we are united. ¹² While I have been with them, I have *completely* protected them by the power you gave me. As a result, only one of them will be eternally separated from you. He is the one who was doomed to be eternally separated from you. *That has happened* to fulfill *what a prophet wrote* in the Scriptures.

¹³ *Father,* now I am about to return to you. I have said these things while I am still *here* in the world in order that my *disciples* may fully experience being joyful, as I have been joyful. ¹⁴ I have given them your message. As a result, those who are opposed to you have hated them, because *my disciples* do not belong to those who oppose you, just as I do not belong to those who oppose you. ¹⁵ I am asking you, not that you take them out of this world, but instead that you protect them from *Satan,* the evil one. ¹⁶ They do not belong to those who are opposed to you, just as I also do not belong to them. ¹⁷ Set *my disciples* apart so that they may completely belong to you, by *enabling them to conduct their lives in accordance with* what is true. Your message is true. ¹⁸ Just as you sent me here into this world, now I surely will be sending them *to other places* in the world. ¹⁹ I set myself apart to completely belong to you, in order that they also may truly dedicate themselves completely to you.

John 17:20-26

THEME: Jesus prayed for future believers.

²⁰ I am praying not only for these *eleven disciples.* I am praying also for those who *will* believe in me as a result of *hearing* their message. ²¹ My Father, *I want* all of them to be united, just as I am united with you because of my relationship with you and as you are united with me because of your relationship with me. I also want them to be united with us. *I want that to happen* so that those who don't know you may know that you sent me. ²² I have honored my disciples just as you honored me, in order that they may be united as we are united. ²³ I want them to be united just as they are united with me and as you are united with me. May they be completely united, in order that those who do not belong to you may know that you sent me and that you have loved them just as you have loved me.

²⁴ *My* Father, I want *the disciples* you have brought to me to *some day* be with me *in heaven* where I will be. I want them to see my greatness. I want them to see the greatness you gave me because you loved me. You gave me that greatness before you created the world.

²⁵ *My* righteous Father, although the people who do not belong to you do not know what you *are like*, I know what you *are like*, and my disciples know that you sent me. ²⁶ I have revealed to them *what* you *are like*, and I will continue to reveal to them *what* you *are like*. I will do that in order that they may love *others* just as you love me, and in order that I may live in them *by my Spirit*."

18

John 18:1-11

THEME: They seized Jesus in a grove of olive trees.

¹ After Jesus finished praying, he went across the Kidron brook, along with us disciples, to a grove *of olive trees*.

² Judas, who was *about to* enable Jesus' enemies to seize him, knew that *he would probably be* there. *He knew that because* Jesus often gathered there with us. ³ So Judas came to that grove, leading a troop of Roman *soldiers* and some Temple guards who had been sent by the Pharisees and chief priests. They were carrying torches and lamps and weapons. ⁴ Jesus knew everything that was about to happen to him. So *as they approached*, he stepped forward and asked them, "Whom are you looking for?" ⁵ They replied to him, "Jesus, the man from Nazareth." He replied, "I am Jesus." Judas, the one who was enabling his enemies to seize him, was with them. ⁶ When Jesus told them "I am Jesus," they lurched backward and fell down on the ground *because of his power*. ⁷ He asked them again, "Who are you looking for?" They said, "Jesus, *the man* from Nazareth." ⁸ Jesus replied, "I told you that I am Jesus. So since I am the one you are looking for, allow these *disciples of mine* to go." ⁹ *This happened* in order that *when they did what he asked them to do*, the words would be fulfilled that he had prayed, 'I will never lose any of those whom God has brought to me.'

¹⁰ Simon Peter had a sword. So he drew it and *tried to kill* the high priest's servant, *but only* cut off his right ear. The servant's name was Malchus. ¹¹ Jesus said to Peter, "Put your sword *back* into its sheath! Don't *you realize* I have to go through what *my* Father wants me to suffer?"

John 18:12-14

THEME: They took Jesus to be questioned by Annas, the former high priest.

¹² Then the troop of soldiers, along with their commander and the Jewish Temple guards, seized Jesus. They tied his hands *behind his back*. ¹³ Then they took him first to Annas, *who was previously the high priest*. He was the father-in-law of Caiaphas. Caiaphas was the high priest that year. ¹⁴ He was the one who *previously* advised the Jewish *Council* that it would be better if one man died for the sake of the people than for all the people of the Jewish nation to die.

John 18:15-18

THEME: Peter denied that he was Jesus' disciple.

¹⁵ Simon Peter and *I* were following Jesus. Because the high priest knew *me*, *his doorkeeper permitted me* to enter the courtyard, ¹⁶ but Peter had to wait outside the doorway. But since I knew the high priest, I went back to the doorway and spoke to the girl who was guarding the doorway. Then *she allowed* Peter to come in. ¹⁷ The servant girl who was guarding the doorway said to Peter, "Surely you are not another disciple of that man *they have arrested*, are you?" He said, "I am not." ¹⁸ It was cold, so the high priest's slaves and Temple guards made a charcoal fire and were standing around it to keep warm. Peter was also standing close to it, warming himself.

John 18:19-24

THEME: The High Priest questioned Jesus.

¹⁹ *While Peter was doing that*, the high priest asked Jesus about his disciples and about what he was teaching people. ²⁰ Jesus replied, "I have always spoken where many people could hear me. I have taught them in the synagogues and in the Temple courtyard, in places where many Jews come together. I have spoken nothing secretly. ²¹ *So* why are you asking me questions *like this illegally*? Ask the people who heard what I taught! They certainly know what I said!" ²² After Jesus said that, one of the Temple guards standing near him slapped him on his face. He said, "That is not the way you should answer the high priest!" ²³ Jesus replied to him, "If I had said something that was contrary *to your laws*, you could have told *me what I said that* was wrong. But I said only what was right, so why are you striking me? ²⁴ Then after they tied Jesus' hands *again*, Annas sent him to Caiaphas, the high priest.

John 18:25-27

THEME: Peter denied two more times that he knew Jesus.

²⁵ As Simon Peter was standing warming himself *near the fire*, someone else said to him, "You are not one of that man's disciples, are you?" He denied *that he was*, and said, "I am not." ²⁶ *Later* one of the high priest's servants, a man who was a relative of the man whose ear Peter had cut off, said to him, "I saw you with that man in the grove *of olive trees*, did I not?" ²⁷ Peter again denied it. Immediately a rooster crowed, *as Jesus had said would happen.*

John 18:28-40

THEME: Pilate the governor questioned Jesus.

²⁸ Then the *Jewish leaders* led Jesus from the *home of* Caiaphas to the headquarters *of Pilate, the Roman governor.* It was before dawn. *Pilate was a non-Jew, and they thought that if they entered his headquarters*, they would become unacceptable to God, and as a result they would not be able to eat *the food during* the Passover *celebration. Because of that, they did not want to enter Pilate's headquarters.* ²⁹ So Pilate came out to *talk to* them. He said, "What law do you say this man has disobeyed?" ³⁰ *They knew Jesus had not disobeyed any Roman law, so they did not want to answer him. Instead,* they said, "If this man were not a criminal, we would not have brought him to you!" ³¹ Then Pilate said to them, "Take him yourselves, and judge him according to your own law!" Then the Jewish *leaders* said, "*No! We want him executed, but we want you Romans to execute him, because* we Jews have no right to execute anyone!" ³² *The Romans executed people by*

nailing them to a cross. So, as a result of what *the Jewish leaders said*, what Jesus had
said previously about the way he was going to die was *about to be* fulfilled.

[33] Pilate then went back inside his headquarters and summoned Jesus. *Because the
Jewish leaders had said that Jesus claimed to be a king*, he said to him *scornfully*, "Are
you the king of the Jews?" [34] Jesus replied, "Are you asking that because you yourself
want to know if I claim to be a king, or because someone else said *that I claim to be their
king*?" [mm] [35] Pilate replied, "**I** am not a Jew, *so how can I understand these matters?* It was
your fellow Jews and your chief priests who brought you to me! What have you done *to
make them want to have you executed*?" [36] Jesus replied, "It is not people in this world
who are *making me* king. If it was people in this world who were making me a king, my
disciples would have fought to prevent the Jewish *leaders* from seizing me. But it is not
someone here in this world who is making me a king." [37] Then Pilate said to him, "So *are
you saying that* **you** are a king?" Jesus replied, "*Yes*, what you have said about my being
a king *is correct*. I was born to become a king, and I came into this world to tell people the
truth *about God*. Everyone who *supports* the truth pays attention to what I say." [38] Pilate
said to him, "*How can anyone know* what the truth is?"

After he said that, he went outside and talked to the Jewish *leaders* again. He said to
them, "I do not find that he has done anything at all for which I should punish him. [39] But
you *Jews* customarily, *every year* during the Passover *celebration*, ask me to release for
you *someone who is in prison*. So would you like me to release for you the *man who you*
Jews *say is your* king?" [40] They shouted again, "No, don't *release* this man! Instead,
release Barrabas!" But Barrabas was *in prison because he was* a revolutionist!

19

John 19:1-16a

THEME: Pilate finally permitted them to crucify Jesus.

[1] Then Pilate took Jesus *inside and had soldiers* strike Jesus with a whip that had pieces
of metal or bone fastened to it. [2] The soldiers also took *some branches with* thorns and
wove them to make *something like* a crown, and put it on his head. They also put a purple
robe on him. *They did these things to ridicule him by pretending he was a king.* [3] Then they
kept coming to him and saying, "Hooray for the King of the Jews!" and slapping him *on his
face*.

[4] Once more Pilate came outside and said to the crowd, "Look! I am bringing him out to
you so that you may know that I do not find him to be guilty of any crime." [5] When Jesus
came out, wearing the crown of thorns and the purple robe, Pilate said to them, "Look at
this *wretched* man!" [6] When the chief priests and Temple guards saw him, they shouted,
"*Command your soldiers to* kill him by nailing him to a cross! Crucify him!" Pilate, *knowing
they could not legally do it themselves*, said to them, "You yourselves take him and crucify
him! As for me, I do not find that he has done anything for which he should be punished."
[7] The Jewish *leaders* replied, "*Our ancestor Moses gave us* a law *that says we must kill
anyone who claims to be God*. This man claims he is the Son of God,"[nn] *so you must have
him executed*." [8] When Pilate heard that, he was more afraid *of what would happen to
himself if he commanded the soldiers to kill Jesus*. [9] So he *took Jesus* back inside the

---

[mm] OR, ...or because Caiaphas said *that I claim to be their king*?"

[nn] OR, ...This man claims that he is God...

headquarters. He said to Jesus, "Where do you *really* come from?" But Jesus did not answer him. [10] So Pilate said to him, "Are you refusing to answer me? Don't you know that I have authority to release you, and I *also* have authority to *have* you crucified?" [11] Jesus replied, "The only authority you have is what has been given to you by God. The *high priest* put me into your hands. *He has done to me what he wanted to do, and you really do not want to do it.* So he is guilty of committing a greater sin *than you are.*"

[12] Because of that, Pilate kept trying to release Jesus. But the Jewish *leaders, threatening to report to the Emperor that Pilate was not going to punish a man who claimed he was a king,* continued to shout, "Anyone who claims that he is a king is opposing the Emperor! So if you release this man, *we will make sure that* the Emperor *learns about it. So think about what the Emperor will do when he* no longer *considers* you his friend!" [13] When Pilate heard that, he brought Jesus out again. He sat down on the seat where he made decisions *about punishing people.* It was called The Stone Pavement. In the Aramaic language its name was Gabbatha. [14] It was almost noontime, on the day they prepared *things for* the Passover *celebration.*[oo]

Pilate said to the Jewish *leaders, ridiculing them,* "Look at your king!" [15] They shouted, "Take him away! Take him away! Have him crucified!" Pilate said to them, "*He is* your **king**! *Do you really want* me to *tell my soldiers to* crucify **him**?" The chief priests replied, "The Emperor is our king! We do not have any other king!" [16] Then *at last* Pilate agreed to do *what they wanted, and he told the soldiers* to crucify Jesus.

John 19:16b-24

THEME: They nailed Jesus to a cross.

Then the soldiers took Jesus away. [17] *As they left,* he himself was carrying the cross *on which they were going to nail him.* They went to a place called The Place of a Skull. In the Aramaic language it is called Golgotha. [18] There, *after removing most of his clothes,* the soldiers nailed him to the cross. They also *nailed* two other *criminals to crosses.* There was one on each side, and Jesus was in the middle.

[19] Pilate also *had them* write *on a board* a notice *that stated why they were executing him,* and fasten it to the cross. *They wrote* 'Jesus of Nazareth, the King of the Jews.' [20] Many Jews were *able to* read this sign, because the place where Jesus was crucified was very close to the city *of Jerusalem, where many people had come for the celebration,* and because they wrote it in three languages, Hebrew, Latin, and Greek. [21] The Jewish chief priests *protested,* saying to Pilate, "Don't write 'the King of the Jews'! Instead, *write,* 'This man said that he is the King of the Jews'!" [22] Pilate replied, "What I *told them to* write is what they have written, *and I won't change it.*"

[23] After the soldiers nailed Jesus to the cross, they took his clothes and divided them into four parts, one part for each soldier. But they kept his cloak *separate.* This cloak had been woven *from top to bottom* from one piece of cloth. [24] So they said to each other, "Let's not tear it. Instead, let's decide by gambling who will get it." So that is what the soldiers did. As a result, these words that *were written* in Scripture were fulfilled:
They divided *most of* my clothes among themselves.
They cast lots for *one piece of* my clothing.

[oo] OR, It was almost noontime, on the day before the Jewish day of rest during the Passover celebration.

John 19:25-27

THEME: Jesus entrusted his mother to John's care.

²⁵ Near the cross where *they had nailed* Jesus stood his mother, his mother's sister, Mary the *wife* of Clopas, and *another* Mary, the woman from *the village of* Magdala. ²⁶ Jesus saw his mother standing there. He also saw me standing near by. Then he said to his mother, "This man *will now be like* your son." ²⁷ And he said to me, "*Treat this* woman as your mother." So from that time I took her to my home *and took care of her.*

John 19:28-37

THEME: Jesus died.

²⁸ Later, Jesus knew that he had now completed everything *that God sent him to do, but he knew that something else that was written in* the Scriptures *had* to be fulfilled. So he said, "I am thirsty!" ²⁹ There was a jar of sour wine there. So someone got a stalk of a *plant called* hyssop and put a sponge *on it. He soaked the sponge in the wine and then* lifted it up to Jesus' lips. ³⁰ When Jesus tasted the sour wine, he shouted, "*I have finished all I came to do!*" Then he bowed his head and *died*, putting his spirit into *God's hands.*

³¹ That was the day they prepared *everything for the Jewish day of rest.* The next day was a special day of rest, *because it was the day of rest during the Passover celebration.* The Jewish *leaders* did not want the bodies *of the three men* to remain on crosses during the day of rest *because leaving bodies hanging overnight would be contrary to their Jewish laws.* So they went to Pilate and asked him *to* command *soldiers* to break the legs *of the three men on the crosses, so that they would die quickly.* Then their *bodies* could be taken down *and buried.* ³² So, *after Pilate gave them permission*, soldiers went and broke the legs of the first man whom they had nailed on a cross near Jesus. Then they broke the legs of the second man. ³³ But when they came to Jesus, they saw that he was dead already. So they did not break his legs. ³⁴ Instead, one of the soldiers pierced Jesus' side with a spear *to make sure Jesus was dead.* Immediately blood *clots* and *other* liquid flowed out, *which showed that Jesus was really dead.* ³⁵ I, *John,* saw this myself, and what I am writing is true. I *know that* I am telling the truth, and I am saying this in order that you may believe *my testimony about Jesus.* ³⁶ These things happened in order that these words would be fulfilled *that are written in* Scripture: 'No one will break any of his bones.' ³⁷ And *they fulfilled* another Scripture passage *that has these words*: 'They will look on the one whom they have pierced.'"

John 19:38-42

THEME: Joseph and others put Jesus' body in a cave.

³⁸ Later, Joseph, from *the town of* Arimathea, *went to Pilate and* asked Pilate to *allow him* to take Jesus' body *down from the cross.* Joseph was a disciple of Jesus, but he did not tell anyone that because he was afraid of the other Jewish *leaders.* Pilate gave him permission, so he went *with others* and took Jesus' body *down from the cross.* ³⁹ Nicodemus went with him. He was the man who previously went to visit Jesus at night. Nicodemus bought an *expensive* mixture of myrrh and aloe *spices to put on the body.* It weighed about 75 pounds. ⁴⁰ They took the body of Jesus and wrapped strips of linen cloth around it, putting the spices in the strips of cloth. They did this according to the Jewish customs *about burying bodies in tombs.* ⁴¹ Close to the place where Jesus was crucified there was a grove *of trees*, and *at the edge of* that grove was a new burial cave. No body had ever been put in that cave *previously.* ⁴² The Jewish day of rest would start *at sunset,*

and they had to finish the burial before then. So, since that cave was nearby, they laid Jesus' body there *and rolled a huge stone in front of the entrance.*

20

John 20:1-9

THEME: On Sunday morning they discovered that Jesus' tomb was empty.

¹Early on Sunday morning, while it was still dark, Mary, the woman from *the village of* Magdala, went to the *burial* cave *with some other women.* She saw that the stone had been removed from the *entrance to the* cave. ²So she ran to where Simon Peter and I *were staying.* She said to us, "They have taken the Lord's *body* out of the tomb, and we don't know where they have put it!" ³So Peter and I started going to the tomb. ⁴We were both running, but I ran faster than Peter and got there first. ⁵I stooped down *at the entrance* and looked inside. I saw the strips of linen cloth lying there *where his body had been laid,* but I did not go inside. ⁶Then Simon Peter, who was running behind me, arrived. He went inside the cave. He *also* saw the strips of linen cloth lying there. ⁷He also *saw the* cloth that they had *wrapped* around Jesus' head. It had been folded and put aside, separate from the linen strips. ⁸Then I also went inside. I saw *those things* and I believed *that Jesus had truly become alive again.* ⁹Before this happened, we did not understand from *what the prophets had written in* the Scriptures, that he had to become alive again after he died.

John 20:10-18

THEME: Jesus appeared to Mary from Magdala.

¹⁰Then *we two* disciples went back to where we were staying. *In the meantime,* Mary *returned to the cave.* ¹¹As she stood outside the cave crying, she stooped down to look inside the cave. ¹²She saw two angels in white *clothing,* sitting at the place where Jesus' body had been laid. One was where his head had been, and the other was where his feet had been. ¹³They said to her, "Woman, why are you crying?" She said to them, "They have taken away *the body of* my Lord, and I don't know where they have put it!" ¹⁴After she said that, she turned around and saw Jesus standing *there,* but she did not know that it was Jesus. ¹⁵He said to her, "Woman, why are you crying? Who are you looking for?" Thinking that he was the gardener, she said to him, "Sir, if you have taken his *body* away, tell me where you have put it. Then I will get it *and bury it properly.*" ¹⁶Jesus said to her, "Mary!" She turned toward him *again and recognized him.* Then she exclaimed in Aramaic, "Rabboni!" which means 'Teacher'. ¹⁷Jesus said to her, "Don't keep clinging to me, because I have not yet returned to my Father. Go to my disciples and tell them, 'I am about to return to my Father and your Father, to the one who is my God and your God'." ¹⁸So Mary went to where we disciples were and told us that she had seen the Lord *alive again.* She also told us what Jesus said that she *should tell us.*

John 20:19-25

THEME: Jesus appeared to many of his disciples.

¹⁹On that Sunday evening *we* disciples gathered together. *We* locked the doors because we were afraid *the Jewish leaders might arrest us. Suddenly* Jesus appeared *miraculously* and stood among us! He said to us, "May God give you *inner* peace!" ²⁰After he said that, he showed us *the wounds in* his hands and his side. We were very happy when we saw

the Lord! [21] Jesus said to us again, "May God give you peace! Just as *my* Father sent me, now I am sending you *to proclaim my message*." [22] After saying that, he breathed on us and said, "Receive the Holy Spirit! [23] If you forgive people for their having sinned, *God will already* have forgiven them. If you do not forgive them, *God* has not forgiven them."

[24] One of us disciples, Thomas, the one whom we called The Twin, was not with us when Jesus appeared to us. [25] When the rest of us told him that we had seen the Lord, he said to us, "If I do not see the marks of the nails in his hands and put my fingers in the place where the nails were, and put my hands into the place in his side *where the soldier thrust the spear*, I will certainly not believe *that he was the one you saw!*"

John 20:26-29

THEME: Jesus appeared to all of his disciples, including Thomas.

[26] A week later we were in *the house* again. This time Thomas was with us. Although *we* had locked the doors, Jesus *again* appeared *miraculously* and stood among us. He said, "May God give peace to you!" [27] Then he *showed* Thomas *his hands* and said to him, "Put your finger here! Look at *the wounds in* my hands! Reach out your hand and put it in *the wound in* my side! Stop doubting! Instead, believe *that I am alive again!*" [28] Thomas answered him, "*You are truly* my Lord and my God!" [29] Jesus said to him, "Because you have seen me, you have believed *that about me*. But God *is truly* pleased with those who have believed *that about me* even though they have not seen me!"

John 20:30-31

THEME: John stated the purpose of this book.

[30] We disciples saw Jesus perform many other miracles, but *I* have not written about them in this book. [31] But these *that I have written about, I* have written about them in order that you may believe that Jesus is the Messiah, the Son of God,[pp] and in order that you may have *eternal* life by trusting in what he *has done for you*.

21

John 21:1-14

THEME: Jesus appeared to seven disciples and enabled them miraculously to catch a lot of fish.

[1] After that, Jesus showed himself to us disciples when we were at Lake Tiberias, *which is another name for Lake Galilee*. This is what happened: [2] Simon Peter, Thomas who was called The Twin, Nathaniel from *the town of* Cana in Galilee, my older brother and I, and two other disciples were together. [3] Simon Peter said to us, "I am going to *try to* catch some fish." We said, "We'll go with you." So we went down *to the lake* and got in the boat. But that night we caught nothing. [4] Early the next morning, Jesus stood on the shore, but we did not know that it was Jesus. [5] He called out to us, "My friends, you haven't *caught* any fish, have you?" We answered, "You are correct, *we haven't caught any*." [6] He said to us, "Throw your net out from the right-hand side of the boat! Then you will find some!" We did that, and we caught so many fish *in the net* that we were unable to pull the net into *the boat!* [7] *But I knew it was Jesus, so* I said to Peter, "It is the Lord!" Peter had taken off his

---

[pp] OR, But *I have written about* these miracles, in order that you may believe that Jesus is the Messiah, the Man who is also God…

cloak *while he was working,* but as soon as he heard *me say* "It is the Lord!" he wrapped his cloak around him and jumped into the water *and swam to shore.* [8] The rest of us came *to the shore* in the boat, pulling the net full of fish. We were not far from shore, only about a hundred yards. [9] When *we* got to the shore, we saw that there was a fire of burning coals there, with a *large* fish on the fire, and *some* bread. [10] Jesus said to us, "Bring some of the fish you have just caught!" [11] Simon Peter got in *the boat* and dragged the net to the shore. It was full of large fish. There were 153 of them! But in spite of there being so many fish, the net was not torn. [12] Jesus said to us, "Come and eat some breakfast!" None of us dared to ask him, "Who are you?" because we knew it was the Lord. [13] Jesus came and took the bread and gave it to us. He did the same with the fish. [14] That was the third time Jesus appeared to us disciples after he was raised from the dead.

John 21:15-19

THEME: Jesus asked Peter three times if he really loved Jesus, and then Jesus told him how he would die.

[15] When we had finished eating, Jesus said to Simon Peter, "John's *son* Simon, do you love me more than these *other disciples do*?" Peter said to him, "Yes, Lord, you know that you are dear to me." Jesus said, "Give to *those who belong to* me *what they need spiritually, like a shepherd provides* food for his lambs." [16] Jesus said to him again, "John's *son* Simon, do you love me?" He replied, "Yes, Lord, you know that you are dear to me." Jesus said to him, "Take care of *those who belong to* me, *like a shepherd takes care of his* sheep." [17] Jesus said to him a third time, "John's son Simon, am I really dear to you?" Peter was grieved because Jesus asked him this three times, *and because the third time he changed the question.* He said, "Lord, you know everything. You know that you are dear to me." Jesus said, "Give to *those who belong to* me *what they need spiritually, as a shepherd provides* food for *his* sheep. [18] Now listen to this carefully: When you were young, you put your clothes on by yourself, and you went wherever you wanted to go. But when you are old, you will stretch out your arms, and someone will fasten them *with a rope,* and they will lead you to a place you don't want to *go.*" [19] Jesus said this to indicate how Peter would die *on a cross* in order to honor God.[qq] Then Jesus said to him, "Keep being my faithful disciple *until you die.*"

John 21:20-23

THEME: Peter asked Jesus what would happen to John.

[20] Peter turned around and saw that I was following them. I was the one who leaned close to Jesus during the *Passover* meal and said, "Lord, who is going to enable your enemies to seize you?" [21] When Peter saw me, he asked, "Lord, what *is going to happen* to **him**?" [22] Jesus said to him, "If I want him to remain *alive* until I return, that is not your concern! You be my *faithful* disciple!" [23] So what Jesus said about me spread among the other believers, and *they thought that Jesus meant* I would not die. But Jesus did not say that I would not die. He said only, "If I want him to remain *alive* until I return, that is not your concern!"

John 21:24-25

THEME: A statement about the truth and accuracy of this document.

[24] *I, John,* am the disciple who has seen all these things and I have written them down.

[qq] OR, …die *violently* in order to honor God.

We *elders of the congregation at Ephesus* know that what *John has written* is true.

[25] Jesus did many other things. If people would write them down in detail, I suppose that the whole world would not have enough space to contain the books that they would write *about what he did.*

The account of the first Christians, which we call the book of

Acts

1

Acts 1:1-3

THEME: Luke referred to the Gospel he had written to Theophilus.

[1] *Dear* Theophilus,

In my first book that I wrote *for you*, I wrote about many of the things that Jesus did and taught [2] until the day on which *God* took him up *to heaven*. Before *he went to heaven*, as the Holy Spirit *guided him*, he told, to the apostles whom he had chosen, *the things he wanted them to know.* [3] After he had suffered *and died on the cross*, he became alive again. As he appeared to them *often* during *the next* forty days, the apostles saw him many times. He proved to them in many ways that he was alive again. He talked *with them* about *how* God would rule *the lives of people who accepted him as their king.*

Acts 1:4-5

THEME: Jesus commanded his apostles to wait for the Holy Spirit.

[4] *One time* while he was with them, he told them, "Do not leave Jerusalem *yet*. Instead, wait *here* until my Father sends *his Spirit to you*, just as he promised *to do*. You have heard me speak *to you* about that. [5] John baptized people in water *because they said they wanted to change their lives*, but after a few days *God* will put the Holy Spirit within you *to truly change your lives.*"

Acts 1:6-9

THEME: Jesus said they would tell about him everywhere, and then he ascended to heaven.

[6] One day when the *apostles* met together *with Jesus*, they asked him, "Lord, will you now become a king over *us* Israelite people *like King David was*?"[a] He replied to them, "You do not *need* to know the time *periods* and days *when that will happen.* [7] My Father alone has decided *when he will make me king.* [8] But, *you do need to know that* the Holy Spirit will make you *spiritually* strong when he comes to live in you. Then, you will *powerfully* tell people about me in Jerusalem and in all *the other places in the district of* Judea, in *the district of* Samaria, and in places far away, all over the world." [9] After he said that, he was taken up *to heaven*, while they were watching. *He went up into* a cloud, which prevented them from seeing him *anymore*.

---

[a] OR, ..."Lord, will you now defeat the Romans and restore the kingdom to us Israeli people?"

Acts 1:10-11

THEME: Angels told the apostles that Jesus would return later.

¹⁰ While *the apostles* were *still* staring towards the sky as he was going up, suddenly two men who were wearing white clothes stood beside them. *They were angels.* ¹¹ *The two of* them said, "You men from *the district of* Galilee, you do not need to stand *here any longer* looking up at the sky! *Some day* this same Jesus, whom *God* took from you up to heaven, will come back *to earth.* He will return in the same manner as you *just now* saw him when he went up to heaven, *but he will not return now.*"

Acts 1:12-14

THEME: The apostles and other believers often prayed together.

¹² Then *after the two angels left*, the apostles returned to Jerusalem from Olive *Tree* Hill, which was about a half mile away from Jerusalem. ¹³ When they entered *the city*, they went into the upstairs room *in the house* where they were staying. *Those who were there included* Peter, John, James, Andrew, Philip, Thomas, Bartholomew, Matthew, *another* James *the son* of Alphaeus, Simon who belonged to the group that wanted to expel the Romans, and Judas *the son* of *another man named* James. ¹⁴ All these apostles agreed concerning the things about which they continually were praying *together. Others who prayed with them* included the women *who had accompanied Jesus*, Mary who was Jesus' mother, and his *younger* brothers.

Acts 1:15-17

THEME: Peter told them why someone must replace Judas.

¹⁵ During those days Peter stood up among his fellow believers. There were *at that place* a group of about 120 of *Jesus' followers*. He said, ¹⁶⁻¹⁷ "My fellow believers, *there are words that King* David wrote in the Scriptures long ago that needed to be fulfilled. The Holy Spirit, *who knew Judas would be the one who would fulfill those words*, told David what to write. ¹⁷ *Although* Judas had been chosen along with *the rest of* us to serve *as an apostle*, Judas was the person who guided the people who seized Jesus.

Acts 1:18-19

THEME: How Judas died.

¹⁸ *The Jewish leaders* gave Judas money when he *promised to* treacherously *betray Jesus. Later, Judas returned that money to them*. When Judas *hanged himself*, his body fell down to the ground. His abdomen burst open, and all his intestines spilled out. *So the Jewish leaders* bought a field *using* that money. ¹⁹ All the people who reside in Jerusalem heard *about that*, so they called that field according to their own *Aramaic* language, Akeldama, which means 'field of blood', *because it was where someone bled and died*.

Acts 1:20

THEME: Peter quoted from the Psalms about Judas.

²⁰ Peter also said, "*I perceive that what happened to Judas is like what the writer of* Psalms *desired to happen*: 'May his house become deserted, and may there be no one to live in

it.[b] And it seems that *these other words that David wrote also refer to Judas:* 'Let someone else take over his work as a leader.'

Acts 1:21-22

THEME: Peter concluded that they needed to choose a man to replace Judas.

[21] "So it is necessary *for us apostles* to choose a man *to replace Judas. He must be one who* accompanied us all the time when the Lord Jesus was with us. [22] *That would be* from *the time when* John *the Baptizer* baptized *Jesus* until the day when Jesus was taken from us up *to heaven*. He must be one who saw Jesus alive again *after he had died*."

Acts 1:23-26

THEME: Jesus' followers prayed and then chose Matthias to replace Judas.

[23] So the *apostles and other believers* suggested *the names of two men who qualified. One man was* Joseph Barsabbas,[c] who *also* had the *Roman* name Justus. The other man was Matthias. [24-25] Then they prayed like this: "Lord *Jesus*, Judas stopped being an apostle. *He died and* went to the place where he *deserved to be. So we need to choose someone* to replace *Judas in order* that he can serve *you as* an apostle. You know what everyone is really like. So *please* show us which of these two men you have chosen." [26] Then they cast lots *to choose between the two of* them, and the lot indicated Matthias. So they considered Matthias *to be an apostle* along with the *other* eleven apostles.

2

Acts 2:1-4

THEME: The Holy Spirit came and enabled the disciples to speak other languages.

[1] On the day when *the Jews were celebrating the festival of* Pentecost, the *believers* were all together in one place *in Jerusalem*. [2] Suddenly *they heard* a noise *coming* from the sky *that sounded* like a strong wind. The noise was heard throughout the entire house where they were sitting. [3] Then they saw *what looked* like flames of fire. These flames separated *from one another*, and *one of them* came down on *the head of* each of the believers. [4] Then all of the believers were completely empowered by the Holy Spirit, and he enabled them to begin speaking other languages *that they had not learned*.

Acts 2:5-13

THEME: Jews from many places were amazed to hear their native languages spoken by the believers.

[5] At that time *many* Jews were staying in Jerusalem *to celebrate the festival of Pentecost. They were people who always tried to obey the Jewish laws. They had come* from many different countries. [6] When they heard that *loud* noise *like a wind*, a crowd came together *to the place where the believers were*. The crowd did not know what to think, because each of them was hearing *something being spoken* in his or her own language. [7] They

---

[b] OR, …'Judge him, Lord, so that neither he nor anyone else may live in his house!'

[c] OR, …*One man was* Joseph, *whom people* called Barsabbas…

were completely amazed, and they said *to each other*, "All these men who are speaking have *always* resided in *the district of* Galilee*, so they would not know our languages!* [8] *We don't understand* how these men can speak our own native languages! *But* all of us hear them *doing that*! [9] *Some of us are from the regions of* Parthia and Media and Elam, and *others of us* reside *in the regions of* Mesopotamia, Judea, Cappadocia, Pontus and Asia. [10] There are some from Phrygia and Pamphylia, Egypt, and the regions in Libya *that are* near *the city of* Cyrene. *There are others* who are *here* visiting *Jerusalem* from Rome. [11] *They include native* Jews as well as non-Jews who have accepted what we Jews believe. And others of us are from *the island of* Crete and from *the region of* Arabia. *So how is it that these people* are speaking our languages, telling us *about* the great things *that* God has done?" [12] All *those people* were amazed, and did not know what to think *about what was happening.* So they asked one another, "What does this mean?" [13] But *some* of them made fun of *the believers.* They said, "*These people are talking like this because* they have drunk too much new wine!"

Acts 2:14-21

THEME: Peter said the prophet Joel foretold what the Holy Spirit would do.

[14] So Peter stood up with the *other* eleven *apostles* and spoke loudly to the *crowd of* people, saying, "*My* fellow-Jews and you *others* who are staying in Jerusalem, listen to me, all of you, and I will explain to you what is happening! [15] *Some of* you think that *we are drunk*, but we are not drunk. It is *only* nine in the morning, *and people here never get drunk at this time* in the day! [16] Instead, *what has happened to us is* the *miraculous* thing that the prophet Joel wrote about *long ago. Joel wrote,*

God says, [17] "During the final days *before I judge all people*, I will give my Spirit generously to people everywhere. *As a result,* your sons and daughters will tell *people* messages from me, the young men among you will see visions *from me,* and the old men among you will have dreams *that I will give them.* [18] During those days I will generously give my Spirit *even* to men and women believers *who are* slaves, so they can tell *people* messages from me. [19] I will cause amazing things to happen in the sky, and I will do miracles on the earth that will show *how powerful I am. Here* on the earth *I will cause war, so that people will bleed and die*, and there will be fire and dark smoke. [20] *In the sky* the sun will *appear* dark *to people,* and the moon *will appear* red *to them. Those things will happen* before the important and amazing day *when I,* the Lord *God, will come to judge everyone.* [21] *Before that time*, all those who ask *me to save them from the guilt of their sins* will be saved."

Acts 2:22-24

THEME: Peter said, "You killed Jesus but God caused him to live again."

[22] Peter continued, "*My fellow* Israelites, listen to me! *When* Jesus from Nazareth *lived* among you, God proved to you *that he had sent him* by enabling him to do many amazing miracles that showed *he was from God.* You yourselves know *that is true.* [23] *Even so*, you *let someone* put this man *Jesus* into the hands of his enemies. *However,* God had already planned for that, and he knew all about it. Then you urged men who do not obey God's laws to kill Jesus. They did that by nailing him to a cross. [24] He suffered terribly *when he died, but God* did not let him continue to be dead, because it was not possible for him to remain dead. God caused him to become alive again.

Acts 2:25-28

THEME: David foretold that the Messiah would rejoice about becoming alive again.

²⁵ "*Long ago King* David wrote *what* the Messiah *said,*
I knew *that* you, Lord *God, would always be* near me. You are right beside me, so I will not be afraid of *those who want to harm me.* ²⁶ Because of that, I joyfully praise *you, O God.* And *I* am completely confident that *you will raise me from the dead.* ²⁷ You will not allow my spirit to remain in the place where the dead are. You will not *even* let my body decay, *because* I am devoted to you and always obey *you.* ²⁸ You have told me *that you will cause my body* to come to life *again.* You will make me very happy *because* you will be with me *forever.*

Acts 2:29-31

THEME: Peter explained that David wrote that the Messiah would become alive again.

²⁹ *Peter spoke* boldly, "My fellow-Jews, I can tell you confidently that *our royal* ancestor, *King* David, died, and that his *body* was buried. And the place *where they* buried his body is *still* here today. ³⁰ So *we know that David was not speaking those words about himself. But* because he was a prophet, *he spoke about the Messiah.* David knew that God had strongly promised him that he would cause one of his descendants to become king like David was king.ᵈ ³¹ David knew beforehand *what God would do,* so he *was able to* say that God would cause the Messiah to live again *after he had died.* He said that God would not let the Messiah remain in the place of the dead, nor let his body decay.

Acts 2:32-35

THEME: Peter said, "Jesus has abundantly given us the Holy Spirit, shown by what you see and hear."

³² "*Jesus is the Messiah, and after he died,* God caused him to become alive *again.* All of us, *his followers,* have seen *and tell people* that Jesus has become alive again. ³³ God has greatly honored him *by causing him to rule* right beside him *in heaven.* Jesus has received the Holy Spirit from *God* his Father, *just as* God promised. *So* Jesus has generously given us the Holy Spirit, *and he has shown that by* what you are seeing and hearing. ³⁴ *We know that David was not speaking about himself* because David did not go up into heaven *as Jesus did. Besides that,* David himself said *this about the Messiah:*
The Lord *God* said to my Lord *the Messiah,* "Rule here beside me, ³⁵ while I completely defeat your enemies."

Acts 2:36

THEME: Peter said, "Know surely that God has made this Jesus both Lord and Messiah."

³⁶ *Peter concluded,* "So, *I want you and* all *other* Israelite people *to* know this for sure: God has caused this Jesus to be both *our* Lord and the Messiah. *But God considers that* you are the ones who nailed him to a cross."

ᵈ OR, ...to *be the Messiah who would* rule *God's people* like David had ruled *them.*

Acts 2:37-40

THEME: Peter told them to repent and said that believers would baptize them.

[37] When the people heard *Peter's words*, they felt very guilty. So they asked him and the other apostles, "Fellow-countrymen, what should we do *so that God will forgive us*?"

[38] Peter *answered* them, "Each of you should turn away from your sinful behavior. Then *we* will baptize you, if *you now believe* in Jesus Christ. Then *God* will give you the Holy Spirit. [39] *God* has promised *to do that* for you and your descendants, and for all *others who believe in him*, even those who *live* far away *from here*. The Lord our God *will give his Spirit* to everyone whom he invites *to become his people*!" [40] Peter spoke much more *and* spoke forcefully to them. He pleaded with them, "*Ask God* to save you *from the punishment he will give to* these evil people *who have rejected Jesus*!"

Acts 2:41-42

THEME: Many people became believers and joined the other believers.

[41] So the people who believed Peter's message were baptized. There were about three thousand *of those who* joined the group *of believers* that day. [42] They continually obeyed the teaching of the apostles, and they very frequently met together *with the other believers*. And they regularly ate *together and celebrated the Lord's Supper*, and prayed *together*.

Acts 2:43-47

THEME: The apostles worked miracles, all the believers shared everything, and the Lord helped them.

[43] All the people *in Jerusalem* were greatly reverencing *God because* the apostles were frequently doing many kinds of miraculous things. [44] All of the believers were united *and regularly met* together. They were also sharing everything that they had with one another. [45] *From time to time some of* them sold *some of* their land and *some of the other* things that they owned, and they would give *some of* the money *from what they sold* to others *among them*, according to what they needed. [46] Every day they continued meeting together in the Temple *courtyard*. And every day they gladly and generously shared their food *with each other*, as they ate together *and celebrated the Lord's Supper* in their houses. [47] *As they did so*, they were praising God, and all the *other* people *in Jerusalem* were *thinking* favorably towards them. *As those things were happening*, every day the Lord *Jesus* increased *the number of people who were being saved*.

3

Acts 3:1-8

THEME: Peter healed a lame man, so the people were amazed.

[1] *One day* Peter and John were going to the Temple *courtyard*. It was three o'clock in the afternoon, at the time when people prayed *there publicly*. [2] There was a man there who had been lame from the time he was born. He *was sitting by* the gate called Beautiful Gate, at the entrance to the Temple *courtyard*. People put him there every day, so he could ask those who were entering *or leaving* the Temple courtyard to give him some money.

³As Peter and John were about to enter *the Temple courtyard*, he saw them and asked them several times to give him some money. ⁴As Peter and John looked directly at him, Peter said to him, "Look at us!" ⁵So he looked directly at them, expecting to get some *money* from them. ⁶Then Peter said to him, "I don't have any money, but what I *can do,* I will *do* for you. Jesus Christ, from *the town of* Nazareth, has authorized me *to heal you*! *So get up and* walk!" ⁷Then Peter grasped his right hand and helped him to stand up. Immediately the man's feet and ankles became strong. ⁸He jumped up and began to walk! Then he entered the Temple *courtyard* with them, walking and leaping and praising God!

Acts 3:9-10

THEME: The people were amazed.

⁹All the people *there* saw him walking and praising God. ¹⁰They recognized that he was the man who used to sit at the Beautiful Gate in the Temple *courtyard* and ask people for money! So all the people there were greatly amazed at what had happened to him. ¹¹As the man clung to Peter and John, all the people were so surprised *that they did not know what to think*! So they ran to them at the place *in the Temple courtyard* that is called Solomon's Porch.

Acts 3:12-16

THEME: Peter explained that Jesus healed the man, and that they should repent.

¹²When Peter saw it, he said to them, "Fellow Israelis, you should not be surprised about what has happened to this man! And you should not stare at us, either! You seem to think that the two of us enabled this man to walk because we ourselves are powerful or because we please God very much! ¹³*So let me tell you what is really going on.* Our ancestors, including Abraham, Isaac and Jacob, worshipped God. And now he has greatly honored Jesus, who always served him. Your *leaders* brought Jesus *to the governor, Pilate,* so that *his soldiers would kill Jesus*. And *God considers that* in front of Pilate you *were the ones who rejected* Jesus *as your king*, after Pilate had decided that he should release Jesus. ¹⁴*Although Jesus* always did what was right and good, you rejected him. *Pilate wanted to release him, but* you urgently asked Pilate to release a murderer! ¹⁵*God considers that* you killed *Jesus*, the one who gives people *eternal* life. But God has greatly honored him by raising him from the dead. Many of us saw *him after that, and now* we are telling *you* about it. ¹⁶But it is because *we two* trusted in what Jesus *could do for this man, that he* made this man, whom you see and know, strong again. Yes, it is because we trusted in Jesus that he has completely healed this man for all of you to see.

Acts 3:17-26

THEME: Peter told them to repent.

¹⁷"Now, my fellow-countrymen, I know that you and your leaders did that *to Jesus* because you *and they* did not know *that he was the Messiah*. ¹⁸However, *your putting him to death* was how God let people do what he had prophesied they would do. *Long ago* he told all the prophets to write *what people would do to the Messiah. They wrote* that the Messiah, whom God *would send,* would suffer *and die*. ¹⁹So, confess *to God* that what you did was wrong, and *ask God to help you* do what pleases *him*, in order that he may completely forgive you for your sins. ²⁰*If you do that*, there will be times *when you will know that* the Lord *God is* helping *you*. And some day he will *again* send back *to earth* the Messiah, whom he appointed for you--Jesus. ²¹Jesus must stay in heaven until the time when God will cause all that he has created to become new. Long ago God promised *to do that, and* he chose holy prophets to tell *that to people*. ²²For *example, the prophet*

Moses said *this about the Messiah*: 'The Lord your God will raise someone up to be a prophet to tell you *words from God. God will send him* as *he sent* me, *and he will be* from among your own people. You must listen to everything that prophet tells you *and obey him*. [23] *Those who* do not listen to *that prophet and obey* him will no longer *belong to* God's people, and *God* will get rid of them'."

[24] *Peter continued*, "All the prophets have told *about what would happen during* these days *in which we are living. Those prophets include* Samuel *and all the others who* later also spoke *about these events* before they happened. [25] You *as well as we* are the people *to whom God sent the Messiah, just like* the prophets said *he would*. And when God strongly promised *to bless* our ancestors, he also surely promised to bless you. He said to Abraham *concerning the Messiah*, '*I* will bless all people on the earth as a result of *what* your descendant *will do*.'" [26] *Peter concluded*, "*So* when God sent *to the earth* his servant Jesus, he sent him first to you *Israelite people* to bless you. *God will* enable you to stop doing what is wicked *and to start doing what pleases him*."

4

Acts 4:1-4

THEME: Jewish leaders arrested Peter and John, but many people became believers.

[1] *Meanwhile, in the Temple courtyard, there were some* priests, the officer who was in charge of the Temple police, and *also some* Sadducee *sect members*. These men came to Peter and John while the two of them were speaking to the people. [2] These men were very angry, because the *two* apostles were teaching the people *about Jesus*. They were telling people that because *God raised* Jesus *from the dead, God* would cause other people who have died to become alive again. [3] So those officials seized Peter and John and put them in jail. *They had to wait* until the next day *to question Peter and John*, because it was already evening, *and it was contrary to their Jewish law to question people at night*. [4] However, many people who had heard the message *from Peter* believed *in Jesus*. So the number of men *who believed in Jesus* increased to about 5,000.

Acts 4:5-7

THEME: Jewish leaders questioned Peter and John about healing the lame man.

[5] The next day *the high priest summoned* the *other* chief priests, the teachers of the *Jewish* laws, and the other members *of the Jewish Council, and they* gathered together *in one place* in Jerusalem. [6] Annas, *the former* high priest, Caiaphas *the current high priest*, two other *former* high priests whose names were John and Alexander, and other men who were related to the high priest *were there*. [7] They *ordered guards to* bring Peter and John in and have them stand in front of them. *Then one of* the leaders questioned *the two of* them, saying, "Who gave you two the power *to heal this crippled man*? And who authorized you to do this?"

Acts 4:8-12

THEME: Peter told them that Jesus healed the man and only Jesus could save people.

[8] So as the Holy Spirit completely controlled Peter, he said to them, "You *fellow Israelites* who rule us and *all of you other* elders, *listen!* [9] Today you are questioning us concerning our performing a good deed for a man who was crippled, and you asked us how he

became healed. ¹⁰ So *we want* you and all *of our other* fellow Israelites to know this: It is because Jesus the Messiah from Nazareth healed him that this man is able to stand before you. *God considers that* it was you who nailed Jesus to a cross, but God caused him to become alive again. ¹¹ *In the Scriptures they wrote this about the Messiah:*

He is *like* the stone that was rejected by the builders.
But that stone became the most important stone in that building.

Jesus is that stone, and you *are those builders who threw away the stone that was the most important one.* ¹² So he alone can save us. *God* has sent only one person into the world who can save us *from the guilt of our sins, and that person is Jesus!"*

Acts 4:13-14

THEME: The Jewish leaders realized that Peter and John had been associating with Jesus.

¹³ The Jewish leaders realized that Peter and John were not afraid of them.^e They also learned that the two men were ordinary people who had not studied in schools. So the leaders were amazed, and they realized that these men had associated with Jesus. ¹⁴ They also saw the man who had been healed standing there with *the two of* them, so they were not able to say anything *to deny what had happened.*

Acts 4:15-18

THEME: The Jewish leaders ordered the two apostles to stop teaching people about Jesus.

¹⁵ So the Jewish leaders ordered *guards* to take Peter, John, and the man outside of the room *where those leaders were meeting. After they did so*, the leaders talked with each other *about Peter and John.* ¹⁶ *One after another* said *in frustration*, "There is really nothing we can do to *punish* these *two* men! Almost everyone living in Jerusalem knows that they have done an amazing miracle, so we can't tell people that it did not happen! ¹⁷ However, *we* must not allow other people to hear about *this miracle.* So we must tell these men that *we will punish them if they* continue to tell other people about this man *who they say gave them the power to do it.*" ¹⁸ So the Jewish leaders ordered *guards* to bring the two apostles *into that room again. After they did so*, they ordered them both that they should never speak about Jesus, and they should not teach *anyone about him again.*

Acts 4:19-20

THEME: Peter and John said that they needed to continue speaking about Jesus.

¹⁹ But Peter and John replied, "Would God think it right for us two to obey you and not to obey him? We'll let you decide what **you** think. ²⁰ *But as for us, we cannot obey you.* We will not stop telling people about the things we have seen *Jesus do* and what we have heard *him teach.*"

Acts 4:21-22

THEME: The Jewish leaders threatened to punish Peter and John, and then released them.

²¹⁻²² Then the Jewish leaders again told *Peter and John* not to disobey them. But all the people *there* were praising God about what had happened *to the lame man. They knew that only God could have enabled Peter and John* to miraculously heal the man, because the man was more than forty years old *and he was lame from birth. They also knew the*

---

^e OR, The Jewish leaders realized that Peter and John spoke boldly.

people would become angry if they punished the two apostles. They could not decide how to punish Peter and John, so *finally* they let them go.

Acts 4:23-28

THEME: The believers talked to God about those who opposed him and them.

²³ After Peter and John had been released, they went to the other believers and reported all that the chief priests and *other Jewish* elders had said to them. ²⁴ When they heard that, they *all* agreed as they prayed to God, and *one of* them prayed, "O Lord! You made the sky, the earth and the oceans, and everything in them. ²⁵ The Holy Spirit caused our ancestor, *King* David, who served you, to write these words:

It is ridiculous that the non-Jews became angry and the Israelite people planned uselessly *against God.* ²⁶ The kings in the world prepared to fight *God's Ruler,* and the *other* rulers assembled together *with them* to oppose *God* and the one whom he had appointed *to be the Messiah.*

²⁷ *We know that what you said long ago was true,* because *king* Herod and the *governor,* Pontius Pilate, and many other people, both non-Jews and the Israelite people, assembled together *here* in this city. *They* planned *to kill* Jesus, who devotedly served you *and* whom you appointed *to be the Messiah.* ²⁸ *Because* you are all-powerful, those people did *only* what you allowed *them to do.* It was what you decided long ago would happen.

Acts 4:29-30

THEME: The believers asked God to help them speak boldly to people about Jesus.

²⁹ "So now, Lord, listen to what they are saying about punishing us! Help us who serve you to very boldly speak messages from you *about Jesus*! ³⁰ *Also,* by your power, miraculously heal *sick people* and do other amazing miracles that will show people your power! Ask Jesus, who always serves you, *to give us the authority to do such miracles!*"

Acts 4:31

THEME: God shook the place where they were, and his Spirit enabled them to speak his words boldly.

³¹ When the believers had finished praying, the place where they were meeting shook. All of them were empowered by the Holy Spirit, with the result that they began to speak boldly the words that God *told them to speak.*

Acts 4:32-35

THEME: The believers shared everything, and the apostles told others about Jesus.

³² The group of people who had believed *in Jesus* were completely agreed in their thoughts and desires. None of them claimed that he *alone* owned anything. Instead, they shared with one another everything they had. ³³ The apostles continued to tell others in a very powerful way *that God* had raised the Lord Jesus from the dead. *People knew that God* was graciously helping all the believers. ³⁴ *Some of* the believers who owned land or houses would occasionally sell *some of* their property. Then they would bring *the money for what they sold* ³⁵ and they would present it to the apostles. Then *the apostles* would give to any *believer* as much money as he needed. So no one among the believers was lacking anything.

Acts 4:36-37

THEME: Joseph Barnabas sold a field and brought the money to the apostles.

³⁶ *For example, there was* Joseph. *He was* a descendant of Levi *and he was born* on *the island of* Cyprus. The apostles called him Barnabas; *in the Jewish language* that name means 'encourager'. ³⁷ He sold one of his fields, and brought the money to the apostles *for them to distribute to other believers.*

5

Acts 5:1-2

THEME: Ananias pretended to give the apostles all the money from selling a field.

¹ But there was one of *the believers* whose name was Ananias, and whose wife's name was Sapphira. He *also* sold some land. ² He kept for himself some of the money *he had received for the land*, and his wife knew he had done that. Then he brought the rest of the money and presented it to the apostles.

Acts 5:3-6

THEME: People were terrified when they saw or heard that Ananias had died.

³ Then Peter said, "Ananias, *it is terrible that* you let Satan completely control you so that you *tried to* deceive the Holy Spirit *and us. You* have kept for yourself some of the money you received for *selling* the land, *pretending that you were giving us all of it.* ⁴ Before you sold that land, it was yours. And after you sold it, you could certainly still have used the money any way you wanted *to.* So why did you *ever* think about doing this *wicked* thing? You were not *merely trying to* deceive us! No, *you tried to deceive* God *himself!*" ⁵ When Ananias heard that, *immediately* he fell down dead. So all *who were there* who heard *about Ananias' death* became terrified. ⁶ Some young men came in, wrapped his body *with a sheet*, and carried it out *and* buried it.

Acts 5:7-11

THEME: Sapphira also died because she lied, and some men buried her beside her husband.

⁷ About three hours later, his wife came in, *but* she did not know what had happened. ⁸ *As* Peter *showed her the money that Ananias had brought*, he asked her, "Tell me, is this the amount *of money you two received for* the land you sold?" She said, "Yes, that's *what we received.*" ⁹ So Peter said to her, "*You both did a terrible thing!* You two agreed to try to determine if you could do that without the Spirit of the Lord *God* revealing *to anyone that you two tried to deceive them*! Listen! *Do you hear the* footsteps of the men who buried your husband? They are right outside this door, and they will carry your *corpse* out *to bury it, too!*" ¹⁰ Immediately Sapphira fell down dead at Peter's feet. Then the young men came in. When they saw that she was dead, they carried her *body* out and buried it beside her husband's *body.*

¹¹ So all the believers *in Jerusalem* became greatly frightened *because of what God had done to Ananias and Sapphira. And* all *the others* who heard *people tell about* those events also *became greatly frightened.*

Acts 5:12-16

THEME: The apostles healed many people, and many people believed in Jesus.

[12] *God was enabling* the apostles to do many amazing miracles among the people. All the believers were meeting together regularly *in the Temple courtyard* at *the place called* Solomon's Porch. [13] All of the other people *who had not yet believed in Jesus* were afraid to associate with the believers, *because they knew if they did anything evil, God would punish them, as well as revealing it to the other believers.* However, those people continued to greatly respect the believers. [14] Many more men and women started believing in the Lord *Jesus*, and they joined the *group of* believers. [15] *The apostles were doing amazing miracles*, so that *people* were bringing the sick into the streets and laying them on stretchers and mats, in order that *when* Peter came by *he would touch them, or* at least his shadow might come upon some of them *and heal them.* [16] Crowds of people were also coming *to the apostles* from the towns near Jerusalem. They were bringing their sick *friends* and those who were being troubled by evil spirits, and *God* healed all of them.

Acts 5:17-21a

THEME: Jewish leaders jailed the apostles, but an angel freed them to teach people.

[17] Then the high priest and all who were with him, members of the *local* Sadducee sect *in Jerusalem*, became very jealous *of the apostles, because many people were accepting the apostles' message.* [18] So on their orders, *the Temple guards* seized the apostles and put them in the public jail. [19] But during the night an angel from the Lord *God* opened the jail doors and brought the apostles outside. *The guards were not aware of what the angel had done.* [20] Then the angel said *to the apostles*, "Go to the Temple courtyard, stand there, and tell the people all about *how God can give them eternal* life." [21] So having heard this, about dawn they entered the Temple courtyard and began to teach the people again *about Jesus.*

Acts 5:21b-24

THEME: The Jewish leaders were perplexed because the apostles were not in jail.

Meanwhile, the high priest and those who were with him summoned the other Jewish Council members. Altogether they made up the entire Council of Israel. *After they all gathered together*, they sent *guards* to the jail to bring in the apostles. [22] But when the guards arrived at the jail, they discovered that the apostles were not there. So they returned to the Council, and *one of* them reported, [23] "We saw that the jail *doors* were very securely locked, and the guards were standing at the doors. But when we opened *the doors and went in to get those men*, none *of them was* inside *the jail!*" [24] When the captain of the Temple guards and the chief priests heard that, they became greatly perplexed, *wondering* what might result from all this.

Acts 5:25-26

THEME: After finding them, the leaders brought the apostles back to question them.

[25] Then someone came *from the Temple courtyard* and *excitedly* reported to them, "Listen *to this*! *Right now* the men you put in jail are standing in the Temple courtyard, and they are teaching the people *about Jesus!*" [26] So the captain *of the Temple guards* went *to the Temple courtyard* with the officers, and they brought the apostles *back to the Council room. But they* did not treat them roughly, because they were afraid that the people would stone them *to death if they hurt the apostles.*

Acts 5:27-33

THEME: Peter and the other apostles said that they must obey God.

[27] After *the captain and his officers* had brought *the apostles to the Council room*, they commanded them to stand in front of the Council members, and the high priest questioned them. [28] He said to them *accusingly*, "We strongly commanded you not to teach people about this man *Jesus*! But *you have disobeyed us, and* you have taught people all over Jerusalem *about him*! Furthermore, you are trying to make it seem that we are the ones who are guilty for that man's death!" [29] But Peter, *speaking for himself* and the other apostles, replied, "We have to obey *what* God *commands us to do,* not what *you* people *tell us to do*! [30] *Yes*, God considers that you are the ones who killed Jesus by nailing him to a cross! But God, whom our ancestors *worshipped*, raised Jesus from the dead. [31] God has greatly honored Jesus. *He has taken him up to heaven! He has authorized him* to be the one who will save us and to rule *over our lives*! *God did this* so that he might enable *us* Israelite *people* to turn away from *our* sinful lives and *that he might* forgive *us for our sins.* [32] We tell people about the things *that we know happened to Jesus*, and the Holy Spirit, whom God has sent to *us* who obey him, is also confirming *that these things are true.*"

Acts 5:33-40

THEME: After beating the apostles, they followed Gamaliel's advice and released them.

[33] When the Council members heard those words, they became very angry *with the apostles*, and they wanted to kill them. [34] But *there was a Council member* named Gamaliel. He was a Pharisee, and one who taught people the *Jewish* laws, and all the *Jewish* people respected him. He stood up in the Council and told *guards* to take the apostles out *of the room* for a short time. [35] *After the guards had taken the apostles out*, he said to the other Council members, "Fellow Israelites, you need to think carefully about what you want to do to these men, *and I will tell you why.* [36] Some years ago *a man named* Theudas rebelled *against the Roman government*. He told people that he was a big shot, and about four hundred men joined *him. But he was killed,* and all those who had been accompanying him were scattered. *So they* were not able to do anything *that they had planned.* [37] After that, during the time when they were taking the census *in order to tax people, a man named* Judas from *the province of* Galilee rebelled *against the Roman government*. He persuaded some people to accompany him. But *soldiers* killed him, too, and all those who had accompanied him went off in different directions. [38] So now I say *this* to you: Don't harm these men! Release them! I say this because if *this is just something* humans have planned, they will not be able to do it. They will fail, *just like Theudas and Judas did*! [39] But, if **God** *has commanded them to do it*, you won't be able to prevent them *from doing it, and* you will find out that you are opposing God!" The other members of the Council accepted what Gamaliel said. [40] They told the *Temple guards to bring the apostles in and flog them. So the guards* brought them *in* and flogged them. Then the Council members commanded them not to speak to people about Jesus, and they freed the apostles.

Acts 5:41-42

THEME: The apostles rejoiced and continued to tell others about Jesus.

[41] So the apostles went out from the Council. They were rejoicing, because *they knew God* had honored them *by letting people* disgrace them for being followers of Jesus. [42] And every day *the apostles went to* the Temple *courtyard* and to *different people's* houses, *and* they continued teaching *people* and telling *them* that Jesus is the Messiah.

6

Acts 6:1

THEME: The believers neglected the Greek-speaking widows.

¹ During that time, many more people were becoming believers. *Some of them were from other countries and spoke only the Greek language, but most of them had always lived in Israel and spoke the Hebrew language.* Those who spoke Greek began to complain about those who spoke Hebrew. They were saying. "When *you Hebrew-speaking believers* distribute *food or money* to widows every day, you are not giving fair amounts to the widows who speak Greek!"

Acts 6:2-4

THEME: The apostles told the other believers to choose men to care for those widows.

² So, *after the* twelve *apostles had heard what they were saying*, they summoned all the *other* believers *in Jerusalem to meet* together. Then the apostles said *to them*, "We would not be doing right if we stopped preaching and teaching God's message *about Jesus* just to distribute food *and money to widows*! ³ So, fellow believers, carefully choose seven men from among you, men whom *you* know the Spirit *of God* controls completely and who have a lot of wisdom. Then we will appoint them to look after this work, ⁴ and we will use our time to pray and to preach and teach the message *about Jesus*."

Acts 6:5-6

THEME: The apostles appointed seven men to care for the widows' needs.

⁵ What the apostles recommended pleased all of the *other* believers. So they chose Stephen. He was a man with a strong faith *in God* and whom the Holy Spirit controlled completely. *They also chose* Philip, Procorus, Nicanor, Timon, Parmenas, and Nicolas, who was from *the city of* Antioch. Nicolas had accepted the Jewish religion *before he had believed in Jesus.* ⁶ They brought these *seven* men to the apostles. Then after the apostles prayed *for those men*, they placed their hands on *the heads of each one of* them *to appoint them to do that work.*

Acts 6:7

THEME: The number of people who were becoming believers increased greatly.

⁷ So *the believers* continued to tell many people the message from God. More and more people in Jerusalem were believing in Jesus. *Among them* were many *Jewish* priests who were believing the message *about Jesus.*

Acts 6:8-10

THEME: People opposed Stephen, but could not refute his arguments.

⁸ God was enabling Stephen to do many things by God's power. He was doing many amazing miracles among the *Jewish* people. ⁹ However, some people opposed Stephen. They were Jews from a group *that regularly met together in a Jewish meeting place* called the Freedmen's Meeting Place. *They were from the cities of Cyrene and Alexandria* and *also* from *the provinces of* Cilicia and Asia. They all began to argue with Stephen. ¹⁰ But

they were not able to prove that what he said was wrong, because God's Spirit enabled him to speak very wisely.

Acts 6:11-14

THEME: People persuaded some men to falsely accuse Stephen.

[11] Then they secretly persuaded *some* men to *falsely accuse Stephen. Those men said,* "We heard him say bad things about Moses and God." [12] So *in that way* they made the *other Jewish* people angry, *including* the elders and the teachers of the *Jewish* laws. Then *they all* seized Stephen and took him to the Jewish Council. [13] They *also* brought in some men who made false accusations about him. They said, "This fellow continually says bad things about this holy Temple and about the laws of *Moses.* [14] Specifically, we have heard him say that this Jesus from Nazareth will destroy this Temple and will tell us to obey different customs than Moses taught our ancestors."

Acts 6:15

THEME: The people saw Stephen's face shining like the face of an angel.

[15] When all *the people* who were sitting in the Council *room heard that, and as they* all stared at Stephen, they saw that his face was *shining* like the face of an angel.

7

Acts 7:1-4

THEME: Stephen started to answer the high priest's accusations by talking about Abraham.

[1] Then the high priest asked Stephen, "Are the things *these people are saying about you* true?" [2] Stephen replied, "Fellow Jews and respected leaders, *please* listen to me! The glorious God *whom we worship* appeared to our ancestor Abraham while he was still *living* in *the region of* Mesopotamia, before he moved to *the town of* Haran. [3] God said to him, 'Leave this land where you and your relatives *are living,* and go into the land to which I will lead you.' [4] So Abraham left that land, *which was also called* Chaldea, and he arrived in *the city of* Haran and lived there. After his father died, God told him to move to this land in which you *and I* are now living.

Acts 7:5

THEME: God promised to give the land to Abraham and his descendants.

[5] "At that time God did not give Abraham any *land here*, not even a small piece of *this* land that would belong to him. God promised that he would *later* give this land to him and his descendants, and that it would *always* belong *to them. However*, at that time Abraham did not have any children *who would inherit it after he died.*

Acts 7:6-7

THEME: God told Abraham that later on he would deliver his descendants from Egypt.

[6] "Later God told Abraham, 'Your descendants will live in a foreign country. They *will live there* for four hundred years, and *during that time their leaders* will mistreat your descendants and force them to work as slaves. [7] But God *also* said, 'I will punish the

people who enslave them. Then, after that, your descendants will leave *that land* and they will *come and* worship me in this land.'

Acts 7:8

THEME: God commanded the ceremony of circumcision for Abraham and his descendants.

[8] "Then God commanded Abraham that he *and every male in his household and all of his male descendants* should be circumcised *to show that they all belonged to God* and that they would obey what he had told Abraham to do. Later Abraham's son, Isaac, was born, and when Isaac was eight days old, Abraham circumcised him. *Later* Isaac's son, Jacob, was born, and Isaac *similarly circumcised* him. And Jacob *similarly circumcised* his twelve sons. They are the twelve men from whom we Jews have all descended.

Acts 7:9-10

THEME: God helped Joseph, so Pharaoh appointed him to govern Egypt.

[9] "*You know that* Jacob's *older* sons became jealous *because their father favored their younger brother* Joseph. So they sold him *to merchants who took him* to Egypt. There he became a slave *of an official who lived there*. But God *helped* Joseph. [10] He protected him from all his troubles and trials. He gave Joseph wisdom; and he caused Pharaoh, the king of Egypt, to think very highly of Joseph. So Pharaoh appointed him to rule *over* Egypt and to look after all of Pharaoh's property.

Acts 7:11-15a

THEME: There was a famine in Canaan, so Jacob's family moved to Egypt.

[11] "*While Joseph was doing that work*, there was a time of famine throughout Egypt and also throughout Canaan, so that people did not have enough food to eat. People were suffering. Jacob and his sons *in Canaan* could not find *enough* food, either. [12] When Jacob heard *a report that* there was grain *for sale* in Egypt, he sent Joseph's older brothers *to go there to buy grain. They went and bought grain from Joseph, but they did not recognize him. Then they returned home*. [13] When Joseph's brothers went to Egypt the second time, *they again bought grain from Joseph*. But this time *he* told them who he was. *And* Pharaoh found out that Joseph's people were Hebrews *and that those men who had come from Canaan were his brothers*. [14] Then after Joseph sent *his brothers back home, they* told their father Jacob *that Joseph wanted* him and his entire family to come *to Egypt. At that time Jacob's family consisted of* seventy-five people. [15] *So when* Jacob *heard that, he and all his family* went to *live in* Egypt.

Acts 7:15b-16

THEME: When Jacob and his sons died, people buried them in Canaan.

"*Later on*, Jacob died *there*, and our *other* ancestors, *his sons, also died there*. [16] *But they* brought the bodies *of Jacob and Joseph back to our land.* They buried *Jacob's body in the tomb that Abraham had bought, and buried Joseph's body* in Shechem in the ground *Jacob* bought from Hamor's sons.

Acts 7:17-19

THEME: An Egyptian king who did not know about Joseph began to oppress the Israelites.

[17] "Eventually, when it was almost time for *God to rescue* our ancestors from Egypt *as* he had promised Abraham to do, they had become very numerous. [18] Another king had began to rule in Egypt. He did not know that Joseph, *long before that time, had greatly helped the people of Egypt.* [19] That king cruelly tried to destroy our ancestors. He oppressed them and caused them to suffer greatly. He *even* ordered them to leave their baby *boys* outside *their homes* so they would die.

Acts 7:20-22

THEME: Moses, who grew up as an Egyptian, spoke and acted powerfully.

[20] "During that time Moses was born, and he was a very beautiful child. So his parents *secretly* cared for him in their house for three months. [21] Then they had to put him outside *the house, but* Pharaoh's daughter *found him and* adopted him and cared for him as *though he were* her own son. [22] Moses was taught all of the wisdom of the people in Egypt, and *when he grew up*, he was very powerful in his speech and actions.

Acts 7:23-29

THEME: Moses killed an Egyptian, so he had to flee to Midian.

[23] *"One day* when Moses was about forty years old, he decided that he would *go and* see his fellow Israelites. *So he went to the place where they worked.* [24] He saw an Egyptian beating one of the Israelites. So he went over to help the Israelite man who was being hurt, and he got revenge on the Israelite man by killing the Egyptian *who was hurting him.* [25] Moses was thinking that his fellow Israelites would understand that God had sent him to free them *from being slaves.* But they did not understand that. [26] The next day, Moses saw two Israelite men fighting *each other.* He tried to make them stop fighting by saying to them, 'Hey, you two are fellow Israelites! *So* stop hurting each other!' [27] But the man who was injuring the other man pushed Moses away and said to him, 'No one appointed you to rule and judge us! [28] Do you want to kill me as you killed the Egyptian yesterday?' [29] When Moses heard that, *he thought to himself, 'Obviously, people know what I have done, and someone will kill me.' He was afraid, so* he fled *from Egypt* to the land of Midian. He lived there *for some years.* He *got married, and he and his wife* had two sons.

Acts 7:30-34

THEME: God commanded Moses to rescue the Jewish people from Egypt.

[30] *"One day* forty years later, *the Lord God appeared as* an angel to Moses. He appeared in a bush that was burning in the desert near Sinai Mountain. [31] When Moses saw that, he was greatly surprised, *because the bush was not burning up.* As he went over to look more closely, he heard the Lord *God* say *to him,* [32] 'I *am* the God *whom* your ancestors worshipped. And *yes, I am* the God that Abraham, Isaac and Jacob *worship.*' Moses *was so afraid that he* began to shake. He was afraid to look *at the bush any longer.* [33] Then the Lord *God* said to him, 'Take your sandals off *to show that you reverence me. Because I am here*, the place where you are standing is sacred. [34] I have surely seen how the people of Egypt are continually causing my people to suffer. I have heard my people when they groan under their *oppression.* So I have come down to rescue them *from Egypt.* Now get ready, because I am going to send you *back* to Egypt *to do that.'*"

Acts 7:35-38

THEME: God sent Moses to lead Israel and tell them of the Prophet who would come.

[35] "This Moses *is the one who had tried to help our Israelite people, but* whom they rejected *by saying,* 'No one appointed you to rule and judge *us!*' Moses was the one God *himself* sent to rule them and to free them *from being slaves. He was the one whom* an angel in the bush *ordered to do that.* [36] Moses was the one who led our ancestors out *of Egypt.* He did many kinds of miracles in Egypt, at the Red Sea, and during the forty years *that the Israelite people lived* in the desert. [37] This Moses is the one who said to the Israelite people, 'God will appoint a prophet for you from among your own people. *He will speak words from God*, just as I *speak his words to you.*' [38] This man *Moses* was *our people's leader* when they gathered together in the desert. It was Moses to whom *God sent* the angel on Mount Sinai to *give him our laws*, and *he was the one who told* our *other* ancestors *what the angel had said.* He was the one who received *from God* words that tell us how to live *eternally, and Moses* passed *them* on to us.

Acts 7:39-43

THEME: Israel rejected Moses, so God rejected them and said he would punish them.

[39] "*However*, our ancestors did not want to obey *Moses.* Instead, *while he was still on the mountain*, they rejected him *as their leader* and decided they wanted to return to Egypt. [40] So they told *his older brother* Aaron, 'Make idols for us who will be our gods to lead us *back to Egypt*! As for that fellow Moses who led us out of Egypt—we don't know what has happened to him!' [41] So, they made an image *out of gold, an image that looked like* a calf. Then they sacrificed *animals and offered other things* to *honor* that idol, and they sang and danced to honor the idol that they themselves had made. [42] So God rejected them. He abandoned them to worship the sun, moon, and stars in the sky. This agrees with the words that one of the prophets wrote that *God said:*

You Israelite *people*, when you *repeatedly* killed animals and offered them as sacrifices during those forty years *that you were* in the desert, you *most certainly* were not offering them to me! [43] *On the contrary*, you carried *with you from place to place* the tent *that contained the idol* representing the god Moloch *that you worshipped.* You also *carried with you* the image of the star *called* Rephan. *Those* were idols that you had made, *and you* worshipped *them instead of me.* So I will *cause you to* be taken away *from your own country. You will be taken far from your homes to regions* even farther than Babylon.

Acts 7:44-47

THEME: The Israelite people worshipped God at the tent Moses built and in the Temple Solomon built.

[44] "While our ancestors were in the desert, they worshipped God at the tent that showed his presence there with them. They had made the tent just like God had commanded Moses *to make it. It was* exactly like the model Moses had seen *when he was up on the mountain.* [45] *Later on*, other ancestors of ours carried that tent with them when Joshua led them *into this land.* That was during the time that they took this land for themselves, when God forced the people *who previously lived here* to leave. So the Israelites were able to take possession of this land. *The tent remained in this land and was still there* when *King* David ruled. [46] David pleased God, and he asked God to let him build a house where *he and* all of our Israelite people could worship God. [47] But *instead, God let David's son* Solomon build a house *where people could worship* God.

Acts 7:48-50

THEME: People can worship God anywhere, not just at certain places.

⁴⁸ "However, *we know that* God is greater than everything, and he does not live in *houses that* people have made. It is like the prophet *Isaiah* wrote. He wrote *these words that God had spoken:*
    ⁴⁹⁻⁵⁰ Heaven is the place from which I rule the entire universe, and the earth is *merely* a stool on which I may rest my feet. I myself have made everything, *both in heaven and on the earth.* So you *human beings, you* really cannot build a house that would be *appropriate* for me. You cannot make a place good enough for me *to live in*!

Acts 7:51-53

THEME: Stephen said that those who were listening to him were opposing God.

⁵¹ "You people are extremely stubborn, not wanting to obey or listen *to God*! You are exactly like your ancestors! You always resist the Holy Spirit *just as they did*! ⁵² Your ancestors caused every prophet to suffer, *including Moses.* They even killed those who long ago announced *that the Messiah* would come, the one who always did what pleased God. *And the Messiah has come! He is the one whom* you *just recently* turned over *to his enemies* and *insisted that* they kill him! ⁵³ You *are the people* who have received God's laws. *Those were laws* that God caused angels to give *to our ancestors.* However, *incredibly,* you have not obeyed them!"

Acts 7:54

THEME: All the people there became very angry with Stephen.

⁵⁴ When the Jewish Council members *and others there* heard all that *Stephen said*, they became very angry. They were *actually* grinding their teeth *together because they were so angry* at him!

Acts 7:55-56

THEME: Stephen said that he could see Jesus standing beside God in heaven.

⁵⁵ But the Holy Spirit completely controlled Stephen. He looked up into heaven and saw a dazzling light from God, and *he saw* Jesus standing at God's right side. ⁵⁶ "Look," he said, "I see heaven open, and *I see* the one who came from heaven standing at God's right side!"

Acts 7:57-59

THEME: The people there threw stones at Stephen.

⁵⁷ *When the Jewish Council members and others heard that*, they shouted loudly. They put their hands over their ears *so they could not hear him, and at once* they all rushed at him. ⁵⁸ They dragged him outside the city *of Jerusalem* and started to throw stones at him. The people who were accusing him *took off* their outer garments *so they could throw stones more easily, and* they put their clothes *on the ground* next to a young man whose name was Saul, *so he could guard them.* ⁵⁹ While they continued to throw stones at Stephen, Stephen prayed, "Lord Jesus, receive my spirit!"

Acts 7:60-8:4

THEME: He asked the Lord to forgive them and he died. The disciples fled, some men buried Stephen, and Saul harassed believers. But the believers preached about Jesus wherever they were scattered.

[60] Then Stephen fell on his knees and cried out, "Lord, do not punish them for this sin!"[f]

Having said that, he died. **8** [1-2] Then some men who revered God buried Stephen's body in a tomb, and they mourned greatly and loudly for him.

On that same day, *people* started severely persecuting the believers *who were living* in Jerusalem. So most *of the believers* fled *to other places* throughout *the provinces of* Judea and Samaria. The apostles were the only *believers who remained in Jerusalem.* [3] While Stephen was being killed, Saul was there approving their murder of Stephen. So Saul *also* began trying to destroy the group of believers. He entered houses one by one, he dragged away men and women *who believed in Jesus*, and then he had them thrown into prison. [4] The believers *who had left Jerusalem* went to various places, where they continued preaching the message *about Jesus*.

Acts 8:5-8

THEME: Many Samaritans heeded Philip's words and rejoiced.

[5] *One of those believers whose name was* Philip went down *from Jerusalem* to a city in Samaria. There he was telling *the people that Jesus is* the Messiah. [6] Many people there heard Philip *speak* and saw the miraculous things that he was doing. So they all paid close attention to his words. [7] For *example, when Philip commanded* evil spirits who controlled many people *to come out of them*, they came out, while those spirits screamed. Also, many people who were paralyzed and *many others* who were lame were healed. [8] So *many people* in that city greatly rejoiced.

Acts 8:9-13

THEME: Philip baptized many Samaritans, including a sorcerer.

[9] There was a man in that city whose name was Simon. He had been doing sorcery for a long time and he had been amazing the people in Samaria *by doing that*. He continually claimed that he was a great person. [10] All the people there, both ordinary and important people, listened to him. *Various ones of* them were saying, "This man works in extremely powerful ways *because* God has caused him to be a great *person*." [11] They continued to listen to him carefully, because for a long time he had astonished them by doing magic. [12] But then they believed Philip's *message* when he preached to them about *how* God desires to rule *the lives of people who believe in him,* and about Jesus being the Messiah. *Philip* was baptizing both the men and the women *who had come to believe in Jesus.* [13] Simon himself believed *Philip's message* and, after *Philip* baptized him, he began to constantly accompany Philip. Simon was continually amazed because he often saw *Philip* doing many kinds of miraculous things.

---

[f]   OR, …"Lord, forgive them for this sin!"

Acts 8:14-17

THEME: Samaritan believers received the power of the Holy Spirit.

[14] When the apostles in Jerusalem heard that *many people throughout* Samaria *district* had believed the message from God *about Jesus*, they sent Peter and John there. [15] When Peter and John arrived in Samaria, they prayed for those *new believers* that the Holy Spirit's *power* would come to them. [16] *Peter and John realized that* the Holy Spirit had not yet begun to empower any of them. They had been baptized *because they had believed* in the Lord Jesus, *but they did not know about the Holy Spirit.* [17] Then Peter and John placed their hands on *the heads of* each person, and they received the *power of* the Holy Spirit.

Acts 8:18-24

THEME: Peter denounced Simon the sorcerer.

[18] Simon saw *things that convinced him* that God had given the Spirit's *power to people* as a result of the apostles placing their hands on them. So he offered *to give* money to the apostles, [19] saying, "Enable me also to do what *you are doing*, so that everyone on whom I lay my hands may receive the Holy Spirit's *power.*" [20] But Peter said to him, "May you and your money go to hell, because you *very mistakenly* thought that you could buy *from us* what God *alone* gives to *people*! [21] God has not authorized you to have any part of this ministry of giving *the Holy Spirit's power,* because he knows that you are not thinking rightly! [22] So stop thinking wickedly *like* that, and plead that the Lord, if he is willing, will forgive you *for* your *wicked* plan! [23] *Turn away from your evil ways*, because I perceive that you are extremely envious of *us,* and you *are* a slave of your *continual desire to do evil!* *God will certainly punish you severely!*" [24] Then Simon answered, "Pray to the Lord *God* that *he* will not do to me what you just said!"

Acts 8:25

THEME: Peter and John preached to many Samaritans.

[25] After Peter and John told *people there* what they knew personally *about the* Lord *Jesus* and declared to them the message about Jesus, they both returned to Jerusalem. *Along the way* they preached the good message *about Jesus to people* in many villages in *the province of* Samaria.

Acts 8:26-28

THEME: Philip met an Ethiopian official.

[26] *One day* an angel whom the Lord *God* had sent commanded Philip, "Get ready and go south along the road that extends from Jerusalem to Gaza." (*That was* a road in a desert area). [27] So Philip got ready and went *along that road*. Suddenly he met a man from *the land of* Ethiopia. *He was* an important official who took care of all the funds for the queen *of* Ethiopia. *In his language people called their queen* Candace. This man had gone to Jerusalem to worship God, [28] and he was returning *home* and was seated *riding* in his chariot. *As he was riding*, he was reading *out loud from* what the prophet Isaiah *had written long ago.*

Acts 8:29-31

THEME: The official could not understand what he was reading.

²⁹ *God's* Spirit told Philip, "Go near to that chariot and keep walking close to *the man who is riding in* it!" ³⁰ So Philip ran *to the chariot and kept running close to it*. Then he heard the official reading what the prophet Isaiah *had written*. He asked the man, "Do you understand what you are reading?" ³¹ He answered Philip, "*No!* I cannot possibly *understand it* if *there is* no one to explain it to me."

Acts 8:31b-35

THEME: Philip preached about Jesus to the official.

Then the man said to Philip, "Please come up *and* sit beside me." *So Philip did that.* ³² The part of the Scriptures that the official was reading was this:
He will *be silent when* they lead him away to kill him,[g]
　like when people lead a sheep *off to kill it.*
As a young sheep is silent when its wool is being cut off,
　similarly he will not protest *when he is made to suffer.*
³³ When he will be humiliated *by being accused falsely,*
　the rulers will not consider him innocent.
No one will possibly be able to tell about his descendants
　because he will be killed
　before he can have any descendants on the earth.

³⁴ The official asked Philip *concerning that passage*, "Tell me, who was the prophet writing about? *Was he writing* about himself or about someone else?" ³⁵ So Philip replied to him and began *to explain* that Scripture passage. He told him the good message about Jesus. *So the official understood it and believed in Jesus.*

Acts 8:36-39

THEME: Philip baptized the official. Then the Spirit took Philip away.

³⁶ While they were traveling along the road, they came to *a place where there was a pond of* water *near the road*. Then the official said *to Philip*, "Look, *there is a pond of* water! Do you know of anything that would prevent *you* from baptizing me?"[h] ³⁸ So the official ordered *the driver* to stop the chariot. Then both Philip and the official went down into the *pond of* water, and *Philip* baptized him. ³⁹ When they came up out of the water, suddenly God's Spirit took Philip away. The official never saw Philip again. But although he never saw Philip again, the official continued going along the road, very happy *that God had saved him.*

---

[g]　This translation uses the future tense because the original passage in Isaiah 53 used a prophetic perfect to make a prophecy about a certain future event.

[h]　Some Greek manuscripts add verse 37, "Philip said to him, 'If you really believe in Jesus, I will baptize you.' The official answered Philip, 'I believe that Jesus is the Messiah and also that he is the Son of God.'"

Acts 8:40

THEME: Philip preached in towns from Azotus to Caesarea.

⁴⁰ Philip then realized *that the Spirit had miraculously taken him to the town of* Azotus. While he traveled around *in that region,* he continued proclaiming the message *about Jesus* in all the towns *between Azotus and Caesarea. And he was still proclaiming* it when he finally arrived in *the city of* Caesarea.

9

Acts 9:1-2

THEME: Saul asked the high priest to authorize him to arrest believers.

¹ Meanwhile, Saul angrily continued to say, "I will kill those who believe *Jesus is* the Lord!" He went to the high priest *in Jerusalem* ² and requested him *to write* letters *introducing him* to *the leaders of* the synagogues in *the city of* Damascus. *The letters asked them to authorize Saul* to seize any men or women who followed the way *that Jesus had taught,* and to take them to Jerusalem *so that the Jewish leaders could judge and punish them.*

Acts 9:3-8

THEME: While Saul was traveling to Damascus, Jesus appeared to him.

³ While Saul *and those with him* were traveling, they were approaching Damascus. Suddenly a *brilliant* light from heaven shone around Saul. ⁴ *Immediately* he fell down to the ground. Then he heard the voice *of the Lord* say to him, "Saul, Saul, stop causing me to suffer *by persecuting those who believe in me*!" ⁵ Saul asked him, "Lord, who are you?" He replied, "I am Jesus, *and* you are causing me to suffer *by hurting my followers*! ⁶ Now instead *of continuing to do that,* stand up and go into the city! *Someone there* will tell you what *I want* you to do." ⁷ The men traveling with Saul *became so frightened that they* could not say anything. *They just* stood there. They only heard the sound *when the Lord spoke,* but they did not see anyone. ⁸ Saul got up from the ground, but when he opened his eyes he couldn't see anything. So the men *with him* took his hand and led him into Damascus. ⁹ For the next three days Saul couldn't see *at all,* and he did not eat or drink anything.

Acts 9:9-19

THEME: Saul could see again after Ananias had put his hands on him.

¹⁰ In Damascus there was *a Jew* named Ananias who believed in Jesus. While *Ananias was seeing* a vision, the Lord *Jesus* said to him, "Ananias!" He replied, "Lord, I *am listening*!" ¹¹ The Lord Jesus told him, "Go to Straight Street to the house that belongs to Judas. Ask *someone there if you can talk to* a man named Saul from *the city of* Tarsus, because, surprisingly, at this moment he is praying *to me.* ¹² *Saul has seen* a vision in which a man named Ananias entered *the house where he was staying* and put his hands on him so that he might see again." ¹³ But Ananias *protested,* saying, "But Lord, many people have told me about this man! He has done many evil things to the people in Jerusalem who believe in you! ¹⁴ And the chief priests have authorized him to come here *to Damascus* to seize all the people who believe in you *and take them to Jerusalem*!" ¹⁵ But the Lord *Jesus* told Ananias, "Go to *Saul*! *Do what I say,* because I have chosen him to serve me in order that he might speak about me both to non-Jewish people and *their*

kings and to the Israelite people. ¹⁶I myself will tell him that he must often suffer greatly because of telling people about me." ¹⁷So Ananias went, and *after he found* the house *where Saul was*, he entered it. Then, *as soon as he met Saul*, he put his hands on him, and he said, "Brother Saul, the Lord Jesus *himself* commanded me to come *to you*. He is the *same* one who appeared to you while you were traveling along the road. *He sent me to you* so that you might see again and that you might be completely controlled by the Holy Spirit." ¹⁸Immediately things like *fish* scales fell from Saul's eyes, and he was able to see again. Then he stood up*, and Ananias* baptized him. ¹⁹After Saul ate some food, he regained his strength. He stayed with the *other* believers in Damascus for several days.

Acts 9:20-22

THEME: People there were astonished that Saul had believed in Jesus.

²⁰Right away he began to preach *to people about Jesus* in the Jewish meeting places *there. He told them* that Jesus is the Son of God.ⁱ ²¹And all the people who heard him *preach* were amazed. *Various ones of* them were saying, "*We can hardly believe that* this is the *same man* who persecuted the believers in Jerusalem! And we know he has come here to tie our hands and take us to the chief priests *in Jerusalem*!" ²²But *God* enabled Saul *to preach to many people even* more convincingly. He was proving *from the Scriptures* that Jesus is the Messiah. Even the Jewish leaders could not think of anything to refute *what he said there in Damacus.*

Acts 9:23-25

THEME: Saul escaped from those who plotted to kill him.

²³Some time later, *after Saul had left Damascus and then returned*, the Jewish *leaders there* plotted to kill him. ²⁴However, *someone* told Saul what they planned *to do*. Day and night those Jews were continually watching *the people passing through* the city gates, so that *when they saw Saul* they might kill him. ²⁵But *one* night some of those whom he had helped *to believe in Jesus* took him *to the high stone wall that surrounded the city*. They *used ropes to* lower him in a *large* basket through an opening in the wall. *So he escaped from Damascus.*

Acts 9:26-28

THEME: Barnabas introduced Saul to other believers in Jerusalem.

²⁶When Saul arrived in Jerusalem, he began trying to associate with other believers. However, *almost* all of them continued to be afraid of him, because they did not believe that he had become a believer. ²⁷But Barnabas took him and brought him to the apostles. He explained to the apostles how, *while Saul was traveling* along the road *to Damascus*, he had seen the Lord *Jesus* and how the Lord had spoken to him *there. He* also told them how Saul had preached boldly about Jesus *to people* in Damascus. *The apostles believed Barnabas and told the other believers about that.* ²⁸So Saul began to associate with the apostles *and other believers* throughout Jerusalem, and he spoke boldly *to people* about the Lord *Jesus.*

ⁱ   OR, …*He told them* that Jesus is the Man who is also God.

Acts 9:29-30

THEME: The believers sent Saul to Tarsus because some Jews tried to kill him.

²⁹ Saul was *also* speaking *about Jesus* with Jews who spoke Greek, and he was debating with them. But they were continually trying *to think of a way* to kill him. ³⁰ When the *other* believers found out that *they were planning to kill him, some of* the believers took Saul down to Caesarea. *There* they arranged for him to go *by ship* to Tarsus, *his home town.*

Acts 9:31

THEME: The church in Israel had peace and many people believed.

³¹ So the groups of believers throughout *the entire regions of* Judea, Galilee, and Samaria lived in peace *because no one was persecuting them any more.* The Holy Spirit was strengthening them *spiritually* and encouraging them. They were continuing to reverence the Lord *Jesus, and the Holy Spirit* was enabling many other people *to become believers.*

Acts 9:32-35

THEME: Because Peter healed Aeneas, many people believed in Jesus.

³² While Peter was traveling throughout those *regions, once* he went to *the coastal plain to visit* the believers *who lived* in *the town of* Lydda. ³³ There he met a man named Aeneas. Aeneas had not been able to get up from *his* bed for eight years, because he was paralyzed. ³⁴ Peter said to him, "Aeneas, Jesus Christ heals you *right now*! Get up and roll up your mat!" Right away Aeneas stood up. ³⁵ Most of the people who lived in Lydda and on the *plain* of Sharon saw Aeneas *after the Lord had healed him*, so they believed in the Lord *Jesus.*

Acts 9:36-37

THEME: Dorcas died.

³⁶ In *the city of* Joppa there was a believer whose name was Tabitha. *Her name* in the Greek language was Dorcas. *Both of those names mean gazelle.* She was continually doing good deeds *for others.* She was helping poor people *by giving them things they needed.* ³⁷ During the time *that Peter was in Lydda*, she became sick and died. *Some women there* washed her body, *according to the Jewish custom, so that the people could bury it.* Then they *covered her body with cloth and* placed it in an upstairs room *in her house.*

Acts 9:38-43

THEME: Peter resurrected Dorcas.

³⁸ Lydda was near Joppa, so when the disciples *in Joppa* heard that Peter was *still* in Lydda, they sent two men to Peter. *When they got to where Peter was*, they repeatedly begged him, "Please come immediately with us *to Joppa*!" ³⁹ So *right away* Peter got ready and went with them. When they arrived *at the house in Joppa*, they took him to the upstairs room *where Dorcas' body was lying.* All the widows *there* stood around him. They were crying and showing him the cloaks and *other* garments that Dorcas had made for people while she was still alive. ⁴⁰ But Peter sent them all out of the room. Then he got down on his knees and prayed. Then, turning toward her body, he said, "Tabitha, stand up!" *Immediately* she opened her eyes and, when she saw Peter, she sat up. ⁴¹ He grasped one of her hands and helped her to stand up. After he had summoned the

believers and *especially* the widows *among them to come back in*, he showed them that she was alive *again*. [42] *Soon* people everywhere in Joppa knew about that miracle, and as a result many people believed in the Lord *Jesus*. [43] Peter stayed in Joppa many days with a man named Simon who made leather *from animal skins*.

10

Acts 10:1-2

THEME: Cornelius was a man who prayed to God and helped people.

[1] *There was* a man *who lived* in *the city of* Caesarea whose name was Cornelius. He was an officer who commanded 100 men in a large group of soldiers from Italy. [2] He always tried to do what would please God; he and his entire household *were non-Jews who* habitually worshipped God. He sometimes gave money to help poor *Jewish* people, and he prayed to God regularly.

Acts 10:3-8

THEME: Obeying an angel, Cornelius sent men to summon Peter.

[3] *One day* at about three *o'clock* in the afternoon *Cornelius saw* a vision. He clearly saw an angel whom God *had sent*. The angel came into *his room* and said to him, "Cornelius!" [4] Cornelius stared at the angel and became terrified. Then he asked *fearfully*, "Sir, what do you want?" The angel answered him, "You have pleased God because you have been praying *regularly to him* and you often give money to *help* poor people. *Those things have been* like a sacrifice *to God*. [5] So now command some men to go to Joppa, and *tell them to* bring back a man named Simon whose other name is Peter. [6] He is staying with a man, *also* named Simon, who makes leather. His house is near the ocean." [7] When the angel who spoke to Cornelius had gone, he summoned two of his household servants and a soldier who served him, one who also worshipped God. [8] He explained to them everything *the angel had said. Then* he told them to go to Joppa *to find Peter and ask him to come to Caesarea.*

Acts 10:9-16

THEME: Peter's vision.

[9] About noon the next day those *three men* were traveling *along the road* and were coming near *Joppa. Meanwhile,* Peter went up on the *flat* house-top to pray. [10] He became hungry and wanted something to eat. While someone was preparing the food, *Peter* saw *this* vision: [11] He saw heaven opened and something like a large sheet was being lowered to the ground.[j] *It was tied at* its four corners *with ropes.* [12] Inside the sheet were all kinds of creatures. *These included animals and birds that the Mosaic laws forbade Jews to eat.* Some had four feet, others crawled on the ground, and others were wild birds. [13] Then *he heard* the Lord say to him, "Peter, stand up, kill *and cook some of these* and eat *their meat*!" [14] But Peter replied, "Lord, surely you don't *really want me to do that*! I have never eaten any *meat* that *our Jewish laws say* is defiled or *something we* must not eat!" [15] *Then Peter heard* God talk to him a second time. He said, "*I am* God, *so* If I have made

---

[j] OR, He saw an opening in the sky and something like a large sheet was being lowered to the ground.

something acceptable *to eat*, don't say it is not acceptable *to eat!*" ¹⁶ *This happened* three *times, so he knew that he had to think carefully about what it might mean.* Immediately *after God had said that the third time, someone* pulled the sheet *with the animals and birds* up into the sky again.

Acts 10:17-23a

THEME: The Holy Spirit commanded Peter to go with the non-Jewish men.

¹⁷ While Peter was trying to understand what that vision meant, the men who had been sent by Cornelius *arrived. They asked people how to get to* Simon's house. *So they found his house* and were standing outside the gate. ¹⁸ They called and were asking if a man named Simon, whose other name was Peter, was staying there. ¹⁹ While Peter was still trying to understand *what* the vision *meant, God's* Spirit said to him, "Listen! Three men *are here who* want to see you. ²⁰ So get up and go downstairs and go with them! Don't hesitate to go with them *because of their being non-Jews*, because I have sent them *here!*" ²¹ So Peter went down to the men and said to them, "*Greetings!* I am *the man* you are looking for. Why have you come?" ²² One of them replied, "Cornelius, who is a *Roman* army officer, *sent us here.* He is a righteous man who worships God, and all of the Jewish people *who know about him* say that he is a very good man. An angel sent from God said to him, 'Tell some men to *go to Joppa to find Simon Peter and* bring him here, so that you can hear what he has to say.'" ²³ So Peter *said he would go with them, and then he* invited them into *the house* for *the night.*

Acts 10:23b-26

THEME: Peter went with the men and met Cornelius.

The next day Peter got ready and went with the men. Several of the believers from Joppa went with him. ²⁴ The day after that, they arrived in Caesarea. Cornelius was waiting for them. He had invited his relatives and close friends *to come, so they were there in his house, too.* ²⁵ When Peter entered the house, Cornelius met him and bowed low in front of him to worship him. ²⁶ But Peter *grasped Cornelius by the hand and* lifted him to his feet. He said, "Stand up! *Don't reverence me!* I myself am only human, *just like you!*"

Acts 10:27-29

THEME: Peter asked why they had sent for him.

²⁷ While he was talking to Cornelius, Peter *and the others* entered *a large room inside the house*. Peter saw that many people had gathered together *there*. ²⁸ Then Peter said to them, "You all know that any *of us* Jews would be disobeying *our Jewish* laws if we associated with non-Jewish people or *if we even* visited them. However, God has shown me *in a vision* that I should not say about anyone that God will not accept him. ²⁹ So when you sent *some men* to ask me to come *here*, I came *right away. I* did not say that I could not go *with non-Jewish people. So, please tell me*, why have you asked me to come *here*?"

Acts 10:30-33

THEME: Cornelius told about his vision.

³⁰ Cornelius replied, "About this time four days ago I was praying *to God* in my house, *as I regularly do* at three o'clock in the afternoon. Suddenly someone whose clothes *shone* brightly stood in front of me, ³¹ and said, 'Cornelius, God has heard your prayers. He has

also noticed that you have *often* given money to *help* poor people, *and he is pleased with that.* ³²So now, send *messengers to* Joppa, to ask Simon whose other name is Peter to come *here.* He is staying near the ocean in a house that belongs to *another* man named Simon, who makes leather. *When Simon Peter comes he will tell you a message from God.'* ³³So I immediately sent *some men who asked* you *to come here*, and *I certainly* thank you for coming. Now we all are gathered *here knowing* God is with us, to hear all the things that the Lord *God* has commanded you *to say. So please speak to us."*

Acts 10:34-38

THEME: Peter reminded them of what they knew about Jesus.

³⁴So Peter began to speak to them. He said, "*Now* I understand that it is true that God does not favor only certain groups *of people.* ³⁵Instead, from **every** group of people he accepts *everyone who* honors him and who does what pleases him. ³⁶*You know* the message that God sent to *us* Israelite people. *He* proclaimed *to us the good news that he* would cause *people* to have peace *with him* because of what Jesus Christ *has done.* This *Jesus is not only Lord over us Israelite people. He* is *also the* Lord *who rules* over **all** *people.* ³⁷You know what *he* did throughout the land of Judea, beginning in Galilee. He began *to do those things* after John had been proclaiming to *people that they should turn away from their sinful behavior before he baptized them.* ³⁸You know that God gave his Holy Spirit to Jesus, *the man* from *the town of* Nazareth, and gave him the power *to do miracles. You also know* how Jesus went to many different places, always doing good deeds and healing *people.* He was continually healing all the people whom the devil was causing to suffer. *Jesus was able to do those things* because God was always helping him.

Acts 10:39-43

THEME: Peter said that God would forgive the sins of all who believe in Jesus.

³⁹"We *apostles* tell people about all the things *we saw Jesus* do in Jerusalem and in the *rest of* Israel. *The leaders in Jerusalem* killed him by nailing him to a cross. ⁴⁰However, God caused him to become alive again on the third day *after he had died.* God *also* enabled *some of us* to see him *so that we would know he was alive again.* ⁴¹God *did* not *let* all the *Jewish* people see him. Instead, he had chosen us *apostles* beforehand to see *Jesus after he became alive again* and to tell others *about him.* We *apostles are the ones* who ate meals with him after he had risen from the dead. ⁴²God commanded us to preach to the people and tell them that Jesus is the one whom he has appointed to *some day* judge *everyone. He will judge all* those who will *still* be living and all those who will have died *by that time.* ⁴³All of the prophets *who wrote about the Messiah long ago* told *people* about him. *They wrote* that if people believe in the Messiah, God would forgive *them concerning* their sins, because of what the Messiah *would do."*

Acts 10:44-48

THEME: The Holy Spirit came to be with the non-Jewish believers.

⁴⁴While Peter was still speaking those words, suddenly the Holy Spirit came down on all *those* who were listening to the message.ᵏ ⁴⁵The Jewish believers who had come with Peter *from Joppa* were amazed that *God* had generously given the Holy Spirit to the non-

---

ᵏ OR, …suddenly the Holy Spirit began to control all *those non-Jewish people* who were listening to the message.

Jewish people as well as to them. ⁴⁶ *The Jewish believers knew that* because they were hearing those people speaking languages *they had not learned* and telling how great God is. ⁴⁷ Then Peter said *to the other Jewish believers who were there*, "Surely all of you would agree that these people should be baptized, *because God* has given them the Holy Spirit just like *he gave him* to us *Jewish believers*." ⁴⁸ Then Peter told those *non-Jewish* people that they should be baptized *to show that they had believed* in the *Lord* Jesus Christ. *So they baptized all of them. After they had done that*, they requested that Peter stay *with them* several days. *So Peter and the other Jewish believers did that*.

11

Acts 11:1-3

THEME: Some Jewish believers criticized Peter.

¹ The apostles and *other* believers who lived in various towns in Judea heard people say that *some* non-Jewish people had believed the message *from* God *about Jesus*. ² So when Peter *and the six other believers* returned *from Caesarea* to Jerusalem, *some* Jewish believers criticized Peter, *because they thought that Jews should not associate with non-Jews*. ³ They said to him, "*You did wrong when* you visited non-Jewish people, and you *even* ate with them!"

Acts 11:4-10

THEME: Peter told about his vision.

⁴ So Peter began to explain exactly *what had happened concerning Cornelius*. ⁵ He said, "I was praying *by myself* in Joppa, and in a trance I saw a vision. I saw that something like a large sheet was being lowered from heaven. *It was tied with ropes* at its four corners, and it came down to where I was. ⁶ As I was looking intently into it, I saw some tame animals *but also animals that our laws forbid us to eat, including* wild animals, snakes, and wild birds. ⁷ Then I heard God commanding me, 'Peter, rise up, kill *some of these*, and *cook and* eat *their meat!*' ⁸ But I replied, 'Lord, *you* surely don't *really want me to do that*, because I have never eaten meat *from any animal* that *our laws say* we must not eat!' ⁹ *But* God spoke from heaven *to me* a second time, saying, '*I am* God, *so* if I have made something acceptable *to eat*, don't say it is not acceptable *to eat!*' ¹⁰ Then *after he had said that the third time*, the sheet with all *those animals and birds* was pulled up into heaven again.

Acts 11:11-17

THEME: Peter said that the Holy Spirit came to be with the non-Jewish believers. Peter accepted those non-Jews as fellow believers.

¹¹ "At that exact moment three men whom *Cornelius* had sent from Caesarea arrived at the house where I was staying. ¹² *God's* Spirit told me that I should be willing to go with them *even though they were not Jews*. These six *Jewish* believers *from Joppa* went with me *to Caesarea*, and then we went into that *non-Jewish* man's house. ¹³ He told us how he had seen an angel standing in his house. The angel told him, 'Tell some *men* to go to Joppa and bring back Simon whose other name is Peter. ¹⁴ He will tell you how you and everyone else in your house will be saved.' ¹⁵ After I started to speak, the Holy Spirit *suddenly* came down on them, just like he had first come on us *during the festival of Pentecost*. ¹⁶ Then I remembered what the Lord had said: 'John caused people to be baptized in water, but

God will cause the Holy Spirit *to enter you and change your lives.*'[17] God gave those non-Jews the same Holy Spirit that he had given to us after we believed in the Lord Jesus Christ. So, *I* could not *possibly* tell God that he did wrong *when he gave them the Holy Spirit*! *He was showing that he had received them!*"

Acts 11:18

THEME: They praised God that he also saves non-Jewish people.

[18] After *those Jewish believers* heard those words, they stopped criticizing *Peter. Instead,* they praised God saying, "Then it is clear *to us that* God has also accepted the non-Jews so that they might have eternal life, if they turn from their sinful behavior *and believe in Jesus.*"

Acts 11:19-21

THEME: Many non-Jews in Antioch believed in the Lord Jesus.

[19] After *people had killed* Stephen, many of the believers left *Jerusalem and went* to other places because people were persecuting them *there in Jerusalem. Some of* them went to *the region of* Phoenicia, some went to *the island of* Cyprus, and others went to *the city of* Antioch *in the province of Syria. In those places* they were continually telling people the message *about Jesus*, but they told only other Jewish people. [20] Some of the believers were men from *the island of* Cyprus and *the city of* Cyrene *in north Africa.* They went to Antioch, and. *although they told other Jews about* the Lord Jesus, they also told non-Jewish people *there.* [21] The Lord *God* was powerfully enabling those *believers to preach effectively. As a result*, very many *non-Jewish* people believed *their message and* trusted in the Lord *Jesus.*

Acts 11:22-24

THEME: Barnabas encouraged the believers at Antioch.

[22] The group of believers in Jerusalem heard *people say that many people in Antioch were believing in Jesus. So* the *leaders* of the congregation in *Jerusalem* asked Barnabas to go to Antioch. [23] When he got *there*, he realized that God had acted kindly toward *the believers. So* he was very happy, and he continually encouraged all of the *believers* to continue to trust completely in the Lord *Jesus.* [24] Barnabas was a good man *whom* the Holy Spirit completely controlled, one who trusted *God* completely. *Because of what Barnabas did*, many people *there* believed in the Lord *Jesus.*

Acts 11:25-26

THEME: Barnabas and Saul taught many believers at Antioch.

[25] Then Barnabas went to *the city of* Tarsus *in the province of Cilicia to try* to find Saul. [26] After he found him, Barnabas brought him back to Antioch *to help teach the believers. So for* a whole year *Barnabas and Saul* met *regularly* with the congregation *there* and taught many of them *about Jesus. It was* at Antioch *that people* first called the believers Christians.

Acts 11:27-30

THEME: Believers in Antioch helped needy believers in Judea.

²⁷ During the time *that Barnabas and Saul were* at Antioch, some *believers who were* prophets arrived there from Jerusalem. ²⁸ One of them, named Agabus, stood up *to speak. God's* Spirit enabled him to tell *the* believers that there would soon be a famine in many countries. (That famine happened when Claudius was the *Roman Emperor.*) ²⁹ So the believers *in Antioch* decided to send *money* to help the believers in *the province of* Judea. Each *of them decided to give as much money* as he was able. ³⁰ They sent *the money* with Barnabas and Saul to the leaders of the congregation *in Jerusalem.*

12

Acts 12:1-4

THEME: Herod had James killed and Peter put in prison.

¹ It was about this time that King Herod *Agrippa sent soldiers* who imprisoned some of the *leaders* of the congregation *in Jerusalem. He did that* because he wanted to make the believers suffer. ² He ordered *a soldier* to cut off the head of *the apostle* James, the older brother of *the apostle* John. ³ When Herod realized that he had pleased the Jewish *leaders by causing James to be killed*, he had Peter arrested *in order to kill him*, too. (This happened during the festival *when the Jewish people ate* bread *that* did not have yeast.) ⁴ After *they* seized Peter, they put him in prison. They arranged for four groups of soldiers to guard Peter. Each *group* had four soldiers. *Every three hours a different group began to guard him while the others rested.* Herod wanted to bring Peter out *of prison and judge him* in front of the *Jewish* people after the Passover *Festival was finished. He then planned to have Peter executed.*

Acts 12:5-11

THEME: An angel freed Peter from prison.

⁵ So *for several days* they kept Peter in prison. But the *other people* in the congregation at *Jerusalem* were praying earnestly for God *to help* Peter. ⁶ The night *before* Herod planned to bring Peter out *from prison to have him executed* publicly, Peter was sleeping *in the prison* between two soldiers, with two chains binding his arms *to the arms of the soldiers. Two other* soldiers were guarding the prison doors. ⁷ Suddenly an angel *from* the Lord *God* stood *beside Peter*, and a *bright* light shone in his cell. The angel poked Peter in the side and woke him up and said, "Get up quickly!" *While Peter was getting up*, the chains fell off from his wrists. *However, the soldiers were not aware of what was happening.* ⁸ Then the angel said to him, "Put on your clothes and sandals!" So Peter did. Then the angel told him, "Wrap your cloak around you and follow me!" ⁹ So, *after Peter put on his cloak and sandals*, he followed *the angel* out *of the prison cell*, but he had no idea that what the angel was doing was really happening. He thought *that he* was seeing a vision. ¹⁰ Peter and the angel walked by the soldiers who were standing on guard at the two doors*, but the soldiers did not see them. Then* they came to the iron gate that *led* out into the city. The gate opened by itself, and Peter and the angel walked out *of the prison.* After they had walked *a ways* along one street, the angel suddenly disappeared. ¹¹ Then Peter *finally* realized that *what had happened* to him was not a vision, but it had really happened. So he said *to himself*, "Now I know for sure that the Lord *God* sent an angel *to help me. He*

rescued me from what Herod intended to do *to me* and *also* from all the things that the Jewish *leaders* expected *Herod would do to me.*"

Acts 12:12-17

THEME: Peter reported to the other believers.

[12] When Peter realized *that God had rescued him*, he went to Mary's house. She was the mother of John whose other name was Mark. Many *believers* had assembled there, and they were praying *that God would help Peter somehow.* [13] When Peter knocked at the outer entrance, a servant girl named Rhoda came to find out *who was outside the door.* [14] *When Peter answered her*, she recognized his voice, but she was so happy and excited that she did not open the door! Instead, she ran back *into the house.* She *excitedly* announced *to the other believers* that Peter was standing outside the door. [15] But *one of* them said to her, "You are crazy!" But she continued saying that it was *really true. Then* they repeatedly said, "*No, it can't be Peter.* It is *probably* the angel *who was guarding him!*"[l] [16] But Peter kept knocking *on the door. So when someone finally* opened the door, they saw that it was Peter, and they were absolutely amazed! [17] Peter motioned with his hand for them to be quiet. Then he told them exactly how the Lord *God* had led him out of the prison. He *also* said, "Tell James, the *leader* of our *congregation,* and our *other* fellow believers." Then Peter *left and* went away to another town.

Acts 12:18-19

THEME: Herod ordered soldiers to kill the guards.

[18] The next morning the soldiers *who had been guarding Peter* became terribly distressed, *because they did not know* what had happened to him. [19] Then Herod *heard about it.* So he *commanded soldiers* to search for Peter, but they did not find him. Then he questioned the soldiers *who had been guarding Peter*, and asked them, *"How did Peter get away when you were there guarding him?" But they couldn't explain it. So* he commanded them to be led away *and executed. Afterwards*, Herod went from Judea down to Caesarea, where he stayed *for some time.*

Acts 12:20-23

THEME: An angel caused Herod to die.

[20] *At that time* King Herod was furiously angry with the people *of* Tyre and Sidon. *Then* some men *who represented those people* came as a group *to Caesarea in order to meet with* Herod. They persuaded Blastus, one of Herod's important officials, to tell *Herod* that the people *in their cities* wanted to make peace *with him. They* wanted to be able to trade *with the people that Herod ruled*, because they needed to receive food from that region. *Herod had commanded the people in the areas he ruled to stop sending food to the people in Tyre and Sidon.* [21] On the day that Herod had planned to *meet with them*, he put on his royal robes. Then he sat on his throne and *formally* addressed *all* the people *who had gathered there.* [22] The crowd repeatedly shouted, "*This man who* is speaking is a god, not a man!" [23] So, because Herod *let the people praise him instead of* praising God, immediately an angel *from* the Lord *God* caused Herod to become seriously ill. *Many* worms ate his intestines, and *soon* he died *very painfully.*

---

[l]   OR, ...It is the angel who has guarded him, and he has come to tell us that Peter has died.

Acts 12:24-25

THEME: Many people heard God's message and became believers. Barnabas and Saul returned to Antioch from Jerusalem.

²⁴ *The believers* continued telling God's message to people in many places, and there were continually more and more people who were believing in Jesus.

²⁵ When Barnabas and Saul finished *delivering the money to help the Jewish believers in Judea*, they left Jerusalem and returned *to Antioch, in the province of Syria*. They took John, whose other name was Mark, with them.

13

Acts 13:1-3

THEME: The Holy Spirit commanded Barnabas and Saul to go on a mission.

¹ Among *the people in* the congregation at Antioch there were those who spoke messages from God and those who taught *people about Jesus. They were* Barnabas; Simeon, who was also called Niger;ᵐ Lucius, from *the city of* Cyrene; Manaen, who had grown up with *king* Herod *Antipas*; and Saul. ² While they were worshiping the Lord and fasting, the Holy Spirit said *to them*, "Appoint Barnabas and Saul to *serve* me and to *go and do* the work I have chosen them *to do!*" ³ So they continued to fast and pray. Then having put their hands on Barnabas and Saul and *praying that God would help them*, they sent them off.

Acts 13:4-5

THEME: Barnabas and Saul preached the gospel in synagogues on Cyprus.

⁴ Barnabas and Saul, guided by the Holy Spirit, went down *from Antioch* to *the port of* Seleucia. From there they went by ship to *the port of* Salamis *on the island of* Cyprus. ⁵ While they were in Salamis, *they went* to the Jewish meeting houses. There they proclaimed the message from God *about Jesus*. John *Mark went with them and* was helping them.

Acts 13:6-12

THEME: Saul-Paul denounced a sorcerer, and an official believed in Jesus.

⁶ The three of them went across the entire island to *the town of* Paphos. There they met a magician named Bar-Jesus. He was a Jew who falsely claimed to speak messages from God. ⁷ He often accompanied the governor *of the island*, Sergius Paulus, who was an intelligent man. The governor sent *someone* to bring Barnabas and Saul to him, because he wanted to hear the word of God. *So Barnabas and Saul came and told him about Jesus.* ⁸ However, the magician, whose name was Elymas *in the Greek language*, was opposing them. He repeatedly tried to persuade the governor not to believe *in Jesus.* ⁹ Then Saul, whose *Roman name was* Paul, empowered by the Holy Spirit, looked intently at the magician and said, ¹⁰ "You are serving the devil and you oppose everything that is good! You are always lying *to people* and doing *other* evil things to them. When are you going to stop *trying to* change the truth about the Lord *God* into a pack of lies? ¹¹ Right

---

ᵐ OR, …Simeon, who was also called Black-man…

now the Lord *God* is going to punish you! You will become blind and not *even* be able to see the sun for a *some* time." At once he became *blind, as though he was* in a dark mist, and he groped about, searching for someone *to hold him by the* hand and lead him. [12] When the governor saw what had happened *to Elymas*, he believed *in the Lord Jesus*. He was amazed by *what Paul and Barnabas* were teaching about the Lord *Jesus*.

Acts 13:13-15

THEME: The synagogue leaders in Antioch asked Paul and Barnabas to speak to them.

[13] *After that*, Paul and the two men with him went by ship from Paphos to *the port of* Perga in *the province of* Pamphylia. *At Perga* John *Mark* left them and returned to *his home in* Jerusalem. [14] Then Paul and Barnabas traveled *by land* from Perga and arrived in *the city of* Antioch near *the district of* Pisidia *in the province of* Galatia. On the Jewish day of rest they entered the Jewish meeting place and sat down. [15] *Someone* read *aloud* from the *books Moses had written. Then someone read from what the other* prophets *had written.* Then the synagogue leaders gave *someone this* note *to take* to Paul and Barnabas: "Fellow Jews, if *one of* you wants to speak a word of encouragement to the people, please speak *now!*"

Acts 13:16-20a

THEME: Paul said that God helped Israel and gave them the land of Canaan.

[16] So Paul stood up and motioned with his right hand *for the people to listen to him*. Then he said, "Fellow Israelis and you *non-Jewish people* who *also* worship God, *please* listen *to me*! [17] God, whom we Israelite people worship, chose our ancestors *to be his people*, and he caused them to become very numerous while they were foreigners living in Egypt. *Then after many years*, God helped them powerfully and led them out of there. [18] *Even though they repeatedly disobeyed him, h*e cared for them for about forty years *while they were* in the desert. [19] He *enabled the Israelite people* to conquer seven tribal groups *who were then living* in Canaan, and he gave their land to us Israelite people for us to possess. [20] *Our ancestors began to possess Canaan* about 450 years after *their ancestors had arrived in Egypt.*

Acts 13:20b-22

THEME: Paul told about God's removing Saul and appointing David to be Israel's king.

"After that, God appointed leaders *to rule the Israelite people. Those leaders continued to rule our people* until the time when the prophet Samuel *ruled them.* [21] Then, *while Samuel was still their leader*, the people demanded that he *appoint* a king *to rule them. So* God appointed Saul, the son of Kish, from the tribe of Benjamin, *to be their king.* He *ruled them* for forty years. [22] After God had rejected Saul *from being king*, he appointed David as their king. God testified about him, 'I have observed that David, son of Jesse, is exactly the kind of man I desire. He will do *everything that* I want *him to do.*'

Acts 13:23-25

THEME: Paul said that God sent David's descendant, Jesus, to Israel to save them.

[23] "From *among* David's descendants, God brought one of them, Jesus, to *us* Israelite people to save us, just as he had told *David and our other ancestors* that he would do. [24] Before Jesus began his work, John *the Baptizer* preached to all of our Israelite people *who came to him. He told them* that they should turn away from their sinful behavior *and*

ask God to forgive them. Then he would baptize them. [25] When John was about to finish the work *God gave him to do*, he frequently said *to the people*, 'You may think that I am *the Messiah whom God promised to send*. No, I am not. But listen! The Messiah will *soon* come. *He is so much greater than I am that* I am not *even* important enough to be his slave.'

Acts 13:26-31

THEME: Paul said that God resurrected Jesus and caused many people to see him.

[26] "Fellow Israelis, you who are descendants of Abraham, and *you non-Jewish people who* also worship God, *please listen! It is* to *all of* us that *God* has sent the message of salvation. [27] The people who were living in Jerusalem and their rulers did not realize that this man *Jesus was the one whom God had sent to save them.* Although messages from the prophets have been read *aloud* every Jewish day of rest, they did not understand *what the prophets wrote about the Messiah. So* the *Jewish leaders* condemned Jesus *to die*, which was just as the prophets predicted. [28] *Many people accused Jesus of doing wicked things*, but they could not prove that he had done anything for which he deserved to die. They insistently asked Pilate *the governor* to order that Jesus be executed. *So Pilate did what they asked him to do.* [29] They did *to Jesus* all the things that *the prophets long ago had* written *that people would do to* him. *They killed Jesus by nailing him to a cross. Then* his body was taken down from the cross and placed it in a tomb. [30] However, God raised him from the dead, [31] and for many days he *repeatedly* appeared to *his followers* who had come along with him from *the province of* Galilee to Jerusalem. Those *who saw him* are now testifying about him to the *Jewish* people.

Acts 13:32-37

THEME: Paul said that God had done what he had promised he would do by resurrecting Jesus.

[32] "*Right* now we *two* are proclaiming to you this good message. We want to tell you that God has fulfilled what he promised to *our Jewish* ancestors! [33] He has now done that for us *who are* their descendants, *and also for you who are not Jews, by sending Jesus.*[n] That is just like what *David* wrote in the second Psalm that *God said when he was sending his Son*,

You are my Son; today I have proven *to people that I really am* your Father.[o]

[34] *God* has raised *the Messiah* from the dead, and will never let him die again. *Concerning that, God* said *to our Jewish ancestors*, 'I will surely help you just as *I promised* David *that I would do.*' [35] So *in writing* another *Psalm, David* said this *to God about the Messiah*: 'Because I am devoted to you and always obey *you, when I die,* you will not let my body decay.' [36] While David was living, he did what God wanted him to do. And when he died, his body was buried *just as* his ancestors' *bodies has been buried*, and his body decayed. *So he could not have been speaking about himself in this Psalm.* [37] *Instead, he was speaking about Jesus. Jesus also died*, but God raised him from the dead, and *so* his body did not decay.

---

[n] OR, ...by causing Jesus to live again.

[o] OR, ...'Today I have shown everybody that you are truly my Son and I am truly your Father.'

Acts 13:38-41

THEME: Paul informed them that God would forgive their sins if they believed in Jesus.

³⁸⁻³⁹"So, *my* fellow Israelis *and other friends*, it is important for you to know that *we* are declaring to you *that God* can forgive you for your sins as a result of *what* Jesus *has done*. Because of *what* Jesus *has done*, *God* considers that everyone who believes *in Jesus* is no longer guilty concerning everything they *have done that displeased God.*[p] *But God* could not do that for you as a result of *your obeying* the laws *that* Moses *wrote.* ⁴⁰So be careful that *God* does not judge you, as one of the prophets said that God would do! ⁴¹The prophet wrote that *God said:*

> You who ridicule *me*, you will *certainly* be astonished *when you see what I am doing*, and *then* I will destroy you. You will be astonished because I will do something *terrible to you* while you are living. You would not believe *that I would do that* even though someone told you!"

Acts 13:42-43

THEME: People asked Paul and Barnabas to speak to them again the next Jewish rest.

⁴²After Paul *finished speaking*, while he and Barnabas were leaving the Jewish meeting house, *many of* the people there repeatedly requested that on the next Jewish day of rest *the two of them* would speak to them *again* about the things *Paul had just told them.* ⁴³After they began to leave *the Jewish meeting house*, many *of them* went along with Paul and Barnabas. They consisted of Jews and also non-Jews who had accepted the things the Jews believe. Paul and Barnabas continued talking to them, and kept urging them to continue *believing the message that* God in his great kindness *forgives people's sins because of what Jesus did.*

Acts 13:44-49

THEME: Many non-Jews believed in Jesus and told others about him.

⁴⁴On the next Jewish day of rest, most of the *people in Antioch came to the Jewish meeting house* to hear *Paul and Barnabas* speak about the Lord *Jesus.* ⁴⁵But *the leaders of* the Jews became extremely jealous, because they saw that large crowds of *non-Jewish people were coming to hear Paul and Barnabas. So* they began to contradict the things that Paul was saying, *and also* to insult *him.* ⁴⁶Then, speaking very boldly, Paul and Barnabas said *to those Jewish leaders*, "*We two* had to speak the message from God *about Jesus* to you Jews first *before proclaiming it to non-Jews, because God commanded us to do that. But* you are rejecting God's message. *By doing so,* you have shown that you are not worthy to have eternal life. *So,* we will go to the non-Jewish people *to tell them the message from God.* ⁴⁷*We are doing that also* because the Lord *God* has commanded us *to do it.* He said to us:

> I have appointed you *to reveal things about me* to non-Jewish people, a message that will be *like* a light to them. *I have appointed* you to tell people everywhere in the world *the way of salvation.*"

⁴⁸While the non-Jewish people were listening *to those words*, they began to rejoice, and they repeatedly said that the message about the Lord *Jesus* was wonderful. And all of the non-Jewish people whom *God* had chosen to have eternal *life* believed *the message about the Lord Jesus.* ⁴⁹*At that time, many of the believers* traveled around throughout

---

[p] OR, …Because of *what* Jesus *has done*, the record has been erased concerning everything that person *has done which displeased God.*

that region. As they did so, they were proclaiming the message about the Lord *Jesus*. And *many more people believed in him.*

Acts 13:50-52

THEME: People expelled the apostles, but the believers continued on.

[50] However, *some leaders of* the Jews stirred up people to oppose *Paul and Barnabas*. The ones they stirred up included the most important men in the city and *some* influential women who had accepted what the Jews believe. *So those non-Jewish people* incited *other people also* to persecute Paul and Barnabas. As a result they expelled the two men from their region. [51] So, as the two apostles *were leaving, they* shook the dust from their feet *to show those Jewish leaders that God had rejected them and would punish them. They left Antioch* and went to *the city of* Iconium. [52] Meanwhile, the believers *in Antioch* continued to rejoice greatly, and they continued to be completely controlled by the Holy Spirit.

14

Acts 14:1-3

THEME: Paul and Barnabas preached the gospel and performed miracles in Iconium.

[1] At Iconium, Paul and Barnabas went as usual into the Jewish meeting place and spoke very convincingly *about the Lord Jesus*. As a result, many Jews and also non-Jews believed *in Jesus*. [2] But *some of* the Jews refused to believe *that message, and* told the non-Jews not to believe it. They told the non-Jewish people that the message *about Jesus* was not true. As a result, *some of* the non-Jews became angry towards the believers *there*. [3] So Paul and Barnabas stayed there a long time, speaking boldly for the Lord, and the Lord Jesus enabled them to do many miracles. In that way he showed *people* that the message about how the Lord saves us in a way we don't deserve was true.

Acts 14:4-7

THEME: Before people could attack the apostles, they escaped to Lystra and Derbe.

[4] The people *who lived* in *Iconium* strongly disagreed among themselves *concerning the message about Jesus*. Some of them agreed with the Jews *who did not believe that message*. Others agreed with the two apostles. [5] Then some non-Jewish people and some Jewish *leaders* talked among themselves about how they could mistreat Paul and Barnabas. Some of the important men in that city agreed to help them. Together, they decided they would stone *Paul and Barnabas to death*. [6] But Paul and Barnabas heard about that, so they quickly escaped to *the district of* Lycaonia. *They went* to Lystra and Derbe and to the area surrounding those towns. [7] *While they were* in that area, they continually told the people the message *about the Lord Jesus*.

Acts 14:8-10

THEME: God enabled Paul to heal a lame man.

[8] *Once while Paul was preaching* in Lystra, a man was sitting there who was crippled in his legs. He was crippled from birth, so he was never able to walk. [9] As he listened to Paul speaking *about the Lord Jesus,* Paul looked directly at him and could see that he believed

that *the Lord Jesus* could make him well. ¹⁰ So Paul called out *to him*, "Stand up!" *When the man heard that*, he *immediately* jumped up and began to walk *normally*.

Acts 14:11-18

THEME: The apostles stopped the people from worshiping them.

¹¹ When the crowd saw what Paul had done, *they thought that Paul and Barnabas must be the gods that they worshipped.* So they shouted *excitedly* in their *own* Lycaonian language, "*Look! These people must really be* the gods *that we worship! They* have made themselves look like people and have come down *from heaven to help us!*" ¹² They began to say that Barnabas was *probably the chief god, whose name was* Zeus. And *they began to say that* Paul was Hermes, *the spokesman for the other gods. They mistakenly thought that* because Paul was the one who had been speaking. ¹³ Just outside *the gates of* the city there was a temple *where the people worshipped Zeus. The priest who was there heard what Paul and Barnabas had done, so he came* to the city gate, where many people had already gathered. He brought *two* bulls with wreaths *of flowers around their necks.* The priest and the other people wanted to kill the bulls *as part of a ceremony* to worship Paul and Barnabas. ¹⁴ But when the apostles, Barnabas and Paul, heard about this, *and understood that the people thought they were gods and wanted to sacrifice the bulls to worship them,* they *were very distressed*, so they tore their own clothes. They rushed among the people, shouting, ¹⁵ "Men, you must not kill those bulls *to worship us! We are not gods*! We are just human beings like you! We have come to tell you some good news! *We have come to tell you about the God who is all-powerful,* who wants you to stop worshiping other gods, because they cannot help you. This true God made the heaven and the earth and the oceans and everything in it. ¹⁶ In the past, all of you non-Jewish people *worshipped whatever gods you wanted to.* God let you worship them, *because you did not know him.* ¹⁷ But he has shown us *that he acts kindly toward us.* He is the one who causes it to rain and causes crops to grow. He is the one who gives you plenty of food, and makes you very happy." ¹⁸ The people heard what *Paul* said, but they still thought they should sacrifice those bulls to worship Paul and Barnabas. *But finally, the people decided not to do it.*

Acts 14:19-20a

THEME: Some Jews incited people to stone Paul at Lystra.

¹⁹ *However*, after that, some Jews came from Antioch and Iconium and persuaded many of the people of Lystra *that the message Paul had been telling them* was not true. The people *who believed what those Jews said became angry with Paul. They let the Jews* throw stones at him *until he fell down, unconscious*. They *all* thought he was dead, so they dragged him outside the city *and left him lying there*. But some of the believers *in Lystra had followed them outside the city.* ²⁰ They came and stood around Paul, *where he was lying on the ground*. And Paul *became conscious! He* stood up and went back into the city *with the believers.*

Acts 14:20b-23

THEME: The apostles revisited believers and appointed leaders.

The next day, Paul and Barnabas *left Lystra and* traveled to Derbe. ²¹ They *stayed there several days, and as they kept telling* the people the good message *about Jesus,* many people became believers. After that, Paul and Barnabas *started on their way back. They* went again to Lystra. *Then they went from there* to Iconium, and *then they went* to Antioch *in the province of Pisidia.* ²² *In each town*, they helped the believers to become strong *spiritually*, and they urged them to keep on trusting in *the Lord Jesus*. They told *the believers,* "It is necessary for us to *endure* persecution before we enter the place where God will rule *over us forever.*" ²³ They appointed leaders for each congregation. *And before they left each town, they gathered the believers together and spent some time* praying and fasting. Then they both entrusted the *leaders and other believers* to the care of the Lord *Jesus*, in whom they had believed.

Acts 14:24-28

THEME: Paul and Barnabas reported to the believers at Syrian Antioch.

²⁴ After Paul and Barnabas had traveled through Pisidia, they went *south* to *the district of* Pamphylia. ²⁵ They *arrived* at Perga *and* preached God's message *about the Lord Jesus to the people there. Then* they went down *to the seacoast* at Attalia. ²⁶ There they got on a ship and went back to *the city of* Antioch *in the province of* Syria. That was the place where they had been appointed to go *to other places* and preach, *the place where the believers* had asked God to kindly help them in the work they had now completed. ²⁷ When they arrived in Antioch, they called the believers together. Then Paul and Barnabas told them all that God had helped them to do, *and how God* had enabled *many* non-Jewish people to believe *in Jesus.* ²⁸ Then they stayed in Antioch with the *other* believers for several months.

15

Acts 15:1-2

THEME: Some Jewish believers said God will save only people who are circumcised.

¹ *Then* some *Jewish* believers went down from Judea to Antioch. They started teaching the *non-Jewish* believers *there, and said, "You must* be circumcised *to indicate you belong to God,* as Moses *commanded* in the laws *he received from God.* If you don't do that, you will not be saved." ² Paul and Barnabas strongly disagreed with those Jews and started arguing *with them. So the believers at Antioch* appointed Paul and Barnabas and some of the other believers to go to Jerusalem, in order to discuss this matter with the apostles and *other spiritual* leaders.

Acts 15:3-4

THEME: Paul and Barnabas reported what God had enabled them to do.

³ After Paul, Barnabas, and the others were given things for their trip by the congregation *at Antioch*, they traveled through *the provinces of* Phoenicia and Samaria. *When they stopped at different places in those provinces*, they reported *to the believers* that *many* non-Jews *in Antioch* had become believers. As a result, all the believers *in those places* rejoiced greatly. ⁴ And when Paul, Barnabas, and the others arrived in Jerusalem, they were welcomed by the apostles, the *other* elders, and the *other members of the* congregation *there*. Then Paul and Barnabas reported the things that God had enabled them to do *among non-Jewish people.*

Acts 15:5

THEME: Some Jewish believers said that non-Jewish believers must obey Moses' laws.

[5] But some of the *Jewish* believers who belonged to the Pharisee sect stood up *among the other believers and* said to them, "The non-Jews *who have believed in Jesus* must be circumcised, and they must be told to obey the laws *that God gave to* Moses."

Acts 15:6-11

THEME: Peter told about non-Jews becoming believers when he preached to them.

[6] Then the apostles and *the other* elders met together in order to talk about this matter. [7] After they had discussed it for a long time, Peter stood up and spoke to them. He said, "Fellow believers, you *all* know that a long time ago God chose me from among you *other apostles, in order that* the non-Jewish people might *also* hear me tell *them* the good message *about the Lord Jesus*, so that they could hear *it* and believe *in him. So Paul and Barnabas are not the first ones to tell non-Jews about Jesus.* [8] God knows *and judges* people according to what they think, *not according to who their ancestors were.* By sending the Holy Spirit to *the non-Jews, just like he had* also done for us Jews, he showed *me and others* that he had accepted them *to be his people.* [9] *God* saved us *Jews* and those *non-Jews* in the same way, making them clean inside simply as a result of their believing *in the Lord Jesus. That was exactly what he had done for us.* [10] *You are wanting to force the non-Jewish believers to obey our Jewish rituals and laws*—laws that God has shown that he does not require them to obey. *Your doing that is like* putting a heavy burden on their necks! So then, stop making God angry by doing that! Both we and our ancestors have never been able to bear *the burden of obeying those laws!* [11] But *we know that it is not because we try to obey those laws that God saves us Jews. On the contrary*, we know it is because of what the Lord Jesus kindly did for us—things that we did not deserve—that *God* saves us. *God saves us Jews* exactly like *he saves* those *non-Jews who believe in the Lord Jesus.*"

Acts 15:12

THEME: Barnabas and Paul reported what God had helped them to do among the non-Jews.

[12] All the people *there* became silent *after Peter had spoken.* Then they *all* listened to Barnabas and Paul, as the two of them told about the many great miracles that God had enabled them to do among the non-Jewish people, *miracles that showed that God had accepted the non-Jews.*

Acts 15:13-21

THEME: James recommended what they should tell the non-Jewish believers.

[13] When Barnabas and Paul had finished speaking, James, *the leader of the group of believers there in Jerusalem*, spoke to them. *He said*, "Fellow believers, listen to me. [14] Simon *Peter* has told you how God previously blessed the non-Jews. God did that by choosing from among them a people who would belong to him. [15] *These* words that *God spoke,* words that were written by *one of* the prophets *long ago,* agree with that:

[16] Later on I will return and I will re-establish the kingdom that David *ruled* and which has been destroyed. My *doing that will be like* rebuilding *a house* that has been torn down. [17] I will do that in order that all other people might seek *me*, God. *I will do that in order that* all the non-Jews whom I have called *to belong* to me might seek me. *You can be certain that this will happen because I,* God, who will do those things, have spoken these words. [18] *I caused my people to know about them* long ago.

[19] *James continued by saying,* "So I have decided *that we* should stop bothering the non-Jewish people who are turning *away from their sins and turning* to God. *We should stop demanding that they obey our rules and rituals.* [20] Instead, we should write *a letter* to them, *one requiring only four things: They should* not eat *meat that has been* offered to idols, they should not have sex with someone to whom they are not married, they should not *eat meat from animals that have been killed by* strangling, and *they should not eat* the blood *of animals.* [21] In many cities, for a very long time people have been proclaiming *the laws that* Moses *wrote, laws prohibiting those things.* And on every Jewish day of rest *those laws* are read in the Jewish meeting houses. *So if the non-Jews want to know more about those laws, they can find out in our meeting houses.*"

Acts 15:22-29

THEME: The church leaders sent messengers with a letter to non-Jewish believers.

[22] The apostles and *the other* elders, along with all the *other* members of the congregation, accepted *what James had said.* They decided to choose men from among themselves and send them, along with Paul and Barnabas, to Antioch, to *let the believers there know what the lead*ers at Jerusalem had decided. So they chose Judas, who was also called Barsabbas, and Silas, who were leaders among the believers *at Jerusalem.* [23] Then they wrote the following letter, *and asked Judas and Silas to take it to the believers at Antioch*: "*We* apostles and *other* leaders who are your fellow believers *send our greetings to you as we write this to you* non-Jewish believers *who live* in Antioch and *other places in the provinces of* Syria and Cilicia. [24] People have told us that some men from among us went *to you,* although we had not told *them to do that.* They troubled you *by telling you things* that confused your thinking. [25] So *while we met together here,* we decided to choose some men and ask them to go to you, along with Barnabas and Paul, whom we love very much. [26] Those two have put their lives in danger because of their *serving* our Lord Jesus Christ. [27] We *have also chosen* Judas and Silas to go to you. They will tell you the same things *that we are writing.* [28] The Holy Spirit has confirmed what we had decided, that you should not be required to obey a lot of burdensome *Jewish* laws. Instead, *we* only *require you to obey* the following instructions,

[29] You should not eat *food that has been* sacrificed to idols.

You should not eat blood from animals.

You *should not eat* meat *from animals have been killed* by strangling.

You should also not have sex with someone to whom you are not married.

Those things *especially offend Jewish believers. So if* you avoid doing them, you will be doing what is right. That is all."

Acts 15:30-32

THEME: The letter and messengers encouraged the believers at Antioch.

[30] The *four* men whom *they* had chosen went *from Jerusalem* down to Antioch. *When* all the believers *there* had assembled together, *Judas and Silas* gave the letter to them. [31] When the believers there read the letter, they rejoiced, *because its message* encouraged them. [32] Judas and Silas, being prophets as *Paul and Barnabas were,* spoke a lot and encouraged the believers *there,* and helped them to trust more strongly *in the Lord Jesus.*

Acts 15:33-35

THEME: Paul and Barnabas continued to teach and preach in Antioch.

[33] After *Judas and Silas* had stayed there for some time *and were ready to return to Jerusalem*, the believers *at Antioch* wished them well, and the believers *prayed that God* would protect *them as they traveled. So the two men* started to go back to the leaders *in Jerusalem* who had asked them to go *to Antioch.*[q] [35] However, Paul and Barnabas continued to stay in Antioch. *While they were there*, they, along with many others, were teaching *people* and preaching to them the message about the Lord *Jesus*.

Acts 15:36-41

THEME: Paul and Barnabas separated, and Paul chose Silas.

[36] After some time Paul said to Barnabas, "Let's go back and visit the fellow believers in every city where we *previously* proclaimed the message about the Lord *Jesus. In that way, we will know* how *well* they are doing spiritually." [37] Barnabas *agreed with Paul, and said that he* wanted to take along with them *again* John, whose other name was Mark. [38] However, Paul *told Barnabas that he* thought it would not be good to take Mark *with them, because* Mark had deserted them when they were previously in *the region of* Pamphylia and had not continued to work with them. [39] Paul and Barnabas strongly disagreed *with each other about that*, so they separated from each other. Barnabas took Mark *along with him, and they got* on a ship and went to *the island of* Cyprus. [40] Paul chose Silas, *who had returned to Antioch, to work with him*. The believers *there* asked the Lord *God* to graciously help *Paul and Silas. Then* the two of them departed *from Antioch*. [41] Paul continued traveling *with Silas* through *the provinces of* Syria and Cilicia. In those places he was helping the congregations to trust strongly *in the Lord Jesus*.

16

Acts 16:1-3

THEME: Paul chose Timothy to work with him and Silas.

[1] Paul *and Silas* went to Derbe *and visited the believers there*. Next *they went* to Lystra. A believer whose name was Timothy lived there. His mother was a Jewish believer, but his father was a Greek. [2] The believers in Lystra and Iconium said good things about Timothy, [3] and Paul wanted to take Timothy with him *when he went* to other places, so he circumcised Timothy. *He did that so that* the Jews who lived in those places *would accept Timothy*, because they knew that his non-Jewish father *had not allowed his son to be circumcised*.

---

[q]   Some Greek manuscripts have for verse 34, "But *just before they left,* Silas decided to stay there *in Antioch.*" Each translator should choose between this text and the implied information that we have given in verse 40. Each should choose the way to translate that seems the most preferable.

Acts 16:4-5

THEME: Paul, Silas and Timothy told believers in Galatia what the church leaders had decided.

[4] *So Timothy went with Paul and Silas,* and they traveled to many other towns. *In each town* they told *the* believers the rules that the apostles and elders in Jerusalem had decided that *non-Jewish* believers should obey.

[5] *God was helping* the believers in those towns to trust more strongly *in the Lord Jesus,* and every day more people became believers.

Acts 16:6-10

THEME: Because of a vision in Troas, Paul went to preach in Macedonia.

[6] Paul and his companions planned to enter *the province of* Asia and preach the message *about Jesus* there, but the Holy Spirit prevented them *from going there. So* they traveled through *the provinces of* Phrygia and Galatia. [7] They arrived at the border of *the province of* Mysia, and they wanted to go *north* into *the province of* Bithynia. But *again* the Spirit of Jesus showed them that they should not *go there.* [8] So they went *west* through Mysia and arrived at *the port city of* Troas. *I, Luke, joined them there.* [9] That night *God gave* Paul a vision in which he saw a man *who was a native* of *the province of* Macedonia. He was standing *some distance away,* and he was earnestly calling to Paul, "*Please* come over *here* to Macedonia and help us!" [10] *The next morning* we immediately got ready to go to Macedonia, because we concluded that God had called us to *go and* preach the good message to the people there.

Acts 16:11-12

THEME: Paul's company went from Troas to Philippi.

[11] So we boarded a ship in Troas and sailed across *the sea* to *the island of* Samothrace. *We spent the night there*, and the next day *we sailed again across the sea and arrived* at *the port of* Neapolis. [12] Then we *left Neapolis and* went *by land* to Philippi. It was a very important city in *the province of* Macedonia *where many* Roman citizens lived. We stayed in Philippi several days.

Acts 16:13-15

THEME: Paul proclaimed the gospel, and Lydia became a believer.

[13] On the first Jewish day of rest *after we arrived*, we went outside the city gate, *down* to the river. We had heard that *Jewish* people gathered to pray there. *When we got there, we saw* some women who had gathered *to pray.* So we sat down and began to tell them *the message about Jesus.* [14] A woman named Lydia was one of those who were listening *to Paul. She was a non-Jewish woman*, from *the city of* Thyatira, *who bought and* sold *expensive* purple cloth. She had accepted what the Jews believe about God. The Lord God opened her heart toward the message that Paul preached, and she believed it. *The members of her household also heard the good message and believed in Jesus.* [15] After *Paul and Silas* baptized Lydia and the others who lived in her house, she invited us to *stay in* her home. She said, "You know that I *now* believe in the Lord *Jesus,* so *please* come and stay in my house." She persuaded us *to do that, so we stayed there.*

Acts 16:16-24

THEME: Paul expelled a demon from a slave girl, so officials imprisoned Paul and Silas.

[16] Another day, while we were going to the place where people regularly gathered to pray, we met a young woman who was a slave. An evil spirit was enabling her to be a ventriloquist and to tell people what would happen *to them*. People paid a lot of money to *the men who were* her bosses, in return for her telling them things that *she said* would happen *to them*. [17] This young woman followed Paul and the rest of us. She continually shouted, "These men serve the God who is the greatest *of all gods*! They are telling you how *to be* saved!" [18] She continued to do that for many days. Finally Paul became irritated. So he turned *toward the young woman* and rebuked the evil spirit *that was in her. He said*, "By the authority of Jesus Christ, I command you to come out of this young woman!" Right away the evil spirit left her. [19] And then, when her bosses knew that she could no longer earn money for them *because she could no longer predict what would happen to people, they were angry*. So they grabbed Paul and Silas and forcefully took them to the public square, to *the place where* the government authorities and *a lot of other people were gathered*. [20] The owners *of the young woman* brought them to the city officials and told them, "These men are Jews, and they are greatly troubling *the people in* our city. [21] They are teaching that we should follow customs that our laws do not allow us Romans to consider *to be correct* or to obey!" [22] Many of the crowd joined *those who were accusing* Paul and Silas, and started beating them. Then the *Roman* authorities commanded *soldiers* to tear the shirts off Paul and Silas and to beat them *with rods*. [23] So the soldiers beat Paul and Silas vigorously *with rods*. After that, they *took them and* shoved them into the prison. They told the jailer to lock them up securely. [24] *Because the officials* had ordered him *to do that*, the jailer shoved Paul and Silas into the cell that was farthest inside. *There, he made them sit down on the floor and stretch out their legs*. Then he fastened their ankles in *grooves* between two large wooden beams, *so that Paul and Silas could not move their legs*.

Acts 16:25-34

THEME: Paul and Silas helped the jailer and his household to become believers.

[25] About midnight, Paul and Silas were praying *aloud* and praising God by singing hymns. The *other* prisoners were listening attentively to them. [26] Suddenly there was a very strong earthquake. It shook the entire jail and its foundation. *The earthquake caused* all the doors *of the jail* to open suddenly, and *caused* all the chains that fastened the prisoners to fall off. [27] The jailer woke up and saw that the doors of the jail were open. He thought that the prisoners had escaped. So he pulled out his sword and was about to kill himself, *because he knew that the officials would kill him if the prisoners escaped*. [28] Paul *saw the jailer and* shouted to him, "Don't harm yourself! We are all here!" [29] The jailer shouted *to someone* to bring torches, *and after they brought them,* he rushed into the jail and knelt down in front of Paul and Silas. *He was* trembling with fear. [30] Then he brought Paul and Silas out *of the jail* and asked: "Sirs, what do I need to do to be saved *from being punished for my sins*?" [31] *They answered,* "Trust in *what* the Lord Jesus *has done for you*, and you will be saved, and the others who live in your house will *also* be saved *if they believe in Jesus*."

[32-34] Then the jailer took Paul and Silas into his house, washed their wounds and gave them a meal. *He woke up all the people in his house, and* Paul and Silas told all of them the message about the Lord *Jesus. They all believed it*. Immediately *after that, Paul and Silas* baptized the jailer and all his family. They were very happy, because now they all believed in God.

Acts 16:35-40

THEME: Paul and Silas encouraged the believers, and then left Philippi.

[35] The next morning, the *Roman* officials ordered *some* police officers *to go to the jail to say to the jailer, "Our bosses* say, 'Let those *two* prisoners go *now*!' " [36] *After the officers went and told that to* the jailer, he *went and* told Paul, "The *Roman* authorities have sent a message saying that *I* should release you and Silas *from prison*. So you *two* can leave *the jail* now. You can go in peace!" [37] But Paul said to the police officers, "The authorities *had us* beaten in front of a crowd before *those authorities* had learned if we had done anything wrong! Then they *ordered us to* be shoved into jail! *But that was not legal, because* we are Roman citizens! And now they want to send us away secretly! No way! We will not accept that! Those *Roman* officials must come themselves and *tell us they are sorry*, and take us out *of jail*." [38] So the police officers *went and* told the city authorities *what Paul had said*. When those authorities heard that Paul and Silas were Roman citizens, they were afraid *that someone would report to their superiors what they had done, and as a result they would be punished.* [39] So those city authorities came to Paul and Silas and told them that they were sorry for what they had done to them. The authorities brought them out of the jail, and repeatedly asked them to leave the city *soon.* [40] After Paul and Silas left the jail, they went to Lydia's house. There they met with her and the *other* believers. They encouraged the believers *to continue trusting in the Lord Jesus*, and then the two apostles left *Philippi.*

17

Acts 17:1-4

THEME: In Thessalonica, Paul convinced many people that Jesus is the Messiah.

[1] Paul and Silas traveled through *the towns of* Amphipolis and Apollonia and arrived at *the city of* Thessalonica. There was a Jewish meeting place there. [2] *On the Jewish day of rest* Paul went into the meeting place, as he usually did. For three weeks *he went there* on each Jewish day of rest. Referring to the Scriptures *about the Messiah*, he spoke to the people who were there. [3] He explained and showed that *the prophets wrote that* the Messiah needed to die and be raised from the dead *afterwards*. He told them: "This man Jesus, whom I am telling you about, is our Messiah. *He died and became alive again, just as the prophets predicted.*" [4] Some of the Jews *there* were persuaded by *what Paul had said,* and began to associate with Paul and Silas. There were also many non-Jewish people there who worshipped God and many important women *who also believed the message about Jesus,* and they began to associate with Paul and Silas.

Acts 17:5-9

THEME: Some Jews there incited people to oppose Paul and Silas.

[5] But *some Jewish leaders* there in Thessalonica became jealous *because many people believed what Paul taught.* So they went to the public square and persuaded some lazy men *who were loitering there* to follow them. *In this way, the leaders of* the Jews gathered a crowd and incited them to become noisy and start a riot *against Paul and Silas.* Those *Jews and others* ran to the house of *a man named* Jason. *He was the man who had invited Paul and Silas to stay at his house.* They wanted to bring Paul and Silas outside to where the crowd *of people was waiting.* [6] They discovered that Paul and Silas were not there, but they found Jason *and grabbed him.* They dragged him and some of the *other*

believers to where the city officials and *many other people were gathered*. The men *who had seized Jason* shouted, "Those *two* men have caused trouble everywhere *they have gone*. Now they have come to our city, ⁷and *this fellow* Jason invited them to stay at his house. All the people *of this sect* oppose what our Emperor has decreed. They say that another person, whose name is Jesus, is *the real* king!" ⁸When the crowd of people *that had gathered* and the city authorities heard that, they became very angry and excited. ⁹*They wanted to put the believers in jail. But instead,* the officials made Jason and the other *believers* pay a fine, and told them they *would give the money back to them if Paul and Silas did not cause any more trouble.* Then the authorities let Jason and those other believers go.

Acts 17:10-12

THEME: In Berea, Paul helped many Jews and non-Jews to believe in Jesus.

¹⁰*So* that same night, the believers sent Paul and Silas *out of Thessalonica* to *the city of* Berea. When Paul and Silas arrived there, they went to the Jewish meeting house, *on a day when people had gathered there.* ¹¹The *Jews* in Thessalonica had not been very willing to listen to God's message, but the *Jews* who lived in Berea were very willing to listen, so they listened very eagerly to the message *about Jesus*. Every day they read the Scriptures *for themselves* to find out if what Paul said *about the Messiah* was true. ¹²As a result, many of the Jewish people believed *in Jesus*, and also some of the important non-Jewish women and many non-Jewish men *believed in him.*

Acts 17:13-15

THEME: Jews from Thessalonica incited people to oppose Paul.

¹³But then the Jews in Thessalonica heard that Paul *was* in Berea and that he was preaching the message from God *about Jesus*. So they went to Berea and *told people there that what Paul was teaching was not true. Thus*, they caused many of those people to get angry *at Paul*. ¹⁴So *several of* the believers *in Berea* took Paul to the coast *to go to another province*. But Silas and Timothy stayed in Berea. ¹⁵When Paul and the other men *arrived at the coast, they boarded a ship and* went to *the city of* Athens. Then Paul said *to the men who had come with him*, "Tell Silas and Timothy to come to me *here in Athens* as soon as they can." Then those men left *Athens and returned to Berea.*

Acts 17:16-17

THEME: In Athens, idols distressed Paul, so he talked to many people about Jesus.

¹⁶In Athens, Paul waited for Silas and Timothy *to arrive. In the meantime, he walked around the city. He* became very distressed as he saw that throughout the city there were many idols. ¹⁷So he went to the Jewish meeting place and talked *about Jesus* with the Jews, and also with the Greeks who had accepted what the Jews believe. He also went to the public square every day and talked to the people *whom he met* there.

Acts 17:18

THEME: When Paul talked about Jesus, he perplexed some teachers.

¹⁸Paul met some teachers who liked to talk about what people should believe. *People called* some of them Epicureans and *they called* others Stoics. They told Paul *what they believed*, and they asked him *what he believed. Then* some of them said *to one another*, "This ignorant person is just talking nonsense!" Others said, "*We think* he is teaching

people about *new* gods that we have not heard about." They said that because Paul was telling them that Jesus *had died and* had become alive again *afterwards. They had not heard that message before.*

Acts 17:19-21

THEME: Athens Council members asked Paul to explain what he had been teaching.

[19] So they took him to the place where the city council met. *When they arrived* there, they said to Paul, "*Please* tell us, what is this new message that you are teaching people? [20] You are teaching some things that startle us, so we want to know what they mean." [21] *They said that because* the people of Athens and also the people from other regions who lived there continually talked about what was new *to them*, or they listened to *others tell* what was new.

Acts 17:22-31

THEME: Paul told them about the God whom they did not know.

[22] Then Paul stood up before the men of the city council and said, "Citizens of Athens, I see that you think it is very important to worship many gods. [23] *I say that* because, while I was walking along and observing the objects *that represent various gods that* you worship, I even saw an altar that had these words *that someone had* carved *on it:* 'THIS HONORS THE GOD *THAT WE* DO NOT KNOW.' So now I will tell you about *that God* whom you worship but do not know.

[24] He is the God who made the world and everything in it. Since he rules over all *beings in* heaven and *on* earth, he does not dwell in shrines that people have made. [25] He does not need to have people make anything for him, because everything that exists belongs to him. He is the one who causes us to live and breathe, and *he gives us* all the things *that we need.*

[26] *In the beginning*, God created one man, and from him God produced all the nations that now live everywhere on the earth. He also decided where each group of people should live and how long they should live *there.* [27] He wanted people to realize that they need him. Then maybe they would seek for him and find him. *God wants us to seek him*, although he is *really* close to each one of us. [28] As someone has said, '*It is only* because he enables us that we live and move and do *what we do.*' And, as some of your own poets have said, 'We are God's children.'

[29] So, because we are God's children, we should not think that he is anything like an image *made* of gold or silver or stone. Those images are designed and skillfully made, *but they are not alive.* [30] During the times when people did not know *what God wanted them to do*, he did not *immediately* punish *them for what they did*. But now God commands all people everywhere to turn away from their evil ways. [31] *He tells us* that on a certain day that he has chosen he is going to judge *all of us people in* the world. He has appointed a *certain* man to judge *us, and that man will judge each of us* fairly. God has shown to all *people that he has appointed that man to judge everyone*, because God raised him from the dead."

Acts 17:32-34

THEME: Some Council members believed in Jesus.

[32] When the men of the council heard *Paul say* that someone had been raised from the dead, some of them laughed scornfully. But others said, "We would like you to tell us more

about this, some other time." [33] After they said that, Paul departed from the council *meeting*. [34] However, some of the people there went along with Paul and became believers. Among those *who believed in Jesus* was a member of the council whose *name was* Dionysius. Also, an *important* woman whose name was Damaris and some other people *who had heard Paul's message also believed in Jesus*.

18

Acts 18:1-4

THEME: In Corinth, Paul helped many people to become believers.

[1] After that, Paul left Athens and went to *the city of* Corinth. [2] There he met a Jew named Aquila, who grew up in *the province of* Pontus. Aquila and his wife Priscilla had recently come from *Rome, in* Italy. *They had previously left Rome* because Claudius, *the Roman Emperor*, had ordered all the Jews to leave Rome. Paul went to see Aquila and Priscilla. [3] Those two made tents *to earn a living*. Paul also made tents, so he stayed with them and they all worked together. [4] Every Jewish day of rest Paul *went* to the Jewish meeting house, where he spoke forcefully to both Jews and non-Jews. He repeatedly tried to persuade them *that Jesus is the Messiah*.

Acts 18:5-8

THEME: Paul helped many non-Jews become believers.

[5] Then Silas and Timothy arrived there from Macedonia. After they arrived, Paul *did not make tents any more. He* used all his time preaching *the message about Jesus in the Jewish meeting house*. He continued to tell the Jews *that he had personally met Jesus and that he knew* that Jesus was the Messiah. [6] But the Jews began to oppose Paul and to say evil things about him. So he shook *the dust from* his clothes *to show them that they were displeasing God. Then* he said to them, "If God punishes you, it will be your own fault, not mine! From now on I will go *and preach* to non-Jewish people!" [7] So Paul left *the meeting house* and went into a house that was next to it, *and preached there*. Titius Justus, the owner of the house, was a non-Jewish man who had accepted what the Jews believe. [8] *After that*, the ruler of the synagogue, *whose name was* Crispus, and all of his family believed in the Lord *Jesus*. Many other people in Corinth who listened *to Paul* also believed *in Jesus*. Then they were baptized. *But there were people who still opposed Paul and his preaching*.

Acts 18:9-11

THEME: Jesus commanded Paul to continue speaking about him, so Paul did that.

[9] One night Paul had a vision in which the Lord *Jesus* said to him, "Do not be afraid *of those who oppose you. Just continue speaking to people about me. Don't stop, [10] because I will help you, and no one will be able to harm you here. Keep telling them about me*, because there are many people in this city who will *believe in* me." [11] So Paul stayed in Corinth for a year and a half, teaching the people the message from God *about Jesus*.

Acts 18:12-17

THEME: Gallio refused to judge Paul.

[12] When Gallio was the *Roman* governor of *the province of* Achaia, the Jewish *leaders* there got together and seized Paul. They took him before the governor *and accused him,* [13] saying, "This man is teaching people *a false religion, leading them* to worship God in ways that are contrary to our *Jewish* laws." [14] When Paul was about to speak *to defend himself*, Gallio said to the Jews, "If this man had acted deceitfully or disobeyed *any of our Roman* laws, I would listen *patiently* to what you Jews *wanted to tell me.* [15] However, you are merely arguing about words and names and your own *Jewish* laws, so you yourselves need to resolve this. I refuse to judge these things!" [16] After Gallio *had said that*, he *commanded that* those Jewish leaders be expelled from the courtroom. [17] Then *the mob* grabbed the ruler of the synagogue, Sosthenes, and beat him, right there in front of the courthouse. Even though Gallio *saw them do this, he* did nothing about it.

Acts 18:18-21

THEME: At Ephesus, Paul parted from Priscilla and Aquila.

[18] Paul stayed on with the believers in Corinth for some time. Then he left the believers there, and went with Priscilla and *her husband* Aquila. They went to *the port of* Cenchrea. There Paul had his head shaved in order to complete a vow that he had taken. Then they boarded a ship and that was headed for *the province of* Syria. [19] They arrived at *the city of* Ephesus, and Priscilla and Aquila stayed there.

Before Paul left Ephesus, he entered the Jewish meeting house and lectured to the Jews. [20] They asked him to stay longer, but he refused. [21] But, as he left, he told them, "I will come back, if God wills." Then *because he wanted to be in Jerusalem to complete the vow*, he *boarded another ship that* sailed from Ephesus *toward Syria*.

Acts 18:22-23

THEME: Paul visited Jerusalem, then he went on to Antioch in Syria and then he returned to visit the believers throughout Galatia and Phrygia.

[22] When the ship arrived at Caesarea, Paul *got off. He* went up *to Jerusalem* and greeted the believers there. Then he went back down to *the city of* Antioch *in the province of Syria.*

[23] Paul spent some time *with the believers* there. Then he left Antioch and traveled to several towns *that he had visited previously,* in *the provinces of* Galatia and Phrygia. He taught all of the believers more *of the message from God about Jesus.*

Acts 18:24-26

THEME: Priscilla and Aquila instructed Apollos about the gospel.

[24] *While Paul was traveling in Galatia and Phrygia*, a Jewish man whose name was Apollos came to Ephesus. He was a native of *the city of* Alexandria. He *spoke eloquently* and he knew the Scriptures thoroughly. [25] *Other believers* had taught him *some things* about how the Lord *Jesus desires people* to conduct themselves, and he taught those things very enthusiastically *to people. He had heard* some of the things that Jesus did and said, and he taught those facts accurately *to people. However, he was teaching incompletely about Jesus, because* he knew only what John *the Baptizer had taught people whom he* baptized. [26] Apollos went to the Jewish meeting house, and he told the people there with great confidence the things that he had learned. When Priscilla and

Aquila heard what he taught, they invited him *to their home*. There they explained more accurately to him the way God *gives people eternal life.*

Acts 18:27-28

THEME: Apollos helped believers in Achaia.

²⁷ When Apollos decided to go to *the province of* Achaia, the believers in Ephesus told him that it would be good for him to do that. So they wrote a letter to the believers *in Achaia saying that they* should welcome Apollos. *So Apollos boarded a ship and went to Corinth.* After he arrived, he greatly helped those whom *God* in his kindness had enabled to believe *in Jesus.* ²⁸ Apollos was vigorously arguing publicly with *the leaders of* the Jews while many other people listened. *By quoting* from the Scriptures, he proved to them that Jesus was the Messiah.

19

Acts 19:1-7

THEME: Paul helped some men to become real believers in Jesus.

¹ While Apollos was at Corinth, Paul *left the places in Phrygia and Galatia* where he had been visiting, and traveled through *the province of Asia* back to Ephesus. There he met some people *who said they* were believers. ² He asked them, "Did you receive the Holy Spirit when you believed *God's message*?" They answered, "No, we have not even heard that there is a Holy Spirit." ³ So Paul asked, "So when you were baptized, what *were you showing*?" They replied, *"We were showing* that we believed what John *the Baptizer* taught." ⁴ Paul said, "John baptized people who turned away from their sinful behavior. He *also* told the people to believe in the one who would come after he *had come*, and that was Jesus." ⁵ So, when those men heard that, they were baptized *to affirm that they believed* in the Lord Jesus. ⁶ After that, Paul placed his hands on their heads *one by one*, and the *power of the* Holy Spirit came upon *each of* them. The *Holy Spirit* enabled them to speak in various languages *they had not learned*, and they also spoke messages *that the Holy Spirit* revealed to them. ⁷ There were about twelve men *whom Paul baptized and who received the power of the Holy Spirit.*

Acts 19:8-10

THEME: Paul helped many people in the province of Asia to hear the gospel.

⁸ For three months after that, Paul entered the Jewish meeting house *in Ephesus on each Jewish day of rest*, and he spoke boldly. He convincingly taught *the people* about how God wanted to rule *their lives.* ⁹ *A few of the people in the meeting house believed the message about Jesus*. But some of them would not believe that message and did not want to *continue to* hear it. While many people were listening, they said many bad things about the way *for people to receive eternal life about which Paul was preaching*. So Paul left them and took the believers with him *to meet in another place*. He taught every day in a lecture hall *owned by a man named* Tyrannus.ʳ ¹⁰ For two years Paul continued to teach

---

ʳ   OR, …Paul went every day to a lecture hall *in which a man whose name was* Tyrannus *also lectured.*

people in that building. In this way, most of the Jews and non-Jews who lived in *the province of* Asia heard the message about the Lord *Jesus*.

Acts 19:11-12

THEME: God enabled Paul to do amazing miracles.

[11] Also, God gave Paul the power to do amazing miracles. [12] *If those who were sick could not come to Paul,* handkerchiefs or aprons that Paul had touched would be taken and placed on sick people. As a result, those sick people would become well, and evil spirits that troubled people would leave.

Acts 19:13-17

THEME: People honored Jesus' name, after Jewish exorcists misused it and failed.

[13] There were also some Jews who traveled around *to where there were people controlled by evil spirits, and* they commanded the evil spirits to leave. *Certain ones of those Jews once* tried to command the evil spirits to come out of people by saying "I command you by the authority of the Lord Jesus, the man about whom Paul preaches, to come out!" [14] There were seven men who were doing that. They were sons of a man named Sceva, a Jew, *who called himself* a chief priest. [15] But *one day as they were doing that*, the evil spirit *refused to come out of that person. Instead, he* said to them, "I know Jesus, and I know *that he has authorized* Paul *to expel demons.* But no one has authorized you *to do anything to me!*" [16] *After saying that, suddenly* the man who was controlled by the evil spirit jumped on the seven Jewish men, *one after another,* knocked all of them down and beat each of them severely. He tore off their clothes and wounded them, causing them to bleed. So, *greatly frightened, they all* ran out of the house. [17] All the people who lived in Ephesus, both Jews and non-Jews, having heard what had happened, were afraid. They honored the Lord Jesus *because they realized he was very powerful.*

Acts 19:18-22

THEME: Many believers confessed their former sins and burned their books of magic.

[18] *At that time*, while other believers were listening, many believers confessed the evil things that they had been doing. [19] Several of those who had *previously* practiced sorcery gathered up their scrolls *that told how to work* magic, and burned them up in a public place. When people added up how much those scrolls had cost, they realized that altogether the amount was fifty thousand valuable silver coins.

[20] As a result, many more people heard the message about the Lord *Jesus,* and the message powerfully *changed their lives.*

[21] After those things had happened, Paul decided he wanted to go to Jerusalem, but he decided that *first* he would visit *the believers in the provinces of* Macedonia and Achaia *again.* Paul said, "After I have been to Jerusalem, I must also go to Rome." [22] He sent two of his helpers, Timothy and Erastus, ahead to Macedonia. But Paul stayed a little longer *in Ephesus,* in *the province of* Asia.

Acts 19:23-24

THEME: Demetrius made silver shrines of the goddess Artemis.

[23] *Soon after that*, some of the people there tried to make a lot of trouble for the people who believed the way *God revealed for us to receive eternal life.* [24] There was a man there

whose name was Demetrius who made little images out of silver. *They were models* of the temple of *a goddess whose name was* Artemis. Demetrius and the other men *who made those little images* earned a lot of money *from selling those images*.

Acts 19:25-31

THEME: Demetrius incited people to shout and to riot.

[25] Demetrius called a meeting of his workmen and also of others who made the little silver images. He said to them, "Men, you know that we earn a lot of money doing our kind of work. [26] Also, you know that this fellow Paul has persuaded many people who live in Ephesus *to no longer buy the images that we make. Now even the people from* many other towns in our province *no longer want to buy what we make*. This fellow tells people that the gods we have made *and worship* are not gods, *and that we should not worship them.* [27] *If people continue to listen to him*, they will soon ruin our business. Besides, people will no longer think that they should *come to* the temple of Artemis *to worship her. People* all over *our province of* Asia and, *in fact*, everywhere, worship *our great* goddess *Artemis. Soon people* may no longer consider that Artemis is great!" [28] All the men there were very angry *with Paul* when they heard what Demetrius said. They began to shout, "Great is the goddess Artemis of us Ephesians!" [29] Many of the other people in the city heard the shouting and went *and joined the crowd. They also became angry at Paul* and began shouting. *Several of* the people seized Gaius and Aristarchus, two men who had been traveling with Paul, *who were from Macedonia. Then the whole crowd of people ran, dragging those men along with them*, to the city stadium. [30] Paul also wanted to go *to the stadium and speak to* the people, but the other believers would not let him go there. [31] Also, some government officials of that province who were friends of Paul *heard what was happening*. So they sent someone to tell him *urgently* not to go into the stadium.

Acts 19:32-34

THEME: The crowd shouted, "Great is Artemis of the Ephesians!"

[32] The crowd of people *in the stadium* continued shouting. Some shouted one thing, and some shouted something different. But most of them did not even know what the meeting was about! [33] One of the *Jews there was named Alexander. Some of* the Jews pushed him to the front of the stadium, *so that he could speak to the crowd of people*. So Alexander motioned with his hands to the crowd, asking them to be quiet. He wanted to tell them that *the Jews* were not responsible *for the riot*. [34] But *many of the non-Jewish people* knew that Alexander was a Jew. *They also knew that the Jews did not worship the goddess Artemis. So the non-Jews there* unitedly *and* repeatedly shouted for about two hours, "Great is Artemis, *the goddess of us* Ephesians!"

Acts 19:35-41

THEME: The city secretary quieted, warned and dismissed the crowd.

[35] Then the city secretary made the crowd stop shouting, and he said to them, "My fellow-citizens, everyone in the world knows that *we* Ephesians guard the temple *where we worship* the great *goddess* Artemis. Also, *everyone knows that we watch over* the *sacred* image *of our goddess* that fell down from heaven! [36] Of course everyone knows that, and no one can say that these things are not true. So you should be quiet now! Don't suddenly do anything foolish.[s] [37] You *should not* have brought these *two* men *here, because they*

---

[s] OR, …So you should be quiet now. Do not suddenly do anything that will cause us trouble.

have not done anything evil. They have not gone into our temples and taken things *from there*. And they have not spoken evil of our goddess. [38] So, if Demetrius and his fellow-workmen want to make any accusations, *they should do it in the right way*. There are courts *that you can go to when you want to accuse someone*, and there are judges *there who have been appointed by the government*. You can accuse *anyone there*. [39] But if you want to ask about something else, *you should ask* for *other officials to* resolve it when *those* officials assemble legally. [40] *And this is certainly not a legal meeting! Resolve this legally* because, if *we don't*, I am afraid *that the governor* will hear about all this noise *you have made* and will say that we were trying to rebel *against the government*. If he would ask me what you were all shouting about, I wouldn't be able to give him an answer." [41] That's what the city secretary said *to the crowd*. Then he told them all to go *home. So they left*.

20

Acts 20:1-6

THEME: After being in Macedonia and Greece, Paul went to Troas.

[1] After the people at Ephesus had stopped rioting, Paul summoned the believers. He encouraged them *to continue to trust in the Lord Jesus. Soon* after that, he told them "Good-bye" and left to go to Macedonia. [2] *After he arrived* there, he visited *each town where there were believers* and encouraged them. Then he arrived in Greece, *which is also called Achaia*. [3] He stayed there for three months. Then he planned to return to Syria by ship, but *he heard that* some of the Jews *in that area* were planning to kill him *as he traveled. So* he decided instead to go *by land, and he traveled* again through Macedonia. [4] The men who were going to travel with him *to Jerusalem were* Sopater, *who was* a son of Pyrrhus, who grew up in of Berea; Aristarchus and Secundus, who were from Thessalonica; Gaius, *who was* from Derbe; Timothy, *who was from the province of* Galatia; and Tychicus and Trophimus, who were from *the province of* Asia. [5] Those *seven* men preceded *Paul and me, Luke, by ship from Macedonia, so* they got to Troas *before we did and* waited for *the two of* us there. [6] *But we two traveled by land as far as* Philippi. After the Jewish festival *when they eat* unleavened bread, we boarded a ship *that was going from Philippi to Troas*. After five days we arrived at Troas and we met the other men who had traveled there *ahead of us*. Then we *all* stayed in Troas for seven days.

Acts 20:7-12

THEME: At Troas, Paul encouraged believers by resurrecting Eutychus.

[7] On Sunday evening, we *and the other believers there* gathered together to celebrate the Lord's Supper *and to eat other food*.[t] Paul spoke to the believers. He continued teaching them until midnight, because he was planning to leave *Troas* the next day. [8] Many *oil* lamps were burning in the upstairs room in which we had gathered, *so the fumes caused some people to become sleepy*. [9] A young man named Eutychus was there. He was seated on *the sill of* an *open* window *on the third story of the house*. As Paul continued talking for a long time, Eutychus became sleepier and sleepier. Finally, he was sound asleep. He fell *to the ground out of the* third story *window. Some of the believers went down imm*ediately and picked him up. *But he was* dead. [10] Paul *also* went down. He lay

---

[t] OR, On the evening of the first day of the week, we *and the other believers there* assembled together to celebrate the Lord's Supper *and to eat other food*.

down and stretched out on top of the young man and put his arms around him. Then he said *to the people who were standing around*, "Don't worry, he is alive *again now!*" ¹¹ Then Paul, *along with the others*, went upstairs again and they ate the Lord's Supper and other food. Afterwards, Paul conversed with the believers until dawn. Then he left. ¹² The *other* people took the young man *home,* and were greatly encouraged about his being alive *again*.

Acts 20:13-16

THEME: Paul and his companions traveled from Troas to Miletus.

¹³ We then went to the ship. Paul did not board the ship *with us in Troas*, because he preferred to go *more quickly* overland to Assos. The rest of us boarded the ship and sailed for Assos. ¹⁴ We met Paul in Assos. He got on *the ship* with us, and we sailed to Mitylene. ¹⁵ The day after *we reached Mitylene*, we *sailed from there and* arrived *at a place* near *the island of* Kios. The day after that, we sailed to *the island of* Samos. The next day we *left Samos and* sailed to *the town of* Miletus. ¹⁶ *On the way to Miletus, the ship passed not very far from Ephesus*. Paul had *earlier* decided that he would not leave the ship and go to Ephesus, because he did not wish to spend *several* days in *the province of* Asia. If possible, he wanted to arrive in Jerusalem by the festival of Pentecost, *and the time of that festival was near*.

Acts 20:17-21

THEME: Paul reminded the Ephesian elders how he had conducted himself and had taught them.

¹⁷ *When the ship arrived at* Miletus, Paul sent *a messenger* to Ephesus to ask the elders of the congregation to come to talk with him.

¹⁸ When the elders arrived, Paul said to them, "You personally know how I *conducted myself among you the entire time* that I was with you, from the first day I arrived *here* in *the province of* Asia *until the day I left*. ¹⁹ *You know how* I was serving the Lord *Jesus* very humbly and how I sometimes wept *about people. You also know how* I suffered because the Jews *who were not believers often* tried *to harm me*. ²⁰ You also know that, as I preached *God's message* to you, I never left out anything that would help you. You know that I taught you *God's message* when many people were present, and *I also went to your* homes and taught it there. ²¹ I preached both to Jews and to non-Jews, telling them *all* that they must turn away from their sinful behavior and ask God *to forgive them. I also told them they should* believe in our Lord Jesus.

Acts 20:22-31

THEME: Paul told them that they would never see him again.

²² "And now note this: I am going to Jerusalem, because *God's* Spirit has clearly shown me that I must go there. I do not know what will happen to me *while I am there*. ²³ But I do know that in each city *where I have stopped*, the Holy Spirit has *led the believers to* tell me that *in Jerusalem* people will put me in prison and will cause me to suffer. ²⁴ But I don't care even if people kill me, if first I am able to finish the work that the Lord Jesus has told me *to do. He appointed me* to tell people the good message that God *saves us* by doing for us what we do not deserve. ²⁵ I have preached to you the message about how God desires to rule *people's lives*. But now I know that today is the last time that you fellow believers will see me. ²⁶ So I want you all to understand that if anyone *who has heard my teaching* dies *without trusting in Jesus*, it's not my fault, ²⁷ because I told you everything

that God has planned for us. [28] *You leaders* must continue to believe and obey *God's message. You must also help* all the other believers for whom the Holy Spirit has made you responsible. Watch over yourselves and the other believers *as a shepherd watches over his sheep.* God bought them with the blood *his Son* poured out *on the cross.* [29] I know *very well* that after I leave, *teachers* of false doctrine will come among you and will do great harm to the believers. *They will be* like fierce wolves that kill the sheep. [30] Even in your own group of believers there will be some who will deceive *other* believers by teaching them messages that are false. They will teach those messages in order that some people *will believe them and* will become their followers. [31] So watch out *that none of you stops believing the true message about our Lord Jesus*! Remember that day and night for *about* three years I repeatedly taught you that message, and I warned you with tears *in my eyes not to believe any other message.*

Acts 20:32-35

THEME: Paul entrusted them to God and to the message about God's goodness.

[32] "*Now as I leave you* I ask God to protect you and to keep you believing the message *that he saves us* by doing for us what we did not deserve. *If you continue believing* the message *that I told you*, you will become *spiritually mature*, and God will give you the blessings he has promised to give to all of those who belong to him.

[33] "*As for myself*, I have not desired anyone's money or *fine* clothing. [34] You yourselves know that I have worked *with my own hands* to earn the money that my companions and I needed. [35] In everything that I did, I showed you that we should work hard in order *to have enough money* to give some to those who are needy. We should remember that our Lord Jesus himself said, 'More blessings *come from God* when we give *to other people what they need* than when we receive *what people give to us.*'"

Acts 20:36-38

THEME: Paul prayed with them and they sadly bade him farewell.

[36] When Paul had finished speaking, he knelt down with all of the elders and prayed. [37] They all cried a lot, and they hugged Paul and kissed him. [38] They were especially sad because he had said that they would never see him again. Then they *all* went with him to the ship.

21

Acts 21:1-3

THEME: Paul, Luke and his other companions traveled from Miletus to Tyre.

[1] *After* we said good-bye to the elders *from Ephesus,* we *boarded the ship and* sailed to *the island of* Cos, *where the ship stopped for the night.* The next day we went from Cos to *the island of* Rhodes, *where the ship stopped again. The day after* that we went to *the port of* Patara, *where the ship stopped.* [2] At Patara we left that ship, and someone told us that there was a ship that would be going to *the region of* Phoenicia. *So* we boarded that ship, and it left. [3] *We sailed until* we could see *the island of* Cyprus. We passed to the south of the island and continued sailing until we got to *the province of* Syria. We arrived at *the city of* Tyre. *The ship was going to stay there several days, because its workers* had to unload the cargo.

Acts 21:4-6

THEME: At Tyre, believers warned Paul not to go to Jerusalem, but he went on.

[4] *Someone told us* where the believers in Tyre lived, so we *went and* stayed with them for seven days. Because *God's* Spirit revealed to them *that bad things would happen to Paul in Jerusalem*, they told Paul that he should not go there. [5] But when it was time *for the ship to leave again*, we *prepared to* continue going *to Jerusalem*. When we left *Tyre*, all the men and their wives and children went with us *to the edge of the sea*. We all knelt down there on the shore and prayed. [6] After we all said good-bye, Paul and we *his companions* got on the ship, and the *other* believers returned to their own homes.

Acts 21:7-9

THEME: Paul and his companions sailed from Tyre to Caesarea.

[7] After we left Tyre, we continued on *that ship* to *the city of* Ptolemais. There were believers there, and we greeted them and stayed with them that night. [8] The next day we left *Ptolemais* and sailed to Caesarea, where we stayed in the home of Philip, who spent his time telling others how to become Christians. He was one of the seven *men whom the believers in Jerusalem had chosen to care for the widows*. [9] He had four daughters who were not married. Each of them *frequently* shared messages that the Holy Spirit had revealed to them.

Acts 21:10-14

THEME: The believers could not persuade Paul from going on to Jerusalem.

[10] After *we had been in Philip's house for* several days, a believer named Agabus came down from Judea and arrived *in Caesarea*. He *frequently* spoke messages that the Holy Spirit had told him. [11] Coming over to where we were, he took off Paul's belt. Then he tied his own feet and hands with it and said, "The Holy Spirit says, 'The Jewish *leaders* in Jerusalem will tie up *the hands and feet of* the owner of this belt, just like this, and they will put him in the hands of non-Jewish people *as a prisoner.*'" [12] When *the rest of* us heard that, we and *other* believers there repeatedly pled with Paul, "Please don't go up to Jerusalem!" [13] But Paul replied, "Please stop crying and trying to discourage me *from going*! I am willing to be put in prison and even to be killed in Jerusalem for *serving* the Lord Jesus." [14] When *we realized that* he was determined *to go to Jerusalem*, we did not try *any longer* to persuade him *not to go*. We said, "May the Lord's *will be done!*"

Acts 21:15-16

THEME: Paul and other believers went from Caesarea to Jerusalem.

[15] After those days *in Caesarea*, we prepared *our things* and *left to* go *by land* up to Jerusalem. [16] Some of the believers from Caesarea also went with us. They took us to stay in the house of *a man named* Mnason. He was from Cyprus, and he had believed *in Jesus* when people were first beginning to hear the message *about him*.

Acts 21:17-26

THEME: Paul agreed with church leaders to perform a Jewish purifying ritual.

[17] When we arrived in Jerusalem, *a group of* the believers greeted us happily. [18] The next day Paul and the rest of us went to speak with James, *the leader of the congregations there*. All of the *other* leaders *of the congregations in Jerusalem* were also there. [19] Paul

greeted them, and then he reported all of the things that God had enabled him to do among the non-Jewish people. [20] When they heard that, James and the other elders said, "Praise the Lord!" Then *one of* them said to Paul, "Brother, you know that there are very many thousands of us Jewish people *here* who have believed *in the Lord Jesus.* Also, you know that we all continue very carefully to obey the laws *that Moses gave us.* [21] *But our fellow Jewish believers* have been told that when you are among non-Jews, you tell the Jewish believers who live there that they should stop obeying *the laws of* Moses. *People say that* you tell *those Jewish believers* not to circumcise their sons and not to practice our *other* customs. *We do not believe that this is what you tell people.* [22] But our fellow *Jewish* believers will certainly hear that you have arrived, *and they will be angry with you.* So *you* need to do something *to show them that what they heard about you is not true.* [23] So do what we tell you. There are four men among us who have made strong vows *to God* about *something.* [24] Go with these men *to the Temple* and *ritually* purify yourself along with them. Then, *when it is time for them to offer the sacrifices to complete that ritual,* pay for what they offer *as sacrifices.* After that, they can shave their heads *to show that they have done what they promised to do. And when people see you in the courtyard of the Temple with those men,* they will know that what they have heard about you is not true. Instead, all of them will know that you obey all our Jewish laws. [25] As for the non-Jewish believers, *we elders here in Jerusalem have talked* about *which of our laws* they *should obey, and* we wrote them *a letter, telling them* what we decided. *We wrote* that they should not eat meat that people have offered as a sacrifice to any idol, *that they should not eat* any blood, and that *they should not eat* meat from animals *which have been killed by* strangling. *We also told them that* no one should have sex with someone to whom he is not married." [26] So Paul *agreed to do what they asked,* and the next day he took the *four* men, and together they ritually purified themselves. After that, Paul went to the Temple *courtyard and* told *the priest* what day they would *finish* purifying themselves *ritually,* and when *they* would offer *the animals as sacrifices* for each of them.

Acts 21:27-30

THEME: Some Jews seized Paul in the Temple courts.

[27-29] When the seven days *for purifying themselves* were nearly finished, Paul *returned* to the Temple *courtyard.* Some Jews from *the province of* Asia saw him there, *and they were very angry with him.* On another day they had seen Paul *walking around* in Jerusalem with Trophimus, who was a non-Jew. Their laws did not permit non-Jews to be in the Temple, and they thought that Paul had brought Trophimus into the Temple *courtyard that day. So* they called out to many other Jews *who were in the Temple courtyard to help them* seize Paul. They shouted, "Fellow Israelites, come and help *us to punish this* man! This is the one who is *constantly* teaching people wherever *he goes that they* should despise the *Jewish* people. *He teaches people that they should no longer obey* the laws *of Moses* nor respect this holy *Temple.* He has even brought non-Jews here into the courtyard of our Temple, causing God to consider it no longer holy!" [30] *People* throughout the city heard that there was trouble *at the Temple courtyard,* and they came running there. They grabbed Paul and dragged him outside of the Temple *area.* The gates *to the Temple courtyard were shut* immediately, *so that the people would not riot inside that area.*

Acts 21:31-32

THEME: Roman soldiers ran to where those Jews were trying to kill Paul.

[31] While they were trying to kill Paul, someone *ran to a fort near the Temple* and told the Roman commander that many people in Jerusalem were rioting *at the Temple.* [32] The commander quickly took some officers and *a large group of* soldiers and ran to *the*

Temple area where the crowd was. When the crowd of people *who were yelling and beating Paul* saw the commander and the soldiers *coming*, they stopped beating Paul.

Acts 21:33-40

THEME: After the commander arrested Paul, soldiers carried him towards the fort.

[33] The commander came to *where Paul was and* seized him. He ordered *soldiers* to fasten a chain to *each of* Paul's *arms*. Then he asked *the people in the crowd*, "Who is this man, and what has he done?" [34] Some of the many people there were shouting *one thing, and* some were shouting something different. Because they continued shouting so loudly, the commander could not understand *what they were shouting. So* he ordered *the soldiers* to take Paul into the barracks *so that he could question him there*. [35] *The soldiers* led Paul to the steps *of the barracks*, but many people continued to follow them, trying to kill *Paul. So the commander told* the soldiers to carry Paul *up the steps into the barracks*. [36] The crowd that followed kept shouting, "Kill him! Kill him!"

[37] As Paul was about to be taken into the barracks, he said *in Greek* to the commander, "May I speak to you?" The commander said, "I am surprised that you can speak the Greek *language!*" [38] "Aren't you that fellow from Egypt who wanted to rebel *against the government not long ago*? Did you not take four thousand violent terrorists *with you* out into the desert, *so our government soldiers couldn't catch you*?" [39] Paul answered, "*No, I am not!* I am a Jew. *I was born* in Tarsus, which is an important city in *the province of* Cilicia. I request you to let me speak to the people." [40] Then the commander permitted Paul *to speak. So* Paul stood on the steps and motioned with his hand *for the crowd to be quiet. And after* the people in the crowd became quiet, Paul spoke to them in *their own* Hebrew language.

22

Acts 22:1-16

THEME: Paul defended his believing in Jesus, but the Jews wanted to kill him.

[1] Paul said, "You *Jewish* elders and my other fellow-Jews, listen to me now while I reply to *those who are accusing me!*" [2] When the crowd of people heard Paul speaking to them in *their own* Hebrew language, they became even more quiet and really listened. Then Paul said to them, [3] "I am a Jew, *as are all of you*. I was born in Tarsus, in *the province of* Cilicia, but I grew up here in Jerusalem. *When I was young, for many years* I studied the laws *that Moses gave to our ancestors*. I was taught by *the famous teacher* Gamaliel. *I have* carefully *obeyed those laws, because* I have wanted to obey God. *I am sure that* many of you also carefully obey *those laws*. [4] *That is why* I previously persecuted those who believe the message that people call 'the Way that *Jesus taught.*'*I continually looked for ways* to kill *them. Whenever I found* men or women *who believed that message*, I *ordered* them to be seized and thrown into jail. [5] The high priest knows this, and so do the *other respected men who belong to our Jewish* Council. They gave me letters to *take to* their fellow-Jews in Damascus. *By means of those letters, they authorized me to* go there and find people who believed in *Jesus. They had written in the letters that I was to bring them* as prisoners to Jerusalem, so that *the leaders here* could punish them.

So I went on my way to Damascus. [6] About noon, my companions and I were getting near Damascus. Suddenly a bright light from the sky flashed all around me. [7] *The light was so bright that* I fell to the ground. Then I heard the voice *of someone* speaking to me *from up* in the sky. *The one who was speaking to me said*, 'Saul! Saul! Why do you do things to harm me?' [8] I answered, 'Who are you, Sir?' He replied, 'I am Jesus from Nazareth. *I am the one* whom you are harming *by doing things to harm my followers*.' [9] The men who were *traveling* with me saw the *very bright* light, *and they heard a voice*, but they did not understand what the voice said to me. [10] Then I asked, 'Lord, what *do you want* me to do?' The Lord told me, 'Get up and go into Damascus! *A man* there will tell you all that *I* have planned for you to do.' [11] *After that, I couldn't see*, because the *very bright* light had had caused me to become blind. So my companions took me by the hand and led me to Damascus. [12] *A couple of days* later, a man named Ananias came to *see* me. He was a man who *greatly respected God and* carefully obeyed *our Jewish* laws. All the Jews living in Damascus said good things about him. [13] He came and stood beside me and said to me, '*My* friend Saul, see *again*!' Instantly I could see! I saw him *standing there beside me*. [14] Then he said: 'The God whom *we worship and* whom our ancestors *worshipped* has chosen you and will show you what he wants *you to do. He has allowed you* to see the righteous one, *the Messiah*, and you have heard him speaking *to you*. [15] He wants you to tell people everywhere what you have seen and heard *from him*. [16] So now don't delay! Stand up, let *me* baptize you, and by praying to the Lord *Jesus, ask God* to forgive you for your sins!'

Acts 22:17-22

THEME: Paul told about the Lord's commanding him to go to non-Jewish people.

[17] Later, I returned to Jerusalem. *One day* I went to the Temple *courtyard*. While I was praying there, I saw a vision *in which* [18] I saw the Lord speaking to me. He said to me, '*Don't stay here*! Leave Jerusalem immediately, because the people *here* will not listen to what you tell *them* about me!' [19] But I *protested and* said to him, 'Lord, they know that I went to many of our meeting houses looking for people who believe in you. I was putting in jail those *whom I found* who believed in you, and I was even beating them. [20] *The people here will remember that* when Stephen was killed because he told people about you, I stood there *watching it all* and approving *what they were doing. I showed my* approval by guarding the cloaks that those who were murdering him *had thrown aside. So if I stay here, the fact that I have changed how I think about Jesus will surely impress those leaders of our people*.' [21] But the Lord said to me, 'No, leave *Jerusalem, because* I am going to send you far away *from here* to non-Jewish people!' "

[22] The people listened *quietly* to what Paul was saying until *he mentioned the Lord sending him to non-Jewish people*. Then they began shouting *angrily*, "Kill him! *He does not deserve to live any longer!*" They said that because they refused to believe that God would save people *unless they became Jews*.

Acts 22:23-29

THEME: Paul said that he was a Roman citizen, so soldiers did not flog him.

[23] While they continued shouting, they took off their cloaks and threw dust into the air *to show their anger*. [24] So the commander ordered *soldiers* to take Paul into the barracks. He told *the soldiers* that they should whip Paul, to make him tell what he had done that made the Jews shout so angrily. *So the soldiers took Paul into the barracks*. [25] Then they stretched his arms out *and tied them* so that they could whip him *on his back. But* Paul said to the officer who was standing nearby *watching*, "*You should think carefully about this!* You will certainly be acting unlawfully if you whip me, a Roman *citizen whom* no one has put on trial and condemned!" [26] When the officer heard that, he went to the commander and said *to him*, "This man is a Roman *citizen*! Surely you would not order *us to whip him!*" [27] The commander *was surprised when he heard that. He himself* went *into*

the barracks and said to Paul, "Tell me, are you really a Roman *citizen*?" Paul answered, "Yes, *I am*." ²⁸ Then the commander said, "*I am a Roman citizen, too.* I paid a lot of money to become a *Roman* citizen." Paul said, "But I was born a *Roman* citizen, *so I did not need to pay anything.*" ²⁹ The soldiers *were about to whip Paul and to ask him questions about what he had done. But when they heard what Paul said, they* backed off immediately. The commander also became afraid, because he realized that Paul was a Roman *citizen* and that he had *illegally ordered soldiers to* tie up Paul's hands.

Acts 22:30

THEME: The commander's soldiers brought Paul to the Jewish Council.

³⁰ *The commander still* wanted to know exactly why the Jews were accusing Paul. So the next day he *had the soldiers* take the chains off Paul. He also summoned the chief priests and the *other Jewish* Council *members*. Then he took Paul *to where the Council was meeting* and ordered him to stand before them *and speak to them*.

23

Acts 23:1-5

THEME: Paul apologized for unknowingly denouncing the high priest.

¹ Paul looked straight at the Jewish council members and said, "My fellow-Jews, all my life I have lived respecting our God, and I do not know of anything I have done that I knew was wrong." ² When Ananias the high priest *heard what Paul said*, he ordered the men who were standing near Paul to hit him on the mouth. ³ Then Paul said to Ananias, "God will punish you *for that*, you hypocrite! You sit there and judge me, using the laws *God gave Moses*. But you *yourself* disobey those laws, because you ordered *these men* to strike me *without having proved that I have done anything wrong!*" ⁴ The men who were standing near Paul *rebuked him. They* said, "Aren't you afraid to insult God's *servant, our* high priest?" ⁵ Paul replied, "My fellow-Jews, *I am sorry*. I did not know that the man *who told one of you to hit me* is the high priest. *If I had known that, I would not have insulted our high priest*, because *I know that* it is written *in our Jewish law*, 'Do not speak evil of any of your rulers!'"

Acts 23:6-10

THEME: The commander rescued Paul from the Council members.

⁶ Paul realized that some of the *Council members* were Sadducees and others were Pharisees. So, *to cause the Pharisees and Sadducees to argue among themselves instead of accusing him*, he called out loudly in the Council *hall*, "My fellow-Jews, I am a Pharisee, just like my father was. I have been put on trial *here* because I confidently expect that *some day God* will raise people from the dead." ⁷ When he said that, the Pharisees and Sadducees started to argue with one another *about whether people who have died will rise again or not*. ⁸ The Sadducees believe that after people die, they will not become alive again. They also believe that there are no angels and no other kinds of spirits. On the other hand, the Pharisees believe *in a resurrection. They also believe* that there are angels and other kinds of spirits. ⁹ So they were divided, and they began shouting at one another *as they argued*. Some of the teachers of the laws *God gave Moses* who were Pharisees stood up and said, "We think that this man has done nothing wrong. Maybe an angel or some other spirit *really* spoke to him *and what he says is true*."

[10] Then the *Pharisees and Sadducees* argued even more loudly *with one another*. The commander *heard the uproar and* was afraid that they would tear Paul to pieces. So he ordered soldiers to go down *from the barracks* and forcefully take Paul away from the Council members and bring him up into the barracks. *So the soldiers did that.*

Acts 23:11

THEME: *The Lord revealed that Paul would tell people about him in Rome.*

[11] That night, *in a vision Paul saw* the Lord *Jesus come and* stand near him. The Lord said *to him*, "*Paul*, take courage! You have told people *here* in Jerusalem about me, and you must tell people in Rome about me, too!"

Acts 23:12-15

THEME: *Some Jews plotted to kill Paul.*

[12] The next morning *some* of the Jews *who hated Paul* met secretly and talked *about how they could kill him*. They promised *themselves* that they would not eat or drink anything until they had killed him. They asked God to curse them *if they did not do what they promised*. [13] There were more than forty men who planned to do that. [14] They went to the chief priests and *Jewish* elders and told them, "God has heard us vow that we won't eat *or drink* anything until we have killed Paul. [15] So *we want* you and the rest of the Jewish Council to go to the commander and ask him to bring Paul down to you *from the barracks.*[u] Tell the commander that you want to question Paul some more. But we will be waiting to kill Paul while he is on the way here."

Acts 23:16-22

THEME: *Paul's nephew warned that some Jews had plotted to kill Paul.*

[16] But the son of Paul's sister heard what they were planning to do, so he went into the barracks and told Paul. [17] *When Paul heard that*, he called one of the officers and said to him, "*Please* take this young man to the commander, because he needs to tell him something *important.*" [18] So the officer took Paul's nephew to the commander. The officer said to the commander, "That prisoner, Paul, called me and said, 'Please take this young man to the commander, because he needs to tell him something *important.*'" [19] The commander took the young man by the hand, led him off by himself, and asked him, "What do you need to tell me?" [20] He said, "*There are some* Jews who have planned to ask you to bring Paul before their Council tomorrow. They will say that they want to ask him some more questions. *But that is not true.* [21] Don't do what they ask you to do, because there are more than forty *Jewish* men who will be hiding and waiting *to attack Paul when he passes by on the way to the Council*. They even vowed to God that they will not eat or drink anything until they have killed Paul. They are ready *to do it*, and right now they are waiting for you to agree *to do what they are asking you to do*." [22] The commander said to Paul's young nephew, "Don't tell anyone that you have told me about their plan!" Then he sent the young man away.

---

[u] OR, So *we request that* you go to the commander and ask him, on behalf of the whole Jewish Council, to bring Paul down to you *from the barracks.*

Acts 23:23-35

THEME: Many soldiers escorted Paul safely to Governor Felix at Caesarea.

²³ Then the commander called two of his officers and told them, "Get a group of two hundred soldiers ready *to travel*. Take along seventy soldiers riding horses, and two hundred other soldiers carrying spears. *All of you must be ready* to leave at nine o'clock tonight, to go *down* to Caesarea. ²⁴ And take along horses for Paul *and those accompanying him* to ride, and safely escort him to *the palace of* Governor Felix." ²⁵ Then the commander wrote a letter *to send to the governor*. This is what he wrote: ²⁶ "*I am* Claudius Lysias *writing to you*. You, Felix, are our governor whom we respect, *and I sincerely send you* my greetings. ²⁷ *I have sent you* this man, *Paul, because certain* Jews seized him and were about to kill him. But I heard that he is a Roman citizen, so I and my soldiers went and rescued him. ²⁸ I wanted to know what those Jews were saying that he had done wrong, so I took him to their Jewish Council. ²⁹ I listened *while they asked this man questions and he answered them*. The things *they* accused him about were entirely concerned with their *Jewish* laws. Paul has not disobeyed any of our *Roman* laws. *So our officials* should not execute him or *even* put him in prison. ³⁰ *Someone* told me that some Jews were secretly planning to kill this man, so I immediately sent him to you, *so that you may give him a fair trial there*. I have also ordered the Jews who have accused him to *go there to Caesarea and* present their *accusations*."

³¹ So the soldiers did what *the commander* ordered them, *taking this letter with them*. They *got Paul and* took him with them during the night *down* to *the town of* Antipatris. ³² The next day, the foot soldiers returned to the barracks *in Jerusalem* and the soldiers who rode horses went on with Paul. ³³ When the men escorting Paul arrived in Caesarea, they delivered the letter to the governor, and they turned Paul over to the governor. ³⁴ The governor read the letter and then said to Paul, "What province are you from?" *Paul answered,* "I am from Cilicia." ³⁵ Then the governor said, "When the people who have accused you arrive, I will listen *to what each of you says,* and then I will judge your case." Then he ordered *soldiers* to guard Paul in the palace that King Herod *the Great had built*.

24

Acts 24:1-9

THEME: Paul defended himself, and Felix promised to judge him.

¹ Five days later Ananias the high priest, *having heard that Paul was now in Caesarea*, went down *there from Jerusalem*, along with some *other Jewish* elders and a lawyer *whose name was* Tertullus. There they formally presented to the governor their accusations against Paul. ² *The governor* ordered *a soldier* to bring Paul in. *When Paul arrived,* Tertullus began to accuse him. He said *to the governor*, "Honorable Governor Felix, during the many years you have ruled us, we have lived well.ᵛ By planning wisely, you have improved many things in this province. ³ *So*, sir, we always gratefully acknowledge everything *you have done* for all *of us,* wherever *you have done those things.* ⁴ But, so that I will not take up too much of your time, I earnestly request that you kindly listen to me very briefly. ⁵ We have observed that this man, *wherever he goes*, causes trouble. *Specifically*, he causes all the Jews everywhere to riot. *Also*, he leads the

---

ᵛ OR, …Honorable Governor Felix, while you have ruled us for many years, we have lived peacefully.

entire group *whom people call* 'the followers of the Nazarene', *a false sect.* ⁶He even tried to do things in the Temple *in Jerusalem* that would defile it. So we seized him.ʷ ⁷But Lysias, the commander at the Roman fort, came with his soldiers and forcefully took him away from us. ⁸Lysias also ordered Paul's accusers to come here and accuse Paul before you. If you question him yourself, you will be able to learn that all these things about which we are accusing him are true." ⁹When the Jewish *leaders who were listening heard that, they* told *the governor that* what Tertullus had said was true.

Acts 24:10-21

THEME: Paul disproved what they had said, but admitted that he was a Christian.

¹⁰Then the governor motioned with *his hand to Paul that* he should speak. So Paul replied. He said, "*Governor Felix, I realize that you have judged this Jewish* province for many years. So I gladly defend myself, confident *that you will listen to me and will judge me fairly.* ¹¹You can *easily* ascertain that not more than twelve days have passed since I went up to Jerusalem to worship *God. That is not enough time to cause a lot of trouble.* ¹²No one *can claim that he* saw me arguing with anyone at the Temple courtyard *because I did not do that. No one can claim that he saw me* stirring up people in *any Jewish meeting house,* or causing trouble anywhere *else* in the city *of Jerusalem, because I did not do that.* ¹³So they cannot prove to you the things about which they are now accusing me. ¹⁴But I admit to you *that this is true*: I do worship the God that our ancestors *worshipped. It is true that* I follow the way that *Jesus taught us,* what the Jewish leaders call a false religion. I also believe everything that was written *by Moses* in the laws *God gave him,* and everything that was written by the *other* prophets. ¹⁵I confidently expect—just as *some of* these men also expect—that *some day God* will cause everyone who has died to become alive again. He will raise from the dead both those who were righteous and those who were wicked. ¹⁶*Because I am confidently waiting for that day,* I always try to do what pleases God and what other people think is right. ¹⁷After *I had been in other places for* several years, I returned to Jerusalem. I went there to deliver some money to my fellow Jews *who are* poor, and to offer sacrifices *to God.* ¹⁸Some *Jews* observed me in the Temple *courtyard* after I had completed the ritual of purification. There was no crowd with me, and I was not causing *people* to riot. ¹⁹But it was some *other* Jews *who had come* from *the province of* Asia *who really caused people to riot. They* should be here in front of you to accuse me, if they thought that I *did* something *wrong.* ²⁰*But if they don't want to do that,* these *Jewish* men who are here should tell you what *they think* I did that was wrong, when I *defended myself* before their Council.ˣ ²¹*They might say that* one thing I shouted as I stood before them *was wrong. What I said* was, 'You are judging me today because I believe that *God* will raise people from the dead.' "

Acts 24:22-23

THEME: Governor Felix adjourned the trial.

²²Felix already knew quite a lot about *what people called* 'the way *of Jesus'.* But he did not let Paul or his accusers continue to speak. *Instead,* he said *to them,* "*Later,* when Commander Lysias comes down here, I will decide these matters that concern you all." ²³Then he told the officer *who was guarding Paul to take Paul back to the prison and* see

---

ʷ Some Greek manuscripts include the sentence: "We would have judged him according to our Jewish Law."

ˣ OR, But since those men are not here, these *Jewish* men who are here should tell you what *they think* I did that was wrong, when I *defended myself* before the Jewish Council.

that Paul was guarded all the time. But he said that Paul was not to be chained, and if his friends came to visit him, *the officer* should allow them to help Paul *in any way they wished*.

Acts 24:24-27

THEME: Felix often talked to Paul, hoping Paul would give him money.

²⁴ Several days later Felix and his wife Drusilla, who was a Jew, came *back to Caesarea after having been away for a few days*. Felix *ordered* Paul to be brought in. Then Felix listened to what Paul *had to say*. Paul spoke about what Christians believe about the Messiah Jesus. ²⁵ Paul explained *to them about what God requires people* to do in order to please him. *He also explained about God requiring people to exercise self-control. Paul also told him that there will be a time when God* will judge *people*. Felix became alarmed *after hearing those things. So* he said to Paul, "That's all *I want to hear* now. When there is a time that is convenient, I will ask you to come *again*." ²⁶ *Felix said that because* he hoped Paul would give him some money for *allowing Paul to get out of prison*. So he repeatedly sent for Paul to come, and Paul *repeatedly went and* talked with him. *But he did not give Felix any money, and Felix did not order Paul's release.*

²⁷ Felix let Paul remain in prison, because he wanted to please the Jewish *leaders and he knew that they did not want him to release Paul*. But when two years had passed, Porcius Festus replaced Felix *as governor*.

25

Acts 25:1-5

THEME: Festus told the Jews to go and accuse Paul at Caesarea.

¹ Festus, *who was now the governor* of the province, arrived in Caesarea, and three days later he went up to Jerusalem. ² In Jerusalem, the chief priests and *other* Jewish leaders formally made accusations against Paul. ³ They urgently asked Festus to do them a favor. *They asked him to order soldiers* to bring Paul to Jerusalem, *so that Festus could put him on trial there*. But they were planning that some *of them* would hide *near the road* and wait *for Paul,* and kill him when he was traveling *to Jerusalem*. ⁴ But Festus replied, "Paul is in Caesarea, and is being guarded *there*. I myself will be going down to Caesarea in a few days. ⁵ Choose some of your leaders to go there with me. *While they are there,* they can make their accusations against Paul."

Acts 25:6-12

THEME: Paul appealed to Caesar, so Festus agreed to that.

⁶ After Festus had been *in Jerusalem* eight or ten days, he went back down to Caesarea. *Several of the Jewish leaders also went there*. The next day Festus ordered that Paul be brought to him *in the assembly hall* so that he could hear Paul's case. ⁷ *After* Paul was brought to *the assembly hall*, the Jewish *leaders* from Jerusalem gathered around him *to accuse him*. They told *Festus* that Paul had committed many crimes. But they could not prove *any of their accusations*. ⁸ Then Paul *spoke* to defend himself. He said, "I have done nothing wrong against the laws of us Jews, and I have not disobeyed the rules concerning our Temple. I have also done nothing wrong against your government." ⁹ But Festus wanted to please the Jewish *leaders, so* he asked Paul, "Are you willing to go up to

Jerusalem so that I can listen as these men accuse you *there*?" [10] But Paul *did not want to do that. So* he said *to Festus,* "*No,* I am *now* standing before you, and you are the judge *whom the Roman* emperor *has authorized. This is the place* where I should be judged. I have not wronged the Jewish people *at all,* as you know very well. [11] If I had done something *for which I* should be executed, I would not plead *that my life be spared.* But none of these things about which they accuse me is *true, so* no one can *legally* surrender me to *these Jews.* So I formally request that the emperor *should judge me at Rome.*" [12] Then after Festus conferred with his advisors, he replied to Paul, "You have formally requested *that I should send you* to the emperor *in Rome. So I will* arrange for you to go *there in order that he can hear your case.*"

Acts 25:13-22

THEME: Festus told King Agrippa about Paul.

[13] After several days, King Agrippa arrived at Caesarea, accompanied by *his younger sister* Bernice. They had come to *formally* welcome Festus *as the new Governor of the province.* [14] King Agrippa and Bernice stayed many days in Caesarea. While *they were* there, Festus told Agrippa about Paul. He said to the king, "There is a man here whom Felix allowed to remain in prison *when his time as governor ended.* [15] When I went to Jerusalem, the chief priests and *the other* Jewish elders made many accusations *against him.* They asked me to condemn him *to be executed.* [16] But I told them if someone has been accused *of a crime, we* Romans do not immediately deliver him *to his accusers.* First, we order him to stand before his accusers and to say whether or not he has done those things. *After that, the judge will decide what to do with* him. [17] So those Jews came *here to Caesarea* when I came, and I did not delay. The day after *we arrived,* after I sat down at the place where I make decisions, I ordered that Paul be brought into *the courtroom.* [18] The Jewish leaders did accuse him, but the things about which they accused him were not any of the *evil* crimes about which I thought *they would accuse him.* [19] Instead, what they argued about with him were some teachings that *some* Jews believe *and others refuse to believe. They argued* about a man whose name was Jesus who had died, *but the man they were accusing, whose name is* Paul, kept saying, 'Jesus is alive again.' [20] I did not know what questions to ask *them, and I did not know how to judge* concerning their dispute. So I asked Paul, 'Are you willing to go *back* to Jerusalem and have the dispute *between you and these Jews* judged there?' [21] But Paul answered, '*No.* I *want you to* request the emperor *in Rome to* judge my case, *and I will just wait here as a prisoner until then.*' So I have ordered that Paul be guarded here until I can send him to the emperor *in Rome.*" [22] Then Agrippa said to Festus, "I myself would like to hear what that man *has to say.*" Festus answered, "*I will order him to come here* tomorrow, and you can hear him."

Acts 25:23-27

THEME: Festus asked King Agrippa to tell him what to write to Caesar about Paul.

[23] The next day Agrippa and Bernice came very ceremoniously to the assembly hall. Some *Roman* commanders and prominent men in the city *of Caesarea* came with them. Then, at the command of Festus, they brought Paul from the prison. [24] Festus said, "King Agrippa, and all *the rest of you* who are here, you see this man. Many Jews in Jerusalem and also here *in Caesarea* appealed to me, screaming that we should not let him live any longer. [25] But *when I asked them to tell me what he had done, and they told me,* I found out that he had not done anything for which he should be executed. However, he has asked that our emperor *should judge his case,* so I have decided to send him to Rome. [26] But I don't know what specifically I should write to the emperor concerning him. That's why I have

brought him here. *I want* you all *to hear him speak*, and I especially want you, King Agrippa, to hear him. Then, after we have questioned him, maybe I will know what I should write *to the emperor about him*. ²⁷ I concluded *that it would be* unreasonable to send a prisoner *to the emperor in Rome without* specifying the accusations against him."

26

Acts 26:1-3

THEME: Paul requested that his hearers would listen to him.

¹ Then Agrippa said to Paul, "You may *now* speak *for* yourself." Paul stretched out his hand *dramatically* and began to defend himself.ʸ He said, ² "King Agrippa, I consider that I am fortunate that today, while you listen, I can defend myself from all the things about which the Jewish leaders are accusing me. ³ I am really fortunate, because you know all about the customs of us Jews and the questions that we argue about. So I ask you, please listen patiently to what I say.

Acts 26:4-8

THEME: Paul told about being a Pharisee who believed that God would resurrect people.

⁴ "Many of my fellow Jews know about how I have conducted my life, from the time I was a child. They know how I lived in the area where I *was born* and *also later* in Jerusalem. ⁵ They have known for many years, and they could tell you—if they wanted to—that *since I was very young* I obeyed the customs of our religion very carefully, just as the *other* Pharisees do. ⁶ Today I am being put on trial because I am confidently expecting that God will do what he promised our ancestors. ⁷ Our twelve tribes are *also* confidently waiting for God to do *for us what he promised*, as they respectfully worship him, day and night. *Respected* king, I confidently expect *that God will do what he promised, and they also believe that! But that is the reason* that these Jewish leaders are accusing me! ⁸ You *people* believe that God can cause those who have died to become alive again, so why *do you refuse to believe he raised Jesus from the dead*?

Acts 26:9-11

THEME: Paul told how he had persecuted Christians.

⁹ "*Formerly* I too was sure that I should do everything I could to oppose Jesus, the man from Nazareth. ¹⁰ So that is what I did *when I lived* in Jerusalem. I put many of the believers in jail, just as the chief priests there had authorized me *to do*. When *the Jewish leaders wanted* to have *Christians* killed, I voted *for that*. ¹¹ Many times I punished the believers *whom I found* in Jewish meeting houses. *By punishing them*, I tried to force them to speak evil *about Jesus*. I was so angry with the followers of Jesus that I even traveled to other cities to *find them and* cause trouble for them.

ʸ OR, …Paul stretched out his hand to salute the king and began to defend himself.

Acts 26:12-18

THEME: Paul told how he had become a believer in Jesus.

[12] "*One day*, I was on my way to Damascus to do that. The chief priests *in Jerusalem* had authorized and sent me *to seize the believers there.* [13] *My respected* king, *while I was going* along the road, at about noon I saw a *bright* light in the sky. It was even brighter than the sun! It shone all around me, and also around the men who were traveling with me. [14] We all fell to the ground. Then I heard the voice of someone speaking to me in my own Hebrew language. He said 'Saul, Saul, stop trying to harm me! You are *hurting yourself by trying to hurt me, like an ox* kicking against *its owner's* goad.' [15] Then I asked, 'Who are you, Lord?' The Lord said to me, 'I am Jesus. You are harming me *by harming my followers.* [16] But instead *of continuing to do that*, stand up now! I have appeared to you to tell you that I have chosen you to serve me. You must tell people about *what I am showing you* as you are seeing me *now*, and about what *I will show you when* I will appear to you again. [17] I will protect you *from those who will try to harm you, both* your own people and *also* those who are not Jewish. I am sending you to them [18] to help them to realize what is true and to stop believing what is false. I am sending you to them so that they may let God control them and not let Satan control them any more. *Then God* will forgive their sins and will accept them as his people because of their trust in me.' *That is what Jesus said to me.*

Acts 26:19-20

THEME: Paul said that he obeyed what Jesus commanded him from heaven.

[19] "So, King Agrippa, I fully obeyed what *the Lord Jesus told me to do when he spoke to me* from heaven. [20] First, I preached to *the Jews* in Damascus. Then *I preached to the Jews* in Jerusalem and throughout *the rest of* Judea. After that I also preached to non-Jews. I preached that they must turn away from their sinful behavior and turn their lives over to God. I told them that they must do things that would show that they had truly stopped their sinful behavior.

Acts 26:21-23

THEME: Paul said that he proclaimed what the prophets had written about the Messiah.

[21] "It is because *I preached* this message *that some* Jews seized me *when I was* in the Temple *courtyard and* tried to kill me. [22] However, God has been helping me *from that time, and he is still helping me* today. So I stand here and I tell all of you, those who are important and those who are not, *who Jesus is.* Everything that I say *about him* is what Moses and the *other* prophets wrote *about long ago, things that they said* would happen. [23] They wrote that *people would cause* the Messiah to suffer and die. They also wrote that he would be the first person to rise from the dead, *also that he would* proclaim *the message that would be like a* light, *and that he would save* both *his own Jewish* people and non-Jewish people."

Acts 26:24-29

THEME: Paul talked to Festus and Agrippa, urging them to become believers in Jesus.

[24] Before Paul could say anything *further* to defend himself, Festus shouted: "Paul, you are crazy! You have studied too much, and it has made you insane!" [25] But Paul answered, "Your Excellency, Festus, I am not raving *insanely*! On the contrary, what I am saying is true and sensible! [26] King Agrippa knows the things *that I have been talking about,* and

I can speak confidently to him *about them*. I am sure that he knows these things, because people everywhere have heard about what happened *to Jesus*." ²⁷ Then Paul asked, "King Agrippa, do you believe *what* the prophets *wrote*? I know you believe it." ²⁸ Then Agrippa *answered* Paul, "*I hope you don't think* that by the few things *that you have just said* you can persuade me to become a Christian!" ²⁹ Paul replied, "Whether it takes a short time or a long time, it does not matter. I pray to God that you and also all of the others who are listening to me today will also *believe in Jesus* like I do, but I don't want you to become prisoners *like I am!*"

Acts 26:30-32

THEME: The officials said that Paul was innocent but must go to Rome.

³⁰ Then the king, the governor, Bernice, and all the others got up ³¹ and left *the room. While* they were talking to one another they said to each other, "There is no reason why we should execute this man or *even* keep him in prison." ³² Agrippa said to Festus, "If this man had not asked the Emperor to judge him, he could have been released."

27

Acts 27:1-8

THEME: Paul and other prisoners sailed from Caesarea to Crete.

¹ When *the Governor and his advisers* decided that it was time for us to get on a ship and go to Italy, they put Paul and some other prisoners into the hands of an army captain whose name was Julius, *to guard us on the journey*. Julius was *an officer* in charge of *a group of* a hundred *soldiers called* 'the Emperor Augustus's Group.' ² So we got on a ship that had come from *the port of* Adramyttium. *The ship* was going to *return there, stopping at* cities along the coast of *the province of* Asia. Aristarchus, *a fellow believer* from Thessalonica in *the province of* Macedonia, went with us. ³ The day after *the ship sailed*, we arrived at *the port of* Sidon. Julius kindly told Paul that he could go and see his friends *who lived there*, so that they could give him whatever he might need. *So Paul visited the believers there.* ⁴ Then the ship left *Sidon*, but the winds were blowing against us, so *the ship* went along *the north* side of *the island of* Cyprus, where it is sheltered *from the wind*. ⁵ After that, we crossed over the sea close to the coast of *the provinces of* Cilicia and Pamphylia. *The ship* arrived at Myra*, in *the province of* Lycia. *We got off the ship there*. ⁶ In Myra, Julius found out there was a ship *there that had come* from Alexandria and would *soon* sail to Italy. So he arranged for us to board, *and we left*. ⁷ We sailed slowly for several days and finally arrived close to the coast, near *the city of* Cnidus. *After that*, the wind *was very strong and* did not allow the ship to move straight ahead *westward. So instead*, we sailed *southward* along the side of *the island of* Crete *that is* sheltered *from the wind*, and we passed *near Cape* Salmone. ⁸ *The wind was still strong, and it prevented the ship from moving ahead fast*. So we moved slowly along the coast *of Crete,* and we arrived at a harbor which was called Fair Havens, near the city of Lasea.

Acts 27:9-20

THEME: Paul warned them not to travel on, but the ship's officials decided to go on anyway.

⁹ Much time had passed, so it would have been dangerous if we had traveled *farther* by ship, *because after that time of the year the sea often became very stormy*. So Paul said to the men *on the ship*, ¹⁰ "Men, I perceive that *if we travel by ship* now, it will be disastrous

for us. A storm may destroy the ship and the cargo, and possibly we will drown." [11] But the officer *did not listen to* what Paul said. Instead, he decided to do what the pilot *of the ship* and the owner of the ship advised. [12] The harbor where the ship had stopped was not a good place to remain during the winter, *when the weather frequently becomes stormy. So most of the people on the ship decided that we should leave there, because they hoped that we* could stay at *the port of* Phoenix during the winter, if we could possibly arrive there. That harbor was open to the sea in two directions, *but the strong winds did not blow there.* [13] Then a gentle wind began to blow *from the south*, and the *crew members* thought that they could travel as they had decided *to do. So* they hoisted *the anchor*, and the ship sailed *westward* along the *southern* shore of Crete. [14] But after a while, a wind that was very strong came across the island *from the north side and hit the ship. That wind was called* "The Northeaster." [15] It blew strongly against the *bow of* the ship. The result was that we could not keep going in the direction *in which we had been going*. So the sailors just let the wind move the ship in the direction *that the wind* was blowing. [16] The ship then passed a small island named Cauda. We passed along the side *of the island that* sheltered *the ship from the wind*. Then *while the ship was moving along*, the sailors lifted the lifeboat up *out of the water* and tied it *on the deck. But the strong wind made it* difficult even to do that. [17] After the sailors *hoisted* the lifeboat onto the ship, they tied ropes around the ship's hull to strengthen the ship. *The wind was pushing the ship*, so the sailors were afraid that it might run onto the sandbanks off the coast of Libya *and get stuck there. So* they lowered the largest sail *so that the ship would move more slowly. Even so,* the wind continued to move the ship along. *The wind and the waves* continued to toss the ship about roughly, so on the next day the sailors began to throw overboard the things that the ship was carrying. [19] On the third *day after the stormy wind had begun to blow*, the sailors threw overboard *most of* the sails, ropes, and poles, *in order to make the ship lighter.* [20] The wind continued to blow very strongly, *and the sky was filled with dark clouds* day and night. We couldn't see the sun or the stars for many days, *so we could not determine where we were. And the wind* continued to blow violently. So we finally thought we would die in the sea.

Acts 27:21-26

THEME: Paul told them an angel from God said that they would all survive.

[21] None of us on the ship had eaten for many days. *Then one day*, Paul stood up in front of us and said, "*Well*, friends, you should have listened to me *when I said* we should not sail from Crete. Then we would have been safe, and the ship and its cargo would be in good condition. [22] But now, I urge you, don't be afraid, because none of us will die. *The storm* will destroy the ship, but not us. [23] *I know this*, because last night God, the one to whom I belong and whom I serve, *sent* an angel *who came and* stood by me. [24] The angel said to me, 'Paul, don't be afraid! You must *go to Rome* and stand before the Emperor there *so that he can judge your case.* Listen! God has determined *that* all those who are traveling by ship with you *will also survive.*' [25] So cheer up, *my* friends, because I believe that God will make this happen, exactly as *the angel* told me. [26] However, *the ship* will crash on some island, *and* we will go ashore *there.*"

Acts 27:27-32

THEME: Paul thwarted some sailors who tried to sneak ashore in the lifeboat.

[27] On the fourteenth night *after the storm had begun, the ship* was still being blown across the Adriatic sea. About midnight, the sailors sensed that the ship was getting close to land. [28] So they lowered *a rope* to measure the depth *of the water.* When they pulled the rope up again, they measured it and saw that the water was one hundred twenty feet deep. They went a little farther and lowered the rope again. *This time*, they found that the water was

only about ninety feet deep. [29] They were afraid that the *ship* might go onto some rocks, so they threw out four anchors from the *ship's* stern and continued to pray that the dawn would soon come *so that they could see where the ship was going.* [30] Some of the sailors were planning to escape from the ship, so they lowered the lifeboat into the sea. In order *that no one would know what they planned to do,* they pretended *that* they wanted to lower some anchors from the *ship's* bow. [31] But Paul said to the army officer and soldiers, "If the sailors don't stay on board, you have no hope of being saved." [32] So the soldiers cut the ropes and let the lifeboat fall into the water.

Acts 27:33-38

THEME: Paul urged them to eat some food, so they did and then lightened the ship.

[33] Just before dawn, Paul urged everyone *on the ship* to eat some food. He said, "For the past fourteen days you have been waiting and watching and not eating anything. [34] So, *now* I urge you to eat some food. We need to do that to stay alive. I *tell you to do that because I know that* none of you will drown." [35] After Paul had said that, while everyone was watching, he took some bread and thanked God *for it. Then he broke the bread and began to eat some of it.* [36] The *rest of us* became encouraged, so we all ate some food. [37] Altogether there were 276 of us on the ship. [38] When everyone had eaten as much as they wanted, they threw into the sea the grain *that the ship was carrying,* and this made the ship lighter.

Acts 27:39-41

THEME: The waves began to break up the ship after it struck a shoal.

[39] At dawn, *we could see* land, *but the sailors* did not recognize *the place.* However, they could see that there was a bay and *a wide area of* sand at the water's edge. They planned that, if possible, they would steer the ship onto *the beach.* [40] *So some of the sailors* cut the anchor *ropes and* let the anchors fall into the sea. At the same time, *other sailors* untied the *ropes that* fastened the rudders, *so that they could steer the ship again.* Then *the sailors* raised the sail at the bow of the ship so that the wind *would blow the ship forward,* and the ship headed towards the shore. [41] But the ship hit a sandbank. The bow of the ship stuck there and couldn't move, and big waves beat against the stern of the ship and it began to break apart.

Acts 27:42-44

THEME: The officer saved Paul and ordered all to go to the shore, so they did that.

[42] The soldiers said *to each other, "Let's* kill *all* the prisoners *on the ship,* so they won't *be able to* swim *away and* escape." *They planned to do that because they were sure* that officials would kill them if they let the prisoners escape. [43] But *Julius,* the commanding officer, wanted to save Paul, so he stopped the soldiers from doing what they planned to do. Instead, he ordered first that everyone who could swim should jump into the water and swim to land. [44] *Then he told* the others *to hold* on to planks or pieces from the ship *and go towards shore. We did what he said, and* in that way all of us arrived safely on land.

28

Acts 28:1-6

THEME: The Maltese thought Paul was a god after a snake did not harm him.

[1] After we had arrived safely *on the shore*, we learned that it was an island called Malta.
[2] The people who lived there received us kindly. They lit a fire and invited us to come and warm ourselves, because it was raining and it was cold. [3] Paul gathered some sticks and put them on the fire. But a snake came out *from the fire to escape* from the heat, and fastened itself onto Paul's hand. [4] *The islanders knew that the snake was poisonous, so* when they saw it hanging from Paul's hand, they said to each other, "Probably this man is a murderer. Although he has escaped from being drowned, *the god who* pays *people back* for their sins is about to cause him to die." [5] But Paul just shook the snake off into the fire, and nothing happened to him. [6] The people were expecting that Paul's body would soon swell up or that he would suddenly fall down and die. But after they had waited a long time, they saw *that the snake* had not harmed him at all. So then the people changed their minds and said *to one another*, "This man is not a murderer! Probably he is a god!"

Acts 28:7-10

THEME: Paul healed many Maltese, so they supplied what he and the others needed.

[7] Near where the people had made the fire, there were some fields that belonged to a man whose name was Publius. He was the chief official on the island. He invited us to *come and stay in* his home. He took care of us for three days. [8] *At that time* Publius' father was lying *in bed* with fever and dysentery. So Paul visited him and prayed *for him. Then* Paul placed his hands on him and healed him. [9] After Paul had done that, the other people on the island who were sick came *to him, and he* healed them, too. [10] They brought us gifts and *showed* great respect for us *in other ways*. When we were *ready* to leave *three months later*, they brought us food and other things we would need *on the ship*.

Acts 28:11-14

THEME: Paul and the others sailed to Puteoli, then went by land towards Rome.

[11] After *we had stayed there* three months, we *boarded* a ship *that was going to Italy, and* we sailed away. The ship had been in *a harbor on* the island during the stormy months. It had come from *the city of* Alexandria. On the bow of the ship there were carved images of the twin *Roman* gods *whose names were Castor and Pollux.* [12] We *sailed from the island and* arrived at *the city of* Syracuse *on the island of Sicily,* and we stayed there three days. [13] Then we traveled on by ship and arrived at *the port of* Rhegium *in Italy*. The next day, the wind was blowing from behind us, *so we sailed along fast*. The day after that, we reached *the port of* Puteoli, *where we left the ship*. [14] In Puteoli we met some believers who invited us to stay with them for a week. *After visiting them,* we *left there and started to travel by land* to Rome.

Acts 28:15-16

THEME: Christians came out from Rome and escorted Paul into that city.

[15] *A group of* believers *who lived in Rome* heard that we *were coming*. So they came out *from Rome* to meet us. *Some of* them met us at *the town called* 'The Market on Appian Road,' and others met us at the *town called* 'The Three Inns.' When Paul saw these

believers, he thanked God and was encouraged. [16] After we arrived in Rome, Paul was permitted to live *in a house* by himself. But *there was always* a soldier there to guard him.

Acts 28:17-22

THEME: The Jewish leaders asked Paul to tell them about Christianity.

[17] After *Paul had been there* three days, he sent a message to the Jewish leaders *to come and talk with him. So* they came, and Paul said to them, "My fellow Jews, although I have not opposed our people nor spoken against the customs of our ancestors, *our leaders* in Jerusalem *seized me. But before they could kill me, a Roman commander rescued me and later sent m*e to Caesarea for Roman *officials to put me on trial.* [18] The Roman officials questioned me and wanted to release me, because I had not done anything for which I should be executed. [19] But when the Jewish *leaders* there opposed *what the Roman authorities wanted to do*, I had to formally request that the Emperor *should judge me here in Rome*. But my reason for doing that was not that I wanted to accuse our leaders about anything. [20] So I have requested you *to come* here so that I can tell you why I am a prisoner. It is because I believe in our Messiah, the one *God long ago promised to send* to us Jews." [21] Then the Jewish leaders said, "We have not received any letters from *our fellow Jews* in Judea about you. Neither have our fellow Jews who have arrived *here from Judea* said anything bad about you. [22] But we want to hear what you think about this *Christian* sect, because we know that in many places people are saying bad things about it."

Acts 28:23-31

THEME: Paul told the Jews that non-Jews would believe the gospel.

[23] So they *talked with Paul and decided that they would come back on another day to hear him. When that day arrived*, they came back to where Paul was staying, and they brought more Jews with them. Paul talked to them from morning till evening. He talked to them about how God wants to rule *people's lives*. He tried to convince them that Jesus *is the Messiah* by reminding them what Moses and the other prophets had written. [24] Some of those Jews believed that what *Paul* said about Jesus *was true*, but others did not. [25] So they began to argue with one another. *Paul saw that some of them did not want to listen to him, so* when they were about to leave, he said, "The Holy Spirit said something to your ancestors. He spoke these words to Isaiah the prophet, *and what he said is also true about you*:

[26] Go to your fellow Israelites and tell them,
"You repeatedly listen and listen to the message of God,
    but you never understand what God is saying.
You repeatedly look at and see the things God is doing,
    but you never understand what they mean."

[27] *God also said to the prophet,*
These people do not understand,
    because they have become stubborn.
They have ears, but they do not understand what they hear,
    and they have closed their eyes because they do not want to see.
If they wanted to obey what I say to them,
    they might understand with their hearts what they see me doing
    and what they hear me saying.
Then they might turn from their sinful behavior and I would save them.

[28] *That is what God said to the prophet Isaiah about our ancestors. But you Jews today do not want to believe God's message.* So, I am telling you that *God* has sent to the non-Jews this message about how he saves people, and they will listen *and accept it!*"[z]

[30] For two whole years Paul stayed *there* in a house that he rented. Many people came to see him, and he received them all gladly *and talked with them.* [31] He preached *and taught people* about how God could rule *their lives,* and he taught them about the Lord Jesus Christ. He did that without being afraid, and no one tried to stop him.

---

[z] Some Greek manuscripts add verse 29, "After Paul said that, the Jewish leaders left, still arguing strongly among themselves."

The Apostle Paul wrote a letter to the Christians at Rome. We call this letter

Romans

1

Romans 1:1-7

THEME: I, Paul, an apostle whom God appointed to proclaim the good message about Jesus Christ, am writing this letter to all you believers who are in Rome. I pray that God will continue to act kindly toward you and grant you peace.

[1] *I*, Paul, who serve Christ Jesus, *am writing this letter*. God chose me to be an apostle, and he appointed me in order that *I should proclaim* the good message[a] that *comes from him*. [2] Long before *Jesus came to earth, God* promised *that he would reveal* this good message by means of what his prophets *wrote* in the sacred Scriptures. [3] This good message is *about the one whom we know as* his Son. As to his Son's physical nature, he was born a descendant of *King* David. [4] As to his divine nature, it was shown powerfully that he is God's own Son.[b] *God* showed this by his Holy Spirit causing him to become alive again after he died. He is Jesus Christ our Lord. [5] He is the one who appointed me *to be* an apostle in a way I did not deserve. He did that in order that *many* non-Jews would honor *him* and would obey him as a result of believing my *message about him*. [6] You *believers* who are living in *the city of* Rome are also among those whom God has chosen to belong to Jesus Christ. [7] *I am writing this letter* to all of *you* whom God loves and whom he has chosen *to become his* people. *I pray that* God our Father and Jesus Christ our Lord will *continue to* act kindly toward you and *will continue to* cause you to have inner peace.

Romans 1:8-15

THEME: I thank God that people everywhere are talking about how you believers in Rome are trusting Jesus Christ. I pray that God will permit me to visit you soon. I want you to know that I have longed to visit you, but things have always prevented me. I am eager to proclaim the good message to you who are living at Rome also.

[8] As I begin *this letter,* I thank my God for all you *believers in Rome*. It is because of *what* Jesus Christ *has done for us that* I *am able to do that*. I thank him because your trusting *in Jesus Christ* is something that people all over *the Roman Empire* are talking about. [9] God, whom I devotedly serve as I *proclaim to people* the good message concerning his Son, knows that I tell the truth when I say that I always mention you whenever I pray. [10] I especially ask God that if he desires *me to visit you,* somehow at last I shall be able to do so. [11] *I pray this* because I long to visit you to help you to become stronger *spiritually*. [12] I long to visit you in order that you and I might encourage each other *by means of our sharing with each other* how each of us trusts in *Jesus.* [13] My fellow believers, **many times**

---

[a] OR, …the gospel…

[b] OR, …that he was God who became human.

I planned to visit you. I certainly want you to know that. *But I have not been able to come to you because things* have prevented me until now. I have wanted to come so that I might help you to mature spiritually, just as *I have helped people* in many other non-Jewish groups *to mature spiritually.* [14] I feel obliged *to proclaim the good message to all non-Jewish people*, to *people who know* the Greek *language and culture* and to those who don't know it, to people who are educated and to those who are uneducated. [15] As a result, what I have eagerly desired is that I might proclaim this good message **to you who are living in Rome also**.

Romans 1:16-17

THEME: I very confidently proclaim the good message about what Christ has done, both to Jews and non-Jews, because by that message God reveals his way of declaring all people righteous.

[16] *That leads me to say that* I very confidently proclaim the good message *about what Christ has done*, because this good message is the powerful *means* God *uses* to save *from the guilt of their sins* all people who trust *in what Christ has done for them*. Specifically, God first saves the Jews *who believe the good message*, and then he saves non-Jews. [17] By means of this good message, God reveals how he erases the record of people's sins,[c] and his doing this is entirely because they trust *in Christ. This is confirmed* by what *a prophet long ago* wrote *that God said*, "Those whose record of sin *I* have erased because they trust *in me* will live *forever*."

Romans 1:18

THEME: God is making it clear to all godless and wicked non-Jewish people that he is angry with them.

[18] From *where God rules in* heaven, he is making it clear to all *non-Jewish* people who show no respect for him and who do wicked things, that he is angry with them *and that they deserve to be punished*. By *behaving* wickedly, they keep other people *from believing what they know* to be true *about God*.

Romans 1:19-23

THEME: Everyone can clearly know what God is like; so no one has a basis for saying, "We never knew about God."

[19] *Everyone* can clearly know what God *is like*, because God himself has revealed to everyone *what he is like.* [20] *People* cannot see what God is like. But ever since he created the world, by means of what he created, he has clearly revealed what he is like. He has made it clear to everyone that he has always been able to do very powerful things. *Therefore we should recognize that* he is God, *completely different from all that he created*. So no one has a basis for saying, *"We never knew about God."* [21] Although *the non-Jews* knew what God *is like,* they did not honor him as God, nor did they thank *him for what he had done.* Instead, they began to think foolish *things about him*, and they became unable to understand *what he wanted them to know.* [22] Although they claimed that they were wise, they became foolish, [23] and they refused to *admit that* God is glorious and will never die. Instead, they made and worshiped idols *that resembled people who* will some day die, and *then they made other idols that resembled* birds and four-footed animals, and they even made idols that resembled reptiles.

---

[c] OR, …God reveals how he declares people no longer guilty for having sinned…

Romans 1:24-27

THEME: So God allowed the non-Jewish people to continue to do disgraceful things that they strongly desired, which resulted in their dishonoring their bodies sexually. He did this because they worshiped idols and things that were created, instead of worshiping God. As a result of both men and women having unnatural sexual relations, they have been punished as they deserve.

[24] So God allowed *the non-Jews* to continue to do the immoral sexual things they strongly desired, things *that their desires were compelling them to do.* As a result, they *began to dishonor each other's bodies *by their sexual actions.* [25] Also, they *chose to worship* false *gods* instead of admitting what is true *about* God. They worshiped and served things *that God* created instead of *worshiping and serving God,* the one who created *everything.* They did that *even though* he deserves to be forever praised *by those whom he created.* May it be so!

[26] So, God allowed *the non-Jews to strongly obey* their shameful *sexual* desires. As a result, many women did not have natural sexual relations *with their husbands.* Instead, they were doing sexual actions with other women. [27] Similarly, *many* men strongly desired to have sexual relations with other men, instead of having natural sexual relations with women.[d] They committed *homosexual* acts with other men, acts that were shameful. As a result, *God has* punished them *by sicknesses* in their bodies, which is what they deserve *because* they *thought* wrongly *that God would not punish them for doing that.*

Romans 1:28-32

THEME: The result of God's letting people become obsessed by their own depraved thoughts was that they themselves began to do all manner of evil things that God says are improper. They even approve of others doing such things.

[28] Furthermore, because they decided that it was not *worthwhile* to know God, he allowed their own worthless thoughts *to completely control them.* As a result, they began doing *evil* things that *God says that people* should not do. [29] They strongly desire to do all *kinds of* unrighteous *deeds.* They strongly desire to do all *kinds of* evil things *to others.* They strongly desire to possess things that *belong to others.* They strongly desire to harm *others* in various ways. *Many non-Jews* are constantly envying *other people. Many* constantly desire to murder *people. Many* constantly desire to cause strife *between people. Many* constantly desire to deceive *others. Many* constantly desire to speak hatefully *about others.*[e] *Many* gossip *about others.* [30] *Many* slander *others. Many* act especially hatefully toward God. *Many* speak or act in an insulting way *toward others. Many* treat others contemptuously. *Many* boast *about themselves. Many* invent new ways to do evil deeds. *Many non-Jewish children* disobey their parents. [31] *Many non-Jews* act in other morally foolish ways. *Many* do not do what they promised *others that they would do. Many* do not *even* love *their own family members. And many* do not act mercifully *toward other people.* [32] Although they know that God has declared that those who do such things deserve to be killed, they not only habitually do these *kinds of evil* things, but they also approve of others who habitually do them.

---

[d]   OR, Similarly, *many* men stopped having natural sexual relations with women.

[e]   OR, ...*Many* constantly desire *to speak harmful things about others, things that are not true.*

2

Romans 2:1-5

THEME: Any one of you Jews who condemns non-Jews for doing evil will be condemned by God, because you also do the same evil things.

¹ *God will severely punish non-Jewish people who habitually do evil deeds, because he has clearly revealed that he is angry with them.* But, *when God judges people,* he will not excuse any one of you Jews *to whom I am writing.* You say that *God should* punish *non-Jews for doing evil deeds.* But when any one of you says that, it is yourself whom you are saying that God should punish, because you do *some of* the same *evil* deeds *that the non-Jews do.* ² We know very well that God is judging fairly when he says he will punish *non-Jewish* people who do such *evil* deeds. ³ So, you who *say God should punish* others for doing evil deeds yet you do evil deeds yourself, you should certainly not think that you yourself will be able to escape from being punished by God. ⁴ Nor should you say, "God is acting very tolerantly and patiently toward me, *so I don't need to turn away from my sin.*" You should realize that God is acting in a kind manner *toward you* in order to encourage you to turn away from your sinful behavior. ⁵ But instead, by your stubbornly refusing to turn away from your sinful behavior, you will be causing God to punish you even more severely. *He will do that* at the time when he shows that he is angry and judges people fairly.

Romans 2:6-11

THEME: Because God is not influenced by a person's status, he will recompense each person according to what that person has done.

⁶ God will recompense each person according to *what that person deserves for* what he or she has done. ⁷ *Specifically,* some people, by persevering in doing good deeds, strive to be highly honored *by God* and to receive a life that will not end. *God will reward them by enabling them* to live forever. ⁸ But some people act in a selfish way and refuse to believe that *what God says is* true, and they do the things *that God says* are wrong. *God will* punish them very severely. ⁹ He will cause everyone who habitually does evil deeds to suffer greatly, *with the result that they will become severely* distressed. This certainly will happen to the Jews *who refuse to accept God's message, because God gave them the privilege to be his special people,* but it will also happen to the non-Jews. ¹⁰ But *God will* greatly reward spiritually every person who habitually does good deeds. He will *certainly* do this for the Jews *because God chose them as his special people,* but he will also do it for the non-Jews. ¹¹ God *will do these things fairly,* because people's status does not influence him.

Romans 2:12-16

THEME: All non-Jews will be eternally separated from God for their sins, and all Jews will be condemned for their sin, because it is only those who have continually obeyed his laws whom God will justify.

¹² Although *non-Jews do not have* the laws *God gave to Moses,* all *non-Jews* who sin will be eternally separated from God. He will *not consider whether or not they knew* the laws he *gave to Moses.* And all the *Jews* who have sinned in spite of knowing the laws *God gave to Moses will also be punished. They will be punished for disobeying* God's laws. ¹³ *It is right for them to be punished because* it is not those who *merely* know God's laws

whom he considers to be righteous. On the contrary, it is only those who continually have obeyed *all of God's* laws whose record of sins God will erase.[f] [14] Whenever the non-Jews who do not have the laws *God gave to Moses* naturally obey those laws, *they prove that* they have a law within their own minds, even though they do not have the laws *God gave to Moses.* [15] They show that they know in their own minds what God *commands in his* laws, as each person's own conscience either accuses or excuses *his behavior.* [16] God *will punish them* at the time when he will judge people according to what they have thought and done. He will judge the non-Jews *even* for the things they have done secretly. He will judge people by *authorizing* Christ Jesus *to judge them.* This is *what I tell people when* I preach the good message to them.

Romans 2:17-24

THEME: It is disgusting that any one of you who has all the advantages of being a Jew would disobey God's law and, by doing so, insult God.

[17] *Now I have something to say to any one of* you *Jews to whom I am writing* who boasts about being a Jew. You trust *that God will save you because you possess* the laws *he gave to Moses.* You boast that *you belong to* God. [18] You know what God desires. Because you have been taught *God's* laws, you are able to know which things are right and to choose to do them. [19] You are certain that you *are able to* show *God's truth to non-Jews,* as guides *show the road* to those who are blind. You are certain that by what you say you show God's way to the *non-Jews who do not understand it,* as a light shows the way to *those who walk in* the darkness. [20] *You are certain that you* can correct *non-Jews, whom you consider* foolish *because of their not understanding God's message.* Because you have in *God's* laws a *written* expression of true knowledge, you are certain that you can teach *people who, being like* children, do not know *God's truth.* [21] *You claim that you have all these advantages because of being a Jew,* so it is disgusting that you who teach other people *that they should obey the laws God gave Moses* don't *obey the laws that you* yourself teach. You who preach that *people* should not steal *things,* it is disgusting that you yourself steal *things.* [22] You who command *people* not to commit adultery, it is disgusting that you commit adultery yourself! You who detest idols, it is disgusting that you rob temples *where people worship idols.* [23] You who boast saying, "*I have God's* laws," it is disgusting that you disobey those same laws. As a result you are insulting **God!** [24] *You must recognize that you are insulting God, about whom* were written *these words in the Scriptures:* "The non-Jews speak evil about God because of *the evil actions of* you *Jews.*"

Romans 2:25-29

THEME: God will consider non-Jews acceptable to him if they obey his laws, and such non-Jews will declare that God is right in condemning those Jews who disobey his laws, because it is only those who are changed inwardly who are true Jews and acceptable to God.

[25] Any one of you who *is* circumcised *to show that you belong to God* can benefit from that if you obey the laws *God gave to Moses.* But if you, *a circumcised person,* disobey *God's* laws, *God will consider that* you who are circumcised are no different *from someone who is* not circumcised. [26] This means that God will certainly consider that even *non-Jews who are* not circumcised can become his people[g] if they obey the things that he commanded in his laws. [27] *If any one of* you disobeys God's laws, even though *you have* the Scriptures

---

[f]   OR, …Rather, it is only those who continually have obeyed *all of* the laws *God gave to Moses* whom God will consider righteous.

[g]   OR, This means that even *non-Jews who are* not circumcised are acceptable to God…

and even though you are circumcised, *God will punish you*. And those people who are not circumcised, but who obey God's laws, *will declare that God is right* in saying that he will punish you. [28] It is not those who perform rituals *to show they are God's people* who are *true* Jews, and it is not being circumcised in their bodies *that causes God to accept them*. [29] On the contrary, we whom *God has changed* inwardly are *true* Jews. And *God has accepted us because we have allowed God's* Spirit to change our hearts, not because we perform rituals. Even if *other* people will not praise us, God will praise us.

3

Romans 3:1-8

THEME: My reply to the objection that there is no advantage in being a Jew or being circumcised is that there is much advantage, especially since God entrusted his promises to us. My reply to the objection that God has not kept his promise is that he certainly has, for his promises are always true. My reply to the objection that it is not right for God to punish us Jews is that it certainly is right, because if God did not judge us Jews, he couldn't judge anyone.

[1] *Someone may object to this, saying,* "If being circumcised does not cause God to accept *us Jews*, there is no advantage in being a Jew *over being a non-Jew*. Being circumcised does not benefit *us Jews at all*!" [2] *I would reply that being Jews does* benefit *us* in many ways. First of all, it benefits us because it was to *our ancestors* that *God* gave his words *that contain his promises*. [3] Many *Jews did not obey God as they promised that they would. Someone might ask,* "Does their not being faithful mean that God will not *bless us Jews* as he promised *he would*?" [4] *I would reply,* "No, it certainly does not mean that. God always does *what he has promised*, even though *people don't*. All those who accuse God *of not keeping his promises to us Jews* are very mistaken!" What *King David wrote about God justly saying he would punish him for his sins applies to those who accuse God of not keeping his promises. What David said to God was,* "So then, everyone must acknowledge that you always tell the truth. You will win the case whenever someone accuses you *of not doing what you have said!*"[h]

[5] So if we *Jews'* being wicked shows that it is right for God *not to bless us*, what shall we conclude? Shall we conclude that it is not right for God to be angry *and punish us Jews*? *I should not be saying these things, but* I am speaking as ordinary humans speak. [6] We should certainly not *conclude that God should not judge us,* because, if God *did not judge us Jews*, it would not possibly be right for him to judge **anyone**! [7] But *someone might object and say to me,* "The fact that God truly *keeps his promises* becomes very clear because of my not doing *what God has commanded*. But the result is that people praise God! So God should no longer say that I should be punished for my sins! [8] *If what you, Paul, say is true*, then we might as well do evil things in order that good things *like that* will result! For example, *then people will praise God!*" Some people speak evil about me by *falsely* saying that I think *such things. God* will fairly punish *people who say such things about me!*

---

[h] OR, …*King David talked about God's justly judging people who sin. David wrote,* "So people will declare that what you have said *about their sin* is right, and you will win the case when you are accused."

Romans 3:9-18

THEME: My reply to a query as to whether God will treat Jews more favorably than non-Jews is no, because the Scriptures make it clear that all people are condemned by God for their sins.

[9] *If someone would ask,* "Shall we conclude that God *will treat us* Jews *more favorably* than he treats *the non-Jews?*" I would reply that we can *certainly not* conclude that! I have already shown you that all people, the Jews and also the non-Jews, have sinned and *so they deserve to be punished.* [10] *The following words* that are written *in the Scriptures support this,*

No person is righteous, not even one!
[11] There is no one who understands *how to live properly.*[i]
There is no one who desires to know God!
[12] Absolutely everyone has turned away from God.
God considers them all depraved.
There is no one who acts righteously, not even one!
[13] What people say is bad, like the smell that comes from a grave that has been
    opened.
By what people say, they deceive people.
They injure people by what they say, just as the poison of snakes injures people.
[14] They are continually cursing others and saying hateful things.
[15] They are eager to murder people.
[16] Wherever they go, they ruin everything and make people miserable.
[17] They do not know how to live peacefully with other people.
[18] They absolutely refuse to reverence God!

Romans 3:19-20

THEME: In summary, no one is able to object to God's condemnation; God has declared everyone guilty.

[19] Furthermore, we know that it is to Jewish people, *who are* required to obey God's laws, that Moses wrote those laws. *We can infer from this that* there is no one, Jew or non-Jew, who is able to say anything *in reply to God's* saying he will punish them for having sinned. God has declared everyone in the world guilty! [20] It is not because people had done the things that God's laws *require* that God will erase the record of their sins,[j] *since no one has done those things completely.* In fact, the *real* result of *our knowing God's* laws is that we know clearly that we have sinned.[k]

Romans 3:21-26

THEME: Now God erases the record of sins of everyone, Jew and non-Jew, who trusts in what Jesus Christ has done for them. God presented Christ as the one who would atone for sins by dying on the cross.

[21] But God's erasing the record of our sins does not depend on our obeying the laws *he gave Moses.* God has now revealed *to us* how he erases the record of our sins *by a different way.* Moses wrote about it in the laws *God gave* him, and the prophets also wrote about it. [22] God erases the record of our sins because we trust in *what* Jesus Christ has

---

[i]   OR, There is no one who understands *God's character.*
[j]   OR, It is not because someone has done the things that God's laws *require* that God will declare him no longer guilty for sin…
[k]   OR, …In fact, it is as a result of *our knowing God's* laws that we realize that we are sinful.

done for us. God does this for every person who trusts *in Christ,* because *he considers* that there is no difference *between Jews and non-Jews.* [23] **All** people have done evil, and all people have failed to accomplish the glorious *goals* that God *set for them.* [24] God erases the record of our sins by acting kindly in paying for our sin, without our doing anything to earn it. Christ Jesus accomplished this *by dying for us.* [25] God showed that Christ was the one who would atone for our sins[i] *with the* blood that *flowed when he died. God forgives* us because of our trusting *in Christ's having died for us. God wanted* to show that he acts justly. *He wanted to do that* because, before *Christ came, God* did not punish *everyone who sinned. So it seemed as though he was not being just.* But he was overlooking their sins during *that time,* [26] because he is patient. *God arranged for Christ to die for us.* By doing that, he now shows that he truly is just, and he shows that he is justly able to erase the record of sins of everyone who trusts in Jesus.

Romans 3:27-31

THEME: So we are prevented from boasting that it was because of our obeying the Mosaic laws. And God will also accept non-Jews on that same basis. And by agreeing that people are declared righteous by their trusting in Christ, we actually confirm the Mosaic laws.

[27] It is not at all because of *our obeying the* laws *of Moses that God erases the record of our sins.* So, there is no way we can boast *that God does that because of our obeying the laws of Moses.* Instead, *it is because of our* trusting *in Christ that God erases the record of our sins.* [28] *We cannot boast about that,* because we conclude that God does not erase the record of our sins because of our obeying the laws *he gave Moses, because it is impossible for us to completely obey them.* He erases the record of our sins because of our trusting *in Christ.* [29] You who are Jews certainly should not *think that it is* only *you* whom God *will accept.* You certainly should *realize that he will accept* non-Jews, too. Of course *he will accept* non-Jews, [30] because, *as you firmly believe,* there is only one God, who will erase the record of Jews' sins if they trust *in what Christ has done,* and who will in the same way erase the record of non-Jews' sins if they trust *in Christ.* [31] So, *if someone should ask concerning the laws God gave Moses,* "By saying *that God erases the record of our sins because of our* trusting *in Christ,* does that mean that those laws now are useless?" *I would reply,* "Certainly not. Instead, we confirm the laws *God gave Moses.*"

4

Romans 4:1-8

THEME: We can draw conclusions from Abraham's life about how God erases the record of our sins. Abraham could not boast about his accomplishing that, because the Scriptures record that it was because he believed what God promised that God erased the record of his sins. God's doing that was a gift, not a reward.

[1] Abraham is the *revered* ancestor of us *Jews.* So think about what we can conclude *concerning Abraham.* [2] If it was because of *Abraham's* doing *good* deeds that the record of his sins was erased, he could then have been able to boast *about that to people,* but he would not *have had any basis to* boast to God *about it.* [3] *Remember that* in the Scriptures it is written that Abraham believed what God *promised,* and as a result, *God* erased the record of his sins. [4] If we receive wages for work we do, those wages are not considered to be a gift. Instead, *they are considered* to be what we have earned. *Similarly, if God erases*

---

[i] OR, God showed that Christ was the one who would forgive our sins…

the record of our sins because we did things to earn God's favor, we would not consider that *God's erasing the record of our sins* was *a gift. Instead, we would consider it as what we had earned.* ⁵But let's suppose we do not do things *to gain God's acceptance.* Suppose we instead trust *in God*, who erases the record of sins of wicked people. Then the erasing of the record of our sins because of our trusting *in Christ* is considered to be a gift to us, *not something we earned.* ⁶Similarly, it is as David wrote *in the Psalms* about people being happy whose record of sins God has erased, even though they have not done things *to earn it. David wrote*:

⁷*God* is pleased with people whose sins *he* has forgiven,
  whose sins he *has decided* to forget.
⁸*God* causes the people whose sins he no longer keeps a record of
  to be happy.

Romans 4:9-12

THEME: This happiness of knowing that God has erased the record of our sins is also for the non-Jews. Remember that it was before Abraham was circumcised—when he was still in effect a non-Jew—that God did that. He later received circumcision simply as a sign of God having erased the record of his sins because of his faith. The result was that he became a spiritual father of all who believe in God as he did, whether they are circumcised or not.

⁹As for our being happy *because God has erased the record of our sins*, it is not something *only* we Jews *can experience*. No, it is also something non-Jews *can experience. What the Scripture* says is that it was because Abraham trusted *in God* that *God* erased the record of his sins. ¹⁰*Think about* when *God erased the record of Abraham's sins. Did it happen* after *Abraham* was circumcised *to be marked as one who belonged to God*, or before he was circumcised? It happened before he was circumcised, not after he was circumcised. ¹¹*Many years later, God commanded that* Abraham *be* circumcised. Abraham's accepting that ritual showed *that he knew that the record of his sins* was erased because he trusted *in God* while he was still, *in effect, a non-Jew because* of not having been circumcised. So we *can understand that* Abraham became like an ancestor to *all* those whose record of sins has been erased because of their believing *in God's promise,* even though some of them were not circumcised. ¹²Likewise, Abraham is the spiritual ancestor of all us Jews who are not merely circumcised, but who, more importantly, *believe in* God's *promise* as our ancestor Abraham did, even before he was circumcised.

Romans 4:13-17a

THEME: It was because Abraham trusted in God that God erased the record of his sins and promised him many blessings. So what God promised is guaranteed to all, both Jews and non-Jews, who trust in God as Abraham did.

¹³God promised Abraham and his descendants that they would receive *the blessings he promised to give to the people in* the world. But when he promised that, it was not because Abraham *obeyed* the laws *that God later gave to Moses.* Instead, it was because Abraham believed *that God would do what he promised he would do.* As a result, God erased the record of his sins. ¹⁴If *we think that* those who obey *God's* laws are the ones who will receive *what he has promised*, it is useless *for us to think he will erase the record of our sins just because we* trust in him, and it is pointless *for us to think that he will give us what he* promised *just because* we trust in him. ¹⁵*Remember that* it is *stated* in God's laws *that he* will punish *people who do not perfectly obey them*, and remember that wherever laws exist, *people* disobey them. ¹⁶So, it is because *we* trust *in God that we will receive what he has promised.* It is *not because we perfectly obey God's laws. He wants*

to erase the record of our sins without our earning it. As a result, he guarantees to give *us* what he now promises, and he guarantees to give them to all people who are *Abraham's spiritual* descendants. *He promises to do that not only for us Jewish believers* who *know* God's laws *and trust in him as Abraham did*, but also for those *non-Jews* who also trust *in him* as Abraham did, *even though they don't know God's laws*. Abraham is the *spiritual* ancestor of **all** us *believers*. [17] What *is written in the Scriptures about what God promised Abraham shows that this is true. God said to him,* "It is in order that you may be the ancestor of many ethnic groups that I have appointed you."

Romans 4:17b-22

THEME: It was because Abraham confidently believed God's promise to give him many descendants, when there was no physical basis for his hoping that this would happen, that God erased the record of his sins.

God *guaranteed that he would give Abraham many descendants*. Abraham confidently believed God *would do that,* [18] even though there was no physical reason for him to hope *that he would have descendants, because he and his wife were too old to bear children.* But God is the one who causes dead people to live again, and who talks about things that do not yet exist as already existing. *God said to Abraham,* "You will have so many descendants that they will be *as impossible to count as the stars.*" And Abraham believed that, and he believed that he would become the ancestor of many ethnic groups. [19] He did not doubt *that God would do what he promised*, even though he knew that his body was already *as incapable of begetting children as if he were* dead because he was about a hundred years old. And *even though he realized that* Sarah had never been able to become pregnant, [20] he did not doubt at all that God *would do what he had* **promised.** Instead, he trusted *in God* very strongly, and he thanked God *for what God was going to do.* [21] He was also very sure that the thing that God promised, God was able to do. [22] *And that is the reason God* erased the record of his sins.

Romans 4:23-25

THEME: The words about God erasing the record of Abraham's sins were also written to assure us who believe in God.

[23] The words *in the Scriptures,* "God erased the record of his sins," are not only about Abraham. [24] They were also written for us whose record of sins *God* will erase. *They were written* for us who believe *God*, the one who caused our Lord Jesus to become alive again after he died. [25] Jesus allowed *men* to execute him so that our evil deeds *could be forgiven*. And *God* caused Jesus to live again because *God wanted to show that because of the death of Jesus he was able to* erase the record of our sins.

5

Romans 5:1-5

THEME: Because God has erased the record of our sins, we have peace with him, we experience his undeserved kindness toward us, we rejoice because we expect to receive his glory, and we even rejoice in suffering because we know the results it brings.

[1] Because we trusted *in Christ*, the record of our sins has been erased. So, we now have a peaceful relationship with God because of *what* our Lord Jesus Christ *has done for us.* [2] Because of *what he has done*, God has also enabled us to begin experiencing his

undeserved kindness to us. Also, we rejoice because we are confidently expecting that God *will gladly show* us how great he is. [3] We rejoice even when we suffer *as a result of our trusting in Christ*, because we know that when we are suffering, the result is that we learn to endure things patiently. [4] And *we know* that when we endure things patiently, the result is that *God* approves of us. And when we *know God* approves of us, the result is that we confidently expect *that he will do great things for us*. [5] And we are very confident[m] concerning the things that we wait expectantly *for*, because God loves us very much. God's Holy Spirit, whom he has given to us, *causes us to understand how much God loves us.*

Romans 5:6-11

THEME: Because Christ died for us ungodly people, he will certainly save us from God's eternal punishment, and so we boast of what he has done for us.

[6] When we were unable to save ourselves, it was Christ who, at the time that God chose, died on behalf of *us* ungodly people. [7] Rarely would anyone die on behalf of another person, even if that person were righteous, although perhaps someone might be courageous enough to die on behalf such a person. [8] Nevertheless, as for God, the way he showed us that he loves us is that Christ died on our behalf while we were still rebelling against God. [9] God has erased the record of our sins because of what Christ *accomplished when* his blood *flowed from his body when he died*. So, it is even more certain that Christ will save us from being punished by God *eternally*. [10] Even though we were acting hostilely towards God, he offered for us to have a peaceful relationship with him as a result of his Son dying for us. So, it is even more certain that Christ will be able to save us because he is alive again. [11] And that's not all! Now we can rejoice about God's *goodness* because our Lord Jesus Christ enabled us to have a peaceful relationship with God.

Romans 5:12-21

THEME: Although the sin of one man, Adam, led to all people dying and God declaring that they deserved to be punished, Christ's righteous act of obedience when he died led to many people experiencing God's kindness and being declared righteous and living eternally, and it will also result in their ruling with Christ.

[12] *What you can learn from what I have written so far is as follows*: All people being sinful is the result of *Adam, the first* man whom *God created, sinning long ago*. Adam died because he sinned. So, **all people** *who have lived since then* die, because *it is as though* **all people** sinned *when Adam sinned*. [13] *People in* the world sinned before *God gave his* laws *to Moses. However, God* does not consider people to be guilty for their sins if there is no law *stating that what they did was sinful*. [14] But *we know* that from *the time* Adam *lived* until *the time* Moses *lived*, all people died. Even people who did not sin exactly like the way Adam *sinned, died. Adam's* sin affected *all people,* just as what *Christ did*, the one who came later, can affect all people. [15] But *the results of God's erasing the record of our sins as* a gift to us are not like *the results of Adam's* sinning. The result of one man, *Adam,* sinning was that many people have died. *It is certain, however,* that many people have abundantly experienced God's undeserved kindness to them. *It is also certain* that they have experienced God's erasing the record of their sins as the result of the undeserved kindness of one man, Jesus Christ. [16] And *there is another way in which God's* freely *erasing the record of our sins* is not like *the results of Adam's* sinning. One person, *Adam,*

---

[m] OR, And we know that we will not be disappointed…

sinned. As a result, *God declared that* all people deserve to be punished. Many people sinned. But what God did was that he erased the record of their sins without their earning it. [17] All people die because of what one man, *Adam,* did. But now many of us experience God's undeserved kindness to us, and we experience his erasing the record of our sins without our earning it. It is also very certain that we will rule *with Christ in heaven.*[n] *This will happen* because of *what* one man, Jesus Christ, *did for us.*

[18] So, because *one man, Adam,* disobeyed *God's law,* that resulted in all people deserving to be punished. Similarly, because one man, *Jesus,* acted righteously by being obedient *to God when he died, that* resulted in God being *able to erase the record of* all people's sins and *enabling them to* live eternally. [19] It was because one person, *Adam,* disobeyed *God* that all people became sinners. Similarly, it is because one person, *Jesus,* obeyed *God when he died* that the record of many people's sins will be erased. [20] *God gave* his laws *to Moses* in order that *people might realize* how greatly they had sinned; but as people sinned more, God continued to show them even more undeserved kindness. [21] He did that in order that, just as people everywhere inevitably sin, *which results in their* dying, people everywhere might inevitably experience God's acting kindly towards them in ways they don't deserve by *erasing the record of their sins. In that way, people* will live eternally because of what Jesus Christ our Lord *did for them.*

6

Romans 6:1-14

THEME: *If someone were to say that perhaps we should continue to sin in order that God may continue to act more kindly toward us, I would reply that we who ought to consider ourselves unresponsive to sinful desires should certainly not continue sinning. We must keep remembering that it is as though our former sinful nature has ceased to function, and it is as though we have become unresponsive to sinful desires, living in a new way. So do not let the desire to commit sin control you. Instead, present yourselves to God to do righteous things.*

[1] Someone might say *in reply to what I have written* that, *since God has acted kindly toward us* in ways we did not deserve, perhaps we should continue to sin in order that he may continue to act even more kindly toward us *and keep on forgiving us.* [2] *I would reply,* No, certainly not! We *ought to consider that our* sinful desires *cannot make us do what they want us to do, just as we can not make* a corpse do what we want it to do. So it is not right that we continue to sin! [3] When we were baptized in order to show we have a relationship with Jesus Christ,[o] our *being baptized was to declare that it was as though* we died with Christ. *I want* you to remember that! [4] So, when we were baptized, *it was as though* we were buried with Christ. *We were baptized* to indicate that *we would not let our sinful desires make us do what they want us to do, just as people cannot make* a corpse *do what they want it to* do. We *were baptized* to *signify that we would* continually conduct our lives in a new way, just as Christ was caused to live again in a new way by the great *power* of God his Father. [5] Because of our close relationship with Christ, we have *separated ourselves from the former way in which we conducted our lives,* just as *Christ was separated from his physical life when he* died. But God will also certainly *enable us to live in a new way, just as he* enabled Christ to live again. [6] We must keep remembering that when Christ died on the cross, *it was as though* our sinful nature *died with him. It has*

---

[n] OR, ...It is also very certain that we will share *the glory of Christ's being* king *in heaven.*

[o] OR, When we were baptized in order to show we are united to Jesus Christ...

lost its power to make us do what it wants us to do. That happened in order that we would not do the sinful *things that our* bodies, which desire to sin, want us to do, and in order that we would no longer have to sin, as slaves *have to do what their masters want.* [7] *We are, as it were, free from* sinful *desires controlling us, just as* anyone who has died is free *from anything controlling him.* [8] Since *it is as though* we died with Christ, we believe that we will continue to live with him. [9] We know that since *God* enabled Christ to live again after he died, he will never die again. Nothing will ever be able to make him die again. [10] When he died, he died once for sinners, and he will never die again; but in regard to his living *again now*, he lives in order to *serve* God. [11] In the same way, you must consider that *it is as though* you have become *unable to do what your* sinful *desires* want, as a corpse *is not able to do what anyone wants it to do.* You must also consider that because of your relationship to Christ Jesus you are living *in a new way* in order to *serve* God. [12] So, don't let the *desire to commit* sin control your bodies, with the result that you do the sinful things you desire to do! *Remember that* your bodies will surely die, *but your spirits will never die.* [13] Don't use any of your body parts do wicked things as you did when you were spiritually dead. Instead, present yourselves to God as people who are alive spiritually. Present all your body parts to God, *to allow him* to use them to *do* righteous things. [14] Don't let a *desire to* sin control you. The laws *God gave Moses* did not enable you *to stop sinning.* But *now* God controls you and kindly helps you *not to sin.*

Romans 6:15-23

THEME: If someone should conclude that people can sin now because they are not obligated to obey the Mosaic laws, I would say, "Certainly not!" Instead, let your minds compel your bodies to act righteously.

[15] I suppose that certain people might think about what I have just said and they might say, "*You say that* the laws *God gave Moses* did not enable us *to stop sinning, but that God is now* treating us with undeserved kindness. *That seems to mean that God permits* us to continue sinning." *My reply to that is no*, we should certainly not continue *sinning!* [16] I want you to remember this: *Slaves* have an obligation to obey *whatever their masters command them to do.* Similarly, if you present yourselves to someone *in order to* obey him, you will be **the slaves** of the person you obey. In the same way, *if you have yielded yourselves to do the* sinful things *you desire*, you are slaves of your sinful desires, and you will be eternally separated from God. *If you have yielded yourselves* to obey *God*, you are slaves of God, and you need to *live* righteously. [17] You were once slaves *to your sinful desires because you did the* sinful things *you desired.* But you began to sincerely obey the new teaching that *you were* taught. I thank God for that. [18] I also *thank God that* you have been freed from *being controlled by a desire to* sin, and that you have become *as though you were* slaves to *living* righteously. [19] I am illustrating what I say *by talking about slavery* because your human nature prevents you from understanding *spiritual truth* easily. *In the past* you willingly did the immoral and unlawful things that *your minds compelled* your bodies to do, *just as* slaves *do what their masters compel them to do.* As a result, you did even more unlawful things. Now, *you need to* willingly allow *your minds to compel* your bodies to *act* righteously, in order that you will behave in a holy way. [20] When you were *like* slaves *because your sinful desires* compelled you to do sinful things, you were not *concerned about behaving* righteously. [21] Nevertheless, you did not benefit at all from *doing* those sinful things that you are now ashamed of, because *doing* those things resulted in your being eternally separated from God. [22] But *God* has freed you from *letting the desire to* sin control you. You have become *as though you were* the slaves of God. So now the result is that God has caused you to completely belong to him and, as a result, you will live eternally. [23] *What people receive for* sinning *is that they are* eternally separated from God. That is *like* wages that *people receive.* But what God gives us is a

gift. What he gives us is that we live eternally because of *our relationship with* Christ Jesus our Lord.

7

Romans 7:1-6

THEME: *You know that after people die, they are freed from being required to obey any law. Similarly, God has freed us from being required to obey all the Jewish rituals and laws.*

[1] My fellow believers, you know about laws. So you certainly know that[p] people have to obey laws *only* while *they are* alive. [2] *For example,* the law requires a woman *to obey and be faithful to her husband as long as he is alive. But if her husband dies, she is freed from having to obey* the law about *remaining married to* her husband. [3] As a result, a woman will be called an adulteress if she lives with another man while her husband is alive. But if her husband dies, she no longer *has to obey* that law. Then she will not be an adulteress if she marries another man. [4] *Likewise,* my fellow believers, *just as people are free from having to obey any law after they die,* God has freed you *and me* from having *to obey* all the Jewish rituals and laws. *That is because it is as though* we died with Christ *when he was crucified.* Now you *and I* belong to someone else, *like a woman who marries again after her husband dies belongs to another man.* Specifically, you *and I* belong to *Christ,* who has been raised from the dead, in order that we may live righteously to *honor* God. [5] When our self-directed nature *controlled* us, desires that led us to sin were acting in our bodies. *Those desires were increased because of our knowing God's* laws. As a result *we did evil things that* caused us to be separated from God. [6] But now we are freed from having *to obey* all the Jewish rituals—*it is as though* we have died. The result is that those rituals do not control us now. So we serve God, not by having *to obey* those rituals, which is the old way, but in the new way, as *God's* Spirit *helps us to serve him.*

Romans 7:7-12

THEME: *My reply to the objection that the laws of Moses are evil because they cause us to sin is that the laws are holy and good; the laws simply reveal that what we are doing is sinful.*

[7] *Someone might object,* saying, "The laws *God gave Moses* must be evil *if our sinful desires are increased because of our knowledge of those laws.*" *I would reply,* they certainly are not *evil, even though our sinful desires are increased because of our knowledge of those laws.* To support my reply, I would say that I, *for example,* realized *what I was doing* was sinful only because *I read what is written in* those laws. For example, I realized that coveting *is sinful* only because it says in those laws, "You must not covet." [8] And because of what that commandment *stated,* my sinful *desire to have things that belong to others* caused me to covet in many ways. *Our desire to* sin is not stirred up when there is no law *that prohibits our doing sinful things.* [9] Formerly, when I did not *know* what God's laws *required,* I used to live *without worrying about what I was doing.* But when I *became aware that God* commanded, *"You must not covet,"* I suddenly realized that I was sinning, [10] and I realized that I was separated from God. The laws that *I thought would enable me to* live *eternally as a result of my obeying them* caused me *to realize that* I was separated from God. [11] *My desire to* sin found a way to deceive me *by making me wrongly think that* I could keep on sinning and at the same time obey God's laws sufficiently *to live eternally,* and *thus my desire to sin* caused me to be separated

---

[p] OR, ...I want you to remember that...

from God. ¹²So we conclude that the laws *God gave Moses* are holy. The commandment *about not coveting, along with all the other commandments*, is also holy, and it is just and good.

Romans 7:13

THEME: My reply to the objection that God's law, being good, causes people to become spiritually dead is, "No, it is our desire to commit sin that causes us to sin and become spiritually dead."

¹³So, *if someone were to object* saying, "*The laws God gave Moses*, which are good, resulted in my being separated from God!" *I would reply*, "Certainly they did not *do that!*" But instead, those *laws*, which are good, stimulated *our desire to commit* sin. I knew the result *of knowing those laws* was that I was separated from God. And also, because I learned what *God had* commanded, *I knew that* what I was doing was truly sinful.

Romans 7:14-25

THEME: The laws came from God's Spirit, but you and I are influenced by our sinful natures. We often do not do the things we desire, and we do the things we detest because of a desire to sin that permeates us and prevents us from doing good, unless Christ frees us from being controlled by these desires.

¹⁴We know that the laws *God gave Moses* came from *God's* Spirit. But as for me, I am *influenced by my* self-directed nature. *It is as though* I have been forced to become a slave of *my desire to* sin. ¹⁵The things that I do, I *often* do not understand. That is, *sometimes* it is *the good things* that I want *to do* that I don't practice. *And sometimes* it is the *evil* things that I detest that I do. ¹⁶Because I *do* the *evil* things that I don't want *to* do, I agree that the laws *of God* are good. ¹⁷So, it is not that I do *evil things because I want to do them*. Instead, *I do evil things because the desire to* sin *causes me to do them*. The desire to sin permeates me. ¹⁸I know that my self-directed nature will not *let me do* anything that is good. I know this because **I want** *to do what is good,* but **I don't do** what is good. ¹⁹I don't do the good things that I want to do. Instead, it is **evil things** that I don't want to do that I do. ²⁰Because I do *evil things* that I don't want to do, it is not that I do *evil things just because I want to*. Instead, *I do them because* my self-directed nature, which permeates me, *causes me to do them*. ²¹I find, then, that what always happens is that when I want to do what is good, there is an evil *desire* present within me that *prevents me from doing good*. ²²With my new inner nature I like the laws of God very much. ²³Nevertheless, I sense that there is a different force that is in my body. It is opposed to what with my mind *I desire to do*, and it puts me inescapably under the control of the sinful *desires* that I have. ²⁴*When I consider this*, I *feel that I* am a very wretched person. I want someone to set me free from the control of what my body *desires*, in order that I might not be separated from God. *I also think that what I have experienced is the same as what all believers experience.* ²⁵I thank God that it is by Jesus Christ our Lord *that we can be free from the control of what our bodies desire*. So then, *with our minds, you and* I, on the one hand, want to obey God's laws. *But then also*, *you and* I *often let* our sinful *desires control us* because of our self-directed nature.

8

Romans 8:1-11

THEME: God will not in any way condemn those who are united to Christ Jesus, because God's Spirit has freed us from the inevitability of sinning and from spiritual death.

[1] God has erased the record of our sins because we trust in what Christ has done for us. So now *God will* not *in any way* condemn and punish us who have a relationship with Christ Jesus. [2] *God's* Spirit causes us to conduct our lives *in a new way* as a result of what Christ Jesus *did for us. And he* has set up a way by which he frees *each of* us from continually being forced to sin[q] and from being separated from God. [3] What *we* could not do *by trying to obey* the laws *of God* because our self-directed nature was too weak *to obey them*, God did. He sent his own Son *into the world in order that his Son might atone* for our sin. His Son took on a human nature that was like *the human nature* of us people who sin. *By sending his Son in this way,* God condemned and punished *his Son who never sinned, instead of punishing us who* sinned. He did that *by making his Son's* body *a sacrifice* for *all our* sin. [4] So we can *now* fulfill all that God required in his laws. We do this, not by acting the way our sinful human nature *desires*, but by living as *God's* Spirit *desires us to live.* [5] People who live according to what their self-directed nature *desires* think about and are concerned about what their self-directed nature *desires*. But people who *live* according to what *God's* Spirit *desires think about and are concerned about* what *God's* Spirit *desires.* [6] Those who think about and are concerned about the desires of their self-directed nature will not live eternally.[r] But those who think about and are concerned about what *God's* Spirit *desires* will live *eternally* and have *inner* peace. [7] Let me explain this. *To the extent that* people think about and are concerned about what their self-directed nature *desires*, they are acting contrary to God. They do not obey the laws of God. In fact, they are not even **able** *to obey his laws.* [8] The people who let their self-directed nature *control them* cannot do what pleases God. [9] But **we** do not have to let our self-directed nature *control us.* Instead, *we can let* God's Spirit *control us,* because he lives within us. If people do not have *living in them* the Spirit *who comes from* Christ, they do not belong to Christ. [10] But if Christ *is living in us by his Spirit, although* our bodies *are certain to* die because we sin, our spirits are alive because God has erased the record of our sins. [11] *God* caused Jesus to live again after he died. And because his Spirit lives in us, *God* will also make our bodies, which *now* are sure to die, live *again after we die.* God, who caused Christ to live again after he died, will make us live again by *causing* his Spirit, who lives within us, *to do it.*

Romans 8:12-13

THEME: We are compelled to live as the Spirit directs, not as our self-directed nature directs, because if we do the latter we will be eternally separated from God, but if we cease doing the latter we will live eternally.

[12] So then, my fellow believers, we must *live as the Spirit directs us.* What we do not have to do is to conduct our lives as our self-directed nature *guides us.* [13] If you conduct your lives the way your self-directed nature *directs*, you will surely not live *eternally.*[s] But if by

---

[q] OR, …he frees *each of* us from obeying our self-directed nature…

[r] OR, …will be eternally separated from God.

[s] OR, …you will surely be *eternally* separated from God.

the power of God's Spirit you quit doing the *sinful* things your bodies *desire*, you will live eternally.

Romans 8:14-17

THEME: Because we who allow the Spirit of God to guide us are God's children, we will also inherit eternal blessings from God.

[14] We who allow **the Spirit of God** to guide us are God's children. [15] *You have showed that this is true*, because you received *from God* a Spirit that is not one that makes you fear *God* again. You are not like slaves *who fear their masters*. On the contrary, we have received a Spirit by whose *work in our hearts God* has adopted us. The Spirit now enables us to cry out *to God*, "*You are my* Father!" [16] The Spirit himself confirms what our spirits *say*, that we are God's children. [17] Because we are *God's* children, we also will some day receive *eternal blessings*. We will receive them from God, and we will *also* receive *them* just as Christ has *inherited them*. But we must suffer *for doing good* as Christ did, in order to receive splendor as he did.

Romans 8:18-25

THEME: Since everything God has created is eagerly awaiting the time when he will reveal who are his true children, I consider that what we suffer now is not worth paying attention to.

[18] I consider that what we suffer during the present time is not worth *paying attention to, because* the future glory that God will reveal to us *is so great.* [19] The *things that God has* created are very eagerly waiting for *the time* when God will reveal *who* his *true* children are. [20] *God* caused the things he created to be unable to achieve *what he had purposed. That was* not because they wanted to *be that way.* On the contrary, *God* made them that way because he wanted them to keep confidently expecting [21] that *he* will free the things that *he* created from their sure decay. *He* will free them in order that *he can give them* the same glory that belongs to his children. [22] We know that until now *it is as though* all *things* that God created have been groaning together, *and they long for that glory, just as a mother having the pains before giving birth to a child* groans *and longs for her baby's birth.* [23] Not only *do those things groan*, but we ourselves also groan inwardly. We who have *God's* Spirit, who is like a partial gift we have received as we await *the future glory, groan inwardly.* We groan while we wait eagerly for the time when we will receive our *full* rights as God's adopted children. That *will include giving us new bodies* when he frees our bodies *from the things that hinder us on earth.* [24] Ever since we were saved, we have continued to confidently expect *that future glory.* Those who already have what they are waiting for do not *need to* wait for it any longer, because those who have something certainly do not continue to wait for it! [25] But because we keep waiting expectantly to receive what we do not yet have, we wait for it eagerly and patiently.

Romans 8:26-27

THEME: God's Spirit helps us when our spirits feel weak. God's Spirit prays for us and God understands what his Spirit intends.

[26] Similarly, *in addition to our continuing to wait for what God will give us, God's* Spirit helps us when *our spirits feel* weak. We do not know what is proper for us to pray. But *God's* Spirit knows, and he prays *with us* even when *we* groan in a way that cannot be expressed in words.[t] [27] *God,* who examines our inner feelings, understands what his Spirit

---

[t] OR, …he prays with us, groaning in a way that cannot be expressed in words.

desires. *What God understands is that* his Spirit prays for *us* who belong to God exactly as God *wants him to pray*.

Romans 8:28-30

THEME: God works out all things in a way that produces spiritual benefits for us who love him. He does this because, having known that we would be saved and thus we would have the character of his Son, he chose us and declared us righteous, and he will surely give us future splendor.

[28] And we know that to us who love God, he works out **all things** that happen *to us* in a way that produces *spiritual* benefits *for us*. He does this for us whom he has chosen, because that was what he planned to do. [29] God knew previously *that we would believe in him*. We are those who God also decided previously would have a character like his Son's character. The result of that is that *Christ is like* a firstborn *son*, and *we who are God's children* are *like* many *younger* brothers and sisters *of Jesus*. [30] And God also summoned us who he decided previously *that we would be like his Son*. And for us whom he summoned, he erased the record of our sins. And for us whose record of sins he has erased, he also will surely give future splendor to us.

Romans 8:31-39

THEME: We must conclude from these things that no one can prevail against us, and absolutely no one and nothing can separate us from Christ's loving us and God's loving us.

[31] So, I will tell you what we must conclude from *all* these things *that God does for us*. Because God *is acting* on our behalf, no one can win against us![u] [32] God did not spare even **his very own Son**. Instead, he turned him over *to people who cruelly killed him,* in order that all we who *believe in him* may benefit *from his death for us*. So, *because God did that,* he will also certainly give us freely everything *that we need to live for him*, in addition to *giving us* Christ. [33] It is God himself who erases the record of our sins. So no one who accuses us *before God* will win against us.[v] [34] *Because* it is Christ Jesus himself who pleads *with God* for us, no one can condemn us *for our sins.*[w] Christ died *for us*, but God raised him from the dead, and he now is at the place of honor *ruling* with God. [35] Absolutely no one and nothing can cause Christ to stop loving us! That could not happen *as a result of someone* afflicting us, or *because someone did things to* harm us, or *because we did* not have anything to eat, or *because we did* not have enough clothes, or *because we lived in* dangerous situations, or *because someone* murdered us. [36] *Such things may happen to us, just as David* wrote *that he said to God*, "Because we are your people, *other people* repeatedly *attempt to* kill us. They consider that we are *just people to be killed, like a butcher considers* that sheep are just *animals* to be slaughtered." [37] But even though all these bad things *may happen to us*, we win completely *over these things because Christ*, who loves us, *helps us*. [38] I am absolutely certain that neither being put to death, nor *what happens to us while* we live, nor angels, nor demons, nor present events, nor future events, nor powerful *forces*, [39] nor *powerful beings* above *the horizon* or below *the horizon*, nor anything else that *God has* created can cause God to stop loving us. *God showed us that he loves us by sending* Jesus Christ our Lord *to die for us*.

---

[u] OR, ...It does not matter if anyone opposes us, since God *is acting* on our behalf!

[v] OR, ...It does not matter if anyone tries to accuse us *before God*.

[w] OR, No one can say that we are still guilty for our sin since it is Christ Jesus himself who pleads *with God* for us.

9

Romans 9:1-5

THEME: I tell you very sincerely that I grieve greatly about most of my fellow Israelites having rejected Christ. I would be willing to be rejected by Christ if that would help them believe in him.

[1] *Now I would like to discuss the fact that most of my fellow Israelites have rejected Christ.* Because of my relationship with Christ I say completely truthfully *what I will now tell you.* I am not lying! My conscience confirms what I *say* because the Holy Spirit *controls it.* [2] *I tell you that* I grieve very greatly and deeply *about my fellow Israelites refusal to believe.* [3] I personally would be willing to let *God* curse me *and, as a result,* Christ *might reject me, if that would* help my fellow Israelites, my natural kinsmen, *to believe in Christ.* [4] We Jews are Israelites, *the descendants of Jacob. God has always considered* us as his children. It was to our ancestors *that he used to appear* gloriously *while they were in the desert.* It was with them that *God made* covenants *several times.* It was to them *that God* gave the laws *at Mount Sinai.* They were the ones *to whom God showed how to* worship him. They were the ones *to whom God* promised many things, *especially that the Messiah would come from our race.* [5] It was our ancestors, *Abraham, Isaac, and Jacob, whom God chose to found our nation.* And, *most importantly,* it was from us Israelites that the Messiah received his human nature. *Nevertheless, most of my fellow Israelites have rejected Christ,* even though he is the one who controls all things! He is God, the one who is worthy of our praise forever! Yes! Yes![x]

Romans 9:6-13

THEME: This does not prove that God has failed to do for Abraham what he promised because, as Scripture illustrates, it is not all who are naturally descended from Jacob or Abraham whom God considers to be his children, but it is those who were born as a result of what God promised whom he considers his children.

[6] *God promised to Abraham, Isaac, and Jacob that their descendants would all inherit his blessings.* But *although most of my fellow Israelites have rejected Christ,* that does not *prove* that God has failed *to do* the things that he promised, because it is not all who are descended from Jacob and who *call themselves the people of* Israel whom *God considers* to be truly his people. [7] And it is also not all of Abraham's natural descendants that *God considers* to be his people. Instead, *God considers only some of them to be Abraham's children. This agrees with what God told Abraham*: "It is Isaac, *not any of your other sons,* whom *I* will consider *to be the true father of* your descendants." [8] That means that it is not all the natural-born descendants *of Abraham* whom God *considers as* his children. Instead, it is those who were born as a result of *believing what God* promised whom *he* considers to be his children. [9] *You know that what God* promised *to Abraham* was this: "About this time *next year* Sarah *your wife* will bear a son *as a result of* my *enabling her."* So Abraham knew that it was not through Ishmael, the son he already had, that God would fulfill what he had promised him.[y] [10] And not only then did he show *that he did not determine who would be his true children according to who their ancestors were. He showed it again* when Rebecca conceived *twins* by our ancestor Isaac. [11-12] Before *the twins, Jacob and Esau,* were born, when neither one had yet done anything good or bad, *God* said to Rebecca *about the twins she was to bear,* "The older one shall later serve the

---

[x] OR, ...Amen!

[y] OR, ...*that his true descendants would come.*

younger one, *contrary to normal custom.*" *God said this* in order that *we might clearly understand* that **the events that God planned** were according to what he himself determined. That is, people's *eternal destiny* does not depend on their ancestry. Instead, their destiny depends on *God,* the one who chooses them. [13] And *this teaching is supported by* what is written *in the Scriptures that God said,* "I favored Jacob, *the younger son.* I did not favor Esau, *the older son.*"

Romans 9:14-18

THEME: As the Scriptures indicate, God's choice of people does not depend on their wishes or efforts. He helps whomever he wants to help, and he makes stubborn whomever he wants to make stubborn. We cannot conclude that God is unjust in choosing the ones he wants to choose.

[14] Someone might ask, "Is God unjust *by choosing the ones he wants to choose?*" *I would reply,* "*He is* certainly not *unjust!*" [15] God told Moses, "I will pity and help anyone I choose!" [16] So, *God chooses people,* not because they wish that *he would choose them* or because they try hard *to do things so that he* will *accept them.* Instead, he chooses people because he himself has mercy *on undeserving ones.* [17] *Moses recorded that God had told* Pharaoh, "This is why I gave you authority: It was in order that I might show *by opposing* you *how exceedingly* powerful I am, and in order that people everywhere would hear about me." [18] So, *we conclude that God* in his kindness helps the ones he wants to act kindly towards. But he makes stubborn the ones *such as Pharaoh* that he wants *to make stubborn.*

Romans 9:19-29

THEME: My reply to anyone's objection to this doctrine is that God has a right to carry out his purposes; he tolerated the people who caused him to be angry, in order that he might disclose how gloriously he acts toward those on whom he intends to have mercy.

[19] *Some of* you may *object to this by* saying to me, "*Because God determines ahead of time everything that people do, that must imply that God wants us to do everything that we do.* No one has resisted what God has willed! So, it would not be right for God to condemn *us for having sinned!*" [20] *I would reply that since* you are *just a* human being, you do not *have any right at all to* criticize God, *saying that what God does is wrong! Just as a potter is the one who creates a clay pot, God is the one who created you.* And a clay pot certainly would not *have a right to criticize* the potter by asking, "Why did you make me this way?" [21] Instead, the potter certainly has the right to *take* some clay, and he forms one lump *of clay* to make one pot that people will honor and *then takes another lump to make another* pot for ordinary purposes. *Similarly, God has the right to carry out what he purposes for people.* [22] Although God desires to show that he is angry *about sin,* and *although he desires to* make clear that he can powerfully *punish people who have sinned,* he tolerated very patiently the people who caused him to be angry and who deserved to be destroyed.[z] [23] *God has been patient* in order that he might make clear how very wonderfully *he treats those* whom he intended to act mercifully towards and whom he prepared ahead of time in order that they might *live* gloriously *in heaven.* [24] That means us whom he chose—not only *us* Jews, but also non-Jews. [25] *These words that* Hosea wrote that *God* said also *support God's right to choose from among both Jews and non-Jews,*

I will declare that many people who were not my people are *now* my people.
I will declare that many people whom *I* did not love before, *I* love now.

---

[z] OR, …who were made to be destroyed.

²⁶ *He also wrote*:

> *What will happen is that* in the places where *God* told them before, 'You are not my
> people,' in those same places *people* will declare truthfully that they are children of
> God, who is completely powerful.

²⁷ Isaiah also exclaimed concerning the Israelites:

> Even though the Israelites are *so many that no one can count them, like* sand *particles
> beside* the ocean, *only* the small part of them will be saved, ²⁸ because the Lord will
> punish completely and speedily the *people who live in that* land, as he said he would
> do.

²⁹ *Also, we can understand from what the prophet* Isaiah said *that God would not save
anyone if he did not show mercy on them,*

> If the Lord, *who controls everything* in heaven, had not *mercifully* allowed some of our
> descendants to survive, we would have become like *the people of the cities of* Sodom
> and Gomorrah, *who were completely destroyed*.

Romans 9:30-33

*THEME: The non-Jews found the way by which God could declare them righteous. The Jews
did not succeed in fulfilling the Mosaic laws. Instead, they tried to find a way to be declared
righteous by the things they did.*

³⁰ We must conclude this: Although non-Jews did not search out *a way by which* God
would erase the record of their sins, they found that way because they trusted *in what
Christ did for them*. ³¹ But although *the people of* Israel sought a basis *by which God would*
erase the record of their sins, they did not succeed in *fulfilling the true purpose of the* laws
God gave to Moses. ³² The reason *they did not succeed* is that they did not trust *God to
provide a way to save them*. Instead, they were trying to do certain things *to gain God's
acceptance. And because they did not expect the Messiah to die, the Israelites* felt
disgusted concerning *Jesus' death, which is like* the stone on which people stumble.
³³ This is just as *a prophet* predicted when he wrote these words *about the Messiah that
God said*:

> Listen! I am placing in Israel *one who is like* a stone on which people will stumble. His
> actions will offend people. Nevertheless, those who believe in him will be very
> satisfied.^{aa}

10

Romans 10:1-4

*THEME: My deep desire and earnest prayer is that God will save the Jews, who do not
understand how to seek him correctly.*

¹ My fellow believers *in Rome*, what I deeply desire and what I pray to God earnestly for is
that he will save *my own people, the Jews*. ² I declare truthfully about them that although
they seek God zealously, they do not understand *how to seek him correctly*. ³ They do not
accept **God's** way of erasing the record of people's sins. They do not *want to* recognize
that way because they want him to do it **their** way. ⁴ They want God to erase the record of
their sins as *a result of their obeying his laws. But* because of what Christ has done, it is

---

^{aa} OR, …Nevertheless, those who believe in him will not be disappointed.

no longer necessary for *people to obey* the laws *God gave Moses in order for God to erase the record of their sins*. Now God will erase the record of sins of everyone who trusts *in what Christ has done*.

Romans 10:5-13

THEME: The message of Scripture is that those who confess publicly that Jesus is their Lord and who believe inwardly that God raised Jesus from the dead will be saved, because God accepts people only because of their faith, Jews and non-Jews alike.

[5] *In regard to the old way*, Moses wrote *concerning people who obey God's laws*, "It is the people who have done *perfectly* the things *that the laws require* who will gain *eternal* life by *doing* them." [6] But those whose record of sins God has erased as a result of their believing *in Christ* can say *to anyone as Moses said*, "You should not say inwardly, 'Someone will have to go up and enter heaven!'" That is to say, someone will have to *go up and* bring Christ down *to bring the message of salvation to us!* [7] "Also, *you should not say inwardly*, 'Someone will have to go down and enter the place where *the spirits* of dead people are!'" That is to say, someone will have to *go down and* bring Christ up *from there to bring the message of salvation to us. You shouldn't say this because Christ has already come down to save us, and has already risen from the dead!* [8] But instead, what *those who believe in Christ* can say is what *Moses also said*, "You can find out about *God's* message very easily. You can speak about it; you can think about it." This is the message that we proclaim, that people must believe *in Christ.* [9] *This message is that* if anyone of you says publicly that Jesus is Lord, and if you believe inwardly that God raised him from the dead, you will be saved. [10] If people believe **inwardly** *that Christ died and that God caused him to become alive again*, the result is that *God will erase the record of their sins. And for those* who state **publicly** *that Jesus is their Lord*, the result is that *God* will save them. [11] *It is written in the Scriptures about the Messiah*, "**Whoever** believes in him will not be disappointed." [12] *God* treats Jews and non-Jews equally well. And he abundantly *blesses* all who ask him *to help them. He is equally* Lord to all people *who believe in him.* [13] *As the prophet Joel wrote*, "The Lord God will save **all** those who ask him to save them."

Romans 10:14-17

THEME: There may be those who object by saying, "If God does not send someone to preach to the Jews, then they cannot ask Christ to save them." My reply to them is that God has sent people to preach about Christ to them, but most of the Jews have not accepted the gospel. However, some Jews have believed in Christ, and many other people are indeed hearing the message.

[14] *In regard to the people of Israel rejecting the gospel,*[bb] *someone might object by saying,* "Well, they certainly cannot ask Christ *to save them* if they haven't *first* believed *in him*. They certainly cannot believe *in him* if they haven't heard about him. And they certainly cannot hear *about him* if someone does not preach to them *about him.* [15] And those who preach to them *about Christ*, certainly cannot preach if *God* does not send them *to preach. God's sending messengers to them would be* just like it is written *in the Scriptures*, 'The arrival of those who preach the good message is wonderful!'" [16] *I would reply in this way to those who hold those ideas: God has indeed sent people to preach the message about Christ.* However, not all *the people of Israel* have paid attention to the good message! *They are like what* Isaiah who said *when he was very discouraged*, "Lord, it seems as if hardly anyone believed what they heard us preach!" [17] *So then, I tell you that people* **have**

[bb] OR, *This raises another problem about the Jews:…*

believed *in Christ* as a result of hearing *the message about him*, and people **are** hearing *the message,* because there are those who are preaching *about* Christ!

Romans 10:18-21

THEME: In reply to a query of whether the Jews have heard or understood about Christ, I would say that, as is supported by the Scriptures, they have heard it and should have understood it, because even the non-Jews, who were not searching for God, understood it.

[18] But if someone were to ask, "Haven't the Israelites heard *the message about God*?" *I would reply that they* certainly have *heard! We know that they have heard from the Psalm that says:*
> The people living all over the world have seen *the stars*, and what they indicate *about God's character has reached people living in* the most remote places in the world!

[19] But someone might ask, *"Is it true that the people of* Israel understood *the message about Christ?" Certainly they understood it, but they rejected it! Remember that Moses first warned his people about their disobeying. He told them that God said,*
> Some of the other people-groups in the world will believe and I will bless them. You will envy them *because you consider that* they are not my people *like you are*. You will become angry with me *because you consider them* to be people who do not understand *your ways.*

[20] Remember also what God boldly told Isaiah,
> The non-Jews who did not seek me will surely come to know me! I will surely reveal *my character* to those who did not ask for me!

[21] But concerning *the people of* Israel, *Isaiah* tells *us that God said*:
> For many years I have held out my arms *in vain* to those disobedient and rebellious people, *to invite them to return to me.*

11

Romans 11:1-6

THEME: God has certainly not rejected all Jews. I am evidence of that. Just as in the past, there is also at the present time a small group of us Jews who have become believers.

[1] Then *if anyone should ask*, "Has God rejected his people *the Jews*?" *I would declare that* he certainly has not *rejected all of us! You can realize that by remembering that* I also belong to the *people of* Israel. I am a descendant of Abraham, and I belong to the tribe of Benjamin, *but God has not rejected me!* [2] No, God has not rejected his people, whom he chose long ago *to bless them in a special way*. Remember what is written in the Scriptures about Elijah when he *mistakenly* complained to God about *the people of* Israel, saying: [3] "Lord, they have killed *all of* **your prophets except me.** They have destroyed **your altars.** I am the only one *who believes in you* who remains *alive*, and now they are trying to kill me!" [4] *Remember that* God answered him like this: "You are not the only one who *believes in me!* I have protected for myself 7,000 *other* men who have not worshiped *the false god* Baal." [5] So, similarly, there is also at this time a small group *of us Jews* who have become *believers. God* has chosen us *to become his people* only because he has acted toward us in ways we do not deserve. [6] Since it is because he acts that way *toward those he chooses, it is* not because they have done good things *that he has chosen them*. If *God chose people because they did good deeds*, then it wouldn't be because he was acting toward them in a kind way they did not deserve.

Romans 11:7-10

THEME: The scriptures confirm that the people of Israel as a whole did not find the way of being declared righteous, although those whom God had chosen did find it.

[7] *Since God chose only some people of Israel, this is what I conclude: Most of the people of* Israel did not find the way for God to erase the record of their sins, even though some were earnestly looking for it. The *people of Israel whom God had* chosen found it, but the rest *of them* were made spiritually insensitive. [8] *Our fellow Jews in these days are* just like *the people about whom Isaiah* wrote,

God caused their senses to be dull.
Up to this very day, *they have* eyes, but they cannot see *spiritually*.
They have ears, but they cannot understand *spiritually*.

[9] And *they remind me of what King* David said, *when he asked God to cause his enemies' senses to be dull,*

Make them *stupid, like animals that are caught in* snares! May *they feel secure because of* the things they enjoy, *but which* will catch them *like* a trap, with the result that you will destroy them. [10] May their ability to perceive *danger* be dulled, so that they will not *become alarmed when there is danger.* Cause them to carry heavy loads on their backs continually *as slaves do!*

Romans 11:11-12

THEME: My reply to a query as to whether the result of the Jews' unbelief is a permanent falling away from God is, "No! God is saving many non-Jews to make the Jews envious and thus seek to be saved."

[11] *Perhaps someone will ask, "When the Jews* sinned *by not believing in Christ, did* it result in their being separated from God *permanently?" I would reply*, No, they are certainly not *separated from God permanently!* What is happening is that because they sinned, *God* is saving non-Jews, in order to cause *the Jews* to envy *the way he blesses non-Jews and so ask Christ to save them.* [12] *When the Jews* rejected Christ,[cc] *the result was that God* abundantly *blessed the other people in* the world *by offering them the opportunity to believe. When the Jews* failed *spiritually, the result was that God* abundantly *blessed* the non-Jews. Since that is true, think how wonderful the blessing to everyone will be when the complete number *of the Jews whom God has chosen will believe in Christ*!

Romans 11:13-16

THEME: I highly esteem the work God has called me to do as an apostle among you non-Jews. I hope that I will make my fellow Jews jealous, and as a result, some of them will be saved.

[13] Now it is to you non-Jews that I am saying *what follows.* I am the one who is the apostle to **non-Jews,** and I highly esteem this work *that God appointed* me to do. [14] But I also hope that *by my labors* I will make my fellow Jews jealous, *with the result that* some of them will *believe, and thus* be saved. [15] *God has rejected most of my fellow Jews because they refused to believe, with the result that* he has caused *many other people in* the world to have a peaceful relationship *with him.* But he will accept *my fellow Jews again when they trust in Christ!* And this is what the result will be: It will be *as though God is making them* alive again after they have been dead! [16] *Just as* the whole lump *of dough* will belong to God if *people offer* to God the *bread baked from* the first part *of it, so the Jews will*

[cc] OR, *When the Jews* sinned…

belong to God because their ancestors belonged to God. And just as the branches of a tree will be good if the root is good, so the descendants of our great Jewish ancestors who belonged to God will also someday belong to God.

Romans 11:17-24

THEME: *You non-Jews who believe in Jesus must not despise the Jews whom God has rejected. You must not become proud, but instead you should worry about yourselves! God will not spare you if you fall away from him, and he will certainly act kindly toward the Jews and accept those who trust in Christ.*

[17] *God has rejected* many of *the Jews, like people* break off *and reject dead* branches *of a tree*. And each of you *non-Jews whom God has accepted is like a branch of* a wild olive tree *that* was grafted among the branches *that were left on a cultivated olive tree. God has caused* you *to benefit from how he blessed our first Jewish ancestors, as branches* benefit from the nutritious sap from the root of a *cultivated* olive tree. [18] However, you *non-Jews* must not despise *the Jews whom God rejected, who are like* the branches that *were broken off from the tree*! If any of you *wants to* boast *about having received blessings from God, remember this: Branch*es do not nourish a root. Instead the root nourishes *the branches. Similarly, you are blessed by God because of the Jews! You must not suppose that they are blessed by God because of you!* [19] If one of you then says, "*God rejected the Jews, like* branches that are broken off *a tree and rejected*, in order that *he might accept us non-Jews, as people* graft in branches of a tree," [20] *I would reply that* this is true. However, it is because the Jews did not believe *in Christ* that *God* rejected them. As for you, it is *only* because you believe *in Christ* that *God has accepted* you! *So none of you* should become proud! Instead, you should be wary *about what could happen* to you! [21] Since God did not spare *the unbelieving Jews who were like a tree's* **natural branches**, he will not spare **any of you** *if you don't keep trusting in him!*

[22] Note, then, that God acts with kindness, but he also acts with severity. He has acted severely toward *the Jews* who have stopped trusting in him. On the other hand, he acts kindly toward each of you *non-Jews only* if you continue *to value his* kindness *to you*. However, *he* will reject you if you do not *keep trusting in him.* [23] And if the Jews believe *in Christ*, God will also *accept them to himself, like the* branches *that are* grafted into *a tree again*, because God is able to do that. [24] Each of you *non-Jews who were previously separated from God has benefited from the ways in which God blessed the Jews. That is like taking branches* that have been cut from a wild olive tree that just grew *without being planted* and, contrary to what is usually done, grafting them into a cultivated olive tree. So, God will much more readily *receive back the Jews because they belonged to him before*! *That will be like* the original branches *that had been cut off* being grafted back into the olive tree on which they *originally belonged*!

Romans 11:25-33

THEME: *I want you to know that all the people of Israel will some day be saved, as the Scriptures say will happen. God still loves them because of their ancestors. It is his purpose to act mercifully towards them as well as toward all non-Jews.*

[25] My *non-Jewish* fellow believers, I want you to understand this truth that God has now revealed *about my fellow Israelites who are refusing to believe.* You should not proudly think *that now God favors you more than he favors them.*[dd] Many *people of* Israel will continue to be stubborn until **all the non-Jews** *whom God has chosen have believed in*

[dd] OR, *…that you understand God's future plans for the Jews.*

Jesus. [26] And then all *the people of* Israel will be saved. *Then these words that* are written *in the Scriptures will be fulfilled:*

The one who sets *his people* free will come from the place where God dwells. Then he will remove the guilt of the Israelite people."

[27] And *as God says:*

The promise that I will make with them is that I will forgive their sins.

[28] In regard to *the Jews rejecting* the good message *about Christ, God treats* them as enemies, and that has benefited you *non-Jews.* But in regard to *their being the people* God chose, *God still* loves them on account of *what he promised* their ancestors. [29] *He still loves them,* having never changed his mind about the privileges he *gave them* and about his choosing *them to be his people.* [30] You *non-Jews* once disobeyed God, but now he has acted mercifully towards you because the *Jews* disobeyed him. [31] Similarly, now they have disobeyed God. The result is that by the very same way in which he acted mercifully towards you, he will act mercifully towards them *again.* [32] God has declared and proved that all people, *both Jews and non-Jews*, disobey his laws. He has declared that because he wants to act mercifully towards **all of us.**

Romans 11:33-36

THEME: I marvel at how great God's wisdom and knowledge are, and his decisions and actions toward us!

[33] *I marvel how* vast and great are God's wisdom and his knowledge! We are completely unable to understand the decisions he has made and *why* he does *what he does!* [34] *I remember the Scripture that says*, "No one has known what the Lord thinks. Absolutely no one has given him advice *about what he should do!*" [35] And, "No one has given anything to God *that he did not previously receive from God!*" So God is not obligated to pay back anything to anyone! [36] God *is the one who created* all things! He is also the one who *sustains all things*! His purpose in creating everything was that *everything he created might praise* him! *May all people* honor him forever! May it be so!

12

Romans 12:1-2

THEME: I appeal to you to present yourselves to God by making yourselves like living sacrifices, which is the appropriate way to serve him. Do not let anything non-Christian determine how you act, but instead let God change your way of thinking.

[1] My fellow believers, since God has acted mercifully *toward you* in so many ways, I appeal to *all of* you that you present yourselves *to him by making yourselves like* holy sacrifices. *Make yourselves sacrifices* that he is pleased with, sacrifices that are living, *not ones that are dead. Since God has done so much for you*, this is the *only* appropriate way to serve him. [2] Do not let anything non-Christian determine how you should act. Instead, let *God* change your *way of life* by making your way of thinking new, in order that you may know what he wants you to do. That is, you will know what is good, and you will know what pleases God, and you will know how to be all that he wants you to be.

Romans 12:3-8

THEME: Do not think you are more important to God than what is right for you to suppose. Instead, think about yourselves sensibly, in a way that corresponds to the abilities God has given to you because you trust in Christ. May we do diligently and cheerfully what God has given us ability to do.

[3] Because God in his kindness has appointed me *to be his apostle,* I say this to all of you: Do not think of yourselves more highly than what is right for you to think. Instead, think *about yourselves* in a sensible way that *corresponds to the abilities* God has given you *because* you trust *in Christ.* [4] Although a person has one body, it consists of many parts. All of the parts are needful for *the body,* but they do not all have the same function. [5] Similarly we, *although we are* many, are *united into* one group because of our relationship with Christ, and we belong to one another. *So, no one should act as though he is more important than the others!* [6] *Instead,* since each one of us can do various things that differ according to the abilities that *God has* given to us, *let's do them diligently and cheerfully!* Those whom *God has enabled* to speak messages from him *should speak* what they believe *God told them, and not add more to it.* [7] *Those whom God has enabled* to serve *others* should do that. *Those whom God has enabled* to teach *his truth* should do that. [8] Those *whom God has enabled to* encourage *his people* should do that.[ee] Those who share *their goods or money with others* should do it sincerely.[ff] Those who govern *the congregation* should do it wholeheartedly. Those who help the needy should do it cheerfully.

Romans 12:9-18

THEME: Love others sincerely in the various ways in which you act toward them.

[9] *The way you must love people is to* love them sincerely! Hate what is evil! Continue to eagerly do what is good *in God's sight!* [10] Love one another as members of the same family do; and in regard to honoring one another, you should be the first ones to do it![gg] [11] Do not be lazy. *Instead,* be eager *to serve God!* Serve the Lord *with enthusiasm!* [12] Rejoice because you are confidently awaiting *what God will do for you!* When you suffer, be patient! Keep praying and never give up! [13] If any of God's people lacks anything, share with them *what you have!* Readily provide hospitality for *travelers who need a place to stay!* [14] *Ask God to* be kind to those who persecute you *because you believe in Jesus! Ask him to* be kind to them; do not *ask him to* cause bad things to happen to them. [15] If someone is joyful, you should also rejoice! If someone is sad, you should also be sad! [16] Desire for others what you desire for yourselves![hh] Do not do things because you want to be *famous!* Instead, be content to do *tasks that others consider that only* unimportant people do.[ii] Do not consider yourselves wise. [17] Do not do evil *deeds* to anyone *who has done* evil to you. Act in a way that all people will recognize as good. [18] Live peacefully with other people whenever it is possible, to the extent that you *can have control over the situation.*

[ee] OR, Those *whom God has enabled to* exhort *his people* should do that.

[ff] OR, Those who share *their goods with others* should do it generously.

[gg] OR, …Take delight in honoring each other.

[hh] OR, …Live harmoniously with each other!
     [Literally. "The same-thing toward one-another you-thinking."]

[ii] OR, …Instead, be content *to associate with unimportant* people.

Romans 12:19-21

THEME: Instead of avenging yourselves, allow God to avenge you; and instead of being overcome by evil done to you, overcome evil deeds by doing good to those who do evil to you, because this is what the Scriptures command.

[19] *My fellow believers* whom I love, do not do evil in return when people do evil to you! Instead, allow *God* to punish them, because it is written *in the Scriptures* that the Lord said, "It is **my** responsibility to take revenge; I am the one who will punish *people who do evil to you.*" [20] Instead of *doing evil to those who have done evil to you, do what the Scriptures teach:* "If your enemies are hungry, feed them! If they are thirsty, give them something to drink! By doing that, you will cause them to feel ashamed *and perhaps they will change their attitude toward you.*" [21] Do not let evil *deeds that others have done to you* overcome you *by making you do evil to them!* Instead, overcome their evil *deeds* by *doing* good *deeds* to them!

13

Romans 13:1-7

THEME: Be subject to civil authorities, because those who oppose them oppose what God has established and will bring punishment on themselves. Do what is good, and then the authorities will commend you. Give to all the authorities what you are obligated to give to them.

[1] Every *believer* must be subject to civil officials, *because* God is the only one *who gives officials their* authority. Furthermore, those officials that exist are ones whom God has appointed. [2] So, whoever resists the officials is resisting what God has established. Furthermore, those who resist officials will bring on themselves the punishment *that God considers fitting.* [3] *God has set up* rulers, not *to cause people who* do good deeds to be afraid. Instead, he has set them up *to cause people who do* evil to be afraid. So, if any of you wants to be unafraid of officials, do what is good! *If you do good*, they will commend you *instead of punishing you.* [4] It is to serve God *by doing their work that every official exists*, in order that they may benefit each of you. If any of you does what is evil, you *will rightfully have reason to* be afraid, because the authority that they have to punish people is very real! The officials exist **to serve God.** That is, they act as God's agents as they punish those who do evil. [5] So, it is necessary for you to be subject *to officials*, not only because they will punish you *if you disobey them*, but also because you know within yourselves *that you should be subject to them*! [6] It is for this reason that you also pay taxes, because the officials are servants of God as they continually do their work. [7] Give to all *the officials* what you are supposed to give to them! Pay taxes to *those who require that you pay taxes.* Pay duties *on goods to those who require that you pay those* duties. Respect *those who ought to* be respected. Honor *those who ought to* be honored.

Romans 13:8-10

THEME: Do not leave any debt unpaid. Your only continual obligation is to love one another, because doing so fulfills all that God's law requires.

[8] Pay all of your debts *when you are supposed to pay them.* The only thing *that is like* a debt that *you* should never stop paying is to love one another. Whoever loves others has fulfilled all that God requires in his laws. [9] *There are many things that God* commanded *in his laws, such as* 'do not commit adultery, do not murder *anyone*, do not steal, and do not desire anything that belongs to someone else.' But the command that sums them all up is

this: 'Each of you must love the people with whom you come in contact, just like you love yourself.' ¹⁰ If you love people with whom you come in contact, you will not do any evil to them. So, whoever loves *others* fulfills all that *God's* laws *require*.

Romans 13:11-14

THEME: Because it is time for us to be fully alert and active, we must quit doing wicked deeds. We must do those things that will help us resist that which is evil, we must live properly, and we must be like Christ.

¹¹ *Do* what I have just told you, especially since you know *the significance of* the time *in which we are living. You know that it is* time for you to be *fully alert and active, like people who have* awakened from sleep, because *the time when Christ will finally* deliver us *from this world's pain and sorrow* is near. That time is *certainly* nearer than when we first believed *in Christ*! ¹² *Our time to live in this world is almost ended, like* a night that is nearly ended. The time *when Christ will return* is near. So, we must quit doing wicked deeds *such as people do* in the darkness, and *we must be doing the things that will help us resist evil, as soldiers who* put on their armor in the daytime *get ready to resist their enemies.* ¹³ We must behave properly, as though the time *when Christ will return were already here.* We must not indulge in drunken carousing. We must not commit any kind of sexual immorality. We must not quarrel. We must not be jealous *of other people.* ¹⁴ On the contrary, we should *be like* the Lord Jesus Christ *so that others will see that we belong to him, in the same way that people* put on *special clothes so that others will see what group they belong to.* We should stop thinking about *doing the things that our* self-directed nature desires.

14

Romans 14:1-4

THEME: Accept those who are not sure whether they are permitted to do certain things. Anyone who thinks it is all right to eat all kinds of food must not despise those who don't think that, and those who don't think it is all right to eat certain foods must not condemn those who do, because God has accepted them.

¹ Accept those who are not sure *whether God will permit them to do certain things that some people think are wrong.* But *when you accept them,* do not argue with them about their opinions. ² Some people believe that God permits them to eat all *kinds of food.* Others believe *that God does not want them to eat certain things, so they* believe that they should not eat meat. ³ Anyone who *thinks it is all right to* eat *all kinds of food* must not despise those who *think it is* not *all right to* eat *all kinds of food.* Anyone who *thinks that it is* not *all right to* eat *all kinds of food* must not condemn those who *think that it is all right to* eat *all kinds of food,* because God himself has accepted those people. ⁴ *God is the master of us all, so he is the one who will decide whether those people have done wrong. Therefore* you have no right to condemn those who eat everything, *because they are also God's servants. And* since God is their master, he is the one who accepts or condemns his servants. And he will accept *believers regardless of whether they eat meat or not,* because he is able to keep them *trusting in him.*

Romans 14:5-9

THEME: Each person should be fully convinced about observing special days, thinking and deciding for himself and not for others. We should try to please God in everything we do.

[5] Some people regard certain days as more *holy* than other *days*. Other people regard all days as *equally suitable for worshiping God*. Each person should be sure *about such matters*, thinking and deciding for himself *and not for others*. [6] As for those who believe that they should worship on a *certain* day *of the week*, it is to *honor* the Lord *that they worship on that day*. And as for those who *think it is all right to* eat *all kinds of food*, it is to *honor* the Lord *that they eat those foods,* as shown by the fact that they thank God *for the food that they eat*. As for those who abstain from *eating certain kinds of* food, it is to *honor* the Lord that they do not eat *those foods*, and they also thank God *for the food they do eat*. *So, doing either of those things is not wrong.* [7] None of us *should* live *merely to please* **ourselves,** and none of us *should choose when or how we will* die, *merely to please* **ourselves.** [8] While we live, *we should be trying to please* the Lord, *not just ourselves*. And when we die, *we should be trying to please* the Lord. So, while we live and also when we die, *we should be trying to please* the Lord to whom we belong. *He is the one we are trying to please, not just ourselves,* [9] because the very purpose for which Christ died and became alive again is that he might be Lord of all people, both of those who have already died and of those who are still living.

Romans 14:10-12

THEME: You should neither condemn nor despise your fellow believers who believe differently about religious regulations from what you do, because it is God who will say whether he approves of what we have done.

[10] **It is disgraceful that you** *who practice certain religious regulations* say that God will punish your fellow believers *who do not practice those regulations. I say this because the time will come when* all of us will stand before God, and **he** will say whether or not he approves *of what we have done*. It is also disgraceful that **you** *who do not practice those regulations* despise your fellow believers *who practice them!* [11] *Remember what* God has said about those who do things that displease him,

Everyone will bow down before me! It is as *certain as the fact that* I live! Everyone will acknowledge *that because I am God*, I have the *right to judge and* punish people!

[12] So, *it is clear that* it is God who will decide *whether or not he approves of* what each of us has done.

Romans 14:13-18

THEME: Instead of condemning each other, decide not to do anything that might lead your fellow believer to sin by following your example and which would then cause others to speak evil of you.

[13] Since *it is God who will judge everyone*, let's stop saying that *God should* punish some of our fellow believers! Instead, we should decide that we will not do anything that would *be an example to* fellow believers *that might cause* them to stop trusting in God. [14] I am absolutely certain on the basis of *my close relationship with* the Lord Jesus that there is nothing that by itself is wrong *to eat*. But if someone thinks it is wrong to eat something, then for that person it is wrong to eat it. *So, you should not encourage him to eat it.* [15] If you *eat* food that **anyone** for whom Christ died *thinks is wrong to eat, you might be encouraging that believer to do something that he believes is wrong. As a result, you might cause that* fellow believer *to stop trusting in God*. He would thus be ruined *spiritually*

simply because you have stopped behaving as one who loves *others should behave!* [16] On the same basis, do not *do something you think is* good if, *as a result, your fellow believer would sin, and then* others would speak evil *of you who say you are Christians*. [17] Letting God rule our lives does not *refer to whether we obey regulations about* eating or drinking *something!* Instead, *it means we must* live righteously, *act* peacefully *towards others*, and be joyful by *the power of* the Holy Spirit. [18] Those who serve Christ *by acting* in such ways please God, and others will also respect them.

Romans 14:19-23

THEME: Try to do what will help fellow believers to be at peace with each other and to grow spiritually. Do not destroy what God has done in others' lives as a result of your eating certain things.

[19] So, we should always eagerly try to *conduct our lives in a way that will cause* peace *among fellow Christians*, and we should try to do what will help each other to mature *spiritually*. [20] Do not destroy the work of God *in the life of any believer by eating certain kinds of* food *that such a person considers wrong to eat! God* permits us to eat every *kind of food*. But if, by your eating *certain kinds of food*, you encourage another person to sin *by doing what he believes is wrong*, you are doing wrong. [21] It is good neither to eat meat nor to drink wine, nor *to do anything else at any time if it* will cause one of your fellow believers to stop trusting in God. [22] Let God tell you *what things are right for you to do, but don't try to force others to accept what you believe! God is* pleased with those who do what they know is right and as a result don't feel guilty *concerning what they have done, because they have done only* those things that they believe are right. [23] But some believers are not certain *that God will approve of their eating a certain kind of food.* So if they eat it, *they think God will punish* them. And *God truly* will punish them, because *they have done things that they* believe *are not right.* Those who do **anything** without being certain *that it is right in God's sight* are sinning.

15

Romans 15:1-4

THEME: We should not be irritated by the practices of those who are uncertain whether God will condemn them for doing certain things that the Mosaic law forbids. Instead, we should do things that please our fellow Christians, because we should follow Christ as our model.

[1] Most of us know *that it is all right for us to do certain things that the laws given to Moses said the Jews shouldn't do. But we* should be patient with those who are unsure *about such things*, and we should not let them irritate us. We should not *simply* please ourselves. [2] Each of us should *do the things that* please the fellow *believers with whom we come in contact, things that will* benefit them. *We should do those things* in order to help them mature *spiritually*. [3] *We should please our fellow believers,* because Christ *has set us an example*. He did not *do things to* please himself. On the contrary, *he tried to please God even when others insulted him,* as it is written *in Scripture that the Messiah said to God*, "When people insulted you, *it was as though* they were also insulting me." [4] *You should remember* that what was written previously *in the Scriptures* was written to teach us, in order that we would be patient and be encouraged *by believing what* is written. If we do that, we can confidently expect *God to do for us all he has promised.*

Romans 15:5-6

THEME: May God enable all of you to live harmoniously with each other.

[5] God is the one who enables us to be patient and who encourages us. *I am asking him that he would* enable *all* of you to live harmoniously with each other, following the example of Christ Jesus. [6] Then, as you are united in what you think and say, you will praise God, *who is the heavenly* father of our Lord Jesus Christ.

Romans 15:7-12

THEME: Accept each other as Christ has accepted you, remembering that what Christ has done was both to help the Jews and to cause non-Jews to praise God.

[7] So *I say to all of you believers at Rome*, accept each other. *If you do that*, people will praise God *as they see you thus behaving like Christ. Accept each other* just as Christ accepted you! [8] I want *you to remember* that Christ *helped us* Jews *by what he did*, in order to show that God is faithful. That is, *his coming as our Messiah* fulfilled what God promised to *our Jewish* ancestors. [9] And *by* acting mercifully *to them and the non-Jews, he also* caused the non-Jews to praise him. *What he has done for the non-Jews* fulfills what is written *in the Scriptures that David said to God*: "So I will praise you *when I am* among the non-Jews, and I will sing to you." [10] *David* also wrote, "Rejoice with us God's people, you who are not our fellow Israelites!" [11] *And Moses wrote in* the *Scriptures*, "Praise the Lord, all *you* non-Jews, and may everyone praise him." [12] And Isaiah wrote *in the Scriptures,* "There will be a descendant of *King* David who will begin to rule the non-Jews, and they will confidently expect him *to fulfill what he has promised.*"

Romans 15:13

THEME: May God make you completely joyful and peaceful in order that you may have abundant hope.

[13] God is the one who causes you to be confidently expecting *him to do what he has promised. I pray* that he will cause you to be completely joyful and have peace as you trust *in him*. And as you do that, by the power of the Holy Spirit you will more and more confidently expect *to receive what God has promised to give you.*

Romans 15:14-16

THEME: I have written frankly to you in this letter because of what God in his kindness commissioned me to do among the non-Jews.

[14] My fellow believers, I myself am *completely* sure that you yourselves *have acted toward others* in a completely good way. You have *acted well* because you have known completely *all that God wants you to know* and because you are able to teach each other. [15] However, I have written to you quite frankly *in this letter* about some things in order to remind you *about those things. I have written this* because God in his kindness has *appointed* me [16] to work for Jesus Christ among the non-Jews. *God has appointed me* to act like a priest as I *proclaim* his good message, in order that the non-Jews *will believe in Christ and be accepted by him. They will be* like an offering *to God* as a result of their being dedicated *to him* by the Holy Spirit.

Romans 15:17-21

THEME: I am happy about my work for God, which I have now completed in this region by proclaiming the gospel in places where people have not heard about Christ.

[17] It follows that, because *of my relationship with* Christ Jesus, I am happy about *my work for God.* [18] I will speak boldly only about the work that Christ has enabled me to do. *I do that work* in order that non-Jews might pay attention to *the message about Christ* as a result of what I have said and done, [19] specifically, by *my performing* many powerful miracles. *I have done those things* as a result of God's Spirit powerfully *enabling me.* As a result *of my doing those things, while traveling* all the way around from Jerusalem to *the province of* Illyricum, I have completed *my work* of proclaiming the message about Christ *in those areas.* [20] As *I proclaim* that message, I am always eagerly trying to proclaim it *in places* where people have not already heard about Christ. I do that in order that, *as I work for God,* I might not *simply be continuing the work for him that someone else already started. I do not want to be like a man who* would build *a house* on a foundation that someone else laid. [21] On the contrary, *my goal is to fulfill* what was written *in the Scriptures about the Messiah:* "Those who did not hear about him previously will perceive *his truth.* Truly, those who have not heard *about him will hear and* understand *his message.*"

Romans 15:22-29

THEME: Because of this work, I have often been hindered from visiting you, but I hope to see you as I journey through your area and I hope that you will give me what I need for my next journey. But now I am about to go to Jerusalem to take funds to God's people there. So later I will visit you in Rome, and I know that Christ will bless us there.

[22] Because *I have attempted to preach the message about Christ in places where they have not heard about him*, I have been hindered many times *from being able* to visit you. [23] But now there are no more places in these regions *where people have not heard about Christ.* Furthermore, for several years I have wanted to visit you. [24] So *I hope to come to see you.* I hope to do that on my way to *the provinces in* Spain. I hope to see you as I journey through *your area*, and I hope that *by whatever you give me* you will help me on my journey to Spain. But before *I go there,* I want to enjoy being with you for just a little while, *although I would like to stay with you much longer.* [25] But *I won't be able to visit you now, because* I am about to go to Jerusalem in order to take money for God's people there. [26] *The believers in the provinces of* Macedonia and Achaia decided to contribute some *money* for those of God's people in Jerusalem who are poor. [27] It was their own decision *to do this, but* truly they owe something to God's people in Jerusalem. The non-Jewish *believers* benefited **spiritually** from Jewish *believers as a result of hearing the message about Christ from them*, so the non-Jews should also help the Jewish believers *in Jerusalem by giving them* money. [28] So when I have finished this *task* by safely delivering all this money *that the believers in Macedonia and Achaia have given*, I will leave *Jerusalem and visit* you *in Rome* on my way to Spain. [29] And I know that when I visit you, Christ will abundantly bless *us.*[jj]

[jj] OR, And I know that when I visit you, Christ will enable *me* to bless *you.*

Romans 15:30-33

THEME: I urge you to pray fervently that God will protect me from the unbelieving Jews in Judea, and that God's people there will accept the money I take to them, and also that I may be refreshed by visiting you. May God be with you all.

[30] Because *we belong to* our Lord Jesus Christ and because the Spirit *of God causes us to* love *each other*, I urge you *all* that *you help me by* fervently praying to God for me. [31] *Pray that God* will protect me from being harmed by the *Jews* in Judea who do not believe *the message about Christ.* Also pray that God's people in Jerusalem will accept the money that I *take* to them. [32] Pray these things in order that I may come to you if God wants me to come, and that I may come joyfully, and that God will refresh my *spirit as a result of my being* with you. [33] *I pray that* God, who *causes us to have* peace, will help you.[kk] May it be so!

16

Romans 16:1-2

THEME: I am introducing and commending Phoebe to you, and I ask you to receive her as a fellow believer and to give her whatever she needs.

[1] *By means of this letter* I am introducing and recommending to you our fellow believer Phoebe. She is a deacon in the congregation in *the city of* Cenchrea. [2] *I am asking* you to receive her because of her relationship with the Lord. *You should do that because* those who are God's people ought to receive *their fellow believers. I am also requesting* you to help her *by giving her* whatever she needs, because she has helped many people, including me.

Romans 16:3-16

THEME: I send greetings to many individuals among the believers there.

[3] Tell Priscilla and *her husband* Aquila that I send greetings to them.[ll] They worked with me for Christ Jesus, [4] and they were even willing to die in order *to save* my life. It is not only I who thank them *for helping me*, but the people in all the non-Jewish congregations also *thank them for saving my life.* [5] Also tell the congregation *that meets* in their house that I send my greetings to them. Tell my dear friend Epaenetus the same thing. He is the first man in *the province of* Asia who *believed* in Christ. [6] Tell Mary, who has worked hard *for Christ* for your benefit, that I send my greetings to her. [7] I also send my greetings to Andronicus and *his wife* Junia,[mm] who are my fellow Jews and who were also *previously* in prison with me. They are respected apostles,[nn] and they became Christians before I did. [8] I also send my greetings to Ampliatus, who is a dear friend because of his relationship with the Lord. [9] I also send my greetings to Urbanus, who works for Christ with us, and to my dear friend Stachys. [10] I also send my greetings to Apelles, whom Christ has approved *because Apelles successfully endured trials.* Tell the *believers* who *live in the house* of Aristobulus that I send my greetings to them. [11] Also tell Herodion, who is my fellow Jew,

---

[kk] OR, ...will be with you.

[ll] OR, Tell Priscilla and *her husband* Aquila that I am thinking fondly of them.

[mm] OR, ...and his sister Julia...

[nn] OR, ...They are well-known apostles...

that I send my greetings to him. Tell the same thing to those who *live in the house* of Narcissus who belong to the Lord. [12] I also send my greetings to Tryphaena and *her sister* Tryphosa, who work hard for the Lord. I also send my greetings to Persis. *We all* love her and she has worked very hard for the Lord. [13] Tell Rufus, who is an outstanding Christian, that I send my greetings to him. *Tell the same thing to* his mother, *who has treated me as though I were her son.* [14] Tell Asyncritus and Phlegon and Hermes and Patrobas and Hermas and the fellow believers who *meet* with them that I am sending my greetings to them. [15] I also send my greetings to Philologus, *to his wife* Julia,[oo] to Nereus and his sister, and to Olympas, and to all God's people who *meet* with them. [16] Greet one another affectionately, but in a pure way, *when you gather together.* The *believers in* all the Christian congregations *in this area send their* greetings to you.

Romans 16:17-20

THEME: Note those who are causing quarrels among you and those who cause people to turn away from God. Avoid them, because they only want to satisfy their own desires and deceive those who do not suspect their motives. If you avoid such people, God will soon crush Satan under your feet.

[17] My fellow believers, I exhort you to watch out for those people who cause divisions among you and who cause people to turn away *from God because they teach things that* are contrary to the message *about Christ* that others taught you. Keep away from such people! [18] They do not serve our Lord Christ! On the contrary, they only want to satisfy their own desires! Also, by all the eloquent things they say they deceive the minds of those people who do not realize *that their teaching is false.* [19] *Believers* everywhere know that **you** have paid attention to *the good message about Christ*, with the result that I rejoice about **you.** But I also want you to be wise, *with the result that* you *do* what is good. I also want you to avoid doing what is evil. [20] *If you avoid people who teach what is false*, God, who causes us to be peaceful, will be crushing Satan *as though he was* under your feet! *I pray that* our Lord Jesus will continue to act kindly towards you.

Romans 16:21-23

THEME: Several of those who are with me send their greetings.

[21] Timothy, who works with me, and Lucius and Jason and Sosipater, who are my fellow Jews, *want you to know that they are* sending their greetings to you. [22] I, Tertius, *one who also belongs to* the Lord, *also want you to know* that I am sending my greetings to you. *I am writing this letter as Paul tells me what to write for him.* [23] I, *Paul,* am staying in the house of Gaius, and the whole congregation *here meets* in his house. He *also wants you to know that* he is sending his greetings to you. Erastus, the treasurer of *this* city, also *wants you to know that* he is sending his greetings to you. Our fellow believer Quartus also sends his greetings to you.[pp]

Romans 16:25-27

THEME: We should forever praise the One who alone is God, who alone is truly wise.

[25] As *I* proclaim *the good message about* Jesus Christ, I *tell about God*, the one who is able to strengthen you *spiritually*. I also proclaim the *truth* that *God* did not reveal in all

---

[oo] OR, …his sister Julia…

[pp] Some Greek manuscripts add verse 24, "May the Lord Jesus Christ continue to act kindly toward you all. Amen!"

previous ages, ²⁶ but which *he* has now revealed. *I, along with others, have proclaimed* what the prophets wrote *about Christ*. We are doing what the eternal God commanded *us to do*. We want the *people in* all ethnic groups to know *Christ* so that they may believe *in him* and obey *him*. ²⁷ *I desire that, by* Jesus Christ enabling us, *we* will forever praise the one who alone is God, who alone is *truly* wise. May it be so!

The Apostle Paul wrote several letters to the Christians at Corinth. We call this letter

1 Corinthians

1

1 Corinthians 1:1-3

THEME: As your apostle, I greet you Corinthian believers, and I desire that God bless you.

¹I, Paul, *am writing this letter.* Sosthenes, our fellow believer, is with *me as I write it.* God appointed me to be an apostle of Christ Jesus because that is what God desired. ²*I am sending this letter* to you who belong to the congregations of God in *the city of* Corinth. *God* has set you apart for himself because of your close relationship with Christ Jesus. God has appointed you to be his people and to live pure lives, just as he has appointed all the people everywhere who belong to him to live pure lives. You and they have trusted in the Lord Jesus Christ. He is their sovereign Lord as well as the sovereign Lord of all of us who have trusted in him.

³We desire that God, who is our *heavenly* Father, and Jesus Christ, who is our sovereign Lord, will continue to act kindly toward you and cause you to experience *inner* peace.

1 Corinthians 1:4-9

THEME: I thank God for you and for all the spiritual abilities he has given you.

⁴I very often thank God concerning you because he has acted toward you kindly, in ways you don't deserve. He has done this because you have a close relationship with Christ Jesus. ⁵That is, *God* has very abundantly helped you spiritually because you have a close relationship with Christ. Specifically, God has abundantly enabled you to speak messages *that his Spirit revealed to you*, and he has abundantly enabled you to know many things that his Spirit revealed to you. ⁶In that way, *he* confirmed to you that what we proclaimed about Christ is true. ⁷As a result, while you wait for our Lord Jesus Christ to return, within your group you truly possess every ability that *God's* Spirit gives *to believers*. ⁸God will also cause you to steadfastly *trust Christ to the very end of your lives*. The result will be that God will not consider you guilty *of any sin* when our Lord Jesus Christ returns to earth. ⁹You can depend on God to do that. He is the one who chose you to become intimately associated with his Son, Jesus Christ, who is our Lord.

1 Corinthians 1:10-17

THEME: Stop creating divisions in your congregations on the basis of which Christian leader you favor.

¹⁰My fellow believers, by the authority of our Lord Jesus Christ I urgently appeal to all of you to agree with one another. What I mean is, stop dividing into groups. Instead, be united concerning what you understand *about spiritual matters* and be united in the decisions you make. ¹¹My fellow believers, *I urge this* because some members of Chloe's

household have told me that you are quarreling among yourselves. [12] Specifically, some of you say, "Paul is the one to whom we *are loyal*," and others say, "Peter is the one to whom we *are loyal*," and still others say, "Christ is the one to whom we *are loyal*." [13] *It is ridiculous that you are quarreling and* dividing up *into groups instead of being loyal to* Christ alone! Christ certainly has not divided himself into parts and distributed them out *to groups of people who oppose each other*! I, Paul, certainly did not die on the cross for you! When you were baptized, you certainly did not promise that you were submitting to **me**! [14] I thank *God* that Crispus and Gaius were the only ones from among you whom I baptized. [15] As a result, no one *else there in Corinth* can say, "Paul baptized me so that I would become submissive to him." [16] Oh yes, *now I remember that* I also baptized the household of Stephanas, but I do not remember baptizing anyone else *there*. [17] Christ sent me not *primarily* to baptize people, but to preach the good message about him. When I did that, he did not want me to use words that human philosophers *consider* wise. I did not want the message about *what Christ accomplished when he was nailed to* the cross to lose its power.

1 Corinthians 1:18-19

THEME: The message about Christ dying on the cross is the means of saving us who believe it.

[18] Those who are perishing spiritually *because they do not believe* the message *about what Christ accomplished when he was nailed to the* cross *consider that message to be* foolish. But to us who are being saved *spiritually because we believe that message*, it *demonstrates that* God acts powerfully *to save us*. [19] *It is like these words of God that* a prophet wrote long ago,

By the things that I will do, I will show that the ideas of those who *think* they are wise
are completely useless.
I will ignore the ideas that they think are so smart.

1 Corinthians 1:20-25

THEME: Some people think that the message about Christ is foolish, but to us whom God has chosen it shows God's power.

[20] So, do you know *what God thinks* about what scholars and philosophers and people who consider themselves to be wise say? *He does not pay attention to what they say, because* he has shown clearly that what unbelievers *think is* wise is *not wise at all. It* is really foolish! [21] God, acting very wisely, made it impossible for unbelievers to know God by doing what they thought was wise. Instead, he was happy to save those who trust *in Christ* as the result of hearing *the message that* was proclaimed to them, a message that others consider to be foolish. [22] The Jews want *people to prove that their message is true by performing* miracles. The non-Jews want to hear only messages that they consider full of wisdom. [23] As for us, we proclaim *the message about what* Christ *accomplished for us when* he was nailed to the cross. That message offends Jews *because they don't think the Messiah will die, and* non-Jews think it is a **foolish** message. [24] But to us whom God has chosen to belong to himself—both Jews and non-Jews—that message shows that God acted powerfully and wisely *by sending* Christ *to die* for us. [25] Keep in mind that *unbelievers may think* God was *acting* foolishly *by doing that*, but the truth is that he was acting more wisely than unbelievers who *think* they are wise. And unbelievers may think that God was *acting* weakly *by sending his Son to die*, but he was acting more powerfully than unbelievers who *think they* act powerfully.

1 Corinthians 1:26-31

THEME: God chose you who were mostly despised people, not important people, to belong to Christ, so you should boast only about him.

[26] My fellow believers, remember what *kind of people you* were when God chose you. *Not many of you* whom he chose were people whom *unbelievers considered to be* wise. Very few of you were considered to be important. Very few of you came from families with a high social standing. [27] Instead, it was *often* those whom *unbelievers considered to be* foolish whom God chose. He did that in order to shame those whom *unbelievers consider to be* wise. It was *often* those *whom unbelievers* considered unimportant whom God chose, in order to shame those whom unbelievers consider important. [28] It was often those who were despised and considered worthless whom God chose, in order to make completely ineffective those *whom unbelievers consider to be important.* [29] *He did that* in order that no one could boast to God about their wisdom or importance. [30] It is because of what God *has done* that you have a close relationship with Christ Jesus. God *accomplished* his wise *plan to save us* by what Christ did for us. As a result of what Christ did, God erases the record of our sins, sets us apart for himself, and frees us from the guilt of *our sins.* [31] So it is **the Lord** we should boast about, *not about our being better than other believers.* We should do as *Jeremiah* wrote *in the Scriptures,*

Those who boast should boast *only* about what the Lord has done.

2

1 Corinthians 2:1-5

THEME: God showed that my message was true by the powerful things he did, not because I spoke in a way that would make people think highly of me.

[1] My fellow believers, when I came to you, I proclaimed to you the message God had revealed to me. But I did not proclaim it using eloquent words that would make people think highly of me, nor did I use brilliant reasoning that unbelievers would think portrayed great wisdom. [2] I did that because I decided that I would speak only about Jesus Christ. Specifically, I told you *what he accomplished for us when* he was killed by being nailed to a cross. [3] Furthermore, when I was with you, I felt that I was not adequate *to do what Christ wanted me to do.* I was afraid *that I would not be able to do it*, and because of that I was trembling very much. [4] When I taught you and preached to you, I did not speak words that *unbelievers would consider* wise in order to convince them that my message was true. Instead, *God's* Spirit showed that it was true by performing miracles. [5] *I taught and preached that way* in order that you might believe *my message*, not because you heard words that people consider to be wise, but *because you realized* God's power.

1 Corinthians 2:6-16

THEME: Unbelievers do not consider my message is one that contains wisdom, because I speak what God's Spirit reveals to me.

[6] I do teach a message that people who are *spiritually* mature *consider to* be wise. But I do not teach a message that unbelievers consider to be wise. I also do not teach a message that unbelieving rulers in the world consider to be wise. *Their opinion does not matter*, because *some day* they will lose their power. [7] Instead, I teach about what God planned *long ago* in his wisdom. It is something that people did not know about previously, because *God* did not reveal it previously. But God determined before he created the world

that he would bring great benefit to us by his wise plan. [8] None of those who rule this world knew that wise plan. If they had known it, they would not have nailed our wonderful Lord to the cross. [9] But *we believers need to remember these words that a prophet* wrote *in Scriptures:*

Things that no one has ever seen,
things that no one ever heard,
things that no one ever thought could happen—
those are the things that God has prepared for those who love him.

[10] God has caused his Spirit to reveal those things **to us believers.** His Spirit can do that because he knows thoroughly the meaning of all things. He even knows the things about God that are very difficult to understand. [11] Only a person himself knows what he is thinking.[a] Similarly, only God's Spirit knows what God is thinking. [12] It was not the ideas that unbelievers teach that we accepted. Instead, it was the Spirit who came from God that we received, in order that we might know the things that God has freely done for us. [13] Those are the things that I tell you about. As I do that, I do not tell you things that someone *whom others thought* was wise taught me. Instead, I tell you truths that *God's* Spirit taught *me*, and I explain those spiritual truths to people whose thinking is guided by God's Spirit.[b] [14] Those who are unbelievers reject the truths that *God's* Spirit teaches us, because they *consider those truths to be* foolish. They cannot understand them, because it is God's Spirit who enables us to evaluate those truths correctly, *and unbelievers do not have God's Spirit.* [15] We who have God's Spirit can judge correctly the *value of* all truths *that the Spirit reveals*, but *unbelievers* cannot evaluate us correctly. [16] As one *of our prophets wrote*, "No human has known what the Lord is thinking; no human is able to instruct him," but we believers **are** able to think *about things in the way that* Christ thinks *about them.*

3

1 Corinthians 3:1-4

THEME: I was unable to teach you difficult concepts because you were controlled by your self-directed nature, as evidenced by your quarreling about which leader you are loyal to.

[1] My fellow believers, *when I was with you*, I was not able to teach you as *I would teach people who are* controlled *by the Holy* Spirit. Instead, *I had to teach you as I would teach* people who are controlled by their self-directed nature. *I taught very simple concepts to you who had recently believed* in Christ, *as a parent would speak very simple words* to an infant. [2] I did not *teach* you *things that were difficult for you to understand, just as a woman does not* give *her baby* solid food *that the baby cannot chew and digest. And just as a woman breast-feeds her baby, I taught you simple spiritual concepts,* because at that time you were not able to understand difficult things. And you are still not able to understand difficult concepts, [3] because you are still controlled by your self-directed nature. Some of you are jealous and quarreling. That shows that your self-directed nature is controlling you! It shows that *you are acting like* unbelievers act. [4] By some of you saying, "I am *loyal to* Paul," and others saying, "I am *loyal to* Apollos," you show that *you are acting like* unbelievers.

---

[a]   OR, Only a person's spirit knows what that person is thinking.

[b]   OR, ...I teach spiritual *truths to* spiritual *people.*

1 Corinthians 3:5-9a

THEME: I preached the gospel to you first, and Apollos followed, but we are both serving God equally.

⁵ So what you really ought to think about Apollos and me is that we are just men who serve God. As a result of our *telling you the message about Christ*, you trusted in him. Both of us are just doing the work the Lord appointed us to do. ⁶ I was *the first one who preached God's message to you. I was like* someone who plants seeds. *Later,* Apollos *taught you more of God's message. That was like* someone who waters plants after they start to grow. But it is God who *enables people to grow spiritually, just as he is the one who* causes *plants* to grow. ⁷ So, *the person who first preaches God's message to people is not important, nor is the person who later teaches people more of God's message important, just as* it is not the person who plants the seeds or the person who waters the plants who is important. Instead, it is God, *who causes plants to grow and who causes people to grow spiritually, who is important.* ⁸ The person *who first preaches God's message to people and the one who later teaches them more of God's message* are both *trying to reach the* same goal. And *God* will reward each of them according to how they served him. ⁹ Remember that Apollos and I are both working together for God. *You don't belong to us.* Just as a field *belongs to its owner, not to those who work in it,* you belong to God, *not to us who work for him.*

1 Corinthians 3:9b-15

THEME: Those who teach believers must examine what they are teaching, because God will reward them only if their teaching is valuable and long-lasting.

Also, a house belongs to its owner. *It does not belong to the man who built it. In the same way, God is the one to whom you belong.* ¹⁰ *Just as* a skilled builder lays a foundation *before he builds a house*, as a result of God kindly helping me, *I was the first one who declared the message about Christ to you. And just as* others build a house on its foundation, there were *others who later taught you more about Christ.* But *just as those who build houses* must be careful about what materials they use to build them, those *who teach God's truth must be careful about what they teach.* ¹¹ Just as people can put in *only* one foundation *for a house, there is only one message we can give to people. That message is about* Jesus Christ. ¹² Furthermore, people can build a house on its foundation *with materials that are valuable and do not burn easily, such as* gold, silver, and expensive jewels. Or they can build a house with *materials that are not valuable and that burn easily, such as* wood, hay, and straw. ¹³ Later it will become clear what kind of material they used to build the house. *In the same way, when people teach*, it will later become clear *what kind of things they taught. God* will make that clear at the time *he judges us.* ¹⁴ When a fire *starts burning a house*, it becomes clear whether the builders used *materials in their* work *that will burn, or materials that will not burn*. Similarly, when God judges us, it will be clear whether we taught others things that were long-lasting and valuable, or not. If *the materials used to* build a house *are materials that* do not burn, the builder will receive a reward. *Similarly, if we have taught others things that are valuable and long-lasting, God will give us a reward.* ¹⁵ If *the things we have taught* are not valuable and long-lasting, *we will not get a reward.* We will be saved *from hell*, but *that is all we will get. We will be like a man who* escapes from a fire *without saving any of his possessions.*

1 Corinthians 3:16-17

THEME: God will destroy anyone who destroys the unity of a congregation.

[16] You need to remember that God *is present among* you *as he was present in the* Temple *in Jerusalem*. God's Spirit lives within you. [17] So, *just as* God will destroy anyone who tries to destroy his Temple, *he will destroy anyone who destroys the unity of a congregation. He will do that* because *he has set* you, *his people, apart for himself, just as he set* his Temple *apart for himself*.

1 Corinthians 3:18-23

THEME: Stop being proud about one Christian leader or another, because we are all just working for your benefit.

[18] Some among you think you are wise because unbelievers previously thought you were wise. Stop deceiving yourselves! *If you really want to be wise, by accepting what God considers to be wise* you should *be willing to let unbelievers consider you to be* foolish. [19] You should do that because things that unbelievers *consider to be* wise, God considers to be foolish. *We can learn from* the Scriptures *what God says about* that,

As to those who think they are wise, he messes up their plans by the mistakes they make!

[20] And *we can learn from* these words *of Scripture,*

The Lord considers as useless the thoughts of *humans who just think they are* wise.

[21] So stop boasting about *how good one Christian leader is or how good another Christian leader is*! All *of us exist as leaders only to help* you! [22] Specifically, don't boast about me, or about Apollos, or about Peter! Everything in the world exists to *benefit* you *believers*. Whether you live or whether you die, the things that are happening now or the things that will happen in the future, are all to bring benefit to you. [23] *You should boast about* Christ, *not about your leaders, because* you belong to him, and Christ belongs to God.

4

1 Corinthians 4:1-7

THEME: Stop judging your leaders' value; do not be proud of one and despise another.

[1] So people ought to consider us *apostles*[c] to be *merely* servants of Christ. God has given to us *the work of* telling others the message that he has now revealed to us. [2] With respect to doing that, those who are given work are required to do that work faithfully. [3] I am not concerned whether you or *the judges in* some court decide whether I have done my work faithfully or not. I do not even judge myself *about that*. [4] I do not think that I have done anything wrong, but that does not prove that I have done nothing wrong. The Lord is the one who judges me. [5] So stop judging any of us before the time *when God judges everyone*! Don't judge us before the Lord comes! He is the one who will reveal the sinful things people have done in secret. He will even reveal people's thoughts. At that time God will praise each person in a way *that each one deserves*.

---

[c] OR, *...Apollos and me...*

[6] My fellow believers, I have *told you* all these things as illustrations of myself and Apollos. I have done this for your sake, so that you may learn *to live according to* the saying, "Do not act contrary to what is written *in the Scriptures*." If you follow that rule, you will not be proud of one *spiritual leader* and despise another. [7] No one has made any of you superior to others. *All the abilities* that you have, you received *from God*. So if you received them all *from God*, why do you boast *thinking* "I got these abilities *from myself, not from God!*"?

1 Corinthians 4:8-13

THEME: *It is disgusting that you are so proud of your spiritual gifts and that you despise us apostles.*

[8] *It is disgusting that you act as though* you have already received everything you need *spiritually*. You act as though you were *spiritually* rich.[d] You act as though you have already begun to rule as kings with Christ. Well, I wish you really were ruling *with him*, so that we *apostles* might also rule with you! [9] But it seems to me that God has put us *apostles* on display at the end of the line. We are like men who have been condemned to die, who have been put in the arena where everyone can see *the wild animals* killing us. And not only people, but even angels, all over the world, *are watching us, as people* watch those who are performing a play *in a theater*. [10] Many people consider us to be fools because *we preach about* Christ, but you proudly think you are wise because of your close relationship with Christ. Many people *consider us* to be unimpressive, but you *proudly* think that you impress others. People respect you, but they don't respect us. [11] Up to this present time we have often been hungry. We have often been thirsty. We have ragged clothes. Often we have been beaten. We *have traveled so much that we* have no regular homes to live in. [12] We work very hard *to earn a living*. When *people* curse us, we *ask God to* bless them. When we are persecuted, we endure it. [13] When *people* slander us, we reply kindly to them. Up to this present time unbelievers *consider us worthless, as though we were* garbage and a rubbish heap.

1 Corinthians 4:14-17

THEME: *Imitate the way I serve Christ.*

[14] I am writing this to you, not to make you feel ashamed, but instead to warn you as *though you were* my dear children. [15] I say this because as *an apostle of* Christ Jesus I *was the first one who* proclaimed the good message to you. As a result, I was the one who enabled you to receive eternal life. So even if there were thousands of Christians who have instructed you, I was the only one who became *like* a father to you. [16] So I urge you to *live for Christ* the way I do. [17] In order to *help you do that*, I am sending Timothy to you. I love him *as though he were* my son. He serves the Lord faithfully. He will remind you of the way I conduct my life *as one who* has a close relationship with Christ Jesus. The way I conduct my life is the same as how I teach *others to conduct their lives* in all the congregations *to whom I have spoken*.

1 Corinthians 4:18-21

THEME: *I hope you will change your thinking so that I don't have to punish you when I come.*

[18] Some of you have become proud, thinking I will not come *to rebuke your congregation about what they are doing*. [19] But if the Lord wants me to come, I will come to you soon. Then I will not *pay any attention to* what those proud people say. Instead, I will find out

---

[d] OR, ...You act as though you had received all *the spiritual gifts you need*.

whether they have God's power. [20] Remember that God *judges whether or not we are letting him* rule *our lives,* not by *listening to how we* talk, but *by seeing if his* power *is present among us.* [21] So what do you prefer? Do you want me to come to you and punish you *because you have not changed your ways*, or shall I come to you and act lovingly and gently toward you *because you have done what I told you to do*?

5

1 Corinthians 5:1-5

THEME: You should expel the man in your congregation who has acted so immorally.

[1] *Now I want to discuss another matter.* It has been reported to me—and I believe it is true—that some people among you have been acting in a sexually immoral way, in a way that is so bad that not even people who do not know about God act that way. People tell me that a man is living with his stepmother.[e] [2] You should be sad about what that man is doing! *You* should have expelled him from your congregation! *But you haven't done that*, so it is disgusting that you are proud, *thinking you are spiritually mature!* [3] As for me, I have already decided *how you should* punish that man. And even though I am away from you, my spirit is with you, and you should do as I would do if I were there with you. [4] *What I have decided is that* when you have gathered together with the authority of our Lord Jesus, and my spirit is with you, and the power of our Lord Jesus *is with you,* [5] you should put that man into Satan's hands for his body to be punished, so that *he will turn away from his sinful behavior* and his spirit will be saved on the day when the Lord *returns.*

1 Corinthians 5:6-8

THEME: Make sure that no one in your congregation is acting immorally or maliciously or wickedly.

[6] It is not good that, *while you are letting that immoral man continue to be in your congregation*, you are boasting *about being spiritually mature.* You know that a small amount of yeast affects all the bread dough *into which it is put. Similarly, one person who continues to sin will have a bad effect on the whole congregation.* [7] So *just as we Jews* expel the old yeast *from our houses during the Passover celebration* so that we may have a fresh batch of dough without yeast in it, *you must expel such evil people from your congregation.* Do *that so that you can truly be holy people,* as *I know* you really are. Remember that Christ sacrificed himself *so that God could spare us from being punished for our sins, just as the Jews sacrificed lambs during* the Passover celebration *so that God would spare them.* [8] So let us celebrate *the fact that God has freed us from being punished for our sins, just as the Jews* celebrated Passover *to celebrate God freeing them from being slaves in Egypt. They made sure that there was* no old yeast in the dough. *They ate bread that* had no yeast in it. *In the same way, let us make sure that there are no people in our congregations who act* maliciously *toward others* or *live* wicked lives. Instead, *make sure that those in our congregations are ones who are* sincere and *speak* truthfully.

---

[e] OR, …with his father's other wife.

1 Corinthians 5:9-13

THEME: Expel wicked people from your congregation.

[9] In the previous letter I wrote to you, I said that you should not associate with sexually immoral people. [10] I did not mean that you should not associate with **unbelievers** who are immoral, or who desire things that belong to others, or who forcefully seize things that belong to others, or who associate with swindlers, or who worship idols. You would have to leave this world *to avoid all people* like that. [11] But now *I am making clear that* when I wrote, I *meant that* you should not associate with those who say they are fellow believers, if they are sexually immoral or if they are covetous and forcefully seize things that belong to others, or worship idols, or slander others, or become drunk. You should not associate with people like that, and you should not even eat with them! [12] It is certainly not my business to judge people who are not believers and who do not belong to *Christian congregations*. But it certainly is your business to judge those who are in *your congregations*. [13] God is the one who will judge those who are not believers. *Do as the Scriptures command:* "Expel the wicked person from your midst!"

6

1 Corinthians 6:1-6

THEME: It is disgusting that you prosecute fellow believers and let judges who are not believers decide your cases.

[1] *Now another matter.* When any of you *believers* accuses another believer about some matter, he takes that matter to judges who are not believers, *for them to decide the case,* instead of asking God's people *to decide it.* That is disgusting! [2] You should keep in mind that *we who are* God's people will *some day* judge those who are unbelievers. So, since you will be judging unbelievers, aren't you capable of judging between *believers who disagree on* small matters? [3] You should keep in mind that we will even judge angels! So we certainly should be able to judge *matters that relate to how we live* here on earth! [4] When you *believers* have a dispute, you choose as judges *to decide your case* people whom the congregation cannot respect *because those judges are not believers.* Why do you do that? [5] I am saying this to make you ashamed. Surely there is someone among you who is wise enough to judge disputes between believers! [6] But instead, some believers *among you* accuse other believers in a legal court. And what is worse, you let unbelievers judge the cases!

1 Corinthians 6:7-11

THEME: God has freed you from your former sinful behavior, so remember that he will exclude from his kingdom those who engage in all kinds of sinful behavior.

[7] The fact that you have **any** lawsuits among you *shows that* you have completely failed *as Christians.*[f] You should *allow other believers* to wrong you *without taking them to court!* You should not accuse them when *they* cheat you! [8] *But you aren't doing that.* Instead, some of you are cheating others and doing wrong to them. *That is bad.* But you are doing that to fellow believers, *and that is even worse!*

---

[f] OR, The fact that you have **any** lawsuits among you *shows that* you have *allowed Satan to* defeat you.

[9] You should keep in mind that wicked people will not become *members of* the group over whom God will rule. Do not deceive yourselves *by thinking wrongly about these matters.* People who are sexually immoral, or who worship idols, or who commit adultery, or who happily allow others to commit homosexual acts with them, or who take the initiative in committing homosexual acts, [10] or who are thieves, or who desire and forcefully seize things that belong to others, or who are drunkards, or who slander others, or who are swindlers, will not be among those over whom God rules. [11] Some of you previously did things like that. But *God* has freed you *from your sinful behavior. He* has set you apart for himself. *He* has erased the record of your sins *because you trusted* in the Lord Jesus Christ and because of what the Spirit of our God *has done for you.*

1 Corinthians 6:12-20

THEME: Because the Lord wants us to use our bodies in ways that please him, we must avoid all sexually immoral acts.

[12] *Some of you may say*, "God allows us to do anything *that he does not forbid.*" But *I would reply, "That is true*, but not everything that God permits us to do is helpful to us." *Yes, as some of you say*, God permits us to do anything *that he does not forbid.* But as for me, I will not let anything make me *its slave; that is, I will not let anything gain control over me in such a way that I will not be able to stop doing it.* [13] *Some of you may also say*, "Food is just for *us to put in* our stomachs, and our stomachs are just for *us to put* food *in.* And since God will do away with food and our stomachs *when he gives us our new bodies, what we do with our bodies sexually does not affect us any more than eating food does." But what you have concluded is wrong, because* the Lord does not *want us to use* our bodies to do sexually immoral things. Instead, the Lord *wants us to use our bodies in ways that please him.* Also, the Lord *wants us to do what is good* for our bodies. [14] God, by his power, caused the Lord *Jesus* to live again after he died, and he will cause us to live again after we die, *which shows that he is very concerned about our bodies.*

[15] You should keep in mind that your bodies belong to Christ. So should I *or any other believer* take our body, which belongs to Christ, and join it *sexually* to a prostitute? Never! [16] When a man has sexual relations with a prostitute, *it is as though* their two bodies become one body. You should never forget that! What *Moses* wrote *about people who join together sexually is*, "The two of them will become *as though they are* one body." [17] But those who are joined to the Lord become one with him spiritually.

[18] Always run away from doing sexually immoral acts. Other sins that people commit do not affect their bodies, but those who commit sexually immoral acts sin against their own bodies. [19] Keep in mind that your bodies are *like* temples of the Holy Spirit. The Spirit, whom God gave you, lives within you. You do not belong to yourselves. You belong to God, [20] *because when his Son died for you it was as though God* paid a price for you. So honor God by *how you use* your bodies!

7

1 Corinthians 7:1-7

THEME: Married people should not deprive their spouses of sexual relations, except under special conditions.

[1] Now *I will reply to* the things you wrote me about.

It is good for people not to get married. ²But since many people are committing sexually immoral acts, *which God detests*, every man should have his own wife *with whom he can have sexual relations*, and every woman should have her own husband *with whom she can have sexual relations*. ³Every man must continue having sexual relations with his wife, and every woman must continue having sexual relations with her husband. ⁴A man's wife does not have the right over her own body *to be the only one to decide about having sexual relations with her husband*. Instead, her husband also has a right *to have a part in that decision*. Similarly, a woman's husband does not have the right over his own body *to be the only one to decide about having sexual relations with his wife*. Instead, his wife also has a right *to have a part in that decision*. ⁵You may deny each other *of having sexual relations* only if you both agree to do that for a short time, in order that you may have more time to pray. Then after that, be sure that you begin having sexual relations again so that Satan will not be able to persuade you *to have sex with someone else* because of your inability to control your sexual desires.

⁶I am telling you these things to say that *God* allows *you to get married, but h*e does not say you **must** *get married*. ⁷I myself wish that all people would stay *single*, as I am. But God has enabled each person to live in different ways. He has enabled some people to *live without getting married*, and he has enabled other people to *get married*.

1 Corinthians 7:8-16

THEME: It is all right to get married, but it is wrong to get a divorce. However, you should not force an unbelieving spouse to keep on living with you.

⁸Now I want to say this to you unmarried people and to you whose spouses have died: It would be good for you to remain *unmarried,* as I am. ⁹But if you cannot control your *sexual desires*, you should get married. It is better to be married *so you can satisfy your sexual desires with your spouse* than to constantly have a burning desire *for sexual relations*.

¹⁰And now I will give a command for *believers who are* married. This is not a command from me alone; it also comes from the Lord Jesus. You married women must not divorce your husbands! ¹¹But if any of you do that, you must remain unmarried, or else you should be reconciled with your husband *and live with him again*. Similarly, men must not divorce their wives.

¹²Now I say this to the rest of you, *to those who became believers after they were married. This is what* I *am saying*, not what the Lord *has commanded*. If someone has a wife who is not a believer, if she is willing to keep living with him, he must not divorce her. ¹³Similarly, if a woman has a husband who is not a believer, if he is willing to keep living with her, she must not divorce him. ¹⁴*I say that* because God has set apart a woman's unbelieving husband because of his wife's *being a believer*, and God has set apart a man's unbelieving wife because of her husband's *being a believer*. If that were not true, *God would consider* their children unacceptable. But, in fact, *God does consider* them to be acceptable to him.

¹⁵However, if a husband who is not a believer or a wife who is not a believer wants to leave, let *him or her* do so. If that happens, the husband or wife who is a believer should not force the other one to stay. God has chosen us in order that we may live **peacefully.** ¹⁶*You who are believers should allow your unbelieving spouses to leave you if they want to*, because you women *who are believers*, there is no way you can be sure that God will

save your husbands if you stay together.[g] Similarly, you men *who are believers*, there is no way you can be sure that God will save your wives if you stay together.[h]

1 Corinthians 7:17-24

THEME: In general, everyone should remain in the status they had before they became believers.

[17] However, everyone should continue in the status the Lord gave them, the status they had when the Lord called them *to belong to himself*. That is the rule I tell people in all the congregations *where I speak*. [18] If a man had already been circumcised when he became a Christian, he should not *try to pretend that he is not* circumcised. If a man had not been circumcised before he became a Christian, he should not become circumcised. [19] *You should not try to change your status that way,* because it means nothing *to God* whether someone is circumcised or not. What is important is that we obey what God has commanded. [20] *Generally,* everyone should remain in the status they had when they became Christians. [21] If you were a slave when you became a Christian, don't be concerned about it. However, if you get an opportunity to be free, take advantage of the opportunity! [22] *Don't worry about previously being a slave*, because those who were slaves before they became Christians, the Lord has freed *from Satan's control*. Similarly, those who were not slaves before they became Christians, *it is as though* they are Christ's slaves *because they must do what he tells them.* [23] *Christ* paid a price to buy you *when he died for you.* So don't *act as if you are people's* slaves *by doing the evil things they tell you to do!* [24] My fellow believers, *I repeat that, in general* each believer, being in fellowship with God, should continue in the status he had before he became a Christian.

1 Corinthians 7:25-28

THEME: It is not sinful to get married, but married people will have a lot of problems.

[25] Now *I will answer your question* about women who have never married. There is nothing the Lord has commanded me *to write about them*, but I am writing this to tell you what I think *is best*, since the Lord *Jesus* has mercifully enabled what I *say* to be reliable. [26] Since there are a lot of distressing events *happening,*[i] I think it is better for people to remain in the status they now have. [27] If any of you *men* are married, don't try to divorce your wife. If any of you are unmarried, don't seek a wife. [28] But if *any of* you *men* get married, you haven't committed a sin *by doing that*. Likewise, if an unmarried woman gets married, she hasn't committed a sin *by doing that*. However, those who get married will have many troubles, *so I am urging you to remain unmarried in order that* you may not experience *such troubles*.

1 Corinthians 7:29-31

THEME: We believers should not devote our time to the affairs of this life.

[29] My fellow believers, this is what I mean: There is not much time left *before Christ returns*. So, from now on those men who are married should *devote themselves to serving the Lord as much* as they would if they were not married. [30] Those who are sad should *devote themselves to serving the Lord as much* as they would if they were not sad. Those

---

[g] OR, So do your best to live peacefully together, because perhaps your husbands will be saved if you stay together.

[h] OR, Similarly, you men *who are believers*, perhaps your wives will be saved if you stay together.

[i] OR, ...soon to come...

who are rejoicing *should devote themselves to serving the Lord as much* as they would if they were not rejoicing. [31] Those who are buying things should *devote themselves to serving the Lord as much* as they would if they did not possess those things. Since this world as it exists now will soon be gone, those who are actively involved in the affairs of this life *should not devote all their time* to be involved in those things.

1 Corinthians 7:32-35

THEME: It is better to remain unmarried, because married people are more concerned about pleasing their spouses than about how to please the Lord.

[32] *Another reason why I encourage you to remain unmarried is that* I desire that none of you be anxious *about the everyday affairs of this life.* Unmarried men are *able to be primarily* concerned about serving the Lord Jesus and trying to please him. [33] But married men are *often* greatly concerned about the affairs of this life. Specifically, they are concerned about pleasing their wives. [34] So their thinking is divided. Unmarried women are *able to be* concerned about serving the Lord. They want to set apart their minds and their bodies for the Lord. But married women are *often* concerned about the affairs of this life. Specifically, they are concerned about how to please their husbands. [35] I am telling you this for your own good. I am not saying it to put restrictions on you. Instead, I am saying it so that you may do what is proper and be able to serve the Lord without being distracted.

1 Corinthians 7:36-38

THEME: It is better for a man to decide his daughter should remain unmarried than that she should get married, but either decision is all right.

[36] *Some of you men have asked about your unmarried daughters. I suggest that* if any man thinks he may be treating his daughter unfairly *by keeping her from marrying*, and if it is already past *the right* time for her to get married, and he thinks she ought to be married, then he should do what he wants to do. He should let her get married. He will not be sinning *by doing that.* [37] But if a man feels absolutely sure *that it is better for his daughter not to get married*, and if nothing is forcing *her to get married*, and if he is free to make his own decision on the matter, if he decides that his daughter should not get married, then he is doing what is right in *keeping her from marrying.* [38] So any man who decides that his daughter should get married is doing what is good, but he who decides that his daughter should not get married is doing something even better.[j]

1 Corinthians 7:39-40-

THEME: Women whose husbands have died are free to get remarried, but only to believers. However, they will probably remain happier if they do not marry again.

[39] Women must remain married to their husbands as long as their husbands are still alive. But if a woman's husband dies, she is free to marry any *unmarried* man she wants to

---

[j]   OR, ...[36] *Some of you men have asked about the women to whom you are engaged to marry.* If any man thinks that he may be treating his fiancée unfairly *by not marrying her*, and if it is already past *the right* time for her to get married, and he wants to marry her very much, then he should do what he wants to do. He should marry her. He will not be sinning *by doing that.* [37] But if a man feels absolutely sure *that it is better* for him not to get married, and if nothing is forcing *them to get married*, if he is free to make his own decision on the matter, if he decides not to get married, he is doing what is right. [38] So any man who decides that he should get married to the woman he is engaged to is doing what is good, but he who decides he should not get married is doing something even better.

1 Corinthians 338

marry, but *she must marry someone who belongs to* the Lord. [40] However, I think that she will be happier if she does not marry again. And I believe that the Spirit of God is *directing me as I say that.*

8

1 Corinthians 8:1-3

THEME: We should not be proud because of knowing the truth about idols.

[1] Now *I will answer what you asked* about eating meat that has been sacrificed to idols. *We know what some of you say, that God has enabled* all of us *to* know *the truth about things such as idols. But often we become* proud because we say we know *all those things.* But instead of being proud about what we know, we should show that we love *our fellow believers by helping them to* become spiritually mature. [2] If anyone thinks he has come to thoroughly know something, he does not yet know it as he should. [3] But as for those who love God, they know that they belong to him.

1 Corinthians 8:4-6

THEME: There are many idols that people think are gods, but there is only one true God.

[4] So *I will tell you* about eating meat that has been sacrificed to idols. We know that it is true—*as you say*—that idols are not really alive. We also know that there is only one true God. [5] It is true that there are gods whom people think live in the heavens or whom they think live on earth. Truly, there are many beings that *people* call gods, and whom *they* call lords. [6] But for us *believers* there is only one true God. He is *our heavenly* Father, who created everything. He is the one we *worship and serve.* Also, for us believers, Jesus Christ is the one and only Lord. He is the one through whom *God* created everything. And It is because of what he *has done* that we have *spiritual* life.

1 Corinthians 8:7-13

THEME: Do not eat meat offered to idols if that would encourage other believers to eat that meat contrary to their conscience.

[7] Nevertheless, some people don't understand *that idols are not alive.* In the past, some among you who are believers now were accustomed to believing that idols *were alive.* As a result, when they eat such meat *now,* they still think that it was sacrificed to an idol *that is alive.* They are not sure *that God allows believers to eat meat that has been offered to idols.* So *when they eat such meat,* they think they have sinned. [8] But God will not think more highly about us *if we eat certain* foods, or if we don't eat *certain foods.* That is, we are not more acceptable to God if we do not eat certain foods, nor are we more acceptable to him if we eat those foods. [9] However, be sure that you don't do anything that God allows you to do, if by doing that you would encourage any of *your fellow believers to do something that* they are not sure *God allows them to do.* As a result, you would be causing them to sin. [10] For example, you know *that idols are not alive.* Suppose you eat *food that has been sacrificed to idols* in a temple *where* idols *are worshipped.* Suppose someone who is not sure God allows us to eat that food sees you eating it. *You* would be encouraging that person to eat it, too. [11] As a result, you who know that *idols are not really alive* might cause that fellow believer, one for whom Christ died, to be ruined *spiritually.* [12] By sinning against fellow believers, causing them to do something they think God does not allow us to do, *it is as though* you are sinning against Christ himself! [13] So if *I, Paul,*

know that by eating a certain food I might cause a fellow believer to be ruined spiritually, I will never eat such food again. I don't want to cause any fellow believer to be ruined spiritually. *And you should do as I do.*

9

1 Corinthians 9:1-2

THEME: As your apostle, I am free to do anything God allows me to do.

[1] I am certainly free *to do all the things God allows me to do. You know th*at I am an apostle. *You know that* I have seen Jesus our Lord. It is a result of **my** work that you *have believed in* the Lord *Jesus.* [2] And even though other people may think I am not an apostle, you certainly should know that I am. *Remember that* your having become Christians *as a result of my telling you about* the Lord confirms that I am an apostle.

1 Corinthians 9:3-7

THEME: Barnabas and I have the same right to receive financial support that the other apostles have.

[3] In order to defend myself, this *is what I say* to those who criticize me *by claiming that I do not act like an apostle*: [4] As for Barnabas and me, certainly we have the right *as apostles* to receive food and drink *from you and other congregations for our work.* [5] The other apostles and the Lord Jesus' *younger* brothers and especially Peter each take along a wife who is a believer *when they travel various places in order to tell people about Christ. And they also have a right to receive support for their wives from the people they work among.* So, Barnabas and I certainly have those same rights. [6] It would be ridiculous to think that Barnabas and I are the only apostles who must work to earn money to pay our expenses *while we are doing God's work!* [7] Soldiers certainly don't pay their own wages. Those who plant a vineyard would certainly eat some of the grapes *from the vineyard.* Those who care for sheep would certainly drink the milk from those sheep. *Similarly, those who tell others about Christ certainly have a right to receive food from the people to whom they preach.*

1 Corinthians 9:8-18

THEME: God's servants have always had the right to receive support from others, but we have not insisted on that right, because we wanted to preach the gospel without charge.

[8] I am saying that not only because people think it is right. I am saying it because it is what *God said* in the laws *he gave Moses.* [9] Moses wrote in one of those laws, "While an ox is threshing *grain,* you must not tie its mouth shut *so that it cannot eat the grain.*" God was not only concerned about oxen *when he gave that law.* [10] He was concerned about us also! Yes, *God caused Moses to* write that *because he was concerned* about us! Someone who plows the ground, confidently expects *to eat some of* the crop *that grows.* Anyone who threshes grain, confidently expects *to eat some of the grain he threshes. Similarly, we who proclaim the message about Christ have the right to confidently expect to receive financial help for our work.* [11] And since we have proclaimed God's message to you, we certainly have the right to receive from you the things we need for our bodies. [12] Since other people *who preached to you* had that right, certainly Barnabas and I have the same right!

However, neither of us insisted *that you give us the things* we have a right *to receive from you*. Instead, we were willing to endure anything in order that we not hinder *anyone from believing* the message about Christ. [13] You should keep in mind that *the priests and servants* in the Temple eat *some of the food that people bring to* the Temple. Specifically, the priests who work at the altar eat some of *the food that the people bring to sacrifice on* the altar. [14] So the Lord has directed that those who proclaim the good message *about him* should receive what they need to live on from *those who hear that* message.

[15] However, I have not asked you to *give me* those things that I have a right *to receive from you*. Furthermore, I am writing this to you, not to ask you to start *giving me financial help now*. I would rather die than *receive help from you*. I don't want anyone to prevent me from boasting *about proclaiming God's message to you without receiving financial help from you*. [16] When I proclaim the message about Christ, I can't boast *about doing it*, because *Christ* has commanded me *to do it*. I would be very miserable[k] if I did not proclaim that message. [17] If I had decided by myself to proclaim it, *God* would reward me. But I did not decide that by myself. I am simply doing the work that *God* entrusted to me. [18] So perhaps you wonder what my reward is. *So I will tell you*. When I proclaim the good message *about Christ*, I don't ask people for financial help. It *makes me very happy not to ask for help, and being happy is the* reward I get. I do not want to use the rights I have *when I proclaim* the good message.

1 Corinthians 9:19-27

THEME: I have adopted the code of conduct of whatever group I have been among, in order to bring more people to Christ.

[19] I am not obligated to do what anyone else thinks I should do. Nevertheless, when I have been with any group of people, I have made myself *do what they believed I should do, just as a slave does what his master wants him to do*. I have done that in order that I might convince more people *to trust in Christ*. [20] Specifically, when I was with fellow Jews, I did the things that Jews *think people should do*. I did that so that I might convince some of them *to trust in Christ*. Although I am now not obligated to obey all the Jewish laws and rituals, when I was with those who believe they are obligated to obey those laws, I did those things they *think people should do*. I did that in order to convince some of them *to trust in Christ*. [21] When I was with non-Jews, I did those things that non-Jews *think people should do*, in order that I might convince some of them *to trust in Christ*. I do not mean that I disobey God's laws. No! I obey the things that Christ commanded us to do. [22] When I was with those who doubt *whether God permits them to do certain things that others disapprove of*, I *avoided doing those things*, so that I might convince some of them *to trust in Christ*. In summary, I have done all the things *that the people I have been with think others should do*, in order that by every possible means I might convince some of them *to trust in Christ*. [23] I do all these things in order that *more people will believe* the message about Christ, and in order that I, along with other believers, may receive the blessings *God promises to give us*.

[24] You certainly know that when people run in a race, they all run, but only one of them wins the race and as a result gets a prize. So, *just as it is* the runner *who exerts himself fully who wins a race, you should exert yourselves fully to do the things God wants you to do*, so that you may receive the reward *God wants to give you*. [25] All athletes exercise their bodies strenuously in many ways. They do that in order to receive a wreath *to wear on their heads as a reward*. Those wreaths fade away, but we will receive a reward that will last forever. [26] For that reason, I *try hard to please God, like a* runner who keeps the goal

---

k   OR, ...*I fear that* God would punish me...

in sight. I *try hard to accomplish what God wants me to accomplish, like* a boxer who tries hard to hit his opponent, and not to miss hitting him. [27] I beat my body *to make it do what I want it to do, as* slaves *do what their masters want them to do*, in order that, after I have proclaimed *God's message* to others, he will not *say that I* don't deserve to receive a reward.

10

1 Corinthians 10:1-5

THEME: Our Jewish ancestors all experienced God's power, but nearly all of them died in the desert because they sinned against him.

[1] My fellow believers, I want to remind you that **all** of our *Jewish* ancestors were under the cloud *by which God miraculously led them and protected them when they left Egypt with Moses.* **All** those ancestors crossed the Red Sea *after God miraculously made the water separate so that they could walk through it.* [2] God caused **all** of them to begin to live under the authority of Moses *when they walked* under that cloud and *walked through the Red Sea.* [3] **All** *those ancestors of ours ate the same food that God* miraculously *provided.* [4] They **all** drank water that *God* miraculously *provided.* That is, they all drank water that God miraculously made flow out of the rock. That rock was *a symbol of* Christ who went with them. *So we conclude that God helped all of those people in many ways.* [5] However, *we also conclude that* God was angry with **most** of them *because they sinned against him. He caused nearly all of them to die, and as* a result their bodies were scattered all over the desert.

1 Corinthians 10:6-13

THEME: What happened to our Jewish ancestors was a warning of what will happen to us if we give in to temptation.

[6] Those things *that happened long ago* became examples to teach us *the following things*: We should not desire to *do* evil things, as those people desired to do. [7] We should not worship idols as many of those people did. *Remember that Moses* wrote, "The people sat down and ate and drank *to honor the golden calf they had just made.* Then they got up to dance *immorally.*" [8] We should not have sexual relations with someone to whom we are not married, as many of them did. As a result God *punished them by* causing twenty-three thousand people to die in only one day. [9] We should not try to see how much we can sin without the Lord punishing us. Some of them did that, and as a result they died because *poisonous* snakes *bit them.* [10] We should not complain *about what God does.* Some of them did that, and as a result an angel destroyed them. *So God will certainly punish us if we sin like they did.*

[11] All those things *that happened to our ancestors long ago* are examples for us. *Moses* wrote those things to warn us *who are living now.* We are the people for whom God has fulfilled *the things he purposed in* the previous periods of time. [12] So *I say this to* those who confidently *think they will always* steadfastly continue to *believe what God said, and who think they will never disobey what he commanded*: Be careful that you do not sin when you are tempted. [13] *Remember that* your desires to sin are the same desires that other people have. But when you are tempted to sin, you can trust God *to help you.* He will not permit you to be tempted more than you are able to resist. Instead, when you are tempted, he will also provide a way *for you* to endure it *without sinning.*

1 Corinthians 10:14-22

THEME: If we participate in demon worship by eating food sacrificed to demons when we eat the Lord's Supper, God will punish us.

[14] So, *I say to* you people whom I love, *avoid* worshiping idols *just as you would* run away from *anything that is dangerous.* [15] It is to people who *say they* are wise that I write. So, **you,** as wise people, judge whether what I am writing *is true.* [16] *During the Lord's Supper, after we ask God to* bless the *juice in the* cup, we give thanks for it *and drink it.* By doing that, we certainly are sharing in what Christ *did for us when* his blood *flowed from his body when he died. During the Lord's Supper, when we break* the bread *and eat it,* we are certainly sharing in what Christ *did for us when* his body *suffered for us on the cross.* [17] Since it is one loaf of bread that we *break and eat during the Lord's Supper, it symbolizes that* we who are many are one group, because we all eat from the one loaf.

[18] Consider *what happens when* the Israelite people *eat the food that the priests* sacrifice on the altar *outside the Temple.* They participate in *what the priests do at* the altar. *Similarly, if you eat food that non-believers have offered to an idol in a temple, you are participating in their worship of the idol there.* [19] By saying that*, I* do not mean that offering food to an idol makes it anything *more than just ordinary food.* Nor do I mean that an idol is anything *more than just an idol.* [20] No! Instead, I mean that what people sacrifice *to idols,* they are sacrificing to demons, not to God. So, *if you eat food that has been sacrificed to idols, you are participating in worshiping the demons that the idols represent.* And I do not want you to participate in worshiping demons! [21] When you drink the juice in the cup *at the Lord's Supper*, you cannot participate in the *blessings* the Lord *Jesus* brought to us and at the same time drink from *the* cup the *wine* people offer to demons! When you eat at the Lord's table, you cannot participate in the blessings the Lord provided when he died for us and at the same time participate in the things that represent demons *by eating food that has been sacrificed to idols!* [22] *If you participate in honoring demons in that way*, you will certainly make the Lord very angry. Remember that you are certainly not stronger than he is, *so you will not escape his punishment if you honor demons in that way*!

1 Corinthians 10:23-11:1

THEME: It is all right to eat food offered to idols, but we should not do so if it would offend those who think it is wrong.

[23] *Some people say,* "God permits *believers to do* anything." But *I say that* not everything people do is beneficial *to them!* Yes, *some people say,* "God permits believers to do all things." But not everything people do helps them to become *spiritually* mature. [24] No one should try to benefit *only* himself. Instead, each person should try to benefit others *spiritually.* [25] *So this is what you should do*: Eat any *food* that is sold in the market. Don't ask questions *to find out if that food has been offered to idols, just* because you think it would be wrong *to eat such food.* [26] *Remember that the Psalmist wrote,* "Everything on the earth belongs to *the* Lord *God because he created it!*" So, *food that has been offered to idols belongs to the Lord, not to the idols.* [27] If a non-believer invites you to a meal, go if you want to, and eat any food that is set before you. Don't ask *whether it was offered to idols, just* because you think it would be wrong *to eat such food.* [28] But if someone says to you, "This is food that was sacrificed *to an idol*," don't eat it, for the sake of the person who told that to you, and also because someone may think it is wrong *to eat such food.* [29] I do not mean that **you** *should be concerned about whether it is all right to eat such food.* What I mean is that you should be concerned about **others** who may think it is wrong to eat such food. Since I know that I am free *to eat such food without God punishing me,* no one should say that what I am doing is wrong just because he himself thinks it is wrong. [30] If

I thank *God* for the food when I eat *food that has been offered to an idol*, no one should criticize me for eating food for which I have thanked God!

[31] So, *in conclusion, I say to you,* when you eat *food*, or drink *something*, or do anything else, do **everything** in order that *people will* praise God. [32] Do not offend Jews or Greeks *who are not believers*, and do not offend members of God's congregations. [33] *Do as I do.* I try *not to offend people.* Instead, I try to please everyone in every way. I do this by not seeking to benefit myself. Instead, I try to benefit many others, in order that they may be saved *from the guilt of their sins.*

11 [1] *Follow my example*, just as I *try to* follow Christ's example.

1 Corinthians 11:2-16

THEME: Women should wear a hair covering while praying or prophesying in a service, but men should not do so.

[2] I praise you because you remember all the things *I taught you* and because you follow the instructions I gave you. You have done just as I told you. [3] *Now,* I want you to know that the one who has authority over every man is Christ, and the ones who have authority over women are men,[l] and the one who has authority over Christ is God. [4] *So if any man wears a covering over* his head when he prays or speaks a message God gave him, he disgraces himself. [5] Also, if any woman does not wear a covering over her head when she prays or speaks a message God gave her, she disgraces herself.[m] That would be acting like *women who are ashamed because* their heads have been shaved. [6] So, if women do not wear coverings over their heads *when they pray or speak messages God gave them*, they should let someone shave their heads *so they will be ashamed.* But since women are ashamed if their hair is *short* or shaved off, they should wear coverings over their heads *when they pray or speak messages God gave them.* [7] Men should not wear coverings over their heads *when they pray or speak messages that God gave them*, because men represent what God is like, and they show how great God is. But women show how great men are.[n] [8] *Remember that God intends for men to have authority over women. We know that* because *God* did not make *the first* man, *Adam,* from the *first* woman, *Eve.* Instead, he made that woman *from a bone he took* from the man. [9] Also, *God* did not create *the first* man *to help* the woman. Instead, *he* created the woman *to help* the man. [10] For that reason, women should wear something *to cover* their heads *as a symbol of their being under their husbands'* authority. They should also cover their heads so that the angels *will see that and rejoice.*

[11-12] However, remember that even though *God created the first* woman from *the first* man, *now* it is women who *give birth* to men. So men cannot be independent of women, nor can women be independent of men. But all things, *including men and women*, come from God. [13] Consider this for yourselves: Is it proper for women to pray to God while they don't have coverings over their heads? [14] Everyone senses that it is disgraceful for men to have long hair. [15] But it is very delightful for women to have long hair, because *God* gave them long hair to be like a covering *for their heads.* [16] But whoever wants to argue *with me about my saying that women should have a covering over their heads when they pray or speak a message from God* should consider the fact that we *apostles* do not *permit* any other custom, and the *other* congregations of God do not have any other custom.

---

[l]   OR, ...are their husbands...

[m] OR, ...she disgraces her husband.

[n]   OR, ...But women show how great their husbands are.

1 Corinthians 11:17-22

THEME When you gather to eat the Lord's Supper, you act selfishly. I cannot praise you for that.

[17] Concerning the matters *about which I will instruct you now*, I do not praise you, because whenever you believers meet together, good *things do not happen.* Instead, **bad things** *happen.* [18] First of all, people have told me that when you gather together as a group *to worship God*, you divide into groups *that are hostile to each other.* To some extent I believe that is true. [19] It seems that you must divide into *groups that despise each other* in order that it might be clear which people among you *God* approves of! [20] When you gather together, you eat the meal *that you say is in memory of the death of* the Lord *Jesus.* [21] But *what happens when* **you** eat it is that each person eats his own meal before *he thinks about sharing his food with anyone else.* As a result, *when the meal is over*, some people are *still* hungry and others are drunk! *So it is not a meal that honors the Lord.* [22] *You act as though* you do not have your own houses in which you can eat and drink *whatever you want to*! Anyone would conclude *that by acting selfishly in this way*, it is God's people whom you are despising, and it is the poor people *in your group* whom you are treating as though they were not important. What shall I say to you about that? Do *you expect* me to praise you *about what you do*? I certainly will not praise you!

1 Corinthians 11:23-26

THEME: The Lord gave us instructions about the significance of the Lord's Supper.

[23] The Lord taught me these things that I also taught you: During the night that Jesus was betrayed,[o] he took some bread. [24] After he thanked God for it, he broke it into pieces. *Then he gave it to his disciples* and said, "This bread *represents* my body, which *I am about to sacrifice* for you.[p] Eat bread in this *way again and again* to remember my *offering myself as a sacrifice for you.*" [25] In the same way, after the meal, he took a cup *of wine.* He *thanked God for it. Then he gave it to his disciples*, saying, "*The wine in* this cup *represents* my blood[q] *that will flow from my body to put into effect* the new agreement *that God is making with people.* Whenever you drink wine in this way, do it to remember that *my blood flowed for you.*" [26] *Remember that* until the Lord *Jesus* returns *to the earth*, whenever you eat the *bread that represents his body* and drink the wine *that represents his blood*, you are telling other people that he died *for you.*

1 Corinthians 11:27-34

THEME: God punishes those who eat the Lord's Supper in a way that does not express the unity of his people.

[27] So, those who eat this bread and drink this wine in a way that is not suitable *for those who belong to the Lord* are guilty of *acting in a way that is contrary to what* our *Lord intended when he offered* his body *as a sacrifice* and his blood *flowed when he died.* [28] Before any believer eats that bread and drinks that wine, he should think carefully about *what he is doing*, [29] because if anyone eats *the bread that represents Christ's body* and drinks *the wine that represents his blood* without recognizing that all God's *people should be united, God will* punish him *for doing that.* [30] Many people in your group are weak and sick, and several have died because of *the way they acted when they ate that bread and*

---

[o] OR, ...During the night that *Judas* enabled *the enemies of* the Lord Jesus to seize him...

[p] OR, ...This bread *is* my body, which *I am about to sacrifice* for you.

[q] OR, ...*The wine in* this cup *is* my blood...

drank that wine. ³¹ If we would think carefully about what we *are doing*, *God* would not judge *and punish* us *like that.* ³² But when the Lord judges *and punishes* us *for acting wrongly*, he disciplines us *to correct us*, in order that he will not *need to* punish us when he punishes *the people who do not trust in Christ.*

³³ So, my fellow believers, when you gather together to eat *food to remember the Lord's death for you*, wait until everyone *has arrived so you can find out who does not have enough food.* ³⁴ Those who are so hungry *that they can't wait to eat until everyone else has arrived* should eat in their own homes *first*, in order that when you gather together God will not judge *and punish them for being inconsiderate of others.*

And when I come *to Corinth* I will give you instructions about other matters *concerning the Lord's Supper.*

12

1 Corinthians 12:1-3

THEME: It is only God's Spirit who enables people to say that Jesus is Lord.

¹ Now, my fellow believers, *I will answer what you asked* about the things God's Spirit *enables believers to do.* I want you to know clearly *about these things.* ² You know that before you became Christians, various things led you to *worship* idols, which are unable to tell you *any of God's message.* ³ So *the first thing* I will tell you now is that it is not the Spirit of God who would cause anyone to say "Jesus deserved to die," and the Holy Spirit is the only one who can enable anyone to say "Jesus is *truly* the Lord."

1 Corinthians 12:4-11

THEME: God's Spirit gives believers special abilities as he desires.

⁴ There are various things *God's* Spirit enables *us believers to do*, but it is that same Spirit *who enables all of us to do them.* ⁵ There are many different ways to serve *the Lord*, but it is the same Lord *whom we all are serving.* ⁶ *We believers* have the power to do many *tasks*, but it is the same God who gives all of us the power *to do* those things.

⁷ *God's* Spirit gives his power to each believer in order to benefit all the other *believers.* ⁸ To some, the Spirit gives the ability to speak with wisdom. To others, the same Spirit gives the ability to know *things he reveals to them.* ⁹ To others, the same Spirit gives the ability to believe *that God will work a miracle.* To others, the Spirit gives the ability to heal *sick people.* ¹⁰ To others, he gives the power *to perform* miracles. To others he gives the ability to speak messages that come directly from God. To others he gives the ability to tell *if a message is really from God or not.* To others he gives the ability to speak messages in languages *they have not learned.* To others he gives the ability to tell the meaning of those messages. ¹¹ It is the same one Spirit who gives all these abilities. He gives whatever abilities he wants to give, to whoever he wants to give them.

1 Corinthians 12:12-31

THEME: A congregation needs all the abilities that God's Spirit gives to its members, but you should especially desire the ones that help others the most.

¹² Although a person's body has many parts, all the parts form just one body. It is the same way *with those who belong to* Christ. ¹³ When we were baptized, the one *Holy* Spirit

caused us to become one group *of believers*. It does not matter if we are Jews or non-Jews. It does not matter if we are slaves or not slaves. *When we believed in Christ*, the one Spirit came to live within all of us.

¹⁴ Our bodies do not have only one part. They have many parts *with different functions*. ¹⁵ If our foot could *talk and* say *to us*, "Because I am not *your* hand, I am not a part of *your* body," it would still be a part of *our* body. ¹⁶ If our ear could *talk and* say, "Because I am not *your* eye, I am not a part of your body," it would still be a part of our body. ¹⁷ If our body were just an eye, we would not be able to hear! If our body were only an ear, we would not be able to smell anything! ¹⁸ But the truth is that God has put all the parts of our bodies together just as he wanted to. ¹⁹ If *our body* had only one part, it would not be a body. ²⁰ But the truth is that there are many parts *in our body*, but it is still only one body. ²¹ That is why if our eye *could talk*, it should never say our hand, "I don't need you!" And if our head *could talk*, it should not say to our feet, "I don't need you!" ²² Instead, the parts of our body that seem to be weaker are the ones that are absolutely necessary. ²³ And the parts that we do not think highly of are the parts we clothe carefully. And we protect carefully those parts that we do not show to people. ²⁴ The parts that are *all right to* show people, we do not need to protect. Instead, **God,** who has put all the parts of our bodies together, causes us to care for in a special way the parts that we think are less important. ²⁵ He does that in order that all the parts of our body will work together harmoniously, and so that all the parts will care for all the other parts equally. ²⁶ If one part of our body hurts, *it is as though* all the parts of our body are hurting. If we pay special attention to one part of our body, *it is as though* all the parts of our body feel pleasure.

²⁷ *Everything I have just said about how the parts of our bodies relate to each other applies to how* all of you who belong to Christ *should relate to each other*. Each of you belongs to him, *but you have not all been given the same abilities and work*. ²⁸ God has placed apostles in our congregations. They are first *in rank*. Next in rank are those who speak messages that come directly from God. Next in rank are those who teach *spiritual truth*. Then there are those who have the power to work miracles, those who have the ability to heal *sick people*, those who have the ability to help others, those who have the ability to govern *the affairs of the congregation*, and those who have the ability to speak messages in languages *they have not learned*. ²⁹ Certainly not all *believers* are apostles. They all do not have the ability to speak messages that come directly from God. They do not all have the ability to teach spiritual truth. They do not all have the power to work miracles. ³⁰ They do not all have the ability to heal people. They do not all have the ability to speak messages in languages *they have not learned*. They do not all have the ability to tell others the meaning of those messages. ³¹ *Certainly not!* But you should eagerly desire to have *the abilities that will help other believers* the most.^r But now I will tell you the best way *to use the abilities God's Spirit has given you*.

13

1 Corinthians 13:1-13

THEME: We should use the abilities God's Spirit has given us in ways that show we love others.

¹ If we could speak *all* the various languages that people *in the world speak* and even speak *the language* that angels *speak*, if we did not love *others, speaking those languages* would be *as useless as beating* a brass gong or clanging cymbals *together*. ² If

---

^r OR, …But you should eagerly desire to have *the abilities God considers* the most important.

we had the ability to speak messages that come directly from God, and if we could understand the plans that he has not yet revealed to others, and if we could know everything *about everything*, and if we believed in God so strongly that we could *do impossible things like* causing mountains to move, if we did not love *others, God would consider all that* to be worthless. ³ If we would give everything we own to poor people, and if we would let others kill us in order that we could boast about *sacrificing our* own bodies, if we did not love *others*, we would not get any reward *from God*.

⁴ *Those who truly* love *others act* patiently and kindly *toward them. Those who truly* love *others* are not jealous *of them*, they do not boast *about what they themselves have done*, and they are not proud. ⁵ *Those who truly* love *others* do not act in disgraceful ways towards them. *They do* not think only of themselves and what they want. *They do* not quickly become angry. *They do* not keep remembering the bad things *that others have done to them*. ⁶ *Those who truly* love *others* do not rejoice when *people do* evil things, but *they do* rejoice when *people act* righteously. ⁷ *Those who truly* love *others* patiently endure *the faults of others. They do* not quickly assume *that others have done something bad. They* confidently expect *that others will act righteously. They* patiently endure *all their own troubles*.

⁸ *We should* never *let anything* stop *us from continuing to* love *others. As for the ability to* speak messages that come directly from God, *some day* that will come to an end. *As for the ability to* speak languages *that we have not learned, our ability to do that* will *also* come to an end some day. And as for the ability to know things that God reveals to us, our *ability to do that* will come to an end *some day because it will not be necessary any more.* ⁹ *God does* not reveal everything to us, and we cannot know everything *he knows*. ¹⁰ But *when everything is* perfect *after Christ returns, things that are* not perfect, *such as the abilities God's Spirit gives us*, will come to an end. ¹¹ When we were children, we talked like children *talk*, we thought like children *think*, we reasoned like children *reason*. But when we grew up, we got rid of our childish ways. *Similarly, you need to get rid of your childish thinking about the abilities the Spirit has given you.* ¹² In this life we do not understand everything fully. *It is like* looking at something *indirectly by seeing it in* a mirror. But when *we get to heaven*, we will *understand everything clearly. It will be like* talking to someone face to face. Now we know only part *of everything God wants us to know*. Then we will know everything *completely*, just as *God* knows us completely. ¹³ So now there are three things *that we must* continue *to do*: To trust *in God*, to confidently expect *to receive what he will give us*, and to love *others*. But the greatest of those three things is loving *others*.

14

1 Corinthians 14:1-25

THEME: Speaking messages that come directly from God will help believers much more than speaking messages in unknown languages.

¹ You must want to love others more *than you love anything else*. But you should *also* eagerly desire the abilities that *God's* Spirit *gives to believers*. And you should desire most of all to have the ability to speak messages that come directly from God. ²⁻³ I say that because those who speak messages that come directly from God *are speaking in languages they and the other believers in the congregation know, and thus* they are able to strengthen them *spiritually* and to encourage and comfort them. But those who speak in languages *they have not learned* are not speaking to people. Instead, they are *only* speaking to God. No one understands them. By *the power of God's* Spirit, they speak

1 Corinthians 348

things that others do not know.^{s} ^{4}Those who speak in languages *they have not learned* are receiving a blessing for themselves, but those who speak messages that come directly from God are giving a blessing to *all the believers in* the congregation.

^{5}I would like you all to have the ability to speak in languages *you have not learned*. But I would like even more for you to have the ability to speak messages that come directly from God. If someone speaks a message in a language that he has not learned, and if no one is there who can explain the meaning, it is not helpful to the congregation. *If believers* speak messages that come directly from God, that is very helpful.

^{6}My fellow believers, suppose I came to you and spoke to you in a language none of you knows *and I did not explain the meaning of what I told you*. Even if I told you something that God had revealed to me, or if I told you some message that had come directly from him, or if I taught you something you needed to know *but spoke in another language*, my message certainly would not help you! ^{7}*Think about* lifeless *musical instruments*, like flutes and harps *for example*. When they are played, if the notes are not played clearly, no one will know what tune is being played. ^{8}If someone playing the trumpet *wants to signal that the soldiers should prepare to fight a battle*, the soldiers certainly will not get ready if *the call to battle* is not played clearly. ^{9}It is the same with you! If you do not speak words that other people can understand, no one will know what you are saying. *It will be as though* you are just speaking to the air! ^{10}There are many different languages in the world, and all of them convey meaning *to the people who know those languages*. ^{11}But if we do not understand the language someone is speaking, *it will be as though* that person is a foreigner to us, and we will be foreigners to him. ^{12}So *I say this to* you: Since you are eager to have the abilities that God's Spirit gives, earnestly desire those abilities that will do the most to help *all the believers in* the congregation!

^{13}So, those who have the ability to speak in languages *they have not learned* should pray that *God will give them the ability to* explain the meaning of what they say. ^{14}If they pray in a language *they have not learned*, their spirits are praying, but they are not using their minds. ^{15}So I will tell you what we should do. *At times* we may pray, *using* only our spirits, *in languages we have not learned. And at other times* we should pray using our minds, *thinking about the words we are praying. Similarly*, at times we may sing using only our spirits, using languages we have not learned, and at other times we should sing using our minds, *thinking about the words we are singing.* ^{16}Suppose any one of you praises God,^{t} only using your spirit *and not using your mind*. Maybe some *will be present who* do not know about *the abilities God's Spirit gives believers*. Since they do not know what you are saying, after you thank God, they will not know when to say "Amen." ^{17}You may be thanking God very well, but you are not helping that other person. ^{18}I thank God that I speak in languages *that I have not learned* more than any of you do. ^{19}But during a worship service, *in order that others will understand what I am saying*, I would prefer to speak five words using my mind, in order that I may teach others, rather than to speak ten thousand words in a language *that that is not understood by the congregation.*

^{20}My fellow believers, stop being like little children in the way you think *about these abilities that God's Spirit gives*! Instead, think about them in a mature way. If you really want to be like little children, do as few wicked things as babies do! ^{21}*When the Jews long ago refused to obey God, he warned them what would happen when he allowed their enemies to punish them.* In the Scriptures, the Lord *God* said:

I will send people from foreign *lands to attack* my people.

Those foreigners will speak strange languages.

---

^{s} OR, …From within *their own* spirit, they speak things that others do not know.

^{t} OR, Suppose any one of you thanks God for what he as done…

In that way, I will warn my people,
   but they will still not pay attention to what I say.

[22] If we speak in languages *that we have not learned*, unbelievers *who are there will realize that the Spirit of God is truly among us.* That will warn them *that they need to fear God.* But believers do not *need such a warning.* [23] Suppose during your worship service everyone started to speak in languages *they have not learned*. If unbelievers or people who do not know *about the abilities God's Spirit gives believers* come in *and hear that*, they will surely think that you are crazy. [24] But if an unbeliever or someone who does not know *about those abilities* comes in while all of you believers are *one by one* speaking messages that come directly from God, everything you *say* will show that person that he is a sinner and that *God* will punish him *if he does not turn from his sinful ways.* [25] He will realize that *God knows the evil things he has done that* other people don't know. Then he will kneel down and worship God and say, "God is truly among you!"

1 Corinthians 14:26-40

THEME: Believers should all be prepared to participate in an orderly way during worship services.

[26] So, my fellow believers, I will tell you what I think you should be doing. When you come together *to worship God*, some of you may have hymns to sing. Others may have something to teach *the congregation*. Others may have *something to say that God has* revealed to them. Others may give messages in languages *they have not learned*. Others will explain the meaning of those messages. Make sure all of these things that you do will make the congregation become more mature spiritually. [27] *It is all right* if two people, or at the most three people, speak in languages *they have not learned*. But they must speak one at a time, and someone must explain the meaning of what the others have said. [28] If *those who wish to speak in a language they have not learned realize* there is no one *there* who will be able to explain the meaning *of what they will say*, they should not speak in that language during the meeting. Instead, they should speak to God by themselves, *somewhere else.*

[29] *During a meeting*, two or three people should speak messages that come directly from God, and others who are there should think carefully about what those people have said. [30] If someone receives a new message directly from God while someone else is speaking, the one who is speaking should stop speaking *and let the other person tell what God has revealed to him.* [31] You can all, one by one, speak messages that have come directly from God, in order to teach others and encourage everyone. [32] Those who speak messages directly from God are in control of their own spirits, *so they can wait for their turn to speak.* [33] Remember that God does not desire things to be done in a disorderly way *during your worship services.* Instead, he desires that everything be done in an orderly way.

Just as it happens in all the other congregations of believers, [34] the women should not be permitted *to interrupt the meeting by* asking *questions*. They must keep quiet. They must be subject *to their husbands.* What Moses wrote *about how God created the first two people* suggests *that women should do that.* [35] If they want to know more about something *a speaker said*, they should ask their husbands when they get home, for it is disgraceful for women to *interrupt a service by* asking *such questions.* [36] *If you don't agree with these things I have been telling you*, remember that the message from God did not first come from you *people in Corinth*. Also, you are not the only ones who have heard it! *Many others have heard it and accepted it, so you should act as the believers in other places act.* [37] Those of you who think they have the ability to speak messages that come directly from God, or think they have some other ability *God's* Spirit gives, should realize that the things I have written about in this letter are things the Lord has commanded. [38] But if they are not willing to accept *my authority*, *God* will not accept them[u]. [39] So, my fellow believers, be eager to speak messages that come directly from God, and do not prevent anyone from speaking in a language *that he or she has not learned.* [40] But make sure *that* **everything** you do *during the worship services* is done in a proper and orderly way!

15

1 Corinthians 15:1-11

THEME: I was not worthy to become an apostle, but the Lord Jesus committed to me the message about his death and resurrection.

[1] Now, my fellow believers, I want to remind you about the message about Christ that I preached to you. It is the message you received and that you have continued to trust firmly. [2] If you keep on firmly *believing* the message that I preached to you, you will be saved. If you do not continue to believe it, your believing *in Christ* was all for nothing!

[3] The most important part of the message I received *from the Lord Jesus*, and what I told you, was this: Christ died to *take away the guilt* of our sins, just as the Scriptures *said he would do.* [4] His *body* was buried. On the third day *after that*, God caused him to become alive again, just as the Scriptures *said would happen.* [5] After that, *Christ* appeared to Peter. Then he appeared to *ten of* the twelve *apostles.* [6] Later he appeared to more than five hundred of our fellow believers. Most of those are still living, but some of them have died. [7] Then he appeared *to his younger brother* James, *who became the leader of the congregation in Jerusalem.* Then he appeared to all of the apostles. [8] Finally, he appeared to me, but I became an apostle in a way that was very unusual. [9] The fact is, I *consider that I* am the least important of the apostles. I do not deserve to be an apostle, because I persecuted God's groups of believers *everywhere I went.* [10] But it is because God in his kindness acted toward me in ways I did not deserve that I became what I am now. And his acting kindly toward me produced a great result, which was that I worked harder *for Christ* than all the other apostles. But it was not that I *was working with my own ability.* Instead, God was helping me in a way I did not deserve. [11] So it does not matter whether it was I *who was preaching or whether it was the other apostles who were preaching.* We all preached *the same message*, and that message is what you believed.

1 Corinthians 15:12-34

THEME: Christ has truly risen from the dead, and he will some day raise all believers.

[12] So now *let me ask you this*: Since *we* have all preached to you that *God* caused Christ to become alive again after he died, no one among you should be saying that *God* will not cause *believers* to become alive again after they die! [13] If *it is true that God* will not cause **anyone** to become alive again, then Christ was not raised from the dead! [14] And if Christ was not raised, then what we preached to you was useless, and your believing *in Christ* is useless. [15] *If it is true that God* will not cause anyone to become alive again after he dies, we have been guilty of lying to you about God, because we told you that God caused Christ to become alive again. [16] But if it were really true that God *will* not cause anyone who has died to become alive again, then *he* did not cause Christ to become alive again either! [17] If it were true that *God* did not cause Christ to become alive again after he died, you have believed in Christ for nothing, *because* God will still *punish* you for your sins.

---

[u] OR, …they will not be accepted *by the congregation.*

[18] And those people who died *while they were trusting* in Christ will go to hell. [19] In this life *many of us have suffered much for Christ* because we confidently expect *that he will reward us in heaven*. If we have confidently expected this in vain, people should pity us more than they pity anyone else!

[20] But *the truth is that* Christ has been raised from the dead, and this guarantees that he will also cause those *believers* who have died to become alive again. [21] What **one man,** *Adam, did affects us all*: We all die. Similarly, what **one man,** *Christ*, did *affects us all:* All *believers* will become alive again. [22] Because of what Adam did, all *of us who are descended* from him die. Similarly, because of what *Christ did*, all of us who have a close relationship with him will be made alive *after we die*. [23] But we must all take our turn. *God raised* Christ first. And when Christ returns, *God will cause* those who belong to Christ to become alive again. [24] Then, after Christ has destroyed all the evil powers that oppose God, *the world* will end. Then Christ will let God, his Father, completely rule over his kingdom. [25] You must realize that Christ must rule over that kingdom until he has completely defeated all his enemies. [26] The last thing that *he* will get rid of is death. *But he certainly will get rid of death, which is like* an enemy *to us*. [27] *From the Scriptures we understand that* God will cause everything to be under Christ's authority. But it is clear that the word 'everything' here does not include God, since God is the one who will cause everything to be under Christ's authority. [28] After everything is put under the authority of God's Son, then he will put himself completely under the authority of God, the one who gave him that authority. Then God will be completely in control of everything, everywhere.

[29] *Now think about this: Some among you* are being baptized on behalf of those who *had never been baptized* before they died.[v] If, *as some people say, God* will not cause *believers* to become alive again, there is no value in those people doing that! If *God* will not cause any *believers* to become alive again, it is senseless to be baptized on behalf of someone who has died. [30] Furthermore, *if God will not cause us believers to become alive again*, it is very foolish for me and the other apostles to be constantly *putting ourselves* in danger *for telling people God's good message*. [31] My fellow believers, every day I *am in danger of* being killed! That is as true as is the fact that I am pleased with you because of your close relationship with Christ Jesus our Lord. [32] *If God will not cause us believers to become alive again after we die*, I will receive no benefit at all *from having opposed those who attacked me so strongly* in *the city of* Ephesus. They were *fighting me like* wild beasts! If we *believers* will not be raised again, we might as well say *as people often say*: "Since tomorrow we are going to die, we might as well enjoy now everything we can. Let's feast and get drunk!" [33] Don't let *yourselves be deceived by those who say God will not cause believers to live again*. If you associate with evil people *who say such things*, they will destroy your good moral way of living. [34] Start thinking correctly again *about these matters*, as you should, and *stop your sinful behavior that has resulted from* your wrong thinking. *I say that* because *it seems that* some among you don't know God, and as a result they *have this wrong thinking*. I say that to make you ashamed.

1 Corinthians 15:35-58

THEME: In heaven we will have glorious indestructible bodies.

[35] But some of you are asking, "How will *God* cause dead people to become alive again? What kind of bodies will they have?" [36] *Anyone who asks such questions is* foolish. You *know that* a seed that is planted in the ground must completely change its form before it sprouts. [37] A seed, such as a wheat seed, is very different from the plant that sprouts from it. [38] God gives everything that lives the form that he desires. He gives each seed its own

---

[v]   OR, ...those who died *before they became believers.*

form. ³⁹ *In the same way*, people, animals, birds, and fish all have flesh, but each one has a different kind of flesh. Also, there are angelic beings in heaven,ʷ and there are people with bodies on the earth. ⁴⁰ The angelic beingsˣ are beautiful in one way, and people on earth are beautiful in a different way. ⁴¹ The sun is bright in one way, and the moon is bright in a different way, and the stars are bright in a different way. And even the various stars are different from each other in how bright they are.

⁴² And it's the same way *with our bodies. The bodies we will have when God causes us* to live again after we die *will not be the same as the bodies we have now*. The bodies we have now will die and decay. *The new bodies we will have* will never die. ⁴³ We despise the bodies we have now, before we die. But our new bodies will be glorious. The bodies we have before we die are weak. But our new bodies will be strong. ⁴⁴ The bodies we have before we die are natural bodies. But our new bodies will be ones that *God's* Spirit *controls.* Just as there are natural bodies, there are bodies that *God's* Spirit *completely* controls.ʸ

⁴⁵ *In the Scriptures* it is written that *when* the first man, Adam, *was created,* he became a living human being. Christ later also became a human being. But *he is different from Adam, because he* became a person who gives us *spiritual* life. ⁴⁶ But our bodies that God's Spirit completely controls are not the bodies we first get. We have our natural bodies first. ⁴⁷ The first man, *Adam*, was created from the dust of the earth. But *Christ*, the one who came later, came from heaven. ⁴⁸ Everyone on earth *has a body* like the first man on the earth had. And in heaven, *everyone will have a body like Christ*, the man who later came from heaven, has. ⁴⁹ Just as *God* gave us bodies like that of the first man on earth, so we *believers will have bodies* like that of *Christ*, who is now in heaven.

⁵⁰ My fellow believers, I want you to know that we cannot go to heaven, where God rules *over everything*, with our physical bodies, because our bodies cannot last forever. They will die and decay. ⁵¹ But I will tell you something that *God* has not revealed *before*: Some of us *believers* will not die. However, *God* will change **all** of us. ⁵² *It will happen* suddenly, as *fast as we can* blink our eyes, when *we hear the sound of God's* trumpet for the last time. When we hear that trumpet, all *the believers* who have died will become alive and will have bodies that *God* will change, bodies that will never decay. ⁵³ And the *bodies of us who are alive at that time* will *also* be changed. These bodies of ours that die and decay must be transformed into *new bodies that* will never die; *it will be like someone* getting rid of *his old clothes* and putting on *new ones*. ⁵⁴ When that happens, what *a prophet* wrote *in the Scriptures* will come true,
　God will completely get rid of death.
⁵⁵ Then death will not completely finish us.
　Death will have no power to hurt us.

⁵⁶ It is because we sin *that we die, and it is because we* have God's laws that we *know we* have sinned. ⁵⁷ But because of what our Lord Jesus Christ *has done*, he enables us to be free *from having to obey God's laws to be saved and to be free of being afraid to die*. We should thank God for that!

⁵⁸ So, my fellow believers whom I love, continue to hold strongly to *the things you believe*. Don't let anything cause you to doubt them. Always be doing enthusiastically the work the Lord *gives you*. And remember that the work you do for the Lord is never in vain, *as it would be if God will not cause us to live again after we die*.

ʷ OR, …Similarly, there are stars and planets in the sky…

ˣ OR, The stars and planets…

ʸ OR, …there are bodies that *God's* Spirit makes alive.

16

1 Corinthians 16:1-4

THEME: You should set aside funds each week for the offering to be sent to believers in Jerusalem.

¹Now *I will reply to another question of yours. You* asked about the money you are collecting *to send* to God's people *in Jerusalem.* Do what I told the congregations in Galatia to do. ²Every Sunday each of you should set aside *at home* some funds *for this purpose*, in proportion to how much *God* has prospered you. Then you should save it up, so that when I arrive there, you will not need to collect *any more money. Choose some men whom you approve of, to take this money to Jerusalem.* ³Then, when I arrive, I will write letters stating that you have authorized these men to take the funds there. ⁴And if *you* think it is appropriate,ᶻ I will go with them.

1 Corinthians 16:5-12

THEME: I plan to spend some time with you. Treat Timothy respectfully when he arrives. Apollos plans to visit you later.

⁵Now I plan to travel through the *province* of Macedonia. I *plan to* come to see you, but I want to go through Macedonia first. ⁶Perhaps I will stay with you for a short while, or I may stay with you for the whole winter, in order that you yourselves can provide some of the things I will need for my next trip. ⁷I don't want to see you just for a short time and then continue my trip. I am hoping to stay with **you** for a while, if the Lord *Jesus* allows me to do that. ⁸But I will stay *here* in *the city of* Ephesus until *after* the *festival* of Pentecost. ⁹*I want to do that* because God has given me a great opportunity *to proclaim his good message here.* As a result of my work here, he is producing great results. I also want to stay here because there are many people here who oppose *my work, and I need to oppose them.*

¹⁰When Timothy arrives *there in Corinth*, treat him respectfully, because he is working for the Lord in the same way that I am. ¹¹Don't let anyone despise him. And when he leaves there, give him some of the things he needs *for his trip here*, and also *ask God to* bless him. I am waiting for him to come along with the other fellow believers *who have been traveling with him.*

¹²*You also asked* about our fellow believer Apollos. I urged him strongly to go back to you with the three fellow believers *who came here from Corinth*. He was not at all willing to go *now*, but he will go later, when he has an opportunity.

1 Corinthians 16:13-24

THEME: I give you my final instructions, greetings from others, and my final blessings.

¹³Be on guard *against anything that would hinder you spiritually*. You have believed *the true message*; continue believing it firmly. Be courageous. Keep strong *in your relationship with God.* ¹⁴Act in a loving *way* in everything *you do.*

¹⁵You know that Stephanas and his family were the first ones *there* in *the province of* Achaia *to believe in Christ*. They have devoted themselves to helping God's people. ¹⁶My

---

ᶻ OR, If *I* think it is appropriate…

fellow believers, I urge you to submit yourselves to them and to people like them who do *God's* work, and who work hard. [17] I was glad when Stephanas, Fortunatus, and Achaicus arrived here *from Corinth*, because *they did things for* me that you were not able to do *because you were not with me.* [18] They comforted and encouraged me, and *I expect that this news* will do the same for you. You should honor *them, and* you should also honor others like them.

[19] The congregations *here* in *the province of* Asia send their greetings to you.[aa] Aquila and *his wife* Priscilla and the congregation that meets in their house send their warm greetings to you because both they and you belong to the Lord. [20] All your fellow believers *here* send their greetings to you. Greet each other affectionately, as fellow believers *should.*

[21] Now I, Paul, *having taken the pen from the hand of my secretary,* write with my own hand to give you my greetings. I do this to show you that this letter really comes from me.

[22] May God curse anyone who does not love the Lord Jesus. May our Lord will come soon!

[23] May our Lord Jesus continue to act in kindness toward you all in ways you don't deserve.

[24] I love all of you who have a close relationship with Christ Jesus.

[aa] OR, …say they are thinking fondly of you.

The Apostle Paul wrote several letters to the Christians at Corinth. We call this letter

2 Corinthians

1

2 Corinthians 1:1-2

THEME: Paul and Timothy greet the Christians in Corinth.

¹ *I,* Paul, who *write this letter to you,* became an apostle of Christ Jesus because God chose me for that. *Timothy, our* fellow believer *is with me. I am sending this* to you who are God's people in the congregation in *the city of* Corinth. *I want* the believers who live in *other places* in *the province of Achaia to also read this letter.* ² May *you experience* God our Father and our Lord Jesus Christ *acting* in kindness toward you and causing you to have *inner* peace.

2 Corinthians 1:3-11

THEME: We thank God that he encourages us in all our troubles so that we are able to encourage you when you suffer. We suffered so much in the province of Asia that we were sure we were going to die, but we learned to trust in God. He saved us from death and he will continue to save us.

³ *We should* praise God, who is the father of our Lord Jesus Christ. He always takes pity on us and helps us, *because he is like* a father to us *and we are like his children.* He always encourages us. ⁴ He has encouraged us whenever we suffered hardships. As a result, we are able to encourage others whenever they suffer hardships, in the same way that God has encouraged us. ⁵ Indeed, just as Christ suffered, we *who serve him* also continually suffer *because we belong to him.* But also, because we *belong to* Christ, God greatly strengthens us *in the same way as he strengthened him.* ⁶ So, whenever we experience sufferings, we *learn how to encourage* you *when you experience sufferings. As a result, you will become more and more the kind of people God* wants you to be. Whenever *God* strengthens us *in our sufferings, he* does so in order that you *may see how he makes us strong when we are suffering. Then, as God* encourages *you in that way,* you will learn to continue patiently *trusting him* when you suffer as we do. ⁷ As a result, we strongly expect that because you suffer in the same way that we do, *God* will encourage you *in the same way that he* encourages us.

⁸ *Our* fellow believers, we want you to know about the trouble we suffered in *the province of* Asia. The trouble *that came upon* us was so very great that it was much more than we were able to endure. As a result, we thought that we would certainly die. ⁹ Indeed, we felt *like a person feels when he has heard a judge say,* "I condemn you to die." But *God allowed us to think that we were going to die* so that we would not rely on our own *strength. He wanted us* instead *to rely* only on his *strength, since he* is the one who *has power to even make* those who have died live *again.* ¹⁰ And *even though* we were *in terrible danger and were* about to die, God rescued us. And he will continue to rescue us *whenever we are in trouble.* We confidently expect that he will continue to rescue us *time*

after time. ¹¹And we are also relying on you to help us by praying for us. *If many people pray for us*, then many people will also thank *God* when *he* kindly answers those many prayers *and delivers us from danger.*

2 Corinthians 1:12-2:11

THEME: You can trust what I tell you. I did not visit you, because I wanted to give you the opportunity to obey the instructions I wrote to you. Now that you have punished enough the man who caused those problems, I urge you to forgive him and to encourage him.

¹²I am pleased *to be able to say* that I have behaved toward all people in an honest and sincere way. I am sure within myself *that this is true.* Above all, I have behaved toward you *in an honest and sincere way, because that is what* God wants us to do. As I have done that, *my thoughts* have not been the thoughts that unbelieving people think are wise. Instead, *I have behaved toward people only as God wants me to, depending on* God in his kindness to help me. ¹³*I say that* because *in all my letters to you* I have always written clearly in a way that you can easily and completely understand *when you* read them. ¹⁴*Previously some of* you, but not all of you, have completely understood *that I am always honest and sincere with you.* But I confidently expect that *soon* you will **all** be fully convinced. Then when the Lord Jesus *returns, you will all be able to say that* you are pleased with me, just as I will *be able to say that* I am pleased with you.

¹⁵⁻¹⁶It was because I felt sure *that all of you were pleased with me* that I was planning to visit you on my way *here* to *the province of* Macedonia. I also planned to visit you again on my way back from here, so that I could *spend time with you* twice, and be able to help you more, and I was hoping that you would *give me things I needed* for my journey to *the province of* Judea. ¹⁷So then even though I *changed my mind later and did not do what* I *first* planned to do, *it was not because I did not have an important reason for changing my plans.* Surely you don't *really think* that I decide on what I am going to do like people who don't know God do. I'm *not like that.* I am not *a person who* says *to people,* "Yes, *certainly I'll do that,*" and then *for no good reason changes his mind and says,* "No, *I won't do it.*"¹⁸Just as surely as God always does what he says *he will do, it is true that I have never said,* "Yes, *I will do this*" when I *really meant* "No." ¹⁹*I follow the example of* God's Son, Jesus Christ. When I along with Silas and Timothy taught you *about Christ,* we told you that he was not *someone who said he* would do *something* and *then* did not *do it.* Jesus Christ never *said to anyone,* "Yes, *I will do what you desire,*" and *then did not do it.* ²⁰*We know that is true,* because everything that God promised to do *for his people,* he has done completely by *sending* Christ *to save us.* That's why we say, "Yes, it is true! *God has done everything he promised to do!*" And we praise him! ²¹Now it is only God himself who causes us, as well as you, to keep on *believing* strongly in Christ. God chose us *to belong to him and to have a close relationship* with Christ. ²²He also sent his Holy Spirit into our lives to mark us as belonging to himself. Also, since he has sent his Spirit to live inside of us, *he wants us to know by this that* he guarantees *to give us every other blessing he has promised.*

²³So now, *let me tell you why I changed my mind and did not visit you as I intended to do*: God himself knows *that what I am telling you is true.* The reason I did not return to Corinth was so that I might not have to *speak to you severely about the wrong you had done.* ²⁴It is not that Silas, Timothy and I want to boss you *and tell you that you must* believe only what we say. *Not at all!* On the contrary, we are working as partners *with you* in order to make you happy. *We don't try to force you to believe everything we believe, because we are sure that you are continuing to* trust *the Lord Jesus Christ* and that you are remaining firmly committed to him.

2

[1] Anyway, I definitely decided that I would not come to visit you again *now. If I had come, I would have spoken severely to you again, and* I would have made you unhappy as I did the last time *I visited you.* [2] *And* if I make you unhappy, there will be none of you to cheer me up, because I will have made unhappy *the only people who can cheer me up!* [3] So, *instead of going to visit you at that time,* I wrote a letter *and sent it to you.* I wrote the way I did so that *you would know what you should do. Then* when I come to visit you, you will not make me unhappy when you should be causing me to rejoice. I was quite sure that all of you *would do what I told you to do in that letter, and because of that* I would be happy and you would be happy, too. [4] I wrote to you *the way I did* because I felt very troubled and distressed about you. I was even crying very much as I wrote. *My purpose in writing was not in order to make you feel bad, but, instead, that you might know how deeply I love you.*

[5] *Now I want to write about the man who* caused all this anguish. *What he did was very wrong, but* I know that it has caused you much more sorrow than it has caused me, because all of you *have been affected in some* measure *by what he did. I* say, "in some measure," *because I don't want to say that he has* done more harm *than he really has.* [6] *Since he has now stopped sinning in that way*, the punishment that nearly all of you *decided was right for him* has continued long enough. [7] So now, instead *of punishing him any longer*, you need to forgive him and deal kindly with him. *If you don't forgive him*, he may become so sad that he will give up *thinking you will ever forgive him.*[a]

[8] For those reasons, I beg you to *forgive him and accept him back into your group, and thus* assure him that you truly love him. [9] *I feel sure that you will do as I ask,* because when I wrote *severely* to you *before,* I did it to test you by seeing whether or not you really would do everything *that I, as your apostle, asked you to do.* [10] So *since you obeyed my instructions before, I feel sure that now you will obey what I am writing in this letter* and forgive the man, as I have done, because I indeed have forgiven him for the wrong thing he did. Anything he needed me to forgive him for, I have forgiven, and Christ knows *that I have forgiven him sincerely. I have done that mainly* to help you *so that you and I will again have fellowship with each other, and the wrongdoer will be restored to fellowship with you.* [11] *I want you to forgive him* so that Satan will not be able to take advantage of *the problems among* us *and make the situation worse.* We know very well how he is always planning to *cause problems among us.*

2 Corinthians 2:12-17

THEME: I did not find Titus in Troas, so I went on to the province of Macedonia. Everywhere we go, God causes people to know Christ through our teaching. We do not teach in order to get money; we teach with sincere motives.

[12] *I will continue by telling you what I did after I wrote to you from the city of Ephesus.* I went to *the city of* Troas to *tell people* the message *about* Christ. *When I arrived there,* I found *many people* who had been prepared by the Lord *Jesus to listen to what I told them about him.* [13] But because my fellow believer Titus had not *arrived with a report from you,* I still felt very anxious and concerned *about you.* So, *after spending only a short time at Troas,* I said 'good-bye' to *the believers who were there* and went to *the province of* Macedonia *to find Titus.* [14] However, *before I tell you any more about that, I want to* thank God *for what he is doing. As a great leader of fighting men causes all his prisoners to take part in his victory parade*, God leads us *who are his workers* to always win out *over Satan because of our close relationship with Christ. God causes people to come to* know Jesus

---

[a]   OR, …he may become so sad that he will give up *believing in Christ.*

Christ as a result of our *teaching his message. That message is like* the smell of perfume.
[15] *When we tell God's message* about Christ, it *spreads out among people* like the smell of
perfume. *Those who believe the message we tell them* are saved *from the guilt of their
sin. But those who reject that message* will be separated from God *forever.* [16] To those
who *are on the way to hell, our message is like* a foul smell *because it is about dying* and
being separated from God forever. *On the other hand, to those who are on the way to
heaven, the message we teach is like* a pure fragrant smell *because we tell them* that they
will live *forever with God. As we think about that, we think* no one can have enough ability
to do such important work *for God!* [17] *You see*, we don't act like so many *others whom you
know. They* teach God's message in a way *they think people will like, and they think*
people will pay them for teaching that way. **We** *certainly don't do that.* On the contrary, *as
servants of* Christ, and knowing that God is watching us, we teach with sincerity *the
message that* God sent us to proclaim.

3

2 Corinthians 3:1-6

THEME: The way you now live proves that we teach the truth about Jesus Christ.

[1] *As I write these things about myself,* I'm not *doing it* to boast about how good I am, *as
some of you say I do.* Some people always carry letters of recommendation with them *that
tell how well they work.* But I don't need *to bring* letters like that *when I come to you.* Nor
do I need to ask you *to write* letters *of recommendation for me when I go to other
congregations.* [2] You yourselves are *like a* letter that recommends my work *for God to
everyone.* People see *how Christ changed* your *lives when you believed the message
I taught you.* Everyone *who knows you* can see *the result of my work for God.* [3] You are
like a letter of recommendation *written by* Christ himself that says good things about *my
work for God.* You show *people by the way you now conduct your lives that God has
changed your lives* as a result of my work *among you. People did* not *find out about you
by* reading *a letter written to them on paper* with *pen and* ink. Instead, *they saw how* the
Spirit of the all-powerful God *has changed your lives.* Nor *did people find out about you by
reading* a letter carved on stone slabs *like the stone slabs God gave to Moses.* Instead, *it
was the change God's Spirit made in* your lives *that they saw.*

[4] *With complete* confidence I *can write these things about the work Silas, Timothy, and
I did among you, because God knows that what I write is true. We are true workers* for
God *because of what* Christ *has done for us.* [5] We, by ourselves, do not have the ability *to
do this work.* None of us *apostles* can say, *"I have changed the lives of these people."*
God is the one *who has given us this ability.* [6] He is the one who enables us to be his
messengers. *He has enabled us to tell people the message* about the new agreement *he
is making with them.* This is not a *message about obeying all the* written laws *of his old
agreement* that he made *with the Jewish people.* Instead, *it is a message about God
giving us his* Spirit. *Previously, God condemned people to be* separated from him forever
if they did not obey his laws. But by *God's new agreement* his Spirit enables people to live
eternally.

2 Corinthians 3:7-11

THEME: Our teaching people God's new message is much greater than the teaching people what Moses taught.

[7] *Moses* taught *the people that if they did not obey God's laws completely they would be* separated from God forever. God wrote *his laws* on stone slabs. *Then he gave them to Moses to teach them to the people. Although God's laws condemned* the people to die, *when Moses brought those laws down from Mount Sinai, God caused Moses' face to shine* with radiance *to show the people that those laws were God's laws.* The radiance was *so bright that* the people of Israel could not keep looking at Moses' face. *They had to look away.* But although the radiance *was bright, it* was slowly fading away. [8] *So, if God showed in such a wonderful way that those laws that condemned them to die were from him,* surely when we teach *people about how God's* Spirit will *change their lives, God will show* in an even more wonderful way *that* it is *his message.* [9] The message *that Moses taught them was wonderful, but when people heard* that message, *they realized that they were sinners and that God* would punish them. But God's message that we *teach is a* much more wonderful message. We teach people that God will erase the record of their sins. [10] *The fact is that, although the work of teaching the people to obey God's laws* was once important, it is not as important now, because it cannot compare with *the work of teaching people that God will forgive them and* enable them to conduct their lives in a way that pleases him. [11] Furthermore, *the message that Moses taught was not a lasting message, just as* the brightness on his face was not lasting and soon faded away. But *when God gives his Spirit to people*, the wonderful work *God's Spirit does in their lives* is much greater *because* it lasts forever.

2 Corinthians 3:12-18

THEME: We teach a message that transforms peoples' lives. So we teach it with great confidence.

[12] We know that the message we teach is a *much greater message than the message Moses taught.* So we *can preach boldly.* [13] We don't *need to put a veil over our faces when we teach people*, as Moses did. Moses put a veil over his face so that the Israelites would not see that the radiance *on his face* soon faded away. *Similarly, the glory of the old agreement has also faded away.* [14] But the Israelites stubbornly refused to *understand that the old agreement would end.* Even now, when they read the old agreement, *they still don't realize that it has ended. It's as if* the veil *that Moses put on his face* is now over their *minds, keeping them from understanding God's true message.* They will *understand that message* only when *they come to trust* in Christ. Then *it will be as though God* has removed the veil. [15] *Throughout all these years*, even until now, when *the Israelites* read *the laws that God told* Moses *to write down, it is as though* a veil is covering their minds. [16] But when any one of them believes in the Lord *Jesus, God* removes that veil. [17] *It is by the power of his* Spirit that the Lord *works in our lives*, and the Lord's Spirit has set us free *from trying to obey all the laws God gave Moses.* [18] *It is as though God* has removed the veil from our faces. We realize how great Jesus is. As we realize that, we are continually being changed to become more and more like Jesus, *so that people can see*, more and more, how great *Jesus is.* It is the Spirit of the Lord who does *this.*

4

2 Corinthians 4:1-6

THEME: We are servants of Jesus. It is Jesus who has shown us how great God is.

¹ So, since God has acted so kindly *toward me* enabling *me to teach* this great *message to people*, I never get *so* discouraged *that I stop teaching it.* ² No, and I have determined that we will be honest in everything we do. We will not *do anything that would cause* us to be ashamed *if people found out about it.* We never try to deceive *you with clever arguments, as some other people do.* We never *try to deceive you* by changing God's message, *as those same people do.* Instead, we always teach *only* the truth *about Christ,* and we teach it clearly. Knowing that God is watching what we do, we *teach his message in an honest way, with the result that* no one can *accuse* us *of being deceitful.* ³ And if, *as some of you say, some people are* not able to understand the message *we teach about Christ, it is not because we don't teach it clearly.* It is because those people *don't want to believe it.* They are on the road to eternal death. ⁴ *Satan, who is* the one *who rules* this world, controls the thoughts of unbelievers. He prevents them from understanding the message about how wonderful Christ is. *They are unable to understand that* Jesus is like God *in every way.* ⁵ That is why, *when we teach people,* we do not boast about ourselves, *as some people say we do.* Instead, *we teach* that Jesus Christ is our Lord. We ourselves are *only* your servants. *We want to honor and obey* Jesus. ⁶ When God *created the world,* he commanded the light to shine *where there was nothing but* darkness. He is the one who has *made his message about Jesus to be like* a light shining into our minds. *God has done that for all of us who believe in Jesus. He has done that so that we will understand that when people saw* Christ, they saw how great God himself was.

2 Corinthians 4:7-15

THEME: As Jesus' servants we suffer, but through our suffering many people will receive eternal life and thank and praise God.

⁷ *This ministry that God has given* us is *like* a very valuable treasure. But we who have that treasure *are as weak as fragile* clay pots. *God has planned it that way* in order that *people* will know that the power *that changes lives* is God's power, and not any power of our own. ⁸ We are continually oppressed in many ways, but *we have* not *allowed that to* stop us *from teaching the message about Jesus Christ.* We often don't know what to do *in difficult situations,* but we never say, "God has abandoned us." ⁹ *We are frequently* persecuted, but *God* never leaves us alone. *Sometimes we are* badly wounded, but *God does* not *allow* us *to* be killed. ¹⁰ *No matter where we go,* we are continually *aware that since people killed* Jesus, *people may* kill us *for teaching his message. But we are willing to go on living this way* in order that *people* will know that Jesus is alive and *that he is directing* us. ¹¹ *So, although* we are *still* alive, we always realize that *some day* we may be killed because *we teach about* Jesus. *God allows us to suffer* to show *people* that Jesus is alive and that he is *strengthening* our bodies that are some day going to die. ¹² So *I conclude that although* we *apostles* are constantly *suffering and may soon* die, *the result of that is that all of* you *have now received eternal* life.

¹³ We are not discouraged. We are like *the person who* wrote *in the Scriptures,* "God, I trusted *in you* and so I keep on speaking *your message.*" We also trust *in God*, so we keep on speaking *his message.* ¹⁴ *We do this* because we know that *although people might kill us, God,* who caused the Lord Jesus to live again after he died, will also cause us to live again *after we die. God will do this because we belong to* Jesus. *And then God*

will bring us, together with you, to be with him. [15] *So I say that* all these things *we suffer* are for your benefit. *We have suffered all this* in order that more and more people, *as a result of hearing that God will* freely *forgive their sins*, will thank *him and praise him, and then* they will greatly honor him *and worship him.*

2 Corinthians 4:16-18

THEME: As our bodies get weaker, God continually makes our inner lives stronger. He will reward us for all that we have suffered.

[16] So, *since we know that as a result of our suffering many people will honor God*, we never get so discouraged *that we stop teaching his message.* Although our bodies are getting weaker, *God* encourages us every day and strengthens us in our hearts. [17] *I know that* all these troubles that *happen to us in this life are* not significant and will not last forever. *When we think of* the glorious things *God is preparing* for us *to enjoy* forever *in heaven*, all *our suffering now* does not matter. [18] That is why we say, "We will not keep thinking about *all the suffering we* are experiencing now. Even though *we* cannot see *all the things that God has prepared for us in heaven*, those are what we should be thinking about." *That is how we should think,* because *all these troubles* that *we* have *now* will last only a short time. But what *we will have in heaven*, that *we* cannot see *now*, will last for ever.

5

2 Corinthians 5:1-10

THEME: God will give all of us new heavenly bodies, and he will reward us according to what we did while we were living in our earthly bodies.

[1] We know that *these bodies* we live in *here in this world are like* tents, *like temporary dwelling places. So we should not be concerned about what happens to our bodies.* We know that if we are killed, God will give us *permanent living places. Those permanent living places* will not be houses that people have made. They *will be new bodies in which we will live forever* in heaven. [2] *Here on earth we suffer.* We often groan because we desire *to go* to heaven *where God* will give us our new *bodies.* [3] When *God gives us our new bodies*, our *spirits will have* bodies to live in *that will last forever.*

[4] *The fact is that* while we are still living in these bodies, we often groan *because we desire to be free from them.* We are not longing to be without a body. Instead, *we groan because* we desire to receive our new bodies in heaven. We long for this to happen so that these bodies that are going to die some day will suddenly be changed *into bodies* that will live *forever.* [5] It is God himself who has prepared us to *receive* these *new bodies.* He is also the one who has guaranteed to us that this will happen. He has guaranteed it by sending his Spirit *to live inside us now.*

[6] So, *since God's Spirit lives in us*, we are always confident *that God will give us new bodies.* We know that as long as we live in our bodies here on *earth*, we are not yet *living together* with the Lord *Jesus in heaven.* [7] While we live *here, we* don't have our *new bodies, but we are* trusting *that God will give them to us.* [8] *Yes, as* I said, we are confident *that he will give us new bodies.* We would much prefer to leave these bodies *in which we are now living,* and be with the Lord *Jesus in our* home in *heaven.* [9] Because of all that, we always want to please *Jesus in everything we do.* Whether we are *still living* here *in these* bodies or whether we have *left* them and are living in our home *in heaven*, we want to

please him. ¹⁰ *And we need to strive to do that* because each one of us *believers* must stand before Christ *to be* judged *by him. At that time* he will *reward each one of* us according to what we have done *while we lived in this world* in these bodies. *He will reward us according to* whether we have done good or whether we have done evil.

2 Corinthians 5:11-6:2

THEME: Christ has shown me how much he loves people. That is why I teach his message with all the strength I have. Therefore I plead with you to believe that God will forgive you because of what Christ did for you.

¹¹ It makes me fearful *to think that some day I will stand before the Lord to be judged.* So I *do everything I can to* convince people *that I teach God's message with sincerity.*[b] God knows very well *how I conduct my life and what I teach,* and I really believe that you also know it, within yourselves. ¹² Once again *I say, in writing this,* I am not just *trying to* make you think highly of me, *as some people will probably say I am.* Instead, I am *telling you in this letter why you have* good reason *to tell those who criticize me* that you think highly of me. *I am telling you this* so that you will know what to say to those *teachers of false doctrine among you.* They are proud *of what they have done,* instead of *making sure* their hearts *are right with God and then being pleased with that.* ¹³ *Some of them say that when God enables me to see visions,* I talk like a crazy person. If *that is so, I want you to realize that I talk that way in order to please* God. On the other hand, if *you think that* I *speak and act* wisely, *that is good. I want you to know that I do* that in order to *help* you. ¹⁴ *I speak and act the way I do* because the love Christ *has for people* influences me *in everything I say and do.* When he died, *he suffered the punishment* for *the sins of* all people. So, we should all *think of ourselves as having* died with him, *being as unresponsive to sinful desires as* a corpse is. ¹⁵ When *Christ* died for the sake of all people, he died in order that *we believers who are alive now* should not conduct our lives in a way that will just *please ourselves.* Instead, *we should conduct our lives in a way that will please* him, *because* he is the one who died for us and was raised to life again.

¹⁶ So, *since I have realized how much Christ loves all people,* I no longer think about people in the way that those who do not believe *in Christ* think about *them.* Before I *was a believer,* I also used to think about Christ in the way other non-believers did. But I don't think of him that way any more. ¹⁷ The fact is that God makes everyone who *trusts* in Christ to be completely different *than they were before.* Their old *way of life* is gone. They now have a *completely* new way of *life.* ¹⁸ This *complete change in people's lives* is all something that God *does.* It is God who made it possible for us to have a peaceful relationship with him. *He was able to do that* because of what Christ *did for us.* Now God *has sent* me, and those *who work* with me, to tell *people that they* can have a peaceful relationship with him. ¹⁹ That is, *he sent us to tell them that,* when Christ *died,* God was *making it possible for all the people of* the world to have a peaceful relationship with him. He no longer keeps a record of the sinful things *believers* have done. The message that *God* has given us *to tell people is how we can have a* peaceful relationship with him. ²⁰ So then, it is I and my companions who are Christ's representatives *in this world. When we tell people the message about Christ,* it is God himself who is pleading with them by means of what we *say.* So, as true representatives of Christ, we plead with you: *Believe God's true message about Christ in order that you may* be reconciled to him.[c] ²¹ *You must believe that even though* Jesus never sinned, God *punished him for all the* sinful things

___

[b] OR, …I *do everything I can to* convince people *that they should believe.*

[c] OR, …*Therefore,* as true representatives of Christ, we plead with you: *Believe God's true message about Christ in order that you may* have a peaceful relationship with him.

that people do, just as if Jesus had done those sinful things himself. And because of our close relationship with Christ, God has erased the record of our sins.[d]

6

[1] *So then*, since I am working together with God *himself*, I say this to you very strongly: Since God has *already* kindly *forgiven you because Christ died for you*, do not now *say* "It does not matter *if I do things just to please myself*." [2] For God said *long ago in the Scriptures*:

> When it is the right time *for me* to help you, *you will ask me to help you*, and I will hear you. Then I will *send* a Savior to help you.

So listen to what I am telling you: Since God *has sent* his Savior, **now** is the time when *God is ready to* save *people from the guilt of their sins*.

2 Corinthians 6:3-10

THEME: In spite of much suffering, we have lived as servants of God should live.

[3] Neither I nor the men *working* with me do anything that would hinder people from trusting in Christ, so no one can accuse *us of not* serving *God in a proper way*. [4] Instead, in everything *that we say and do*, we show people that we serve God faithfully. We patiently endure *all the things that happen to us. People cause us* many troubles, as a result of which we have anxiety *and often do not know what to do*. [5] We have at times been beaten *and bound with* chains in prison. *Angry crowds of* people have rioted, *wanting to kill us*. We have kept on working *for God until we had no more strength to work*. We have had many sleepless nights, and we have *often been without food*. [6] *All that we think about and all that we do, is* pure *in God's sight*. Knowing *how God wants us to conduct our lives, we do what pleases him*. We are patient *with those who oppose us*. We are kind *to all people. We depend on* the Holy Spirit *to help us*. We love people sincerely *as God wants us to love them*. [7] We faithfully teach *the true* message *about Christ*, and God *gives us* his power *as we teach it*. *Like soldiers* using weapons *in a battle*, we, by *living* righteously, *defend God's message and refute those who attack it*. [8] *We serve God faithfully* whether *people* praise us or *whether they* despise us, whether *people say* bad things *about us* or *whether they say* good things *about us. We keep teaching* the truth *even though some people say that* we are deceiving *people*. [9] *Some people* know *well that we are true servants of God, and yet others*, who know us, refuse to *believe that. People have often tried to* kill us, yet we are still alive. *We have often* been beaten, but we have not been killed. [10] Although we are often very sad *because people have rejected our message*, we are always happy *because of all that God has done for us*. Even though we are poor, we make *it possible for* many people to be *spiritually* rich. Yes, it is true that *in this world* we have nothing *valuable*, but, *because we belong to God's family*, all *that God has* belongs to us.

2 Corinthians 6:11-13

THEME: I ask you to accept us and love us as we love you.

[11] You *fellow believers* in Corinth, *I have been* completely honest with you. *I have told you exactly how we feel about you, that* we love you very much. [12] We are not *treating you as though we don't* love you, but you are *treating us as though you don't* love us. [13] In return

---

[d] OR, …God has declared us no longer guilty for our sins.

for our loving you, will you not love *us* just as *much as we love you?* I am writing *to you* as if you were my own children.

2 Corinthians 6:14-7:1

THEME: Do not get involved with people who do not honor God.

[14] Do not team up with anyone who does not trust *in Christ. I say this* because we who *trust in Christ and do* what is right should not be *interested in doing things* with wicked people. Or *to say it in another way*, just as light and darkness never go together, so *those who belong to Christ and those who belong to Satan should never join together.* [15] There is no agreement of any kind between Christ and Satan. *So,* a believer has no common interests with an unbeliever. [16] *Just as* no one would *dare to bring* idols into the Temple *in Jerusalem*, believers should never join with those who worship idols. *I say that* because *the Holy Spirit lives in us, and so* we are *like* the Temple of the all-powerful God. *It is just* as God himself said *in the Scriptures,*

I will live in *my people.*
I will always be helping them.
They will say to me, "You are our God," and
I will say to them, "You are **my** people."

[17] *In another place in the Scriptures we read that* the Lord said,
Get away from those who do evil;
keep yourselves separated from them.
Do *nothing sinful that would make you* unacceptable to me.
Then I will welcome you *as members of my family.*

[18] *The Lord also said,*
I will *care for you* as a loving father *cares for his children,*
and *it will be as though* you are my own sons and daughters.
I, the all powerful Lord, am saying this *to you.*

7

[1] My friends, whom I love, since God made these promises *to accept us as his children,* we must stop doing anything that is sinful. We must not do sinful things with our bodies, and we must not *think* sinful thoughts. *Because* of our great reverence for God, we must strive to *live* a completely pure life. By doing that we will become the kind of people he wants us to be.

2 Corinthians 7:2-4

THEME: I love you all and I have great confidence in you.

[2] *So, as I just wrote*, I want you to love me.[e] I have never done anything wrong to any of you. I have not *done anything to* harm any one of you spiritually or financially. Nor have I tried to get money *from you* for myself. [3] *It is true that some people among you have said that I have done such things.* In spite of that, I am not trying to make you all feel ashamed because, *just as* I wrote before, I will continue to love you all very much, whether I live with you or die with you. [4] I have great confidence in you. I am very pleased with you. *You* have

---

[e]   OR, …love us who are true apostles of Christ.

greatly encouraged me, so that I am now very happy in spite of all the hardships I *have endured*.

2 Corinthians 7:5-16

THEME: Titus told me that my letter caused you to repent, and so now I am very happy.

⁵ Now *I will return to what I was saying about trying to find Titus*. When I *left Troas and* came *here to the province of* Macedonia, I still did not find rest for my body. Instead, everywhere we went, *people were constantly* causing us trouble. *And not only that*, but I was greatly concerned *about you all*. ⁶ But God, who always encourages his people when they are discouraged, encouraged us by *sending* Titus back to us. ⁷ I was encouraged by *seeing* Titus*, but when I heard how* you had encouraged him, that encouraged me even more. He told me how much you wanted *to see me*. *He told me* that you were very sorry *you had made me so unhappy. He also told me* that you are very eager for me *to continue to serve as your apostle. When Titus told me those things,* I was very, very happy.

⁸ Even though what *I wrote* in my letter distressed you, I am not sorry *that I wrote it*. For a while I was sorry that I had written it, *because I knew that it would distress you*. Now *Titus has also told* me that it did distress you *when you read it*, but you were distressed only for a short time. ⁹ *So now* I am happy *that I wrote it*. I am not happy that you were distressed, but *I am happy* because, when you became distressed, you became sorry for what you had done and *you asked God to forgive you. What I mean is that you became sorry in the way God wanted you to be sorry, so my making* you sorry did not harm you at all. ¹⁰ *The fact is that* when God causes *us to be* truly sorry for having sinned and we turn from our sinful behavior, then God saves us *and will not punish us for the sinful things we have done*. And no one is ever sorry about that. *On the other hand*, the people who do not trust *in God* may be sorry *for the sinful things they have done*. But *if they do not turn from their sinful behavior and ask God to forgive them*, they will remain separated from him forever. ¹¹ But *think about what happened when you read my letter*. God caused you to be truly sorry *for what you had done.* You eagerly *wanted to do what was right,* and you wanted to show God*ᶠ* that you had done the right thing. You were angry *about what had happened*, and you were worried *that God would punish you if the situation continued.* You also wanted me *to visit you to encourage and help you*. You wanted me to know *that you really do accept me as your apostle, and that you punished the wrongdoer as I told you to do. By doing* all of those things, you have shown *me* that you have done what is right in this matter. ¹² So, even though I wrote that *severe* letter to you, I did not *write it just* so that *you would punish* the man who had done what was wrong. Nor *did I write it* for the benefit of the person whom *he* had wronged. Instead, *I wrote it* so that, when you *read the letter*, God would enable you to realize how much you really do respect *my authority*. ¹³ So, *because you listened to me and did what I asked you to do*, I was encouraged. Not only was I encouraged, but I was *also* very happy to see how happy Titus was *when he arrived here. He told me that* his mind was put at ease because *he saw* that you all *had a good attitude toward me*. ¹⁴ I had told Titus that I was pleased about you. And *I* did not need to be ashamed *for having boasted about you like that, because you did what I knew you would do*. Just as everything I have taught you *and written to you* has been the truth, in the same way the good things that I told Titus about you were also true. ¹⁵ Now he thinks *back* happily on how you all *were willing to* do *what I asked you to do*. He is *also happy about the way you* treated him with great respect. *When he thinks about those things*, it *makes* him love you even more *than he did when he was with you*. ¹⁶ *As for me*, I am very

---

ᶠ   OR, …You wanted to show me…

happy *because now* I am certain I can depend on you *to do what you know God wants you to do.*

8

2 Corinthians 8:1-15

THEME: The believers in Macedonia have already collected the money they are going to send to the believers in Jerusalem. You should also finish collecting the money that you are preparing to send, and have it ready to send to Jerusalem soon.

[1] Now, my fellow believers, I want to tell you *the results of* God's *acting* kindly *in the lives* of *the believers in* the congregations here in *the province of* Macedonia. [2] Even though *the believers here* have been enduring great suffering at the hands of unbelievers, the believers are always rejoicing very much. *Although they* are very poor, *they gave* very generously *to help other believers.* [3] *I know that is true*, because I have seen for myself that they not only gave *money* they were able *to give*, they gave *so much money that they did not* even keep enough *to buy what they needed for themselves*. Without anyone telling them *to share their possessions,* [4] they themselves kept asking us to let them participate in what *other believers* are doing in *sending a gift of money to* God's people *in the province of Judea.* [5] I thought *that they would just give a little of their money, but* they did much *more than that!* First, they told the Lord *Jesus* that they wanted to do *what pleases him. After that, they told* me that they wanted to do *whatever I thought was good, because they were sure that* would be what God *wanted them to do.* [6] So, since Titus was the one who *helped you to* start *gathering the money* for your gift, I urged him to also *help you* to finish *collecting the rest of* your generous and loving gift. [7] You are doing very well in so many *other* ways. *God's Spirit enables you to* believe that *God* will *do miracles. His Spirit has given you the ability to* tell *God's message to others. His Spirit makes you able to* know things he reveals to you. You eagerly *want to help people*, and you love us very much. *So now*, try to do well in getting your generous *gift of money ready to send to Judea.*

[8] I am not commanding you *to do this*. But, *because I have seen how believers in* other *places* are eager *to help believers who do not have enough to live on*, I want you in the same way to show that you love others sincerely. [9] You already know *what* our Lord Jesus in his great kindness *did for you.* Everything *in heaven* belonged to him. But in order to benefit you, *he left all of those things behind and became a human being. Here on earth he had* very few possessions *of his own.* But because he became poor that way, he was *able to cause* **you** to become *spiritually* rich. [10] So, *as you think of our Lord's example, I will tell you* what I think you should do in this matter *of giving funds. As you know*, last year, because of your desire *to give money to help God's people in Judea*, you started *collecting money.* [11] So now you should finish *collecting* the money that you began *to gather.* In that way *everyone will know that you are just* as ready to finish *collecting this gift* as you were to begin collecting it. Give what you are able to give. [12] *Keep in mind that* if you really want to *give something to help others*, whatever any one of you is *able to give* will be pleasing *to God. God does not expect his people to give more* than they can afford to give. [13] I don't mean that *you should give so much to help others that* you yourselves don't have what you need. No, what I want is that *both you and others* equally *have what you need.* [14] Right now, when you have plenty and *the believers in Judea* don't have all they need, *with your gift you will enable them to have enough. It could turn out that some day* when you don't have all you need and they have more than they need, they will *be*

able to help you. Then everyone's needs will be supplied.⁹ ¹⁵ *If that happens, the result will be like it is written in the Scriptures about the time when God provided manna for his people,*

"If someone gathered a lot *of manna*, he still did not have more than he needed *because he shared with someone who did not have enough.* And if someone gathered only a little *manna*, that person still had all he needed *because someone who gathered more than he needed shared some manna with him.*"

2 Corinthians 8:16-9:5

THEME: I am sending Titus to you along with two other believers to help you get your gift ready. They are all well-respected and trustworthy men, so treat them well. It will be good if you have your gift ready to send to the province of Judea by the time I arrive in Corinth.

¹⁶ *So now I am sending Titus to visit you again.* God has caused him to be just as eager *to help you prepare your gift* as I am. I thank God that it is so. ¹⁷ *He is going there,* not just because we urged him to go, but because he himself is very eager *to visit you again.* ¹⁸ I am sending with Titus another believer *whom you know well.* All the groups of believers *in this area* think highly of him because he has *faithfully taught* the good message *about Christ.* ¹⁹ Not only that, but he was appointed by the congregations *in this area* to go there with us *when we take* the generous gift of money *to the believers in Jerusalem. We are taking this* gift to honor the Lord *Jesus* and to show them that we all *very much* want to *help them.*

²⁰ *The believers have* given money generously. So, *by sending that fellow believer along with Titus* to take the money *to Jerusalem*, we are trying to make sure that no one will accuse us *of taking some of the money for ourselves.* ²¹ I *say that* because we are trying to make sure that we do what is right in the sight of the Lord *God*, and also in the sight of people. ²² Furthermore, there is also another believer *here* whom we are sending *to you* along with the two men *I have just mentioned.* Many times I have seen his good work *for the Lord*, and I know that he is eager *to serve the Lord.* Now, because he knows for sure that you *want to join other believers in giving this gift*, he is even more eager than he was before *to go with the others.* ²³ As for Titus, *I have chosen him because* he is my partner, and he has worked faithfully with me *to help you.* As for the other two men, the congregations *in this area* are sending them as their messengers. These two honor Christ *by everything they do.* ²⁴ So then, show them that you truly love *them*, and *in that way* help their congregations to understand *why* we are always saying such good things about you.

9

2 Corinthians 9:1-5

THEME: You and I will be ashamed if your gift is not ready when I arrive.

¹ Now *I want to write* more about the gift *of money* that *you and other believers are preparing to send* to the believers *in Judea. On the one hand*, I don't *really* need to *keep on writing to you about it*, ² because I already know that you really do want to give this help. In fact, I have been boasting *about you*, telling the *believers here in* Macedonia that *you people in the province of* Achaia have been ready to help, beginning from last year. As a result, because you are very eager to help *the believers in Judea*, you have made most of *the believers here in Macedonia also want* to give a gift. ³ However, I am sending

---

⁹ OR, ...In that way each will share alike.

these *three* believers in order that *they will be able to help you finish collecting the money. Then when I and others arrive later, the people with me will see for themselves that* the things I have been boasting about you are true. *I want* you *to have your part of the gift* ready *for us to take to Jerusalem*, just as I have been telling them that you were ready. [4] When I come, if any of *the believers from* Macedonia come with me, *I do not want them to find that your gift is* not ready. If that were *to happen*, I would be very ashamed, and you yourselves would be even more ashamed. [5] So that is why I felt it was necessary to urge these *three* believers to go *and visit* you before I *come. In that way, they would be able to help you finish* collecting the generous gift that you said you would give. *If you do that, not only will* the gift be ready *by the time we arrive, but everyone will see that you have given because you really want to give, and* not because anyone has forced you to give.

2 Corinthians 9:6-15

THEME: If you give generously and willingly, God will always continue to bless you so that you will have enough to continue giving generously, and your generosity will cause many other people to give praise and honor to God.

[6] Don't forget this: "*Farmers* who sow only a few *seeds* will not reap a large *harvest*, but those who sow a lot *of seeds* will reap a large *harvest.*" *Similarly, if you give just a little to help others, God will give you only a few blessings. But if you give willingly and cheerfully to help people, you will receive in return many blessings from God.* [7] Each of you should decide within yourself how much you should give, *and then give that amount.* You should not *be thinking to yourself*, "*I really* don't want to give this money." *And you should* not give *just* because someone tells *you to give. Rather, you should give willingly and cheerfully*, because God loves those who give cheerfully. [8] Moreover, God can enable you to *give to others cheerfully. If you give that way*, God will *in return* give you many good blessings. He will do that so that at all times you will always have all that you need. Indeed, you will have even more *than you need. As a result, you will be able to do* many more good things *to help others.* [9] *Those who give willingly and cheerfully will be rewarded like the man about whom* it is written *in the Scriptures,*

He generously *helps others,*
　he gives to those who are poor.
God will keep in mind the good things he did,
　and reward him with good things forever.

[10] *God always* gives seeds to farmers to plant, and also gives them food to eat. *So, in the same way, God will* always make it possible for you to have enough money, so that you will be able more and more to generously *help those who are in need.* [11] *God* will *give you* many blessings in many different ways as a result of your generosity in *helping others. Furthermore, the* generous *gift you are getting ready for* us *to take to the believers in Judea* will be the cause of *many people* giving thanks to God.

[12] *Also remember that* when you give money to help God's people, you not only give them what they need, but also, *because of that, many people will* thank God very much *for you and for what you have done.* [13] As a result of your giving *money to help others*, they will praise God, not only because you have believed the good message about Christ, but also because you have *generously given some of your possessions* so that they and other *believers will all have their needs supplied.* [14] In addition, when they pray for you, *asking God to bless you, they will remember how grateful they are* that God *caused you to give* very willingly and cheerfully. [15] *Finally, we should all* thank God *because he gave us the greatest gift of all when he sent his Son to rescue us from the guilt of our sin.* That is a gift too wonderful for words!

10

2 Corinthians 10:1-6

THEME: I Paul say to you, "Do not listen to those who say that I am afraid to rebuke you when I am with you and that I behave like people do who are not believers."

[1] Now I myself, Paul, appeal to you in a gentle and humble way, like Christ *would. Certain people among you have falsely accused me by saying*, "When *Paul* is with you, he is humble *and speaks gently* to you, but when he is away from you, *in the letters he writes to you* he threatens *to punish* you." *Those people claim that I don't have authority over you as an apostle.* [2] I strongly plead with you, *"Please don't listen to people who talk like that!" I strongly plead with you to not do that,* so that when I am there *with you* I will not *need to* speak severely *to you* in the same severe way as I *plan to* speak to those people who think that I behave like people who are not believers. [3] *Remember that* although I am *human like everyone else* in the world, I don't fight *against those who oppose me* in the way that people who are not believers fight those who oppose them. [4] *I will tell you what I mean by that: Just as soldiers use* various weapons *to fight their enemies, I fight against those who* oppose God's message, but I do it in a different way. I don't *use human arguments and clever talk* like unbelievers do. Instead, *I fight against my opponents* by the powerful means God *has given me.* With that power *I destroy their arguments against God's message and against me, just as soldiers destroy* the fortresses *of their enemies.* [5] *Specifically*, I show that the *human* arguments they use to deceive *people are completely wrong.* When they *proudly say things that* keep other people from knowing God, *I show them that they are completely wrong. I also enable people to* change their ways of thinking so that they think about everything as Christ *wants them to.* [6] I am also ready to discipline everyone *among you* who has not obeyed *the teachings of Christ. I will do this* as soon as you *who truly want to obey Christ show me that* you are *going to* obey him completely.

2 Corinthians 10:7-11:6

THEME: Those who teach what is false must come to realize that I also belong to Christ and that God has given me authority over you. I worry that they will deceive you and that you will stop being faithful to Christ alone.

[7] *I want you to understand what is* happening among you. There are certain *people there who are telling you that* they know for sure that they are Christ's *representatives and that I am not.* Those people should realize that I *represent* Christ just as much as they do. [8] *I say that* because the authority the Lord gave me *as his apostle* is to help you to become mature believers, not to destroy your *faith in Christ.* So even if I were to boast a little more than I have *already done, no one would be able to make me* ashamed *by proving that Jesus has not given me that authority.*[h] [9] I do not intend to make you afraid of me by the letters I *write to you.* [10] *I say that* because some people are saying, *"When Paul writes* letters, he says severe things *in order to make you obey him*, but when he is here with you, *people look at him and say* he is weak, and he certainly is not a skillful speaker." [11] The *people who say* such things should think carefully about this: The kind of *severe* person that *you think* me to be when you read my letters is exactly the kind of person I will be when I come. *I will do what I wrote that I would do.*

---

[h] OR, …proudly talk a little more than I have *already talked* about the authority the Lord gave me *as his apostle*, he gave me that authority in order to help you to become mature believers, not to keep you *from knowing more about Christ.*

¹² *Those who oppose me* tell others how good they are. *Well, if they really were superior to me*, I would not be so bold as to say that I *was equal to them, or* to compare myself with them. *But in fact, they are not superior to me.* They make up their own standards *about what God's servants should be like*, and then they look at themselves and decide *whether or not they meet those standards. By doing that, they show that* they are foolish. ¹³ But as for me, I will not boast about *working among people living in* areas other than the areas *God assigned me to work in.* But *it is right for* me to say that *I have worked* in the areas God assigned to me. *And since those areas* include the one where **you** live, ¹⁴ *when I talk about working among you,* I am not boasting *about working in an area where God did not give me the right to work. What those who oppose me say about my not having authority to be your apostle might be true* if I had not already come all the way to your area. *But that is not true,* because I was the one who first brought the message about Christ to you. *I came before they did*!

¹⁵ Also, *my opponents* boast about work that others have done *as if it were their own work.* It is improper for them to do that, but I don't do as they do. I confidently expect that as you trust more and more *in the good message that I preach*, you will increasingly *agree that God has given me the right to* work *as Christ's representative* among you. ¹⁶ Then I will be able to go to places beyond where you *are.* I will be able to tell the good message about Christ *to people in areas where no one has yet gone to tell that message.* And *I will be able to talk about the work I myself have done in those areas*, instead of boasting about work that someone else has already done *as if it were my work.* ¹⁷ *I try to do according to what Jeremiah wrote in the Scriptures*,

If anyone wants to boast *about something*, he should boast *only* about what the Lord God has done.

¹⁸ *You can see, then, that* it is not those who tell you what great things they have done, *as my opponents do*, whom you should accept *as apostles.* Instead, you *should accept as true apostles only* those whom the Lord commends.

11

¹ *But now, because my opponents are saying that Christ sent them to you as his representatives and that he did not send me*, please be patient with me *while I say a few things that may sound as if I am praising myself, like* a foolish person *would do. You have been putting up with those who teach what is false;* now then, put up with me *too.* ² I really do care about *what happens to* you, *in the same way that* God cares about *what happens to you. Just as a father wants his daughter to be sexually pure when he presents her to the man she will marry,* I *want you to belong* to Christ *alone and to no other.* I want to present you *to him* as people who remain faithful to him *only, and who have not believed the deceitful message of those who are teaching what is false.* ³ However, just as *Satan, when he* cunningly *appeared as a* snake, deceived Eve's thinking *and caused her to disobey the Lord God*, I am concerned that *those teachers* will cause you to think wrongly so that you will no longer *be faithful to* Christ alone. ⁴ *I say that* because some people have come among you who are teaching *their own thoughts about* Jesus. They *are saying about him* things that are *entirely* different from what I taught you. *They are encouraging* you to receive a *powerful* spirit who *would come to live in you*, but it is not the same *Spirit* you received *from God when you believed in Christ.* They preach *what they call* a good message, and you accept *their message, even though it is not the same as the good message about Christ that you heard from me. And* you have gladly accepted them and their message. *You should not do that!* ⁵ I consider that none of those *men, even though they think of themselves as being* extra-special apostles, are in any way greater than I am. ⁶ *Yes, I admit that* I am not an eloquent speaker, but I do know *God's message.* I have

made that clear to you by everything *I have done among you and by all that I have taught you.*

2 Corinthians 11:7-15

THEME: You are mistaken if you think that I do not love you because of my refusal to accept money from you for my teaching. I will go on doing that to prevent those false apostles among you from boasting that they work in the same way I do.

[7] *I refused to accept money* from you as pay for teaching you God's message about Christ. It is ridiculous for you to think that was wrong! *I know that by teaching you without pay,* I made myself seem unimportant to you. *But actually, I did it* to honor you. [8] *Some people might say that it was as though* I was robbing other congregations because I accepted money from them in order that I might work among you. [9] Furthermore, when I was *there* with you and had no *money to buy things I needed,* I did not cause any difficulty to any *of you by asking you for money,* because our fellow believers who came from *here in* Macedonia brought enough *money for me to buy everything* I needed. So I have not put any burden on you *by asking you for money,* and I never will. [10] *And just as sure as you know that* everything Christ says is true, *you can be sure that what* I say *to you now is true.* Wherever *I go* there in *the province of* Achaia, *I do not let you believers in Corinth pay me for doing God's work among you.* And no one will be able to prevent me from boasting *about that.* [11] No one should wrongly think that it is because I don't love you that *I don't take pay from you.* God knows *that you really are very dear to me.*

[12] There are *some men there among you* who would like to be able to say boastfully that they *work among you* in the same way I do. So then, in order to make it impossible *for them to say that,* I have *refused to accept pay from you,* and I will continue doing that. [13] Those men are lying *when they say they are* apostles. They work deceitfully. *Even though they say they work for God, they are working only for themselves.* They try to make people think that Christ *sent them* as his apostles, *but they don't really represent him.* [14] I am not surprised *that they act like that,* because Satan himself causes people to think *he has come* as a shining messenger *from God.* [15] So it shouldn't surprise *you* if these men, who *really* serve *Satan, do good deeds in order* to make you think they *serve God.* Some day God will *punish them* according to what their *evil* deeds deserve.

2 Corinthians 11:16-12:10

THEME: Since you seem to listen to those who boast, I too will boast. I will boast about being a Jew (as those others do), and I will boast about having suffered greatly for Christ, and about an extraordinary vision which God gave me. Although God then caused me to suffer an affliction, he promised that he would help me and strengthen me.

[16] I say again: I don't want anyone *among you* to think that my *boasting about myself* is like the boasting of foolish *people.* But even if anyone *thinks that, listen to* what I *have to say anyway, just as you listen to those false apostles.* They really *speak* foolishly! Listen to me while I also boast a little. [17] About the things that I am *going to tell you,* boasting confidently *about myself, surely you know they are not the kind of things* that the Lord *Jesus* would say. Instead, *I will speak* as a foolish *person would speak.* [18] Because many *among you* are boasting *about their own work,* as unbelievers do, I will also boast *about myself and my work.* [19] *I am sure that you, who think that you are so wise, will accept what I say* because you gladly *accept the* false teachers and the foolish things *that they say.* [20] When people *treat* you as if they were your bosses, you gladly submit *to them. You think it's okay when others* make you provide a living for them. You think it's okay *when people* take control over you, when they boast about themselves, *or when they insult you by*

slapping you in the face. [21] I agree that I wasn't bold enough to treat you in such ways. *So then do you think that* I should feel ashamed of myself?

So now, talking like a person who does not have any sense, I will boldly tell you *some things about myself, just as those false apostles do.* [22] Do *they tell you* they are Hebrews *and can speak in the Hebrew language*? Well, the same *is true of* me. Do they *tell you that they* belong *to God's people*, the nation of Israel? Well, I can say the same thing. *Do they tell you that* they are descendants of *our great* ancestor Abraham? Well, he is my ancestor too. [23] *Do they tell you how much* work they have done for Christ? Now I am talking like a crazy person. Well, I work for Christ much more *than they do. I have been* in prison many more times *than they have. Many times I* have been beaten very severely *because of believing in and obeying Christ.* Many times I almost died *because of serving Christ.* [24] On five occasions Jewish *religious leaders* lashed me 39 times with a whip. [25] On three occasions *Roman* officials beat me with wooden sticks. On one occasion *a large crowd of people* threw stones at me *to kill me.* On three occasions the ship *I was traveling in* was wrecked *and sank. On one of those occasions* I was *floating* in the water a night and a day *before I was rescued.* [26] In my frequent travels *I have often risked losing my life. For example*, sometimes I have been in danger *crossing* rivers. *I have been* in danger *traveling in places* where there were bandits. *At times I have faced* danger among people of my own nation, *the Jews*, and *at other times I faced* danger from those who are not Jews. *I have been* in danger in cities, and I have been in dangerous situations in barren areas. I have been in dangerous situations *when I was traveling in ships. I have faced* danger among people who falsely *claim to be* fellow believers. [27] I have worked very hard *to earn a living*, and often I did not sleep. At times I was hungry and thirsty, and at times I did not have enough time to eat. Sometimes I was cold *because* I did not have enough clothes *to wear.* [28] Besides all that, I have constant and deep concern for all the congregations *that I have helped to begin.* [29] *Every time I hear about a fellow believer* who is not strong *spiritually*, I sympathize with him *and try to help him. Every time I learn about a fellow believer* who causes *another believer* to do something wrong, that makes me very angry.

[30] Since *it seems* necessary for me to *continue* boasting *about myself*, I will boast about things that *caused some people to think of me* as being weak. [31] God, who is the Father of our Lord Jesus, and who is the one *we should* praise forever, knows that I am not lying *about this.* [32] *Once when I was* in *the city of* Damascus, the governor whom King Aretas *had appointed* to rule *part of his area told his soldiers* to guard *the gates of* the city so they could seize me *if I tried to leave.* [33] But *my friends* enabled me to escape *by* putting me in a large basket and lowering me *to the ground by a rope* through an opening in the *city* wall. *That was really humiliating!*

12

[1] *It seems that* it is necessary for me to go on boasting *about myself.* Although *I* don't *think my telling you about* this will help *you to accept me as Christ's representative to you*, I *will say this anyway.* I will tell you about visions the Lord *gave a certain man* and about things he supernaturally revealed *to that man. I will tell you this because some of the people among you boast that it was in visions that they received their teachings.* [2] The man I will tell you about is one *who believes* in Christ. Fourteen years ago he was taken up into the highest heaven, *the place where God is.* I don't know whether he went there *in his physical body* or whether he was outside of his body *at that time and only his spirit went.* Only God really knows. [3-4] But he was *suddenly* taken up to *a place called* Paradise, *that wonderful place where God lives. I repeat that* I don't know whether his body *went there* or just his spirit. Only God knows *that. While he was there, God* told him some things that he

does not allow *human beings* to tell *others about.* [5] I will proudly talk about that person. However, I will not be boasting *as* I say that I *am the one who saw and heard those wonderful things.* I will talk only about the things that *cause others to think of* me as a weak *human being like everyone else.* [6] But even if I should choose to boast *to you about such wonderful things that happened to me*, I would not be *speaking like* a fool, because I would be telling you the truth. But I will not *boast about such things*, because I don't want any of you to think highly of me *just because of the things that have happened to me.* Instead, *I want you to decide what kind of person I am by the way you see* me *conducting my life* and by what you hear me teach. [7] In order that I might not become proud because of those many wonderful things *that Christ* revealed to me, *God permitted* Satan to send a messenger *to humble me.*[i] *What he did to me was painful, like* a thorn pricking my body. [8] Three times I prayed to the Lord about it, begging him to take it away from me. [9] But he said to me, "*No, I will not take this away from you. Instead*, I will kindly help you, and that will be all you need, because it is *when you are* weak that I *can* best *work* powerfully *to help you.*" So because of *what the Lord said to me*, I will very gladly boast about *the things that make* me *seem* weak, so that *people may see* that it is Christ who empowers me *to serve him.* [10] For that reason, *whenever I am* weak, or *when people* insult me, *or when I have to endure* hardships, or *when I am persecuted*, or *when I am in* distressing *situations*, I am content because *I am serving* Christ. *I can say that* because at any time when I myself am weak, that is the *very* time when *Christ* powerfully *helps me.*

2 Corinthians 12:11-18

THEME: When I was with you, I did things that showed you that I am truly Christ's representative. But I still will not take pay from you when I come to visit you again. And those people are wrong who say that I tricked you by sending Titus to get money for myself from you.

[11] It has been foolish for me *to talk about myself like this*, but it is you who forced me to do it. Truly *if the Lord would not help me*, I would be worthless, *as my opponents say I am.* But none of the men whom you *wrongfully think* are great apostles are greater in any way than I am. So it would have been proper for you to say good things about me. [12] *You should have done that, because* when I was with you *I* repeatedly did the things that showed you that *I am truly* an apostle, such as performing many miracles. [13] And I have *certainly treated* you as well as *I treated* the other congregations *that I helped to start. Or do you think that* by not asking you *to pay me for my work*, I was not treating you as well as I treated the other congregations? It is foolish for you to *think that it* was wrong for me not *to ask for pay from you for my work, and therefore I should ask* you to forgive me for that!

[14] Now listen! It is time for me to come to you for a third *visit. When I come,* I *still* will not insist that you *pay me for my work*, because I don't want *any of* your *money!* What I want is for you *to love and appreciate me.* It is not *normally the duty of* children to save up *money to provide for the needs of* their parents. Instead, it *is the duty of* parents to *provide* for their children. Similarly, *it is not your duty to provide for me. Instead, it is my duty to provide spiritual help for you because you are my spiritual children.* [15] So, on my part, *as a good parent would do*, I will be very happy to use everything I have and do everything I possibly can *in order to help you.* And since I love you very much, I will be very disappointed if *you* don't love me a little bit, too.

[16] *You all* know that I did not depend on you *to provide for my needs.* However, *there are some who accuse me, saying that* I was very clever and got money from you by tricking you. [17] But did I ever do that? No! I never asked any of the men I sent to you *to get money*

---

[i] OR, ...Satan sent his personal messenger *make me sick.*

from you *and bring it to me!* [18] Titus went *and visited you because* I urged him to do so. I also sent the other believer *whom you know* to go with Titus. *You know that* Titus did not trick *you in order to get money from you. And you certainly know that* he and I have always acted in exactly the same *honest* way *towards you.*

2 Corinthians 12:19-13:10

THEME: I am worried that when I visit you I will find that many of you are still sinning. I pray that God will help you turn from your sinful behavior, so that I will not have to discipline you when I come.

[19] If you have been thinking while *reading this letter* that I have *just* been *saying these things to* defend myself *against those who accuse me, you are wrong.* I have been saying *these things honestly, knowing* that God is listening *to me. I also speak as one who has a close relationship* with Christ. Everything I do and *everything I say is* to *help you* whom I love to grow *spiritually.* [20] *I have written this way to you* because I worry that when I come *to visit you,* I will find that *some of* you are *not conducting your lives the way* I want you *to.* If that is so, *when I get there* you will see that I will have *to act* in a *very severe way toward you, and I am sure* you don't want that. Specifically, I am afraid that *some of you* may be quarreling, or that you are being jealous *of each other,* or that you quickly *demonstrate your* anger, or that you are acting selfishly, or that *some of* you are saying bad things about others, or that you are spreading false rumors about each other, or that you are acting proudly, or that you are *doing things* in a disorderly manner. [21] *I feel anxious about you. I worry that* when I visit you again, God, the one whom I *serve,* will make me feel ashamed of you *when I see that* you *still are not behaving as believers should.* Then I will feel very sad about *some of* you who were sinning previously and have not turned from your sinful behavior. *Some of you* may still have impure *thoughts. Some of you* may be having sexual intercourse with those to whom you are not married. *And some of you* may be doing other shameful things.

13

[1] *In the Scriptures, it is stated that when one person* accuses *another of wrongdoing, you must not believe his* accusation *right away. First, you must listen to at least* two or three people who actually saw what happened. Okay, this will be the third time I will visit you! [2] When I visited you the second time, I warned you *that I was going to punish all the wrongdoers among you. And now* I am *warning you* again while I am still away *from you.* When I visit you this third time, I will punish those who were sinning *at the time I visited you* before *and who are still sinning,* and I will *punish* the others *who have been sinning since then, unless they have turned away from their sinful behavior.* [3] Because you have demanded proof that Christ is speaking *through me when* I *speak to you, I will show you that I speak to you as his apostle. Christ* does not approve of your sinful behavior. On the contrary, he will powerfully *discipline you.* [4] *It is true that* Christ *seemed to be* weak when he was crucified. But *it is also true that* he *now* lives because God *worked* powerfully to *make him alive again. Similarly,* as I *serve* God, I also am a weak human *being as Christ was.* But I am also *joined with* Christ *who is now alive again.* And with his *authority* I will use God's power *to discipline* you.

[5] *On your part,* each of you should ask yourself: "*Do I* believe *God's message about Christ?*" Each of you should *test yourselves to* make sure that you truly do *believe* in Christ *and thus truly belong to him,* and that *his Spirit lives* within you. When you test yourselves *in that way,* I am sure that you will say *to me,* "Yes, of course we *belong to* Christ!" [6] I am *also* certain that you will know that I *belong to Christ just as you do.* [7] But

because I don't want to have to punish you, I am praying to God that he will help you not to do anything evil *that would cause me to punish you. I pray this*, not in order that when people *who say I am not your apostle* see *the success of my ministry among you, they will have to agree* that I do have authority from Christ. Instead, *I pray this because I want* you to do what is right, even though that might mean that *my opponents would think* that I don't have authority from Christ, *since I would not have an opportunity to show my authority to discipline you.* [8] *If you do what is right, I will not discipline you, because it would* not *be right for me to do that if you are living the way you should, in* agreement with God's true *message. My responsibility is to help people to know and obey God's* true *message.* [9] I am happy *whenever I see that* your *faith in Christ is strong and that you are living in obedience to him, and because of that I do not have to show my authority to discipline you. It does not matter to me if that makes people think I don't have any authority.* Indeed, what I am praying for is that *God* will *help* you to completely *live for him.* [10] That is why I am writing these things while I am still away from you. *What I want is that* when I visit you, *you will already be conducting your lives as God wants you to*, and so I will not have to *discipline you* severely, as the *Lord Jesus Christ gave me* the authority to do. The authority I have from the Lord is to help you become *spiritually* mature believers, not to cause you to stop *trusting in him.*

2 Corinthians 13:11-14

THEME: I finish my letter with some advice. All of us here send you our greetings, and I pray that God will bless you.

[11] Finally, my fellow believers, *I say to you*, rejoice. Completely *change your ways*, and do what I have urged you *to do*. Be united in what you think *about the matters about which I have written to you.* Live peacefully *with each other. If you do those things*, God, who *enables you to* love *each other* and be peaceful, will bless you. [12] Greet each other affectionately as *fellow members* of God's family *should.* All God's people *here* send you their greetings. [13] *I pray that* the Lord Jesus Christ will act in kindness *toward* all of you, that God will *show all of you how much he* loves you, and that the Holy Spirit *will cause you to have good* fellowship *with him and with each other.*

The Apostle Paul wrote a letter
to the Christians in the province of Galatia.
We call this letter

Galatians

1

Galatians 1:1-5

THEME: I, Paul, as God's chosen apostle, am sending this letter to the churches in Galatia and I am asking God's blessings on you all.

¹ *I*, Paul, *write this letter to you. I remind you that I am* an apostle. That is not because a group of people *appointed me*, nor because a human being *sent me to be an apostle*. Instead, Jesus Christ and God, *our heavenly* Father, who caused Jesus to become alive again after he died, have *appointed me and* sent *me to be an apostle.* ² All the fellow believers *who are here* with me *approve of this message that I am writing. I am sending this letter* to the congregations *which are* in *the province of* Galatia. ³ *I pray that* God, our Father, and the Lord Jesus Christ will kindly give *you inner* peace. ⁴ Christ offered himself *as a sacrifice* in order that *he might remove the guilt for* our sins. He did that to enable us to quit *doing the evil things that people* do *who do not know him. He did all that* because God, who is our Father, wanted him to do it. ⁵ *I pray that people will* praise God forever. May it be so!

Galatians 1:6-10

THEME: I am disappointed that you are believing a message which is not the good news about Christ, and I ask God to eternally punish those who are teaching such a message.

⁶ I am very disappointed that so soon *after you trusted in Christ* you have turned away from *God.* He chose you so that *you might have what* Christ freely gives. I am also disappointed that so soon you are believing a different *message, one which some say is* "good news." ⁷ That message is not a true message. *What is happening is that* certain persons are confusing you. They are desiring to change the good message *about Christ and are creating another message.* ⁸ But even if we *apostles* or an angel from heaven would tell you a message that is different from the good message that we told you *before*, we should be punished *forever.* ⁹ As I told you previously, so now I tell you this once more: Someone is telling you *a message that he says is* a good message, but it is a message that is different from *the good message* that I gave you. That person should be destroyed forever! ¹⁰ *When I say that,* I am not wanting **people** to approve me, *contrary to what some have said about me.* It is God's approval that I desire. *Specifically, I don't say and do* things just to please people. If it were still people whom I was trying to please, then I would not be *at the same time* one who *willingly and completely* serves Christ.

Galatians 1:11-12

THEME: It was Jesus Christ, not any human, who revealed the message I proclaim.

[11] My fellow believers, I want you to know that the message about Christ that I proclaim is not one that some person *created.* [12] I did not receive this message from a human *messenger,* and no *human being* taught it to me. Instead, Jesus Christ revealed it to me.

Galatians 1:13-24

THEME: For seventeen years after God showed his Son to me, I had no contact with the apostles.

[13] People have told you how I conducted my life formerly when *I practiced* the Jewish religion. They told you that I continually did very harmful things to the groups of believers that God *established*, and that I tried to get rid of them. [14] I practiced the Jewish religion more thoroughly than many *other Jews* who were my age. I much more enthusiastically tried to get others to obey the traditions of my ancestors. [15] Nevertheless, before I was born, *God* set me apart. He chose me *to live eternally,* something I did not deserve. [16] Because he revealed to me that *Jesus* is his Son, I *wanted* to tell others the message about his Son in regions where non-Jews live. But I did not immediately go to any human beings to gain *an understanding of that message. I received it directly from Christ!* [17] I did not *immediately* go to Jerusalem *for that purpose* to those who were apostles before I was. Instead, I went away to *the region of* Arabia*, a desert area*. Later I returned once more to *the city of* Damascus. [18] Then three years after *God revealed this good message to me*, I went up to Jerusalem to meet Peter. But I stayed with him for *only* fifteen days, *which was not long enough for him to teach me thoroughly about Christ*. [19] I also saw James, who is the brother of our Lord *Jesus and the leader of the believers there in Jerusalem, but* I did not see any other apostle. [20] God knows that what I am writing to you is completely true! [21] After *I left Jerusalem*, I went to *the regions of* Syria and Cilicia. [22] *At that time people in* the Christian congregations that are in *the province of* Judea still had not met me personally. [23] They just heard *others say about me* repeatedly, "*Paul*, the one who was formerly doing harmful things to us, is now telling the *same message* that we believe, the message that formerly he was trying to cause people to stop believing!" [24] And they praised God because of *what had happened to* me.

2

Galatians 2:1-10

THEME: Finally, when I returned to Jerusalem and told Peter, James, and John what was the message I always proclaim, they agreed that Barnabas and I were preaching the same message and serving the Lord just as they were.

[1] After fourteen years passed, I went up again to Jerusalem with Barnabas. I took Titus also. [2] But *I tell you that* I went up there because of what God revealed to me. *It was not because someone asked me to come.* I talked privately to those who are considered to be your leaders. I told them what that good message was, the message I was preaching to non-Jews. I did that in order that what I was doing and what I had done might not become useless *as a result of people rejecting my message because they thought I was teaching something that was not true.* [3] But *even though the leaders of the believers usually insisted that when non-Jews trusted in Christ they must be circumcised*, they did not even insist that Titus, who was with me, be circumcised, even though he was a Greek. [4] *I talked to*

them *privately* because some people *were* pretending that they were fellow believers, and were associating with the true believers. They did that to observe closely what we do because we are free *from having to obey all the Jewish rules and rituals* because of our close relationship with Christ Jesus. Those people wanted to make us slaves *of those rituals by convincing us that we cannot trust Christ solely, but that we must also obey all the Jewish rituals.* ⁵But not even briefly did we do what they wanted *regarding circumcision. We resisted them* so that the truth of the message about Christ might continue to *benefit* you. ⁶The *leaders in Jerusalem,* whom your new teachers respect, did not add anything to what I preach. *And I would add that* whatever status those leaders had did not influence me, because God does not favor certain persons more than others. ⁷No, those leaders did not add to the message I preach. Instead, they understood that God had given the good message to me so that I might proclaim it to the non-Jews, just as God had given the good message to Peter so that he might proclaim it to those who are Jews. ⁸That is, just as God had authorized Peter to be an apostle *to bring God's message* to the Jews, he also had empowered me to be an apostle to *bring his message to* the non-Jews. ⁹And *those leaders* knew that God had kindly given me this special work. So James, Peter, and John, the ones whom your new teachers *respect because they are* leaders *of the believers,* shook hands with *Barnabas and me to show that they agreed that we were serving the Lord just as they were, and that we were preaching the same message.* They also agreed that we were the ones whom God was sending to *tell his message to* non-Jews, but that God was sending them to *tell his message to* Jews. ¹⁰They merely urged that we still remember to help the poor *fellow believers who live in Jerusalem, and* that is exactly what I was eager to do.

Galatians 2:11-21

THEME: Later I rebuked Peter for not behaving according to the gospel, in that he was encouraging non-Jews to adopt Jewish *laws and rituals.*

¹¹But *later, while I was in the city of* Antioch, after Peter came there, I told him directly that what he was doing was wrong. ¹²*This is what happened:* Peter *went to Antioch and started* eating regularly with non-Jewish believers there. Later, there were certain *Jewish believers who claimed they* were sent by James, *the leader of the congregations in Jerusalem, who* came *to Antioch.* But when *those* men came, Peter gradually quit *eating* with the non-Jewish believers and wouldn't associate with them. He was afraid that the Jewish *believers from Jerusalem would criticize him for associating with non-Jews.* ¹³Also, the other Jewish *believers in Antioch* acted insincerely along with *Peter.* The result was that they convinced even Barnabas to *stop associating with the non-Jewish believers!* ¹⁴But when I realized that they were not acting according to the truth of the message about Christ, *when* all *the fellow believers there* were present, I told Peter *the following:* "Although you are a Jew, *you often conduct yourself* like non-Jews *do by disregarding Jewish laws about food. When you are among non-Jews,* you do not customarily conduct yourself like a Jew. So now it is wrong that you are causing non-Jews *to think that they must obey all* the Jewish rites and customs!" ¹⁵Some of us *believers* were born as Jews. We were **not born as non-Jews.** *We Jews have always considered non-Jews to be* **'sinners'** *because they don't obey the Jewish ceremonial laws.* ¹⁶But we have come to know that it is not because someone obeys the laws *God gave to Moses* that *God* erases the record of that person's sins. *God erases the record of a person's sins only if that person trusts in what Jesus Christ has done.* Even we Jews *decisively* trusted **Christ Jesus.** We did that so that God would erase the record of our sins because of our trusting Christ, and not because of our obeying the laws *God gave Moses. God has said that* he will *never* erase the record of people's sins just **because of their obeying those laws.** ¹⁷Furthermore, because we *Jews* desired that God would erase the record of our sins because of our relationship with Christ, *it means* we realized *that* we ourselves were

sinners *like non-Jews, whom we called* sinners, *because we also were not obeying the Jewish ceremonial laws. But we certainly cannot conclude* that it is Christ who causes us to sin. No, Christ certainly does not *cause anyone to sin.*

[18] So if I should again believe *that God would erase the record of my sins because of my obeying the laws he gave Moses, I would be like a man who* rebuilds an old building that he tore down. It would *soon* be clear that I am one who disobeys those same laws *that God gave Moses.* [19] When *I realized that I could not earn God's favor* by *obeying* the laws *he gave Moses, I decided not to respond to what those laws demanded, just as* a dead person *does not respond to anything.* Now I live to *serve* God. [20] *It is as though* I was with Christ when he was crucified.[a] No longer am I *directing the way I live as I did before I believed in Christ.* Now Christ *is directing how* I *live. And whatever I do* now while I am alive, I do it trusting in God's Son. He is the one who loved me and offered himself *as a sacrifice* for me. [21] I am not rejecting *as useless* what God *did for me that I did not deserve, as my opponents are doing. I fully accept that God saved me by acting kindly towards me.* If it is because people *obey the* laws *God gave Moses* that God erases the record of their sins, then Christ died for nothing.

3

Galatians 3:1-5

THEME: You received the Holy Spirit and now experience his working among you because you trusted in Christ, not because you obeyed the laws God gave Moses.

[1] You *believers who live in the province of* Galatia are very foolish! Someone must have put an evil spell on you! I clearly explained to you *what* Jesus Christ *accomplished when* he was crucified. [2] *So* I want you to tell me one thing: *Do you think that* it was because you obeyed the laws God gave Moses that you received the *Holy* Spirit? *Don't you know that* it was because *you* trusted in *Christ when you* heard *the good message concerning* him? [3] You are acting so foolishly! You first *became Christians* as a result of God's Spirit *working within you.* So do you now think it is by means of your own human efforts that you will continue *to grow spiritually*? [4] Keep in mind that *if what God has done for you was because of your obeying the laws God gave Moses and* not because of your trusting in Christ, when you suffered *because of being Christians*, you suffered many things needlessly! *I certainly hope that you did not suffer like that* needlessly. [5] *When God now* generously gives to you his Spirit and performs miracles among you, *do you think it is* because you obey the laws *God gave Moses? Surely you know that* it is because you trusted in *Christ* when you heard *the good message about* him!

Galatians 3:6-12

THEME: It is those Jews and non-Jews who trust Christ who are Abraham's spiritual descendants, because those who seek to be justified by obeying the Laws God gave Moses are condemned by God.

[6] *What you have experienced is* as *Moses wrote in the Scriptures about* Abraham. *He wrote that Abraham* trusted God, and as a result, *God* erased the record of his sins.[b] [7] You must realize, therefore, that it is those who trust *in what Christ has done who* are

---

[a] OR, Now I live to *serve* God: *It is as though* my *old way of life ended when* Christ died on the cross.

[b] OR, ...and as a result, he was considered as being righteous.

considered to be Abraham's descendants *because they trust in God as Abraham did.*
[8] Furthermore, God planned beforehand that it was *when* non-Jews trusted *him* that he
would erase the record of their sins. *Moses wrote in* the Scriptures this good message that
God told Abraham: "Because of *what* you *did*, I will bless *people in* all nations." [9] So *we
can conclude that* it is those who trust *in what Christ has done* whom *God* blesses. That
includes *all non-Jews and Jews who trust him*, along with Abraham, the one who trusted
him *long ago.* [10] That is, God will eternally punish all those who mistakenly think *that he will
erase the record of their sins if they obey* the laws *he gave Moses.* What is written in the
Scriptures is that *God* will eternally punish everyone who does not continuously and
completely obey all the laws *that Moses wrote.* [11] But God *has declared that* if he erases
the record of anyone's sins, it will not be as a result of *that person's obeying* the laws *he
gave Moses. This is evident from the Scriptures that say,* "Those whose record of sins
God erases because they trust in him will live *spiritually.*" [12] But *when God gave* his laws *to
the Jews, he did* not *state that a person must* trust *him.* Instead *he stated that* it is those
who obey *all his laws, continuously and completely*, who will live.

Galatians 3:13-14

*THEME: Christ was condemned instead of us, so that God might bless the non-Jews similar to
how he blessed Abraham, and so that we might receive the Spirit.*

[13] *Even though we humans have not continuously and completely obeyed God's law,*
Christ rescued us from being punished eternally. Christ rescued us by means of his being
the one God condemned instead of God condemning us. What is written *in the Scriptures*
shows that is true. It is written, *"God has already* decided he will punish eternally those
who are executed for their crimes and whose bodies hang on a tree." [14] Christ rescued us
in order that as a result of what Christ Jesus *has done, God might bless the non-Jews,
similar to* how he blessed Abraham. And because of our trusting *Christ*, we receive the
Holy Spirit *whom God* promised *to give to us.*

Galatians 3:15-18

*THEME: By giving his laws to the Jews, God has not canceled what he promised to Abraham
much earlier concerning Abraham's descendant, Christ. As God gave his blessings to Abraham
just because he promised to do so, so he freely gives his blessings to us.*

[15] My fellow believers, I will now *illustrate* by referring to human *relationships. After an
agreement is confirmed and* signed *by two people*, no one can reject it or add to it. [16] *God*
declared to Abraham and his descendant that he was promising *to give blessings to
Abraham. The words which God spoke were not "and your* descendants." *He was not*
referring to many people. Instead, he was referring to one person, who is Christ, *because
the words God spoke were,* "and your descendant." [17] This is what I am saying: *God* gave
the laws *to the Jews* 430 years after *he declared to Abraham what he was promising to do
for him*, so those laws do not cancel the agreement *with* Abraham that God himself had
previously agreed *to establish.* [18] Remember that if it is because *we obey God's* laws *that
he gives us* what *he has* promised, then it is not *just* because he *has* promised *that he
gives those things to us.* God freely gave to Abraham *what he had promised to give him,
just* because *God had* promised *to give it. Similarly, it is not because we obey God's laws
that God gives to us what he has promised.*

Galatians 3:19-25

THEME: God gave his laws to supervise us sinful Jews until Christ, Abraham's promised descendant, would come.

[19] So, *if someone should ask*, "Why *did God later give* his laws *to Moses*?" *I would reply that* it was to show *people* how sinful they are. *Those laws were valid* until *Jesus came. He was* the descendant that God *was referring to when he made* the promises to Abraham. God *gave his laws to Moses* by causing angels to *tell them to him. Moses was the* mediator, *the one who told the laws to the people.* [20] Now *when* a mediator *functions*, one *person* is not *speaking with another* directly; but God *made his promises directly to Abraham.*

[21] *If someone should ask, "When God gave his* laws *to Moses* long *after he told Abraham* what he was promising *to give him, was he* changing his mind?" *I would reply that God* certainly did not *change his mind when he did that!* If God had given a law that could enable people to live *eternally*, then it actually would be because of people *obeying that* law that God would erase the record of their sins. [22] But instead, *what we read in* the Scriptures is that God *caused all people to be unable to escape being punished for their sins*, just as *people* in prison *are unable to escape. God did that in order that he might give what he promised to those who trust Jesus Christ, just* because they trust him. [23] Before *God revealed the good message concerning* trusting *in Christ*, the laws God gave Moses were *confining us Jews as* prisoners *in jail are* confined. *We* were unable to escape *obeying those laws.* This was so that *we might believe* the good message *concerning Christ, the message which God was going to* reveal. [24] *Like a father supervises his immature son by appointing a* servant to look after him, *God* was supervising us *by means of* his laws until Christ came. He did this in order that he might erase the record of our sins because we trust *Christ.* [25] But *now that God* has revealed the message *concerning trusting in Christ*, the laws *God gave Moses* are no longer supervising us *Jews.*

Galatians 3:26-29

THEME: Because of our relationship with Christ we are Abraham's spiritual descendants.

[26] Now all of you *Jews and* non-Jews have become God's children because you trusted Christ Jesus. [27] That is, you who *began a relationship* with Christ when you were baptized identified yourselves as belonging to Christ. [28] *If you are believers, it does not matter to God if you are* Jews or non-Jews; slaves or not slaves; males or females, because all of you are one *kind of person because of your relationship* with Christ Jesus. [29] Furthermore, since you belong to Christ, you are *considered to be* Abraham's descendants *because you trust God as Abraham did*, and, you will receive all that God has promised.

4

Galatians 4:1-7

THEME: You are no longer like slaves. You are children of God and heirs of what he has promised.

[1] Now I *will further* discuss *children and heirs*: An heir is a person who will *later* control all that his father has. But as long as the heir is a child, others *control* him, so that he is just like a slave. [2] Until the *day that* his father *previously* determined, *other* persons supervise

him and manage his property. ³Likewise, when we were^c *like* young children, we had to obey rules and rites which concerned external and material things. These rules controlled us like *masters control their slaves.* ⁴But exactly at the time *that God had previously determined*, he sent *Jesus*, who was his Son,^d into the world. Jesus was born to a *human* mother. He had to obey the laws *God gave Moses.* ⁵God sent Jesus to redeem us who had to obey *all those* laws. God wanted us all to receive from *him* the status of being his children. ⁶Furthermore, we know that we are God's children because God sent his Spirit, who is intimately related to his Son, to live in our hearts. *His Spirit enables us to* pray fervently, "Daddy! Father!" *This shows that we are God's children.* ⁷So *because of what God has done*, no longer are you *like* slaves. Instead, *you* are children *of God.* Furthermore, since *you are God's* children, he has also made you to be those who will receive all he has promised.

Galatians 4:8-20

THEME: I plead with you to do as I did when I was with you, and not obey all the Jewish rules and rituals.

⁸When you did not have a relationship with God, you served gods that actually did not exist. You were their slaves. ⁹But now you have come to know God. Perhaps *it would be better to say that* now God knows you. *So now you are acting foolishly!* You are again believing *that by obeying* rules and rites *you will benefit spiritually! Those rules are* ineffective and inadequate! You are wanting to *obey them* again like slaves obey their masters. ¹⁰You *non-Jews* are carefully practicing *Jewish rules and rituals about Jewish days of rest* and *about the first day of each* month and *about special* seasons and years.

¹¹I worry about your *mistaken ideas. I do not want* to have *so* strenuously served among you in vain. ¹²My fellow believers, I strongly urge you to do as I do. *Stop thinking you have to obey Jewish rules and rituals. When I was with you,* I *did not obey all the Jewish rules and rituals*, just as you *were not obeying them.*

At that time you treated me entirely justly. ¹³You know that the first time I told the good message to you was when *I went to your area to regain my health, because I was physically weak.* ¹⁴*Although* you might have *despised me because* I was physically weak, you did not despise me or act contemptuously toward me. Instead, you welcomed me like *you would welcome* an angel from God. *You welcomed me* like *you would welcome* Christ Jesus! ¹⁵I am disappointed that you have forgotten *that then* you *declared that you were* pleased with *me.* I can testify that at that time you *would have done anything to help me.* You would have gouged out your eyes *and* given them to me, *if that would have helped me!* ¹⁶So I am very disappointed that you *now* act as though I have become hostile to you *because I have kept on* speaking the true *message about Christ* to you. ¹⁷Those *who are insisting on following Jewish rules* are eagerly showing *interest in* you, but *what they are doing is* not good. They even want you not to associate with *me and other genuine* believers, because they want you to eagerly show *interest in* them, and *not in us.* ¹⁸But *just as* it always feels good when others show they appreciate you, *I would like you to* always *appreciate me*, and not just when I am with you. ¹⁹You *who are like* my children, *once* again I am very worried concerning you, *and I will continue to* be worried until Christ's *nature is developed* in you exclusively *and wholeheartedly, as children* become developed *in their mothers' wombs.* ²⁰But I do wish that I could be with you now and that I might talk *more gently with you*, because I don't know *what to do about* you.

---

^c OR, Likewise, when we *Jews* were…

^d OR, …*Jesus*, the man who was also God…

Galatians 4:21-31

THEME: Because of our relationship with Christ we are not subject to Mosaic law. Being Abraham's spiritual descendants, we are free from such bondage.

[21] Some of you desire *to obey all the laws* God gave Moses. *I say that* you *should* consider *the implications of what Moses wrote in* the Scriptures. [22] *He* wrote that Abraham became the father of two sons. His female slave *Hagar* bore one son, and his *wife Sarah*, who was not a slave, bore the other. [23] Also, *the sons differed in that Ishmael*, the *son born to* the female slave, was born naturally, but *Isaac*, the *son born to* his wife who was not a slave, was born *miraculously* as a result of what *God* had promised *Abraham.* [24] *I am telling you this* as an illustration. These *two women* symbolize two agreements. The first *agreement involved obeying the laws God gave Moses* at *Mount Sinai. Since that agreement forces those who accept it to keep obeying all its rules, it is like a slave mother whose* children are slaves. *So* Hagar, *the female slave, symbolizes* this *agreement.* [25] Also, the *word* 'Hagar' is *associated with* Mount Sinai *which is in the land of* Arabia. *Hagar, the female slave, also* represents *the city of* Jerusalem as it is today. Jerusalem is *like* a slave *mother, and those who live there are like* her slave children *because they all must obey the laws God gave Moses.* [26] But there will be a *new* Jerusalem in heaven, and we *who are going there* are free *from having to obey all the Jewish laws.* We *who belong to that city consider it* our mother *city because we are God's true children.* [27] *Our new city will have more people than those who live in Jerusalem now. It will be just as* Isaiah foretold about *the people whom he expected would come back to Jerusalem from exile. He expected that they would be more numerous than those who were taken into exile. He* wrote:

> *You who live in Jerusalem, you will* rejoice! Now you have no children, like a barren *woman* who does not bear *children! But some day you will* shout *with joy* without restraint, *even though now you are few, like a woman who* cannot give birth *to children, and you* feel deserted. *You will be very happy* because *you will have many children who will come to you. Those children will be* more than *the children* any woman with a husband *could have given birth to.*

[28] Now, *my* fellow believers, you have become children *of God as a result of believing* God's promise to us, just as Isaac *was born as a result of Abraham believing what God promised him.*

[29] *Also, long ago Abraham's son* Ishmael caused trouble for *Abraham's son* Isaac, who *was conceived* supernaturally. In the same way, now *those who think that we must obey the laws God gave Moses to be saved are causing trouble for those who are trusting Abraham's descendant, Christ.* [30] But these are the words in the Scriptures: "The son of the *woman* who was not a slave will inherit *what his father has.* The female slave's son will certainly not inherit those things. So send away from *this place* the female slave and her son!" *That means that you should expel from your groups those who insist that we obey all the laws God gave Moses.* [31] *My* fellow believers, *Hagar symbolizes the laws God gave Moses. But we are not those who must obey all those laws. So* we are not *the* spiritual descendants of *Hagar, the* female slave. *Sarah's descendants are those who were born as a result of believing what God promised to Abraham. So we are the spiritual* descendants of *Sarah, the woman* who was not a slave.

5

Galatians 5:1-6

THEME: Reject the false teaching that you must be circumcised. Do not become enslaved to rules and rituals again, otherwise Christ will not benefit you at all.

¹ It is in order that we might conduct our lives without being obliged *to obey all the Jewish rituals* that Christ freed us *from being condemned because of disobeying those rituals.* So you must firmly *reject the false teaching that you must be circumcised.* Do not *live like slaves again by letting others force you to obey those rules and rituals again.* ² Consider very carefully what I, Paul, *an apostle,* now tell you: If you are permitting yourself to be circumcised, then what Christ *has done for you* will not benefit you at all. ³ All of you who suppose that God has accepted you because you have been circumcised, I solemnly declare again to that you must *perfectly* obey all of the laws *God gave Moses!* ⁴ Those of you who suppose that God will erase the record of your sins because you obey the laws *God gave Moses,* you have separated yourselves from Christ. You have abandoned God's *true method of saving you, which is* erasing the record of your sins because of his kindness, *not because you deserve it.* ⁵ But we are eagerly awaiting *what God will do* for us whose record of sins has been erased. We await it because God's Spirit assures us that we can expect it, and because we trust in Christ. ⁶ As for us who have a relationship with Christ Jesus, God is not concerned whether we are circumcised or not. Instead, God is concerned that we trust *in* Christ, with the result that we love others.

Galatians 5:7-12

THEME: Although someone has confused you, I am sure that you will not accept his false teaching, and that God will punish him.

⁷ You were progressing well *spiritually.* You should not have let someone influence you so that *now you* don't believe the true *message about Christ!* ⁸ *God,* the one who chose you, is not the one who is persuading you to think like this! ⁹ *Remember that this false doctrine that a few people are teaching will affect all of you, just like* a little *yeast* causes all of the dough to swell up. ¹⁰ *Nevertheless,* because of my relationship with the Lord, I am certain that you will think only as I do *about forcing people to obey rules and rituals.* Furthermore, *God* will punish anyone who is confusing you, even if he is an important person. ¹¹ But, my fellow believers, *although someone claims that I am proclaiming that men must be circumcised, I certainly am not still proclaiming that. Remember that the Jews are still persecuting me.* If I were still proclaiming that men must be circumcised *in order for God to accept them,* the Jews would not be persecuting me. *They would not be persecuting me because* then *they* would no longer be offended. *They are offended because I proclaim that Christ, the Messiah, died on* the cross. ¹² I *would even* wish that those who are disturbing you *by insisting that men be circumcised* would also emasculate themselves, *with the result that they would be expelled from your congregations!*

Galatians 5:13-15

THEME: Although you are free from having to obey Jewish rules, don't do what your self-directed nature desires. Instead, love and serve each other.

¹³ My fellow believers, *God* chose you so that *you might live* without having to *obey rules and rituals.* But *don't assume that because* you are free *from having to obey rules and rituals,* you are permitted to *do what your* self-directed nature *desires.* Instead, as you love

each other, constantly serve each other. [14] Keep in mind that we can sum up all of the laws *that God has* given us in one law, which is: "You must love each person you come in contact with, just like *you love* yourself." [15] But you are attacking and injuring each other *by the things you say*. I warn you! *If you continue doing that*, you will totally ruin each other *spiritually!*

Galatians 5:16-18

THEME: Let God's Spirit direct you, and then you will not do what your self-directed nature desires.

[16] *So* I tell you this: Constantly let *God's* Spirit direct you. *If you do that,* you will certainly not do the things your self-directed nature wants *you to do*. [17] Your self-directed nature opposes *God's* Spirit, but also his Spirit opposes your self-directed nature. These two are always fighting with each other. The result is that you don't *always* do the *good* deeds that you truly want *to do*. [18] But when God's Spirit directs you, you *are able to do what pleases God,* now that you are no longer obligated to practice *all* the laws *God gave Moses*.

Galatians 5:19-24

THEME: Those who think evil thoughts and do evil things will not receive the blessings of God's rule, but God's Spirit produces many good qualities in our lives.

[19] How *people think and* act because of their self-directed nature is *already* familiar *to you*. These are *some of the things they do: People* are sexually immoral. *People* commit unnatural sexual acts. *People* act indecently. [20] *People* worship false gods *and* things *that* represent those gods. *People* perform sorcery. *People* are hostile *to others. People* quarrel *with each other. People* resent other people's status. *People* behave angrily. *People* try to get others to think highly of them and do not consider *the feelings of* others. People do not associate *with some people; they* associate only with those who agree *with them*. [21] *People* want what others have. *People* get drunk. *People* participate in wild parties. And *they do other* things like these. I warn you *now*—just as I warned *you previously*—that the ones *who constantly* act *and think* like this will not receive *what* God *has for his own people when he begins* his rule over us. [22] But *these are the things God's* Spirit causes *us to do*: We love *others*. We are joyful. We are peaceful. We are patient. We are kind. We are good. We are *ones whom* others can trust. [23] We are gentle. We control our behavior. And there is no law that says we should not *think and act like that!* [24] Furthermore, we who belong to Christ Jesus have *stopped obeying* our self-directed nature, and we have *stopped doing* all the evil things we desire to do. *It is as though* we nailed them to the cross!

[25] Since *God's* Spirit has made us *spiritually* alive, we should *conduct our lives the way he directs us*. [26] We should not be saying how great we are. We should not be making ourselves more important than others. We should not envy each other.

6

Galatians 6:1-6

THEME: Gently correct anyone among you who is sinning, and help each other without thinking you are better than others.

[1] My fellow believers, if *you* discover that a person *in your congregation* is sinning, *those of* you whom *God's* Spirit *is directing and empowering* should gently correct that person. *Furthermore, each of* you *who corrects someone should* be very cautious, in order that you might not *sin in the same way when* you are tempted. [2] *When there are those who have* problems, you should help each other. By doing that, you will complete what Christ requires. [3] Keep in mind that those who *refuse to help others because they think they are more important than others, although they are* really *not* more important, are deceiving themselves. [4] Each *of you* should *constantly* test *what you yourself are doing and thinking and see if you can approve of it.* Then you can boast because of what you yourself *are doing and thinking*, and not boast that what you are doing is superior to what others *are doing.* [5] Keep in mind that you must each perform your own *individual* tasks. [6] *You* who are being taught *God's truth* should share your various material things with your teachers.

Galatians 6:7-9

THEME: We should not tire of doing good. Instead, we should do good to everyone, especially to believers.

[7] You should not deceive yourselves. *Remember that* no one ever outwits God. *Just as* farmers will reap exactly the kind *of crop* they sow, *God will reward people according to what they have done.* [8] *God* will punish eternally all those who do what their self-directed nature urges them to do. But all those who please *God's* Spirit will live forever *with God* because of what *God's* Spirit does for them. [9] We should not tire of doing what pleases God, because *eventually*, at the time *God* has determined, we will receive a reward, if we don't give up *doing the good things that we have been doing.* [10] So whenever we have opportunities, we should do good to all people. But particularly we should do good to all those who believe *in Christ.*

Galatians 6:11-16

THEME: Some people want you to be circumcised only so that they will not be persecuted for proclaiming what Christ accomplished for us on the cross, but what Christ did for us is the only thing I will boast about.

[11] *I am now writing this last part to you in my own handwriting. Notice the large letters with which I am now writing. I am doing this to emphasize the following:* [12] *Some Jewish believers are trying to force you to perform certain rituals so that other Jews will think*

highly of them. They are insisting that you be circumcised. They are doing that only so that other Jews will no longer persecute them for proclaiming that God will save us because of our trusting in what Christ accomplished when he died on the cross. [13] *The reason I say that is that the ones who are insisting that you be circumcised do not themselves fully obey the laws God gave Moses. No, what they want is for you to be circumcised so they can boast to those who would persecute them that they persuaded you to do that.* [14] *I myself, however, strongly desire never to boast about anything like that. The only thing I will boast about is what our Lord Jesus Christ accomplished by dying on the cross. Because of what Christ did on the cross, I no longer am interested in the things that are valued by those who do not trust Christ, and those people are no longer interested in me.* [15] *I will boast about Christ dying on the cross because God is not concerned whether people are circumcised or are not circumcised. Instead, he is concerned only that people conduct their lives in a completely new way.* [16] *I pray that God will give inner peace and act kindly towards all who will conduct themselves according to this new way of life.*

It is all those who conduct themselves according to this new way of life who are now truly God's people, as the Jews previously were.

Galatians 6:17

THEME: I have suffered enough for declaring the truth about Jesus, so do not trouble me again.

[17] Finally, I say that people have caused me to suffer for declaring the truth about Jesus, and as a result I have scars on my body. Your new teachers don't have scars like mine! So don't trouble me about these matters again!

Galatians 6:18

THEME: I pray that God will act kindly within your lives.

[18] My fellow believers, I pray that our Lord Jesus Christ will kindly accomplish what he desires within you. May it be so!

The Apostle Paul wrote a letter to the Christians at Ephesus. We call this letter

Ephesians

1

Ephesians 1:1-2

THEME: I am writing this to you people of God in Ephesus, asking God to bless you.

¹ I, Paul, am an apostle whom God appointed to represent Christ Jesus because that is what God wanted. *I am writing this letter* to you who are the people of God in *the city of* Ephesus. *You are people who* faithfully trust in Christ Jesus and who have a close relationship with him. ² *I pray that* God our Father and Jesus Christ our Lord will continue to act kindly toward you and cause you to have *inner* peace.

Ephesians 1:2-14

THEME: We should praise God for having chosen and redeemed us, for having revealed his plan to unite all things under Christ, and for causing Christ to rule over all his people.

³ Praise God, the Father of our Lord Jesus Christ! Because of our relationship with Christ, he has blessed us spiritually in every way by giving us blessings that come from heaven. ⁴ Before God created the world, he chose us to be his people because of the relationship *we would have* with Christ. God chose us so that *he could consider* us to be completely holy. Because *God* loves *us*, ⁵ he decided long ago that he would adopt us to be *as though we were* his own children because of what Jesus Christ *has done*. He decided to do that because it pleased him. ⁶ He wanted us to praise him for acting extremely kindly toward us, in a wonderful way that we did not deserve, because of our relationship with his beloved Son.

⁷ When the blood of Christ *flowed from his body when he died, it was as though* he paid a price to free us *from the guilt of our sins*. That provided a way for God to act very kindly toward us, and to forgive us for having sinned. ⁸ He acted extremely kindly toward us and enabled us to become wise about many things and to understand his truth. ⁹ He has enabled us to know the things that he has planned, things that he had not yet revealed to anyone. He did that because he wanted to do it, and because he had planned to do it by means of the things Christ would do. ¹⁰ God planned that at the time *he appointed*, he would unite all things[a] in heaven and all things on earth, and cause Christ to be the one who will rule them. ¹¹ Because of our close relationship with Christ, God has also chosen us Jews to receive what he has promised us. He decided long ago to do that. It was exactly what he planned. He accomplishes everything exactly as he plans and desires. ¹² He chose us so that we Jews, who confidently expected Christ *to do great things for us* before *the non-Jews did,* will praise him for his greatness. ¹³ You *Ephesians* also heard the true message, the good message about how God saves you. *People* put their seal on

---

ᵃ OR, …all beings…

something to show that *it belongs to them.* And when you believed *in Christ,* God *showed that you belong to him by giving you* the Holy Spirit as he promised to do. The Holy Spirit was *like* a seal *that showed you belong to God.* ¹⁴ The Holy Spirit is *also like* a deposit. That is, he is the guarantee that you and *we will receive* all that God has promised to give us, at the time when God will give to those who belong to him everything *Christ* paid *for them to have. God showed that you and we belong to him* so that we all would praise him for his greatness.

Ephesians 1:15-23

THEME: I thank God for your faith. I pray that you will understand more about how powerfully God works on our behalf, just as he did when he raised Christ from the dead and made him ruler over everything.

¹⁵ Because of *what God has done for you,* and because people have told me that you continue to trust in the Lord Jesus and that you love all those who belong to God, ¹⁶ I thank God for you constantly. I mention you constantly, whenever I pray. ¹⁷ *I pray* that God, who is the glorious Father of our Lord Jesus Christ, will cause his Spirit to make you wise, and that his Spirit will reveal *God to you* so that you may fully know him. ¹⁸ And I pray that God will enable you to understand his truth, so that in your hearts you may know the things that we believers should confidently expect to receive, because of God having chosen us *to be his people.* And I pray that you will know how God will bless his people in a very wonderful way *when we finally receive* all that he has promised to give us. ¹⁹ And *I pray that* you will know how very powerfully *God acts* for us who continue to trust *in Christ.* He works powerfully for us, ²⁰ just as he acted powerfully for Christ when he caused him to become alive again after he died and put him in the place of highest honor in heaven. ²¹ *There in heaven,* Christ is the supreme ruler over every powerful spirit having every level of authority. His rank is much higher than any of them will receive, not only now, but forever. ²² God has caused all beings to be subject to Christ, and he has also appointed Christ, who rules over all things, to rule over all believers. ²³ We believers *relate to Christ like the parts of a person's* body *relate to its head.* Christ demonstrates all his power *among us* in the same way he demonstrates it throughout the whole universe.

2

Ephesians 2:1-10

THEME: Formerly we were all spiritually dead and were certain to be punished by God, but he acted very kindly toward us and saved us freely as a result of our faith in Christ.

¹ Formerly, because you were habitually sinning, you were *spiritually* dead. ² You were living in the same *evil* way as those people who oppose Christ live. That is, you were doing the *evil* things that Satan *wanted you to do.* He rules over evil spiritual beings that no one can see. He is also the spirit who now powerfully controls the people who disobey God. ³ Formerly, we all used to disobey God, just as those people do. We did the things that our self-centered nature wanted us to do. We habitually did those *evil* deeds that our bodies and our minds wanted to do. When we were living that way, it was certain that *God* would punish us, just as he will certainly punish all other *evil* people.

⁴ But God always acts very mercifully, and he loves us very much. ⁵ As a result, even when we were *spiritually* dead because of habitually sinning, he enabled us to receive *spiritual* life because of our relationship with Christ. *Don't forget this: It is only* because God has acted so kindly toward you—in a way that you did not deserve—that you have been saved

from the guilt of your sins! [6] And *it is as if* God gave us spiritual life at the time he caused Christ Jesus to come to life again after he died. And *it is as if* God caused us to sit *and rule* with Christ in heaven. [7] He did all this so that he might show to everyone at all times in the future that he has acted in an extremely kind way because of what Christ Jesus *did for us.*

[8] It is *only* by *God* acting *toward you* in a way that you did not deserve that he has saved you as a result of your trusting *in Christ*. You did not save yourselves. His saving you was his gift to you. [9] He did not save any of you because of anything you yourselves did. The result is that no one can be proud of what they have done *to save themselves*. [10] It is God who has made us what we are now. Because of our relationship with Christ Jesus, he has enabled us to receive *spiritual* life, in order that we should conduct our lives habitually doing the good deeds that God previously planned for us to do.

Ephesians 2:11-22

THEME: God brought you Gentiles into his family so that now you and Jewish believers both share the same blessings and form one group. You now have peace with each other and can come to God in prayer with the help of the Holy Spirit.

[11] You *Ephesians* are not Jews, having been born into non-Jewish families. The Jews *insult you by* calling you 'those who are not circumcised.' They *proudly* call themselves 'we who are circumcised.' *They have been* circumcised *to indicate that they are God's people, but* that has *only* changed their bodies, *not their hearts*. [12] You should constantly remember these things: Formerly you did not have any relationship with Christ. You did not belong to the people of Israel, the people chosen by God. You did not share in the things God promised in his agreements *with his people*. You did not confidently expect *that God would save you*. You were *living* in this world without *knowing* God. [13] But now, because of your relationship with Christ Jesus, God considers you, who had no relationship with him, as members of his family. That is because *you trusted in what Christ accomplished when* his blood *flowed from his body when he died on the cross.*

[14] Christ himself *has caused us Jewish and non-Jewish believers* to have peace *with each other*. He has made *our two groups* into one *group. Just as people* tear down a wall that separates *groups of people*, he has destroyed the hatred *between Jews and non-Jews.* [15] By dying *for us on the cross* he made it no longer *necessary to obey* all the *Jewish* laws and rituals *in order to be saved*. He did that in order to enable the two *groups* to become one new group because of our relationship with him. The result was that he has caused us to have peace *with each other*. [16] By *dying on* the cross he caused both Jews and non-Jews to have a peaceful relationship with God. In that way he caused us to no longer be enemies *with God.*[b] [17] He came *to earth* and proclaimed that you *non-Jews,* who did not have a relationship with *God*, and *we Jews*, who *considered that we were part* of God's *family*, can *all* now have peace *with God*. [18] *We know he has done that* because we both, *Jews and non-Jews*, are *now* able to approach God the Father by the help of his Spirit, because of what Christ *has done.*

[19] So *God no longer treats* you *non-Jews* as *people treat* foreigners and strangers. Instead, along with all God's people, *it is as though* you have become citizens of a country that he rules over, and *as though* you have become members of the family *of which he is the father.* [20] *Just as people* build a building on a foundation, *God has joined you into one group that originated* from what the apostles and prophets *taught*. Christ Jesus is the *most important member of that group, just as a* cornerstone *is the most important part of the*

---

[b] OR, …In that way he caused us to no longer be enemies *with each other.*

foundation of a building. [21] Just as *a builder might* join together all the parts of a building to make it a temple that *will* be dedicated to the Lord, *God is continually causing all of* you who have a relationship with *Christ to be united, so that you will become one holy group.* [22] And because of your relationship with Christ, *God* is joining you *non-Jewish believers* together with *Jewish believers* to be *like* one building in which his Spirit lives.

3

Ephesians 3:1-13

THEME: I am in prison because of doing the work God appointed me to do, the work of telling non-Jews that Christ is the source of great spiritual blessings for them.

[1] Because *God has done all this for* you non-Jews, I, Paul, *pray for you. I want you to know that it is because I serve* Christ Jesus for your sake that I am in prison. [2] You have heard how God acted very kindly toward me, appointing me *so that I would proclaim the good message to you non-Jews.* [3] God revealed to me the message that he had not revealed to others. When you read what I have already written briefly, [4] you will know that I understand clearly that message about Christ. [5] Formerly, *God* did not reveal that message to anyone, but now his Spirit has revealed it to his holy apostles and prophets.[c] [6] That message, which he has now revealed, is that because of their relationship with Christ Jesus, non-Jews as well as Jews will receive the *great spiritual blessings that God has* promised, as we all form one group *as a result of our believing* the good message *about Christ.* [7] God acted toward me in a way I did not deserve, and chose me *to do the work of* telling others this good message, and he powerfully enables me *to do that.*

[8] Although I am the least *worthy* of all God's people, God kindly *appointed* me to proclaim to the non-Jews the message about the great spiritual blessings *they can receive* from Christ, [9] and to enable everyone to understand clearly how God accomplished what he had planned. God, who created everything, *has now revealed* this message, which he never revealed to anyone before. [10] What he intended was that all believers would be the ones who would reveal to all the ranks of spiritual beings in heaven that what God had planned was wise in every way. [11] That is what God had always planned, and it is what he accomplished by means of what our Lord Jesus *has done.* [12] Because of what Jesus has done and because of our relationship with him, *when we pray,* we can approach God confidently and without being afraid. [13] So I ask you not to be discouraged because of all I am suffering for you *here in prison.* You should feel honored that I am *willing to* suffer *these things.*

Ephesians 3:14-21

THEME: I pray that God's Spirit will empower you, that you will experience how great is Christ's love for you and that God will make you all he intends you to be.

[14] Because *God has done all this for you,* I kneel *and pray* to *God our* Father. [15] He is the one who is *like* a father of all *the believers* in heaven and those who are still on the earth. [16] I pray that, using his unlimited resources, he will cause you to be strengthened by his Spirit in your hearts, with all *God's* power. [17] That is, I pray that because of your trusting in Christ, his *Spirit* may live in your hearts.[d] And I pray that because you love *Christ* firmly

---

[c] OR, …has revealed it to people who tell messages that come directly from God.

[d] OR, …he may live in your hearts.

and faithfully, you, [18] along with all other believers, will be able to know how very much Christ loves *us all*. [19] I want you to experience how very deeply he loves us, even though it is not possible for us to understand fully *his love for us*. And I pray that God will enable you to have a full measure of all the qualities that he himself has.

[20] According to *God's* power that is working within us, he is able to do far greater things than we could ask him to do, or even that we might think he can do. [21] Because of our relationship with Christ Jesus, may all us believers praise him forever. May it be so!

4

Ephesians 4:1-16

THEME: Conduct your lives in a way that shows you are God's people. Do all you can to keep all the believers united. Remember that Christ has given various abilities to each of us who are his people, so that we may be united, grow spiritually, and become like him.

[1] So I, who am in prison because *I serve* the Lord *Jesus*, urge you, whom God has chosen *to be his people, to do these things*: Conduct yourselves as *God's people* should. [2] Always be humble, and don't demand your own rights. Be patient *with each other* and endure each other's irritating behavior because of your love for each other. [3] Since *God's* Spirit has caused you to be united *with one another*, do all you can to remain united by acting peacefully *toward each other*. [4] *All we believers form just one group*, and there is only one *Holy* Spirit, just as *God* chose you so that you all might confidently keep expecting the same things *that other believers do*. [5] There is only one Lord, *Jesus Christ*. We all believe the same *teaching about him. It was to show that we belong to him* alone that *we were* baptized. [6] There is one God, who is the *spiritual* Father of all *of us believers*. He *rules* over all his people; he enables all his people *to do powerful things,*[e] and his *Spirit lives* in all his people.

[7] Christ has freely given to each one of us spiritual gifts, just as he decided to give them. [8] *When Christ gave gifts to his people, it was similar to what the Psalmist said about God receiving tribute money from those he had conquered,*
    When he ascended to heaven, he gave as gifts to friends
    the things *he had taken* from the people he captured.

[9] The words 'he ascended' must imply that Christ had also previously descended to the earth. [10] Christ, who descended *to earth*, is also the one who ascended to the most exalted position in heaven, so that he might show his power throughout the universe. [11] He appointed some people to be apostles. He appointed some people to be prophets, *ones who reveal messages directly from God*. He appointed some to be evangelists, *ones whose work is to tell others the message about Christ*. He appointed some to lead and teach *the congregations*. [12] *He appointed all of these* in order that they would prepare God's people to do *God's* work, so that all the people who belong to Christ might become *spiritually* mature. [13] He wants all of us *believers* to be united *because* we all believe in the Son of God and *because* we all know *him*. He wants us to become spiritually mature; that is, he wants us to be all that God wants us to be, *just as* Christ was *all that God wanted him to be*. [14] Then we will no longer be *spiritually immature*, as little children *are immature*. We will no longer be constantly *changing what we believe, as* waves of the sea are *constantly changing when the wind blows and* tosses them back and forth. We will not

---

e   OR, ...he sustains all his people.

allow people who teach *what is false* and who scheme cleverly to deceive us. [15] Instead, by loving *others* as we conduct our lives according to *God's* truth, we will become more and more like Christ in every way.[f] He is the one who controls *all his people, just as a person's* head *controls his* body. [16] He *enables all those who belong to him to mature spiritually. They will become mature spiritually* by loving each other and by all of them doing the work *that God wants them to do. That is just like* a person's body *grows stronger, as* each part of the body is joined to the others by the ligaments and as each part functions properly.

Ephesians 4:17-32

THEME: You should conduct yourselves in a way that matches your new character; so stop doing the harmful things that unbelievers do, and do good to one another.

[17] By *the authority of* the Lord *Jesus*, I strongly tell you to no longer conduct yourselves in the way that unbelievers do. The futile way in which they think *controls the way they conduct their lives.* [18] They are unable to think clearly *about what is right and what is wrong.* Because they have decided that they do not want to know about God and because they stubbornly refuse to *listen to his message*, they do not have the *eternal* life that God *gives us.* [19] The result is that because they have ceased to care *about what is right and what is wrong*, they have deliberately committed themselves to doing the shameful things that their bodies desire, and they commit all kinds of immoral acts, and continually are eager to do more of those kinds of things.

[20] But when you learned *about* Christ, you did not learn *to behave* that way. [21] I am sure that you heard the message about *Christ*, and that because you are people who have a close relationship with him, you have learned the true *way to conduct our lives* that Jesus *showed us.* [22] *You were taught {I taught you}* that you must put aside your evil nature*; that is, that you must not behave like you formerly did.* Your evil desires deceived you, making you want to do evil things and causing you to think that *doing that was good for you*, and that was destroying you *spiritually.* [23] Others taught you that instead, you must let *God's* Spirit change the way you think, [24] and that you must start being the new persons that God made you to become. That is, your *behavior* must be righteous and truly/genuinely devout.

[25] So stop lying to one another. Instead, since we all belong to just one group *of believers*, speak truthfully to each other. [26] If you get angry, don't sin *as a result of* getting angry. Stop yourself from being angry before the end of each day, [27] so that don't allow the devil to make you do evil. [28] Those who have been stealing must not steal any longer. Instead, they should work hard to earn their living by their own efforts, so that they may have *something* to give to those who are needy. [29] Don't use foul language. Instead, say only things that are suitable and helpful, things that will help people *spiritually.* [30] *God has given you his* Spirit to confirm that some day *God will claim all* you people *whom Christ has* redeemed, *just like people confirm that something belongs to them by* putting their seal on it. So do not cause God's Holy Spirit to be sad *by the way you talk.* [31] Don't be resentful at all towards others. Don't become angry in any way. Never shout abusively at others. Never slander others. Never act maliciously in any way. [32] Be kind to one another. Act mercifully toward each other. Forgive each other, just as God has forgiven you because of *what* Christ *did for you.*

---

[f]   OR, Instead, by loving *others* as we speak in a loving manner what is true, we will become more and more like Christ in every way.

5

Ephesians 5:1-6

THEME: Imitate God, do everything in a way that shows love, and do not let anyone persuade you to live immorally, because God will punish those who disobey him.

[1] Imitate God, because *you know that* he loves you *and considers you* his children. [2] Do everything in a way that shows you love *others,* just as Christ loved us and willingly died for us. He offered himself *to God as a sacrifice* that was very pleasing to God, *just as Jewish priests offered* sweet-smelling *animal* sacrifices to God. [3] Don't commit any kind of immoral act, and don't desire more things than you need. Don't *act in such a way that others could* even spread rumors about the way you behave, because it is not appropriate for God's people to do such things. [4] Don't use obscene language. Don't talk foolishly. Don't use vulgar language, because such language is not appropriate for God's people. Instead, tell people how much you thank *God for all he does for you.* [5] You can be sure of this: No person who is sexually immoral or who acts indecently will be among those people whom God and Christ rule over *in heaven.* Neither will those who desire more things than they need. Such persons worship their possessions *instead of worshiping God.* [6] Don't let anyone deceive you by suggesting that *God will* not *punish people who commit such sins*, because God certainly will punish those who habitually disobey him *by doing such things.*

Ephesians 5:7-6:9

THEME: Live righteously. Expose the evil deeds that people do, because when you do that, the people who do those evil things will come to know the truth.

[7] So don't commit the same kinds of deeds that such people do. [8] Remember that formerly you *did not know God's truth, in the same way that those who* are in darkness *don't know what is around them.* But now *it is as though* you are in the light *because you know God's truth* because of your relationship with the Lord *Jesus.* So do those things that those who know God's truth should do. [9] Keep in mind that *just as* light produces *things that are good, those who know God's truth should do the things* that are good, righteous, and honest. [10] And as *you do that*, try to find out what pleases the Lord. [11] Don't do the worthless deeds that the people who are in *spiritual* darkness do. Instead, let others know those people's deeds are worthless. [12] Although it is shameful for God's people to even discuss *among themselves* the evil deeds that evil people do secretly and habitually, [13] when *God's people rebuke them for their deeds, it will be clearly seen how evil their deeds really are, just as* everything exposed to the light becomes visible. [14] *And just as* something on which a light shines reflects that light, *those who have come to know God's truth reveal that truth to others.* That is why *we believers* say this:

> You who are sound asleep, wake up!
> *Be like* dead people who are coming alive again!
> Christ will *cause you to know God's truth,*
>   *just as a* light which shines *causes people to know what is in the darkness.*

[15] So be very careful how you behave. Do not behave as foolish people do. Instead, behave as wise people do. [16] Use your time carefully, because in these days *people do* extremely evil *deeds.* [17] Because of that, don't be foolish. Instead, understand what the Lord *Jesus* wants you to do, *and do it!*

[18] Don't become drunk by drinking *any kind of* alcoholic drinks, because people are unable to control their behavior when they are drunk. Instead, let *God's* Spirit control your

behavior at all times. [19] Sing to each other Psalms, sing *other* songs *the congregation knows*, or songs *God's* Spirit *gives you*. Sing these Psalms and other songs sincerely to *praise* the Lord *Jesus*. [20] At all times thank God, who is our *heavenly* Father, for everything, because of what the Lord Jesus Christ *has done for you*. [21] *Humbly* submit to each other because you reverence Christ, *who is our example of humility*.

Ephesians 5:22-6:9

THEME: I am giving you instructions about how husbands and wives, children and parents, and slaves and their masters should behave toward each other.

[22-23] Since husbands have authority over their wives, just as all of us believers form one group *under the authority of* Christ, you women must submit yourselves to *the authority of your* husbands in the same way that you submit to the Lord *Jesus*. He is the one who saves us who are his people *from the guilt of our sins*. [24] Just as all we believers submit to *the authority of* Christ, the women must submit completely to the *authority of* their husbands.

[25] Each of you husbands must love your wife as Christ loved all of *us who would become* believers, with the result that he willingly died for our sake, [26] in order that he might set us apart for himself. That is, by *revealing his* message *to us,* he wanted to *remove the guilt of our sins, just as people remove dirt from something* by washing them. [27] *Christ did that* so that he might cause all of us believers to be a glorious group of people that belong to him, people who are completely pure, without any moral flaws, when he gathers us to his presence. [28] In the same way, each man ought to love his wife as he loves his own body. Men who love their wives, *it is as though* they love themselves. [29-30] This is shown by the fact that we never hate our own bodies. Instead, we feed and care for them, just as Christ also cares for all of us believers. We have become one group that belongs to him. [31] *What is written in the Scriptures about people who marry is this,*

When a man *and woman marry*, they should permanently leave their fathers and mothers. They should be joined *as husband and* wife, and the two of them shall become *as though they were* one person.

[32] It is very difficult to *completely* understand the meaning of these things that God has now revealed to me, but *I am telling you that* these words *also* refer to *the relationship between* Christ and all of us who belong to him. [33] However, as for you, each man must love his wife in the same way as he loves himself, and each woman must respect her husband.

6

[1] You children, since you have a close relationship with the Lord *Jesus*, you must obey your parents, because it is right *for you to do* that. [2] God commanded *in the Scriptures,*
Greatly respect your father and mother.

That is the first *law that God* commanded in which he also promised *something*. He *promised,*
[3] If you do that, you will prosper, and you will live a long time on the earth.

[4] You parents,[9] don't treat your children so severely that they become angry. Instead, bring them up by instructing them and by disciplining them in *the way* the Lord *Jesus wants you to*.

---

[9] OR, You fathers…

[5] You slaves, obey *your masters* here on the earth very respectfully and sincerely, just as you obey Christ. [6] Obey them not only when they are watching you, and not only to cause them to think highly of you. Instead, obey them as *though you were* slaves of Christ, *instead of being slaves of your masters*. Do enthusiastically what God wants *you to do.* [7] Serve *your masters* zealously, as you would serve the Lord *Jesus*, not just as you would serve *ordinary* people. [8] Do this because you know that *some day* the Lord Jesus will reward each person for whatever good *deeds* that person has done. He will reward people who are slaves and people who are not slaves.

[9] You bosses, just as your slaves *should serve you well*, you similarly must treat them well. Stop threatening *to beat* them *if they don't do their work well*. Don't forget that the one who is their Lord and your Lord is in heaven. *He is the one who will tell you and your slaves whether he approves of what you and they have done*, and he does not judge some people differently than he judges others.

Ephesians 6:10-20

THEME: Always relying on the Lord to strengthen you, make use of every spiritual resource God provides to resist the devil and all his powerful evil spirits.

[10] Finally, at all times rely completely on the Lord *Jesus* to strengthen you *spiritually* by his mighty power. [11] *Just as soldiers* put on all their armor *to help them fight*, you should *use every spiritual resource that God provides for you*, in order that you may successfully resist the devil when he cleverly tries *to oppose you.* [12] Remember that the fighting we believers do is not against human beings. Instead, we are fighting against evil spirits who rule and have authority over all that is evil in the world. We are fighting against evil spirits in heavenly places.[h] [13] So, *just as soldiers* put on all their armor, *you must use well all the spiritual resources that God provides for you*. Do that so that you may be able to successfully resist the devil and all his powerful evil spirits every time they attack you. Also do it in order that when you have done all you can to resist their *attacks*, you will still be ready to resist them *when they attack you* the next time.

[14] You must be ready to firmly *resist the devil and his evil spirits, just as soldiers must be ready to resist the enemy. Be ready for that by doing these things: To be strong spiritually*, hold firmly to *God's* truth, just as soldiers prepare to stand firm against their enemies by fastening their belts around their waists. Act righteously *in order to protect yourself against demonic attacks, just as soldiers* put on breastplates *to protect their chests against their enemies' attacks.* [15] *Be ready to tell others the good message about how they can have* peace *with God, just as soldiers prepare to* stand firm *against their enemies* by putting their boots on. [16] In addition, keep trusting firmly *in the Lord. That will enable you to protect yourselves from anything that Satan*, the evil one, *may do to harm you spiritually, just as soldiers* carry shields *to protect themselves against* the arrows that have flaming tips *that their enemies shoot at them.* [17] And *rely on the fact that God* has saved you, *in order to protect yourselves against demonic attacks, just as soldiers* put on helmets *to protect their heads from attacks by their enemies.* And be ready to use *the weapon that God's* Spirit *has given you*, which is the message of God, *in order to fight against demonic powers, just as soldiers* hold their swords *to fight against their enemies.* [18] As you are doing all these things, keep praying *to God* at all times, and requesting him *for your needs and the needs of others;* and let his Spirit *direct how and what you pray*. In order to pray like this, always be spiritually alert, and always be persistent in praying for all God's people. [19] And *specifically* pray for me. Pray that God will tell me what I should say whenever I speak, so that I may boldly tell others the good message about Christ. People did not know that

---

[h]   OR, …We are fighting against evil spirits who are everywhere.

message before, *but God has now revealed it to me.* [20] I am a representative *of Christ as I tell this message to others, and* I am in prison *because I have done just that.* Pray that when I tell *others about Christ*, I will speak without being afraid, because that is the way I ought to speak.

Ephesians 6:21-24

THEME: I am sending Tychicus to tell you what is happening here and to encourage you. I pray that God will give you peace and love for each other, and that he will continue to show his kindness to you all.

[21] In order that you may know about *what is happening* to me and what I am doing, I am sending Tychicus *with this letter*. He will tell you everything *that is happening here*. He is a fellow believer whom we love very much, and he serves the Lord *Jesus* faithfully. [22] That is the reason I am sending him; I want you to know how we are, and I want him to encourage you.

[23] *I pray that* God our Father and the Lord Jesus Christ will cause all of you fellow believers to have *inner* peace, and will *enable you to* love *each other* and to continue trusting *in Christ*. [24] I pray that God will continue to act kindly to *you and* to all *others* who love our Lord Jesus Christ and who will never stop loving him.

The Apostle Paul wrote a letter to the Christians at Philippi. We call this letter

Philippians

1

Philippians 1:1-2

THEME: I, Paul, write this letter to all of you at Philippi who are God's people. May God our Father and Jesus Christ our Lord bless you.

¹ *I,* Paul, and Timothy, *who is with me, are* men who serve Christ Jesus. *I am writing this letter* to all *of you who are* pastors and deacons in *the city of* Philippi, and to the rest of God's people *there who have a close relationship* with Christ Jesus. ² *We both pray that* God, *who is* our Father, and Jesus Christ, *who is our* Lord, *will continue to* show their kindness to you and *will give* you *inner* peace.

Philippians 1:3-8

THEME: I thank God and rejoice because, from when you first believed until now, you have been working together with me to make known the good message.

³ I thank my God whenever I think about you. ⁴ Every time I pray *for* all of *you,* I pray for you joyfully. ⁵ *I thank God and rejoice* because you have been *working* together with me to *make known* the good message about Christ. *You started doing that* when you first *believed that message, and you have continued doing it* until now. ⁶ I am completely confident that God, who has begun to perform in you what is good,[a] will continue to do that until he finishes doing it on the day Christ Jesus *returns.* ⁷ During this time that I have been a prisoner and during the times I have defended the good message about Christ and showed that it is true, all of you have been sharing with me in this work *that God* in his kindness gave *to me to do. So* indeed it is right that I feel joyful about you all, because you are very dear to me. ⁸ God *can* verify that Christ Jesus causes me to *love and* long for all of you very much, *just as* Christ loves *you.*

Philippians 1:9-11

THEME: I pray that God will enable you to know how to love one another more and more in a proper way, and to completely understand how you should believe and conduct your lives.

⁹ And what I pray *for you* is that *God will enable* you to truly know and discern how to love *one another* more and more in a proper way in every situation. ¹⁰ *And I pray that he will enable* you to completely understand *how you should believe and how you should conduct your lives. I pray this* so that you may be *spiritually* pure and faultless[b] on the day Christ *returns,* ¹¹ *and so that* you may conduct your lives completely righteously as a result of

---

[a] OR, I am completely confident that since God has begun to perform in you what is good, he…

[b] OR, …be completely faultless…

Jesus Christ *enabling you to live that way,* in order that *people will* honor God and praise him[c] *when they see you living that way.*

Philippians 1:12-14

THEME: I want you to realize that as a result of my imprisonment many more people have heard the good message about Christ.

[12] My fellow believers, I want you to know that the *troubles* I have experienced *have not prevented me from proclaiming the good message to people. Instead, these things I have experienced* have enabled even more people to hear the good message about Christ. [13] All the military guards who are stationed here *in Rome* and many other *people in the city* know that I am a prisoner because *of proclaiming the good news* about Christ. [14] Also, most of the believers *here now* proclaim the message from God more courageously and fearlessly *because* they trust the Lord *more firmly to help them. They trust the Lord more* because *they have seen how he has helped me* during the time I have been a prisoner *here.*

Philippians 1:15-18a

THEME: Even though some believers proclaim the message about Christ because they are antagonistic toward me, at least they are proclaiming Christ, and so I rejoice.

[15-16] Some people proclaim *the message about* Christ *as I do* because they are happy *with my work.* They proclaim *the message about* Christ because they love *me and because* they know that *God* has placed me *here* to defend that message. [17] Others proclaim *the message about* Christ because they envy *me* and oppose *me.* They want to exalt themselves *above me. They proclaim the message about Christ out of* wrong motives. They *wrongly* assume *that because many people are following them, I will be jealous, and that as a result,* I will feel more miserable *here* in prison. [18] But it does not matter! It does not matter whether *people proclaim the message about Christ* out of wrong motives, or out of right motives. The important thing in either case is that *the message about* Christ is being proclaimed. And so I rejoice!

Philippians 1:18b-26

THEME: I will continue to rejoice because I know that I will remain completely victorious spiritually, because I earnestly expect to boldly honor Christ, whether I live or die.

Furthermore, I will continue to rejoice, [19] because I know that the outcome of these *troubles I am experiencing* will *be that some day God will* say that he approves *of what I have done.*[d] *This will happen* as a result of your praying for me, and *as a result* of God's Spirit, whom Jesus Christ gave me, helping me. [20] *I know it will happen* because I very confidently expect that in no way will I be reluctant *to honor Christ.* Instead, just as I always *have done,* I will continue now also to very boldly honor Christ by means of all that I do, whether by *the way I* live or *by the way I* die.

[21] As for me, *as long as* I live, *I am living to honor* Christ. But if I die, it will be better *for me than if I continue to live, because then I will be completely united with him.* [22] On the other hand, if I continue to live, I will continue to serve *Christ* effectively. As a result, I don't know whether I prefer *to live or to die.* [23] I'm not sure which of those two *I prefer.* I long to leave

---

[c] OR, …in order that *people will* praise God very much…

[d] OR, …*that the Roman authorities* will set me free.

this world and *go to* be with Christ, because that will be very much better *for me.*
[24] Nevertheless, it is more important that I remain alive *than that I go to be with Christ,
because* you still need *me to help you.* [25] Since I am convinced of this, I know that I will
remain *alive* and *that I will come to* be with you all. *As a result*, you will come to believe *in
Christ* more firmly, and *so* you will rejoice. [26] You will rejoice very greatly because of Christ
Jesus *bringing* me *to be with you again.*

Philippians 1:27-30

*THEME: Conduct yourselves just as you learned in the message about Christ, unitedly and
fearlessly resisting those who oppose you and the gospel, since God is helping you in all your
struggles.*

[27] Most importantly, as fellow *believers in Christ*, conduct yourselves just as *you learned
you should do when you heard* the message about Christ. Do that so that whether I come
and see you, or whether I am away from you and people tell me about you, *I will be made
happy.* In either case, I will learn that you are, in a united and cooperative manner,
resisting *those who oppose the message about Christ. I will know* that you are not
allowing others to influence you to believe a message that is different from the good
message *about Christ.* [28] And *I will know* that you are not at all afraid of the people who
oppose you. Your not being afraid will signal to them that *God* will certainly punish them
severely, but it will give you the assurance that you will be saved eternally. It is God who is
doing *all* this. [29] Remember that he has not only enabled you to believe in Christ, but *he*
has also allowed you to suffer for the sake of Christ. [30] *As a result,* you are *having to* resist
those who oppose the good message, just as you saw that I *had to* resist *such people
there in Philippi*, and just as you hear that I *still have to resist such people here* now.

2

Philippians 2:1-4

*THEME: Since Christ loves and encourages us, and the Holy Spirit fellowships with us, make
me completely happy by agreeing with one another, loving one another, and humbly serving one
another.*

[1] Since Christ encourages us, since he loves us and comforts us, since God's Spirit has
fellowship with *us, and* since *Christ* is very merciful to us, [2] make me completely happy *by
doing the following things*: Agree with one another, love one another, be closely united to
one another, *live* harmoniously with one another. [3] Never try to selfishly make yourselves
more important than *others* or boast *about what you are doing.* Instead, be humble, *and in
particular*, honor one another more than you honor yourselves. [4] Each one of you should
not *only* be concerned about your own affairs. Instead, each of you should also be
concerned *with helping* each other.

Philippians 2:5-11

*THEME: You should have the same attitude that Christ Jesus had. He willingly gave up his
divine privileges and humbled himself, willingly obeying God, even though it meant being
disgraced by dying on a cross. As a result, God exalted him to the highest position, to be
acknowledged by the entire universe as the supreme Lord.*

[5] Your attitude should be the same as that of Christ Jesus. [6] *Although* he has the same
nature as God, he did not insist on keeping all the privileges of being equal with God.

[7] Instead, he *willingly* gave up his divine privileges. He became a human being and chose to act like a *humble* servant. When he had become a human being, [8] he humbled himself *even more. He* obeyed *God* even to the extent of *being willing to* die. *He was even willing to* die on a cross, *which was a very shameful way to die.* [9] As a result, God raised him *to a position in heaven that is* higher than any other *position.* God bestowed upon him a rank that is above every *other* rank.

[10] *God did that* so that every being in heaven and on earth and under the earth would worship Jesus, [11] and so that every person would declare that Jesus Christ is Lord. *As a result of everyone doing that,* God, *his* Father, will be honored.

Philippians 2:12-13

THEME: Since you have always obeyed God, continue to try to do the things that are appropriate for people whom God has saved, and he will enable you to do them.

[12] My dear friends, as you consider this, since you have always obeyed *God,* each of you, with much reverence toward him, should try to do the things *that are proper for those who have been* saved. *You should do them* not only when I am with you. *Instead, you should try* even more *to do them* now, when I am not with you. [13] *You are able to do them because* God causes you to desire to do what he wants you to do, and he also enables you to do what he wants you to do.

Philippians 2:14-16

THEME: Always obey God and your leaders, and never complain against them or argue with them, so that you may be perfect children of God, witnessing by life and word to the ungodly people among whom you live.

[14] Do everything *God or the leaders of your congregation ask you to do.* Never complain about what they want you to do, or argue with them. [15] Behave in that way so that you may be completely faultless and may be perfect children of God while you are living in the midst of people who are wicked and do very wicked things. As you live among them, show them clearly *the way they ought to conduct their lives,* just as the sun, moon, and stars *show clearly to us the road we should take.* [16] Tell them the message that *God can enable them to* live eternally. *I ask you to do that* so that I may be able to rejoice on the day Christ *returns, knowing* that my hard work among you was not in vain.

Philippians 2:17-18

THEME: Because I and all of you dedicate ourselves together to do God's will, even if I am to be executed, I will rejoice, and you should also rejoice.

[17] Perhaps *the Roman authorities* will execute me, *and my blood will pour out just like the priest* pours out wine when he offers it to God. *As for you,* you believe *in Christ firmly.* As a result, you have given yourselves completely to God to do what he wants, *just as a priest* offers a sacrifice *completely to God. Because I dedicate myself wholly to God* together with you, even if *I am executed,* I will greatly rejoice, *because I am giving myself wholly to God,* and because you all *are giving yourselves wholly to him.* [18] In the same way, you too should rejoice *because you are giving yourselves wholly to God,* and you should rejoice because I *am giving myself wholly to him.*

Philippians 2:19-24

THEME: I confidently expect that the Lord Jesus will enable me to send Timothy to you soon. Timothy genuinely cares for your welfare, not his own interests. I am confident that the Lord will also enable me to come to you soon.

[19] My relationship with the Lord Jesus *leads me* to confidently expect that *he will enable me* to send Timothy to you soon, so that *you will be encouraged by the news he tells you about me. But* I also expect that *when he returns to me and* tells me the news about you, I will be encouraged! [20] *Keep in mind that* I have no one *else* like him who genuinely cares for you. [21] All the others *whom I have considered that I could send* are concerned *only* about their own affairs. They are not concerned with things Jesus Christ *considers important.* [22] But you know that Timothy has proved that he *serves the Lord and others faithfully. You know* that he has served *the Lord closely together* with me in *proclaiming* the message about Christ, as though he were my son *and I were his* father. [23] So then he is the one I confidently expect to send *to you* as soon as I know what will happen to me. [24] And I am confident that the Lord will enable me also to come *to you* soon.

Philippians 2:25-30

THEME: Since Epaphroditus longs to see you and is distressed, I am sending him back to you. So welcome him very joyfully. Honor him and all people like him. He nearly died while serving me on your behalf.

[25] I have concluded that it is *really* necessary that I send Epaphroditus *back* to you. He is a fellow believer and my fellow worker, and he *endures difficulties together with me, just as* soldiers *endure difficulties together.* You sent him *to me* to help me when I was in need. [26] *But I have concluded that I must send him back to you,* because he has been longing to see you all. Furthermore, he has been *very* distressed because *he knows that* you heard that he was sick. [27] Indeed, he was so sick that he almost died. However, *he did not die.* Instead, God pitied him and he also pitied me, *and as a result he healed him. God pitied me* because he did not want me to be even more sorrowful than I already was. [28] So I am sending him *back to you* as quickly as possible, in order that you will rejoice *when you see him again* and in order that I will be less sorrowful. [29-30] So welcome him very joyfully *just as believers* in *our* Lord *Jesus should welcome one another. He has been* working for Christ by helping me in your stead. *You couldn't help me because you were far away.* He knew he might die as a result of helping me, and *truly* he nearly did die. So honor *him, and honor all* those who are like him.

3

Philippians 3:1

THEME: Continue to rejoice. It is not tiresome for me to mention this again and it is also a safeguard for you.

[1] *Now there are* other things *I want to write about.* My fellow believers, continue to rejoice because *you belong to* the Lord. *Although* I will *now* write to you about the same matters *I mentioned to you before, this is* not tiresome for me, and it will protect you *from those who would harm you spiritually.*

Philippians 3:2-4a

THEME: Beware of the unholy people who would harm you spiritually by insisting that you must be circumcised in order to become God's people.

[2] Beware of the *people who insist that you must be circumcised to become God's people! They are dangerous* evildoers, *as dangerous as wild* dogs. *They will harm you spiritually!* [3] *They think that they are God's people because they are circumcised.* But **we**, *not they*, are the ones who are *truly God's people*, *whether or not we are* circumcised. We care about the ones whom God's Spirit *enables to* worship *God.* We are the ones who praise Christ Jesus *because he has enabled us to become the people of God.* We do not believe *that God will consider us his people as a result of what has been done to our* bodies. [4] *We do not trust in those things to make us acceptable to God*, although I could very well do that.

Philippians 3:4b-6

THEME: Since I was circumcised properly and have a purely Hebrew ancestry, and since I kept the Jewish laws blamelessly, I could rely upon what I have done and who I am better than anyone else could, if it were beneficial for salvation.

In fact, if I could benefit from it for my salvation, I could rely upon what I have done and who I am more than anyone else could. *Consider this*: [5] *I was* circumcised when I was one week old. I am from the race of Israel. I am from the tribe of Benjamin. I am completely Hebrew in every way. *During the time I was* a member of the Pharisee *sect*, I *strictly obeyed* the laws *that God gave Moses.* [6] I was *so* zealous *to make people obey those laws that* I caused the people who believe in Christ to suffer *because I thought they were trying to abolish those laws. Indeed,* as far as my obeying those laws is concerned, no *one could* have accused *me of* disobeying any of them.

Philippians 3:7-11

THEME: I consider worthless all these advantages that I once supposed would benefit me, and I consider everything else to be worthless as well, because I only want to know Christ, to be united with him, and to be made righteous through trusting in him alone.

[7] Nevertheless, all such things as those—things that I used to *consider to* be useful to me—I now consider worthless, because *I want to know* Christ. [8] More than that, I consider all things to be worthless, as I think about how great it is to know Christ Jesus my Lord. Because *I want to know* him *better,* I have rejected all *other* things as worthless. I consider them *as useless as* rubbish, in order that I may have *a close relationship with* Christ, [9] and in order that I may completely belong to him. God did not erase the record of my sins as a result of *my obeying* the laws *he gave Moses.* Instead, it is because I have trusted in Christ *that God* has declared the guilt for my sins to be cancelled, and thus he has declared me to be righteous. *It is* God *himself who* has done that, *and it is only* because I have trusted *in Christ.* [10] *I want* to know Christ *better and better. I want* to continually experience *his working* powerfully in my life, *just as God worked powerfully when he* caused Christ to become alive after he died. *I also want to be continually willing* to suffer *in order that I may obey God*, just as Christ suffered *in order that he might obey God. I also want* to be completely willing to die for *Christ*, just as he died for me, [11] *because I expect that, as a result of God's goodness,* he will cause me to live again after I have died.

Philippians 3:12-16

THEME: Since you desire to be perfected, and since you have my example of not considering myself to be already perfect, but of constantly striving to become more and more like Christ, follow my example.

¹²I don't claim that I have already become completely like Christ Jesus. I have not yet become all that God intends me to be. But I earnestly try to become *more and more like Christ*, because he chose me *so that I might become like him*. ¹³My fellow believers, I certainly don't consider that I have already become completely like Christ. But *I am like a runner. A runner does not look backward*. Instead, he leans forward as he runs straight toward the goal *to win the prize. In the same way*, I don't think about what I have already done. ¹⁴Instead, I concentrate only on *continuing to become more and more like Christ, right up to the end of my life*. As a result, because of my relationship with Christ Jesus, God will summon me to receive a reward from him *in heaven*. ¹⁵So all of us who are *spiritually* mature should think this *same way*. If any *of you* do not think this same way regarding what *I have written here*, God will reveal this to you. ¹⁶What is important is that we must live according to what *God has already revealed to* us.

Philippians 3:17-21

THEME: Imitate me and those who live as I do. Remember that there are many people who are bad examples, as shown by their lustful behavior and by their wanting to do what their bodies desire. But as for us, Christ will transform our weak bodies to be like his glorious heavenly body.

¹⁷My fellow believers, *all of* you should unitedly imitate me, and observe the people who conduct their lives as I do, *so that you may imitate them also*. ¹⁸*Keep in mind that* there are many people *who say they believe in Christ* who act in *ways that show* that they are opposed to *the teaching about* Christ *dying on* the cross. I have told you about these people many times *before*, and now I am sad, even crying, as I tell you *about them again*. ¹⁹*God* will severely punish them. The things their bodies desire have become *like* gods to them. They are proud of the things they should be ashamed of. They think only about what unbelievers think about. ²⁰*But remember* that we are citizens of heaven. And we eagerly wait for our Savior, the Lord Jesus Christ, *to return* from there. ²¹By the power that enables him to put everything under his own control, he will change our weak bodies to become like his glorious body.

4

Philippians 4:1

THEME: You encourage me very much! And I urge you to continue to trust in the Lord.

¹My fellow believers, I love you and I long for you. You make me happy, and *your spiritual maturity is for me like* a reward *given to those who win a race*. Dear friends, on the basis *of all that I have told you*, continue to believe firmly in the Lord according to what I have just taught you.

Philippians 4:2-3

THEME: I urge Euodia and Syntyche to be reconciled with each other. Help them in this because they have both proclaimed the good news faithfully together with me and my other fellow workers.

[2] I urge *you*, Euodia, and I urge *you*, Syntyche, to again have a peaceful relationship with each other, *because you both have a relationship with* the Lord. [3] And, my faithful comrade[e], I ask you to help them *to again have a peaceful relationship with each other*, because they have *faithfully proclaimed* the message *about Christ* together with me, *while many people* opposed us. They have faithfully proclaimed that message together with Clement and the rest of my fellow workers, whose names *are* in the book *that lists the names of all the people who will* live *forever*.

Philippians 4:4-7

THEME: The Lord is near. Always rejoice, and be gentle to everyone. Don't worry about anything, but pray to God instead. As a result, God will grant you profound peace.

[4] *Because all of you have a relationship with* the Lord, always rejoice! I say again, rejoice! [5] *Behave in such a way that* everyone can know that you have a gentle attitude. The Lord is near![f] [6] Don't worry about anything. Instead, in every situation, pray *to God*, tell him what you need, and ask him *to help you*. Also thank *him for what he does for you*. [7] As a result, God will enable you not to worry *about anything*.[9] *That is*, he will cause you to have *inner* peace *because of your relationship with* Christ Jesus. You won't be able to understand *how you can be so peaceful in such difficult circumstances!*

Philippians 4:8-9

THEME: Continually think about everything that is good and praiseworthy. Practice everything you have learned from me. As a result, God will be with you and give you inner peace.

[8] My fellow believers, there is one more thing *I want you to do*. Whatever is true, whatever is worthy of respect, whatever is right, whatever is morally pure, whatever is pleasing, whatever is admirable, whatever is good, whatever *deserves* praise, those are the things that you should continually think about. [9] The things that I have taught you and that you have learned from me, the things you have heard me *say* and that you have seen me *do*, those are the things that you should do. As a result *of your doing those things*, God, who *causes us to* have *inner* peace, will bless you.

Philippians 4:10-14

THEME: I rejoice greatly because you have once again demonstrated your concern for me by giving to meet my needs, although it is true that Christ enables me to be content in every situation.

[10] I rejoice greatly *and thank* the Lord because now, after some time, *by sending money to me* you have once again shown that you are concerned about me. Indeed, you were concerned about me all the time, but you had no opportunity *to show it*. [11] I am not saying this because *I am worried that I will* lack things *that I need*. In fact, I have learned to be

---

[e]   We do not know who Paul was addressing. However, it appears that Paul expected a certain person would know how to facilitate the reconciliation of these two woman.

[f]   OR, ...The Lord is coming soon!

[9]   OR, ...God will protect your minds *in every way*.

content in whatever *situation* I am. [12] I know how *to be content when* I don't have what I need, and I know how *to be content when* I have plenty. I have learned how *to be content* in any and every *situation*. I have learned how *to be content when* I have enough to eat, and I have learned how *to be content when* I don't have enough. I have learned how *to be content when* I have plenty *of what I need,* and I have learned *how to be content when* there are things I lack. [13] I am able to cope with every situation because *Christ* gives me the strength to do it. [14] Nevertheless, you did very well in that you *gave me money* while I *have been going through* these hardships.

Philippians 4:15-17

THEME: You Philippians know that in the early days when I preached the good news in your region, you were the only congregation that sent me gifts. It's not that I desire your gifts, but I desire that God will abundantly bless you for aiding me.

[15] *My friends there at Philippi,* you yourselves know that during the time I first *proclaimed* the message about Christ *to you*, when I left there to go to *the province of* Macedonia, you were the only group of believers who *sent me* funds so that I could *proclaim that message* to others just as I had done for you. [16] Even *when I was* in *the city of* Thessalonica, you sent *money* to me two different times in order to *supply* what I needed. [17] It's not that I want to receive money from you. What I want is that *God* will abundantly bless you for *helping me.*

Philippians 4:18-20

THEME: I have received your very generous gift. God is very pleased with this gift, and he will abundantly supply your every need also. Let's praise him forever!

[18] I have received a very generous *gift from you,* and *as a result,* I have plenty. I have an abundant supply *of what I need, because* I have received from Epaphroditus the money you *sent to me*. God considers your gift very acceptable, and he is very pleased with it. *It is like* fragrant incense *offered to God.* [19] *Moreover,* God, *whom* I *serve*, has an unlimited supply *of everything that we need*. And as a result, because of your relationship with Christ Jesus, he will completely supply everything **you** need. [20] *So* praise God our Father forever and ever! Amen!

Philippians 4:21-22

THEME: All of God's people here, including those who serve God with me and those who work in the emperor's palace, join me in greeting each one of God's people there.

[21] Greet *for us* all of God's people *there in Phillipi, that is, all those who have a relationship with* Christ Jesus. The fellow believers who *serve God together* with me here send their greetings to you.[h] [22] All of God's people *here* send their greetings, especially the *ones who work* in the palace of the emperor.

Philippians 4:23

THEME: May the Lord Jesus Christ bless you.

[23] *I pray that our* Lord Jesus Christ *will continue to* act kindly toward all of you.

---

[h] OR, …The fellow believers who *serve God together* with me here say they are thinking fondly of you.

The Apostle Paul wrote a letter to the Christians at Colossae. We call this letter

Colossians

1

Colossians 1:1-2

THEME: I, Paul, am sending this letter to you who are God's people in Colossae. We pray that God will bless you.

[1] I, Paul, *am writing this letter to you.* Our fellow believer Timothy *is with me.* I am an apostle who represents Christ Jesus, because that is what God wanted. [2] *I am sending this letter* to you in *the city of* Colossae who are God's people and our faithful fellow believers, to you who have a close relationship with Christ. We pray that God our Father[a] will act in kindness to you and will give you *inner* peace.

Colossians 1:3-8

THEME: We thank God for you very often that you believe in Christ Jesus and that you love all God's people.

[3] Very often we thank God, the Father of our Lord Jesus Christ, as we pray for you, [4] because we have heard that you believe in Christ Jesus, and that you love all God's people. [5] You do that because you are confidently expecting to receive what God is reserving for you in heaven. You heard about that previously when you heard the true message, the message *about Christ.* [6] It was proclaimed to you, just as it has been proclaimed in many countries. That true message is changing the lives of more and more people, just as it has changed your lives since you heard it and truly experienced that God acts kindly towards us in ways we don't deserve. [7] That is the message Epaphras taught you. We love him. He serves Christ together with us and works for Christ faithfully for your benefit. [8] He told us that you love all God's people, which is what God's Spirit *has enabled you to do.*[b]

Colossians 1:9-12

THEME: We have been praying very often to God for you. We pray that you will truly know all that he wants you to do, so that you will conduct yourselves as his people should.

[9] So, ever since we heard *this good report* about you, we have been praying very often for you. We pray that you will truly know all that God wants *you to do*—that you will become very wise, and that you will become spiritually perceptive. [10] The goal of our prayers is that that you will conduct yourselves as the Lord's *people should,* and that you will please the Lord in every way. We have been praying that you will be doing every sort of good deed

---

[a] Some Greek manuscripts add, "and our Lord Jesus Christ".

[b] OR, ...you love all God's people spiritually.

and that you will be getting to truly know God, more and more. [11] *And we pray that God* will greatly strengthen you *spiritually,* to the extent of his mighty power, so that you will always be steadfast and patient *when you experience difficulties,* while *at the same time* you will be rejoicing. [12] *And we pray that you will be continually* thanking God our Father, because he has qualified you so that you[c] also will obtain what he will give to his people in heaven.

Colossians 1:13-20

THEME: God has caused us to be ruled by his Son, who existed before, and ranks above, everything that has been created.

[13] God has rescued us *spiritually* so that the evil one no longer rules us. God has transferred us spiritually so that *now* his Son, whom he loves, rules us. [14] Because of our relationship with his Son,[d] God has redeemed us. He has forgiven our sins. [15] **God's Son reveals perfectly what God, his Father,** whom no one can see, **is like**. God's Son existed before, and ranks above, everything that God has created. [16] When God created everything that is on the earth, he did it by having his Son do it. His Son created everything that we can see, and also everything that is in heaven that we cannot see. His Son created all ranks of important spirit beings. And he ranks above everything, because God created everything by means of the work of his Son, and to praise his Son. [17] He ranks above everything because he existed before anything else existed, and because God uses him to sustain everything. [18] And *God's Son ranks above everything*, since it is he who rules over his people as our heads control our physical bodies, because he causes his people to live *spiritually*. He is the first one who rose from the dead, which was in order that he would become the most important in every way. [19] *He reveals perfectly what God his Father is like*, because it is in him that his Father chose to dwell completely. [20] God caused his Son to rule us, because he chose to reconcile to himself everything that is on earth and in heaven by what his Son did, so that everything might honor his Son. God chose to reconcile everything to himself by means of his *Son's* blood that *flowed from his body when he died on the cross*.

---

[c] OR, ...qualified us so that we...

[d] OR, Because of what his Son did...

An alternative arrangement of the sentences of Colossians 1:13-19:

When Paul arranged these ideas, he separated pairs of clauses that are related closely, instead of joining them. We have rearranged the concepts so that those directly related clauses or sentences are joined together

[13] God our Father has rescued us *spiritually* so that we are no longer ruled by the evil one, and God has transferred us spiritually so that we are ruled by his Son, whom he loves. [14a] By means of what his Son did, we have been redeemed by God. [14b] Our sins have been forgiven by him. [20] God has done this because he chose to reconcile to himself, by means of his Son, everything that is on earth and that is in heaven, in order that his Son might be honored. God chose to reconcile everything to himself by means of his Son's blood *that flowed from his body when he died on the cross.* [15b] God cannot be seen by anyone, [15a] **but his Son reveals perfectly what God—his Father—is like** [19a] because it is in his Son that the Father chose [19b] to dwell completely. [15c] God's Son ranks above everything [15d] that has been created, [16] because it was by means of him that God created everything that is on the earth and can be seen by people, and also everything that is in heaven and cannot be seen by people. All types of important spirit beings were created by means of him, because everything that has been created by God has been created by means of his Son. And his Son ranks above everything, because everything has been created by God to honor him. [17] He ranks above everything because he existed before anything else existed, and because God uses him to sustain everything. [18] His Son ranks above everything because it is he who *rules over his people, just as* our heads *controls our physical bodies, because he causes his people to live spiritually.* He is the first one who rose from the dead, which was in order that he would become the most important in every way.

Colossians 1:21-23

THEME: As for you, God our Father has now reconciled you to himself.

[21] As for you, although formerly God considered you as his enemies, and although you were formerly hostile to him because of your evil thoughts and deeds, [22] in spite of that, he has now reconciled you *to himself. He did that* as a result of his Son's physical death. He did it so that you will be completely holy when he brings you into his presence. [23] But he wants you to continue to believe the message about Christ. He wants you to continue to be stable and to continue to confidently expect to receive what you heard about when you first heard that message. That message has been proclaimed to people in very many places; and I, Paul, have also become one who proclaims it.

Colossians 1:24-29

THEME: I am completing what Christ appointed me to do—that I should endure suffering physically for the benefit of his people. And I proclaim the previously unrevealed message about Christ to every class of people.

[24] At the present time I am rejoicing that I am suffering for your benefit. In suffering for you, I am completing what Christ *has decided* that I should suffer physically for the benefit of all

believers, *who are as dear to him as* his own body. [25] I myself became one who serves God's people, because God gave me a responsibility to you *who are non-Jews*. I became one who serves God's people, to make known to you non-Jews the whole message from God. [26] We did not know this message previously; God concealed it from those *who lived in all* the previous ages, but he has now revealed it to his people. [27] God has now chosen to reveal to his people that he will greatly bless the non-Jews. This message declares that Christ, *by means of his Spirit*, will live in you who are non-Jews, with the result that you confidently expect to share in *God's* glory. [28] We proclaim the message about Christ *to every class of persons*. We warn them, and specifically, we teach everyone with great wisdom. We do this so that all those who have a close relationship with Christ may be all that God wants them to be when we present them to Christ. [29] In order that I may *achieve this*, I am working hard, exerting myself as a result of Christ's empowering me mightily.

2

Colossians 2:1-5

THEME: I am exerting myself very greatly on your behalf so that you will truly know the message about Christ, in order that no one will be able to delude you.

[1] In particular, I want you to realize that I am exerting myself very greatly on your behalf, on behalf of believers in *the city of* Laodicea, and on behalf of all other believers who have not met me personally. [2] I am doing this so that they and you may be strengthened spiritually, as you are united in loving each other. And I am doing this in order that they and you will fully and thoroughly understand the message that God has now revealed; that is, so that they and you will truly know the message from God about Christ, [3] who alone is able to cause them and you to understand thoroughly this very important message. [4] I am telling you this so that no one will be able to deceive you by persuasive arguments. [5] Even though I am absent from you physically, I am very concerned about you. At the same time, I am rejoicing because I know that you are united and that you believe firmly in Christ.

Colossians 2:6-7

THEME: Conduct yourselves as befits those who are united to Christ Jesus our Lord.

[6] In a way that is consistent with *the message* you received about Christ Jesus, who is our Lord, conduct yourselves as you should, because of the close relationship you have with him. [7] Continue believing and practicing what you were first taught about him. Continue to do this more and more. Continue to be sure about all true teaching, just as *Epaphras* taught it to you. And continue thanking *God* very much *for all he has done for you*.

Colossians 2:8-15

THEME: Make sure that no one influences you to become their disciples by teaching you a false religious philosophy. You are spiritually complete because of being united to Christ.

[8] Make sure that no one influences you to become their disciples by teaching you a religious philosophy that is valueless and false. It is a false philosophy because it teaches what mere human beings think, and because it teaches elementary regulations *that are concerned merely with what is external*, and because it teaches what is contrary to the true teaching about Christ. [9] *Make sure that you are not influenced by such teaching, because* it is in Christ's body that God lives completely. [10] And you are spiritually complete because of the close relationship you have with Christ, who rules over every *other* being

that rules. [11] Because of your close relationship with him, it is as though you have been circumcised spiritually. This does not mean that you have been circumcised physically, but it means that Christ has completely removed your entire self-directed nature. [12] And when you were baptized, *it was as though* you *had died and* were buried by God with Christ, and *it was as though* God caused you to live again with Christ as a result of your believing that God acted powerfully when he raised Christ from the dead. [13] *Before you* non-Jews *trusted in Christ,* you were *spiritually* dead because of your sins. You were uncircumcised spiritually; that is, your self-directed nature controlled you. In spite of that, God caused you to become alive *spiritually* with Christ. God forgave us all our sins. [14] *It was just as though* he canceled the document that stated the charges against us and that said he would punish us. And *it was just as though* he removed that document by nailing it to the cross *when Christ was nailed on the cross.* [15] And God defeated the *evil* spirit beings that rule, and he demonstrated it publicly. He triumphed over them as a result of what *Christ did.*

Colossians 2:16-19

THEME: Disregard those who condemn you for disobeying certain regulations and for not worshipping God in the way they insist you should.

[16] So don't pay any attention to those who say God will punish you because you eat *certain foods* and drink *certain drinks,* or because *you don't celebrate* special *yearly* festivals or celebrate the time when the new moon *appears* or the weekly Jewish days of rest. [17] *Disregard what such people say,* because those *regulations concerning food and drink and festivals* are *only* like a shadow *that is cast by something that is approaching. They merely symbolically represent* the real spiritual blessings that Christ *has given.* [18] Don't pay attention to those who say that God will punish you because *you don't worship him in the way* they say *you should.* They insist that you should humiliate yourselves and that you should worship the angels. Disregard what such people say, because they base their authority on things that they have never seen. They are proud without reason because their self-directed nature *controls* what they think. [19] They don't teach the true teaching about Christ. *Christ is the one who causes all of his people to develop spiritually as God plans that we should develop, just as* our heads direct how our bodies grow, as they are held together by the joints and ligaments.

Colossians 2:20-23

THEME: Do not submit to elementary regulations, which are concerned merely with what is external.

[20] *It is as though* you died with Christ. So *you no longer have to obey* elementary regulations *that are concerned merely with what is external, just as a dead person no longer has to do anything.* So, don't submit to regulations [21] such as 'Don't handle *certain things,*' 'Don't taste *certain things,*' 'Don't touch *certain things.*' [22] The things they refer to cease to exist when we use them. *So don't submit to such regulations,* because they are based on what mere human teachers command and teach. [23] *Don't obey such regulations* because they only cause people to do what their self-directed nature wants. *Those regulations* seem to be wise because they *urge people to* worship in a way that seems right *to those teachers. They urge* people to humiliate themselves and to treat their bodies harshly. But those regulations don't help people at all to not do the sinful things they *naturally* desire.

3

Colossians 3:1-4

THEME: Be constantly desiring what is associated with heaven.

¹You now are alive *spiritually*, and *it is as though God caused you to become alive* when he caused Christ to become alive again. So be constantly desiring what is associated with heaven, where Christ is. There *in heaven* God has given him supreme authority and the highest honor. ²Be constantly desiring the blessings God has prepared for you in heaven. Don't be constantly wanting *to do the evil deeds that people on* earth do, ³because you have *ceased to behave as you formerly did. It is as though you have* died *to that way of life.* You now live *spiritually* together with Christ in *the presence of* God; and *it is as though that life is hidden because* people cannot see it. ⁴When Christ, who causes you to live *spiritually*, is publicly revealed, then God will also reveal you publicly together with Christ, *and you together with Christ will be* glorious.

Colossians 3:5-11

THEME: Do not do what is evil.

⁵*Get rid of your evil practices, as though they were enemies whom* you were killing.ᵉ Do not practice sexual immorality. Don't commit unnatural sexual acts. Don't desire to do things like that, and don't desire *to do anything that is* evil. Don't desire to have more things than you need, because if you do that, you are making material things your god. ⁶*Remember that* God will punish those who disobey him by doing things like that. ⁷Formerly you did such things when you were disobeying God. ⁸Now, however, don't do any of these evil deeds *any more*: Don't get angry in any way. Don't act maliciously. Don't slander people. Don't talk abusively to people. ⁹Don't lie to one another. Don't do those things, because you have disposed of your former evil nature, and you have *stopped doing what you did when you had that* nature, ¹⁰and you have acquired a new nature. God is causing your new nature to become more and more like his own nature. He created your new nature so that *you might* truly *get to* know *him*. ¹¹As a result of that, it is not *important whether you are a* non-Jew or a Jew, or whether you are circumcised or not, or whether you are a foreigner or uncivilized, or whether you are a slave or not. *What is important is* Christ. He is supremely important in every way.

Colossians 3:12-14

THEME: Do what is good. In particular, love one another.

¹²Since God has chosen you, since God has reserved you for himself, and since God loves you, be compassionate to one another. Be kind to one another. Be humble. Be meek.ᶠ Be patient with one another, ¹³and don't get uptight when others do things that irritate you. Forgive one another, if one of you has a grudge against another. Just as the Lord *Jesus freely* forgave you, you also *must freely forgive one another.* ¹⁴And what is more important than all of these is that you love one another, because by doing that you will be perfectly united together.

ᵉ OR, *Get rid of your doing evil,* like dead people do not do what is evil.

ᶠ OR, ...Be considerate toward one another.

Colossians 3:15-16

THEME: Continue to be at peace with one another. Be constantly thanking God. Continue getting to know thoroughly the message about Christ.

[15] Since God chose you to be at peace *with one another* in your local congregations, let that peace which Christ gives control your hearts, and be constantly thanking God. [16] Continue to let the message about Christ govern all you think and do, as you very wisely teach and warn one another with psalms and hymns and spiritual songs,[g] singing to God sincerely and gratefully.

Colossians 3:17

THEME: Do everything in the manner that those who belong to the Lord Jesus should.

[17] Whatever you say, and whatever you do, do all of this in the manner that those who are representatives of the Lord Jesus *should,* constantly thanking God our Father as you ask the Lord Jesus to take your prayers to God.

Colossians 3:18-19

THEME: Wives, be subject to your husbands. Husbands, love your wives.

[18] You women, be subject to your husbands. That is what you should do because you have a close relationship with the Lord *Jesus.* [19] You men, love your wives. Don't be harsh with them.

Colossians 3:20-21

THEME: Children, obey your parents in every circumstance. Parents, do not over-correct your children.

[20] You children, obey your parents in every circumstance, since the Lord *God* is pleased when you do that. [21] You parents,[h] don't correct your children more than you need to, lest they become discouraged.

Colossians 3:22-4:1

THEME: Slaves, obey your masters in every circumstance, sincerely and wholeheartedly. Masters, treat your slaves justly and fairly.

[22] You slaves, obey your earthly masters in every circumstance. Don't obey them only when they are watching you, like those who *merely* wish to impress their masters favorably. Instead, obey them sincerely. Do that out of reverence for the Lord *Jesus.* [23] Whatever *work* you do, work at it wholeheartedly, like those who are working for the Lord *Jesus.* Don't work like those who are working *merely* for *their* employers, [24] because you know that it is the Lord who will properly repay you. That is, you will receive what God has promised. *Remember that* it is Christ who is the real master whom you are serving. [25] And God will judge impartially any of you who keeps doing wrong. He will judge you according to what you have done.

---

[g] OR, …songs which God's Spirit *gives you…*

[h] OR, You fathers…

4

[1] You masters, treat your slaves justly and fairly, since you know that you have a master who is in heaven *who will say whether he approves of what you have done.*

Colossians 4:2-4

THEME: Pray to God persistently. And pray that God will give me opportunities to declare the message about Christ.

[2] Pray to God persistently, and at the same time be alert and be thanking him. [3] Since I am in prison because *I declared the message about Christ* that God has now revealed, pray also for me. Pray that God will give me opportunities to speak, so that I can declare his message. [4] Pray for me that *God will enable me to* make his message known publicly. I need to do that, because I am obliged to declare it.

Colossians 4:5-6

THEME: Always speak wisely and graciously to those who do not believe in the Lord Jesus.

[5] Act wisely towards those who don't believe in the Lord Jesus. Use every opportunity to do that. [6] In particular, always speak graciously and in a pleasant way *to those who don't believe in the Lord Jesus.* As a result, you will come to know how to answer each one of them.

Colossians 4:7-9

THEME: Tychicus will tell you all that has been happening to me.

[7] Tychicus will tell you all that has been happening to me. He is a fellow believer whom we love and who helps me faithfully and serves the Lord *Jesus* together with me. [8] The reason I am sending Tychicus to you *with this letter* is so that he will know how you are and so that he can strengthen you *spiritually.* [9] I am sending him to you with Onesimus, who is a faithful fellow believer whom we love and who is your fellow townsman. Those two will tell you all about what has been happening here.

Colossians 4:10-14

THEME: My fellow workers here greet you.

[10] Aristarchus, who is in prison with me, and Mark, who is a cousin of Barnabas, send you their greetings.[i] Since I have instructed you about Mark, if he comes to you, welcome him. [11] Jesus, who is also called Justus, also sends you his greetings. These three men are the only Jewish *believers* who are working with me to teach people to submit to God as their king, and all three have comforted me. [12] Epaphras, who is your fellow townsman and who serves Christ Jesus, sends you his greetings. He prays earnestly for you very often. *He prays* that you will be spiritually mature and that you will be fully convinced about all that God wants *you to do.* [13] *He prays this* because he is deeply concerned for you, and for the believers who live in *the cities of* Laodicea and Hierapolis. I can assure you that this is true *of him.* [14] Luke, our beloved doctor, sends you his greetings, and Demas does, too.

---

[i] OR, ...say they are thinking warmly about you.

Colossians 4:15-17

THEME: Obey these instructions.

¹⁵ Tell the fellow believers who live in *the city of* Laodicea that we send them our greetings. *Tell* Nympha[j] and the congregation *that meets* in her house that we send them our greetings. ¹⁶ After someone reads this letter *publicly* to you, have it read to the congregation that is in Laodicea. And as for the *letter that I wrote to the congregation in* Laodicea, make sure that it is also read publicly. ¹⁷ Say to Archippus, "Make sure that you complete the task that God appointed you to do, since you have a close relationship with the Lord Jesus."

Colossians 4:18

THEME: I, Paul, am penning this myself in order that you may know that this letter was sent by me. Remember to pray about the fact that I am in prison.

¹⁸ I, Paul, send you my greetings. *Having taken the pen from my scribe, I am now writing this myself in order that you may know that I have truly sent this letter. Remember to pray about the fact that I am in prison. I pray that our Lord Jesus Christ will continue to act in kindness towards you all.*

---

[j] Some Greek manuscripts have Nymphas, a man's name. [Nympha is a name for a woman.]

The Apostle Paul wrote letters to the Christians at Thessalonica. We call this first letter

1 Thessalonians

1 Thessalonians 1:1

THEME: I, Paul, greet you believers who are in Thessalonica

[1] *I*, Paul, *am writing this letter.* Silas and Timothy *are with me. We are sending this letter* to you who are the congregation *of believers* in *the city of* Thessalonica. We all *worship* God[a] our Father and *our* Lord Jesus Christ. *We three pray that God, our Father, and Jesus Christ, our Lord, will continue to* act kindly toward you and *will continue to* cause you to have *inner* peace.

1 Thessalonians 1:2-10

THEME: We always thank God for you all. We continually remember the way you live as believers and we know that God chose you. The Holy Spirit enabled us to powerfully tell you the good message, and although people persecuted you greatly, you were joyful. As a result, you inspired all the believers in Macedonia and Achaia to trust in God firmly, as you do.

[2] We always thank God for you all *when* we mention you while we pray.[b] [3] *We thank God because* we continually remember that you work *for God because* you trust *in him* and you earnestly help people because you love them. You also endure *it when people cause you to suffer.* You endure it because you confidently expect that our Lord Jesus Christ *will soon return from heaven to rescue you!* [4] My fellow believers whom God loves, we *also thank him since* we know that he chose you *to become his people.* [5] We know that he chose you because the Holy Spirit *helped us to speak* to you powerfully, and he strongly assured *us that he was powerfully working in you by means of* the message about Christ that we *told you. When* we told that message to you, we did not speak only words. *You yourselves know that,* because you know how we spoke and how we conducted our lives when we were with you, in order that *we might help* you. [6] We also *know that God chose you* because we have now heard that you have endured your troubles when *people* caused you to suffer very much *because you believed in Christ.* You endured just as the Lord *Jesus Christ* endured, and in the same way that we did *when people caused us to suffer.* At that time you were joyful because the Holy Spirit caused you to be joyful! [7] As a result *of your joyfully enduring your troubles*, all the believers who live in *the provinces of* Macedonia and Achaia *have heard how firmly you trust God. So they know that they should firmly trust in God* as you do. [8] Other people have heard you tell the message *from* the Lord *Jesus.* Then they also have proclaimed the message to people who live throughout Macedonia and Achaia. Not only that, but *people who live* in many faraway places have heard that you trust in God. As a result, we do not need to tell people *what God has done in your lives.* [9] People *who live far from you are telling others what happened when we were with you.* They also report that you stopped *worshiping things that your ancestors considered to be* gods, and now you worship God. *As a result*, you

---

serve the God who is all-powerful and who is the real God. ¹⁰They tell us that now you wait expectantly for his Son *to return to earth* from heaven. You firmly believe that God raised him to life again after he died. You believe also that Jesus will rescue *all of* us *who trust in him* from *God's* punishing us.

2

1 Thessalonians 2:1-12

THEME: You and God know it is true that we behaved in a very virtuous, upright, and irreproachable manner toward you. You know also that we continually exhorted, encouraged, and urged that you behave in the way that God's people should.

¹My fellow believers, you know that our time with you was very effective. ²Although *people in the city of* Philippi previously mistreated us and insulted us, as you know, our God caused us to be courageous. As a result, we told you the good message *that originates from* God, even though some *people in your city* also strongly opposed *us*. ³When we exhorted you *to obey God's message*, we did not speak to you an untrue message. *Instead, we spoke* a true *message*. We don't *want to gain something for ourselves by* immoral means. We don't try to deceive *you or other people*. ⁴On the contrary, we tell God's message because he trusted us to do that, because he examined us and he considered us *to be acceptable to tell people* the message about Christ. As we teach people, we don't say what they like to hear. Instead, *we say what* God *wants us to say, because* he examines everything we think and what we desire. ⁵We never flattered *you*, as you know. We were never greedy, so we never needed to use words to make you think we were not greedy. God knows that is true! ⁶We never tried to get people *to honor us*, ⁷although we could have demanded *you to honor us*, because we are apostles *who represent* Christ. On the contrary, we were gentle when we were among you, as a mother *gently* takes care of her own children. ⁸So, because we love you, we were delighted to personally tell you the good message that God gave us. But also we were delighted to lovingly do all we could do to help you because you had become very dear to us. ⁹My fellow believers, you remember that we worked very hard *in order to support ourselves while we were with you*. We worked day and night in order that we would not have to ask any one of you to give us what we needed, *while* we proclaimed to you the good message that God gave us. ¹⁰You know it is true—and God knows it is true—that we acted in a very virtuous, upright, and irreproachable manner toward you believers. ¹¹You know also that *we lovingly acted toward* each one of you as a father *lovingly acts toward* his own children. ¹²*Specifically, we* kept strongly exhorting and pleading with you that you conduct your lives in the way that God's people should, *because* he has invited you to become his people over whom he will wonderfully rule.

1 Thessalonians 2:13-16

THEME: We continually thank God also that you accepted as true a message that does not originate from human beings. Rather, you accepted as true the message that originates from God, and the result was that people caused you to suffer as Christ did.

¹³We continually thank God also because when you heard the message *that* we told to you, you accepted it as the true message, the good message that God gave us. We did not invent it. *We also thank God* that he is changing your lives because you trust this message. ¹⁴My fellow believers, we *know that you sincerely believed the message from God,* because the way you acted was just like the way *the congregations* in Judea acted.

They also *worship* God, *and they have a close relationship with* Christ Jesus. Specifically, you endured it *when* your own countrymen *mistreated you because you believed the message from God,* in the same way that those *Jewish believers in Judea* endured it *when* the Jews *who do not believe in Christ mistreated them.* [15] *Unbelieving Jews are* the ones whom God considers guilty *for* killing the Lord Jesus, as well as *for killing* many prophets. Other unbelieving Jews forced us to leave *many towns.* They really make God angry; and *they are* opposed to *what is best for* all human beings! [16] *Specifically*, when we tell *the good message* to non-Jewish people in order *that God* will save them *spiritually*, these *unbelieving Jews* try to prevent us from doing that. Because they continually sin more and more, they are almost reaching the limit *that has been set by God*! *God* is about to punish them, at last, for all their sins!

1 Thessalonians 2:17-20

THEME: It is because of you that we are pleased and joyful. So when people forced Silas, Timothy and me to be separated from you for a short time, we strongly desired to be with you.

[17] My fellow believers, when for a short time *those people forced us to be separated* from you, *we felt like parents* whose children had all died. *Although* we were far away from you, *we were still* very much *concerned about you,* and we strongly desired to be present with you. [18] *You should know that* we wanted to return to you. Indeed I, Paul, *tried to return* twice. But *we did not return, because* each time Satan prevented us *from returning.* [19] *We were strongly desiring to be with you*, because you *are the ones about whom we are proud and are joyful!* It is because we are confident that you *will remain faithful to the Lord* that we *will be* joyful! You are the ones who we confidently expect *will keep strongly trusting in God!* It is because you *will remain faithful* that we *will* be proud *of the work we have done when* our Lord Jesus *examines what we all have done, at the time* he comes back *to earth!* [20] Indeed, it is because of you that *even now we* are pleased and are joyful!

3

1 Thessalonians 3:1-5

THEME: When I could no longer endure worrying about you, I sent Timothy to you in order to find out whether or not you were still trusting in God.

[1] As a result of that, when I could no longer endure *worrying about you*, I decided that *Silas and I* would stay behind alone in *the city of* Athens, [2] and we two sent Timothy *to you. You know that he is* our close associate and also works for God by *proclaiming* the message about Christ. *Silas and I sent him* in order that he would encourage you to continue to strongly trust *in Christ.* [3] We did not want any *of you* to consider turning away from Christ as a result of *people* causing you to suffer. You know that *God has* planned that *we who trust in him will suffer like that.* [4] Remember that when we were present with you we kept telling you that *people* would cause us to suffer. And because that is what happened, you know that *what we said* was true! [5] *I was* afraid that *Satan*, the one who tempts us, had caused you *to stop trusting in Christ. If that had happened*, our work among you would have been for nothing! *So* I sent *Timothy to you* in order to find out whether or not you were *still* trusting *in Christ.* I sent him because I could no longer endure *not knowing about your spiritual condition.*

1 Thessalonians 3:6-10

THEME: Now Timothy has just returned and has told us the good news that you still trust in Christ. As a result, we have been cheered up, and we cannot thank God adequately for what he has done for you. Very frequently we ask God that we will be able to visit you and help you to trust him more strongly.

[6] Now Timothy has just returned to Silas and me from being with you, and he has told us the good news that you *still* trust *in Christ* and that you love him.[c] He told us also that you always happily remember us, *and that* you strongly desire that we visit you, just as we strongly desire to visit you. [7] My fellow believers, *even though* we are suffering very much because of what people are doing to us here, we have been cheered up because *Timothy told us about* your *still* trusting *in Christ.* [8] In our situation we feel very encouraged that you continue to strongly *trust* in the Lord *Jesus.* [9] I cannot thank God enough for *what he has done for* you! I greatly rejoice concerning you *when I pray to* our God! [10] I constantly and fervently ask *God* that *we will be able* to visit you and that *I will be able* to help you to trust *in God* more strongly!

1 Thessalonians 3:11-13

THEME: We pray that God will help us return to you and that the Lord Jesus will help you to love each other and other people more and more, just as we love you more and more.

[11] *We pray to* God our Father and to our Lord Jesus that they will clear the way so that we can return to you. [12] As for you, we *pray that* the Lord *Jesus* will help you to love each other and other people more and more, just as we *keep loving* you more and more. [13] *We pray* that *our Lord Jesus* will strengthen your purpose *to do what pleases God.*[d] We pray that God our Father will enable you to conduct your lives in a way that is pure and that *no one* can *justly* criticize so that when Jesus comes back *to earth* accompanied by all those who belong to him, he will be pleased with you.

4

1 Thessalonians 4:1-2

THEME: Just as we told you previously, we strongly urge you to increasingly conduct your lives in a way that will please God.

[1-2] Now, my fellow believers, *I want to write* about some other matters. Because we all have a close relationship with the Lord Jesus, we strongly urge you to conduct your lives in a way that pleases God. We taught you to live that way, and you know we did that as a result of what the Lord Jesus *told us to say.* We know you are living that way, but *we strongly urge* that you live that way even more.

---

[c] OR, ...that you love each other.

[d] OR, ...strengthen you spiritually.

1 Thessalonians 4:3-8

THEME: God wants you, by your behaving in a sexually pure way, to show that you completely belong to him.

³ God wants you to live pure lives that will show that you completely belong to him. He wants you to avoid doing any sexually immoral acts. ⁴ *That is, he wants* each one of you to know how to control your own sexual desires. He wants you to live pure lives that all people will see as good. ⁵ You must not lustfully desire *to do* immoral acts as unbelievers *do* who do not obey God. ⁶ *God wants each one of you to control your sexual desires in order that* none of you sin against your fellow believer and take advantage of him or her by doing that. Remember that we strongly warned you previously that the Lord *Jesus* will punish all *those who do* sexually immoral acts. ⁷ When God chose us *believers*, he did not want us to *be people who* behave in a sexually immoral way! On the contrary, *he wants us* to be *people who* behave in a morally pure way. ⁸ So I warn you that those who disregard *this teaching of mine* are not just disregarding a human being! On the contrary, *they are* disregarding God, *because God commanded it! Remember that* God sent his Spirit, who is **holy**, *to live* in you!

1 Thessalonians 4:9-12

THEME: We urge you to increasingly love each other, to strive to work at your own occupations, and not meddle in others' affairs.

⁹ *I want to urge you* again *that you should* love *your* fellow believers. You don't really need anyone to write you about that, because God has already taught **you** *the way* to love each other, ¹⁰ and because you already are *showing that you love* your fellow believers *who live* in other places *in your province* of Macedonia. Nevertheless, my fellow believers, we urge you to increasingly *love each other.* ¹¹ *We urge you* also to eagerly try to attend to your own affairs and to not meddle with the affairs of others. We urge you also to work at your own occupations *to earn what you need to live.* Remember that we taught you previously to live that way. ¹² If you do these things, unbelievers will *see and* acknowledge that you behave decently, and you will not have to depend on others *to supply what you need.*

1 Thessalonians 4:13-18

THEME: God will cause to live again those believers who died and will bring them to the sky with Jesus. Encourage each other by telling this message.

¹³ My fellow believers, we also want you to understand well *what will happen* to our fellow believers *who now* are dead. *You must not be like* unbelievers. They *grieve very much for people who die because* they don't confidently expect *people to live again after they die.* ¹⁴ We *believers* know it is true that Jesus died and that he rose *to live* again. So *we know well that* God *will cause believers* who have died *to live again. We know that he* will cause them to go *to heaven* with Jesus as a result of God's *commanding them to arise and come to him.*ᵉ ¹⁵ *I write this* because the Lord *Jesus* revealed *to me* that which I now tell you. *Some of you may think that* when the Lord *Jesus* comes back, he will consider that we *believers* who are still living will be superior to those *believers* who have died because *we will meet Jesus first. That is certainly not true!* ¹⁶ The Lord *Jesus* himself who will descend from heaven. *When he comes down, he* will command all of *us believers to rise.* The chief angel will shout *with a loud* voice, and *another angel* will blow a trumpet for God. Then,

---

ᵉ   OR, ...*We know that he* will cause them to come *to heaven* with Jesus as a result of Jesus' *commanding them to arise and* come.

the first thing that will happen is that the people who *trusted* in Christ who have died will live again. [17]After that, *God* will powerfully take up into the clouds all of us *believers* who are still living *on this earth*. At the same time, *he will take up* those *believers who have died*, in order that *we all* might together meet the Lord *Jesus* in the sky. As a result of that, we *all* shall be with him **forever**. [18]Because *all of this is true*, encourage each other by reminding each other of this teaching.

5

1 Thessalonians 5:1-8

THEME: We believers should be prepared for the time the Lord Jesus returns and not be like unbelievers, who will be unprepared. We must be vigilant and self-controlled.

[1]My fellow believers, *I want to tell you more* about the time period *when the Lord Jesus will come back. Really*, you don't need that I write to you about that, [2]because you yourselves know accurately *about it already! You know* that the Lord *Jesus will return unexpectedly.*[f] *People will not expect him, just like no one knows when* a thief *comes unexpectedly* at night. [3]*At a future time* many people will say, "*All is* peaceful and *we are* safe." Then suddenly he will come to punish them severely! Just as a pregnant woman who *experiences* birth pains *cannot stop those pains*, those people will definitely not *have any way to* escape *their punishment*. [4-5]*Just as people* in darkness *are unaware of what is happening around them, most people are not aware of what is about to happen to them.* Just as a thief *comes unexpectedly for people who are unaware, that time of punishment will come on people when they are not expecting it*. But you, my fellow believers, are people who are very much aware of what is going to happen. As a result, you will be expecting those things to happen. All of us *believers* are people *who do what is right, as people usually do when it is* daytime. We are not *people who do bad things, as some people do when it is* dark. [6]So we believers must be aware of what is happening. We must watch carefully, *as people who are awake are watchful for a thief*. We must be self-controlled, as people who are not drunk control what they do. People who sleep *are unaware of what is happening, and unbelievers are like that.* [7]It is at night when people *are unaware of what is happening because they* are asleep, and it is at night when people become intoxicated *and they do very wrong actions*. [8]But because we believers are people who *should do what is right*, we must be self-controlled, *as people in the daytime are usually sober and able to control what they do. As Roman soldiers protect themselves by* putting on breastplates and helmets, we *believers* must *protect ourselves by continuing to* trust and love *the Lord Jesus* by continuing to confidently expect that he will save *us from God's punishing us at the time he will punish other people.*

1 Thessalonians 5:9-11

THEME: God has destined us believers to be saved from future punishment and to be able to live together with our Lord Jesus after he returns. Since this is true, encourage each other.

[9]When God chose us, he did not plan for us to *be people whom he will severely* punish. On the contrary, *he decided* that he would save us because of *our trusting in what* our Lord Jesus Christ *has done for us*. [10]Jesus died *to atone* for our *sins* in order that we might be able to live together with him, whether we are alive or whether we are dead *when*

---

[f] OR, *...will return when some people are unprepared.*

he returns to earth. [11] Because *you know this is true*, continue to encourage each other, as indeed you now are doing.

1 Thessalonians 5:12-13

THEME: Recognize as leaders those people who care for and instruct you; highly esteem and love them. Live peacefully with each other.

[12] My fellow believers, we *three* ask that you recognize *as leaders* those people who work hard for you. *Specifically*, respect those who lead you as fellow believers who have a close relationship with the Lord *Jesus*. They warn you *to stop doing wrong.*[g] [13] That is, we *ask that you* consider those people to be very important and that you love them, because they work *hard to help you*. We also urge you to live peacefully with each other.

1 Thessalonians 5:14-15

THEME: Warn believers who will not work, and encourage and help those who need it. Be patient with all people. Do good deeds to them all, including those who do evil deeds to you.

[14] My fellow believers, we urge that you warn *believers* who will not work *in order to earn money to buy the things they need to live. Tell them that they are behaving wrongly.* We urge you to encourage *believers* who are fearful,[h] that you help all people who are weak *in any way*. We also urge you to be patient with everyone. [15] Make sure that none *of you* does evil deeds to anyone *who has done* evil to you. On the contrary, you must always aim to do good *deeds* to fellow believers and to everyone else.

1 Thessalonians 5:16-18

THEME: Always rejoice, pray, and thank God.

[16] Be joyful **at all times**, [17] pray **continually**, [18] and thank *God* **in all** *circumstances*. God wants you *to behave* like that *because of what* Christ Jesus *has done for you.*[i]

1 Thessalonians 5:19-22

THEME: Evaluate all messages that people claim the Holy Spirit gave them. Accept authentic messages and obey them.

[19] Don't *refuse the urging from God's* Spirit *when he is working among you; that would be like* throwing water on *a fire.* [20] *Specifically*, don't despise messages that the Holy Spirit reveals to someone *and reject them automatically.* [21] On the contrary, evaluate all *such messages*. Accept the authentic *messages and obey them.* [22] Don't obey any kind of evil message.

---

[g] OR, They instruct you *to do what is right.*

[h] OR, ...who are discouraged...

[i] OR, ...*because* you have a close relationship with Christ Jesus.

1 Thessalonians 5:23-24

THEME: We pray that God will cause you to be distinct people who behave right in every way, and I am sure that he will do this.

[23] *We pray to* God that he will change you to become more and more like his people should be. He is the one who causes *his people* to have *inner* peace. *That is, we pray* that he will help you so that in all that you think, in all that you desire, and in all that you do, you will be without fault. We ask him that he will keep doing that *until* our Lord Jesus Christ comes back *to earth*. [24] *Since God* has invited you *to be his people, you can* **certainly** trust him to keep on doing that.

1 Thessalonians 5:25-28

THEME: Pray for us. Affectionately greet all your fellow believers, and make certain that someone reads this letter aloud to all of them. May the Lord bless you.

[25] My fellow believers, pray for me and for Silas and for Timothy. [26] *When you gather together as believers*, greet each other affectionately, as fellow believers *should*. [27] Make certain that you read this letter to all the believers *who may be absent when you read it at first, knowing that* the Lord *Jesus* wants you to do it. [28] *I pray that* our Lord Jesus Christ *will continue to act* kindly toward you.

The Apostle Paul wrote letters to the Christians at Thessalonica. We call this second letter

2 Thessalonians

1

2 Thessalonians 1:1-2

THEME: We three, Paul, Silas, and Timothy, are sending this letter to the congregation of God's people in Thessalonica. We pray that God will continue to bless you with his kindness and inner peace.

¹ *I*, Paul, *am writing this letter*. Silas and Timothy *are with me. We are sending this letter* to *you* who are the congregation *of God's people* in *the city of* Thessalonica. You belong to God our Father, and you belong to Jesus Christ our Lord. ² *We pray that* God our Father and Jesus Christ our Lord *will continue to* act in kindness toward you, and *will continue to cause you to have inner* peace.

2 Thessalonians 1:3-4

THEME: We thank God very frequently that you are believing in the Lord Jesus more and more.

³ *Our* fellow believers, we thank God very frequently for you because we believers ought *to thank God for each other, and* specifically, it is appropriate *that we should thank God for you. We thank him* that you are believing in *the Lord Jesus* more and more, and that each one of you is loving *each of* the others more and more. ⁴ As a result, **we** keep telling the *other* congregations who *worship* God that we are proud of you. *We tell them* that you are being steadfast and that you *continue* believing *in the Lord Jesus*, even though you frequently suffer as a result of people causing you trouble.

2 Thessalonians 1:5-10

THEME: God will judge all people justly. He will publicly declare that you are worthy to enter the place where he will rule his people forever.

⁵ *Your being steadfast* shows *us* clearly that God will judge *all people* justly. He will publicly declare that you are worthy to be his people and to be in the place where he will rule *forever, because* you also suffer for *telling others about letting* God rule your lives. ⁶ *God will certainly cause trouble for* the people who are troubling you, because he *considers* it just to punish them for doing that to you. ⁷ He also *considers* that it is just to reward you who are being troubled, by giving you relief *from your suffering*. He will do that for both you and us when our Lord Jesus descends from heaven, together with his powerful angels and with blazing fire. ⁸ *Then* our Lord Jesus *will* punish those people who don't *want to* know him and *those* who refuse to obey his message. ⁹ *Our Lord Jesus* will forbid them from ever coming near to him and near to the glory which he has *because he is so*

powerful.[a] He will punish those people by destroying them forever. [10] *The Lord Jesus* will do this when he comes *back from heaven* at the time *God has chosen*. As a result, all we who are his people will praise him because of *what he has done for us.* And all we believers will marvel at our Lord because of *what he has done. And you will be there, too,* because you believed what we testified to you.

2 Thessalonians 1:11-12

THEME: We are praying very frequently for you that God will consider you worthy to receive that to which he summoned you.

[11] In order that you might *praise Jesus like that,* we are praying very frequently for you. We pray that *you will be able to demonstrate to* our God that **you** are worthy *to receive* that which he chose *you to receive.* We pray also that he will powerfully enable you to do good in every way that you desire, and that he will also enable you to do powerfully every *good* deed *that you do because* you believe *in Jesus Christ.* [12] *We pray this because we want* you to praise our Lord Jesus, and we want him to honor you. This will happen because God, whom we *serve,* and our Lord Jesus Christ will continue act kindly toward you, doing for *you* things that you don't deserve.

2

2 Thessalonians 2:1-3a

THEME: Do not be quickly troubled in mind or alarmed by any message stating that the Day of the Lord has already come.

[1] Now *I want to write to you* about the time when our Lord Jesus Christ will return and when *God* will gather us together to *where Jesus* is. My fellow believers, I urge you [2] to think calmly *about any message* that *claims* that the Lord has *already* come again. Don't be shaken or alarmed by any such message. *It does not matter* if *it is a message that someone claims was revealed by God's Spirit*, or if *it is some other message that someone* has spoken, or whether *it is a message that someone claims that* I wrote in a letter. [3] Don't allow anyone to deceive you in any way *with the result that you believe any such message.*

2 Thessalonians 2:3b-5

THEME: The Lord will come only after that time when the man who will sin very greatly appears.

The Lord will not come *immediately.* First, *many people* will rebel *against God.* The result of their rebelling will be that *they will accept the message of* the man who will sin very greatly *against God.* [4] He will be the *supreme* enemy *of God.* He will *proudly* exalt himself above everything that *people* consider to be God and above everything that people worship. *Because of wanting people to worship him,* he will *even enter* God's Temple and sit down *there to rule!* He will publicly proclaim that he himself is God! But *God* will *certainly* destroy that man! [5] I am sure you remember that I kept telling you these things while I was still with you.

---

[a]   OR, …the glory which is manifested by his might.

2 Thessalonians 2:6-8

THEME: This man will be revealed by God when he who is now preventing him from being revealed will have been removed by God.

⁶ You also know that there is someone^b that is preventing this man *from revealing himself*. He is being restrained *now* so that he can reveal himself at the time *God has appointed*. ⁷ *Although Satan* is already secretly causing *people* to reject *God's* laws, this man will be prevented *from revealing himself* until the one who is blocking him will be removed by *God*. ⁸ It is then that *God will allow* this man, who *completely* rejects *God's* laws, to reveal himself. Then the Lord Jesus, by what he commands, will destroy him. Jesus, by his own glorious arrival, will cause him to become *completely* powerless.

2 Thessalonians 2:9-12

THEME: When this man is present, he will completely deceive those who will perish.

⁹ But *before Jesus destroys this man*, Satan will give him very great power. As a result, he *will do all kinds of supernatural* signs and amazing deeds that will make it seem as though *God has enabled him to do them*. ¹⁰ And by doing wicked *deeds* he will completely deceive those who are doomed to go to hell. *He will deceive them* because they will have refused to love the true *message*. So they will not be saved. ¹¹ God, by his power, will cause this man to easily deceive them, so that they will believe what *this man* falsely claims *about himself*. ¹² The result will be that *God* will *justly* condemn everyone who did not believe the true *message* and gladly chose *to do* what is wicked.

2 Thessalonians 2:13-14

THEME: God chose you and summoned you in order that you should be saved and share in Christ's glory.

¹³ *Our* fellow believers, whom our Lord *Jesus* loves, we thank God very frequently for you. It is appropriate for us to do that, because God chose you from the beginning *of creation* to save *you* as a result of *your* believing the true *message* and as a result of *God's* Spirit setting you apart *for God*. ¹⁴ *We thank God that* he chose you as a result of our *proclaiming* the message about Christ *to you*, in order that you might share some of the glory our Lord Jesus Christ has.

2 Thessalonians 2:15

THEME: Continue believing the teaching that we committed to you.

¹⁵ So, *our fellow believers, continue to be steadfast concerning what you believe*; that is, continue believing the *true* teaching that we committed to you by speaking to you and by *writing* a letter *to you*.

2 Thessalonians 2:16-17

THEME: We pray that our Lord Jesus Christ himself will encourage you and cause you to continue doing and speaking what is good.

¹⁶ *We pray for you to* our Lord Jesus Christ himself and to God, our Father. God loves us and encourages us and causes us to confidently expect *to receive* the eternal things *he*

---

^b   OR, ...something...

has promised to give us as a result of Christ acting in kindness toward us, in ways we don't deserve. [17] We pray that God and Jesus together will encourage you! And we pray that they will enable you to continue doing and saying what is good in God's sight!

3

2 Thessalonians 3:1-2

THEME: Pray that more and more people will believe the message about our Lord Jesus.

[1] As for the other matters, our fellow believers, pray for us that more and more people will hear our message about our Lord Jesus. Pray that they will believe this message, just as you have done. [2] Pray also for us that God will rescue us from the very evil people here who cause us to suffer. Pray like that because they and many others refuse to believe our message.

2 Thessalonians 3:3-5

THEME: Our Lord Jesus will cause you to continue to be steadfast and he will protect you from the evil one.

[3] Remember that our Lord Jesus is trustworthy! So we are sure that he will cause you to continue to be steadfast. We are also sure that he will protect you from Satan, the evil one.[c] [4] Because of your close relationship with our Lord Jesus, we are confident that you are obeying what we have commanded you, and we are confident that you will obey what we are commanding you in this letter. [5] We pray that our Lord Jesus will enable you to continue knowing that God loves you. We pray also that the Lord will cause you to continue being steadfast.[d]

2 Thessalonians 3:6-11

THEME: We command you to disassociate yourselves from every fellow believer who refuses to work.

[6] Our fellow believers, we command you—with the authority that our Lord Jesus Christ has given to us—that you stop associating with any fellow believer who is lazy and refuses to work. That is, you must keep away from those who are not conducting their lives in the manner that we taught you. [7] We tell you this because you yourselves know that you ought to conduct your lives as we did. We did not just sit around without working while we were living among you. [8] We did not eat others' food if we did not pay them for it. Instead, we worked very hard to support ourselves. We worked hard day and night, in order that we would not depend on any of you to supply what we needed. [9] We have always had the right to depend on you for money, but instead, we worked hard in order to be an example for you, in order that you should conduct your lives as we did. [10] Remember that when we were there with you, we kept commanding you that if any fellow believer refuses to work, you should not give him food to eat. [11] We command you this again now, because someone has informed us that some of you are just sitting around without working at all! Not only that, but some of you are interfering with what other people are doing!

---

c   OR, ...will protect you from evil.

d   OR, ...will cause you to be steadfast as he was steadfast.

2 Thessalonians 3:12

THEME: We command the believers who are not working to support themselves by settling down and working.

¹² We command the believers who are not working and urge *them* by the authority of our Lord Jesus Christ that they settle down and support themselves by working.

2 Thessalonians 3:13

THEME: You others, do not stop doing what is right because you are discouraged.

¹³ Fellow believers, don't ever get tired of doing what is right!

2 Thessalonians 3:14-15

THEME: Publicly identify fellow believers who do not obey what we have written in this letter, and do not associate with them.

¹⁴ If there are *fellow believers who refuse to work* and don't obey what I have written in this letter, *publicly* tell the congregation about them. Then don't associate with them, in order that they may become ashamed. ¹⁵ Don't regard them as being *your* enemies; instead, warn them as *you would warn your* other fellow believers.

2 Thessalonians 3:16a

THEME: I pray that our Lord Jesus himself will give peace to you always and in every situation.

¹⁶ *I pray that our* Lord *Jesus* himself, who *gives inner* peace *to his people*, will give *inner* peace to you always and in every situation.

2 Thessalonians 3:16b-18

THEME: In closing, I pray that our Lord Jesus will continue to bless you all. I, Paul, am greeting you and I am writing this part myself so that you may know that it truly comes from me.

I *pray that our* Lord *Jesus will continue to* help you all. ¹⁷ Now, having taken the pen from my scribe, I, Paul, am sending my greetings you as I write this part myself. I do this in all my letters so that you may know that it truly comes from me. This is the way I always end my letters. ¹⁸ I pray that our Lord Jesus Christ will continue to act kindly to you all.

The Apostle Paul wrote letters to his assistants. We call this letter

1 Timothy

1

1 Timothy 1:1-2

THEME: This letter is from me, Paul, to you, Timothy. May you be blessed with kindness and mercy from God and Christ Jesus.

¹ *I*, Paul, *am writing this letter. You know that* I am an apostle. I *represent* Christ Jesus because God and Christ Jesus commanded me *to do the work of an apostle*. God is the one who saved us, and Jesus is the one *whose return* we are confidently waiting for. ² *You*, Timothy, *are like* a true son *to me because you* trusted *in Christ after I told you about him. I pray that* God, who is our Father, and Christ Jesus, who is our Lord, will *continue to act* in kindness and mercy toward you, and *may they give you inner* peace.

1 Timothy 1:3-20

THEME: Defend and promote the true Christian doctrine. Teach it and live by it. Also I instruct you how to strengthen the congregation, which upholds the truth.

³ *I urge you now*—just as I urged you when I was about to go to *the province of* Macedonia—that you remain there in *the city of* Ephesus. Stay there so that you can command certain people not to teach false *doctrines*. ⁴ And tell people to not continually give their attention to stories *that tell about our ancestors*, stories in which there are genealogies that *seem to be* endless. *You must command your congregation not to think that these stories are valuable,* because *whenever people think* that, they *just* start arguing uselessly about things, instead of *teaching* God's plan, which *is concerned with* what we believe.ª ⁵ I commanded you *to teach them* to have pure desires and to *know within themselves that God* approves of what they do, and to sincerely believe *the true doctrine*. By doing that, *they will* be filled with love *for God*. ⁶ There are some people who have turned away from these true teachings. As a result, they *just* discuss what is useless. ⁷ They desire to teach the laws *God gave to Moses*, but they don't understand what they are really saying nor the subjects about which they speak so confidently.

⁸ We know that the laws *God gave to Moses are* good *for us* if we consider correctly *what God intended those laws for*. ⁹ We must remember that God did not give Moses those laws in order *to condemn* righteous people. By those laws he *condemns people who act as though there were no* laws, and who refuse to obey *anyone. By them he condemns* those who don't revere God and those who sin habitually. *He condemns* those who refuse to perform rituals that are pleasing to God and who show no respect for religion. *He condemns* those who murder their fathers and who murder their mothers and who murder *other* people. ¹⁰ *He condemns* those who are sexually immoral and those who are

---

ª OR, …which *we know because* we trust in Christ.

homosexuals. *He condemns* those who kidnap people to make them slaves. *He condemns* those who lie and those who promise something strongly but don't do what they promised. He condemns every other action that is contrary to our true teaching. [11] This is what we teach people when we tell them the glorious message about Christ that our awesome God *has revealed* and that he gave to me to teach.

[12] I am grateful to Christ Jesus our Lord, who enabled me to do this work, because he considered that I could be trusted. So he appointed me to *serve him.* [13] Formerly I used to say evil things *about him,* I caused *his people* to suffer, and I acted very cruelly toward them. But *Christ acted* kindly to me since I did those things, not knowing that I was doing wrong, because I did not believe *in him.* [14] Our Lord kindly did for me what I did not deserve, so that I now believe *in Christ Jesus,* and I love him *because I belong to him.*[b]

[15] *Something that all we believers* say is certainly true and worthy for us to fully accept is that Christ Jesus came into the world in order to save sinful people *so that God would not punish them for their sins.* As for me, I *consider that I have sinned* more than all others. [16] Yet *Christ* Jesus acted mercifully to me so that he might demonstrate *to people that he is perfectly patient with them.* He demonstrated that by being patient with me, who have sinned in worse ways than all the others. He wanted what he did for me to be an example *of patience* to people who would *later* believe in him and as a result would live forever.

[17] I desire that people honor and praise the only *true* God forever! Even though no one can see him, he is the King who rules for all time, who will never die! Amen! [18] Timothy, you *are like* a son *to me.* So, based on what *someone* previously prophesied about you, I am instructing you *to strongly oppose those who teach false doctrines. You should oppose them like* soldiers strongly oppose *those who attack their countrymen.* [19] Continue to believe *the true doctrine* and do only what you know to be right! Remember that some people have pushed aside the true doctrine. As a result, they no longer believe what is true. [20] Among the ones who have done that are Hymenaeus and Alexander, whom I put in the hands of Satan, so that *when Satan punishes them* they may learn not to teach wrong doctrine.

2

1 Timothy 2:1-3:16

THEME: I instruct you how people should conduct themselves who belong to God's family and who uphold the truth.

[1] The first thing[c] I am urging *you to tell your congregation* is that *Christians* should continually ask *God* for *what they need.* They should also pray to God *for all other people,* and they should be thanking *God.* [2] Specifically, they should pray for rulers and for all *other people* who are in positions of authority, so that *God will help them to rule. As God enables the rulers to rule well*, we can live very peaceably as we conduct ourselves *as we should*, doing all that is right and proper *in the sight of God and others.* [3] It is good *to pray like that, and* it pleases God, who saves us, when we pray like that. [4] He desires to save all people. *He wants* everyone to fully know *and accept* his true *message.* [5] He is the *only* one *true* God! And there is *only* one person who talks to God on behalf of people. That person is Christ Jesus, who *himself became* a man. [6] He gave his *life as a sacrifice* in order to

---

[b]   OR, ...and I love others *because I belong to him.*

[c]   OR, The most important thing...

ransom all *people*, which showed at the proper time *that God desires that all people be saved.* [7] As for **me**, I was appointed by him to declare *this message* and to be an apostle. I am telling the truth *about God appointing me.* I am not lying! He appointed me to teach the non-Jews that they should believe his true message.

[8] I desire that in every place *where believers worship*, the men who pray publicly should be men who are not practicing sin. When they pray, they should not be angry[d] *with anyone*, and they should not doubt *that God will answer their prayers.* [9] *I would like that* the clothing that women wear be modest and sensible. I want them to not fix their hair in fancy ways, nor wear gold *jewelry*, nor pearls, nor expensive clothing *to make themselves attractive.* [10] Instead, they should be doing things that women who claim to worship God should do; that is, they should be doing good deeds. [11] Women must learn to *listen* quietly *during the worship services* and to fully subject themselves *to the leaders of the congregation.* [12] I don't permit women to teach *men spiritual truth publicly*, and I don't permit them to have authority over men. Instead, *I desire* that women *listen* quietly *during the worship services,* [13] because God made Adam first, and afterwards he made Eve, [14] and also, it was *Eve*, not Adam, whom *Satan* deceived. As a result of the woman being deceived, she sinned. She did what God had told her not to do. [15] But even though she did that, now God will save women as they bear children if they continue to trust *him,* if they continue to love others, if they continue to live *more and more* acceptably to God, and if they continue to be modest.

3

[1] Those who aspire to be elders[e] *in the congregation* desire a noble task. [2] *Since that is a task others should respect*, overseers must *conduct themselves* in such a way that *no one* can truly find fault with them. Specifically, they *must be* faithful to their wives. They must think clearly *about what they do.* They must be sensible. They must control their behavior. They must be dignified. They must welcome and care for guests. They must be able to teach *God's truth* well. [3] They must not be drunkards. They must not be quick to fight *those who make them angry.* On the contrary, they must be gentle and not be quarrelsome. They must not be greedy. [4] They must lead and care for their own households well. For example, they must be men who are obeyed and completely respected by their children, [5] because those who don't know how to manage well the people who live in their own homes certainly cannot care for God's congregation. [6] They must not be ones who have just recently *trusted in Jesus*, because *if you choose ones* like that, they might become conceited *because you chose them so soon.* And as a result of their being conceited, God will condemn them like he condemned the devil *for being conceited.* [7] Moreover, *elders must conduct their lives* in such a way that non-Christians will speak well of them, because *if they conduct themselves* that way, people will not say evil things about them, and the devil will not catch them *like people catch animals* in a trap.

[8] *Those whom you choose to serve as* deacons likewise *must be ones who conduct their lives suitably. Specifically,* they must be serious. They must be sincere. They must not like to drink a lot of alcohol. They must not be greedy. [9] They must sincerely believe the message that *God* has now revealed *to us.* [10] *The same as you do for the elders*, you must examine *the character of the deacons before you appoint them to serve.* Then if they are without fault, let them serve as deacons. [11] Their wives[f] likewise *must conduct themselves*

---

[d] OR, ...should not quarrel...

[e] OR, ...a bishop...

[f] OR, The women who are deacons...

suitably. *Specifically, they must be* serious. They must not speak evil about people. They must not drink a lot of alcohol. They must be faithful in everything they do. [12] Deacons must be faithful to their wives, and they must lead well and care well for their children and *the rest of* the people in their homes. [13] Because if deacons serve well, they will be respected and they will be able *to speak* very confidently about what they believe concerning Christ Jesus.

[14] Although I hope to come to you soon, I am writing these things to you *now,* [15] so that if I am delayed, you will know how believers should conduct their lives *and you will be able to teach them regarding that. I am referring to* all those who are members of God's family, all the congregations that belong to the all-powerful God, all those who uphold the true *message.* [16] It is certainly true that *the message God* has now revealed is very wonderful! From it, we learn this spiritual truth which we say about *Christ.*[g] *We affirm concerning Jesus Christ that,*

He is the one who appeared *on the earth* in a human body.
God's Spirit showed *that he was truly the Messiah.*[h]
Angels saw him.
People preached about him in *many* nations.
People in *many parts of* the world believed the message about him.
God took him up into heaven.

4

1 Timothy 4:1-16

THEME: Take heed that you conduct yourself well and that you teach the true doctrine.

[1] God's Spirit has clearly told us that in later times some people will stop believing *what all of us* believe. Instead, they will listen to *evil* spirits who deceive *people. They will also believe the false* doctrines that *they receive from* those evil spirits. [2] The people who teach those false doctrines are liars! And they don't feel at all guilty *when they teach such things!* [3] For example, they forbid *believers* to marry *because they say that it makes us unacceptable to God.* They also command people to abstain from *eating certain* foods. But God created such foods for us eat! We who believe *in Christ* know the true *doctrine,* and we thank *God for the food he gives us. That is why we* can eat it. [4] We can eat all kinds of food because all food that God has created is good. We should not refuse to eat certain kinds of food if we thank *God for the food* when we eat it. [5] It is acceptable *to God for us to eat it* because God *long ago* said *that all things he made are good*, and also because we pray, asking *God to bless it*, when we eat it.

[6] When you teach these things to your fellow believers, *you will be showing that* you, whom Christ Jesus *appointed*, are serving them well. You will have become strong *spiritually* by holding fast to the true message *we all* believe. [7] You must completely reject godless, silly stories *from your ancestors that old people tell*. Keep training yourself in godly behavior. [8] *Some people say*, "Physical exercise helps us in some ways." But *I say that* what *really* benefits us very much is to conduct our lives in a godly way, because *if people live in a godly way, their godly living* will benefit them both in their present life and in their future life *in heaven.* [9] Those are words that are absolutely true, and everybody

---

[g] OR, We affirm this doctrine to be true and very important. It is what shows us how to live in a godly manner. It is what God has now revealed, even though it was not known *before.*

[h] OR, ...*God's Spirit showed that he always acted righteously.*

should accept them! [10] This is the reason we work so hard *for others*, because we confidently expect that God, who is all-powerful, *will do the things he has promised*. He is the one who *wants to* save all people, *so he protects them*. He certainly *protects us* who believe *in Christ!* [11] Command these things and teach these things.

[12] *Timothy*, by the way you conduct your life, show the believers *in your congregation* how they should conduct their lives. Specifically, speak *good things*, conduct yourself *well*, love *people*, trust *God*, and be pure in every way. Then no one will *have any reason to* belittle you because of your being young. [13] Until I come, be sure to read *the Scriptures to the congregation* and to exhort them *to obey the Scriptures* and to teach them. [14] Don't neglect *to use* the *abilities that God* gave you as a result of *the* prophecies *given to you* when the elders laid their hands on you *to commission you*. [15] Do the things *that I have told* you to do! Do them sincerely and wholeheartedly so that everyone may see that you are growing *in you ability to serve God and the congregation*.

[16] Be careful to *conduct* yourself as you should, and continue *to teach the good* doctrine. If you continue to do that, *God* will save you and the people who listen to you.

5

1 Timothy 5:1-25

THEME: I instruct you how to act toward different groups in the church.

[1] Don't rebuke older men. Instead, exhort them *respectfully* as you would exhort your father. Exhort younger men *gently* as you would exhort your brothers. [2] *Exhort* older women *respectfully* as *you would exhort* your mother. *Exhort* younger women *gently* as *you would exhort* your sisters, but act in a completely proper way as you do that.

[3] *Make sure the congregation* respects widows who have no one to care for them. *The congregation should respect them by taking care of them.* [4] If a widow has children or grandchildren, these *children or grandchildren* should learn that they are to respect their own family first. By doing that, they can repay their parents and grandparents *for taking care of them when they were young*, because doing that pleases God. [5] The widows who are really alone, and have no one *to help them,* confidently expect that God *will help them.* So night and day they pray, earnestly asking *God to help them and others*. [6] But widows who just want to have a lot of pleasure are *spiritually* dead, even though they are *physically* alive. [7] And tell *the congregation* that *the children or grandchildren should take care of the widows in their families,* so that *no one* can say the believers are doing things that are wrong. [8] Those who don't take care of those who live in their own homes, and especially if they don't take care of their own families, have denied what we believe and *we should consider them to be* worse than people who don't believe *in Christ at all.*

[9] *You have a list of* widows *who will do work for the congregation and receive funds*. Put a woman's name on that list *only if* she is more than sixty years old, and if she was faithful to her husband. [10] *Put women's names on that list only* if it is known that they have zealously done every kind of good deed, if they have helped *children* who were afflicted, if they have brought up their own children *properly*, if they have welcomed and cared for guests, and if they have humbly served other believers. [11] As for younger widows, don't put their names on that list, because they *promise to do work for the congregation, but instead of doing that, they usually* want to marry *again* when they have strong desires. [12] If that happens, they will become guilty of not having done what they had promised *to do for the*

congregation.[i] [13] In addition, they generally become lazy. Specifically, as they *just* go about from house to house they also begin to gossip and meddle *in other people's affairs*, saying things they shouldn't say. [14] So, *instead of your putting the names of younger widows on the list*, I advise *you to tell them* to marry again, that they should bear children, manage their homes *well*, and not do anything about which an enemy could say bad things. [15] *I say this* because some *younger widows* have stopped *obeying Christ* and are obeying Satan.

[16] If any woman who believes *in Christ* has widows *in her household*, she should take care of them. The congregation should not be burdened by having *to take care of their needs*. The congregation should take care of the widows who truly *have no one to care for them*.

[17] *Each congregation* should pay well the elders who lead *well*. *The congregation should* greatly honor them, especially those who preach and those who teach. [18] *Long ago Moses* wrote in the Scriptures, "While an ox is threshing *grain,* you must not tie its mouth shut *so that it can't eat the grain*," and *Jesus said*, "Those who work should be paid by those they work for." *So we know that congregations should support their elders.*

[19] When someone accuses an elder *about doing wrong*, accept what that person says only if there are *at least* two or three persons who testify they saw the elder do that wrong.

[20] But as for any *elder* who repeatedly sins, rebuke him in front of the whole congregation, so that the rest *of the elders* will be afraid *to sin*.

[21] I solemnly tell you that God and Christ Jesus and the holy angels know everything you do. *So keep that in mind as you* obey these commands *about elders*! *As you consider what others say about an elder*, don't quickly decide that he has done wrong. And treat all the elders equally.

[22] Don't be in a hurry to lay your hands on a man *to set him apart as an elder. Wait until you find out how he conducts his life,* because *God will consider* that you are responsible if *you approve* a person who sins. Keep your life pure in every way. [23] *And Timothy*, no longer drink *only* water, but instead use a little wine *also*, because *that may help to cure* your stomach's frequent illnesses. [24] *I tell you not to set apart elders hastily, because* some people *sin secretly*, so that it is not known what they have done until after someone examines them.[j] On the other hand, some people sin openly, so that people know what they have done before anyone examines them. [25] Similarly, although *some people* do good deeds openly, with the result that people know what they have done, some people *do good deeds secretly*, yet the good deeds they have done cannot remain secret, either.

6

1 Timothy 6:1-21

THEME: Live according to the Christian doctrine, and complete what I have commanded.

[1] As for slaves *who are believers, teach them that they* should consider that it is right for them to honor their masters in every way. If they do that, people will not speak evil about God, and they will not speak evil about that which *we apostles* teach, *because they will see that the slaves are being respectful toward their masters*.

---

[i] OR, ...promised *Christ that they would do.*

[j] OR, ...it is not known what they have done before God judges them.

[2] *Slaves* who have masters who believe *in Christ* must not be disrespectful to their masters just because their masters are fellow believers. Instead, they should serve *their masters* even better, because *their masters* are fellow believers whom *God* loves and who benefit when *the slaves* serve them well.

As you teach these things *to your congregation*, exhort *people* to do them.

[3] Some people teach things that are different. What they teach does not agree with the correct teaching that our Lord Jesus Christ *taught.*[k] They don't teach that we should conduct our lives in a godly way. [4] Such people are very proud and don't understand anything. Instead, they have a distorted desire to *argue about unimportant* matters and about certain words. As a result, *people who listen to them* envy *others*. They quarrel *with others and with one another.* They say bad things about *others. They* suspect that *others* have evil *motives*. [5] Their whole way of thinking has become completely wrong *because* they have rejected the true *doctrine*. As a result, they *mistakenly* think that by practicing religion they will gain a lot of *money*.

[6] *We* truly do gain great *benefit* if we conduct our lives in a godly way, and if we are content *with what we have.* [7] We brought nothing into the world *when we were born*, and we can't take anything out *of it when we die,* [8] so if we have food and clothing, we should be satisfied with those. [9] But some people strongly desire to be rich. As a result, they *do wrong things to get money, and this will cause them to* be caught, just like animals get caught in traps. They foolishly desire many things, and those desires cause them to get hurt. And God will completely reject *them!* [10] All kinds of bad things will happen to people who desire to have a lot of money. Because some people longed for money, they have stopped believing the doctrine *that all of us believe,* and they have caused themselves a lot of grief.

[11] But as for you, a man who *serves God*, keep completely away from such love of money. Decide that you will do what is right, and that you will be godly. Decide that you will trust *God*, and that you will love *others*. Endure *difficult circumstances*. Always be gentle *with people.* [12] Try earnestly and with all your energy to live in accordance with what you believe. *Continue to do your tasks well so that* you will know for sure that you will live eternally. Remember that *God* chose you to *live with him*, and in the presence of many elders you affirmed *that you trust in Christ.*

[13] God, who gives life to all things, knows everything you do. Christ Jesus also knows everything you do. He strongly affirmed what was true *when he was on trial* before Pontius Pilate. [14] I command you that as you keep all that in mind, in every way hold fast to what Christ has commanded us. Hold those teachings fast in a way that our Lord Jesus Christ cannot criticize you about. Hold them fast until he comes again. [15] *Remember that God* will *cause Jesus to return* at the proper time. God is awesome! He is the only Ruler! He rules over all other rulers! [16] He is the only one who will never die, *and he lives in heaven in* light *that is so bright that* no one can approach it! He is the one whom no person has ever seen and whom no person is able to see! My desire is that all people will honor him and that he *will rule* powerfully forever! May it be so!

[17] Tell *the believers* who are rich here in this present world that they should not be proud, and that they should not trust in their riches, because they can't be certain *how long they will have them.* Teach them that they should not *trust in their wealth. Instead, they should trust* in God. He is the one who abundantly gives us everything we have so we can enjoy it. [18] Also, tell them that their good deeds must be as plentiful *as their money.* They should share very generously with others *what they have.* [19] If they do that, *Jesus will give them a*

---

[k] OR, …the correct teaching that is about our Lord Jesus Christ.

great reward. It will be as though they are storing up *in heaven* much treasure for themselves that will be a good *basis on which they can rely for receiving a great reward in* the future.[1] By doing this they will have the life that is the real life.

[20] Timothy, faithfully proclaim the true message *Jesus* has given *to you*. Avoid *people who want to* chatter about things that God considers unimportant. Avoid *people who claim they have* 'true knowledge' but who say things that are opposed to *our true teaching.* [21] *Reject completely the teaching such people give. Remember that* some people who claim *to have this 'knowledge'* have stopped believing what *all of us* believe.

May God continue to act in kindness toward you all.

---

[1] OR, …a good *basis which will be as solid as* the foundation *of a house.*

The Apostle Paul wrote letters to his assistants. We call this letter

2 Timothy

1

2 Timothy 1:1-2

THEME: This letter is from me, Paul, to you, Timothy.

[1] *I, Paul, am writing this letter. I am* an apostle whom Christ Jesus chose because that is what God wanted. He chose me *to tell people that God* has promised *that they will* live *eternally* as a result of their having a close relationship with Christ Jesus. [2] *I am writing to you*, Timothy, whom I love *as if you were* my own son. *I pray that* God our Father and Christ Jesus our Lord will *continue to act* with kindness to you, be merciful to you, and *give you inner* peace.

2 Timothy 1:3-5

THEME: I thank God that you sincerely believe in Christ Jesus.

[3] I thank God *for all he has done for you*. I serve him, and my ancestors *served him, too. I serve him* in a manner I know to be right. *I thank him* as I *pray* repeatedly *for you* night and day. [4] *While I am thanking God for you*, I very much want to see you because I remember how you cried *when we separated. I want to see you* so that I will be filled with joy. [5] *I thank God because* I remember your sincere faith *in Christ Jesus*, the faith that your grandmother, Lois, and your mother, Eunice, *had before you. And yes*, I am very sure that you also have that same kind of faith.

2 Timothy 1:6-7

THEME: So I remind you to do fervently what God has enabled and assigned you to do.

[6] Because *I am sure of your faith in him*, I remind you to do fervently what God has assigned you to do and what he has enabled you to do. *God assigned* you to do it when I laid my hands *on you to indicate that he had chosen you to do his work.* [7] Remember that God has put *his Spirit* within us. *His Spirit does not cause us to be* afraid. Instead, *he causes us to be* powerful *to work for God*, and he helps us to love *others* and *to* control what we say and do.

2 Timothy 1:8-14

THEME: Never be ashamed, either of the message or of me, but be willing to endure with me whatever we suffer because we tell the good news.

[8] So never be ashamed[a] to tell others the message about our Lord. And don't *be ashamed* of me, *even though I am* a prisoner *because I preach about* him. Instead, *be willing to* suffer as I do as you proclaim the message about Christ. *Endure what you will suffer* by letting God empower *you to endure it.* [9] *God* saved us and chose us to conduct our lives in a pure way. It was not our doing good deeds *that caused him to do for us what we did not deserve.* Instead, before he created the world he planned to *be kind to us* as a result of what Christ Jesus *would do for us.* [10] Now, as a result of our Savior Christ Jesus having come, God has shown *that he acts kindly toward us. Christ Jesus* has declared that death will not defeat us! He has also revealed that, as a result of *our hearing and accepting* the message *about Christ, we* will live *forever in bodies that will* not decay! [11] Christ chose me to go as an apostle to many places and proclaim that message to people. [12] So, even though I suffer *here in this prison*, I am not ashamed *of being here,* because I know *Christ Jesus*, the one whom I have trusted. I am sure that he is able to keep safe the good message he has entrusted to me.[b] I am sure that he will reward me *when he comes again*.

[13] Be sure that you tell others the same correct message that you heard from me. *And as you tell it*, keep trusting *in Christ Jesus,* and keep loving others as Christ Jesus *enables you to do.* [14] Don't let anyone persuade you to change the *good message that* God has entrusted to you. Allow the Holy Spirit who lives in us to *direct what you say*.

2 Timothy 1:16-18

THEME: Many people have turned away from me, but Onesiphorus often refreshed me and was not ashamed of me.

[15] You know that *almost* all *the believers* in *the province of* Asia have turned away from me, including Phygelus and Hermogenes. [16] *But I pray that* the Lord will be kind to the family of Onesiphorus for the following reasons: Often he refreshed me and, *even though* I was a prisoner, he was not ashamed *to admit he was* my *friend.* [17] On the contrary, when he came to *the city of* Rome, he diligently searched for me until he found me. [18] *I pray that* the Lord will be kind to him on that day *when he will judge people.* And how much Onesiphorus served *me* in *the city of* Ephesus, you yourself know very well.

2

2 Timothy 2:1-2

THEME: Let God empower you; and entrust the message to trustworthy people.

[1] You *are like a* son to me. So I urge you to *let God* empower you *spiritually* as a result of Christ Jesus acting kindly toward you. [2] *As you let God do that*, keep in mind that *the message* you heard from me is the same message that other people have declared to you, and entrust that message to people whom you can trust, people who will be competent to teach others.

---

[a] OR, So never be reluctant…
     OR, Therefore, always be eager…
[b] OR, …the things I have entrusted *to him*.

2 Timothy 2:3-13

THEME: Endure with me what we suffer for Christ Jesus.

[3] Endure as I do what we suffer for Christ Jesus, like good soldiers *endure what they suffer.* [4] *You know that* soldiers, in order to please their captain, don't become involved in civilian affairs. *So, like soldiers, don't let anything distract you as you serve Christ Jesus!* [5] *You also know that* athletes who do not obey the rules of the contest don't win any prize. *So, like athletes, discipline yourself to do all that Christ Jesus has commanded, so that God will reward you!* [6] *You also know that* hard working farmers ought to be the first to have a share of the crop. *So, like farmers, work hard for Christ Jesus and expect that God will reward you!* [7] Think about what I have just written because, *if you do*, the Lord will enable you to understand everything *you need to understand.* [8] *Endure everything by* remembering how Jesus Christ *endured suffering.* Remember that God raised him from the dead and *affirmed him to be king as* his ancestor *King* David was. Those are things I tell to people when I tell them the message about Christ. [9] I am suffering *here in prison* because *some people oppose* the good message *I tell.* They have even put me in chains as if I were a criminal. Nevertheless, nothing is preventing *others from proclaiming* the message from God. [10] So I *willingly* endure all *that I am suffering* for the sake of those *whom God has* chosen. *I do this* in order that Christ Jesus will save them, too, and that they will be forever with *him in the* glorious *place where he is.* [11] *Endure everything as you remember* that these words *that we all say*[c] *are trustworthy:*

Since we *have stopped behaving as we did in the past*, and now are acting as though we died when he died,
    we shall also live with him.
[12] Since we are patiently enduring *what we suffer*, we shall also rule with him.
But if we say that we don't *know him*, he also will say that he does not *know* us.
[13] If we are unfaithful *to him*, he himself will *treat us just as he* promised to do,
    because he always does what he says he will do.

2 Timothy 2:14-15

THEME: Remind teachers about the things I have told you and charge them not to quarrel. Be sure that you yourself are the kind of person that God will approve of.

[14] *Those whom you appointed to teach others*, keep reminding them about these things *I have told you.* Tell them strongly that, since God knows what they are doing, they must not quarrel about words,[d] *because, when teachers quarrel, it helps* no one, *and because, when they quarrel, they spiritually* destroy those who hear them.

[15] Do your best to be the kind of person that God will approve of. *Be like* good workmen as you teach the true message accurately. If workmen work well, they will not need to be ashamed *of what they do.*

2 Timothy 2:16-19

THEME: Have nothing to do with godless and foolish talk.

[16] Stay away from *those who* talk in godless and foolish ways, because *those who talk foolishly* will become even more ungodly, [17] and their message will harm people like

---

[c] OR, *...that we teach people...*

[d] OR, Tell them strongly that God *will judge them for everything wrong they do, and therefore* they must not quarrel about words...

cancer does. *You know* Hymenaeus and Philetus. They are *two* people *who talk in that manner.* [18] *They* teach a wrong message; *that is*, they say *wrongly that God will not raise dead people because* he has already given us *spiritual* life. *They claim that is the only new life we will receive. By saying that*, they cause some people to quit believing *in Christ.* [19] But *in spite of them, the congregations of* God are strong. *They are like* a strong foundation on which is written: "The Lord knows the people who really belong to him," and "Every person who calls Jesus 'Lord' must stop living a wicked life."

2 Timothy 2:20-22

THEME: Avoid the bad things that some young people desire to do. Do good instead.

[20] In a wealthy person's house there are not only utensils made of gold and of silver, but also utensils made of wood and of earth. The gold and silver *utensils are used* at special *occasions,* and the others are used at ordinary *occasions. Similarly, in a congregation there are those who are ready to do great things for the Lord Jesus, and there are those like the false teachers who are not.* [21] So those who stop doing what is evil will be able to *work well for the Lord. They will be like* utensils used at special *occasions*, set apart for and especially useful to the owner *of the big house. They will be like fine utensils* that are ready to do any kind of good work. [22] *Because that is so*, you must avoid doing the wrong things that *many* young people desire to do. Instead, you must earnestly do things that are right, you must believe *the true teaching*, you must love *God and others, and you must continually be at* peace with those who ask the Lord *to help them and who are* pure in every way.[e]

2 Timothy 2:23-26

THEME: Do not discuss foolish questions, but gently instruct those who oppose the true message.

[23] Do not join in talking *with anyone who* foolishly *wants* to argue about matters that are not important. *Don't talk with them*, because you know that *when people talk about foolish things*, they start to quarrel. [24] But those who serve the Lord must not quarrel. Instead, they should be kind to all people, they should be able to teach *God's truth well*, and they should be patient *with people.* [25] *That is, they should* gently instruct those who oppose *the true message. They should do that* because perhaps God will cause those people to completely change their thinking, so that they will accept *and believe* the true *message.* [26] Then they would get free from *what is like* a trap *set by* the devil. The devil has deceived them so that *they would do* what he wants *them to do.*

3

2 Timothy 3:1-9

THEME: Realize that evil people will cause the last days to be difficult. Avoid such people.

[1] You need to realize that during the last days *before Christ returns, evil people will make* it difficult *for us believers to conduct our lives as we should.* [2] This is because *such evil* people will be habitually loving themselves and loving money. They will habitually boast *about themselves*, they will be proud, and will often say bad things *about others. They* will

---

[e] OR, *...and who serve Jesus* faithfully.

disobey *their* parents. They will not be thankful, nor will they respect *anything that is good.* ³They will not *even* love their own family, nor agree with *anybody.*^f They will tell lies against people. They will not control what they say and do, nor allow anyone to control them. They will not love *anything that is* good. ⁴They will betray others and act foolishly. They will be very proud of themselves, and they will love to please themselves instead of loving God. ⁵*And, although they* pretend that they worship God, they will not let *God's Spirit* work powerfully *in their lives.* Don't associate with such people,⁹ ⁶because some such *people, even now,* subtly persuade foolish women to let them enter their houses, and then they deceive those women *so that they control those women's thoughts. Those women* have been burdened with sins and they have been led to do the many *evil* things that they strongly desire to do. ⁷*Even though* they are always *wanting to* learn new things, they are never able to recognize what is true. ⁸Just as Jannes and Jambres *long ago* very much opposed Moses, so also some *people* now oppose the true *message. Those* people have only evil thoughts. God rejects them *because they don't* believe *what is true.* ⁹Nevertheless, they will not continue to succeed, because most people will understand clearly that such people are foolish, just as people also realized *clearly that Jannes and Jambres were foolish.*

2 Timothy 3:10-17

THEME: Continue to believe what you have learned and been assured of.

¹⁰But as for you, you have fully known what I taught. You have known *and imitated* the way I conducted my life, and what I was trying to do. You have trusted *God as I do. You have been* patient as *I am.* You have loved people as I have, and you have endured as you suffered like I have suffered. ¹¹*You know how I endured many times when people* harmed me. *People* caused me to suffer in *the cities of* Antioch, Iconium, and Lystra. *But even though they caused me to suffer, I endured it; and every time they did those things to me,* the Lord rescued me. ¹²Indeed, *you know that* for us who want to live in a manner that pleases God, there will always be people who will cause us to suffer because we *have a close relationship with Christ Jesus.* ¹³Evil people who deceive others will teach things that are more and more wrong. *They will* deceive other people, and *those who hear them will* deceive others. ¹⁴But you, in contrast, must continue *to believe* what you have learned and have been assured of. *I know you are confident it is true because* you know that you have learned it from all *of us who taught you God's truth.* ¹⁵From *the time when you were* a child you have known the holy Scriptures. *You now know that* they enabled you to become wise so that *you know* you are saved because of your trust in Christ Jesus. ¹⁶God inspired everything *that is written* in the Scriptures, and the Scriptures are all useful to teach *us what is true*, to cause us to know *when we are* wrong and then to correct us, and to train us to do what is right. ¹⁷They are useful to help us who *serve* God to be ready to do all that we ought to do. By means of the Scriptures, God gives us what we need in order to do every *kind of* good deeds.

---

^f   OR, ...*they never forgive anyone.*

⁹   OR, ...Do not let such people join *with your congregation...*

4

2 Timothy 4:1-8

THEME: I solemnly charge you to preach the true message and to do everything you ought to do.

[1] Christ Jesus *is going to come back and* judge both those who will still be living *at that time* and those who will have died. He will judge them *concerning what rewards they deserve, and* he will rule everyone. So, *knowing that* he and God are watching *everything we do,* I solemnly command you [2] to proclaim the *true* message to people. Always be ready *to proclaim it* whether people want to hear it or not. Refute *people who are saying things that are not correct.* Rebuke them when they do wrong. Tell them what they ought to do. Be very patient as you teach them. [3] *Do these things* because a time will come when people will not listen to good teaching. Instead, they will bring in many teachers for themselves who will tell them just what they want to hear. *The reason they will bring in such teachers is* that they want to do the evil things that they desire. [4] That is, they will not listen to what is true, but will listen instead to strange stories *from their ancestors.* [5] *Furthermore, I command* you to always control your thoughts and actions. *Be willing* to endure hardships. Your work should be telling people the message *about Christ Jesus.* As you serve *the Lord,* do everything that *God has told* you to do.

[6] *Timothy, I say these things to you because* I feel *as though I will soon be executed. It is as though my blood will be poured out* as a sacrifice on the altar. *I know* that it is the time for me to die. [7] *As to telling people the* good *message and defending it,* I have exerted myself thoroughly, *like a boxer does. As to doing the work God gave me to do,* I have completed it, *like a runner who has finished* the race. *As to* what we believe, I have been loyal to it. [8] *So, like they award* a prize *to the winner of a race,* the Lord, who judges rightly, will give me a reward *because I have lived* righteously. He will give me that reward at the time *he judges people.* And not only *will he reward* me, but he will also reward all those who very much want him to return.

2 Timothy 4:9-15

THEME: Do your best to come to me soon.

[9] Do your best to come to me soon. [10] *I say that* because Demas has left me. He wanted very much *the good things he might enjoy* in this world right now, and so he went to *the city of* Thessalonica. Crescens *went to serve the Lord* in *the province of* Galatia, and Titus went to *the district of* Dalmatia. [11] Luke is the only one *of those who were helping me* who is still with me. *And when you come,* bring Mark with you, because he is useful to help me in my work. [12] Tychicus *cannot help me because* I sent him to *the city of* Ephesus. [13] And when you come, bring the coat that I left with Carpus in *the city of* Troas. Also, bring the books, but most of all *I want* the parchments *on which some important things are written.*

[14] Alexander, the man who makes idols from metal, did many harmful things to me. The Lord will punish him for what he did. [15] So you, too, must beware of him. *He will try to destroy your work if he can,* because he very much opposes the message that we proclaim.

2 Timothy 4:16-18

THEME: The Lord will rescue me from everything evil and bring me safely to heaven.

[16] When I first defended myself *in court here*, no one came along *to help defend* me. Instead, they all left me. *I pray* that *God* will forgive them *for that*. [17] Nevertheless, the Lord was with me and strengthened me. He enabled me to fully preach the message, and all the non-Jewish people *in the court* heard it.[h] And *the Lord* rescued me *from great danger, as if I were taken* out of a lion's mouth. [18] *Because of that, I am sure that* the Lord will rescue me from everything that is truly evil and will bring me safely to heaven, where he rules. Praise him forever! Amen!

2 Timothy 4:19-22

THEME: Greet my friends there. Your friends here greet you. May the Lord bless you.

[19] Greet *for me* Priscilla, *her husband* Aquila, and the family of Onesiphorus. [20] Erastus stayed in *the city of* Corinth. I left Trophimus in *the town of* Miletus because he was sick. [21] Do your best to come to me before winter. Eubulus, Pudens, Linus, Claudia, and many other fellow believers *in this city* send their greetings to you. [22] *I am asking* the Lord to *help you in* your spirit, *Timothy,* and to act kindly toward all *you believers there.*

---

[h] OR, …and people from many nations heard it.

The Apostle Paul wrote letters to his assistants. We call this letter

Titus

1

Titus 1:1-4

THEME: I, Paul, have been appointed by God as his servant and as an apostle of Jesus Christ to lead God's people to know, believe, and practice the true teachings. I write this letter to you, Titus. May God continue to bless you.

[1] I, Paul, *am writing this letter to you, Titus. God appointed me to be* his servant and *to be* an apostle *who represents* Jesus Christ. *God appointed me to teach* those whom he has chosen *to be his people,* to have a *correct* belief *in him.* He wants me to teach them the true *teachings about God,* so that they will learn to conduct their lives in a godly manner. [2] *As a result of my teaching these things, they* confidently expect that God will cause them to live forever. God, who never lies, promised before he created the world that *his people* would live forever. [3] Then, at the time he *chose,* he revealed *to us his* message. *Specifically,* God our Savior gave this message to me, and he trusted me to proclaim it. [4] Titus, *I am writing this letter* to *you. You are like* a true son *to me because I led you to* believe the same *teachings about Christ that I believe. I pray that God our Father and Christ Jesus our Savior will continue to* act with kindness toward you and will cause you to have *inner* peace.

Titus 1:5

THEME: I want you to teach the believers and to appoint elders.

[5] When I *asked you* to stay on *the island of* Crete, I wanted you to do these things: *to teach the believers what they need to know so that they* can understand correctly the *spiritual* matters about which some are teaching wrong things, and to appoint elders *in the congregation* in each town in the manner I told you.

Titus 1:6-9

THEME: Appoint as elders men whom no one can justly criticize.

[6] *When you appoint men as elders*, you must choose men whom no one can *justly* accuse of *habitually* doing what is wrong.[a] Specifically, appoint men who have been faithful to their wives. Appoint men whose children faithfully obey *their parents. Do not appoint men whose children habitually* do all the things their bodies urge them to do, or who refuse to obey their parents. [7] Leaders *of the congregation* must be *men* who are known to habitually do what is good, because it is on God's behalf that they will direct *the congregation. They must* not be arrogant. They must not easily become angry. They must

---

[a] OR, …you must choose men of whom everyone speaks well.

not *be men who* drink a lot of alcohol. They must not *be men who react* violently *when they are angry. They must* not *be men who are* greedy for money.* [8] Instead, they must be men who welcome and take care of guests. They must be devoted to *doing* what is good. They must do *what God considers* to be right. They must be completely dedicated to God. They must be men who do what their minds tell them is right to do *and not what their emotions urge them to do.* [9] They must firmly believe in the message *about Jesus Christ* exactly as *we* taught it, so that they will be able to teach *the believers* what is correct and to urge *them to follow it. If they firmly accept our message*, they will be able to convince those who oppose *what is correct that they are wrong*.

Titus 1:10-16

THEME: Since there are many deceivers teaching what is false, who do not even know God themselves and are unable to do any good thing, you must rigorously convince the believers who follow false teachings that they are wrong, so that they will come to firmly believe in the correct teachings.

[10] I say this because there are many *people who oppose the correct teachings*. They refuse to obey those in authority. They talk on and on, saying what helps no one, and they deceive people. The Jewish *believers who insist we must obey all their Jewish rituals are the ones* especially *doing this.* [11] *You and the leaders whom you appoint* should prevent such people from teaching *the believers*. They are causing whole families to stop believing in the correct teachings *because of the wrong ideas* they are teaching. *They are teaching people only* in order that people will give them money, *which is a very* shameful *thing to do.* [12] A man from *the island of* Crete whom *they consider* a prophet said, "*My fellow Cretans are always lying to one another! They are like dangerous* wild animals! They are lazy and always eat too much!*" [13] The words that this man said *about the Cretan people* are *still* true, *especially about Cretans being liars*. So rigorously convince *the Cretan believers* that those *false teachings* are wrong. Tell them to *firmly* believe in the correct teachings. [14] *Teach them that* they should no *longer* listen to the stories the Jews made up. *Especially* tell them to refuse to obey those who reject our true teachings, because those people are teaching things that only come from human beings, *not from God.* [15] *Believers should reject those teachings, because* no *food that we eat* can make us unacceptable to God if we are pure *in our hearts*. But if people are evil *within themselves* and do not trust *in Christ Jesus*, there is no *ritual* that can make them acceptable to God. Such people's way of thinking has been ruined. They do not even feel guilty *when they do what is evil.* [16] Even though they claim to know God, by what they do they *show that they* don't know him.* [b] They don't obey *God*, and they are unable to do anything *that he considers* good. So *God considers them to be absolutely* disgusting!

2

Titus 2:1-10

THEME: Teach and urge the believers to behave in a manner that is consistent with the correct teachings, so that people will perceive that the teachings about God our Savior are very good.

[1] But as for you, *you must* teach *the believers* what is consistent with the correct teachings. [2] *Tell* the older men that they should control themselves in all situations, *that they should behave in such a manner* that all people will respect them, and that they should control

---

[b] OR, Even though they claim to know God, they *show they* reject his true teaching by what they do.

what they say and do. Tell them that they should firmly believe in the correct teachings, that they should sincerely love others, and that they should always be steadfast. [3] Similarly, *tell* the older women that they should behave in a reverent manner that shows they are devoted to God. *They should* not slander others, and they should not be addicted to *drinking* a lot of alcohol. Tell them that they should teach *the younger women* what is good, [4] so that they will love their husbands and their children. [5] They should teach the younger women to control what they say and do, and to be pure *in every way*, to be good workers at home, and to be submissive to their husbands. *The younger women should behave like this* so that no one will speak against the message about God. [6] As for the younger men, urge them also to control themselves *in all they say and do.* [7] And you yourself must continually do what is good, so that others will see how they should behave. Teach *the believers* sincerely and seriously. [8] Teach what is correct and what no one can *justly* criticize. *Do this* so that *when the believers conduct their lives in a proper manner*, those who oppose *us* will be disappointed because there will be nothing bad that they can *justly* say about us. [9] As for slaves, *urge them* to be submissive to their masters in everything. They should please *their masters, and they should not refuse to obey them.* [10] They should not steal *things that belong to their masters*. Instead, they should always be completely honest, and thus *show that they can* be completely trusted. They should behave like this so that *as a result of the good conduct of Christian slaves, people* will perceive that the teachings about God our Savior are very desirable.

Titus 2:11-14

THEME: God showed great kindness to us by sending Jesus Christ to earth in order that he might save all people. God graciously trains us to behave in a godly manner.

[11] *The believers should conduct themselves in a good manner* since God did for us what we don't deserve, *sending Jesus Christ to earth* in order that he might save all people. [12] God teaches us how to stop doing what he dislikes, and to stop desiring the things that ungodly people desire. He wants us to be self-controlled and to do what is right and to do what he is pleased with while we live in this present age. [13] *Don't forget that* we are waiting expectantly for that which will make us very happy *indeed*! We are expectantly waiting for our great God and Savior, Jesus Christ, to come gloriously! [14] He is the one who *willingly* gave himself *as a sacrifice* on our behalf to set us free from all sinful behavior! Since we are his very own people, he wants us to get rid of all our evil ways. He also wants us to be *people who* are eager to do what is good.

Titus 2:15

THEME: Teach these things with full authority. Urge the believers to do them, and correct those believers who do not do them.

[15] Teach *the believers* these things! Urge *them to do them!* Correct *those who don't do them! As for you, you have* full authority *to do this*, so don't allow anyone to disregard you!

3

Titus 3:1-2

THEME: Remind the believers to act appropriately toward authorities and kindly toward everyone.

¹Remind *the believers* that they should submit to all those who rule them or have authority over them, and that they should obey them. They should be ready to do anything that is helpful. ²They should never say bad things about anyone, they should not quarrel, they should be patient *when others irritate them, and they should* always treat all people as important.

Titus 3:3-7

THEME: God acted kindly toward us and mercifully saved us, even though formerly we were behaving sinfully.

³*Remind the congregations about these things,* because formerly we *believers* ourselves were also foolish, just as *all people who do not believe in Christ are foolish. We* did not obey God's message. *We let* others deceive us. We spent all our time doing what is evil, and couldn't stop ourselves from doing all the things our bodies enjoyed. We were envying others. We were causing people to hate us, and we were hating one another. ⁴⁻⁵Even though we were behaving sinfully like this, God saved us! God our Savior *treated us* kindly and lovingly, *and saved us!* He did this, not because we did things that are right, but just because he *wanted to be* merciful to us! He washed *us inwardly and gave* us a new way of living as a result of the Holy Spirit changing us inwardly. ⁶*Because we trusted in* Jesus Christ our Savior, God put the Holy Spirit within us *in order to* wonderfully *change us.* ⁷He wanted to erase the record of our sins, even though we did not deserve that, and he wants us to receive all that *he desires* to give us. *These are the things we* confidently expect to receive when we live *with him* eternally.

Titus 3:8a

THEME: I want you to confidently teach this trustworthy message to the believers in order that they will be constantly concerned with doing what is good for others.

⁸These words that *I* have said are trustworthy. So I want you to confidently teach the things *I have written about in this letter* to those who have trusted in God, so that they will be constantly devoting themselves to doing deeds that are good and helpful for others.

Titus 3:8b-11

THEME: Have nothing to do with foolish disputes about genealogies and about the Jewish laws. Do not allow divisive people who have turned away from the true teachings to influence the believers.

These *teachings* are beneficial and profitable for *all* people, ⁹but there are people who foolishly dispute *with you, wanting you to believe* senseless *myths based on your ancestors'* genealogies. They argue and quarrel *with you, insisting that you obey* the Jewish laws. Keep *completely* away from them, because *arguing about such things* is not profitable *for anyone. It is absolutely* worthless! ¹⁰Those people, *by teaching things that are false,* are causing others to turn away from the true teachings. You must warn them *that God will judge them if they continue doing that. If they don't stop,* warn them one more time. *If they still don't stop*, then no *longer* allow *them to influence the believers.* [11] You will know clearly that such persons have *deliberately* turned away *from the true teachings*. They know they are doing what is sinful, *but they deliberately keep on doing it.*

Titus 3:12-14

THEME: Make every effort to come to me at Nicopolis. Help Zenas and Apollos on their journey. All the believers should likewise learn to devote themselves to doing good deeds for those who need help.

[12] I *expect to* send either Artemas or Tychicus to you. *As soon as one of them arrives,* make every effort to come to me *quickly* at *the town of* Nicopolis, because it is there that I have decided to *go and* stay during the winter *season.* [13] As for Zenas, the expert in laws, and Apollos, *when they are both ready to leave the island of Crete*, help them as much as you can so that they will have everything *they need as they travel.* [14] Moreover, our *fellow believers* also should learn to devote themselves to *doing* good deeds *for people* who need help so that they, our fellow believers, will live very useful lives.

Titus 3:15

THEME: Everyone who is with me greets you and the other true believers there. May our Lord Jesus Christ continue to show great kindness to all of you.

[15] *As I finish this letter*, everyone who is with me wants me to send greetings to you.[c] We send our greetings to those *there* who love us and believe *as we do*. May our Lord Jesus Christ continue to show great kindness to all of you.

---

[c] OR, ...everyone who is with me says they are thinking about you.

The Apostle Paul wrote a letter to a friend. We call this letter

Philemon

Philemon 1-3

THEME: I, Paul, am writing this letter to you, Philemon, and to those with you. May God bless you.

¹ *I*, Paul, am a prisoner *who serves* Christ Jesus. *I am here* with Timothy, our fellow believer. *I am writing this letter* to *you*, Philemon, our dear *friend* and fellow worker. ² *I am also writing* to *your wife*, Apphia, and to Archippus, *who is like* our fellow soldier *because he serves Christ steadfastly as we do.* I am also *writing this* to the congregation *that meets* in your house. ³ *I pray that* God our Father and our Lord Jesus Christ *will continue to* show great kindness to you all and *will continue to* cause you to have *inner* peace.

Philemon 4-7

THEME: I thank God and rejoice greatly because you have shown that you love God's people.

⁴ I always thank my God when I pray for you, because I hear *people say that* you love all God's people ⁵ and that you continue to trust in the Lord Jesus. ⁶ I pray that as a result of knowing all the good things *that God has done for* us, you may be effective *in influencing others* as you share with them what you believe, so that *they will honor* Christ. ⁷ I have rejoiced greatly and have been greatly encouraged because you, my dear friend, have acted lovingly toward God's people by encouraging them.

Philemon 8-11

THEME: Because I know that you love God's people, instead of commanding you, I am requesting you to do what you ought to do for my spiritual son Onesimus.

⁸ So *I have a favor to ask of you.* I am completely confident *that I have authority* to command you *to do* what you ought to do, because *I am an apostle of* Christ. ⁹ But because *I know that you* love *God's people*, I am requesting this instead of *commanding you to do it.* It is I, Paul, an old man and now also a prisoner *because I serve* Christ Jesus, *who am requesting it.* ¹⁰ I am requesting that you *do something* for someone *who has become like* my own son *because I told him about Christ here in* prison. *His name is* Onesimus. ¹¹ Although *his name, as you know, means 'useful',* formerly he was useless to you. But now he is useful both to you and to me!

Philemon 12-16

THEME: I am sending Onesimus back to you. He is as dear to me as my own self, and he will now be even dearer to you than he is to me.

¹² Although Onesimus is *as dear to me as* my own self, I am sending him back to you. ¹³ I would like to have kept him with me, so that he might serve me on your behalf, while I am in prison here *because of my preaching* the message *about Christ.* ¹⁴ Nevertheless, because *I had not yet asked you and* you had not yet permitted me *to keep him here with me*, I decided not to *keep him here. I decided that I should* not do anything without your permission. *I decided that you should help me only if you* really want to help me.

[15] Perhaps the reason *God permitted* Onesimus to leave you for a little while was that *he would believe in Christ, and as a result* you would have him back with you forever! [16] *You will no longer have him only* as a slave. Instead, *you will have him* as *someone who is* more than a slave. *You will have him* as a fellow believer! He is especially dear to me, but he certainly will be more dear to you *than he is to me, because now he* not only belongs to you but he also belongs to the Lord.

Philemon 17-19

THEME: If you consider me to be your partner, receive Onesimus as you would receive me. I guarantee to repay you whatever Onesimus owes you.

[17] So, if you consider me to be your partner *in God's work*, receive him as you would receive me. [18] If he has wronged you in any manner or if he owes you anything, charge that to me *so I can repay you.* [19] *I, Paul, am now writing this in my own handwriting: I will repay you what he owes you! Although I might mention to you that you owe me even more than Onesimus may owe you, because it was the result of my telling you about Christ that God saved you.*

Philemon 20

THEME: Please encourage me in this matter, just as you encourage other believers in Christ.

[20] Yes, my dear friend, because you and I both have a relationship with the Lord, I want you to do this for me. Encourage me *by receiving Onesimus kindly, just as you encourage others who believe* in Christ.

Philemon 21

THEME: I have written this letter to you, confident of your compliance with my request.

[21] I have written *this letter* to you confidently, *knowing that you will do what I am requesting you to do. In fact*, I know that you will do even more than what I am requesting.

Philemon 22

THEME: Also, keep a guest room ready for me.

[22] Also, keep a guest room ready for me, because I confidently expect that as a result of your prayers *for me, I* will be released *from prison and will come* to you all.

Philemon 23-25

THEME: My other fellow workers greet you. May the Lord Jesus Christ bless you spiritually.

[23] Epaphras, who is *suffering hardship* with me in prison because of *his serving* Christ Jesus, sends his greetings to you.[a] [24] Mark, Aristarchus, Demas, and Luke, who are my *other* fellow workers, also send their greetings to you. [25] *I pray that* the Lord Jesus Christ *will continue to* work with kindness in all of your lives.

---

[a] OR, ...wants you to know he is thinking fondly about you.

The letter that was written to Jewish believers.
We call this letter
Hebrews

1

Hebrews 1:1-3

THEME: God formerly communicated with our ancestors through the prophets, but now he has communicated with us through his Son, who is just like him.

¹Long ago God communicated frequently with our ancestors by giving messages to the prophets. He did that in various ways. ²But now when this final age *is beginning*, God has communicated with us *through* his Son.ª *God appointed him to possess everything that truly belongs to God. God also appointed* him to create the universe. ³He manifests God's glory. He represents exactly *what God is like*. He sustains everything by means of his powerful words. When he had *cancelled* the *guilt of* our sins, he sat down in heaven *to rule* at the place of highest honor with God.

Hebrews 1:4-14

THEME: God's son is greater than the angels.

⁴By doing that he *showed that he* was very much greater than the angels, to the same extent that his relationship *to God, as God's Son,* is more excellent than the relationship the angels *have to God.* ⁵*We know that* because *in the Scriptures* God is never reported as saying to any angel *these words, which he said to his Son*:
    You are my Son! Today I have *declared to everyone* that I am your Father!

And he said in another Scripture passage,
    I will be his Father, and he will be my Son.

⁶And *we know that God's Son is greater than the angels, because in* another *Scripture passage it is written what God said about his esteemed Son*, when he was about to send him into the world:
    All my angels must worship him!ᵇ

⁷*About the angels, God only says,*
    I make the *angels* who serve me *to be changeable*ᶜ *like* winds and flames of fire.

⁸But on the other hand, *in the Scriptures he said* to his Son,
    You are *also* God! You will rule forever,
        and you will reign righteously over your kingdom.
    ⁹You have loved *people's* righteous *deeds* and you have hated *their* lawless *deeds*.
    So I, your God, have given you more joy than I have given anyone else.

ª OR, …God has communicated with us by means of what the man who was also God *said and did.*

ᵇ OR, …All God's angels must worship him *when he comes again.*

ᶜ OR, …*I* make the *angels* who serve me *to be swift and forceful…*

[10] And *we also know that God's Son is superior to angels because in the Scriptures it is written that* someone said to God's Son,

Lord, it was you who created the earth in the beginning.
You also made *the rest of* the universe.[d]
[11] *Even though all the things you created* will perish, you will keep on living *forever.*
They will all wear out as clothing *wears out.*
[12] You will dispose of them as one rolls up an *old* coat *to discard it.*
Then, you will exchange *all that is in the universe for something new*, as someone puts on a new garment *in exchange for an old one that he discards.*
But you *are not like what you created,*
because you stay the same, and you live forever!

[13] *We also know that God's Son is greater than the angels because God never* said to any angel *what he said to his Son*,

Rule with me, while I put all of your enemies completely under your control!

[14] The angels are *only* spirits who serve *God. God* sends them *to earth* to help the people who will receive what *he will give to* those he has saved.[e] *God* sends them *to earth* to help us people whom he has saved.[f]

2

Hebrews 2:1-4

THEME: We will not escape God's punishment if we ignore such a great message of salvation.

[1] So, *since it is true that God's Son is greater than the angels*, we must pay very close attention to what we have heard *from God's Son,* lest we drift away from it, *as a boat drifts when no one guides it.* [2] *God's laws that* were spoken by angels were valid, and God justly punished all who transgressed and disobeyed them. [3] So we will certainly not escape *God's punishment* if we ignore such a great *message about how he* saves us! This *new message* was first spoken by the Lord *Jesus.*[g] Then it was confirmed to us by those who heard *what he told them.* [4] God also confirmed to us *that this message was true* by *enabling believers to do* many things that showed his power, to do other miraculous things, and *to do other things* by the gifts that the Holy Spirit distributed to them according to God's desire.

Hebrews 2:5-9a

THEME: God has determined that Christ, not angels or people, will rule everything.

[5] God has not determined that the angels will rule over everything. *Instead, he has determined that Christ* will rule in the new world that *God* will *create. That is the new world* about which I am writing. [6] Someone spoke to *God about this* somewhere *in the Scriptures*, saying,

There are no people who are worthy enough for you to think about them!
No humans are *worthy enough* for you to care for them!

---

[d] OR, …You also made the *things in* the sky.

[e] OR, …those *whom* he will save.

[f] OR, …*whom* he will save.

[g] OR, …The Lord *Jesus* first spoke this *message.*

[7] You have caused people to be for a little while inferior in rank to angels.
But you have greatly honored people, as *kings are honored with* a crown.
[8] You have put everything under their control.

God has determined that people will rule over everything. That *means nothing will be omitted from their control.* But now, at this present time, we perceive that people do not yet have authority over everything. [9] But we do know about Jesus, *who truly has authority over everything!*

Hebrews 2:9b-13

THEME: Jesus, the creator of everything, is the one who died for us, makes us holy, and proclaims us to be his brothers and sisters.

For a little while Jesus became inferior *in rank* to angels in order to die on behalf of all people. He became inferior *in rank* when he suffered *and* died, as God in his kindness *planned*. But now he has been *honored by being* crowned *as kings are*. [10] It was fitting that *God* made *Jesus* perfect. God was enabling many people who would belong to him to share his glory. He *is the one who* created all things, and *he is the one* for whom all things *exist. He perfected Jesus* by causing him to suffer *and die*. It is because of what *Jesus did that God* is able to save people. [11] *Jesus*, the one who sets people apart for God, along with the ones whom he sets apart *for God*, belong to God's family. *As a result, Jesus* gladly proclaims them to be his own brothers *and sisters*. [12] *The Psalmist wrote what Christ said to God about us becoming his brothers and sisters, in these words:*
I will proclaim to my brothers how awesome you are![h]
I will sing praise to you in the midst of the congregation!

[13] And a prophet wrote *in* another *Scripture passage what Christ said about God*:
I will trust him.

And in another *Scripture passage, Christ said about those who are like his* children:
I and the ones that God has given me are here.

Hebrews 2:14-18

THEME: It is Jesus, not angels, who became a human being to help us as our High Priest.

[14] So, since those *whom God calls his* children are all human beings, Jesus also became a human being *just like them*. The devil has the power to cause people *to be afraid* to die, but Christ became a human being so that by his dying he might make the devil powerless. [15] *Jesus did that* to free all of us who are like slaves all of our lives because we cannot escape being afraid to die. [16] Because *Jesus became a human being,* it is not angels that he wants to help. No, it is we who trust God as Abraham did, whom he wants to help. [17] So, *since he came to help humans, not angels*, he had to be made exactly like *us whom he calls* his own brothers *and sisters*. This was so that he could be a high priest who *acts* mercifully *to all people* and who acts faithfully in matters that pertain to God, so that people who had sinned would no longer be guilty. [18] *And* because he suffered *as a human being*, and was also tempted *to sin as we are,* he is able to help us when we are tempted.

---

[h] OR, …I will proclaim to my brothers what you have done.

3

Hebrews 3:1-6

THEME: Our high priest, Jesus, deserves more honor than Moses does.

[1] My fellow believers, *God* has set you apart and has chosen you, just as he chose me. So, consider Jesus. *He is God's* messenger to us. He is also the high priest whom we say we believe in. [2] He faithfully *served God,* who appointed him, just as Moses faithfully *served* God's people. [3-4] Just as every house is made by someone, Jesus made everything, and he is God. So God has considered Jesus to be worthy of *people* honoring him more than they honor Moses, just as the one who makes a house deserves that people honor him more than honoring the house *he made.* [5] Moses very faithfully *served God as he helped* God's people, just as every servant *faithfully serves his master.* The result was that Moses testified about what Jesus would say later. [6] But Christ *faithfully serves God as he helps* his own people, just as a *son helps his own family.* And we are God's people if we continue to confidently *believe in Christ* and proudly wait for *what God will do for us.*

Hebrews 3:7-8

THEME: Do not stubbornly rebel against God as your Jewish ancestors did.

[7] The Holy Spirit *caused the Psalmist to write these words in the Scriptures:*
Now, when you hear God speaking to you, [8] don't stubbornly *refuse to obey him, as the Israelites stubbornly disobeyed him* when they rebelled against *him* in the desert. *At that time, God said to them,* "They tried to determine how many *things that displeased me they could do* in the desert *without me punishing them.* [9] Your ancestors repeatedly tested *whether I would be patient with them, even though* for forty years they saw all the amazing things I did. [10] So I became disgusted with the people who saw those things, and I said *about them,* 'They are constantly disloyal to me and they don't understand how I *want them* to conduct their lives.' [11] As a result, because I was angry with them, I solemnly declared, 'They will not enter *the land of Canaan* where I would let them rest!'"

Hebrews 3:12-15

THEME: Be careful that you do not stop trusting in Christ.

[12] Accordingly, my fellow believers, beware that none of you wickedly stops trusting *in Christ.* That would cause you to reject the all-powerful God. [13] Instead, each of you must encourage each other every day, while *you still have* the opportunity, so that no one of you may become stubborn *with the result that* you sin.[i] [14] *We must do that,* because we benefit in *all* Christ *has done* only if we firmly keep trusting *in him* from the time when we first confidently *trusted in him* until *the time when* we die. [15] *We can do this* by paying attention to *what the Psalmist wrote in that Scripture passage in which* God said:
Now, when you hear me speaking *to you,* do not stubbornly disobey me as *the Israelites stubbornly disobeyed me* when they rebelled *against me.*

---

[i] OR, …may stubbornly reject God as you deceive yourselves, *with the result that* you sin.

Hebrews 3:16-19

THEME: It was their Jewish ancestors for whom God did great things who rebelled against God.

[16] *Think about* who it was who rebelled against him, even though they heard him speaking to them. It was not people who had not experienced God's power. Instead, it was all those people whom Moses led miraculously out of Egypt. [17] And *you must remember* who it was that God was disgusted with for forty years. It was those same people who had sinned like that, and whose bodies as a result lay where they died in the desert. [18] And *you must remember* who *it was God was describing when* he solemnly declared, "They will not enter the land where I would let them rest." It was those Israelites who disobeyed God. [19] So, from that example we perceive that it was because they did not trust *in God* that they were unable to enter *the land where they would have rested.*

4

Hebrews 4:1-5

THEME: The Israelites failed to enter the place where they could rest; we must beware of acting like them.

[1] *The Israelites did not enter the place where they would have rested.* But *God* has still promised us that we can start to experience *spiritual* rest. So we must beware *of the possibility* that *God* may consider that some of you have failed to start to *rest as the Israelites could have rested.* [2] We have heard the message *about Christ*, just as *the Israelites* heard *what God had promised.* But *just as* the message did not benefit *most of* those who heard it because they did not believe it as *Joshua and Caleb did, it won't benefit us eternally if we don't keep believing it.* [3] We who have believed *in Christ* are able to rest *spiritually. We know that is true,* because God said:

Because I was angry with them, I solemnly declared, "They will not enter *the land where* I would let them rest."

God said that even though he ceased his work *of creation* after he created the world. [4] What someone wrote somewhere *in the Scriptures* about the seventh day *after he had spent six days creating the world,* supports that,

Then, on the seventh day, God rested from his work *of creating everything.*

[5] But note again what God said about the Israelites *in the passage that I quoted previously,*
They will not enter *the land where* I would have let them rest.

Hebrews 4:6-10

THEME: Scripture supports the claim that there is a time when God's people will rest eternally.

[6] Some people experience that *spiritual rest. But* those *Israelites* who first had the good message preached to them *about what God had promised them* did not enter *that place of resting,* because they refused to believe God. [7] *But God* appointed another time *for us to rest.* That time is now! *We know that is true because* much later than when *the Israelites rebelled against God in the desert,* he caused *King* David to write what I have already quoted,

Now, when you understand what God is saying *to you*, don't stubbornly disobey him.

[8] If Joshua had led the Israelites to enter the place of resting, God would not have spoken later about another *time when we could rest. So we know that God was speaking about*

another time when some people would rest spiritually. [9] So, just *as God rested on* the seventh day *after he had finished making everything,* there remains a time when God's people will rest eternally. [10] Specifically, whoever starts to rest *spiritually* with God has ceased doing things *to gain God's favor*, just as God ceased doing his work *of creating everything.*

Hebrews 4:11-13

THEME: We must beware of being insincere about trying to enter the place of eternal rest.

[11] God destroyed the *Israelites because they disbelieved his message.* So we must strive to experience his *spiritual* rest lest he destroy any of us for not believing *his message.* [12] *Beware of being insincere about doing this,* because the message God *has given us* very powerfully penetrates our thinking more than a two-edged sword *penetrates flesh.* It penetrates *deeply* into our souls and spirits, as *a sharp sword can penetrate* into our joints and marrow. *His message* exposes *to us* all our thoughts and all our desires. [13] God knows everything about everyone. Everything is completely exposed to him, *and he is* the one who will say whether or not he approves of what we have done.

Hebrews 4:14-16

THEME: Let us come boldly to Christ our high priest to receive his gracious help.

[14] We have a great high priest who ascended through the heavens *when he returned to God's presence.* He is Jesus, God's Son. So let us firmly profess *what we believe about him.* [15] Our high priest can indeed compassionately deal with us who tend to sin easily, because he also was tempted *to sin* in every way that we are *tempted to sin,* and yet he did not sin. [16] So, let us come boldly to *Christ,* who rules *from heaven* and does for us what we don't deserve, in order that we might experience *his acting* mercifully *toward us*, and in order that we might experience his kindly helping us whenever we need *it.*

5

Hebrews 5:1-10

THEME: Christ learned to be a compassionate high priest by obeying God as he suffered.

[1] Every *Jewish* high priest was chosen by *God* from among *ordinary* men. They were appointed to come before him on behalf of their people. *Specifically, God appointed them to* bring gifts *to him on behalf of the people,* and in order to sacrifice *animals to him* for people who sinned. [2] The high priests could deal gently with those who ignorantly sinned, since they themselves tended to sin easily. [3] As a result, they had to offer something to God for themselves for their own sins, just as *they had to offer something to God* for *God's* people who sinned. [4] Furthermore, no one honors himself *by appointing himself to become a high priest.* Instead, God chose each man *to become a high priest,* as he chose Aaron *to be the first high priest.* [5] In the same way, Christ also did not honor himself by appointing himself to become a high priest. Instead, God *appointed him by* saying to *him what he never said to any other priest,* what the Psalmist wrote in the Scriptures,

You are my Son! Today I have declared that I am your Father!

[6] And he also said *to Christ what the Psalmist wrote* in another *Scripture passage,*

You are a priest eternally in the same way that Melchizedek was a priest!

⁷When Christ lived on the earth, he prayed to God and he tearfully cried out loudly to him. He asked *God,* who was able to help him, that he would not *fear the sufferings just before* he died. As a result, God listened to him, because Christ reverently submitted *to what God wanted him to do.* ⁸Although Christ is *God's own Son,* he learned to obey *God* by suffering *before he died.* ⁹*By doing that he has now* become fully qualified *to be our high priest. As a result, he is the one who saves* eternally all who obey him. ¹⁰Furthermore, God has designated him to be *our* high priest in the way that Melchizedek was a high priest.

Hebrews 5:11-14

THEME: You are not ready for more advanced spiritual truth.

¹¹Although there is much to say *to you* about *how Christ resembles Melchizedek*, this is hard *for me* to explain *to you* because you now understand things so slowly. ¹²*You became Christians long ago. So* by now you should be teaching *spiritual truths to others.* But you still need someone to teach you again the truths that God has revealed. *I am talking about* the truths we teach people *when they* first *believe in Christ.* You need *those elementary truths* like babies need milk. You are not *ready for advanced teaching which is like* the solid food *which mature people need.* ¹³Remember that those *who are still learning these elementary truths* have not become familiar with *what God* says concerning becoming righteous. They are *just like* babies *who need* milk! ¹⁴But *the more advanced spiritual truth* is for people who are *spiritually* mature, *in the same way that* solid food is for *people who are physically* mature. Spiritually mature people can tell the difference between what is good and what is evil, because they have trained themselves *to keep doing that.*

6

Hebrews 6:1-8

THEME: If you believers later reject the message about Christ, God will reject you.

¹So, let's not keep *discussing* the elementary principles about Christ. Instead, let's proceed *to the teaching that will make us spiritually* mature. Let's not *be people who always need someone to teach them* the elementary truths *about Christ that are like* a foundation. *I am referring to the teaching that people who do sinful* things, things that *those who are spiritually* dead do, must turn away from their sinful behavior. *I am referring to the teaching* that people must believe in God. ²*I am referring to the teaching about what* various *Jewish and Christian* rituals for purifying people *signify. I am referring to the teaching about how elders enable people to receive spiritual gifts by* laying hands *on them. I am referring to the teaching that God will* raise people from the dead. And *I am referring to the teaching that God* will judge *some people and punish them* eternally. ³*Instead of continuing to discuss these elementary truths,* we will *go on to give people mature teaching*, if God allows it. ⁴*Let me explain why it is important to do that. Some* people have at one time fully understood *the message about Christ.* They have experienced *a relationship with Jesus Christ* that God gave *to them.* They have received the Holy Spirit the same as *others have.* ⁵They have experienced that God's message is good. And by what they have experienced *now*, they know how *God will work* powerfully in the future. If those people reject *the message about Christ*, it will not be possible for anyone to persuade them to turn away from their sinful behavior again! ⁶What those *believers who later renounce the message about Christ do is as though* they themselves are nailing the Son of God to a cross again! They are causing others to publicly despise

Christ. [7] Keep this in mind: It is land on which rain has frequently fallen and on which plants grow that is useful for the people who prepare the land that God has blessed. *Similarly, it is those believers who have received many good things from God and who do good things that please God, whom God will bless.* [8] But *what will happen to believers who do things that do not please God will be like what happens to land* on which *only* thorns and thistles grow. *Such land* is worthless. It is almost to being land that God will curse, and eventually he will burn *its vegetation.*

Hebrews 6:9-12

THEME: But God will not overlook all you have done for him.

[9] Although I am writing *to you* like this as a *warning*, I am certain that you whom I love *are doing* better than that. Specifically, I am certain that *you are doing* the things that are appropriate *for those whom God* has saved. [10] Since God is always just, he will not overlook all you have done *for him. He will also not overlook your showing your* love for him by the way you helped your fellow believers and *by the way you still* help them. *Instead, God will reward you for doing good deeds.* [11] I strongly want each of you to diligently continue to fully expect to receive *what God has provided for you,* until you finally *receive all that you have confidently expected to receive.* [12] I don't want you to be lazy. *Instead, I want* you to imitate those who, by their patience and continuing trust in *God,* are receiving what he promised *to give them.*

Hebrews 6:13-20

THEME: Our confidence is in God because he promised to bless us, and he made an oath to confirm that he would.

[13] When God promised to *do things for* Abraham, he said that he would punish himself *if he did not do that,* because there was no one of greater importance to ask to punish him *if he did not do it.* [14] He said *to Abraham,* "I will certainly bless you and I will certainly increase *the number of* your *descendants.*" [15] As a result, after Abraham patiently waited *for God to do what he promised,* he obtained what *God* promised him. [16] *Keep in mind that when people promise something,* they ask a more important person to punish them if they don't do what they promise. Furthermore, when someone asks God to punish him *if he does not tell the truth,* no one doubts him anymore. [17] So, when God wanted to demonstrate very clearly to the people who would receive what he had promised that he would not change what he had purposed *to do,* he solemnly guaranteed that he would declare himself guilty if he did not do what he promised. [18] He did that to strongly encourage us as a result of our *knowing* that *God has done* two things that cannot change: *Namely, he promised to bless us, and he solemnly declared that he would declare himself guilty if he did not do it.* We *know* that God, who did those things, cannot lie. We have fled *to God* so that we might continue confidently to expect to receive what he promised *to give us.* [19] *That confident expectation is like* an anchor that *holds us fast. The one we confidently expect to help us is Jesus, who* goes into *God's very presence, just as the high priests went* behind the curtain into the innermost *part of the tent in the wilderness.* [20] Jesus went *into God's presence* ahead of us to *help* us, when he became a high priest eternally in the way that Melchizedek was high priest.

7

Hebrews 7:1-3

THEME: There are ways in which Melchizedek was like God's Son.

¹ *Now I will say more about* this *man* Melchizedek. He was the king of *the city of* Salem *and was* a priest of God, the one who is greater *than anyone else*. He met Abraham who was returning *home* after *he and his men* had defeated the *armies of four* kings. Melchizedek *asked God to* bless Abraham. ² Then Abraham gave to him one tenth of all *the spoils he received from the battle. Melchizedek's name* means firstly 'king *who rules* righteously,' and since Salem means 'peace', he was the 'king *who rules* peacefully.' ³ *In the Scriptures there is* no *record of who his* father *was*, nor *is there any record of who his* mother *was*, nor *is there any record of who his* ancestors *were*. There is no *record of when he was* born, nor *is there any record of when he* died. *For these reasons, it is as though* he continues to be a priest forever, and for this reason he is like God's Son.

Hebrews 7:4-10

THEME: Melchizedek was greater than Abraham.

⁴ You can realize how great this *man Melchizedek was* from the fact that Abraham, *our famous* ancestor, gave him one tenth of the spoils *from the battle*. ⁵ According to the laws *God gave Moses*, the descendants of *Abraham's great grandson* Levi, who were priests, should take tithes from *God's* people who were their relatives, even though those people also were Abraham's descendants. ⁶ But this man *Melchizedek,* who was not among the descendants *of Levi*, took tithes from Abraham. He also *asked God to* bless Abraham, the man to whom *God* promised *many descendants*. ⁷ We know for certain that it is the more *important people* who *ask God to* bless the less important people. *And Melchizedek blessed Abraham. So we conclude that Melchizedek was greater than Abraham.* ⁸ In the case of *the priests who are descendants of Levi*, men who will die some day receive tithes. But in the case of *Melchizedek it is as though God* testifies that he was still living, *since there is no record in Scriptures about his death.* ⁹ And it was as though Levi himself, and *all the priests descended from him* who received tithes *from the people*, paid tithes *to* Melchizedek. And when Abraham paid tithes, it *was as though Levi and all the priests descended from him* acknowledged that the work Melchizedek did as a priest was greater than the work Levi did, ¹⁰ since *the sperm from which all those priests were eventually born* was still in Abraham's body when Melchizedek met Abraham.

Hebrews 7:11-19

THEME: The former Jewish priests were not adequate, so a new one like Melchizedek had to come.

¹¹ *God* gave his laws to his people at the same time he gave regulations about the priests. So, if what the priests descended from Levi could have provided a way for God to completely *forgive* people *for disobeying those laws*, certainly no other priest like Melchizedek would have been necessary. Instead, priests who were descended from Aaron, *Levi's descendant, would have been adequate.* ¹² *But we know they were not adequate, because a new type of priest like Melchizedek has come.* And since *God* has appointed a new type of priest, he also had to change the regulations *concerning how priests were appointed.* ¹³ *Jesus*, the one about whom *I am saying these* things, is a descendant of someone else, *not a descendant of Levi*. None of the men *from whom*

Jesus descended ever served as priests. [14] *We know that* since it is obvious that it is from *the tribe of* Judah that our Lord was descended. Moses never said that any of Judah's descendants would *become* priests. [15] Furthermore, *we know that the priests descended from Levi were inadequate, because* it is even more obvious that another priest has appeared who is like Melchizedek. [16] He became a priest, but not because *he fulfilled* what *God's* law required *about being a descendant of Levi*. Instead, he has the kind of power that *enabled him to* live *again after he was* killed. [17] *We know this* because *God* confirmed it in *the Scripture passage in which he said to his Son*,

You are a priest eternally in the same way that Melchizedek was a priest!

[18] On the one hand, God canceled his previous commandment *concerning the priests* because it failed in every way to enable anyone *to become all that God intended*. [19] Remember that no one was able to become all that God intended *by obeying* the laws *God gave Moses*. On the other hand, *God caused that we could* confidently expect better things *than we could expect by obeying God's laws. He did that by his establishing Christ as priest*. Now by means of *Christ sacrificing himself for us* we can come near to God.

Hebrews 7:20-25

THEME: Jesus lives eternally as a high priest to plead with God for us.

[20] Furthermore, *when God appointed Christ, it was when he* solemnly declared *that Christ would be a priest*. When *God appointed former* priests, it was not by his solemnly declaring *that they would be priests*. [21] However, when he *appointed Christ to be a priest*, it was by these words that *the Psalmist wrote in Scripture*:

The Lord has solemnly declared *to the Messiah*, and he will not change his mind,
"You will be a priest forever!"

[22] Because of that, Jesus guarantees that *the new* covenant will be better *than the old one*.

[23] And formerly, the priests could not keep serving *as priests*, because they all died. So there were many priests *to take the places of the ones who died*. [24] But because *Jesus* lives eternally, he will continue to be a high priest forever. [25] So, he can completely and eternally save those who come to God by *trusting in what* Christ *has done for them*, because he lives forever to plead *with God* to help them.

Hebrews 7:26-28

THEME: Jesus is the kind of high priest we need because he was sinless.

[26] Jesus is the kind of high priest that we need. He was holy, he did no wrong, and he was innocent. *God has now* separated him from *living among* sinners, and *has now taken him* up to the highest heaven. [27] *The Jewish* high priests need to sacrifice *animals* day by day *as well as year by year*. They do this, firstly, *to atone* for their own sins, and then *to atone for other* people *who have sinned. But because Jesus never sinned*, he does not need to do that. The only thing *he needed to do to save people* was to sacrifice himself once! [28] *We need a high priest like* him, because *Moses* wrote in the laws *God gave him* that men who *easily* tended *to sin* would be appointed to be priests. But *God* solemnly *declared* after *he had given* his laws *to Moses* that *he would appoint* his Son *to be a high priest. Now his Son* has forever become all that God intends him to be.

8

Hebrews 8:1-6

THEME: The rituals performed by the Jewish high priests were only a model of what Jesus our high priest does in heaven.

¹ The main point of *all* that *I* have written is that we have a high priest like that. He has sat down to rule with God at the place of greatest honor in heaven. ² He ministers in the true holy place, the place that *Moses'* tent *represented*. The Lord set up the true place of worship. No human *set it up*.

³ Every high priest was appointed to offer *to God* gifts and sacrifices *for people who sinned*. So, since *Christ became a high priest*, he also had to offer something. ⁴ Since there are already *Jewish* priests who offer gifts as God's laws *require*, if Christ were *now living* on the earth, he would not be a high priest. ⁵ The *Jewish* priests perform rituals that are only models of *what Christ would do in heaven. God* instructed Moses specifically how to make the tent *where the priests should perform the rituals. What he said implies to us that those rituals were only models. God said*:

Be sure that you do the rituals according to the models that I showed you *while you were* on Mount Sinai!

⁶ But, as it is now, *Christ* ministers in a more excellent way *than the Jewish priests do*. Likewise, the *new* covenant he established *between God and people* is better *than the old one. When God established the new covenant*, he promised us better things *than the laws God gave Moses did*.

Hebrews 8:7-13

THEME: The first covenant was not adequate, so God needed a new one.

⁷ If that first covenant had been perfectly adequate, God would not have thought he needed another *covenant to replace it*. But *it was not adequate, so he needed a new one.* ⁸ Because God found *the Israelites* guilty *of not obeying the first covenant, he wanted a new covenant. This is what a prophet wrote about that*:

The Lord says, "Listen! There will soon be a time when I will make a new covenant with the people of Israel and the people of Judah. ⁹ That covenant will not be like the covenant I made with their ancestors when I led them out of Egypt, *like a father leads a child* by the hand. They did not continue to *obey* my covenant, so I rejected them," says the Lord. ¹⁰ "This is the covenant that I will make with the Israelites, after *the first covenant has ended*," says the Lord: "I will cause them to understand my laws, and I will cause them to obey them sincerely. I will be their God, and they will be my people. ¹¹ *As a result*, no one will *need to* teach a fellow citizen or tell his fellow kinsmen, '*You need to* know the Lord,' because all *my people* will know me: *my people* of every status *will know me*. ¹² I will mercifully *forgive them for* the wicked things they have done. I will no longer *consider* them to be *guilty for their* sins."

¹³ Since God spoke about a new *covenant*, he considered the first *covenant* to be no longer in use, and that it would soon disappear, just *as anything that* gets old *will disappear*.

9

Hebrews 9:1-5

THEME: A description of the man-made sanctuary that accompanied the first covenant.

¹To continue: In the first *covenant, God* regulated how people *should perform* rituals, and *he instituted* a man-made sanctuary. ²*That sanctuary* was a tent that *the Israelites* set up. In its outer room there was the lampstand and the table *on which they put* the bread that *the priests* presented *to God. That room* was called 'the holy place.' ³Behind the curtain inside *the holy place* there was *another* room. That was called 'the very holy place.' ⁴It had an altar *made from* gold, *for burning* incense. *It also had the chest that they called* the chest of the covenant. All its sides were covered with gold. In it was the golden pot containing *pieces of the food they called* manna. *That was the food with which God miraculously fed the people before they entered the promised land.* In the chest there was also Aaron's walking stick that budded *to prove he was God's true priest.* In the chest were also the stone tablets *on which God had written* the ten commandments. ⁵On top of *the chest* were *figures of* winged creatures *that symbolized God's* glory. Their *wings* overshadowed the chest's lid, where *the high priest sprinkled the blood* to *atone for those who had sinned. I* do not *need* to write about these things in detail now.

Hebrews 9:6-10

THEME: Offerings made under the first covenant were not able to remove a sense of guilt for sin.

⁶After all those things were prepared *in the two rooms of the tent*, the *Jewish* priests habitually went into the outer *room of the* tent to perform their rituals. ⁷But into the inner room, only the high priest *went*, once a year. He always took the blood *of animals they had slaughtered.* He offered them *to God* for his own *sins* and for the sins other people had committed. They included sins they did not realize *were sinful.* ⁸By those things the Holy Spirit indicated that *just as God* did not reveal the way *for ordinary people* to enter into the inner room while the outer room still existed, *similarly he did not reveal the way for ordinary people to enter the presence of God while the Jewish system of offering sacrifices was in effect.* ⁹*The things that the priests did inside the outer room* symbolized *what was true* during the time *the first covenant was in effect.* According to *the first covenant,*ʲ *priests* offered gifts and other sacrifices to God. But *by offering them,* the people who brought them were unable to make themselves feel that they were no longer guilty for having sinned. ¹⁰*They brought those gifts and made those sacrifices* only according to *regulations concerning* things to eat and drink, and *rules that required people to* wash various things. *God* declared those regulations about our bodies were to be in effect until *he put into effect the new covenant*; that was a better system.

Hebrews 9:11-14

THEME: Christ redeemed us by offering his own blood as a sacrifice.

¹¹But when Christ came as our high priest, *he brought* the good things that are now available. When he appeared, *he went into God's presence in heaven. That is like a* very great and perfect tent not made by humans; that is, it is not part of the world *God* created. It was better *than the tent Moses set up here on earth.* ¹²*When a high priest went into the*

ʲ OR, *...In that outer room...*

inner room in the tent each year, he took goats' blood and calves' blood *to offer as a sacrifice*. But Christ did not *do that. It was as though* he went into that very holy place only once, taking his own blood with him. By doing that, he eternally redeemed us. [13] The priests sprinkled on people goats' blood and bulls' blood and *the water that has been filtered through* the ashes of a *red* heifer that has been *completely burned. By doing that ritual, they can ritually* cleanse those who are *ceremonially* unclean. Furthermore, performing those rituals enabled people to have fellowship with God again. [14] *So, because we know what* Christ *accomplished when* his blood flowed *when he died for us*, we will be very certain that we are not guilty *for having* done those things *that those who are spiritually* dead do. *As a result*, we can serve the all-powerful God. *The priests always offered to God animals* with no defects. In the same way, when Christ offered himself *as a sacrifice* to God, he was sinless. He did that as a result of *God's* eternal Spirit *helping him*.

Hebrews 9:15-22

THEME: Christ has put the new covenant into effect with his own blood.

[15] *By shedding his blood and* dying, *Christ* set free from the penalty for their sins even those who disobeyed the *conditions of* the first covenant.[k] So, *because the old covenant could not make anyone perfect*, now Christ establishes *between God and people* a new covenant. He does that in order that those whom God has chosen may eternally have *the blessings that God* has promised them. [16] A covenant *is like a will. In the case of a will, in order to put its provisions into effect*, someone must prove that the one who made it has died. [17] A will goes into effect *only when the one who makes the will* has died. It is not in effect when the one who made it is still alive. [18] And so *God* put the first covenant into effect only by means of *animals'* blood that was shed *when they were slaughtered*. [19] After Moses had declared to all the Israelites everything God commanded in the laws *God gave him*, he took calves' and goats' blood *mixed* with water. He *dipped into it* scarlet wool *tied around* a sprig of hyssop. Then he sprinkled *with some of the blood* the scroll itself containing God's laws. Then he sprinkled *more of the blood on all the* people, [20] saying to them, "This is the blood *which puts into effect* the covenant that God commanded you to *obey*." [21] Likewise, he sprinkled with the blood the tent and every object that they used in performing rituals. [22] It was by *sprinkling* blood that they *ritually* cleansed almost everything. That was what God's laws *prescribed*. If blood is not shed *when people offer a sacrifice, God* can not forgive *the person who is making the sacrifice*.

Hebrews 9:23-28

THEME: The Jewish priests kept offering the blood of animal sacrifices every year, but Christ sacrificed himself once to take away our guilt.

[23] So it was necessary for *the priests* to cleanse by rituals like that the things that symbolized what Christ does in heaven. But God has to *consecrate* the *people who will enter* heaven *by means of* better sacrifices than those. [24] Christ did not enter a sanctuary made by humans. That one only represented the true *sanctuary*. Instead, he entered heaven itself, in order to now be in God's presence to *plead with* God for us. [25] The *Jewish* high priest enters the very holy place once every year, taking blood that is not his own, *to offer it as a sacrifice*. But when Christ entered heaven, it was not in order to offer himself repeatedly like that. [26] *If that were so*, he would have needed to suffer *and shed his blood* repeatedly since *the time when God* created the world. But instead, in this final age, *Christ* has appeared once in order that by sacrificing himself he could cause *people* to no longer

---

[k]   OR: …those who disobeyed *during the time of* the first covenant.

be *guilty for their* sins. ²⁷ All people must die once, and after that *God* will judge them *for their sins.* ²⁸ Likewise, when Christ *died, God* offered him once to be a sacrifice, to punish him instead of the many *people who had* sinned. He will come *to earth* a second time, not *to sacrifice himself again for those who* have sinned, but to *complete* his saving those who expectantly wait for him.

10

Hebrews 10:1-4

THEME: *The blood of animals can never take away the guilt for sin.*

¹ Just as a shadow vaguely represents the thing it is a shadow of, the laws that God *gave Moses* only poorly represent the good things that were to come later. Those laws were not all the good things themselves that God has promised. So, by offering the same kinds of sacrifices every year, people who approach God can never become all that God intends them to be. ² If God had removed the guilt for having sinned of those who brought the sacrifices, they wouldn't feel that they were still guilty. So they would certainly have stopped offering those sacrifices! ³ But rather, the fact that they offer those sacrifices each year reminds them that they are still guilty for their sins, ⁴ because no blood of animals, such as bulls or goats, can remove the guilt of those who have sinned.

Hebrews 10:5-10

THEME: *Christ set us apart for God by offering his own body once as a sacrifice.*

⁵ So, as *Christ* was coming into the world, he said *to his Father about offering himself as a sacrifice for people's sin, in words that the Psalmist wrote,*
    It is not sacrifices and offerings that you have wanted,
        but you have prepared for me a body *to serve you.*
    ⁶ Animals that are completely burned up as sacrifices have not pleased you,
        and *other sacrifices that atone* for those who have sinned have not pleased you.'
    ⁷ Then *because of this,* I said, "My God, here I am!
    I have come *here* in order to do what you want me *to do,*
        just as they have written about me in the Scriptures."

⁸ First he said, "You have certainly not wanted sacrifices and offerings and animals like the ones that *the priests* have completely burned up, and other *offerings to atone for* those who have sinned. They have not pleased you." *He said that even though* they offered all those things according to the laws *God gave Moses*! ⁹ Then, *concerning his offering himself as a sacrifice to atone for people's sin,* he said, "Listen, I have come *here* to do what you want me *to do!*" Thus Christ got rid of the first *way of atoning for sin,* in order to establish the second *way of atoning for* sin. ¹⁰ Because of Jesus Christ *doing what God* wanted him to do, *he* has set us apart for God by offering his own body *as a sacrifice, one that was completely sufficient to cancel all of our sins.*

Hebrews 10:11-18

THEME: *Scripture supports the claim that Christ made one sacrifice that will be adequate forever.*

¹¹ As every *Jewish* priest stands daily *in front of the altar*, he performs rituals and offers the same kind of sacrifices that could never remove *the guilt from anyone who* sinned. ¹² But

Christ one time offered a sacrifice that *will be adequate* forever! Then he sat down *to rule* with God at the place of highest honor. ¹³ From now on, he is waiting for *God* to completely subdue *all* his enemies. ¹⁴ By offering himself once, he has provided that those whom *God* has set apart will be eternally made all that God intends them to be. ¹⁵ The Holy Spirit also confirms to us *that that is true*. First the Lord says:

¹⁶ When the time *of the first covenant* with my people has finished,
I will make a new covenant with them. I will do like this for them:
I will cause them to understand my laws, and I will cause them to obey them sincerely.ⁱ

¹⁷ Then *he said*:
I will forgive them for their sins,
and I will *consider* them to be no longer *guilty for* having sinned.

¹⁸ When *God* has forgiven someone's sins, that person does not *need to make* any more offerings *to atone for his sin!*

Hebrews 10:19-25

THEME: Let's come to God and let him make us pure and help us to hold fast to his truth and do things that please him.

¹⁹ So, my fellow believers, because we *trust in what Jesus accomplished by shedding* his own blood *for us*, we can confidently go into *God's very presence* that was *symbolized* by the very holy place *in the tent*. ²⁰ He enabled us to go into *God's presence* by making a new and effective way. He *offered* his body *as a sacrifice* for us *in order that nothing would stop us* from entering *God's presence, just as* the curtain *of the very holy place prevented people from entering God's presence*. ²¹ Christ is a great priest *who rules over us, who are* God's people. ²² *Just as the priests* were sprinkled *with blood* to symbolize that they were no longer guilty for having sinned, we also no longer are *guilty for having done* evil. *Just as the priests ceremonially* washed their bodies with pure water *to prepare themselves to serve God*, we are allowing *God* to continually make us pure in every way. So, we must approach *God* sincerely by confidently trusting *in him*. ²³ We must unwaveringly keep professing *what we believe. Since God* faithfully *does all* he promised *to do,* we must confidently expect *him to keep his promises*. ²⁴ *Since God* faithfully *does all* he promised *to do*, we must consider how each of us can stimulate the others, in order that *each one* will love the others, and in order that each one will do good deeds. ²⁵ We must not cease gathering together *to worship the Lord*, as some people have done. Instead, each one of us must encourage the others. *We must do that* all the more because we know that the day *that the Lord will return* is near.

Hebrews 10:26-31

THEME: If we have known and then rejected the message about Christ, God will surely punish us.

²⁶ *We must do those things,* because if we deliberately sin habitually after we have known the true *message about Christ*, no other sacrifice will remove our guilt for having sinned in this way. ²⁷ Instead, we must fearfully expect that *God will* judge us, and then he will angrily *destroy* his enemies in a furious fire. ²⁸ They mercilessly killed everyone who rejected the laws *that God gave* Moses when *at least* two or three people testified that they had done that. ²⁹ *That was severe punishment*. But *Christ* is God's Son.ᵐ His blood,

---

ⁱ OR, …I will cause that they understand my laws, and I will cause that truly know them.

ᵐ OR, …But *Christ* is the man who is also God.

by means of which *he put into effect* the new covenant, is sacred. Because of *Christ shedding* his blood, *God* freed us from our guilt. So, you can be sure that anyone who shows contempt for *those truths* and who insults the Spirit of God, who acts with kindness toward us in a way we don't deserve, deserves to be punished even worse than that! [30] *We can be sure of that*[n] since we know that God said, "I myself will get revenge on those who sinned, and I will give them the punishment they deserve." And *Moses wrote*, "The Lord will judge his people." [31] It will be a terrible thing if the all-powerful God seizes and punishes you!

Hebrews 10:32-39

THEME: Remember how you accepted persecution because of your faith in Christ, and do not be discouraged if you are persecuted now.

[32] Recall the former times when you *first* understood *the message about Christ*. You endured a hard struggle and *continued to trust him* when you suffered *for your faith in Christ*. [33] At times people publicly insulted you and persecuted you. At other times you showed great concern for those who were treated like that. [34] You not only were kind to those who were in prison *for their faith in Christ*, but you also accepted it joyfully when *unbelievers* took away your possessions. You accepted it because you yourselves knew very well that you have eternal possessions *in heaven* that are much better *than those they took from you!* [35] So, don't become discouraged *when you are persecuted*, because *if you continue to trust in God*, he will greatly reward you. [36] You must patiently continue *to trust in him* in order that, because of your doing what God wants you to do, he will give you what he has promised. [37] *You must do that* because *a prophet wrote* in the Scriptures *that God said about the Messiah*,

In just a short time the one *I promised* would come will surely come;
    he will not delay coming.
[38] But those I have summoned, who *act* righteously, must continually live trusting in me,
    because if they, in a cowardly manner, cease *to trust in me*, I will be angry with them.

[39] But we are not ones who in a cowardly manner cease *to trust in God*, with the result that God will destroy us. Instead, we are ones who trust in him, with the result that *God* will save us eternally.

11

Hebrews 11:1-3

THEME: Because of our faith we confidently expect to receive God's promises.

[1] It is because people trust *God* that they are sure that they will receive the things that they confidently expect *God to give them*. They are also certain *that they will see those things happen*, though no one sees them yet. [2] It was because our ancestors believed in God that *he* commended them. [3] It is because we trust God that we understand that God formed the universe by commanding *that it exist*. The result is that that the things that we see now were not made from anything that already existed.

---

[n] OR, *We need to think about that carefully…*

Hebrews 11:4

THEME: Because of his faith Abel made a better sacrifice than his brother Cain did.

[4] It was because *Adam's son* Abel trusted God that he sacrificed something better to God than what *his older brother* Cain offered to God. Because Abel did that, when God spoke well about what he sacrificed, God declared that Abel was righteous. And although Abel is dead, we still learn from him *about trusting God.*

Hebrews 11:5-12

THEME: Because of their faith God blessed Enoch, Noah, and Abraham.

[5] It was because Enoch believed *God that God* took him *up to heaven*. The result was that he did not die. No one found him, because he was taken up from the earth *to heaven*. Before *God* took him away, *he* testified that Enoch pleased him well. [6] It is possible for people to please God only if they trust God, because anyone who wants to come to God must first believe that God exists and that he rewards those who seek *to know* him.

[7] It was because Noah trusted *God* that after *God* warned him about a flood that had not yet happened, Noah *showed that he* revered God by building a huge ship to save his family. By doing that, he *showed all the people who did not believe him that they deserved God's* condemnation. He became one whom God declared to be righteous because of his trusting in God.

[8] It was because Abraham trusted God that when *God* called to him, he obeyed *God,* left *his own country,* and went to a place that God would give him. Abraham left his own country, even though he did not know where he would be going. [9] It was because Abraham trusted God that he lived as though he was a foreigner in a land that *God* had promised *to give him*. Abraham lived in tents, and his son Isaac and his grandson Jacob did also. God promised to give them the same things that he promised to give to Abraham. [10] Abraham was waiting to live in a city *in heaven* that would remain forever. It was a city that God would build. [11] It was because Abraham trusted God that God gave Abraham strength so that he was able to produce a son. Even though his wife Sarah was beyond the time *when women bear children*, *God* promised *to give her a son*, and Abraham considered that God would keep his promise. [12] So, though Abraham was too old to have children, from that one man people descended who are as many in number as the stars in the sky and as countless as the grains of sand along the shore, *just as God promised him.*

Hebrews 11:13-16

THEME: All these people who had faith in God died without receiving what God promised.

[13] It was while they still trusted in God that all those people died. Even though they had not yet received the things that God had promised to give them, *it was as though* they saw those things in a distance. They were glad *to kno*w about what he promised. It was as though they admitted that they were not from this earth, but that they were only here temporarily. [14] As for those people who say such things, they clearly show that they long for *a place that will become* their true native land. [15] If they had been thinking about *that place being* the place from which they had come, they would have taken the opportunity to return there. [16] But, instead, they desired a better *place in which to live*; that is, they desired *a home* in heaven. So, God has prepared a city for them to live *with him*, and he is pleased for them to say that he is their God.

Hebrews 11:17-31

THEME: It was because they trusted God that he blessed Abraham, Isaac, Joseph, Moses, the Israelite people, and Rahab.

[17] It was because Abraham trusted *God* that he *was ready to* kill his son Isaac as a sacrifice when *God* tested him. This same man to whom *God* promised *to give him a son* was going to sacrifice *that same son*, the only son *whom his own wife had borne!* [18] It was to him that God said, "It is *only* from Isaac that I will consider your family to descend." [19] Abraham considered that *to fulfill that promise*, God could make *Isaac* live again *even if* he had died *after Abraham sacrificed him!* The result was that when Abraham did receive Isaac back *after God told him not to harm Isaac*, it was as though he received him back after he died.

[20] It was because Isaac trusted God that he *prayed for God to* bless *his* sons Jacob and Esau after *Isaac died*.

[21] It was because Jacob trusted God that, as he was dying, he *prayed that God would* bless each of the sons of *his own son Joseph*. He worshipped God as he leaned upon his walking-stick *before he died.* [22] It was because Joseph trusted God that, when he was about to die *in Egypt*, he anticipated the time when the Israelites would leave Egypt; and he instructed *his people that they should carry* his bones *with them when they left Egypt.*

[23] It was because Moses' father and mother trusted God that they hid *their son Moses* for three months shortly after he was born, because they saw that the child was beautiful. They were not afraid of *disobeying* what the king of Egypt had commanded, *namely, that all the Jewish male babies must be killed.* [24] The daughter of the *king, whom they called* Pharaoh, *raised* Moses, but when he had grown up it was because he trusted God that he refused to *accept the privileges that would have been his if people* considered that he was the son of the king's *own* daughter. [25] He decided that it was better for others to mistreat him for a time along with the Israelite people, than to temporarily enjoy living sinfully *in the King's palace.* [26] This is because he decided that if he suffered for the Messiah, it would be worth far more *in God's sight* than owning all the treasures of Egypt *that he would receive as Pharaoh's heir. His decision was based on* looking forward to the time when *God would give him* an *eternal* reward. [27] It was because he trusted God that he left Egypt. He was not afraid that the king would be angry *on account of his doing that.* He kept going because *it was as though* he kept seeing *God*, whom no one can see. [28] It was because Moses believed *that God would save his own people* that he instituted the festival called Passover. He did that *by commanding the people to kill lambs and* sprinkle their blood *on their* doorposts. They did that in order that *the angel who* causes people to die would not kill the oldest male Israelites *when he killed the oldest sons in each Egyptian family*.

[29] It was because they trusted God that when the *Israelite* people walked through the Red Sea it was as though they walked on dry land! But, when the *army of* Egypt also attempted to *cross that same water*, they drowned, because *the sea came back and flooded them!*

[30] It was because the *Israelite* people trusted God that the walls around *the city of* Jericho collapsed, after the Israelites marched around the walls for seven days.

[31] Rahab *had been* a prostitute, but because she trusted God, she did not perish with those *inside Jericho* who disobeyed *God. Joshua sent some spies* into the city to find ways to destroy it, but God saved her because she welcomed those spies *peaceably*.

Hebrews 11:32-38

THEME: Some who trusted God gained great victories and others were tortured and killed.

[32] I cannot tell you about others *who trusted in God*. It would take too much time to tell about Gideon, Barak, Samson, Jephthah, David, Samuel, and the *other* prophets. [33] It was because they trusted God that some of them *did great deeds for him*. Some conquered lands ruled by powerful men. Some ruled *Israel* and justly *punished those men and nations who rebelled against God*. Some obtained *from God* the things that he promised to give them. Some forced lions to keep their mouths shut. [34] Some escaped from being destroyed by fire. Some of those people escaped from *being killed with* a sword. Some of those *people who trusted God* were made strong again after they had once been weak. Some became powerful when they fought wars. Some caused foreign armies to run away from them. [35] Some women *who trusted God* received *their relatives* back again when *God raised them from the dead*.

But *others who trusted God* were tortured until they died. They were tortured because they refused to agree when *their captors said, 'We will* release you *if you deny that you believe in God.' They refused to do that*, because they wanted to live with God forever, which is better than *continuing to live on earth* after having almost died. [36] Other *people who trusted God* were mocked; *some had their backs* cut *open by being struck* with whips. Some were chained and put in prison. [37] *Some* of those believers were stoned to death.° Others were cut completely in two. Others were killed with swords. Others of these people who trusted God wandered around the land *wearing garments made only of* skins from sheep and goats. They did not have any money. They were continually oppressed and tormented. [38] *The people on earth who caused those who trusted in God to suffer were so bad that* they did not deserve *to live with people* like those *who trusted God. Some who trusted God* wandered in deserts and mountains. Some lived in caves and in other *large* holes in the ground.

Hebrews 11:39-40

THEME: Only when we are together with all these people who trusted God will we receive all God has promised.

[39] Although *God* commended all these people for their trust in him, God did not give them all that he promised them *while they were alive*. [40] God knew ahead of time that what he would give us and them *later* would be better than giving them immediately what he promised. What God intends is that only when they and we are together will we be all that God intends us to be.

12

Hebrews 12:1-2

THEME: Since we know so many people with faith like that, let us put aside anything, especially sin, which hinders us, and let us strive to achieve God's will and concentrate on Jesus.

[1] We *know about* many people like that *who showed they trusted in God*. They are like a crowd of spectators *who are* cheering for us inside a stadium. Knowing that, we must put away all the things which hinder us, *as runners put aside everything heavy that would*

°   Some Greek manuscripts add, "Men tortured others continuously."

hinder them. Especially we must put away sinful actions that *hinder us, as runners* set aside clothes they don't need that would entangle them. We must *wholeheartedly strive to achieve what God has planned for us, as people* in a race wholeheartedly run the course that is before them. [2] And we should *keep our minds on* Jesus, *as runners* keep their eyes on *the goal.* He is the one we should imitate concerning his perfect trust in God. *When he died on* the cross he endured great suffering, instead of *thinking about the things he would* rejoice about *later.* He disregarded the disgrace *of dying that way.* He is now sitting at the place of highest honor at the throne *where God rules.*

Hebrews 12:3-6

THEME: Do not become discouraged when you are suffering as you struggle against evil.

[3] Jesus patiently endured it when sinful people acted so hostilely against him. Compare yourselves with him, so that you do not give up *your faith* or become discouraged. [4] While you have struggled against *the temptation to* sin, you have not yet shed your blood *and died because of resisting evil, as Jesus did.* [5] Don't forget these words *that Solomon spoke to his son, that are the same as* God would exhort you as his children,

My child, pay attention when the Lord is disciplining you,
and don't be discouraged when the Lord punishes you,
[6] because it is everyone whom he loves whom the Lord disciplines,
and he punishes everyone whom he accepts as his child.

Hebrews 12:7-11

THEME: Since our sufferings are to discipline us, if we haven't experienced God's discipline we are not his true children. We should accept God's discipline since it is always to help us.

[7] It is in order that God may discipline you that he requires you to endure the disagreeable things that happen to you. God is treating you as a father treats his children *when he disciplines you.* All fathers discipline their children. [8] So, if you haven't experienced God disciplining you just as he disciplines all his other children, you are *not true children of God. You are like* illegitimate children; *no father disciplines them.* [9] Furthermore, our natural fathers disciplined us *when we were young,* and we respected them for doing that. So we should certainly more readily accept God our spiritual Father disciplining us, with the result that we live eternally. [10] Our natural fathers disciplined us for a short time just as they considered right, but God always disciplines us to help us. He does it so that we may be holy, as he is. [11] During the time that God is disciplining us, that does not seem to be something about which we should rejoice. Instead, it is something that pains us. But later it causes those who have learned from it to be peaceful and to live righteously.

Hebrews 12:12-17

THEME: Renew yourselves spiritually; go forward in your Christian life; try to live peacefully with everyone; seek to be holy; guard against bitterness; do not be immoral; and do not refuse to listen to God.

[12] So, *instead of acting as though you were spiritually exhausted*, renew yourselves *spiritually.* [13] Go straight forward *in your Christian life*, so that any believer who is uncertain about his faith *will follow you* and not become useless to God. Instead, he will be spiritually restored as an injured and useless limb is restored. [14] Try to live in peace with all people. Seek to be holy, because no one will see the Lord if they are not holy. [15] Beware that none of you falls away from trusting in God's kindly doing for us what we did not

deserve.[p] Be on guard lest any of you *act evilly towards others*, because that will *grow like*
a root *grows into a big plant*, and the result *of yo*ur doing that will be that many believers
will sin and become unacceptable to God. 16 Make sure that no one is immoral, or
irreligious as Esau was. He exchanged his rights of being a firstborn son for only one
meal. 17 You know that after he did that, he wanted to receive *what his father would*
promise to give him if he blessed him. But *his father* refused his request. And Esau found
no way to change what he had done, even though he sought tearfully to do that.

Hebrews 12:18-24

THEME: You have not experienced the terrifying things your ancestors did; you have come to Christ and benefited from his shedding his blood for you.

18 In coming *to God* you have not *experienced things like what the Israeli people*
experienced at Mount Sinai. *They* approached *a mountain that God told them* not to touch.
They approached a blazing fire, and it was gloomy and dark and there was a hurricane.
19 They heard a trumpet sounding, and they heard *God* speak. The result was that those
who heard it pleaded for him not to speak to them like that again. 20 When *God*
commanded them saying, “If *a person or* even an animal touches this mountain, *you* must
stone him *to death*,” they were terrified. 21 Truly, because Moses was terrified after seeing
what happened *on the mountain*, he said, “I am trembling with fear!” 22 Instead, *it is as*
though you have come to *the presence of God in heaven. That is like what your ancestors*
did when they came to worship God on Zion Hill, in Jerusalem, in the city of the all-
powerful God. You have come[q] to where there are countless angels, who are rejoicing as
they have gathered together. 23 You have joined all the believers *who have privileges like*
first-born sons, whose names *God* has written down in heaven. You have come to God,
who will judge everyone. You have come to where the spirits of God’s people are, people
who lived righteously *before they died* and who now have been made perfect *in heaven*.
24 You have come to Jesus, who arranged a new covenant *between us and God*. You have
accepted *what he accomplished when* his blood flowed *when he died on the cross. His*
doing that made it possible for God to forgive us. That is better than the blood of Abel,
*who just w*anted revenge because his brother Cain murdered him.

Hebrews 12:25-29

THEME: Let us be in awe before God who will punish us if we reject him.

25 Beware that you do not refuse to listen to *God* who is speaking to you. The Israelite
people did not escape *God’s* punishment when *Moses* warned them here on earth. So we
shall surely not escape *God’s punishment* if we reject him when he warns us from heaven!
26 The earth shook then when he spoke *at Mount Sinai*. But now he has promised, “I will
shake the earth again, one more time, but I will shake heaven too.” 27 The words “again,
one more time” indicate that *he* will shake things *on earth*, meaning he will set aside all
that *he* has created, in order that the things *in heaven* that nothing can shake may remain
forever. 28 So, let us thank God that we are becoming members of a kingdom that nothing
can shake. Let us worship God in a way that pleases him by being greatly in awe before
him. 29 Remember that the God we *worship* is like a fire that burns up everything *that is*
impure!

---

[p] OR, Beware that none of you are ones who have never experienced God kindly saving him.

[q] OR, …You are coming to…

13

Hebrews 13:1-3

THEME: Love one another, be hospitable, and help imprisoned and other mistreated believers.

¹Continue to love your fellow believers. ²Don't forget to be hospitable to needy travelers. Remember that by being hospitable, some people have entertained angels without knowing it. ³Remember *to help* those who are in prison *for their faith*, as though you were in prison with them. Remember those who are being mistreated *because they are believers. As you do that,* consider that you are also alive, *and you could suffer as they do.*

Hebrews 13:4-6

THEME: Respect the marriage relationship, and avoid covetousness.

⁴You must keep sacred the marriage relationship in every way, and you must keep sexual relations pure, because God will surely condemn those who act immorally and those who act adulterously. ⁵Live without constantly coveting money, and be content with the things you possess, remembering what *Moses* wrote *that God* has said *about supplying what you need,*
I will never leave you.
I will never stop providing for you.

⁶So we can say confidently *as the Psalmist said*:
Since the Lord is the one who helps me.
I will not be afraid!
People can do nothing to me *that will deprive me of God's   blessings.*

Hebrews 13:7-9

THEME: Remember the manner of life of your former spiritual leaders and imitate their faith; since Christ never changes, don't be diverted to strange teachings.

⁷Your spiritual leaders used to tell you the message of God *before they died.* Remember how they conducted their lives. By considering how they died,ʳ imitate their faith *in Christ.* ⁸Jesus Christ *is* the same now as he was previously, and he will be the same forever. ⁹*So*, don't let anything divert you with the result that you believe various teachings *that are contrary to God's truth.* It is good to let God act kindly toward us so that we may be strengthened spiritually. *Obeying rules about* various foods, rules that have not benefited those who obeyed them, will not benefit us.

Hebrews 13:10-12

THEME: Let us stop practicing Jewish sacrifices and rituals, and go to Jesus to be saved, since we do not have a city like Jerusalem where we must offer sacrifices, but instead we wait for a future everlasting heavenly city.

¹⁰We have *Jesus.* All those who continue to observe the Jewish rituals of sacrifice have no right to obtain the benefits of his sacrifice. ¹¹After the high priest brings into the most holy place the blood of animals *they have sacrificed to atone* for sins, they burn the bodies of

---

ʳ OR, …By considering what resulted from how they lived…

those animals outside the city. [12] Similarly, Jesus suffered *and died* outside the gate *of Jerusalem* in order that he might make *us*, his people, holy by *shedding* his own blood *to atone for our sins.*

[13] So, we must abandon *performing Jewish* sacrifices and rituals *in order to be saved*, and we must go to Jesus *to be saved*. As we do that, we should *be willing to* let others reproach us just as people reproached him. [14] Here on earth, we believers don't have a city *such as Jerusalem where we must* continually *offer sacrifices*. Instead, we are waiting for a future *heavenly* city *that will last forever.*

Hebrews 13:15

THEME: Since Christ sacrificed himself for us, let our continual praise of God be our sacrifice.

[15] With *the help of* Jesus, let's continually praise God. That will be something we can sacrifice *to him instead of our sacrificing animals only at specific times.* Specifically, let's say openly *that we have trusted* in Christ.

Hebrews 13:16

THEME: Let us do good deeds and share with others, since this too will be a sacrifice pleasing to God.

[16] Be continually doing good deeds *for others*, and be continually sharing *with others the things you have*, because doing things like that will *also* be *as though you are offering* sacrifices that will please God.

Hebrews 13:17

THEME: Obey and submit to your spiritual leaders.

[17] Obey your *spiritual* leaders and do what they tell you, since they are the ones who are guarding your *spiritual* welfare. *Some day* they will have to stand before God so he can say if he approves of what they have done. Obey them so that they can do their work joyfully and not have to do it sadly, because if you cause them to do it sadly, that will certainly not help you at all.[s]

Hebrews 13:18-19

THEME: Pray for me that God will quickly remove the things that hinder my coming to you.

[18] Pray for me. I am certain that I have not done anything that displeases God. I have tried to act honorably *toward you* in every way. [19] I urge you earnestly to pray that *God* will quickly remove the things that hinder my coming to you.

Hebrews 13:20-21

THEME: May God equip you with everything good that you need, and may Christ be praised forever.

[20] Jesus *provides for us, protects us, and guides us as* a great shepherd does for his sheep. And God, who gives us *inner* peace, raised our Lord Jesus from the dead. By doing that, God ratified his eternal covenant with us by the blood *that flowed from Christ*

---

[s] OR, …they won't be able to help you at all.

when he died on the cross. ²¹ So I pray that God will equip you with everything good *that you need in order* for you to do the things that he desires. May he accomplish in us the things that he considers pleasing, as a result of Jesus Christ *doing this for us*. May Jesus Christ be praised forever. Amen.

Hebrews 13:22

THEME: Patiently consider what I have written in this short exhortation.

²² My fellow believers, since this is a short letter that I have written to you, I appeal to you to consider patiently this exhortation I have given you.

Hebrews 13:23

THEME: Since Timothy has been released from prison, he will accompany me when I go to see you.

²³ I want you to know that our fellow believer Timothy has been released *from prison*. If he comes here soon, he will accompany me when I go to see you.

Hebrews 13:24

THEME: Greet your spiritual leaders and all other believers; the believers who are from Italy send you their greetings.

²⁴ Tell all your *spiritual* leaders and all the *other* fellow believers *in your city* that I am sending them my greetings.ᵗ The believers *in this area who have come* from Italy *want you to know they* are sending you their greetings.

Hebrews 13:25

THEME: May God act graciously to you all.

²⁵ *I pray that* you will continue to experience God's kindness toward you all.

ᵗ OR, …I am thinking fondly about them.

James, the brother of Jesus, wrote a letter to Jewish believers. We call this letter

James

1

James 1:1

THEME: I, James, am writing this letter to Jewish people who trust in the Lord Jesus who are scattered throughout the world. Greetings!

¹ *I*, James, am a servant of God and the Lord Jesus Christ. *I am writing this letter* to *all* the Jewish people *who trust in Christ* who are scattered throughout the world. *I send my* greetings *to all of* you.

James 1:2-4

THEME: When you experience difficulties that test whether or not you will continue to trust God, rejoice greatly and keep on bravely enduring them in order that you may become all that God intends you to be.

² My fellow believers, rejoice greatly, *even* when you experience various kinds of difficulties. ³ *God sometimes allows you to experience difficulties in order to* test whether or not you will continue to trust *him. Whenever that happens, you need to* realize more and more that *if you continue to trust him*, you will be able to bravely endure difficulties. ⁴ Keep on enduring difficulties *bravely by trusting God more and more firmly* in order that you may become all he intends you to be,ᵃ not lacking any *good quality that you need to conduct your life as God wants you to.*

James 1:5-8

THEME: If you want to have wisdom to know what to do when difficulties come, ask God to help you, and firmly trust him.

⁵ *In order to endure difficulties well*, if anyone of you does not know have wisdom *to know what to do*, he should ask God *to show him what he should do, because* God wholeheartedly helps all people *who ask* and does not scold *anyone for asking. If anyone asks*, God will give him wisdom to know *what he should do.* ⁶ But *when you* ask *God*, you should firmly trust him. You should not doubt *his willingness to help you*, because people who keep doubting God are *changeable,* like a wave of the sea that is blown back and forth by the wind. ⁷ Indeed, people *who doubt* should not think that the Lord will do anything *that they request him to do,* ⁸ *because they are* people who cannot decide *if they will commit themselves to God, and they are* undecided in all they do.

ᵃ OR, …you may become *spiritually* mature and complete…

James 1:9-11

THEME: Believers who are poor and those who are rich should both value highly what God has done for them, rather than focusing on their material resources that will disappear.

[9] Believers who are poor should be happy *that God* considers them very valuable.[b] [10] And *believers* who are rich should be happy *that* they have humbled themselves *in order to trust in Jesus Christ,*[c] because they *and their riches* will pass away just as wild flowers *wither.* [11] When the sun rises, the scorching hot wind dries plants and their flowers fall and they are no longer beautiful. In the same way, rich people will die while they are busy working, *leaving behind their riches.*

James 1:12

THEME: God blesses those who bravely endure difficulties; he will reward them by causing them to live eternally.

[12] *God* is pleased with the people who *patiently* endure difficulties. And when, *by patiently enduring difficulties,* they have proved *that they truly trust him,* he will give them *eternal* life. That is the reward he has promised to those who love him.

James 1:13-15

THEME: If people are tempted to do evil, they should not think that it is God who is tempting them. It is their own evil desires that are tempting them to do evil.

[13] If people are tempted to do what is evil, they should not think that it is God who is tempting them, because *God is totally good.* He never tempts anyone *to do evil,* nor can *anything* ever tempt him to *do* evil. [14] But people strongly desire to do what is evil, *and as a result* these desires stimulate them to want to do what is evil. [15] Then *because* of their desire to do what is evil, they proceed to do it. And when they have become people who *habitually* do what is evil, they will be separated from God forever *if they do not turn away from their evil behavior.*

James 1:16-18

THEME: Stop thinking wrongly that God tempts you to do evil, because God does only good for us.

[16] My fellow believers whom I love, stop deceiving yourselves, *thinking that God does what is evil.* [17] *The truth is that God,* our heavenly Father, does only what is good *for us, in order to help us become* all he intends us to be. He is not like all the things *in the sky* that he created to give light*, because they* change*; that is, they don't shine the same all the time.* But God never changes. *He is always good.* [18] *And because* of his desire *to help us,* he gave us *spiritual* life as a result of our *trusting in his* true message. So now we have become the first ones of *all the people* that he created *to be totally dedicated to him.*

---

[b] OR, And *believers* who are poor should be happy *that God* has exalted them *spiritually.*

[c] OR, But the rich person *can only* take pride *in the fact that God* will humble him *when he judges everyone…*

James 1:19-20

THEME: Every one of you should eagerly pay attention to God's message and should not speak hastily or be quick to get angry.

[19] My fellow believers whom I love, you know[d] that everyone of you should be eager to pay attention to *God's true message*. You should not hastily speak *your own thoughts*, or be quick to get angry, [20] because when we *get* angry, we don't do the righteous things that God *wants us to do*.

James 1:21-25

THEME: So stop doing all kinds of evil, and do what God commands in his message instead of just listening to it. God approves of those who do what he wants them to do.

[21] So, stop doing all kinds of evil, and **humbly** accept the message that *God* planted in your hearts, *because* he is able to save you *if you accept his message.* [22] Do *what God commands in* his message. Don't just listen *to it, because people who just listen to it and don't obey it* think wrongly *that God will save them.* [23] Some people hear God's message but don't do *what it says.* They are like people who look at their faces in a mirror. [24] Although they look at themselves, they go away *from the mirror* and immediately forget what they look like. [25] But other people look closely at *God's* message, which is perfect and which sets people free *to voluntarily do what God wants them to do.* And if they continue *to examine God's message* and don't just hear it and then forget it, but do *what God tells them to do*, God will bless them because of what they do.

James 1:26-27

THEME: Those who show compassion on people in need and who do not think or act immorally are those who truly worship God and receive his approval.

[26] Some people think they worship God rightly, but they habitually speak evil talk. Those people are wrong in thinking *that they worship God rightly.* The fact is *that they* worship God **in vain**. [27] *One of the things that God has told us to do* is to take care of orphans and widows who suffer hardship. *Those who do that and* who do not think or act immorally like those who do not obey God truly worship God, *who is our* Father, and God approves of them.

2

James 2:1-11

THEME: Stop honoring some people more than others, because by doing that, you are disobeying God's law that we should love one another.

[1] My fellow believers, *because* you trust our Lord Jesus Christ, the one who is glorious, stop honoring some people more than you honor others. [2] *For example*, suppose a person who wears gold rings and fine clothes enters your meeting place. Then suppose a poor person who wears shabby clothes also comes in. [3] And *suppose* you show special attention to the one dressed in fine clothes by saying, "Sit here in this good seat!" and you say to the poor one, "Stand there, or sit on the floor!" [4] Then, you have obviously caused

---

[d] OR, My fellow believers whom I love, I want you to know…

divisions in the congregation,[e] and you are using evil *motives* to evaluate *people.* [5] Listen *to me*, my fellow believers whom I love. God has chosen poor people whom *unbelievers think of as possessing* nothing of value, *in order that he might bless them* abundantly *because* they trust *in him*, and in order that they will enter the place where *he* will rule *forever.* That is what he has promised to those who love him. [6] But you dishonor the poor people. Think about it! It is the rich people, *not the poor*, who are oppressing you! It is *the rich people* who forcibly take you to court *to accuse you in front of judges!* [7] And they are the ones who speak evil against Jesus Christ, the one who is worthy *of praise,* the one to whom you belong! [8] *God has commanded you* in the Scriptures that each of you must love other people like you love yourself. That commandment was *also given* by *Jesus our* King. If you *are loving others,* you are doing what is right. [9] But if, *on the other hand,* you honor some people more than others, you are sinning. And because you *don't do what God commanded us to do,* he condemns you because you disobey his laws.

[10] Don't forget that those who disobey only one of God's laws, even if they obey all *his other* laws, *God considers them* to be *as guilty as anyone who has disobeyed* all *of* God's *laws.* [11] For example, *God* said, "Don't commit adultery," but he also said, "Don't murder *anyone." So* if you don't commit adultery but you murder someone, you have become a person who disobeys *God's* laws.

James 2:12-13

THEME: Continually act mercifully toward others, because God will not act mercifully to those who do not act mercifully toward others.

[12] Continually speak and act in such a way *toward others* as people should who will be judged by the law that sets us free *from being punished us for our sins.* [13] *Speak and act like that,* because when *God* judges us, he will not show mercy toward us if we haven't shown mercy *to others.* But when we *show* mercy *to others, we can rejoice*, because *our being* merciful *shows we are acting like people whom God* has mercifully saved from being judged.[f]

James 2:14-17

THEME: Anyone who says he trusts in Jesus Christ but does not act compassionately toward others is not truly trusting in Jesus.

[14] My fellow believers, *there are some people who say*, "I trust *in the Lord Jesus Christ,"* but don't do good deeds *to other people.* Their saying that will certainly not do them any good! *God* will certainly not save *people who say they believe but don't do good deeds!* [15] *To illustrate*, suppose a fellow believer, either a man or a woman, is consistently lacking clothing or lacking food for each day. [16] And suppose one of you says to him or her, "May *God* bless you and supply the clothing and food that you need," but you don't give him or her the things he or she needs. That would be no help *to him!* [17] *Similarly, those who* don't do good deeds *to help others, what they have said about* trusting *in Christ* is good for nothing! They don't *really trust in Christ.*

---

[e] OR, Then you have obviously been inconsistent…

[f] OR, …But when we *show* mercy *to others, we can rejoice*, because God will judge us mercifully.

James 2:18-26

THEME: But someone may claim that some people are saved because they trust in God and other people are saved because they do good to others. In answer to that, the inadequacy of faith without good deeds is demonstrated by the example of demons. And from the examples of Abraham and Rahab we can see that only by obeying God and doing good to others can people prove that they truly trust in God.

[18] But someone may say *to me*, "*God saves* some people only *because* they trust *in him,* and *he saves* others *because* they do good deeds *to people.*" *I would answer that person*, "*You can't* prove to me that anyone truly trusts *in God if* he does not do good deeds *to others!* But by doing good deeds *to others* I will prove to you that I truly trust *in God!* [19] *Think about it!* You believe that there is only one God, and you are right *to believe that.* But the demons also believe that, yet they tremble, *because they know that God is going to punish them.* [20] Also, you foolish person, I will prove to you that *if someone says,* 'I trust *in God,*' but does not do good deeds, *what that person says* will not benefit him. [21] It was certainly *because of* what our *revered* ancestor Abraham **did,** when he *prepared to* sacrifice his son Isaac, that *God* considered him to be a righteous, *obedient* person. [22] You can see that he was not only trusting *in God,* but he was also doing *what God told him to do,* and *you can see* that he was able to trust *in God more* completely because of having done *what God told him to do.* [23] And *so it happened just as it is written in the* Scriptures: "Because Abraham truly trusted in God, *God* considered him to be righteous," and *it is also* stated *in the Scriptures,* "He was 'God's friend.'" [24] *From the example of Abraham,* you can see that it is because people **do good deeds** that *God* considers them to be righteous, and not **only** because they trust *in him.* [25] Similarly, it was certainly *because of* what Rahab **did,** that *God* considered her to be a righteous, *obedient* person. Rahab was *previously* a prostitute, but she cared for the Israelite men who came *to spy out the land* and *helped them to escape by* sending them home on a different road.

[26] Remember that when people's spirits *permanently leave their* bodies*, their bodies* are dead *and useless.* Similarly, *as for those who say,* "I trust *in God,*" but don't do *things to help others, what they say about trusting in God* is useless.

3

James 3:1-12

THEME: Not many of you should become teachers, because God will judge teachers with greater severity than he will judge others. You should all strive to speak rightly, because what you say has a powerful effect on others, and it is often destructive and hypocritical.

[1] My fellow believers, not many of you should *desire to* become teachers *of God's truth, because* you know *that God* will judge us, who teach, more severely *than he will judge others.* [2] It is true that we **all** in many ways do what is wrong. But those who always control what they say will be all that God intended them to be. They will be able to control all their actions. [3] *To illustrate*, if we put *a small* bit into the mouth of a horse to make the horse obey us, we can make the horse turn *and go where we want it to.* [4] Think also about ships. *Although* a ship may be very large and *although* it can be moved by strong winds, by *turning* a very small rudder we can direct the ship wherever we want *it to go.* [5] Similarly, *although* our tongues are very small, *if we don't control them* we can *harm* **many** people by what we proudly say. Think *also* about how *just* a **small flame** can set a **large forest** on fire. [6] *Just as a fire damages a forest*, when we say things that are evil, *we harm many people.* What we say reveals that there is much evil within us. What we say contaminates

all we think and do. *Just like a flame easily* sets on fire *the whole surrounding area*, what we say can cause *others* to want to do evil. It is the devil himself who causes us to speak what is evil. [7] Indeed, although people are able to tame all kinds of wild animals, birds, reptiles and creatures that live in the water, and people have tamed them, [8] no person on his own is able to tame his tongue *and control what he says*. And when people speak evilly, *it shows that* they are uncontrolled and wicked. *As* the poison *of a snake kills people, we harm others* by what we say. [9] We use our tongue to praise God, who is our Lord and Father, but we also use our same tongue to ask God to do evil to people. *That is very wrong, because* God made people like himself. [10] With our same mouth we praise God, but we wish evil *on other*s. My fellow believers, this should not be! [11] Surely bitter water and good water don't come out of the same spring. [12] My fellow believers, a fig tree can't produce olives. Nor can a grapevine produce figs. Neither can a salty spring produce good *water. In the same way, we should speak only what is good, and we should not speak what is evil.*

James 3:13-18

THEME: If you are jealous of others and self-seeking, don't boast that you are wise. Instead, demonstrate that you are truly wise by doing good and by acting peaceably and compassionately toward others.

[13] If any of you thinks that *you are* wise and know a lot, you should always act in a good way to show people that your good deeds are the result of *your being truly* wise. Being wise *helps us to act* gently *toward others.* [14] But if in your hearts you are intensely jealous and always want to have your own way, you should not say *that you are wise, for by boasting like that,* you are saying that *what God says about you* is not true. [15] Those who have such *attitudes are* not wise in the way God *wants them to be.* Instead, they are only thinking and acting as *ungodly people do.* They think and act according to their own *evil* desires. They do what the demons *want them to do.*[9] [16] *Keep in mind that* people who have such attitudes are unruly and *do* all kinds of evil things. [17] But *when people* are wise in the way **God** *wants them to be*, they are pure in every way, which is very important *in his* sight. They also *live* in peace with *others*, they are considerate of others, they are willing to yield to *the wishes of* others, they have compassion *on others,* and they do all kinds of good things *for others. The way they treat others does not* depend on others' status, and they are sincere *in all they do.* [18] Those who *live in* **peace** *with others* cause the *others to also live in* peace, with the result that they all live together, *acting* righteously.

4

James 4:1-3

THEME: You are fighting among yourselves because of your evil desires, and you are never getting what you want because you pray with wrong motives.

[1] Now I will tell you why you are fighting among yourselves and quarreling with each other. It is because each of you *wants to do the evil things you enjoy doing.* You keep on wanting to enjoy things that are opposed *to what God wants you to do.* [2] There are things you *very much* desire to have, but you don't get *those things, so* you *want to* kill *those who hinder you from getting them.* You desire what *other people have,* but you are unable to get *what you desire, so* you quarrel and fight *with one another.* You don't have *what you*

---

[9] OR, ...They think and act as demons *do.*

desire because you don't ask *God for it.* [3] *And even when* you do ask *him,* he does not give you *what you ask for* because you are asking **for the wrong reason.** *You are asking for things* in order that you may use them just **to enjoy yourselves.**

James 4:4-6

THEME: You are unfaithful to God and are behaving as evil people do, so you have become God's enemies, but he wants to help you. He opposes the proud, but he helps those who are humble.

[4] *Like* a woman who is unfaithful to her husband, you *are being unfaithful to God.* Those who are behaving as evil people do are hostile toward God.[h] Perhaps you don't realize that. So if anyone chooses to act as evil people do, he becomes an **enemy of God.** [5] Surely you don't think that **it is for no reason** that *God told us in* the Scriptures that he eagerly desires that his Spirit, who lives in us, will help us to love *God* only! [6] No, *he has a reason for desiring that.* It is that he in his kindness *to us* wants very much to help us. That is why *King Solomon* wrote *in the Scriptures,* "God opposes **those who are proud,** but he helps those who are **humble.**"

James 4:7-10

THEME: So submit yourselves to God and resist the devil. Stop doing wrong and thinking wrong thoughts. Be sorry for having sinned. Humble yourselves before God, and he will honor you.

[7] So submit yourselves to God. Resist the devil, and *as a result* he will run away from you. [8] Come near *spiritually* to God, and *as a result* he will come near to you. You who are sinners, stop doing what is wrong and do only what is good. You who can't decide *whether you will commit yourselves to God,* stop thinking wrong thoughts, and think only pure thoughts. [9] Be sorrowful and weep *because of the wrong you have done.* Don't laugh, *enjoying just what you yourselves selfishly desire.* Instead, be sad *because you have done what is wrong.* [10] Humble yourselves before the Lord, and *as a result* he will honor you.

James 4:11-12

THEME: Stop speaking evil against one another and thus condemning each other. Only God has the right to condemn people.

[11] My fellow believers, stop speaking evil against one another, *because* those who speak evil against a fellow believer and *thus* condemn *one who is like* a brother *to them* are really speaking against the law *that God gave us to obey. In this law, God commanded us* to *love others,* and those who speak evil against fellow believers are, *in effect,* saying *by what they do* that we don't have to do what *God* commanded. If you say that you don't have to obey those commands, you are not obeying God's law. Instead, you are claiming that you *have the authority* to condemn *others.* [12] *But in fact,* there is only **one** who *has the authority to* tell *people* what is right to do and to condemn *them, and that is God.* He alone is able to save *people* or to destroy *them. So,* **you** certainly have no right to condemn people!

---

h   OR, …Those who love *the evil pleasures of* this world are hostile to God.

James 4:13-16

THEME: You should not boast about what you will do in the future, because life is transitory. Instead, you should plan to do whatever God wants you to do, because boasting about what you want to do, rather than considering the will of God, is sinful.

[13] *Some of you* are *arrogantly* saying, "Today or tomorrow we will go to a certain city. We will spend a year there, and we will buy and sell things and make a lot of money." Now, you listen to me! [14] *You shouldn't talk like that, because* you don't know what will happen tomorrow, and you don't know *how long* you will live. Your life *is short, like* a mist that appears for a short time and then disappears. [15] Instead of *what you are saying*, you should say, "If the Lord wills, we will live and do this or that." [16] But what you are doing is boasting about all the things that you arrogantly *plan to do*. Your boasting like that is evil.

[17] So if anyone knows the right thing that he ought to do, *but* he does not do it, he is **sinning**.

5

James 5:1-6

THEME: The rich people who oppress you should weep because they will suffer much. God will punish them because they have unjustly caused others to suffer.

[1] Now *I have something to say to* the rich people *who don't believe in Christ and who oppress you.* Listen *to me,* you rich people! You should weep and wail *loudly* because you will experience terrible troubles. [2] Your wealth *of various kinds* is *worthless, as though it were* rotted. Your fine clothes are *worthless, as though they were* ruined by termites. [3] Your gold and silver are *worthless, as though they were* corroded. *When God judges you,* this worthless wealth of yours will be evidence that you are guilty *of being greedy,* and as rust and fire *destroy* things, *God* will severely punish you. You have *in vain* stored up *wealth* in a time when *God* is about to *judge you.* [4] Think *about what you have done.* You have not paid wages to the workmen who have harvested your fields for you, *with the result that* those reapers are crying out *to God for him to help them. And God*, the all-powerful Lord, has heard their loud cries. [5] You have lived in luxury, just to have pleasure *here* on earth. *Just as cattle fatten themselves, not realizing that* they will be slaughtered, you have *lived just for pleasure, not realizing that God will severely punish you.* [6] You have *caused* innocent people to be condemned. You have caused some people to be killed. *And even though* those people had not done anything wrong, they were not *able to* defend themselves against you. *My fellow believers, that is what I say to the rich people who oppress you*!

James 5:7-11

THEME: So wait patiently for the Lord Jesus Christ to return and judge all people fairly. Do not complain against each other, lest Jesus judge you when he returns. From the examples of the prophets and Job, we know that God blesses and rewards those who patiently endure suffering.

[7] So, my fellow believers, *although rich people cause you to suffer*, be patient until the Lord *Jesus Christ* comes *back*. Remember that when farmers *plant a field*, they wait for their valuable crop to grow. They have to wait patiently for the rain *that comes* at the planting season and for more rain *that comes* just before the harvest season. They wait *for* the crops *to grow and mature before they can harvest them.* [8] *Similarly,* **you also** should wait

patiently and be strong in your faith in the Lord *Jesus*, because he is coming *back* soon *and will judge all people fairly.* [9] My fellow believers, don't complain against each other, lest you be condemned *and punished by the Lord Jesus*. It is **he who will judge** us, and he is **ready to appear**. [10] My fellow believers, as an example *of how to be patient*, consider the prophets whom the Lord *God sent long ago* to speak his messages. *Although people caused* them to suffer much, they endured it patiently. [11] And we know that *God* approves of those who endure *suffering for him*. You have heard about Job. You know that *although he suffered much,* the Lord *God* finally brought good *to Job because* he **endured** *that suffering.*[i] *And from that we know* that the Lord is very compassionate and kind.

James 5:12

THEME: Do not say, "If I am lying, may God punish me." Instead, always tell the truth, lest God condemn you.

[12] Also, my fellow believers, *I want to say* something important *about how you talk. If you say you will do something*, don't say, "If I don't do it, may *God in* heaven punish me." Don't even say, "If I don't do it, may *someone here on* earth punish me." Don't say anything like that. Instead, if you say 'Yes,' then *do what you said you would do.* If you say 'No,' then don't *do it.* Otherwise, *God* will condemn you.

James 5:13-18

THEME: Whatever your circumstances are, pray trusting in God, and he will certainly help you, both physically and spiritually. So confess your sins to each other and pray for each other, because God answers prayer.

[13] Those of you who are experiencing trouble should pray *to God for help. Those who* are cheerful should sing songs of praise *to God.* [14] Those who are sick should call the leaders of the congregation *to come to pray for them.* The leaders should put *olive* oil on them and, with the Lord's authority, pray. [15] And if they truly trust *in the Lord* when they pray, the sick people will be healed. The Lord will heal them. And if they have sinned *in a way that caused them to be sick, if they confess what they did that was wrong, the Lord* will forgive them. [16] So, *because the Lord is able to heal the sick and to forgive sin*, tell each other the sinful things you have done, and pray for each other in order that *God* may heal you *physically and spiritually.* If righteous people *pray and* asks *God to do something, God* will act powerfully and will certainly do it. [17] *Although the prophet* Elijah was an ordinary human being like us, he earnestly prayed that it would not rain. *As a result*, it did not rain for three and a half years. [18] Then he prayed again, *asking God to send rain*, and *as a result God* sent rain, and plants *grew and* produced crops *again.*

James 5:19-20

THEME: If anyone turns away from God's true message, you believers should urge him to once again obey God so that his many sins will be forgiven.

[19] My fellow believers, if anyone of you stops obeying the true message *from God*, someone from among you should persuade that person to once again do *what God has told us to do.* [20] *If he stops doing what is wrong*, the one *who persuaded him* should realize that *because* he has enabled the person who was sinning to stop doing what is wrong,

---

[i]   OR, …*Because* he **continued** *to trust God,* the Lord *God* finally brought good *to Job.*

God will save that person from being separated from him forever, and will forgive *his* many sins.

The Apostle Peter wrote letters to his fellow believers. We call this letter

1 Peter

1

1 Peter 1:1-2

THEME: I am writing this letter to Jewish believers who have been scattered throughout five provinces in Asia Minor. I wish them God's blessings.

¹ I, Peter, who *have been commissioned by* Jesus Christ to be an apostle, *am writing this letter* to you believers whom God has chosen to belong to him. *You are living* in *the Roman provinces of* Pontus, Galatia, Cappadocia, Asia, and Bithynia. *Just as the Jews who long ago lived in Israel were* scattered *to other countries far from their homes*, you now live *far from* heaven, *which is your true home.* ² God our Father chose you according to what he himself decided previously. His Spirit has set you apart in order that you would obey Jesus Christ. And *just as Moses* sprinkled *the Israelites with blood when God established the old covenant, Jesus wanted to establish his new covenant with you* with the blood *which flowed from his body when he died.* May God act with great kindness to you, and may he give you much *inner* peace.

1 Peter 1:3-12

THEME: God has done great things for you. Although you are now enduring trials to test your faith, you are rejoicing about your salvation. That salvation is something the prophets who lived long ago did not fully understand.

³ Praise God, who is the Father of our Lord Jesus Christ! It is because of his great mercy to *us that he has given us new life.* Because he has caused Jesus Christ to become alive again after he died, he has enabled us to live very confidently, fully expecting to receive the things *that he has promised to give us.* ⁴ He has enabled us to expect to receive an absolutely imperishable inheritance that he has preserved in heaven for us. ⁵ God, by his mighty power, is guarding you as you trust in Jesus. *He is keeping you safe so* that he may, at the end of the time in which we now live,[a] completely deliver us *from Satan's power.* ⁶ You rejoice because of what will happen then, but now you are grieving for a short time as *God is allowing* you to be tested, *as tests precious metals are tested to see if they are pure. These trials you are experiencing are necessary* ⁷ to prove that you really do trust in Jesus, to prove that your faith *in him* is genuine. And that is more valuable than gold, *which does not last forever even* though it is purified *by being put it in a hot* fire. As a result of your passing the test *and proving that your faith is genuine,* God will honor you very highly when Jesus Christ comes again. ⁸ You love *Jesus,* although you have not seen him. Although you do not see him now, you rejoice very much ⁹ because you are experiencing the result of your believing in him; that is, *God* is saving you *from the guilt of your sins.*

ᵃ OR, ...so that he may, when Jesus returns...

¹⁰ As for those who *long ago* spoke messages that God had revealed to them about the way God would show his kindness to you, they investigated very carefully about how God would save you. ¹¹ They inquired into whom the Spirit of Christ that was in them was referring to, and what time he was talking about, when he told beforehand that the Messiah would suffer *and die*, and that glorious things would happen *to him and to us* afterwards. ¹² *God* told to them that it was not for their own sake that he was revealing these things to them, but that it was for your sake. It was these things *that were being proclaimed to you* by those who told you the message *about Christ*. They declared them to you because the Holy Spirit whom *God* sent from heaven *enabled them to do so*. And even angels would like to know more about these *truths about how God saves us*.

1 Peter 1:13-25

THEME: You must live holy and reverent lives and love each other, because Christ has bought you and given you a new life.

¹³ So, *prepare your minds as people* fasten their belts around their waists *to prepare to work*. *What I mean is that* you should discipline your minds, and by doing that, live in full and confident expectation of the good things *God will* in his kindness *do for you* when Jesus Christ returns *from heaven*. ¹⁴ *And because you ought to obey your heavenly Father* as children *ought to* obey their fathers *here on earth*, don't do the evil deeds that you used to desire to do when you did not know *God's truth*. ¹⁵ Instead, just as God, the one who chose you, is holy, you also must be holy in everything you do, ¹⁶ because it is written *in the Scriptures that God said*, "You must be holy because I am holy."

¹⁷ And since you call the one who impartially judges what each one does 'Father,' conduct yourselves reverently during the time you are living here on earth. *While you are living here, you are* like exiles *because you are away from your true home in heaven.* ¹⁸ *Conduct your lives reverently* because you know that *God* bought you to free you from your useless life-style that you learned from your ancestors. He paid something more enduring than the things that will not last forever, things like gold and silver. *God* bought you to free you from your useless life-style that you learned from your ancestors. ¹⁹ It was with the precious blood of Christ *that flowed from his body when he died that he bought you. Christ's death was a perfect sacrifice for us, like* the lambs that *the Jewish priests sacrificed were* perfect, without any blemishes or spots. ²⁰ On the one hand, he was chosen *by God* before the world was created. But on the other hand, it was not until now, *when the time in which we are living* will soon end, that *God* revealed him for your sake. ²¹ Because of what Christ has done, you are trusting in God, who caused him to become alive again after he died, and greatly honored him. As a result, God is the one in whom you are trusting and confidently expecting *to do great things for you*.

²² Because you have been made pure by obeying the truth, with the result that you sincerely love your fellow believers, continue to love each other earnestly and sincerely. ²³ *I ask you to do this, because now you have* a new life. It was not *by means of* something that will perish that you received this new life. Instead, it was *by means of* something that will last forever; namely, by the life-giving and enduring message of God. ²⁴ *We know this is true* because, *as Isaiah wrote*,

All people *will perish*, like grass *perishes*.
And all the greatness of humans is *only temporary*,
    like the flowers *that grow up* in the grass.
The grass withers and the flowers die,
    ²⁵ but God's message lasts forever.

This message *that lasts* is the message *about Christ* that was proclaimed to you.

2

1 Peter 2:1-10

THEME: Do not act maliciously or act hypocritically. God is joining you together into a holy group indwelt by his Spirit, to do deeds that are pleasing to him.

[1] So, don't act maliciously in any way or deceive others. Don't try to make others think you have qualities you don't really have, and don't envy others. Don't ever slander anyone. [2] Just as newborn babies *long for their mothers'* pure milk, you should long for *God's* spiritual *truth,* so that by learning it you may become *spiritually* mature. *You need to* do this until the day when God *will* deliver you completely *from all the evil in this world.* [3] *You need to do this* because you have experienced the Lord's goodness to you.

[4] You have come to the Lord Jesus. He is *like the cornerstone of a building, but he is* living, *not lifeless like a stone.* He was rejected by *many* people, but God chose him and *considers him* to be very precious. [5] *And like men* build houses with stones, *God* is causing you to be joined together into a group in which *God's* Spirit *lives,* in order that you, *like* priests *who offer* sacrifices, might *do deeds* that are pleasing to God because of what Jesus Christ *did for us.* [6] *What Isaiah wrote* in the Scriptures *shows us this is true.* He wrote *these words that God* said:

Pay attention to this: I am placing in Jerusalem *one who is like* an extremely valuable cornerstone, and those who believe in him will never be disappointed.

[7] So, *God will* honor you who believe in *Jesus.* But those who *refuse to* believe in him *are like the builders* that this Scripture *talks about*:

The stone that the builders rejected has become the cornerstone.

[8] And *it is also written in the Scriptures*,

He will be like a stone that causes people to stumble,
    and like a rock that people trip over.
Just as people are injured when they stumble over a rock,
    people who disobey the message *about Jesus are injured spiritually*,
    and that is what *God* determined would happen to them.

[9] But you are people whom God has chosen. You are *a group that represents God like* priests do, and you rule with God like kings. You are a holy group of people. You are people who belong to God. This is in order that you might proclaim the virtues of *God. He has* called you from *your former ways, when you were ignorant of his truth,* into the marvelous *understanding that he gives us. He has called you* out of *spiritual* darkness into *spiritual* light. [10] *What the prophet Hosea wrote is true of you*,

Formerly, you were not a people *who had a relationship with God,*
But now you are God's people.
At one time *God* had not acted mercifully toward you,
But now he has acted mercifully toward you.

1 Peter 2:11-12

THEME: Avoid obeying your self-directed natures. Behave in a good way among unbelievers.

[11] You people whom I love, I urge you to consider that you are like foreigners *whose real home is in heaven,* and as a result, avoid doing the things that your self-directed nature desires, because those desires fight against your souls. [12] Keep behaving in a good way among those who don't know God. *If you do that,* although they may accuse you of doing

what is evil, they will see your good behavior, and at the time when God comes *to judge people*, they will say that what God does is right.

1 Peter 2:13-17

THEME: Submit yourselves to human authorities, and act as servants of God should.

[13] For the sake of the Lord *Jesus*, submit yourselves to every human authority. That includes submitting yourselves to the king, who is the most important authority, [14] and to governors, who are sent by the king to punish those who do what is wrong and to commend those who do what is right. [15] What God wants is for you to do *only* what is good so that foolish people who do not know *how Christians behave* will be unable to say things *to condemn you.* [16] Conduct your lives as though you were free *from having to obey authorities,* but don't think 'Since I am free from having to obey authorities, I can do what is evil.' Instead, act as servants of God *should.* [17] Act respectfully toward everyone. Love all your fellow believers. Revere God, and honor the king.

1 Peter 2:18-25

THEME: You slaves must submit yourselves to your masters, even if they mistreat you. Imitate Christ in the way he in which suffered unjustly.

[18] You slaves *who are believers*, submit yourselves to your masters with complete respect for them. Submit yourselves not only to those who *act in a* good and kind way towards you, but also submit yourselves to those who *act in a* harsh way *towards you.* [19] You should do that because God is pleased with those who, knowing that he is aware of what is happening to them, endure the pain they suffer *because of being treated unjustly by their masters.* [20] But God will certainly not be pleased with you if you do something that is wrong and as a result you are beaten! But if, instead of doing wrong, you do what is good, and as a result of that, you suffer for doing what is good, and you endure that suffering, God will commend you. [21] *Suffering is part of God's plan for you. It is one of his reasons for* choosing you. When Christ suffered for you, he left you an example, in order that you would imitate what he did. [22] *Remember how Christ behaved,*
He never sinned, and he never said anything to deceive people.
[23] When *people* insulted him, he did not insult them in return.
When people caused him to suffer, he did not threaten *to get revenge.*
Instead, he left his case in the hands of *God, who always* judges justly.
[24] He himself endured *the punishment for* our sins in his body *when he died* on the cross,
    in order that we would stop sinning[b] and begin living righteous *lives.*
It is because he was wounded that your *souls have been saved from being sinful,*
    as people's bodies are healed *from being sick.*
[25] Truly, you were like sheep that had gone astray, but now you have returned to *Jesus,*
    who cares for your souls *as* a shepherd *cares for his sheep.*

---

[b] OR, …in order that we would no longer respond to sinful desires…

3

1 Peter 3:1-6

THEME: You women should submit yourselves to your husbands, even if they are not believers, and make your hearts beautiful with qualities that will not fade away.

[1] You women *believers*, just as *slaves should submit themselves to their masters,* submit yourselves to your husbands. Do that in order that if any of them do not believe the message *about Christ,* they may become believers without *it being necessary for* you to say anything to them *about their relationship to God.* [2] *They will believe in Christ* when they see that you respect them and that your way of life is pure. [3] Do not be *trying to make* yourselves beautiful outwardly, such as by your hair *style* or by wearing gold jewelry and fine clothes. [4] Instead, make your hearts *beautiful* with qualities that will not fade away. Have a humble and quiet attitude, which is something God considers to be very valuable. [5] The devout women who lived long ago who trusted in God made themselves beautiful *by having attitudes* like that, and by being submissive to their husbands. [6] Sarah, for example, obeyed *her husband* Abraham and called him 'my master'. You will be *as though you are* her daughters if you do what is right and are not afraid *of what your husbands or anyone else may do to you because you are believers.*

1 Peter 3:7

THEME: You men must live in an appropriate way with your wives, so that nothing will hinder your prayers.

[7] You men *who are believers*, just as your wives should respect you, you should live in an appropriate way with them. Treat them respectfully, realizing that they are *usually* weaker than you are, and realizing that they share with you the gift *that God* in his kindness *has given to you, which is eternal* life. Do this so that nothing will hinder you from praying.[c]

1 Peter 3:8-12

THEME: Agree with each other, love each other, be humble, and bless those who do evil to you instead of retaliating.

[8] To conclude *this part of my letter*, I say to all of you, agree with each other *in what you think*. Be sympathetic *toward each other*. Love *each other as* members of the same family *should*. Act compassionately *toward each other*. Be humble. [9] *When people do* evil things to you or insult you, don't do evil things to them or insult them in return. Instead, *ask God to* bless them, because that is what *you have been chosen by God* to do, in order that you may receive a blessing *from him.* [10] *Consider what the Psalmist wrote about the proper way of living,*

As for those who want to enjoy life
  and experience good *things happening to them every* day,
  they must not speak what is evil or speak words that deceive others.
[11] They must *continually* turn away from *doing what is* evil,
  and must do what is good *instead.*
They must have a deep desire
  to see people *live in* peace toward each other;
  they must zealously *urge people to live in* peace,

---

[c] OR, …nothing will hinder God from answering when you pray.

¹² because the Lord sees what righteous people do
and he appreciates what they do.
He listens to righteous people when they pray *and he answers them.*
But he is opposed to those who do evil.

1 Peter 3:13-22

THEME: Do good to others, even if you suffer for doing it, as Christ did.

¹³ If you are eager to do good deeds, *most people* will not harm you. ¹⁴ But even if you suffer because of *doing* what is right, *God* will bless you. *Do as Isaiah wrote*: 'Don't be afraid of people who threaten you, and don't worry about what they *might do to you.*' ¹⁵ Instead, acknowledge in your hearts that Christ is the one who is in complete control *of your lives.* Always be ready to answer everyone who asks that you tell them about what you confidently expect *God to do for you.* ¹⁶ But answer them humbly and respectfully, and make sure that you do nothing wrong, in order that those who speak evil about you may be ashamed when they see the good way in which you are conducting yourselves because of your relationship with Christ. ¹⁷ *It may be God's will for you* to suffer for doing what is good. But it is better to do that, *even you suffer for doing them*, than to do evil deeds and suffer *for doing that.* ¹⁸ *I say that* because Christ died once for the sake of people who have sinned. He was a righteous person who died for unrighteous people. He died in order that he might bring us to God. *During the time he had* an ordinary body, he was killed, but *God's* Spirit caused him to become alive again. ¹⁹ The Spirit also helped him as he went to proclaim *God's victory to the evil* spirits whom God had imprisoned *in the heavens.*^d ²⁰ Long ago, during the time that Noah was building a big boat, *those evil spirits* disobeyed God when he waited patiently *to see if people would turn from their evil behavior.* Only a few people were saved *in that boat.* Specifically, *God* brought only eight persons safely through the waters *of the flood, while all the others drowned in it.* ²¹ That water, *by means of which eight people were saved when God punished the other people,* represents *the water in which we are* baptized *to show that God has* saved us *from punishment.* The water in which we are baptized does not remove dirt from our bodies. Instead, *it shows that* we are requesting *God to assure us* that he has removed our guilt *for having sinned.* And because Jesus Christ became alive again after he died, *we know that God accepted his sacrifice for us and thus was able to remove our guilt.* ²² Christ has gone into heaven and is ruling in the place of highest honor, next to God, now that all the evil and powerful spirit beings have been made subject to him.

4

1 Peter 4:1-6

THEME: Think as Christ did when he suffered, and conduct your lives as God wants you to, not doing the immoral things you used to do.

¹ So, because Christ suffered in his body, you also must think the way he did *when he was willing to suffer,* because those who suffer in their bodies *because of belonging to Jesus* have stopped sinning *the way they used to sin.* ² As a result, during their remaining time here on earth, they don't do the things that sinful people desire to do, but instead they do the things God wants them to do. ³ *I say that to you* because you have already spent too

---

^d OR, …to proclaim *God's victory to the* spirits of those who had died, and who were in the place where the spirits of dead people are.

much of your time *here on earth* doing what the people who do not know God like to do. In the past you committed all kinds of sexually immoral acts, you got drunk and then participated in orgies, you caroused *with others*, and you *worshiped* idols, which is abominable. ⁴ *Because you used to do those things*, *your friends* are surprised that you do not join with them any more when they participate in that kind of wild behavior *that is rushing to destroy them like* a flood. As a result, they speak evil about you. ⁵ But *God* is ready to judge the people who are living *now* and the people who have died, and he is the one who will decide whether he approves of what they have done. ⁶ That is the reason the message *about Christ* was preached to believers who have now died. *That message was preached to them* in order that even though *sinful* people might judge them *and say they are guilty*, God's Spirit would *enable them to* live *eternally*.

1 Peter 4:7-11

THEME: Keep thinking sensibly. Love each other earnestly. Provide hospitality to others. Use your spiritual gifts well. Do kind deeds with all the energy you have.

⁷ It is almost the time when all things on this earth will come to an end. So, keep thinking sensibly and control your thoughts, so that you can pray *clearly*. ⁸ Most important of all, love each other earnestly, because if we love others, we will just ignore many of the sinful things *they do to us*. ⁹ Provide food and a place to sleep for those *who come to your community, and do it* without complaining. ¹⁰ Each believer should use the spiritual gifts that God has given them to serve others. They should use well the various gifts that God in his kindness has given them. ¹¹ Those who speak *to the congregation* should do that as though they are speaking the *very* words of God. Those who do kind deeds to others should do it with the strength that God gives them, in order that God may be honored as Jesus Christ *enables us to do so. I pray that we will* praise God and give him the authority *to rule over us* forever. May it be so!

1 Peter 4:12-19

THEME: Do not be surprised about your sufferings for being Christians, and don't be ashamed when that happens. Instead, commit yourselves to God.

¹² You whom I love, do not be surprised about the painful things you are suffering *because you belong to Christ. Those things are testing you like people test metals by putting* them in a fire. Don't think that something strange is happening to you. ¹³ Instead, rejoice that you are suffering the same kinds of things that Christ endured. Rejoice *in your sufferings*, in order that you may also be very glad when Christ returns and reveals how glorious he is. ¹⁴ If you are insulted because you believe in Christ, *God is* pleased with you, because it shows that the Spirit of God, the Spirit who reveals how great *God is*, lives within you. ¹⁵ If you suffer, do not let that suffering be the result of your being a murderer or a thief or as a result of doing some other evil deed, or as a result of interfering in someone else's affairs. ¹⁶ But if you suffer because of being a Christian, do not be ashamed about it. Instead, praise God that you are suffering because of belonging to Christ. ¹⁷ I say that because the time has now come for God to start judging people, and first he will judge those who belong to him. Since he will judge us believers first, how terrible will his judging be for those who do not obey the good message that comes from him! ¹⁸ *That will be as it is written in the Scriptures:*

> *Many* righteous people *will have to suffer*
>   many *difficult trials before being taken to heaven.*
> So ungodly and sinful people will surely have to suffer
>   *much severe punishment from God!*

[19] So, those who suffer because of its being God's will that they suffer *because of being Christians* should commit themselves to God, the one who created them and the one who always does what he promises to do. And they should continue to do what is right.

5

1 Peter 5:1-7

THEME: You elders must care for your congregations with enthusiasm, not being greedy for money or acting like bosses. Instead, be examples to them.

[1] *Now I will say this to those among* you who are elders in the congregations: I also am an elder. I am one *of those* who saw Christ when he suffered, and I am also one who will share some of the glory Christ has in heaven. [2] *I appeal to you elders* to take care of the people in your *congregations* as shepherds *take care of their* flocks of sheep. Do this, not because you must do it, but instead do it willingly, as God desires. Don't be greedy to get a lot *of money for doing it,* but do it enthusiastically. [3] Don't act like domineering *bosses over* the people whom God has entrusted to you, but be examples to them by the way in which you conduct your lives. [4] *If you do that,* when Jesus, who is like our chief shepherd, appears, he will give each of you a glorious reward. That reward will be like the wreaths *that are given to victorious athletes,* but your reward will never wither *like wreaths do.*

[5] *Now I will say this to* you young men *and women.* You must subject yourselves to *the authority of* the leaders *of the congregation.* And all of you *believers* should act humbly toward each other, because *this proverb is true,*
God opposes people who are proud,
    but he treats with kindness those who are humble.

[6] So, realizing that God has great power *to punish proud people,* humble yourselves in order that he may honor you at the time *he has determined.* [7] Since he takes care of you, let him take care of all the things you are worried about.

1 Peter 5:8-11

THEME: Resist the devil by always being alert and trusting in Christ's message, remembering that believers everywhere are also suffering as you are.

[8] Always be alert with your full attention, because the devil, who is your enemy, is going around, looking for people *to destroy. He is* like a lion who roars as it prowls around, seeking someone to *kill and* devour. [9] You must resist him by continuing to firmly trust in *Christ and his message,* remembering that your fellow believers all over the world are experiencing similar sufferings *that the devil is bringing to them.* [10] God is the one who in his kindness helps us in every *situation,* and *he is the one* who chose us to share his eternal glory *in heaven* because of our relationship with Christ. *And* after you have suffered for awhile *because of things people do to harm you,* he will remove your spiritual defects, he will strengthen you *spiritually,* and he will support you *emotionally.* [11] *I pray that* he will *rule* powerfully forever. May it be so!

1 Peter 5:12-14

THEME: I have written this short message to encourage you. The believers here, including Mark, greet you. May God give you inner peace.

¹² Silas has written this letter *for me as I have dictated it to him.* I consider him to be a faithful fellow believer. I have written this short letter to you to encourage you, and I want to assure you that *what I have written* is a true message about the things God in his kindness does for us. Continue to firmly believe this message.

¹³ In *this city which is sometimes referred to as* 'Babylon', the believers, whom *God* has chosen *to belong to him* just as he chose you, send you their greetings. Mark, who is *like* a son to me, also *sends his greetings to you all.* ¹⁴ Greet each other with a kiss *on the cheek* to *show how* you love *each other. I pray that God will give inner* peace to all of you who have a relationship with Christ.

The Apostle Peter wrote letters to his fellow believers. We call this letter

2 Peter

1

2 Peter 1:1-2

THEME: I, Simon Peter, am writing this letter to you whom God has caused to believe in Christ just as we apostles believe in Christ. I pray that God will bless you greatly.

¹I, Simon Peter, *am writing this letter to you. I* serve Jesus Christ, and am an apostle *appointed by* him. *I am sending this letter to you* whom God has caused to believe *in Christ* just as he *caused us apostles to believe in Christ.* You and we have equally been given the privilege of believing in Jesus Christ. He *is* God, he is righteous, he is the one we *worship,* and he is our Savior. ²*I pray that God* will continue to act with kindness towards you, and give you a deep *inner* peace, because you *truly* know God and Jesus who is our Lord.

2 Peter 1:3-4

THEME: God has given us everything that we need to receive eternal life and to live godly lives.

³*God* has given us everything *we need* to receive *eternal* life and to live godly *lives.* He gives us all that by the power of being God, and he has also given it to us as a result of our knowing him. He is the one who by his own glorious and perfect *nature* chose us *to be his people.* ⁴By means of this *glorious and perfect nature* he has promised us *that he will do* very great and priceless things *for us. He has also promised* you that by *believing what he has promised* you will be able to act *righteously*, just as God acts *righteously.* He has also promised that you will be free from being morally depraved, and not *be like* those who do not believe in Christ are, because of their desire to do what is evil.

2 Peter 1:5-11

THEME: Exert yourselves to the utmost to develop a stable Christian character.

⁵Because God has done all that, by exerting yourselves strenuously, make sure that you not only believe *in Christ*, but that you are also living morally good lives. And make sure that you are not only living morally good lives, but that you also know *what God desires.*[a] ⁶And make sure that you not only know *what God desires,* but that you also control what you say and do. And make sure that you not only control what you say and do, but that you are also steadfast *when you are caused to suffer.* And make sure that you are not only steadfast, but that you are also godly. ⁷And make sure that you are not only godly, but that you also have a concern for your fellow believers, as brothers and sisters *ought to have* for each other. And make sure that you not only have a concern for your fellow

---

[a] OR, …but that you also behave wisely.

believers, but that you love *others.* [8] If you do those *things,* and if *you do them* more and more, that demonstrates that knowing our Lord Jesus Christ is producing good results in your lives. [9] If these *qualities* are not present in people, it means they are *not aware of the importance of these things, just as* blind people *are not aware of what is around them.* They *think only about earthly matters, just as* a shortsighted person *sees clearly only things that are near.* It seems that they have forgotten that God has forgiven them for their former sinful lives. [10] Instead of *acting like those people,* try to confirm by the way you conduct your lives that you are among those *God* has chosen to be his people. If you do that, you will certainly never become separated from God, [11] and *God* will very warmly welcome you into the place where our Lord and Savior Jesus Christ will rule forever.

2 Peter 1:12-15

THEME: I intend to keep reminding you very frequently about these matters.

[12] I intend to keep on reminding you very frequently about these *matters,* even though you *already* know them and are firmly convinced that they are true. [13] I consider it right that I should help you *to continually think about these matters* by reminding you *about them* as long as I am alive, [14] because I know that I shall die soon, just as our Lord Jesus Christ clearly has revealed to me. [15] Moreover, I shall make every effort *by writing these things down* to enable you to remember them at all times after I have died.

2 Peter 1:16-21

THEME: You can be sure that these matters are true, because we apostles ourselves witnessed that our Lord Jesus Christ is supremely great, and also because what the prophets say about him is completely reliable.

[16] We *apostles* told you that our Lord Jesus Christ *acts* powerfully and that he is coming back *some day.* We were not basing *what we told you* on stories that we had cleverly invented. Instead, we told you what we ourselves saw with our own eyes, that *the* Lord Jesus is supremely great. [17] God, our Father, greatly honored him when God's great glory surrounded him, and God said, "This is my Son, whom I love very much; I am very pleased with him." [18] We ourselves heard God *say* that from heaven, when we were with *Christ* on that holy mountain. [19] We also have what the prophets *wrote about Christ long ago,* which is completely reliable. You should pay attention to *what they wrote,* because *what they wrote enables you to discern whether what is taught to you is true or whether it is false,* like a lamp that is shining in a dark place *enables people to see where they are going. You should pay attention to what they wrote* until *our Lord Jesus Christ comes back and enables* you *to know God fully, which will be like when* a day dawns and the morning star rises *and we can see it clearly.* [20] It is important that you realize that without *the help of God's Spirit,* no one can interpret by himself *the meaning of* what the prophets wrote *in the Scriptures,* [21] because no human beings decided *to make those prophecies.*[b] On the contrary, those who spoke *messages from God* did so because it was the Holy Spirit who caused them to do *it, and so we must also have the help of the Spirit to interpret their meaning.*

---

[b]   OR, …because no Scripture originated with the prophet himself.

2

2 Peter 2:1-3

THEME: There will be false teachers among you who will behave wickedly and who will entice you to behave in the same way they do. God will certainly destroy them.

[1] Just as there were false prophets among the *Israelite* people *long ago*, so there will also be teachers of false doctrine among you. They will enter *your congregations* without you realizing *that they are false teachers,* and they will injure some people spiritually by what they teach. Specifically, these false teachers will even deny *that* the Lord *Jesus died to* pay for *the guilt of our sins.* As a result, they will soon destroy themselves *spiritually, and God will also punish them.* [2] And many *people* will behave in an extremely immoral manner, imitating the extremely immoral manner in which *these teachers of false doctrine* behave. As a result, *unbelievers* will discredit the true message. [3] Because *the teachers of false doctrine* want a lot of things that other people have, *they think that* by telling you stories they themselves have made up, they will get money from you. *God decided* long ago *that he would* punish them, and he has not fallen asleep! *He will most certainly* destroy them.

2 Peter 2:4-10c

THEME: It is certain that God knows how to rescue those who are godly, and that he knows how to keep those who are unrighteous until the time when he will punish them.

[4] God destroyed the angels who sinned. He threw them into the worst place in hell and confined *them there* in darkness to keep them there until he judges *and punishes them.* [5] He also destroyed *the people who lived in* the world long ago. He saved *only* eight of them, including Noah, who was a righteous preacher. God saved them when he destroyed by a flood *all* the ungodly people *who were living then.* [6] He also condemned the cities of Sodom and Gomorrah, destroying them by burning them completely to ashes. *By doing that* he gave a warning to those who afterwards would live in an ungodly manner. [7] But he rescued *Abraham's nephew,* Lot, who was a righteous *man. Lot* was greatly distressed because the people *in Sodom* were doing such immoral deeds. [8] That righteous *man's* soul was tormented day after day because of seeing and hearing those wicked people behave in such a lawless *manner when he was* living among them. [9] And since the Lord God *preserved Lot, you can be sure that* he knows how to rescue godly people from their sufferings, and *he is able* to keep ungodly *people whom he has started to* punish even now, until the time when he will *bring their* judgment to completion *and punish* them. [10] *He will be especially hard on* those *ungodly teachers of false doctrines* who do the things that their self-directed nature desires and by which they are defiled. Those *teachers of false doctrines* despise *all beings who* rule *over them.*

2 Peter 2:10d-16

THEME: Because those false teachers will behave wickedly and will entice people to do the same things they do, God will destroy them.

Because of the extreme arrogance of *those teachers of false doctrines*, they are not afraid to insult glorious beings *in heaven.*[c] [11] In contrast, angels do not insult *the false teachers* when they are accused by those teachers while the Lord God is watching, even though

---

[c] OR, …glorious beings who rule over people.

the angels are much more powerful *than the teachers of false doctrines.* ¹²Because those *teachers of false doctrines are* like animals that cannot reason things out, they say evil things about *spiritual* things concerning which they know nothing. *As a result,* God will destroy them like *people* destroy *animals, animals* that are born only in order to be captured and destroyed. ¹³God will punish *those false teachers* in return for the unrighteous things they have done. It even pleases them to carouse in the daytime *as well as at night.* And as they indulge themselves just like they want to while feasting with you, they *defile you greatly, as* stains and blotches *defile a clean garment.* ¹⁴They *want to commit* adultery *with every woman* they look at. They never stop seeking opportunities to sin. They entice those who are *spiritually* unstable *to join them. Because of their ever-increasing* greed for more and more things, they are doomed *to eternal punishment.* ¹⁵They have rejected good moral standards. They have imitated *what the prophet* Balaam the son of Bosor *did long ago.* He, *acting very* unrighteously, wanted *the enemies of the Jews* to pay him if he *asked God to curse the Jews.* ¹⁶God rebuked him for having done that which was wrong *and for* behaving very foolishly. And even though donkeys don't speak, *God used* a donkey to hinder Balaam *by enabling it to* speak to him with a human voice.

2 Peter 2:17-22

THEME: Because those false teachers will entice people to behave wickedly, God has reserved darkest hell for them.

¹⁷These *teachers of false doctrines deceive people by promising what they cannot fulfill,* as dried-up springs *deceive people by causing them to expect to get water from them.* They *deceive people* just as clouds that are blown along by strong winds *deceive people by causing them to expect rain, but no rain falls.* So, God has reserved the darkness of hell *for those teachers of false doctrines.* ¹⁸By boasting proudly as they make speeches that are worthless, they lure *into sin* people who have recently *become believers and* have ceased to do the things that wicked people do. They lure them by encouraging them to *do the* evil deeds that their self-directed nature *urges them to do.* ¹⁹*The teachers of false doctrines* tell people that they are free *to do whatever they want to, even though* they themselves are *like* slaves *because their own self-directed nature forces them to do* sinful deeds. *Keep in mind the implications of these well-known words: 'Whenever a person is controlled by something, it is as though* that person has become a slave of what controls him.' ²⁰Those *teachers of false doctrines* learned about our Lord and Savior Jesus Christ. As a result, they stopped doing those deeds that defile *people spiritually.* Since they have begun to do *those evil deeds again,* with the result that they are unable to stop doing such deeds, they are in a worse condition than *they were before they knew Jesus Christ.* ²¹*Because God will severely punish them,* it would have been better for them if they had never known what it means to conduct their lives in a righteous manner. It is too bad that they knew *how to conduct their lives in a righteous manner,* but they rejected the things that God commanded people to do, the things that *we apostles* taught them.ᵈ ²² *The way they are behaving again* is just like these well-known sayings: '*They are like* dogs that return *to eat* their vomit, and *they are like* sows that have washed and then wallow *again* in the mud.'

ᵈ OR, ...the things that *Christ* taught them.

3

2 Peter 3:1-2

THEME: I am writing this letter to you in order to stimulate you to remember what the holy prophets said and what our Lord and Savior commanded.

[1] This letter that I am now writing to you whom I love, is the second *letter* that I have written to you. *I have written both* these *letters to you in order that* by reminding you *about the things you already know, I may* stimulate you to think sincerely *about those things.* [2] *I want you* to remember the words that the holy prophets spoke long ago, and also to remember what our Lord and Savior commanded, things that we, your apostles, told you about.

2 Peter 3:3-10

THEME: Although certain people will ridicule the idea that the Lord Jesus Christ is going to come back, the reason he has not yet come back to judge people is that God is being patient with people; but Jesus will certainly come back and judge people.

[3] It is important for you to understand that in the time *immediately* before Christ comes back, there will be people who will ridicule *the idea of his coming back. Those people will do whatever* evil deeds they wish to do. [4] They will say, *"Although it is was* promised *that Christ* will come back, *nothing has happened that would indicate* that he is coming back. Indeed, since the Christian leaders of previous years died, everything *has remained the same.* Things are as *they always have been* since God created *the world!"* [5] *They will say that because* they deliberately overlook *the fact* that God, by commanding long *ago that it should be so,* caused the heavens to exist, and he caused the earth to come up out of water and be separate from the water. [6] And God, *by commanding that it should be so,* later destroyed the world *that existed* at that time, by causing the earth to be flooded with water. [7] Furthermore, *God, by* commanding *that it should be so,* is preserving the heavens and the earth *that exist* now, and *he* is preserving them until the time when *he* will judge ungodly people, and at that time *he* will destroy the heavens and the earth by burning them. [8] Dear friends, I want you to understand well that the Lord *God is willing to wait a long time to judge the people in the world! How much time passes before* the Lord God *judges the world does not matter to him! He considers* that one day *passes no more quickly than* a thousand years, and *he also considers* that a thousand years *passes as quickly as* one day *to us!* [9] *So, you should not think that because Christ has not yet come back to judge people,* the Lord God is slow in doing what he promised. Some people think that this is so, *and they say that Christ never will come back.* But *you should understand that the reason Christ has not yet come back to judge people is that* God is being patient towards you, because he does not want anyone to perish. Instead, he wants everyone to turn away from their sinful behavior. [10] Although *God is being patient, at* the time *that he has appointed,* the Lord *Jesus Christ* will *certainly* come back *to judge people.* He will come back *unexpectedly*, like a thief *comes unexpectedly.* At that time there will be a great roaring sound. The heavens will cease to exist. The elements will be destroyed by fire, and the earth *that God made* and everything on it *that people have made* will disappear.[e]

---

[e] OR, …the earth that he has made and everything on it that people have made will be burned up.

2 Peter 3:11-13

THEME: You certainly ought to behave in a godly manner, because God will destroy everything and because only those people who are righteous will live in the new heavens and on the new earth.

[11] God will certainly destroy all these things like *I just said*, so you certainly know how you ought to behave. You ought to conduct your lives in a godly manner [12] while you eagerly look forward *to Christ* returning on the day God *has appointed*, and you should try to make that day come soon. Because of what *God will do on that day,* the heavens will be destroyed. The elements will melt and burn up. [13] Although *all those events will happen, we rejoice because* we are waiting for the new heavens and new earth *God* has promised. The *only people who will be* in the new heavens and on this new earth will be *people who are righteous.*

2 Peter 3:14-18a

THEME: Do all you can to live in a godly manner. Guard against those who would entice you to doubt what you now firmly believe.

[14] So, dear friends, because you are waiting for these things *to happen,* do all you can *to live in a godly manner, in order that Christ* will see that you *are* completely pure *and that you are living* peacefully *with each other.* [15] And think about this: Our Lord *Jesus Christ is* patient *because he wants* people to be saved. Our dear brother Paul also wrote with wisdom to you *about these same matters,* because God caused him to understand *these things that will happen.* [16] In the *letters* Paul wrote there are certain things that are difficult to understand. People *who are spiritually* ignorant and unstable interpret these things wrongly, as they also interpret the other Scriptures wrongly. The result is that they will destroy themselves *spiritually,* and *God* will punish them. [17] So, dear friends, *since you already know about these false teachers,* guard against them. Do not let these wicked people deceive you by telling you things that are wrong, with the result that you yourselves begin to doubt *what you now firmly believe.* [18] *Instead, live in such a manner that you* experience more and more the kindness of our Lord and Savior Jesus Christ *to you,* and that you get to know him *better and better.*

2 Peter 3:18b

THEME: I pray that Jesus Christ will always be honored.

I pray that Jesus Christ will be honored both now and forever! [f]

---

[f]　Some Greek manuscripts add "Amen" at the end.

The Apostle John wrote a letter to his fellow believers. We call this letter

1 John

1

1 John 1:1-4

THEME: We apostles proclaim to you the message about the One who has lived eternally, so that you may be joined together with us and we may be completely happy.

[1] *I, John, am writing to you about* the one who existed before *there was anything else!* He is the one we *apostles* listened to *as he taught us!* We ourselves actually saw him! We looked at him and touched him! *He is the one who taught us* the message that *enables people to have eternal* life.[a] [2] Because he came here *to the earth* and we have seen him, we proclaim to you clearly that the one we have seen is the *one who* has lived *eternally*. He was *previously* with his Father, but he came to live among us. [3] We proclaim to you the *message about Jesus*, the one whom we saw and heard, in order that you may have a close relationship with us. The ones we have a close relationship with are God our Father and his Son Jesus Christ. [4] I am writing to you about these things so that you will be convinced that they are true, and as a result we may be completely joyful.

1 John 1:5-2:2

THEME: We should continue to be morally pure, because God is morally pure and he is able to forgive our sins on the basis that Jesus died to acquit us of the guilt of all our sins.

[5] The message we heard from Christ and proclaim to you is this: God is *pure in every way. He never sins. He is like* a *brilliant* light that has no darkness at all. [6] If we claim to have a close relationship with *God,* but *we live in an impure manner, that is like* living in *evil* darkness. We are lying. We are not conducting our lives according to *God's* true message. [7] But conducting our lives *in a pure manner,* as God is *pure in every way, is like living* in God's light. If we do that, we have a close relationship with each other. Not only that, but *God* acquits us of *the guilt of* all our sins because *he accepts* what his Son Jesus did for us *when his* blood *flowed from his body when he died. So we should conduct our lives according to God's standard of purity.* [8] Those who claim they never behave sinfully are deceiving themselves, and refusing *to accept as* true *what God says about them.* [9] But God will do what he says he will do, and what he does is *always* right. So, if we confess to him that we *have behaved* sinfully, he will forgive *us for* our sins and will free us from *the guilt of* all of them. *Because of that, we should confess to him that we have behaved sinfully.* [10] *Because God says everyone has sinned,* those who claim they have never behaved sinfully talk *as though* God lies! They reject what God says *about us!*

---

[a] OR, …to live *spiritually.*

2

¹You who are very dear to me, I am writing this to you *to say*, 'Don't sin!' But if any of you *believers* sin, *God can forgive you because* we have Jesus Christ, who is the righteous one, who speaks to the Father on our behalf *and asks him to forgive us.* ²*Remember that Jesus Christ* voluntarily sacrificed *his own life for us, so that as a result God forgives* our sins. *Yes, God is able to forgive* our sins, but not only ours! *He is* also *able to forgive* the sins of people everywhere!

1 John 2:3-6

THEME: We ought to live as Christ lived, obeying what God commands us to do. We would then be loving God in the manner he wants us to.

³*I will tell you* how we can be sure that we have a close relationship with *God. If we* obey what he commands *us to do, that shows us that we have a close relationship with him. So we must always obey what he commands us to do.* ⁴Those who say, "I have a close relationship with God," and don't obey what *God* commands *us to do,* are liars. They are not conducting their lives according to *God's* true message. ⁵But those who obey what *God* commands them to do are the people who love God in the manner he wants us to. *I will tell you* how we can be sure that we have a close relationship with God: ⁶If we say we are conducting our lives as God wants us to, we ought to *conduct our lives* as Christ *did.*

1 John 2:7-11

THEME: We ought to love our fellow believers in order to continue behaving like people living in the light.

⁷Dear friends, I am not writing a new *additional* command to you. Instead, I am writing to you a command that you have had since you first *believed in Christ.* That command is *part of* the message you have *always* heard. ⁸Nevertheless, *I can say that* the command I am writing to you is *indeed* a new command. *It is new because* what Christ *did* was new, and what you *are doing* is new, because *you have ceased to live in a morally impure manner* and *are now truly living in a pure manner. That is like* no longer *living in* darkness. Instead, *it is like* living where brilliant light is already shining. ⁹Those who claim that they are *morally pure, like people* living in the light, but who hate any of their fellow believers, are still *behaving in a morally impure manner, like people continually living* in darkness. ¹⁰But those who love their fellow believers *are continuing to behave like people* who are living in the light. They are people who please *God. So you should love your fellow believers.* ¹¹But those who hate any of their fellow believers are still *behaving in a morally impure way, like people who are living* in darkness. They don't know that they will eventually destroy themselves *eternally.* They have become *spiritually* blind, *unaware of spiritual truth.*

1 John 2:12-14

THEME: I am writing all these matters to you because I know that God has forgiven your sins and also because you have come to know the Father and Christ, who has always existed, and because you have overcome the evil one.

¹²⁻¹³I am writing *this* to you *whom I love as though you were my* little children, to you who are *spiritually mature people who are like* fathers, and to you *spiritually vigorous people who are like* young men. Remember that *God* has forgiven your sins on account of what Christ *has done.* You have come to know *Christ, the one* who always existed. You have

overcome the evil one, *Satan*. [14] *I will say it again*: I have written *this* to you because you have come to know the Father, because you have come to know *Christ, the one* who always existed, because you are *spiritually* strong, because you continue to *obey* God's word, and because you have overcome the evil one, *Satan*.

1 John 2:15-17

THEME: Do not esteem the evil manner in which other people in the world live, since you want to live forever.

[15] Don't desire *to conduct your lives in the evil manner in which other people in* the world *conduct their lives,* and don't love anything that *the evil people* in the world *consider to be good*. Those who desire *to conduct their lives in the evil manner in which other people of* the world *conduct their lives* don't *really* love God their Father *at all*. [16] Keep in mind that all *the evil human desires* in the world *consist of things such as these*: *People* desire to do *what* their self-directed nature *strongly desires*. *People* desire *to possess* whatever appeals to their senses. *People* boast about the material things they possess. *Such evil patterns of behavior* don't originate from the Father! Instead they originate from *the godless people in* the world! [17] The *godless people in* the world, along with what they desire, will disappear, but those who do what God wants *them to do* will live forever!

1 John 2:18-25

THEME: You know that it is now the final period of this age when there are liars who deny that Jesus is God's Chosen One. But you have the power of God's Spirit and you know what is true and what is false. So continue to live according to the true message that you heard when you began to believe in Christ, in order that you may continue to live united both to God's Son and to the Father.

[18] *You who are very dear to me*, it is *now* the final period *before Jesus returns*. Just as you heard *from us apostles* that a person who opposes Christ is going to come, so now there are *already* many people who oppose Christ. That is why we know that it is the final period *of this age*.[b] [19] The *people who oppose Christ* refused to remain in our congregations, but they never *really* belonged with us. If they had belonged with us, they would have remained with us. But because *they left, everyone* can clearly know that none of them were fellow believers. [20] But as for you, you have been given the power of *God's Spirit, which comes from Christ,* the Holy One.[c] *As a result*, you all know *how to distinguish false teaching from the true message*. [21] I am writing *this letter* to you, not because you don't know *what is God's* true message, but because you do know *what it is*. You also know that no false message originates from *God, who is the source of all* truth. [22] The *worst* liars are the ones who deny that Jesus is the Messiah. They are *the ones we told you about*, the ones who oppose Christ. They refuse to acknowledge that *God is* the Father and that *Jesus is his* Son.[d] [23] If anyone refuses to acknowledge that *Jesus is God's* Son, he does not have a relationship with the Father. But those who acknowledge that *Jesus is God's* Son, *not only have a relationship with God's Son, but they* have a relationship with the Father also. [24] *So*, as for you, you must continue to conduct your lives according to *the true message* that you heard when you began *to believe in Christ*. If you continue to *do that*, you will continue to have a close relationship with both *God's* Son and the Father. [25] And what God told us is that *he will cause us* to live forever!

---

[b]   OR, ...final period *before Jesus returns.*

[c]   OR, ...*which comes from God* the Holy One.

[d]   OR, ...*Jesus is* the one who is also God.

1 John 2:26-27

THEME: Continue to live according to what you were originally taught by God's Spirit.

²⁶ I have written this to you *to warn you* about those *who want to* deceive you *concerning the truth about Christ.* ²⁷ As for you, God's Spirit, whom you received from Christ, remains in you. So you don't need anyone to teach you *anything else that they might claim is the truth.* God's Spirit is teaching you all *of God's truth that you need to know.* God's Spirit is truthful, and he never says anything that is false. So continue to conduct your lives in the way that *he originally* taught you.

1 John 2:28-29

THEME: Continue to live united to Christ, so that you will be confident that he will accept you when he returns.

²⁸ Now, *while teachers of false doctrine are trying to persuade you to accept their teaching, I urge* you who are very dear to me to continue to *have a close relationship with* Christ. *We need to do that* in order to be confident *that he will accept us* when he comes back again. If we do that, we will not be ashamed *when we stand* before *him* when he comes. ²⁹ Since you know that *Christ* always does what is right, you know that all those who continue doing what is right are the ones who have become children of God.

3

1 John 3:1-10

THEME: Do not allow anyone to entice you to sin, because you are God's children, and his children maintain themselves free from evil behavior by not continuing to sin as the devil's children do.

¹ *Think about* how much our Father loves us! He allows us to be called his children! *And it is indeed true that* we are *his children. But people in* the world *who are unbelievers* have not understood *who* God *really is.* So they don't understand *who we are,* that we *are God's children.* ² Dear friends, even though at present we are God's children, *he* has not yet made clear *to us* what we will be like in the future. However, we know that when *Christ* comes back again, we will be like him, because we will see what he is really like. ³ *So,* all those who confidently expect *to see what Christ is really like when he returns* must maintain themselves *morally* pure in every way, just like Christ, who is pure in every way. ⁴ But everyone who continues sinning is refusing to obey *God's* laws, because that's what sin is, refusing to obey *God's* laws. ⁵ You know that Christ came in order to completely remove *the guilt for* our sins. You know also that he never sinned. ⁶ Those who keep *doing what* Christ desires do not continue sinning repeatedly. But those who repeatedly sin have not understood *who Christ is,* nor have they had a close relationship with him. ⁷ *So I urge you* who are very dear to me, don't let anyone deceive you *by telling you that it is all right to sin.* If you continue doing what is right, you are righteous, just as Christ is righteous. ⁸ *But* those who continue sinning are like the devil, because the devil has always been sinning since *the world* began. *And* the reason God's Son became a human being was to destroy what the devil has done. ⁹ People don't continue sinning repeatedly if they have become children of God. Instead, they to live according to *the good life and character that God produced in them.* They cannot continually sin, because God has caused them to become his children. ¹⁰ Those who are God's children are clearly distinguished from those who are the devil's children. *The way we can know who are Satan's children is this*: Those

who don't do what is right are not God's children. *Specifically*, those who don't love their fellow believers are not *God's children. Instead, they are Satan's children.*

1 John 3:11-18

THEME: Because we have been changed from being spiritually dead people to being spiritually alive, we should love each other genuinely by helping our fellow believers who are in need.

[11] The message you heard when you first *believed in Christ* is that we should love each other. [12] *We should* not *hate others* as did *Adam's son* Cain, who belonged to *Satan,* the evil one. *Because Cain hated his younger brother*, he murdered him. I will remind you about why he murdered his brother: It was because Cain habitually behaved in an evil way, and *he hated his younger brother* because his *younger* brother *behaved* righteously. [13] You shouldn't be surprised, my fellow believers, when *unbelievers* hate you. [14] We know that we have been changed from *being spiritually* dead to *being spiritually* alive. We know this because we love our fellow believers. Those who don't love *their fellow believers* are still *spiritually* dead. [15] As for those who hate *any of* their fellow believers, *God considers them to be* murderers. And you know that murderers don't have eternal life. [16] The way we have come to know *how to truly* love *our fellow believers is by remembering* that Christ voluntarily gave his life for us. So, *when any of* our fellow believers *are in need, we should be willing to help them. We should even be willing to* die for them. [17] Many *of us* have the material things we need in this world. If we become aware that any of our fellow believers are in need and *if we* refuse to *give them what they need*, it is clear that we don't love God *as we claim we do.* [18] *I say to* you whom I love dearly, let's not merely say that *we love our fellow believers!* Let's genuinely love them by doing things *to help them!*

1 John 3:19-24

THEME: We must believe in God's Son and love each other in order to be confident that we have a close relationship with God and that we will receive what we ask from him.

[19] By means of *truly loving our fellow believers* we can be sure that we are *conducting our lives according to* the true message. *As a result*, we will not feel guilty *when we talk* to God. [20] We can *pray with* confidence, because *although* we might feel guilty *about our sins*, God is more worthy to be trusted than our feelings. He knows everything *about us*. [21] Dear friends, when we don't feel guilty *because of our sins*, we can *pray* to God confidently. [22] Then, when we request *something from him,* we receive it because we do what he commands *us to do* and what pleases him. [23] *I will tell you* what he commands *us to do: We must* believe that Jesus Christ is his Son.[e] *We must* also love each other, just as he commanded *us to do.* [24] Those who do what God commands are ones who have a close relationship with God, and God has a close relationship with them. *I will tell you how* we can be sure that God has a close relationship with us: It is because *we have* his Spirit, whom he gave to us, that we can be sure that God has a close relationship with us.

---

[e] OR, ...*We must* believe that Jesus Christ is the one who is also God.

4

1 John 4:1-6

THEME: Continue to test the teachings you hear to know whether or not they are from God. You should test them by whether or not they acknowledge that Jesus Christ came in human form and also by what kind of people listen to that kind of teaching.

¹ Dear friends, many people are teaching *false messages*. So, don't trust every *message someone claims God's* Spirit *gave him*. Instead, think carefully about the teachings *you hear,* in order to know whether they are from God or not. ² *I will tell* you how to recognize *teachings that come from* the Spirit of God: Those who affirm that Jesus Christ came *from God* to become a human *like us* are *teaching messages* that are from God. ³ But those who don't affirm *that about* Jesus are not *teaching messages* from God. *They are teachers who* oppose Christ. You have heard that people like that are coming *to be among us*. Even now they are already here!

⁴ As for you who are very dear to me, you belong to God, and you have refused *the false messages* those people *teach*, because *God,* who enables you *to do what he wants*, is more powerful than *Satan,* who enables godless people *to do what he wants*. ⁵ As for *those who are teaching what is false*, they are godless people. Because of that, they teach what godless people want to hear. That is why the godless people listen to them. ⁶ As for us, *because* we belong to God, whoever has a close relationship with God listens to us. *But* those who do not belong to God don't listen to us. That is how we can know whether *the things people are teaching* are true, or whether they are *false and* leading *people* astray.

1 John 4:7-11

THEME: Let us love each other. God shows us what real love is.

⁷ Dear friends, we should love each other, because God *enables us* to love *each other*, and because those who love *their fellow believers* have become God's children and have a close relationship with him. ⁸ God's *nature* is to love *all people*. So, those who don't love *their fellow believers* do not have a relationship with God. ⁹ I will tell you how God has shown us *that he* loves us: He sent his only Son[f] *to live* on the earth to cause us to live *eternally* as a result of *our trusting in what* he *accomplished for us by dying for us*. ¹⁰ And God has shown *us what real* love is: It is not that we loved God, but that God loved us and sent his Son to sacrifice *his life* in order that our sins *might be forgiven*. ¹¹ Dear friends, since God loves us like that, we certainly ought to love each other!

1 John 4:12-21

THEME: In order to be assured that we are living according to God's character, we must love God and our fellow believers, because God loved us first.

¹² No one has ever seen God. *Nevertheless*, if we love each other, *it is evident that* God lives within us and that we love others just as he *intends for us to do*. ¹³ *I will tell you* how we can be sure that we have a close relationship with God and that God is living within us: He has put his Spirit within us. ¹⁴ We *apostles* have seen God's Son, and *we tell people* that the Father sent him to save *the people in* the world *from being punished for their sins*. ¹⁵ *So* those who affirm that Jesus is the Son of God, God is living within them, and they

---

[f]   OR, …He sent the one who was also God…

have a close relationship with God. ⁶We have experienced the way God loves us and we believe that he loves us. *As a result, we love others. Because* God's *nature* is to love people, those who continue to love *others* have a close relationship with God, and God has a close relationship with them. ⁷We *should* love others completely. And if we do that, when the time comes for *him to* judge us, we will be confident *that he will not condemn us.*⁹ *We will have that confidence* because of our *conducting our lives* in this world as Christ did. ⁸We will not be afraid *of God* if we *truly* love *him,* because those who love *God* completely cannot possibly be afraid *of him. We would be* afraid only *if we thought he would* punish us. So if people are afraid *of God, that shows* they are not loving *God* completely. ⁹We love *God and our fellow believers* because God loved us first. ²⁰ *So* those who say, "I love God" but hate a fellow believer are lying. Those who don't love one of their fellow believers, whom they have seen, certainly cannot be loving God, whom they have not seen. ²¹Keep in mind that this is what God has commanded us: If we love him, we must also love our fellow believers.

5

1 John 5:1-5

THEME: Those who believe that Jesus is God's Anointed One are people who have been caused to live spiritually, and they love their fellow believers. They obey God's commands and overcome the evils of human society.

¹All those who believe that Jesus is the Messiah *have truly* become children of God. And everyone who loves *a man who is* someone's father will *be expected to* love that man's children as well. *Similarly, those who love God, who has caused them to become his children, should love their fellow believers, whom God has also caused to become his children.* ²The way we can be sure that we *genuinely* love God's children is this: We are loving them when we love God and do what he commands *us to do.* ³Indeed, our obeying what God commands *us to do* is *the same as* loving him. And it is not burdensome for *us to do* what God commands *us to do.* ⁴All of us whom God has caused to become his children have been able to successfully resist doing what the people *who live in* opposition to God do. It is only by trusting *in Christ* that we are able to resist doing what people in the world who are opposed to God do. ⁵*I will tell you* who are the ones who are able to resist doing what the people who are opposed to God do. It is those who believe that Jesus is God's Son.

1 John 5:6-12

THEME: Jesus came from God to earth. Those who believe in and live united to him have eternal life.

⁶*Think about* Jesus Christ. He is the one who came *to earth from God. God showed that he had truly sent Jesus when Jesus was baptized* in water and *when Jesus'* blood *flowed from his body when he died. God made this clear* not only *when Jesus was baptized,* but also when Jesus' blood flowed *from his body when he died. And God's* Spirit declares *truthfully that Jesus Christ came from God.* The Spirit always *speaks what* is true. ⁷There are three *things* by which we know *that Christ came from God.* ⁸*Those three things are: What God's* Spirit *tells us,* what God said when Jesus was baptized *in* water, and *Jesus'* blood *which flowed from his body when he died on the cross.* These three things all tell us the same thing, *that Jesus came from God.* ⁹We *usually* believe what other people say.

---

⁹ OR, …we will be confident *that we have a relationship with him.*

But what God says is more *reliable than what people say*. So *we must believe* what God has said about his Son.[h] [10] Those who trust in the Son of God know within their hearts that *what God* says *about his Son is true. But* those who refuse to believe that *what* God says is true are saying that God is a liar, because they refuse to believe what God has said about his Son. [11] This is what *God* says *to us*: "I have given eternal life to you *who believe in my Son!*" We will live forever if we have a close relationship with his Son. [12] Those who have *a close relationship with God's* Son have *already* begun to live *forever. But* those who do not have a relationship with God's Son have not begun *to* live *forever*.

1 John 5:13-21

THEME: We have a close relationship with God because we are united to his Son. Because of that relationship, we have eternal life.

[13] I have written this *letter* to you who believe that Jesus is God's Son so that you may know that you have eternal life. [14] Because we have a close relationship with him, we are very confident that he hears us when we ask him *to do anything* that is in accordance with his will. [15] *And* since we know that he hears us whenever we make requests, we *also* know that *it is as though* he has *already* done what we requested him *to do*.

[16] Those who see one of their fellow believers sinning in a way that does not result in eternal separation from God should ask *God to help that fellow believer*, and *as a result* God will help that fellow believer and enable him to live *eternally. But some people* sin *in a manner that causes them* to be separated from God eternally. I am not saying that *you should* ask *God to help* people who sin like that. [17] Everyone who does what is wrong is sinning, but there are some sins that do not cause a person to be separated from God eternally. [18] We know that if God has caused a person to become his child, that person does not continue sinning. Instead, the Son of God protects him so that *Satan*, the evil one, does not harm him *spiritually*. [19] We know that we belong to God, and *we know* that the evil one controls all *the evil people in* the world. [20] We also know that God's Son has come *to us*, and *we know* that he has enabled us to know the one who is really God. So now we have a close relationship with *God because* we belong to Jesus Christ, the one who is the Son of God. Jesus Christ is truly God, and *he is the one who enables us to have* eternal life.

[21] *I say to* you who are very dear to me, guard yourselves from *worshiping* gods that have no real power!

---

[h]   OR, …what God has said about the one who is also God.

The Apostle John wrote another letter to his fellow believers. We call this letter

2 John

2 John 1-3

THEME: I, the Elder, write to the congregation and to all the members. I love you and know that God the Father and his Son will bless us.

[1] *You all know me as* the *chief* Elder. *I am writing this letter* to all of you in your congregation. *God* has chosen *you,* and I love you truly! Not only do I myself love you, but all those who know *and accept the* true message *that Jesus taught* also love you! [2] *All of us believe God's* true message. It is in our *hearts,* and we will continue *to believe it* forever! [3] God the Father and Jesus Christ, who is his Son,[a] will continue *to act toward us* in kindness and mercy *because they* love *us. They will enable us to have inner* peace, *because we believe* their true message.

2 John 4

THEME: I am happy that some of your members are living just as God commanded us to live.

[4] I am very happy because I learned that some of you are conducting your lives in a manner that is consistent with *God's* true message. You are conducting your lives just as our Father *God* commanded us *to do.*

2 John 5-6

THEME: Continue to love each other just as God commanded us to love when we first began to believe his true message.

[5] And now, dear congregation, *there is something that* I am requesting you *to do.* I am writing this not to command you to do something new, but *to continue doing* what God commanded when we first began *to believe his true message. What he commanded* is that we love each other. [6] And we are truly loving *God* when we are conducting our lives in accordance with whatever he commands *us to do.* What he commands us to do is to continue *to love one another.* That is exactly what you heard when you first began *to believe God's true message.*

2 John 7-11

THEME: Be on your guard against teachers of false doctrine, so that you will receive your complete reward of being with God eternally. Do not welcome or encourage any of these false teachers in any way.

[7] Many people who deceive *others have left your congregation and* have now gone out among other people *in your area.* They are the ones who do not acknowledge that Jesus Christ became human. They are the very ones who deceive *people* and oppose *what we*

---

[a] OR, …who is the man who is also God…

teach about Christ. ⁸ *So* be sure *that you don't let those teachers deceive you!* If you let them deceive you, you will lose *the reward* which we, *together with you,* have been working for, and you will not receive the complete reward *of being eternally united to God!* ⁹ Those who change what Christ taught and don't continue *to believe* what he taught, they do not have *a relationship with* God. *But* those who continue to believe *what Christ* taught have *a close relationship with* both the Father *God* and with his Son. ¹⁰ When anyone comes to you who teaches something different from *what Christ* taught, don't welcome him into your homes! Don't *encourage him by* wishing him well *in any way!* ¹¹ *Keep in mind that* if you are encouraging people like that, *God will punish you* along with them for the evil that they do.

2 John 12-13

THEME: Instead of writing much more to you, I expect to come and talk directly with you. The members of your sister congregation greet you.

¹² *Even though* I have much *more that I want* to tell you, I have decided not *to write it* in a letter. Instead, I expect to be with you *soon* and talk directly with you. Then we can be completely joyful *together.* ¹³ Your fellow believers *here*, ones whom *God* has also chosen, send their greetings to you.

The Apostle John wrote a letter
to a fellow believer.
We call this letter

3 John

3 John 1-4

THEME: I, the Elder, write to you, Gaius, whom I truly love. I ask God that all may go well with you, just as your soul does well. I am happy because of the way you live.

[1] *You know me as* the *chief* Elder. *I am writing this letter to you,* my dear friend Gaius, whom I truly love. [2] *Dear* friend, I ask *God to enable things to go* well for you in all respects, *specifically,* to keep you physically healthy just as you are spiritually healthy. [3] I am very happy because some fellow believers have come *here* and told me how you conduct your life in accordance with the true message. You are *conducting your life* in a manner *that is consistent with God's* true message. [4] I am very happy when I hear that people whom I helped to believe in Christ[a] are living that way!

3 John 5-6

THEME: Continue receiving the visiting fellow believers, as you have been doing.

[5] Dear friend, you are *serving Jesus* faithfully whenever you do things to help fellow believers, *even those you* don't know, who are traveling *around doing God's work.* [6] *Some of* them have reported before the congregation *here how* you have showed love *to them.* You should continue to help such people in their travels in a way that is pleasing to God.

3 John 7-8

THEME: Especially provide for them financially.

[7] When those fellow believers went out *to tell people about Jesus*, the people who don't believe in Christ did not give them anything *to help them.* [8] So we *who believe in Christ* ought to give food and money to such people to help *them as they teach others God's* true message.

3 John 9-10

THEME: Because Diotrephes does not recognize my authority, I will publicly expose what he does in opposing us.

[9] I wrote *a letter* to the congregation *telling them to help those fellow believers*. However, Diotrephes does not *pay any attention to what* I wrote, because he desires to be in charge of *the congregation.* [10] So, when I arrive *there* I will *publicly* expose what he does: He tells others evil nonsense about us *in order to* harm *us by what he* says, and he isn't content with just doing that. He himself refuses to receive the fellow believers who are traveling around doing God's work, and he also stops those who want to receive them by expelling them from the congregation.

---

[a] OR, …when I hear that my *spiritual* children…

3 John 11

THEME: Do not imitate a bad example; imitate good ones.

¹¹ Dear friend, don't imitate a bad *example like that*. Instead, *keep imitating* good *ones*. *Remember that* people who do good deeds are *spiritual children* of God, *but* those who do *what is* evil don't have fellowship with God.

3 John 12

THEME: You will do well to receive Demetrius, who is highly recommended.

¹² All *the believers who know Demetrius* say that he *is a good person*. The fact *that he conducts his life in a way that is consistent with God's* true *message* shows *that he is a good person*, and we also say the same thing *about him*. You know that what we say *about him* is true. *So it will be good if you welcome him and help him. He is the one who will be bringing this letter to you.*

3 John 13-15

THEME: Instead of writing more, I expect to visit you soon, and we will speak directly with one another. Our mutual friends here send their greetings to all of you.

¹³ When *I began* to write this letter, I had much more *that I intended* to tell you. But *now* I don't want to write *it* in a letter. ¹⁴ Instead, I expect to *come and* see you soon. Then we will talk directly with one another. ¹⁵ *I pray that God will enable* you *to experience inner* peace. Our friends *here* send you their greetings.ᵇ Tell our friends *there* that we send our greetings to them.

ᵇ OR, …Our friends *here* say they are thinking fondly of you.

514

Jude, a brother of Jesus, wrote a letter to his fellow believers. We call this letter

Jude

Jude 1-2

THEME: I, Jude, a servant of Jesus Christ and brother of James, write to you who are chosen, loved, and protected by God.

¹ *I am* Jude. I *serve* Jesus Christ *like* a *voluntary* slave. I am a *younger* brother of James, *the leader of all the congregations. I am writing* to you whom *God* has chosen *to belong to him. You are* loved by God *our* Father and protected by Jesus Christ.ᵃ ² *I pray that* you will continue to *experience* very much *God acting* mercifully toward you, *causing you to have inner* peace, and loving *you*.

Jude 3-4

THEME: Proclaim the truth we believe, and strongly defend it against those who oppose it.

³ You whom I love, although I was very eager to write to you about the salvation we all share, now I realize it is necessary *for me* to write to you to exhort you to defend the *truth about Christ* that we believe. *Jesus and his apostles* gave that truth once for all to us who belong to God, *and we must not let it be changed.* ⁴ Some people falsely *teach that because* God in his kindness does for us what we don't deserve, it does not matter if we continue to sin. *Those people show by their behavior* that they don't want to admit that Jesus Christ *is* our only Master and Lord. *It was written* long ago that *God* would condemn such ungodly people. But some *of those* people have entered *like crawling snakes* into your congregations *and oppose the truth about Christ, so you must oppose them.*

Jude 5-8

THEME: The way God destroyed three groups illustrates that he will destroy these ungodly people in your midst.

⁵ Although you previously knew all these things, *there are certain things about* which I desire to remind you. *Don't forget that although* the Lord rescued *his people* from *the land of* Egypt, he later destroyed most of those same people, ones who did not believe *in him.* ⁶ And there were *many* angels to *whom God assigned positions of authority in heaven.* But they did not continue to rule with authority *in those positions.* Instead, they abandoned the place that *God* gave them to live *in heaven.* So God has put those angels in chains forever in the darkness *in hell. They will stay there* until the great day when *God* will punish them. ⁷ Similarly, the people who lived in *the cities of* Sodom and Gomorrah and the nearby cities committed sexual immorality. They sought all kinds of sexual relations that differ *from what God permits. So God destroyed their cities. What happened to those people and those angels* shows that *God will* punish in the eternal fire *of hell* people such as the ones who teach false doctrines. ⁸ Similarly, these *ungodly people in your midst* also defile their own bodies *by living immorally,* because *they claim that God*

ᵃ OR, ... *You are ones* whom *God* has protected *to present* to Jesus Christ.

revealed in visions *that they should act that way.* They refuse to *allow* anyone to have authority over them, and they revile *God's* glorious *angels.*

Jude 9-10

THEME: Those teachers of false doctrine revile the spiritual beings that they do not understand. But God will destroy them.

[9] When the devil argued with the chief angel Michael about *who would take away* the body of *the prophet* Moses *to bury it,* Michael did not *do as these false teachers do. Even though Michael has much more authority than they do*, he did not disrespectfully revile Satan and accuse him. Instead, he *only* said, "*I desire that* the Lord *God* will rebuke you!" [10] But the ones *in your midst who teach false doctrine* revile the *spiritual* beings that they don't understand. They also *do the things they desire*, things that they know instinctively are wrong, things that they just do without thinking *about the consequences,* like animals *do.* So they destroy themselves. *But they will also be punished by God.*

Jude 11-13

THEME: Because the teachers of false doctrine do wicked things, God will condemn them to hell. They are dangerous, useless, spiritually dead, restless, without shame, and unreliable.

[11] *God will do* terrible things to the teachers of false doctrine! They conduct their lives *wickedly* like Cain, *who murdered his brother.* They devote themselves to *doing* wrong things *like* Balaam, who *tried to induce God's people to sin in order to get the money that was offered to him.* They will perish like Korah, who rebelled *against the authority God gave to Moses.* [12] Those teachers of false doctrine are *as dangerous to you as* hidden rocks on a reef *are to a boat.* When you gather together *to eat the meals that promote Christian* love and fellowship, they *join you and* carouse shamelessly, looking out *only* for themselves *and not for others. Because they don't do anything to help others*, they are *as useless as* clouds that are blown along by the wind but that don't *produce* any rain. *They are as disappointing as* trees that don't produce fruit in the autumn *as expected.* They are not only *spiritually* dead themselves, *but they are* not *able to cause others to be* alive *spiritually, just like* trees that have been uprooted and *as a result* are unable to produce any fruit. [13] They are *restless, like* the pounding waves of the ocean. *Just as* waves produce foul-smelling *foam on the shore, those teachers of false doctrine do* shameful *deeds. We can't depend on them to show us how to conduct our lives, just as we can't depend on* meteors *to show us the way when we travel.* God has reserved intense darkness for them forever *in hell.*

Jude 14-16

THEME: Enoch prophesied that the Lord will condemn people like the wicked teachers of false doctrine. They grumble, are discontent, and are arrogant flatterers.

[14] Enoch, the sixth *person in the line of people descended* from Adam, prophesied this about those *teachers of false* doctrine: "Listen carefully to this: The Lord will certainly come with a countless number of his holy *angels* [15] to judge everyone, and to punish all wicked and ungodly people for all the ungodly things they did in an ungodly way, and for all the harsh things that ungodly sinful people have spoken against him." [16] Those *teachers* of *false* doctrine grumble *about the things God does.* They complain about *what happens to them.* They do the sinful things their *bodies* desire. They talk boastfully. They flatter people just in order to get *those people to give them the* things they want.

Jude 17-19

THEME: The apostles predicted that wicked people like the teachers of false doctrine would come. They divide believers, are self-directed, and devoid of God's Spirit.

¹⁷ But you people whom I love need to remember the things that the apostles of our Lord Jesus Christ predicted. ¹⁸ They told you, "In the final period of time *in which we live*, there will be people who will laugh at *the truths God has revealed*. They will do the ungodly things their *bodies* desire." ¹⁹ *That describes* the teachers of false doctrine *well, because* they are the ones who cause divisions among *believers*. They do what their own desires tell them to do. The Spirit *of God* does not live within them.

Jude 20-21

THEME: Believe the truth more firmly, pray by the power of the Spirit, and keep expecting God's mercy.

²⁰ But you people whom I love, establish yourselves firmly in the very sacred *truths* you believe. Pray by *letting* the Holy Spirit empower you. ²¹ Keep conducting your lives in *a way that is appropriate for those whom* God loves. Keep constantly expecting that our Lord Jesus Christ will *act* mercifully toward you. Keep expecting that until *the time when we start* living eternally *with him*.

Jude 22-23

THEME: Mercifully help those who are not certain what to believe, save those who are in danger of being influenced by the teachers of false doctrine, and pity those completely convinced by them.

²² Mercifully *help* those who are not certain *what teaching they should believe*. ²³ Snatch others from *the influence of those who teach what is false, as you would rescue* things by snatching them *from* a fire. Pity those *whom the teachers of false doctrine have completely convinced,* but beware *you are not influenced by them*. Detest *doing or even thinking about the sins those people commit, just as you would detest* not only filthy things but the clothes that were stained by those things.

Jude 24-25

THEME: God, who is able to keep you from being condemned for your sin and to present you guiltless before him, was great and ruled before time began, is still like that, and will remain so forever.

²⁴ God is able to keep you from ceasing to trust in him,ᵇ and he is able to present you before his glorious presence. *In his presence*, there will be nothing *for which you will* be condemned, and you will be rejoicing greatly. ²⁵ He is the only true God. He has saved us as a result of what Jesus Christ our Lord *did for us*. God was glorious and great and mighty and *ruled* with great authority before time began. *He is still like that*, and he will *remain like that* forever! Amen!

ᵇ OR, …keep you from sinning…

Jesus showed the Apostle John a vision. We call John's account

Revelation

1

Revelation 1:1-3

THEME: John urged people to read this book, listen carefully to it, and obey it.

[1] *This book tells the message* that God revealed to Jesus Christ. God revealed it to him so that he might reveal to his servants the *events* that must happen soon. Jesus communicated *this message* to *me*, his servant John, by sending his angel to me. [2] *By writing it down I*, John, am truthfully reporting everything that I saw *and heard*, the message from God that Jesus Christ *communicated to me.* [3] *God is* pleased with those who read *this book to their congregation*, and he is pleased with those who listen carefully to it and obey what *he has commanded by means of* this prophetic message that *I* have written down. *So read this message, pay close attention to it, and obey it*, because *these things that Jesus has revealed* will happen soon.

Revelation 1:4-8

THEME: John said he was writing to believers in the seven congregations in Asia. He prayed that God would bless them. He said that Christ is coming to judge rebellious people and to bring in his kingdom.

[4] *I*, John, am *writing this* to *you believers in* the seven congregations *that are located* in *the province of* Asia. *I pray that God the Father, God's Spirit, and Jesus Christ* will act kindly toward you and cause you to have *inner* peace. *God the Father is* the one who is, who has always existed, and who will always exist. The Spirit *of God, who* is in front of God's throne, has *all power.*[a] [5] Jesus Christ has faithfully told *people about God.* He is the first one whom God raised from the dead *to show that he will also raise us who trust him.* Jesus Christ is the one who rules the kings of the earth. He is the one who loves us. He is the one who has cancelled the guilt for our sins by his blood *which flowed from his body when he died on the cross.* [6] He is *the one who* has caused us to become people over whose lives God rules, and he has made us to be priests *who serve his* God and Father. *As a result of this, we acknowledge that* Jesus Christ is eternally divine and eternally powerful. Amen!

[7] Listen! Christ will surely come in the midst of the clouds *to judge the rebellious people of earth*, and everyone will see him *come.* Even those who *are responsible for* piercing *and killing* him *will see him come. People from* all people-groups on earth will mourn because he *will punish them.* Indeed, may it be so. [8] The Lord God declares, "I am the one who began *all things*, and I am the *one who will cause all things to* end." He is the one who is, who has always existed, and who will always exist. He is the Almighty One.

---

[a] OR, …The Spirit *of God is symbolized by* seven spirits who are in front of God's throne.

Revelation 1:9-20

THEME: Christ appeared to John and commissioned him to write down the vision he was about to give him, and to send it to the seven congregations of Asia.

[9] I, John, your fellow believer, am suffering as you *are* because of our letting Jesus rule our lives. You and I are steadfastly enduring *trials* because of our relationship with him. I was exiled to the island of Patmos because *I proclaimed* God's message and told *people about* Jesus. [10] *One day God's* Spirit took control of me. It was on the day *of the week* when *we believers worship* the Lord *Jesus.* [11] *When that happened*, I heard behind me someone *speaking to me as loudly and as clearly* as a trumpet. He was saying *to me*, "Write on a scroll what you see, and send it to seven congregations. Send it to *the congregations* in *the city of* Ephesus, in the *city of* Smyrna, in *the city of* Pergamum, in *the city of* Thyatira, in *the city of* Sardis, in *the city of* Philadelphia, and in *the city of* Laodicea." [12] *In this vision* I turned in order to see who had spoken to me. When I turned, [13] I saw seven golden lampstands. In the midst of the lampstands there was *someone* who looked like one who came from heaven. He wore a robe that reached to his feet, and he wore a gold band around his chest. [14] The hair on his head was white, like white wool *or* like snow. His eyes were *shining brightly* like a flame of fire. [15] His feet *looked* like brass that glows *as it is being* purified in a furnace. *When he spoke,* his voice *was* like the sound *made by* a great volume of *swiftly tumbling* water. [16] In his right hand he held seven stars. A sharp two-edged sword extended from his mouth. His face *shone as bright* as the sun shines *at midday.* [17] When I saw him, I fell down at his feet *and was unable to move or speak*, as though *I were* dead. But he laid his right hand on me and said to me, "Stop being afraid! I am the one who began *all things* and the *one who will cause all things to* end. [18] I am the one who always lives. Though I died, I am alive and will live forever! I have *the power to cause people* to die, and I have authority over the place where all the dead *are.* [19] So write down the *vision* you are seeing. Write about the *conditions* that exist now, and the *events* that are about to occur afterward. [20] The meaning of the seven stars that you saw in my right hand and of the seven golden lampstands *you saw is this*: The seven stars *in my hand represent the leaders who are like* angels *who watch over* the seven congregations, and the *seven* lampstands *represent* the seven congregations."

2

Revelation 2:1-7

THEME: Christ exhorts the congregation at Ephesus to repent and to begin again to love him and each other.

[1] *He also said to me*, "Write *this message* to the leader of the congregation in *the city of* Ephesus: '*I* am saying these things *to you. I am* the one who firmly holds the seven stars in my right hand. *I am* the one who walks among the seven golden lampstands. [2] I know all you do: You are laboring *for me* intensely, and you are continuing *to serve me* steadfastly. *I know* that you cannot tolerate people *who teach what is* evil, and that you investigated people who falsely claimed to be apostles, and you found that they were lying. [3] *Yes,* you continue *to serve me* steadfastly. *Even when people persecuted you*, you continued to serve *me* because of *your faith* in me, and you have not become too tired *to keep on serving me.* [4] Nevertheless, I have *this complaint* against you: You no longer love *each other and me* as you did when you first *trusted in me.* [5] *So I tell you to* remember how you used to love *me and each other, and* to *realize* that you no longer love *us* as you did. *I tell* you to turn away from your sin *of not loving me and each other*, and to start loving *again*

as you did at first. If you don't turn away from your sinful behavior, I will come *to judge* you and cause your group to cease to be a Christian congregation. [6] But you have the following good quality: The Nicolaitans *teach you believers that God will not punish you if you worship idols or if you act immorally*. However, you hate such teaching, just as I do. [7] Everyone who wants to understand my message must listen carefully to the message that *God's* Spirit speaks to the congregations. To everyone who overcomes *Satan*, I will give the right to eat *fruit* from the tree *that gives* eternal life, the tree that is in God's garden.'"

Revelation 2:8-11

THEME: Christ exhorts the congregation at Smyrna not to fear what they will suffer, but to trust in him, even if they must die because of it.

[8] "Write *this message* to the leader of the congregation in *the city of* Smyrna: *'I am* saying these things *to you. I am* the one who began *all things* and *who will cause all things to* end. I am the one who died and became alive *again*. [9] I know that you are suffering *because of what unbelievers do to you*, and that you lack *material possessions*. But *I also know that* you are *spiritually* rich. *I know* that people slander you. They say that they are Jews, but I do not *consider them to be Jews. I consider that* they *belong to* the assembly that Satan *controls!* [10] Do not be afraid of any of the things that you are about to suffer. Indeed, the devil is about to *put* some of you in prison, in order to tempt you *to deny that you believe in me*. For a short period of time you will suffer *because of what will be done to you*. Continue to trust in me, *even if* you are killed *for your faith in me*. As a result, I will *reward you with* eternal life*, just as people reward victorious athletes by putting* wreaths *on their heads*. [11] Everyone who wants to understand must listen carefully to the message that *God's* Spirit speaks to the congregations. *After* those who conquer *Satan die, they will live with God.* They will never suffer again, *even though many others* will suffer *as though they* died a second time.'"

Revelation 2:12-17

THEME: Christ exhorts the congregation at Pergamum to stop listening to what the Nicolaitans teach.

[12] "Write *this message* to the leader of the congregation in *the city of* Pergamum: *'I am* saying these things *to you. I am* the one who has the sharp two-edged sword. [13] I know where you live: It is where Satan controls *people. I know* that you firmly believe in me. You did not deny that you believe in me, not even in the time Antipas, my faithful witness, *was alive*. He was killed in your city, where *people* habitually obey Satan. [14] Nevertheless, I have this *complaint* against you: You permit some of your *members* to teach things like Balaam *taught long ago. He* taught Balak to persuade the Israelite people to sin. He taught them to eat food that had been offered to idols and to practice sexual immorality. [15] Because of that teaching, some of *your members* are practicing what the Nicolaitans teach, *which is like what Balaam taught.* [16] So, you must stop doing *this*. If *you* don't stop doing *it*, I will come to you without delay. With the words I will speak I will fight against those *who believe this false teaching*, and I will *condemn them to punishment.* [17] Everyone who wants to understand must listen carefully to the message that *God's* Spirit speaks to the congregations. To everyone who conquers *Satan*, I will give *blessings that will be like* the *food called* manna *that is* hidden *in a jar.*[b] I will also give them a white stone on which *I will* engrave a new name, one that no one but the ones who receive it will know.'

---

[b]   OR, …hidden *in heaven.*

Revelation 2:18-29

THEME: Christ rebukes the congregation at Thyatira for tolerating a teacher who encourages sexual immorality and for eating food offered to idols. He warns those who participate in these things that he will punish them unless they repent, and he exhorts the rest of the members of the congregation to remain loyal to him.

[18] "Write *this message* to the leader of the congregation in *the city of* Thyatira: *'I*, the Son of God,[c] am saying these things *to you. I am* the one whose eyes *shine* like a flame of fire, and whose feet *shine* like fine brass. [19] I know that you love *me and each other*, and that you trust *in me.* I know that you serve *others* and that you steadfastly endure *various trials. I know* that you are doing these things more now than *you did* in the past. [20] Nevertheless, I have this complaint against you: You tolerate the woman *among your members who is like the wicked queen* Jezebel *who lived long ago.* That woman says she is a prophetess, but by her teaching she is deceiving my servants. She is urging them to practice sexual immorality and to eat food offered to idols. [21] Although I gave her time to turn away from *her sexual immorality and pagan practices*, she did not want to stop *doing them.* [22] Take notice *that, as a result,* I will cause her to become very ill. I will also cause those *who act immorally as she does* to suffer greatly, if they don't stop *doing* what she does. [23] Some *have become* her children by accepting *what she teaches*; I will certainly get rid of them. As a result, all the congregations will recognize that I am the one who finds out what everyone thinks and desires. I will reward each of you according to what you have done. [24] But I have something to say to commend the rest *of you believers* in Thyatira. *It is good* that you don't follow that *false* teaching. *It is good that you reject* what the *false teachers* call their 'secret *practices,'ones* that Satan *actually inspired.*[d] I will not impose upon you any other burden *than that which you already have.* [25] Just keep *believing firmly in me, and obey me* until I come. [26] As for those who conquer *Satan* and who keep[e] on doing what I command until they die, I will give them my authority, just as I myself received it from my Father. *They will exercise that authority* over the nations *that rebel against God.* [27] They will exercise authority over them *severely, as if they were striking them* with an iron rod. They *will destroy evildoers* just as *people* shatter clay pots. [28] I will also give to *everyone who conquers Satan a share in the glory like* the morning star has. [29] Everyone who wants to understand must listen carefully to the message *God's* Spirit speaks to the congregations.'

3

Revelation 3:1-6

THEME: Christ exhorts the congregation at Sardis to wake up and repent. The members of the congregation who are worthy will live with him.

[1] "Write *this message* to the leader of the congregation in *the city of* Sardis: 'I am saying these things *to you. I am* the one who can give *people* all the power of God's Spirit,[f] and *I am the one* who has the seven stars. I know everything you have done. Though you

---

c   OR, ...I, the one who am also God...

d   OR, ...*It is good that you reject* what those false teachers *facetiously* call 'the secret *practices that* Satan *inspires'.*

e   OR, As for those who conquer *Satan* and *because* they keep...

f   OR, ...*I am* the one who has the seven spirits of God *that symbolize the powers of God's Spirit*...

appear to be alive *spiritually, you are so weak spiritually that it is as if* you were dead. ² *Become aware of your spiritual need as though you were* awaking *from sleep*, and strengthen *yourself spiritually, because you are so useless that you are like someone who is* about to die. *You must do this* because I know that nothing that you do is satisfactory in the sight of my God. ³ So then, keep remembering how you received *God's message* when you first heard it. Obey it continually, and turn away from your sinful behavior. If *you don't become aware of your spiritual need and turn away from your sinful behavior*, I will come to you *when you are not expecting me*, as a thief *does*. You will never know at what time I will come to *judge* you. ⁴ Nevertheless, *there* in Sardis you have a few members who *have not been doing what is wrong. It is as though they* have not soiled their garments. As a result, since they are worthy *to live with me,* they will live with me *and will be pure in every way, like someone dressed* in *pure* white *clothing*. ⁵ Everyone who conquers *Satan* I will dress in these same white garments,⁹ and I will never erase their names from the book *which records the names of the people who have eternal* life. Instead, as my Father and his angels are listening, I will acknowledge that they *belong to me*. ⁶ Everyone who wants to understand must listen carefully to the message that *God's* Spirit speaks to the congregations.'"

Revelation 3:7-13

THEME: Christ exhorts the congregation at Philadelphia to continue to obey his word and to be faithful. He promises that some Jews will acknowledge that he loves the congregation, and he also promises that he will keep the congregation from spiritual harm during the period of testing.

⁷ "Write *this message* to the leader of the congregation in *the city of* Philadelphia: 'I am saying these things *to you. I am* God's holy one, the true one. *Just as King* David had authority *to allow people to enter the ancient city of Jerusalem, so I have the authority to allow people to enter the new city of Jerusalem. I am* the one who opens *doors* so that no one can close them, and who closes doors so that no one can open them. ⁸ I know everything you have done. Be aware that I have opened before you a door that no one can close. *I know that although* you do not have *many believers in your congregation,*ʰ you have obeyed what I say, and you have not denied *that you believe in* me, ⁹ *even though I am aware that* some of your people meet together with those who follow Satan. They claim to be Jews, but I know that they are not true Jews. They are lying. I will cause them to come to you and to bow down *humbly* at your feet and to acknowledge that I love you.

¹⁰ Because you have paid attention to the message to endure *suffering* patiently, I will keep you *safe from those who will try to harm you spiritually* during the period that is about to come. At that time *God will cause rebellious people* on the earth to suffer, so that I can determine *whether they will turn away from their sins or not*. ¹¹ I am coming soon. *So* continue to hold fast to the *truths* you have received, so that no one can cause you to lose the reward *that God has reserved for* you. ¹² I will make everyone who conquers *Satan* secure. They will be *firm like* the pillars in the Temple of my God, and they will remain there forever. I will mark them with the name of my God, *showing that they belong to him. I will also mark them* with the name of the city of my God, *showing that they will live there. That city is* the New Jerusalem, the city that will descend out of heaven from my God. *I will also mark them* with my new name, *showing that they belong to me.* ¹³ Everyone who

---

⁹ OR, Everyone who conquers *Satan* will be *spiritually pure, as though* they were dressed in these white garments…

ʰ OR, …*I know that although* you do not have much *spiritual* strength…

wants to understand must listen carefully to the message that *God's* Spirit speaks to the congregations.'

Revelation 3:14-22

THEME: Christ exhorts the congregation at Laodicea to repent of neglecting fellowship with him and of failing to accept his provision for their spiritual needs. He wants to restore fellowship with any member of the congregation who will respond to his call.

[14] "Write *this message* to the leader of the congregation in *the city of* Laodicea*: 'I* am saying these things *to you. I am* the one who guarantees *all of God's promises.* I am the one who testifies reliably and accurately. I am the one by whom God created *all things.* [15] I know everything you have done: You *neither deny that you trust in me nor are you zealous in loving me. You are like water that is* neither cold nor hot. I wish that you were either cold or hot! [16] Because you are neither enthusiastic about me nor concerned about your lack of spiritual growth, I am about to *reject* you, *as if* I were spewing *lukewarm water* out of my mouth. [17] You are saying, *'Because we have all that we need spiritually,* we are *like* rich *people who* have acquired a lot of wealth. We lack nothing!' But you don't realize that you are *lacking spiritually in so many ways that you are like* people who are very wretched and pitiful, who are poor, blind, and naked. [18] I advise you *to obtain from me all that you need spiritually, as though you were* buying from me gold that has been refined by fire, so that you may be *truly* rich *spiritually. Let me make you righteous, as though you were* buying from me white garments in order that you might wear clothes instead of being naked and ashamed. *Let me help you to perceive spiritual things, as though* you were buying from me eye salve in order to anoint your eyes so that you might see.'[i] [19] *Since* I rebuke and correct all those whom I affectionately love, *I urge you* earnestly to turn away from your sinful behavior. [20] Be aware that *I am calling each one of you to respond to me* as though I *were* standing at *your* door and knocking. I will come to all those who hear my voice and respond to me, and I *will fellowship* with them *as friends do when they* eat together. [21] I will permit everyone who conquers *Satan* to sit *and rule* with me on my throne, just as I conquered *Satan* and am now sitting *and ruling* with my Father on his throne. [22] Everyone who wants to understand must listen carefully to the message that *God's* Spirit speaks to the congregations.'"

4

Revelation 4:1-11

THEME: A throne was in heaven with one sitting on it. He was in the midst of every creature and object in heaven. The elders and the living creatures worshiped him as God, the Mighty Creator.

[1] After these things I, *John,* saw *in the vision that* there was a door open in heaven. The one whose voice was like a *loud* trumpet, the one *who had spoken to me* previously, said *to me,* "Come up here! I will show you events that must occur later." [2] Immediately I experienced that *God's* Spirit *was controlling me in a special way.* There was a throne there in heaven, and on the throne someone was sitting *and ruling.* [3] His appearance

---

[i] Commentaries says that John was probably referring to things that people knew about the city of Laodicea. If it is desired to make this clear, one could translate for this verse "*Although you have many rich people there,…Although many clothes are made and sold there, …Although there is a famous eye doctor there…*"

shone like a *brilliant crystalline* jasper *jewel* and like a *brilliant red* carnelian *jewel*. Around the throne was a rainbow that *shone like a brilliant green* emerald *jewel*. [4]Around the throne there were twenty-four other thrones. On these thrones twenty-four elders were *sitting*. They were wearing *pure* white garments and had golden crowns on their heads. [5]From the throne there came lightning and rumblings and thundering. Seven torches of fire were burning in front of the throne. They *represent* the Spirit of God who has all *power*.[j] [6]In front of the throne *there was what looked* like an ocean *made of* glass. It was *clear,* like crystal. On each of the four sides of the throne there was a living *creature*. Each one was covered with eyes in front and behind. [7-8]The first living *creature* was like a lion. The second was like an ox. The third had a face like a man's face. The fourth was like an eagle that was flying. Each of the four living *creatures* had six wings. They were completely covered with eyes, all around *their bodies* and under *their wings*. Day and night they continually sing,

"Holy, holy, holy is the Lord God, the Almighty One.
He is the one who has always existed,
who is now, and who will always exist."

[9-10]The living *creatures praise*, honor, and thank the one who sits on the throne, the one who lives forever. Whenever they do that, the twenty-four elders prostrate themselves before the one who sits on the throne, and they worship him, the one who lives forever. They lay their crowns in front of the throne and sing,

[11]"Our Lord and God, you are worthy *of* praise,
you are worthy to be honored,
and *you are worthy that all beings* acknowledge
that you are the powerful one,
because you *alone* created all things.
Moreover, because you purposed *that they should exist,*
you created them, and *as a result* they exist."

5

Revelation 5:1-14

THEME: When the Lamb took the scroll from the one on the throne, the whole created universe worshiped him, the one who is the worthy Redeemer. The twenty-four elders and the four living creatures acknowledged that he alone was worthy to open the seals on the scroll.

[1]I saw that there was a scroll in the right hand of the one who was sitting on the throne. The scroll had writing on its outside as well as on its inside, and it was sealed with seven seals. [2]I saw a strong angel who was announcing in a loud voice, "Who is worthy to break the seals of the scroll and then to open it?" [3]But no *created being* in heaven nor any *created being* on the earth nor any *created being* under the earth was able to open the scroll and see what *was written* on it. [4]I cried loudly because there was no one worthy to do that. [5]But one of the elders said to me, "Don't cry *any longer!* Look, *the one who is called* the Lion from the Tribe of Judah, *the Messiah, who is* the descendant of *King* David, has overcome *Satan! As a result, he is worthy* to break the seven seals on the scroll and open it!" [6]Then I saw *Jesus, the one who is like a sacrificial* lamb, standing there. He stood near the throne, in the midst of the four living *creatures* and the elders. It appeared that he had been killed, *but he was alive again*. He had seven horns, and he

---

[j] OR, ...*These represent the Spirit of God who is also symbolized as* seven spirits.

had seven eyes that symbolize the Spirit of God who has all kinds of power.[k] *He sends God's Spirit out into all the earth.* [7] Jesus came and took the scroll from the right hand of the one who sits on the throne. [8] When he took it, the four living *creatures* and the twenty-four elders prostrated themselves before *Jesus,* the *one who was like a* lamb, *to worship him.* They each had a harp, and they had golden bowls full of incense that *represents* the prayers of God's people. [9] The living *creatures* and the elders sang a new song. They sang,

"You are worthy to receive the scroll and to open its seals,
because *you were* killed,
and because you redeemed *people* for God
from every tribe, language, people-group, and nation
with the blood that *flowed from your body when you died.*
[10] You have caused them to become a people over whom our God rules
and to become priests *who serve* him,
and they will rule on the earth."

[11] As I *continued to* look, I heard the voices of many angels around the throne and around the living *creatures* and the elders. There were millions of them, a *crowd so large that no one could count them.* [12] They were singing in a loud voice,

"The *One who is like a* lamb, who was killed *and who became alive again,*
is worthy that *all created beings* acknowledge—
that he is infinitely powerful,
that he is infinitely rich,
that he is infinitely wise,
that he is infinitely strong,
and that he is worthy *of being* honored and praised by *all created beings!*"

[13] I also heard every creature in heaven and on the earth and under the earth and in the ocean, every creature in all those places, saying,[l]
"*May we* forever praise and honor the one who sits on the throne!
May we forever praise the *One who is like a* lamb!
May they reign with complete power forever!"

[14] The four living *creatures* said, "Amen!" Then the elders prostrated themselves and worshiped *God and Jesus.*

6

Revelation 6:1-8

THEME: When the Lamb opened the first four seals of the scroll, the four living creatures called forth four mounted horsemen who brought judgment to the people on earth.

[1] I saw that *Jesus, the one who is like a* lamb, opened the first of the seven seals *of the scroll.* Then I heard one of the four living *creatures* say in a voice *as loud* as thunder, "Come!" [2] Then I saw a white horse *come out.* The one who sat on it had a bow *and arrows. God* gave him a crown *to show that he was a king.* Then the one who conquers *people* went out to continue to conquer. [3] When the *one who was like a* lamb opened the second seal, I heard the second living *creature* say, "Come!" [4] Then a red horse came out.

---

[k] OR, ...the Spirit of God, who is also symbolized as seven spirits.
[l] OR, ...singing...

God allowed the one sitting on it to take away peace, so that people would kill each other. *For this purpose* he was given a large sword. [5] When *the one who is like a* lamb opened the third seal, I heard the third living *creature* say, "Come!" This time, I saw a black horse *come out*. The one who sat on it had a pair of balance scales in his hand. [6] I heard a voice *that sounded* like *it was coming from* among the four living *creatures*. It was saying *to the man on the horse*, "A quart of wheat *will cost so much that* a man must work a whole day to earn enough money to buy it, and three quarts of barley will sell for the same price. But don't cut off *the supply of olive* oil or the wine!" [7] When the *one who is like a* lamb opened the fourth seal, I heard the fourth living *creature* say, "Come!" [8] This time I saw a pale horse *come out*. The one who was sitting on it is named '*The one who causes* death,' and he was accompanied by *the one named 'The place where dead people go'*. *God* gave them both authority over one quarter of the people on earth to incite them to kill each other with weapons. He also gave those two the authority to kill people by famine, by epidemics, and to be *attacked* by wild animals.

Revelation 6:9-11

THEME: When the Lamb opened the fifth seal, the souls of dead believers appealed to God to judge those who killed them, but God told them to rest a bit longer.

[9] When the *one who is like a* lamb opened the fifth seal, I saw under the altar[m] *in heaven* the souls of *God's servants* who had been killed because of *believing* God's message, and because they told others *the message about Jesus*. [10] They appealed loudly *to God* saying, "Sovereign Lord, you are holy and true. How long *will it be* before you judge *and punish* the people on earth who murdered *us*?" [11] *God* gave to each of them a long white robe, and *he* told them to rest a little longer, because there were still *people* who had served *the Lord* with them who would be killed. There were still those whom *God knew would be killed in just the same way* that others had been killed.

Revelation 6:12-17

THEME: When the Lamb opened the sixth seal of the scroll, the upheaval in the sky and on the earth caused all the rebellious people on earth to hide because they knew the time of God's judgment had come.

[12] I saw that when *the one who is like a* lamb opened the sixth seal, the earth shook violently. The sun became as black as pitch. The whole moon became *red* like blood. [13] The stars fell to the earth *in great numbers*, just like unripe figs fall *in the wintertime* when shaken by a strong wind. [14] The sky split open and *rolled up on either side,* just like an *old* scroll rolls up *on both sides when it is split in two*. Every mountain and island moved out of its place. [15] *As a result, all the rebellious people* of the earth, *including* kings, high-ranking people, generals, the rich, the powerful, along with every*body else*, whether slave or free, hid themselves in caves and in between the *tall* mountain rocks. [16] They shouted to the mountains and to the rocks, "Fall on us and hide us so that the one who sits on the throne will not be able to see us, and *so that* the *one who is like a* lamb will not be able to punish us! [17] This is the great day on which they will punish us, and no one will be able to survive!"

---

[m] OR, …I saw at the base of the altar…

7

Revelation 7:1-8

THEME: An angel ascended from the east and commanded the four angels stationed in four directions to continue restraining the destructive winds until God's servants had been sealed.

[1] After this I saw four angels. One was standing at the north, one at the east, one at the south, and one at the west. They were restraining the winds that blew from all directions, to keep them from blowing *destructively* on the earth or on the ocean or *even* on any tree. [2] I saw another angel ascend from the east. He was carrying the seal of God, who is all-powerful. *He intended to put God's mark on a special group of people to protect them.* The angel called out with a loud voice to the four angels to whom *power* had been given to harm the earth and the ocean, [3] saying *to them,* "Don't harm the earth or the ocean or the trees until we have marked the servants of our God on their foreheads." [4] *Then the angel and his fellow angels marked all God's servants.* I heard the number of people who *were* marked. *The number was* one hundred and forty-four thousand. They were from all the tribes of Israel. *They symbolized the complete number of people whom God would protect.* [5] *The angels* marked twelve thousand people from the tribe of Judah, twelve thousand from the tribe of Reuben, twelve thousand from the tribe of Gad, [6] twelve thousand from the tribe of Asher, twelve thousand from the tribe of Naphtali, twelve thousand from the tribe of Manasseh, [7] twelve thousand from the tribe of Simeon, twelve thousand from the tribe of Levi, twelve thousand from the tribe of Issachar, [8] twelve thousand from the tribe of Zebulun, twelve thousand from the tribe of Joseph, and twelve thousand from the tribe of Benjamin.

Revelation 7:9-12

THEME: The triumphant crowd stood before the throne in heaven and acknowledged that their deliverance had come from God and the Lamb. Then the angels, the elders, the living creatures, and a huge crowd of people worshiped and praised God.

[9] After these things I saw a huge crowd. There were so *many people* that no one would be able to count them. *They were* from every nation, every tribe, every people-group, and every language. They were standing before the throne and before *Jesus, the one who is like a* lamb. They were wearing white robes, and held palm branches *to wave* with their hands *in order to celebrate.* [10] They shouted loudly, "O our God, you who sit on the throne, and *Jesus, you who are like a* lamb, *you two* have delivered *us from Satan's power!*" [11] All the angels were standing around the throne and around the elders and the four living *creatures.* They all bowed down before the throne with their faces *to the ground* and worshiped God. [12] They said, "That is true! *We* praise, thank, and honor *you,* our God, forever! *We acknowledge* that you are completely wise, the powerful one, who is able to do all things forever! May *everyone acknowledge* it is so!"

Revelation 7:13-17

THEME: One of the elders explained to John about the saints who are dressed in white robes.

[13] Then one of the elders asked me, "These *people* who are wearing white robes, *do you know* who they are, and where they come from?" [14] I answered him, "*No,* sir, *I don't know. But surely* **you** know *who they are!*" He said to me, "These are the people who *have been persecuted. They believed that Jesus, the one who is like a* lamb, *atoned for sin when* his blood *flowed from his body when he died. Because of that, it is as though* they have

washed their robes and have made them white. [15] That is why they are in front of God's throne, and they serve him day and night in his *heavenly temple. God*, the one who sits on the throne, will shelter them. [16] *As a result*, they will never again be hungry. They will never again be thirsty. The sun will never again beat on them, nor will any heat *scorch them.* [17] This is because the *one who is like a* lamb who is there at the throne will *look after them, just as* a shepherd *takes care of his sheep.* He will guide them *to the source of eternal life, just as a shepherd leads his sheep* to springs of water *where they can drink to stay* alive. God will *cause them to no longer be sad. It will be as if he were* wiping away all tears from their eyes."

8

Revelation 8:1-5

THEME: *After the Lamb opened the seventh seal, there was thunder, flashes of lightning, and an earthquake.*

[1] When Jesus, the *one who is like a* lamb, opened the seventh seal, there was no sound at all in heaven for a very short time.[n] [2] I saw the seven angels who stand in front of God. A trumpet was given to each of them. [3] Another angel, who had a golden container for burning incense, came and stood at the altar. *He was given* a large quantity of incense to offer, with the prayers of all God's people, on the golden altar that is in front of *God's* throne. [4] He then threw *this incense on the altar*. The smoke of the *burning* incense along with the prayers of God's people went up to God. [5] *Next*, the angel took the incense burner and filled it with *coals of* fire from the altar. He threw *the contents of* the incense burner onto the earth. Thunder sounded and rumbled, lightning was flashing, and the earth shook.

Revelation 8:6-12

THEME: *The successive trumpet blasts by each of the first four angels resulted in great catastrophes on the earth and in the sky.*

[6] The seven angels, *each* of which had *one of* the seven trumpets, prepared to blow them. [7] When the first angel blew his trumpet, hail and fire mixed with blood poured down on the earth. *As a result*, a third of *everything on the surface of* the land was burned up. A third of the trees were also burned up, as well as *a third of* all the green grass. [8] When the second angel blew his trumpet, something like a huge mountain burning with fire fell into the ocean. *As a result*, a third of the ocean became *red like* blood, [9] a third of the living creatures in the ocean died, and a third of the ships *in the ocean* were destroyed. [10] When the third angel blew his trumpet, a huge star, burning like a torch, fell from the sky into a third of the rivers and into *a third of* the water-springs. [11] The name of the star was Bitterness. *As a result*, the water in a third *of the rivers and springs* became bitter, and many people died from *drinking* the water because it had become bitter. [12] When the fourth angel blew his trumpet, *God* struck the sun, the moon, and the stars, so that they lost a third of their light. The *sun* did not shine during a third of the day, and *the moon and stars did not shine during a third* of the night.

---

[n] OR, …there was silence in heaven for about a half an hour.

Revelation 8:13

THEME: An eagle announced that rebellious people on earth would suffer greatly.

[13] As I watched, I heard an eagle that was flying high in the sky, shouting in a loud voice, "Terrible things will happen to *rebellious* people who live on the earth as a result of *what will happen when* the three remaining angels blow their trumpets! And they are about to blow them!"

9

Revelation 9:1-12

THEME: When the fifth angel sounded his trumpet, locusts with stings like scorpions came on the earth and attacked the rebellious people.

[1] The fifth angel blew his trumpet. Then I saw *an evil angel. He was like* a star that had fallen from the sky to the earth. He was given the key to the shaft *that descended to* the underworld. [2] When he opened that shaft, smoke arose from it like smoke from a great burning furnace. The smoke prevented *anyone from seeing the light of* the sun and the sky. [3] Locusts came out of the smoke onto the earth. *They were given* power *to sting people* like scorpions *sting.* [4] *God* told the locusts not to harm the grass of the earth, nor any plant, nor any tree. *He said that they should sting* all the people who did not have a mark on the forehead, a mark *that showed they belonged to him.* [5] However, *God* did not allow the locusts to kill those people. Instead, *he* allowed them to continue torturing them for five months. The pain they felt was like the pain a scorpion causes when it stings someone. [6] During that time, *the pain will be so bad that* those people will want to find a way to die, but they will not find any. They will long to die, but they will not be able to. [7] The locusts looked like horses ready for battle. They had on their heads what looked like golden crowns. Their faces were like human faces. [8] They had *long* hair like the *long* hair of women. Their teeth were *strong,* like lions' teeth. [9] They wore metal breastplates. *When they were flying,* their wings made a noise like a roar made when many horses *pull chariots as they are* rushing into battle. [10] They had tails like *tails of* scorpions *by which they* stung *people.* Their power to harm people during those five months was in their tails. [11] The king who ruled over them was the angel of the underworld. His name in the Hebrew language is Abaddon. In the Greek language it is Apollyon. *Both of* those names *mean 'Destroyer'.*

[12] That ended the first terrible event. *Be aware that* two tragic events are still to come.

Revelation 9:13-21

THEME: When the sixth angel blew his trumpet, a third of the rebellious people on earth died. But the rest of the rebellious people did not repent of their worship of idols or of their evil practices.

[13] The sixth angel blew his trumpet. Then I heard a voice from the four corners of the golden altar that is in God's presence. [14] The voice was saying to the sixth angel, the one who had *just blown* the trumpet, "Release the four angels who are bound at the great River Euphrates." [15] The four angels were released, those who had been kept ready for that *exact* hour of that day, of that month, of that year. They were released so that they might enable *their troops to* kill a third of the *rebellious* people. [16] The number of the troops riding on horses was two hundred million. *I know that because* I heard *someone say* how

many there were. [17] In the vision I saw what the horses and the *beings* that rode them looked like. The riders *wore* breastplates that were *red* like fire, dusky blue *like smoke*, and *yellow* like sulfur. The heads of the horses were like the heads of lions. From their mouths came fire, smoke, and *fumes of burning* sulfur. [18] Those three things, the fire, the smoke, and the *burning* sulfur, killed a third of the *rebellious* people. [19] The power of the horses is in their mouths and in their tails. Their tails have heads like snakes, by which they harm people. [20] The rest of the *rebellious* people, those who were not killed by the fire and smoke and burning sulfur, did not turn from their sinful behavior. *They did not stop worshiping* the idols that they had made with their own hands. They did not stop worshiping demons, and they did not stop worshiping idols *made* of gold, of silver, of bronze, of stone, and of wood, *even though the idols* can neither see nor hear nor walk. [21] They did not stop murdering people, or practicing sorcery, or acting in sexually immoral ways, or stealing *things*.

10

Revelation 10:1-7

THEME: John saw a mighty angel coming down out of heaven and holding a small open scroll. When the angel shouted, the thunders responded, but a voice from heaven prohibited John from recording what they said. The angel affirmed that the living Creator of the universe would no longer delay in completing his purpose for his creation.

[1] *In the vision* I saw another mighty angel, *surrounded* by a cloud, coming down out of heaven. There was a rainbow over his head. His face *shone* like the sun. His legs looked like pillars of fire. [2] He had in his hand a small scroll that was open. He set his right foot on the ocean and his left foot on the land. [3] He shouted something with a loud voice, a voice like the roar of a lion. When he shouted this, it thundered seven *times*, speaking *words I could understand*. [4] When it thundered *like that*, I was about to write *the words that I* heard, but a voice from heaven said to me, "Keep secret what the thunder said! Don't write it down!" [5] Then the angel whom I had seen standing on the ocean and the land raised his right hand toward heaven, [6] and he asked the one who lives forever, the one who created heaven and everything that is in it, *who created* the earth and everything that is in it, and *who created* the ocean and everything that is in it, to affirm that what he said was true. *He said that he* would surely no longer delay *what he had planned*. [7] He said that when the time *came* for the seventh angel to blow his trumpet, *he* would complete God's secret plan, just as he announced *long ago* to his servants, the prophets.

Revelation 10:8-11

THEME: The heavenly voice told John to take the open scroll from the angel and eat it. When he had eaten it, he was commanded by God to prophesy again about all people.

[8] The one whose voice I had heard from heaven spoke to me again. He said, "Go and take the open scroll from the hand of the angel who is standing on the ocean and on the land." [9] So I went to the angel and asked him to give me the little scroll. He said to me, "Take it and eat it. In your mouth it will *taste* sweet like honey, but it will make your stomach bitter." [10] I took the little scroll from the angel's hand and ate it. In my mouth it *tasted* sweet like honey, but when I had eaten it, *it* made my stomach bitter. [11] The one whose *voice spoke from heaven said to me*, "You must prophesy again about many people-*groups*, many nations, *speakers of* many languages, and many kings."

11

Revelation 11:1-14

THEME: Christ told John to mark out his worshipers from the nations, and he appointed two witnesses to prophesy to the nations for a limited time. When they finished witnessing, the beast from the underworld killed them, causing the nations to enjoy temporary victory. God resurrected his witnesses, took them to heaven, and punished the nations. Survivors feared and acknowledged God as awesome.

[1] *An angel gave* to me a reed similar to a measuring stick. He said *to me, "Christ says this: Go* to the temple *where people worship* God, measure it and the altar *in it,* and count the people who worship there. [2] But don't measure the court outside *of the temple,* because *it* has been given to *the* non-Jewish *people. As a result,* they will trample *Jerusalem* for forty-two months. [3] I will appoint my two witnesses, and they shall speak for me for one thousand two hundred and sixty days. They will wear *rough* clothes made from goat's hair *to show they were sad about people's sin.'"* [4] These *witnesses are the ones* represented by the two olive trees and the two lamp stands that are in the presence of the Lord *who rules* the earth. [5] If any enemy tries to harm those *witnesses,* fire will come from their mouths and destroy them. If people want to harm them, *the two witnesses* will certainly kill them in the same way. [6] Those *witnesses* will have authority over the sky in order to keep rain from falling during the time that they are speaking for God. They also will have authority to cause water *everywhere* to become *red like* blood, and *authority* to strike the earth with all kinds of plagues, as often as they want to. [7] When they have finished testifying *to people,* the beast that comes up from the underworld will attack them, overcome them, and will kill them. [8] The dead bodies of the *two* witnesses will lie in the street of the great city where their Lord was crucified, the city which is symbolically named Sodom or Egypt, *because its people are very evil.* [9] Individuals of many people-*groups,* tribes, language *groups,* and nations will look at their dead bodies for three and a half days. But they will not allow *anyone* to bury their bodies. [10] When the *rebellious* people who live on the earth *see that the witnesses are dead,* they will rejoice and celebrate. They will send gifts to each other, because these two prophets had *sent plagues that* tormented the *rebellious* people on the earth. [11] But after three and a half days, God will cause them to breathe again and live. They will stand up, and. the people who see them will be terrified. [12] The *two witnesses* will hear a loud voice from heaven saying to them: "Come up here!" Then they will go up into heaven in a cloud. Their enemies will see them *as they ascend.* [13] At that same time there will be a great earthquake, as a result of which a tenth of *the buildings in* the city will collapse, and seven thousand people will die. The rest of the people will be afraid and *acknowledge* that the God *who rules in* heaven is awesome.

[14] That will be the second terrible event. *Be aware that* the third tragic event will come soon.

Revelation 11:15-19

THEME: When the seventh angel sounded his trumpet, voices from heaven declared that the Lord God and his Messiah now govern all people, and the elders declared that the time had come for God's final judgment. With the heavenly sanctuary open, lightning flashed, thunder reverberated, the earth shook, and large hail fell.

[15] Then the seventh angel blew *his trumpet.* Voices in heaven shouted loudly, "Our Lord *God* and the Messiah *whom he has appointed* can now govern *all the people in* the world,

and *he* will continue to rule them forever!" [16] The twenty-four elders who sat on their thrones in God's presence bowed down low and worshiped him. [17] They said,

"Lord God, you are the Almighty One!
You are the one who has always existed!
You are the one who exists now!
You will always exist!
We thank you that you have defeated with your power
    everyone who has rebelled against you,
    and you now rule *over all the people in the world*.
[18] The *unbelieving people of* the nations were angrily raging *at you*.
As a result, you have become very angry *with them*.
You have decided that this is the appropriate time
    for *you* to judge *all* the dead *people*.
You have also decided that it is the time for you
    to reward *all* your servants, *both* the prophets
    and the rest of your people who reverence you,
    whether they were socially significant or *socially* insignificant.
    All of them!
You have also decided it is the time for you to destroy
    the people who are destroying *others on* the earth."

[19] Then God's Temple in heaven was opened and *I* saw in the Temple the sacred box that contains God's covenant. Lightning was flashing, it was thundering and rumbling, the earth shook, and large hail *fell from the sky*.

12

Revelation 12:1-6

THEME: When the royal woman gave birth to a kingly son, she fled to safety and care in a place in the wilderness prepared by God.

[1] Then something very unusual appeared in the sky. It was a woman, whose *appearance and* clothing were as bright as the sun. The moon was under her feet. On her head was a crown *made* of twelve stars. [2] She was pregnant. Because she was about to give birth, she cried out in pain. [3] Then something else very unusual appeared in the sky. It was a huge red dragon. It had seven heads and ten horns. On each of its heads was a royal crown. [4] The dragon's tail dragged a third of the stars from the sky and threw them to the earth. The dragon set himself in front of the woman who was about to give birth, in order that he might eat her child as soon as it was born. [5] She gave birth to a son, who *is destined* to rule all the nations with *complete authority as if he was using* an iron rod. *God* snatched away her child and took him to *rule from* his throne. [6] The woman fled to a desert. She has a place there that God has prepared for her, in order that *the angels* may take care of her for a thousand, two hundred and sixty days.

Revelation 12:7-12

THEME: There was a battle in heaven in which Michael and his angels fought the dragon. The dragon and his angels were thrown out of heaven to earth. A loud voice from heaven declared the victory and the sovereignty of God.

[7] There was a battle in heaven. Michael and the angels he *commanded* fought against the dragon. The dragon and his angels fought back *against Michael and his angels*. [8] But the

dragon did not win the battle. *God* did not allow the dragon and his angels to stay in heaven any longer. ⁹The huge dragon was thrown out *of heaven*. The dragon is the ancient serpent, *the one* who is called the Devil and Satan. He is the one who deceives *people all over* the earth. He was thrown to the earth, along with all his angels. ¹⁰Then I heard *someone* in heaven shout loudly, saying,

"Now our God has saved *his people* by his power, and he rules *all people!*
Now his Messiah, who is the *supreme* ruler *appointed by God*,
    has authority *to rule all people*,
because *our God* has thrown out *of heaven* the one who accuses our fellow believers!
The dragon is the one who accuses them day and night before our God,
    saying that they have sinned and ought to be punished.
¹¹ *Our fellow believers* overcame him because they never stopped trusting *Jesus,*°
    the One who is like a lamb;
    they trusted in what accomplished when his blood *flowed down.*
Even though those believers wanted to live,
    they were willing to let people kill them *for speaking truly about him.*
¹² So, all you *angels* living in heaven, rejoice!
But terrible things will happen to you *ungodly people who live* on the earth
    and on the ocean, since the devil has come down to you!
He *is* very angry because he knows that he has only a short time
    during which he can harm people."

Revelation 12:13-18

THEME: When the dragon pursued the woman who had borne the male child, he was thwarted, so he prepared to fight against her other offspring.

¹³When the dragon realized that he had been thrown down to the earth, he pursued the woman who had given birth to a son. ¹⁴But the woman was given two wings like the wings of a very large eagle, in order that she might fly to a desolate place. That is a place *God* has prepared for her. There *God's angels* took care of her for three and one half years. The serpent, *that is, the dragon*, was not able to reach her there. ¹⁵The serpent poured water like a river from his mouth in the direction of the woman, so that the water might sweep her away. ¹⁶But the ground helped the woman *by* opening up and swallowing the river that the dragon poured out from his mouth! ¹⁷Then the dragon was very angry with the woman, so he went away to fight against *the people who are like* the rest of her offspring. They are the people who obey God's commandments and who tell other people about Jesus. ¹⁸The dragon stood on the ocean shore.

13

Revelation 13:1-10

THEME: A beast rose from the ocean. It received power and authority from the dragon. All people worshiped that beast for forty-two months; that is, all people who were not recorded in the book of life.

¹ *In my vision* I saw a beast coming up out of the ocean. It had ten horns and seven heads. On each *of* its horns there was a royal crown, and on *each* of its heads there was a name that insulted *God*. ² The beast that I saw was like a leopard, but its feet were like the feet of

---

° OR, …they never stopped telling people about *Jesus*…

a bear, and its mouth was like the mouth of a lion. The dragon gave the beast *power*. From his own throne he also gave it authority *to rule people*. ³ One of the heads of the beast had been wounded, causing the beast to die. But the wound was healed *and it came to life again. As a result nearly* all *the people of* the earth marveled at the beast and became his disciples. ⁴ They worshiped the dragon, because he had given to the beast authority *to rule people*. They also worshiped the beast, saying, "No one is *as powerful* as the beast! No one would dare to fight against it!" ⁵ The beast was allowed to speak proudly and to insult *God. It was also* allowed to exercise authority *over people* for forty-two months. ⁶ It spoke in order to insult God, to insult his name, to insult the place where he lives, and to insult the people who live there in heaven. ⁷ *It was* allowed to fight against God's people and to conquer them. *It was* allowed to have authority *to rule* over every tribe, over every people-*group*, over *speakers of* every language, and over every nation. ⁸ Most of the *people* living on earth worshiped it. They were ones whose names were not written in a book by the *one who is like a* lamb, the one who had been killed. Since the beginning of the world *he registered in it the names of the people who* will have *eternal* life. ⁹ Everyone who wants to understand must listen carefully to *this message from God*: ¹⁰ If *God has determined* that some people will be captured by their *enemies*, they will be captured. If *God has determined that* some people will be killed with a sword, they will be killed with the sword. So God's people *must be* steadfast, and be faithful *to him*.

Revelation 13:11-18

THEME: Another beast appeared, having the same authority to rule people that the first beast had, and it caused people on earth to worship the first beast. People made an image of the beast, and the beast had everyone killed who refused to worship the image. It caused all people to be marked with the name of the first beast. The number of the beast's name is 666.

¹¹ I saw another beast, which was coming up from the earth. It had two small horns *on its head* like a sheep has. But it spoke *things to deceive people* like the dragon does. ¹² While the first beast watched, it used all the *same* authority *to rule people that the first beast had*. It made the people who live on the earth worship the first beast, that is, the one who was healed of the wound that had caused it to die. ¹³ The second beast performed awesome miracles, even causing fire from the sky to fall to earth while people watched. ¹⁴ He performed miracles on behalf of the *first* beast. By doing that he deceived *many* people on the earth so that they *believed that they should worship the first beast*. The second beast told the people living on earth to make an image of the *first* beast, the one that *people* had killed with a sword and that then came back to life again. *But this happened only because God* allowed *it to happen*. ¹⁵ The image of the *first* beast was allowed to breathe, in order that it might speak. It commanded that whoever refused to worship its image should be killed. ¹⁶ *The second beast* required also that *the beast's name* be marked on the right hand or on the forehead of everyone, those of little *social importance* and those of great *social importance*, the rich and the poor, free *people* and slaves. *Everyone!* ¹⁷ They did this in order that no one could buy *anything* or sell *anything* if they did not have the mark, which represents the name of the beast or the number of its name. ¹⁸ You must *think* wisely to understand *the meaning of the mark*. Anyone who thinks wisely should calculate from the number of the beast what the man's name is. That number is six hundred and sixty-six.

14

Revelation 14:1-5

THEME: John saw the Lamb standing on Mt. Zion with 144,000 redeemed people, who were marked with God's seal. They were singing a new song that only the redeemed could sing.

¹But then I saw the *one who is like a* lamb standing on Mount Zion *in Jerusalem*. With him were 144,000 *people*, on whose foreheads his name and his Father's name had been written. ²I heard a sound from heaven, as *loud* as the sound of a huge waterfall[p] and *as loud as* mighty thunder. The sound I heard was like *the sound that* is made when people are playing their harps. ³The 144,000 people were singing a new song *while they stood* in front of the throne, in front of the four living *creatures*, and in front of the elders. Only the 144,000 *people*, the ones who have been redeemed from among the people on the earth, could learn that song. No one else could learn the song *they sang*. ⁴Those 144,000 are the people who are *spiritually pure, like* virgins *are morally pure*. They have not defiled themselves *by worshiping any false god*. They are the ones who accompany Jesus, the *one who is like a* lamb, wherever he goes. They *represent all those who have been* redeemed for God from among the people *of earth, in order that he might offer* them to God and to *himself.* ⁵*Those people* never lie when they speak, and they never act immorally.

Revelation 14:6-13

THEME: An angel announced that God's judgment had destroyed the wicked cities symbolized as Babylon. Another angel declared individual judgment on worshipers of the beast, who symbolizes the head of this world power. The saints are called to remain steadfast.

⁶I saw another angel flying between the sky and heaven. He was bringing *God's* eternal good message *to earth*, to proclaim it to people who live on the earth. He will proclaim it to every nation, *to every* tribe, *to speakers of every* language, and *to every* people-*group*. ⁷He said in a loud voice, "Reverence God and honor him, because it is now time for him to judge *people!* Worship *God, because he is* the one who created the heaven, the earth, the ocean, and the springs of water." ⁸Another angel, the second one, came after him, saying, "The very evil *cities*[q] *represented by* Babylon are completely destroyed! *God* has punished *their people because* they *have persuaded people of* all the nations *to forsake God, just as a prostitute* persuades *men* to drink *strong* wine and *as a result* commit sexual immorality." ⁹Another angel, the third one, came afterward, saying in a loud voice, "If people worship the beast and its image and *allow* its mark to be put on their foreheads or on their hands, ¹⁰God will be angry with them and punish them very severely. They will be tormented in burning sulfur in the presence of his holy angels and in the presence of the *one who is like a* lamb. ¹¹The smoke *from the fire* that torments them will rise forever. *They will* be tormented continually, day and night. *That is what will happen to* the people who worship the beast and its image and who allow its name to be marked on them." ¹²So, God's people, those who obey what God commands and who trust in Jesus, must faithfully continue *obeying and trusting him.* ¹³I heard a voice from heaven saying, "Write *this: God will* now *abundantly* bless for the rest of *their lives* the people who have a close relationship with the Lord *Jesus.*" *God's* Spirit says, "Yes, *after they die* they will no longer

---

[p] OR, I heard a sound from heaven which was as *loud* as the sound of a wide river of rushing water...

[q] OR, ...The very evil *city*...

have difficulties. Instead, they will rest, and *the record of the good deeds* that they have done will go with them."

Revelation 14:14-20

THEME: One like the One who came from heaven sat on a cloud, holding a sharp sickle. An angel from the sanctuary commanded him to harvest the earth. Another angel was commanded to reap the fruit of the vine of the earth. He threw the fruit that he harvested into the winepress of God's anger. When the winepress was trodden, the flow was like a flood of blood on the earth.

[14] Then I was surprised to see a white cloud, and on the cloud *someone* was sitting who looked like the One who came from heaven. He *was wearing* a golden crown on his head. In his hand *he held* a sharp sickle. [15] Another angel came out of the Temple *in heaven*. In a loud voice, *speaking figuratively about gathering people for judgment*, he said to the one who was sitting on the cloud, "The time has come to reap *the grain on earth*, so with your sickle *reap* the *grain*, because the grain on earth is ripe." [16] The one who was sitting on the cloud forcefully gathered together *all the people* on earth, *as a farmer* reaps grain with his sickle. [17] Another angel came out of the sanctuary in heaven. He also held a sharp sickle. [18] From the altar came another angel, the one who takes care of the fire *of the altar*. Also *speaking figuratively about gathering the wicked people for judgment and punishment*, he said in a loud voice to the angel who held the sharp sickle, "With your sharp sickle cut off the clusters of grapes together in the vineyards on the earth! Then gather the clusters of grapes together, since the grapes are ripe!" [19] So *just like a man would* cut off with his sickle the clusters of grapes in his vineyard, an angel forcefully *gathered the wicked people* of earth. Then he threw them into the huge place where God will angrily punish them. [20] *The wicked people* were trampled on *in* the winepress outside the city. The blood that came out from the winepress flowed *in a stream so deep that it reached* to the bridles of the horses, *and extended* 180 miles.

15

Revelation 15:1

THEME: John saw in the sky a marvelous sign of the seven angels responsible to inflict the seven last plagues.

[1] Something else very unusual *appeared* in the sky. I saw seven angels, whose duty it was to *punish rebellious people* with seven different plagues.[r] God is so angry *with rebellious people that* this is the last *time he will punish them with the purpose of giving them an opportunity to turn away from their sinful behavior.*

Revelation 15:2-4

THEME: John saw the victors over the beast respond to God's judgment of rebellious people on earth by singing God's praise for his mighty deliverance and righteous judgment.

[2] I saw what looked like an ocean *made of* glass and mixed with fire. And I saw the people who overcame the beast *by not worshiping it* or its image, or *allowing its agent to mark them with* the number that corresponds to the beast's name. They were standing by the ocean *that looked like it was made* of glass. They had harps *for praising* God. [3] They were

---

[r]   OR, …whose duty it was to inflict hardship upon *rebellious people* in seven different ways.

singing a song *like* God's servant Moses *sang long ago.* They sang *like this to praise Jesus, the one who is like* a lamb,

"Lord God Almighty, whatever you do is powerful and marvelous!
You always act righteously and truthfully.
You are king forever!
[4] O Lord, everyone will fear you and honor you, because you alone are holy!
People of all nations will come and worship you,
because *you* show *everyone* that you have judged *everyone* righteously."

Revelation 15:5-8

THEME: John saw angels being given the seven bowls of judgment in the heavenly sanctuary, which became filled with the smoke of God's unapproachable glory.

[5] After this, I saw in heaven an open door in the Temple *that* the tent *the Israelites pitched in the desert represented, the tent in which* the Ten Commandments *were placed.* [6] The seven angels *who had the bowls containing* the seven plagues came out of the Temple. The angels were dressed in clean, white linen *garments,* and they wore gold bands around their chests. [7] One of the four living *creatures* gave *each of* the seven angels a golden bowl, filled with *wine. That wine symbolized* that God, who lives forever, would severely punish *rebellious people.* [8] The Temple was filled with smoke *that symbolized* the presence of the glorious and all-powerful God. No one was able to enter the Temple until the seven angels finished *pouring out* the seven plagues.

16

Revelation 16:1-9

THEME: Four angels emptied their judgment bowls.

[1] *In the vision* I heard *someone* in the Temple speak in a loud voice to the angels *who had the seven bowls.* He said, "Go *from here* and pour out on the earth *the liquid in* the seven bowls. *This will show that* God is angry with *rebellious people and will punish them."* [2] So the first angel went and poured out on the earth *the wine that was in* his bowl. *As a result* horrible and painful sores broke out on the people whom the beast's *agents* had marked and who worshiped its image. [3] The second angel poured out on the ocean *the wine that was in* his bowl. *As a result* the *water in the ocean stank like the blood* of a person who has died. *As a result,* every living creature that was in the ocean died. [4] The third angel poured out on the rivers and water springs *the wine that was in* his bowl. *As a result the water in the rivers and springs* turned into blood. [5] I heard the angel *who has authority over* the waters say *to God,* "O God, you exist and have always existed. You are the holy one. You judge people justly. [6] *The rebellious people* murdered your holy people and prophets. So you are just in punishing them by giving them blood to drink. This is what they deserve!" [7] Then I heard *an angel* respond *from* the altar, "Yes, Lord God, you who are almighty, you punish *people* rightly and justly!" [8] Then the fourth angel poured out on the sun *the wine that was in* his bowl. *He* enabled the sun to scorch *people* with fiery *heat.* [9] Because people were severely burned by the intense heat, they said evil things about God, *because* he had the power *to strike people with* plagues like those. But they refused to turn away from their evil behavior and refused to honor him.

Revelation 16:10-16

THEME: Two more angels emptied their judgment bowls on the earth. Demons gathered armies to fight against God. But Jesus warned his people to watch faithfully for his imminent coming. The battle was ready to begin at Armageddon.

¹⁰ When the fifth angel poured out on the throne of the beast *the wine that was in* his bowl, it became dark in the kingdom that the beast *ruled. As a result, the beast and the people it ruled* were biting their tongues because *of suffering intense* pain. ¹¹ They insulted God *who rules in* heaven, because their sores were so painful. But they refused to stop doing the *evil* things they were doing. ¹² The sixth angel poured out on the huge river Euphrates *the wine that was in* his bowl. *As a result, the river's* water was dried up to prepare a path for the rulers from the eastern *countries to cross it with their armies.* ¹³ I saw evil spirits that looked like frogs. One came out of the mouth of the dragon, one from the mouth of the beast, and one from the mouth of the false prophet. ¹⁴ Those spirits were demons who were *able to* perform miracles. They went out to the rulers of the whole world, in order to gather their *armies* together to the battle *they will fight* on the great occasion when Almighty God *punishes his enemies.* ¹⁵⁻¹⁶ The evil spirits will gather the rulers at a place that is called in the Hebrew *language* Armageddon.

I heard the Lord Jesus say, "*You must* listen carefully to *me*: I am coming unexpectedly, like a thief. *So,* I will be happy with those who stay alert and *keep on living righteously so that they will not be ashamed*, just as a person keeps his clothes *on* so that he will not be ashamed when *people* see him walking around naked." *I heard the Lord Jesus say,* "*You must* listen carefully to *me*: I am coming unexpectedly, like a thief. I will be happy with those who stay alert and *keep on living righteously so that they will not be surprised and ashamed, like a person who keeps on his clothes while sleeping so that he will not be awakened* naked *and be ashamed.*"

Revelation 16:17-21

THEME: After the seventh angel emptied his bowl, God punished the very evil city symbolized by Babylon and destroyed other cities, and great disasters followed.

¹⁷ The seventh angel poured out into the air *the wine that was in* his bowl. *As a result, someone* said with a loud voice from the Throne in the temple, "*The time for God to punish rebellious people* is *about to be* finished!" ¹⁸ When the angel emptied his bowl, lightning flashed, there were rumblings and thunder, and the earth shook. It shook more violently than it has ever shaken since people first *lived* on earth. ¹⁹ And *as a result*, the very evil city *symbolized by Babylon* split into three parts. *God also* destroyed cities in *other* nations. God did not forget that *the people of* the very evil *city symbolized by* Babylon *had sinned very much.* So he *caused the people with whom* he was furiously angry *to drink* a cup of very *poisonous* wine *that represented his punishment.* ²⁰ Also *as a result of the earthquake*, every island disappeared, and the mountains became flat land. ²¹ Also *as a result of the angel's emptying his bowl*, huge hailstones, each weighing about 100 pounds, fell from the sky onto the people. Then people insulted God because *he had caused* the terrible plague of destructive hail to fall on them.

17

Revelation 17:1-2

THEME: One of the seven angels offered to show John how God will punish the very evil city represented by a prostitute with whom the rulers of people on earth have been seduced to act immorally and idolatrously.

¹One of the seven angels, who had *one of* the seven bowls, came to me. He said to me, "Come *with me* and I will show you how *God* will punish the very evil *city that is represented by* a prostitute, a city in which there are many *streams of* water. ²*It is as though* the rulers of earth have acted immorally *and idolatrously* with the people of the city, and they *have persuaded people* who live on the earth to act immorally *and idolatrously* with them, *just as a prostitute persuades men to become* drunk from the *strong* wine *she gives them that results* in their committing immorality."

Revelation 17:3-6

THEME: When the angel took John to a wilderness, he saw an immoral woman who was drunk with the blood of God's people. The sight caused John to react with great bewilderment.

³Then, as *God's* Spirit *controlled me*, the angel carried me away to a desolate area. There I saw a woman who was sitting on a red beast. Someone had written names all over the beast. They were names that insulted *God*. It had seven heads and ten horns. ⁴The woman *I saw* was wearing purple and red *clothes*, and gold, precious stones, and pearls were fastened to her *clothes and her body*. She held in her hand a golden cup that was full of *a liquid that represents* the detestable, idolatrous things and filthy immoral things that she *does*. ⁵This name that has a hidden *meaning* was written on her forehead: "*This woman is* Babylon the very evil *city! She acts like* the mother of all the prostitutes on the earth. She teaches them to *act* immorally and to worship idols." ⁶I saw that the woman had become drunk as a result of drinking the blood of God's people, those who had told others about Jesus. When I saw her I was very bewildered.

Revelation 17:7-18

THEME: The angel revealed the meaning of what John had seen, identifying as ruling entities both the beast which amazed people and his seven heads and ten horns, and the angel declared that they would be overcome by the Lamb and defeated. The angel identified the prostitute representing the very evil city that dominates people, and he declared that it would be destroyed.

⁷The angel said to me, "Don't be bewildered! I will explain to you the mystery of the woman and of the beast on which she rides, the beast that has the seven heads and the ten horns. ⁸The beast that you saw *lived* previously. Eventually God will destroy him, but now he is dead. He is *about to* come up from the underworld. *When* the beast who had previously lived, and who then had died, reappears, the people who live on the earth will be amazed. *They are people whose* names were not in the book in which are written the names of people *who will* have eternal life. *The angels have been writing those names in a list* from the beginning of the world. ⁹Those who *think* wisely *can understand* this: The seven heads *of the beast* on which the woman sits *symbolize* the seven hills *of the city that woman represents*. They also *symbolize* seven rulers. ¹⁰Five *of those rulers* have died. One is *still alive*. The seventh *ruler* has not yet come. When he comes, he must remain for *only* a short *time*. ¹¹The beast that *lived* before and then was not *alive* will be the eighth *ruler*. He will be *evil like* the seven *rulers were, but God* will surely destroy him.

¹² The ten horns that you saw *represent* ten rulers who have not yet begun to rule. They will receive authority to rule *people* together with the beast *for only a short time, as if it were* for one hour. ¹³ Those *rulers* will all desire to do the same thing. *As a result* they will give to the beast their right *to rule* and their authority *to rule*. ¹⁴ The rulers and the beast will fight against *Jesus,* the *one who is like a* lamb. He will defeat them, because he is Lord *who rules over all other* lords and the King *who rules over all other* kings. Those who are with him *and helping him* are the ones whom *God* has chosen, and who remain faithful *to him*." ¹⁵ The angel said to me, "The waters that you saw where the prostitute sits represent people-*groups*, multitudes *of people*, nations, and *speakers of many languages*. ¹⁶ The ten horns that you saw *represent rulers*. They and the beast will hate *the people in the city* that the prostitute *represents*. As a result, they will *take away everything that is in the city as if* they were leaving it naked. They will *destroy it as if* devouring flesh, and they will burn it with fire. ¹⁷ They will do that because God has caused them to decide to do what he wants them to do. As a result, they will let the beast have their power to rule until *they* fulfill what God has said. ¹⁸ The prostitute that you saw *represents* the very evil city *whose leaders* rule over the kings of the earth."

18

Revelation 18:1-3

THEME: A powerful angel descended from heaven and announced that the cities represented by Babylon were about to be completely destroyed because of their immorality and idolatry.

¹ After this I saw another angel, who had great authority, coming down from heaven. The earth became bright *because* he was shining so intensely. ² He shouted with a mighty voice, "*God is about to* completely destroy all the very *evil* cities *that* Babylon *represents*.ˢ As a result, all *kinds of* evil spirits will live there, and all *kinds of* foul and detestable birds will live there. ³ *God will destroy those cities* because *their rulers have persuaded* the people of all nations to act highly immorally *and idolatrously with the people of those cities, just as* a prostitute persuades men to drink strong wine and then commit fornication with her. The rulers of the earth have also acted immorally *and idolatrously* with the people of those cities. The merchants of the earth have become rich *because the people of those cities* strongly desired the luxuries *of the world*."

Revelation 18:4-5

THEME: John heard Jesus tell God's people to flee out of those cities.

⁴ I heard *Jesus* speak from heaven. He said, "My people, flee from *those cities*, in order that you may not sin as the people *of those cities* do. If you sin as they do, I will punish you as I will punish them. ⁵ *It is as though* their sins have piled up to heaven, and God remembers them, *so now he must punish them*."

Revelation 18:6-8

THEME: Jesus sentenced the cities represented by Babylon to destruction

⁶ *To the angels whom God assigned to punish those cities*, Jesus said, "Pay the people of those cities back to the same extent that they harmed *other people*. Indeed, cause them to

---

ˢ   OR, …*God is about to* completely destroy the city that Babylon *represents.*

suffer twice as much *as they caused other people to suffer.* [7] To the same extent that they have honored themselves and lived to do just the things they wanted to do, to that extent torment them and cause them to grieve. *Do that because* in their minds they think, 'We rule as queens! We are not widows, and we shall never mourn *as widows do!* [8] So in one day great calamities will come upon them. *The people in those cities* will die, others will mourn for them, people will be hungry *because there will be no food,* and *their cities* will be burned up. The Lord God is able to punish those cities *like that,* because he is mighty."

Revelation 18:9-19

THEME: Earth's kings, merchants, and maritime traders mourned the loss of those cities.

[9] The kings of the earth who have acted immorally *with people of those cities* and have lived self-indulgently with the people of those cities will weep and lament for them when they see the smoke of the fire that is burning them. [10] They will stand far away *from those cities,* because they will be afraid *that they will suffer just as the people of those cities* are suffering. They will say, "Terrible things will happen to the awesome and mighty cities *represented by* Babylon! *God* will punish them suddenly and swiftly!" [11] The merchants of the earth will weep and will mourn *for those cities,* because no one will ever again buy the things they have *to sell to the people in those cities.* [12-13] *They sell ornaments made* of gold, silver, precious stones, and pearls. They sell *expensive fabrics made of* fine linen and silk, *expensive fabrics dyed* purple and crimson. They sell all kinds of *rare* wood, all kinds of items *made of* ivory, costly wood, bronze, iron, and marble. They sell cinnamon, other spices, perfume, frankincense, wine, olive oil, fine flour, and grain. They sell cattle, sheep, horses, and chariots. They even sell human beings to become slaves. [14] *The merchants will say,* "The good things you people longed to have are gone! You have lost all your luxurious and splendid *possessions!* They will be gone forever!" [15] The merchants *who sold* these things and who had become rich by *supplying them* for your *cities* will stand far away, because they will be afraid *that they will suffer just as* the people *of those cities* are suffering. They will weep and mourn, [16] and they will say, "Terrible things have happened to the awesome cities! *They were like queens* who dressed themselves in *clothes made of* fine linen *fabric* and expensive fabrics dyed purple and crimson, and who were adorned with gold, precious stones, and pearls. [17] But suddenly and swiftly *God* has destroyed those expensive things." Every ship captain, all people who travel by ship, all sailors, and all others who earn their living *by traveling on* the ocean will stand far away *from those cities.* [18] When they see the smoke of the fire that is burning those cities, they will shout, "No *other* cities have ever been so awesome!" [19] They will throw dust on their heads *to show that they are sad,* and they will shout, weep, and mourn. They will say, "Terrible things have happened to the awesome cities, the cities that made all people who own ocean-going ships become rich by *carrying* their costly merchandise! *God* has suddenly and swiftly destroyed those cities!"

Revelation 18:20-24

THEME: All of God's people who live in heaven are called to rejoice since God has pronounced judgment on the cities represented by Babylon.

[20] Then someone spoke from heaven saying, "God has justly punished the people of *the cities represented by* Babylon because they acted evilly toward you! So you who live in heaven, rejoice over what has happened to those cities! You who are God's people— including the apostles and the prophets—rejoice!"

[21] Then a mighty angel picked up a boulder the size of a large stone for grinding grain, and he threw it into the ocean. Then he said, "O you people in the awesome cities represented by Babylon, your cities will be destroyed so that they will disappear just like that stone

disappeared in the ocean! Your cities will be gone forever! [22] In your cities there will never again be anyone playing harps, singing, playing flutes, and blowing trumpets. There will no longer be any craftsman making things. There will never again be people grinding *grain at* the mill. [23] No lamplight will ever again shine. There will never again be the *happy* voices of a bridegroom and his bride. *God will destroy your cities* since your merchants were the most *deceiving* men in the world. You persuaded them to deceive *people of* all nations. [24] You are also *responsible for killing the* prophets and *others* of God's people. Indeed, you are the ones who are guilty for the deaths of all *God's people* who have been killed on the earth!"

19

Revelation 19:1-8

THEME: After the destruction of Babylon, John heard a huge crowd praising God for saving his people and announcing the marriage of the one who is like a Lamb.

[1] After these things I heard *what sounded* like a huge crowd in heaven. They were shouting,
   "Hallelujah![t] He has saved *us!*
   He *is* glorious and mighty!
   [2] *Praise him* because he judges truly and justly!
   He has punished the very evil *cities that are like a* prostitute,
      because their people persuaded the *other people of* earth
      to *act* immorally *and idolatrously* like they do.
   Praise him because he has punished them for murdering his servants!"

[3] *The crowd* spoke a second time saying,
   "Hallelujah! The smoke of *the fire that is burning* those cities will rise forever!"

[4] The twenty-four elders and the four living *creatures* prostrated themselves and worshiped God, who sits on the throne. Then they said, "*It* is true! Hallelujah!" [5] Someone spoke from the throne and said, "All you who are his servants, praise our God! All you who reverence him, *whether you are socially* significant or insignificant, praise him! *Everyone!*" [6] I heard something like the noise of a huge crowd *of people*, like the sound of a great volume of water tumbling swiftly, and like the sound of loud thunder. They were shouting,
   "Hallelujah, because the Lord God, the Almighty One, reigns! [7] Let's rejoice, let's be *extremely* glad, and let's honor him,
      because it is now *time for Jesus*, the *One who is like a* lamb,
      to *be united permanently with his people,*
      which will be like a man marrying *his bride*,
      and because those who belong to him have prepared   themselves.
   [8] *God* has granted to them that *they should be completely pure,*
      like a bride who dresses in fine linen, bright and clean."

Fine *bright and clean* linen represents the righteous acts of God's people.

---

[t]   OR, ...They were shouting, "Praise God!..."

Revelation 19:9-10

THEME: God will abundantly bless the people who have been invited to celebrate the marriage of the Lamb. Only God should be worshiped. All his servants are on an equal basis.

⁹ Then the angel said to me, "Write *this: God will abundantly* bless the people whom *he* has invited to the feast *that celebrates Jesus, the one who is like a* lamb, *permanently uniting with his people, like someone marrying a wife*." He also said *to me*: "These words that God *declares* are true!" ¹⁰ I *immediately* prostrated myself at his feet in order to worship him. But he said to me, "Don't *worship me!* I am *just* your fellow servant and the fellow servant of your fellow believers who tell people about Jesus! You should worship God, since it is the Spirit of God who gives the power to tell others about Jesus!"ᵘ

Revelation 19:11-16

THEME: John saw heaven open and saw the one whom he described as King of kings and Lord of lords mounted on a white horse.

¹¹ I saw heaven open, and I was surprised to see a white horse. *Jesus*, the one who was riding on the horse, is called 'Trustworthy and Genuine.' He judges *all beings according to* what is right, and fights righteously *against his enemies*. ¹² His eyes *shone like* a flame of fire. There were many royal crowns on his head. A name had been written *on him*. Only he knows *the meaning of the name*. ¹³ The cloak he was wearing was drenched with blood. His name is *also* "The one who tells us what God is like."ᵛ ¹⁴ The armies of heaven were following him, riding on white horses. They were wearing clothes *made of* clean white linen. ¹⁵ *The words* he speaks *will be like* a sharp sword, in order to strike *the rebellious people of* the nations. He himself will rule them *powerfully, as though he had* an iron rod. He will crush *his enemies just as a person crushes grapes in a* winepress. *He will do this on the behalf of* God Almighty, who is furiously angry *with them because of their sins*. ¹⁶ On his cloak close to his thigh a name had been written, which is 'King who *rules over all other* kings and Lord who *rules over all other* lords.'

Revelation 19:17-21

THEME: An angel invited all flesh-eating birds to feast on the flesh of people who were killed by the rider on the white horse. When the beast and the false prophet gathered kings with their armies against the rider and his army, the beast and the false prophet were thrown into the lake of fire. The sword of the rider killed rebellious people, and the birds gorged themselves on their flesh.

¹⁷ I saw an angel standing in *the light of* the sun. He called loudly to all the *flesh-eating* birds flying high in the sky, "Come and gather for the great feast God *is providing for you!* ¹⁸ *Come* and eat the flesh of all *God's enemies who are dead*—the flesh of kings, of army commanders, of *people who fought* powerfully, of horses and of the *soldiers* who rode them, *and the flesh of all other kinds of people*, whether *they were* free or slave, *socially* insignificant or significant. All kinds!" ¹⁹ Then I saw the beast and the kings of earth with their armies gathered together to fight against the rider on the horse, and against his army. ²⁰ The beast and the false prophet were captured. The false prophet is the one who had performed miracles in the beast's presence. By doing that he had deceived the people who had accepted the beast's mark *on their foreheads* and who worshiped its image. The beast and the false prophet were thrown alive into the lake of fire that burns

---

ᵘ OR, …since everyone who tells others about Jesus is truly speaking the words of God!

ᵛ OR, …His name is *also* "The Word of God".

with sulfur. ²¹ The rider on the horse killed the rest *of their armies* by *his words, which were like* a sword that extended from his mouth. All those birds gorged themselves on the flesh of *the people whom he had killed*.

20

Revelation 20:1-3

THEME: John saw an angel coming down from heaven. He seized, bound, and imprisoned the dragon for a thousand years.

¹ I saw an angel coming down from heaven. He had the key of the bottomless pit, and he was carrying a large chain in his hand. ² He seized the dragon. That dragon is the ancient serpent, the devil, that is, Satan. The angel bound him with the chain. That chain could not be loosed for a thousand years. ³ The angel threw him into the bottomless pit, shut *the door of the pit*, locked it, and sealed it. He did that in order that Satan might no longer deceive *the people of the* nations, until those thousand years have ended. After that *time*, Satan must be released for a short time *to do what God has planned*.

Revelation 20:4-6

THEME: John saw the thrones of the martyrs who lived again and had authority to judge people. Those martyrs are the first people whom God will cause to live again. They will reign with Christ during the thousand years.

⁴ I saw thrones on which people were sitting. *They were given authority* to judge *other people*. I also saw the souls *of people* whose heads had been cut off because of *their telling people about* Jesus and declaring God's message. They were ones who refused to worship the beast or its image, and who refused to be marked, either on their foreheads or on their hands. They came to life again, and they ruled with Christ *during those* thousand years. ⁵ They were the ones who lived again after the first resurrection. The rest of *the people who* had died did not live again until after those thousand years. ⁶ God will be pleased with those who live again this first time. He will *consider* them holy. They will not die a second time. Instead, they will be priests *who serve* God and Christ, and they will reign with *Christ* during those thousand years.

Revelation 20:7-15

THEME: When Satan is released, he will deceive the nations in order to assemble them to fight against God and his people. God will send fire to burn up the rebellious nations. He will cause Satan to be thrown into the lake of fire for everlasting punishment.

⁷ When the thousand years have ended, Satan will be released from his prison. ⁸ He will go out to deceive the *rebellious* people in nations all over the earth. *These are the nations that the prophet Ezekiel called* Gog and Magog. Satan will gather them to fight against *God's people*. There will be *so many of them fighting against God's people that no one will be able to count them*, just as *no one can count the grains of* sand on the ocean shore. ⁹ They will march over the whole earth and will surround the camp of God's people *in Jerusalem*, the city that *God* loves. Then *God will send* fire down from heaven, and it will burn them up. ¹⁰ The devil, who had deceived those people, will be thrown into the lake of burning sulfur. *This is the same lake* into which both the beast and the false prophet had been *thrown. As a result*, they will continually suffer severely forever.

¹¹ Then I saw a huge white throne on which *God* was sitting. He *was so awesome that* the earth and the sky disappeared from his presence completely; they were completely destroyed. ¹² I saw that the people who had died *but now lived again* were standing in front of the throne. *They included people of* every social status! The books *in which God records what people do* were opened. Another book was opened, which is *called the Book* of Life, *in which God has written the names of people who have eternal life. God* judged the people who had died *and now lived again* according to what they had done, just as *he* had recorded it in the books. ¹³ *The unbelievers who were buried* at sea *became alive again in order to stand before God's throne.* Everyone who had been buried on the land^w *became alive again, in order to stand before the throne. God* judged each one of them according to what each one had done. ¹⁴ All the unbelievers—those who had been in the place where they waited after they died—*were thrown into the burning lake.* The burning lake is *the place in which people* die the second time. ¹⁵ The people whose *names* were not in the book, the one *where God* has written *the names of people who* have *eternal* life, *were also thrown into the burning lak*e.

21

Revelation 21:1-4

THEME: John saw a new heaven, a new earth, and New Jerusalem, where God will dwell permanently with his people.

¹ Then I saw a new heaven and a new earth. The first heaven and the first earth had disappeared, and the oceans no longer existed. ² I saw *God's* holy city, which is the new *city of* Jerusalem. It was coming down out of heaven from God. *The city* had been prepared *and decorated* as a bride is decorated *beautifully in order to marry* her husband. ³ I heard a loud voice that spoke from the throne *of God,* saying, "Take note! Now God will live with people. He will live *right in the midst of* them! They will be his people. God himself will be with them, and he will be their God. ⁴ *As a result*, he will *cause them to no longer be sad. It will be as though he will* wipe every tear from their eyes. *None of them* will ever again die or mourn or cry or suffer pain, because the former things *that make us sad* will have passed away."

Revelation 21:5-8

THEME: God declares that he has made everything new and that everything has been accomplished. He declares himself to be the beginning and the end, and so he will provide abundant eternal life to all who seek him, but punishment in the lake of fire will be the lot of all the wicked.

⁵ Then *God*, who sits on the throne, said, "Look! I am *now* making everything new!" He said *to me*: "Write these things *I have told you*, since you can trust *that I will certainly make them happen*." ⁶ He said to me, "I have completed *all these things*! I am the one who begins all things and the one who will cause all things to end. To everyone who is *spiritually* thirsty, I will freely give water from the spring *that causes people* to live *forever*. ⁷ I will give this to every person who is victorious over *the evil powers*.^x I will be their God, and they shall be my children. ⁸ But those who are cowardly, who do not believe *in me*,

---

^w OR, …Every person who was waiting in the place where dead people stay…

^x OR, I will give these things to every person who is victorious over *Satan.*

who do detestable things, who are murderers, who sin sexually, who commit sorcery, who worship idols, and every liar, will *all suffer* in the lake that burns with fire and sulfur. *Anyone who suffers in that lake* will be dying the second time."

Revelation 21:9

THEME: One of the seven angels of the seven bowls offered to show to John the Bride of the Lamb.

⁹ One of the seven angels, holding one of the seven bowls that had been full of *the liquid causing* the seven last plagues, came and said to me, "Come *with me* and I will show you *the people who have permanently united with Christ, the one who is like a* lamb! They will be *like* a bride *for him.*"

Revelation 21:10-14

THEME: An angel showed John the city of God, the New Jerusalem, which was coming down out of heaven from God, shining with his glory, having a huge wall with twelve gates and twelve huge foundation stones.

¹⁰ Then, while *God's* Spirit *controlled me*, the angel carried me to the top of a very high mountain. He showed me *God's* holy city, *the New* Jerusalem. It was coming down out of heaven from God. ¹¹ It was shining with his glory. The city was shining like a very precious jasper stone *shines, and* was clear like crystal. ¹² *Around the city* was a very high wall that had twelve gates. An angel was at each gate. The names of the twelve tribes of Israel were written over the gates. *Each gate had the name of one tribe.* ¹³ Three gates were on the east *side*, three were on the north *side*, three were on the south *side*, and three were on the west *side.* ¹⁴ The wall of the city had twelve foundation *stones*. On each foundation *stone was* the name of one of the twelve apostles of *Jesus, the one who is like a* lamb.

Revelation 21:15-17

THEME: The angel guide measured the city and its wall.

¹⁵ The angel who was speaking to me carried a golden measuring rod, in order to measure the city, its gates, and its wall. ¹⁶ The city was square *in shape*; it was as long as it was wide. After the angel measured the city with his rod, *he reported that it was* 1500 miles long, and that its width and height were each equal to *its length.* ¹⁷ He measured its wall *and reported that it was 220 feet thick.*ʸ The angel used the *kind of* measuring rod that people *normally use.*

Revelation 21:18-27

THEME: John described the composition of the city, its wall, its foundations, its gates, and its street, emphasizing the extreme value of each part.

¹⁸ The *city* wall was made of *something like the green stone we call* jasper. The city *itself* was *made of something like* pure gold *that looked* like clear glass. ¹⁹ The foundations of the wall of the city were beautifully made with *wonderful stones like* precious stones *on earth*. The first foundation *stone was a crystalline stone like* jasper, the second *foundation stone was a blue stone like* sapphire, the third *foundation stone was a green stone like* agate, the fourth *foundation stone was a green stone like* emerald, ²⁰ the fifth *foundation*

ʸ OR, *...220 feet high.*

stone was a brown and white layered stone like sardonyx, the sixth *foundation stone was a red stone like* carnelian, the seventh *foundation stone was a yellow stone like* chrysolite, the eighth *foundation stone was a green stone like* beryl, the ninth *foundation stone was a yellow stone like* topaz, the tenth *foundation stone was a green stone like* chrysoprase, the eleventh *foundation stone was a blue stone named* hyacinth, the twelfth *foundation stone was a purple stone named* amethyst. ²¹ The twelve gates *of the city* were *something like huge* pearls. Each gate was like *it was* a single pearl. The *ground of* the main plaza of the city^z *appeared to be* pure gold *that looked* like clear glass.

²² There was no temple in the city. The Lord God Almighty *himself*, and the *One who is like a* lamb, are *there, so there was no need for* a temple. ²³ The people in that city will not need the sun or the moon, because the glory of God will *shine on* the city, and *the One who is like a* lamb will provide its light. ²⁴ The people of the nations will live with the light of the city *shining upon them*. And the kings of the earth will bring their wealth into the city *to honor God and the One who is like a lamb*. ²⁵ The gates of the city will not be shut *at the end of the day as they could be*, because there will be no night there. ²⁶ The *people of the* world will also bring their wealth into the city to honor *God and the One who is like a lamb*. ²⁷ No one who is morally impure, no one who does deeds *that God considers* detestable, no one who tells lies, will ever enter that city. Only those *people who* have *eternal* life will be there, those whose names are written in the book belonging to the *One who is like a* lamb.

22

Revelation 22:1-5

THEME: God will supply abundant life in the city. His servants will worship him face to face. No one will be there whom God would curse. God's servants will reign forever and ever.

¹ The angel showed me the river of water *that causes people who drink from it* to live *forever*. The water was sparkling and clear like crystal. The river was flowing out from the throne where God and the *one who is like a* lamb *were sitting*. ² It flowed down through the middle of the *main* street of the city. On each side of the river were trees *having fruit that causes people who eat it* to live forever. *The trees* bear twelve *crops* of fruit,^{aa} one crop each month. The *people of the* nations *use* the leaves of the trees *as medicine* in order that they may be strengthened. ³ There will never be *any one or anything there that God* will curse. The throne of God and of the *one who is like a* lamb will be in the city. And his servants will worship him there. ⁴ They will see him face to face, and his name will be written on their foreheads. ⁵ There will never again be night. *God's servants* will not need the light of a lamp or the light of the sun, because the Lord God will shine his light upon them. And they will reign forever.

Revelation 22:6-7

THEME: God verified the revelation of his message to his servants in which he showed them what must happen soon.

⁶ The angel said to me: "These words that *God has revealed to you* are true, and he will certainly fulfill them. The Lord God who *inspires* the prophets sent his angel to show the

---

^z OR, ...The streets of the city...

^{aa} OR, ...*The trees* bear twelve *kinds* of fruit...

people who serve him the events that must happen soon." ⁷ *Jesus says to all his people,* "Listen carefully to me! I am coming quickly; *God will abundantly* bless everyone who obeys the message that *has been written* in this book."

Revelation 22:8-11

THEME: John attested that he has himself heard and seen all these things. He was told to tell others the revelation because its fulfillment was near, and everyone should be ready.

⁸ I, John, am the one who heard and saw *in a vision* these things *that I have written down.* When I had heard and seen *them,* I immediately knelt down at the feet of the angel who was showing them to me, in order to worship him. ⁹ But he said to me, "Don't *worship me!* I am *just* your fellow servant! I am also the fellow servant of your fellow believers who are the prophets, and a fellow servant of those who obey the message in this book. Worship God!" ¹⁰ He also said to me, "Don't keep secret the message about what *God* has foretold in this book, because it is almost time for him to *fulfill this message.* ¹¹ *Since that will soon happen, if* those who act in an evil manner *wish to* continue to act that way, *that is up to them. God will soon pay them back for that. If* those who are vile *wish to* continue to be vile, *that is up to them. God will soon pay them back for that.* Those who are *acting* righteously should continue to act righteously. Those who are holy should continue to be holy."

Revelation 22:12-16

THEME: Jesus announced that he had sent his angel to bear witness to the congregations about all that John had seen. He authoritatively identified himself as the Descendant of King David and as the Messianic Morning Star.

¹² *Jesus says to all people*: "Listen! I am coming soon! And I will pay back and reward everyone according to what each one has done. ¹³ I *am* the one who begins all things and the one who will cause all things to end. I am before *all things* and I am at the end *of all things.* ¹⁴ *God* is very happy with the people who wash their robes*, making themselves spiritually clean,* because they will be able to *eat the fruit of* the tree *that enables people* to live *forever,* and because they will *be able* to enter the gates into the *holy* city. ¹⁵ Very certainly, all those people who continue to want to do evil will never at all see that city, neither will those who are practicing sorcery, people who sin sexually, murderers, idol worshippers, and all people who enjoy telling lies and are continual liars.

¹⁶ "I, Jesus, sent my angel in order that he might say to you who are in the congregations *that all* these things *are true.* I am the descendant of *King* David *whom the prophets promised would come.* I am the one *that Moses promised would come,* the *one who is like* the bright morning star."

Revelation 22:17

THEME: God's Spirit and the bride invite all who desire to drink the living water to come and drink, and they invite all who hear to extend the invitation to others.

¹⁷ *God's* Spirit and *his people who are like* the bride *of Christ* say *to each one who desires to believe,* "Come!" Let whoever hears *this* also say *to each one who desires to believe,* "Come!" The *spiritually thirsty people should come!* Everyone who desires the water *that enables people to* live *forever* should take it as a free gift!

Revelation 22:18-19

THEME: Jesus warned about what would happen to anyone who adds to the message of the book or who distorts any message of its revelation.

[18] "*Jesus says, "I solemnly* warn everyone who hears the message about what *I* have told *John* in this book *as follows*: Those who add anything to this message, God will cause them to suffer from the plagues that are described in this book. [19] Those who distort any of the message about what *I* have told John in this book, God will not give them the right *to eat fruit from* the tree *which enables people* to live *forever*. He will also not give them the right *to enter* God's city. *Both these things* are described in this book."

Revelation 22:20

THEME: Jesus declares that he is certainly coming soon.

[20] *Jesus*, who says that *all* these things are true, says, "Certainly I am coming soon!" *I, John, reply*, "May it be so! Lord Jesus, come!"

Revelation 22:21

THEME: John closes with a prayer that Jesus may continue to bless all God's people.

[21] *I pray that our* Lord Jesus *will continue to* act kindly to all *of you who are God's people.* May it be so!